Right-Wing Resurgence

Right-Wing Resurgence

How a Domestic Terrorist Threat is Being Ignored

Daryl Johnson

ROWMAN & LITTLEFIELD PUBLISHERS, INC.
Lanham • Boulder • New York • Toronto • Plymouth, UK

Published by Rowman & Littlefield Publishers, Inc.
A wholly owned subsidary of The Rowman & Littlefield Publishing Group, Inc.
4501 Forbes Boulevard, Suite 200, Lanham, Maryland 20706
www.rowman.com

10 Thornbury Road, Plymouth PL6 7PP, United Kingdom

British Library Cataloguing in Publication Information Available

Library of Congress Cataloging-in-Publication Data

Johnson, Daryl, 1969-
  Right wing resurgence : how a domestic terrorist threat is being ignored / Daryl Johnson.
    p. cm.
  Includes bibliographical references and index.
  ISBN 978-1-4422-1896-3 (cloth : alk. paper) — ISBN 978-1-4422-1897-0 (ebook)
  1. Radicalism—United States. 2. Terrorism—United States. 3. Internal security—United States. 4. National security—United States. I. Title.
  HN90.R3J64 2012
  363.325—dc23

                                                                    2012016574

∞™ The paper used in this publication meets the minimum requirements of American National Standard for Information Sciences—Permanence of Paper for Printed Library Materials, ANSI/NISO Z39.48-1992.

Printed in the United States of America

This book is dedicated to those who have died,
and who will yet perish, from right-wing extremist violence.

A special thanks to my wife—my eternal companion; extended family and friends; members of the former Department of Homeland Security domestic terrorism team; federal, state, and local law enforcement personnel; many of my peers at the DHS; Mark Potok and staff members at the Southern Poverty Law Center; the Anti-Defamation League; and many others throughout government and the private sector who supported me during a time of personal crisis—one of the most difficult life challenges I have ever faced.

Contents

Foreword

Daryl Johnson is a man of true principle. A sober and careful individual, Johnson nevertheless made a decision in 2011 to go public with explosive criticisms of the Department of Homeland Security and its backing away from pursuing intelligence on the very real threat from the radical right. Speaking as the DHS's former lead analyst of non-Islamic domestic terrorism, his words carried great weight.

I first met Daryl at a conference on extremism in 2000, nine years before the leak of a key report of which he was the lead author—"Rightwing Extremism: Current Economic and Political Climate Fueling Resurgence in Radicalization and Recruitment"—sparked howls of outrage from the political right. I found him to be deeply knowledgeable, a smart analyst who was on top of what was happening in the country and not afraid to call them like he saw them. In the years that followed, we met several more times, and my impression never changed.

As is recounted in this volume at length, the 2009 leak of Johnson's report was almost immediately picked up in the right-wing blogosphere, where its analysis and measured warnings were rapidly twisted into what was described, in essence, as a left-wing government attack on all conservatives. Rush Limbaugh claimed the report portrayed "standard, ordinary, everyday conservatives as posing a bigger threat to this country than Al Qaeda terrorists." Right-wing columnist Michelle Malkin called it a "hit job on conservatives," an "embarrassingly shoddy piece of propaganda." Gay-bashing televangelist Pat Robertson said the DHS report "shows somebody down in the bowels of that organization is either a convinced left winger or somebody whose sexual orientation is in question." Twenty conservative groups sponsored ads calling for the ouster of DHS secretary Janet Napolitano.

Napolitano, after briefly defending the report, caved. It was withdrawn, and the secretary apologized to the American Legion, which had objected to the report's pointing out that extremists were seeking to recruit returning war veterans.

It's hard not to wonder if any of these people actually read Johnson's report. The reality is that it was a perfectly sober document that correctly attributed the rise of radical right-wing groups to the election of a black president and the ailing economy—findings that were remarkably similar to what independent research at the Southern Poverty Law Center also discovered. It rightly pointed out that some extremists were driven by a single issue, such as abortion or immigration. And its suggestion that certain extremists were seeking out veterans of the wars in Iraq and Afghanistan was entirely borne out by independent SPLC findings. It is completely false that it demonized all conservatives as potential Timothy McVeighs.

But DHS's reaction was one of political cowardice. Johnson says the DHS deliberately mischaracterized the report as having gone outside authorized channels—even though he personally met with Napolitano to discuss it before release. Even worse, he says the department effectively dismantled his unit. A dismayed Johnson finally left the agency in 2010, followed by most of the members of his team.

That was after events showed just how prescient the report had been. In April 2009, just days after it was leaked, a Florida man "severely disturbed" by the election of Barack Obama murdered two Okaloosa County sheriff's deputies who were trying to arrest him. In May of that year, an antiabortion zealot in Kansas murdered Dr. George Tiller. The next month, a longtime neo-Nazi gunned down a guard at the U.S. Holocaust Memorial Museum before being shot himself. In the months that followed, there were a large number of similar events, including the arrests in 2010 of members of antigovernment militias in Alaska and the Midwest in separate plots that involved the murder of large numbers of police officers.

At the same time, the numbers of radical-right groups were climbing steadily, according to research by the Southern Poverty Law Center. Hate groups rose from 926 in 2008 to 1,002 in 2010, but the truly explosive growth came in the so-called "Patriot" groups, whose members generally believe the federal government plans to impose martial law and eventually force the country into some kind of socialistic global government. From a mere 149 groups in 2008, the Patriot groups skyrocketed to 824 by 2010—an almost unbelievable 450 percent rise in just two years.

It's shocking, in retrospect, how easily the political right was able to thwart intelligence work on the radical right in this country. Based on deceptive propaganda and twisted descriptions of Johnson's report, it essentially ended, up to the time of this writing, any official attempt to analyze the radical right. That's despite the fact, as Johnson noted in an interview for the magazine I edit at the SPLC, that his critics "would have been shocked to know that I personify conservatism. I'm an Eagle Scout. I'm a registered Republican. I'm Mormon. In fact, I was helping the Boy Scouts with a fund-raiser when I heard the report being attacked on the news."

What is the practical effect of the lack of intelligence from DHS? Are the police departments and other law enforcement agencies that used to get serious analytical reports on the radical right from DHS genuinely suffering?

Bob Paudert thinks so. Paudert is the former chief of police of West Memphis, Arkansas. On May 20, 2010, Paudert's son and another officer working for him were murdered during what appeared to be a routine traffic stop by a father-son team of "sovereign citizens"—people who believe most federal tax and criminal laws don't apply to them. Paudert says his officers knew nothing of the sovereign movement, and so had no idea what was going on when the father and son showed them bogus registration papers—only to pull out a heavy weapon seconds later. Paudert says if his department had been properly alerted and trained—something he believes was the job of the federal government—"my son would still be alive today."

"These incidents are beginning to add up," Johnson said of recent terror plots in his interview with the SPLC magazine. "Yet our legislators, politicians, and national leaders don't appear too concerned about this. So my greatest fear is that domestic terrorists in this country will somehow become emboldened to the point of carrying out a mass casualty attack, because they perceive that no one is being vigilant about the threat from within. This is what keeps me up at night."

And that is precisely what worries me, too.

—Mark Potok

1

The Leak

It was 10:16 p.m. EST on Saturday, April 11, 2009. I had finished a long day helping the Boy Scouts with their annual fund-raiser. It had rained most of the day, which left me wet, hungry, and exhausted. The fund-raiser had sapped my energy. So, like most nights, I was fast asleep at this hour.

This Saturday night, like many before it, was filled with the sound of millions of fingertips busily typing on computer keyboards throughout the country. Many people were awake at this hour—actively viewing websites, typing messages, and carrying out all manner of personal business.

Rarely do I stay up late at night. Weekday mornings come early in Washington, D.C. Long commutes are a fact of life here. I learned early in my federal career that making the simple mistake of sleeping in—if only for a few extra minutes—can add an extra hour or more to an already arduous journey to and from work each day.

Most people give little thought to what's going on in the world around them as they sleep. Many of us tune in to the morning news to get caught up on the previous day's events and overnight developments. But on this night, I wish I had stayed awake. Perhaps I should have paid more attention to the Internet chatter that night as someone in cyberspace was plotting against me.

An unknown, angry person had a "beef" with the government. They had grown increasingly upset after receiving and reading an official assessment from the Department of Homeland Security (DHS) concerning an alleged resurgence in right-wing extremist activity within the United States. Political rage and paranoia likely fueled their anger.

They registered an Internet moniker, "SayItLoud." The message, dated Saturday, April 11, 2009, at 10:16 p.m., is titled, "Question of Some Urgency For Mods [Moderators] Or Others In The Know."[1]

This anonymous individual (who has yet to be identified) obviously felt the need "to sound the alarm." They felt a civic duty to warn the public. But their warning was not a rational one. It was not tipping the public to an imminent threat or anything physically dangerous. Rather, the supposed "warning" was a rally call, meant to incite others (supporters and political allies) into an antigovernment fervor. The message was a warning to "Patriots," a general phrase used to describe fanatical Americans obsessed with preserving their constitutional rights. I have little doubt that this anonymous person was growing increasingly fearful and paranoid. They likely believed that the new administration, led by America's first African-American president, had a preconceived agenda to usurp the U.S. Constitution, replacing it with a Marxist government.

Earlier in the week, the DHS had issued an official intelligence assessment about the resurgence of right-wing extremism in the United States. The assessment cited the recent economic downturn, the unprecedented election of an African-American president, and the return of military veterans unable to fully integrate into American society as reasons for this resurgence. On April 7, 2009, the assessment had been officially disseminated to many federal, state, and local law enforcement agency throughout the country. It warned of a possible increase in extremist-related criminal activity and violent acts as a result of a combination of these factors as well as polarizing national issues that fueled the radicalization and recruitment of extremists into antigovernment and racist groups. How do I know this? I am the author of that assessment and I was astounded to learn that it took less than four days for it to leak.

"I have a PDF that has very, very important information, but it is too long to copy. Can I just put up a link to the PDF? Thanks," the message began. Other users soon joined in the discussion. Some appeared inquisitive and expressed curiosity.[2]

At 10:23 p.m., SayItLoud returned to the forum and posted again—a second message thread with more specific information. The message reads, "Rodger Hedgecoke [sic] a radio talk show host has posted a report from the Dept [sic] Of Homeland Security that is titled below. If you click on the link to his show, click the Tea Party tab and look for the HSA link it will go to a report that is from DHS. It is chilling. Read the PDF. Are we still America?"[3]

Precisely four minutes later, SayItLoud returned to his first message and provided an update. "It is up. It is about the Dept [sic] of Homeland Security and a new report and right wing extremism from the Roger Hedgecock website . . . . There is critical info in the PDF. Do what you like."[4] This latest post led to a discussion thread between SayItLoud and four other users, who debated the contents of the DHS report, its authenticity and merits.

Soon the anonymous author became noticeably abrupt, remarking in frustration, "What really pisses me off is that it isn't Islamic terrorists who are training in camps as we sit here reading so that they can creat [sic] terror and havoc in the USA or the Aztlan[5] or Mecha[6] who are teaching kids on the border that the southwest is theirs and that they are planning on taking it by bloodshed if necessary or groups like the ELF [Earth Liberation Front] that blow shit up in the name of animal saving . . . that isn't who they deem a threat. It is Americans who want our borders secured and illegals [sic] to go the hell home and want our immigration laws enforced. It is Americans who hate killing babies in the womb . . . I daresay most Christians and many from other religions as well would fit into that category [sic]. It is Americans who are concerned about our economy and the riots that would start if it gets worse that are going out to stock up on weapons to defend their families. It is Americans who are angry about the outsourcing of our manufacturing to China, Mexico and India. THAT is who they are worried about? Are you KIDDING me?"

A person using the anonymity of the Internet had undermined the DHS, by betraying the very government for whom they likely worked. Their actions were clearly disloyal to the intelligence and law enforcement communities to which they likely belonged. A clandestine coward, whose identity remains veiled in secrecy, had somehow rationalized that leaking a sensitive government document was in the public's best interest. They were wrong and acted irrationally and recklessly. They may very well be responsible for radicalizing a large number of Americans who misunderstood the assessment's intent and true purpose—to warn law enforcement of a likely resurgence in domestic right-wing terrorism and associated violent criminal activity that would surely translate into loss of life.

A few hours earlier that same day, a separate anonymous message had been posted on a different Internet forum. This message, posted at 7:24 p.m., appeared on an extremist forum found on the Oath Keepers website. The Oath Keepers is a secretive, obscure antigovernment extremist organization that had yet to announce its presence publicly. It is not known whether this earlier message was the work of the same anonymous individual or another person.

The message title read, "Subject: SHOCKING New DHS Report!! Concerned Americans and activists are now Dangerous Right Wing Extremists!"[7] It began, "Hello brothers, this just came in here in San Diego, California. It looks like Washington has heard of the Oath Keepers, more lies coming from the anti American left wing communist . . . [it is a] brand new confidential report from FBI and DHS dated April 7th and leaked by a DHS insider to Roger Hedgecock. YOU are now a dangerous terrorist according to the Obama Administration. Read this shocking report . . . FORWARD THIS TO EVERY AMERICAN!"[8]

A person, or perhaps persons unknown, had obviously leaked a sensitive but unclassified DHS assessment titled "Rightwing Extremism: Current Economic and Political Climate Fueling Resurgence in Radicalization and Recruitment." The report contained a law enforcement information handling notice admonishing recipients not to release the information to the media, general public, or over nonsecure Internet servers. It also warned, "Release of this information could adversely affect or jeopardize investigative activities."[9]

The anonymous Oath Keeper concluded the message to other extremists in the movement, "Kudos to Roger for exposing this on his radio show yesterday and today. I had my friend at DHS view this document today and he believes it is real . . . Looks like the Southern Poverty Law Center and the ACLU are now writing Federal Intelligence reports full of La Raza[10] and Mexican lies and propaganda."[11]

Coincidentally, I had received a very odd feedback form on Friday, April 10, 2009—from one of my DHS colleagues at the Office of Intelligence and Analysis (I&A). The feedback concerned the assessment I had authored that was just released through our Production Management Division. The feedback had negative overtones and questioned the definition of right-wing extremist that was cited in a footnote on the second page of the assessment. It also contained similar discussion points and themes as the two aforementioned anonymous postings.

I was not accustomed to receiving negative feedback from my coworkers concerning products that I had written. It was highly unusual for a DHS employee to submit a formal feedback form to our production management branch concerning a product written by his own office. This strange event had upset me at the time. But after I wrote a response to this individual, I brushed it off. It was several weeks later before I revisited this incident and came to realize that this single event—the negative feedback from a peer—may have some potential significance related to this egregious security breach.

On April 11, 2009, the day on which the DHS assessment was leaked, the Oath Keepers had not yet announced their existence publicly. Movement organizers, however, were busily preparing for their national debut on the Lexington Green in the small, historic town of Lexington, Massachusetts, on April 19, 2009—just a week away. The location for the Oath Keepers opening ceremony was purposefully selected for its historic and symbolic significance as the exact site that marks the onset of the American Revolutionary War. It is also symbolic of the "minutemen" of the American Revolution as well as the unorganized militia that fought in that war. It was no coincidence that men who saw themselves as today's minutemen and who also had ties to the modern militia movement would gather together at the Lexington Green in 2009 to proclaim their anger and disdain for the federal government and its new administration.

The Oath Keepers portray themselves as a civic-minded organization that caters to current and former members of the military and law enforcement. Their name is taken from the oath of office that each of them took as public servants when they began their military or law enforcement career—an affirmation to "support and defend the Constitution against all enemies foreign and domestic . . . so help me God."[12]

Federal civil servants are required to take an oath of office by which they swear to support and defend the U.S. Constitution. The U.S. Constitution not only establishes a system of government, it also defines the role for the federal workforce—"to establish Justice, ensure domestic tranquility, provide for the common defense, promote the general welfare, and secure the blessings of liberty."[13]

The actual oath of office for federal employees can trace its history to Article 2 of the U.S. Constitution, where the president of the United States is required to take an oath—to "preserve, protect, and defend the Constitution of the United States."[14] Article 4 requires that all other government officials, the military, and the state also take a similar oath. Article 4, however, does not provide specific language, but vaguely states that government employees "shall be bound by oath or affirmation to support the Constitution."[15] Article 6 was later passed into law by the first Congress, which implemented a simple written oath stating, "I do solemnly swear or affirm (as the case may be) that I will support the Constitution of the United States."[16]

Today's wording used in the oath of office for federal employees is found in the United States Code, Chapter 33, Title 5, Section 3331. The specific wording for this oath reportedly dates back to the American Civil War and contains what is called the Ironclad Oath.[17]

The Ironclad Oath, adopted by Congress in 1862, required a two-part test for federal employees.[18] The first part was referred to as a "background check." It involved a process of determining whether or not an individual supported the Union or subverted it through the Confederacy. The second part involved a person's future performance—meaning what they would swear to do in the future. This process involved reciting an oath to clearly and publicly state an individual's accountability to the government and the American people. In 1873, Congress limited the oath of office process to the second part of the Ironclad Oath, thus eliminating the need for the background check. Today background checks are only conducted for those government employees who need security clearances, have law enforcement responsibilities, or handle sensitive government information as part of their government employment. In 1884, Congress adopted the specific wording that the government uses today in its swearing-in ceremonies.[19]

Today military service members, police officers, intelligence professionals, and other government personnel take this "oath of office" as they enter the workforce. Their oaths are not only statements of loyalty to the U.S. Constitution from a legal standpoint, but they are also an expression of allegiance both to government and to those holding executive office, such as a governor or the president of the United States. Under federal law, betraying one's oath could be considered an act of treason.

Like police officers and military servicemen, I have taken this oath on four separate occasions as I transitioned from one government agency to another. I had sworn to protect the nation, specifically our constitutional principles, against all enemies—foreign *and* domestic.

A month earlier, in March 2009, I had received a preliminary tip from a local law enforcement contact about a new possible extremist group called Oath Keepers. At the time, no one in my extended network of law enforcement and intelligence community contacts had ever heard of them. However, upon further research, I and a few others suspected that the Oath Keepers represented a new strain of antigovernment activism—a physical manifestation of the mounting antigovernment fervor we had seen boiling over the past ten months. We also suspected the Oath Keepers may have had ties with other, well-known forms of antigovernment extremism, such as the Sheriff's Posse Comitatus (an antigovernment movement in the United States defunct since the 1980s) and the modern-day sovereign citizen and militia movements. At first, we had little information to help us assess the group. Besides a few clues gathered from the Internet, we really had no idea who the Oath Keepers were or what they represented, but it wouldn't take long for our initial suspicions to be confirmed.

On April 19, 2009, the Oath Keepers publicly unveiled their core beliefs, supporters, and leadership at a ceremony held at the Lexington Battle Green in Lexington, Massachusetts. Oath Keeper speakers would include Richard Mack, Guy Cunningham, Walter Reddy, and Edwin Viera Jr. Each of these individuals is known for his outspoken views and antigovernment activism. Some have ties to the modern militia movement, while others are iconic figures who were associated with antigovernment extremism during the 1990s.

The Oath Keepers are not a traditional threat such as organized crime, violent gangs, or terrorist groups. They represent internal operational security and counterintelligence threats—things we had not seen in this country for several decades. The Oath Keepers mission appears to subvert the U.S. government through secretive infiltration; the covert monitoring of law enforcement, military, and intelligence information; and, if necessary, unauthorized disclosure of sensitive information to their membership, affiliated groups, and the general public. Of course, they're not interested in just any type of information. They are likely looking to exploit information that can be politically charged or generate public speculation and criticism to further their unique, conspiratorial view of the United States and world events.

The Oath Keepers leadership and membership are very open about their unquestionable, unwavering loyalty and support to the organization's goals rather than their allegiance to those government agencies that they represent. According to their own propaganda found on the Internet, the Oath Keepers acknowledge they "are in a battle for the hearts and minds of our own troops. To win that battle, Oath Keepers will use written and video testimony of active duty military, veterans (especially combat vets), and peace officers to reach, teach, and inspire our brothers in arms in the military and police to fulfill their oaths and stand as guardians of the Republic."[20]

I soon learned firsthand that the Oath Keepers not only represent a rising tide of antigovernment sentiment sweeping the nation, but they signify the greatest internal counterintelligence threat facing this nation since the world wars. Despite having no real ties to violent activity, the Oath Keepers pose a significant and potentially dangerous threat to the military, law enforcement, and intelligence community. Whenever you have a group of armed individuals, who have been entrusted and empowered to enforce the law, take a subversive stance against the very establishment that has instilled that power and authority, there is a serious need for identifying those associated with this potential threat, conducting a vulnerability assessment, and implementing countermeasures.

Neither I nor my colleagues had noticed the preliminary Internet chatter late that Saturday night, April 11, 2009, nor the Sunday morning conservative talk-radio programs concerning the report. However, by Monday morning, April 13, 2009, the number of media stories about the report was growing by the hour.

I was busy completing a few outstanding deliveries related to a Boy Scout fundraiser when I first heard the news on Monday morning. I happened to catch the term "right-wing extremism report" during a thirty-second news sound bite on a local radio station.

At the time I heard this news item, I wasn't particularly concerned. Previous reports I had written at DHS, as well as many other reports from I&A, had been leaked to the media in the past. Prior leaks had not generated too much controversy, just political dialogue. Of course, the media had almost always taken a negative spin regarding Homeland Security and its mission. So this leak was "par for the course."

By Tuesday, April 14, 2009, the media and public's reaction to the DHS report news was rising to a feverish hype. The report was being dissected, analyzed, and scrutinized by all major television news networks and national radio programs, including networks that provide twenty-four-hour coverage. Almost all major newspapers were featuring articles about it. I soon became concerned.

Roger Hedgecock, a freelance writer for *World Net Daily*, and Stephen Gordon, a writer for the *Liberty Papers*, were credited with breaking the story. Within a day, the story was picked up by the lunatic fringe with Alex Jones's *Info Wars* and a host of other conspiratorial-minded journalists providing their opinions.

Hedgecock is the primary source behind revealing the story of the DHS right-wing extremism report to the public.[21] During an interview with DHS assistant secretary Sean Smith, Hedgecock acknowledged receiving the report on Friday, April 10, 2009—three days after it was officially disseminated to federal, state, and local law enforcement and other government agencies.[22]

Hedgecock also wrote an article for *World Net Daily*, a small conservative media company that has generated controversy for its articles of questionable credibility, such as published stories that supported the position that President Barack Obama is not a U.S. citizen as well as other articles that questioned the truth behind the September 11 terrorist attacks.[23,24,25]

Hedgecock's article has a catchy title: "Disagree with Obama? Gov't Has Eyes on You."[26] It immediately drew interest from unsuspecting readers. The title contains the false and outlandish premise that the DHS monitored individuals and groups that "disagree with Obama."

Hedgecock attempted to paint a dark and menacing picture by quoting actual text from the report, which had been taken out of context. He made no mention of the report's scope note located on the first page in italics that provides DHS context to the type and definition of "right-wing extremism." The report's scope note also contained language about the assessment's purposes, such as "facilitate a greater understanding of the phenomenon of violent radicalization in the United States" and to provide information to "law enforcement officials so they may effectively deter, prevent, preempt, or respond to terrorist attacks against the United States."[27]

Furthermore, the key findings section elaborates on the types of "right-wing extremists" about whom the DHS report is concerned. Terms such as "domestic right-wing terrorists"; "acts of violence"; "threats"; "violent antigovernment groups"; "confrontations"; "attack planning"; "violent acts"; "terrorist groups"; "Oklahoma City bombing"; "lone wolf extremists capable of carrying out violent attacks"; "violence against the government"; and "boost their violent capabilities" make it very clear to whom DHS is referring when the term "right-wing extremism" is used.[28] It is apparent that Roger Hedgecock either forgot to read the report's scope note and key findings (the first two and half pages of the document) or deliberately chose to ignore them.

After extracting some of the report's more ambiguous language, such as the definition of right-wing extremism, Hedgecock went on the attack. His primary argument focused on potential extremist recruitment of military veterans. "Most disgusting of all, it [the DHS right-wing extremism report] targets veterans for increased law enforcement scrutiny . . . . What's the evidence for this? None," he says.[29]

Hedgecock launched into another outburst, stating, "The assessment admits that membership in 'right-wing extremist' groups is in decline and asserts that no increase in such violence has been detected."[30] The report does not say "membership in right-wing extremist groups is in decline." Again, the report's key findings section contains phrases including "rightwing extremists may be gaining new recruits"; right-wing extremist groups "are focusing their efforts to recruit new members, mobilize existing supporters, and broaden their scope and appeal"; and that proposed firearms restrictions and weapons bans would likely "attract new members into the ranks of rightwing extremist groups."[31] Such statements hardly hint at a declining membership. Language in the report predicts an anticipated rise in violence, so of course "no increase in such violence has been detected." The report accurately predicted a rise in right-wing extremism violence, which was manifested during the course of the year following the report's release. This increase in right-wing extremism violence has remained consistent. The country may have yet to see the worst of it.

Hedgecock lobbed another accusation, stating, "This report smacks of profiling and harassing American citizens based on their political views, and specifically based on their opposition to the Obama administration's proposals."[32] This statement is absurd and not true.

"Under Obama, 'Homeland Security' has become an instrument of oppression of opposing points of view," Hedgecock alleged.[33]

In contrast, Stephen Gordon's article for the *Liberty Papers* was poorly written and less sophisticated than Hedgecock's piece. It appeared under the headline "Homeland Security Document Targets Most Conservatives and Libertarians in the Country."[34] A caption under a photo of an alleged Tea Party gathering cited "Thousands of racists and terrorists rally at Cincinnati Tea Party."[35] It was an interesting and sensational headline, but misleading and shoddy journalism, because the DHS report never used either term anywhere in the entire document.

Gordon's article was over the top. Much like Hedgecock's insinuations, Gordon took statements from the DHS report completely out of context. For example, Gordon stated, "According to this new Homeland Security report, all it takes to fit the terrorist profile is to have general anti-government feelings or prefer local/state government to federal control over everything."[36] The report neither said nor implied this. Gordon took the DHS definition of a right-wing extremist found in the footnote of the report's second page completely out of context. The report made clear that DHS is concerned about violent antigovernment groups and potential terrorists. Gordon even weaved the misleading thought that this definition somehow equates to a "terrorist profile," although DHS was attempting to provide a definition for clarity purposes. Perhaps the definition was poorly worded and too vague. In hindsight, the definition of right-wing extremist should have incorporated the aspects of supporting, endorsing, and conducting criminal acts and violence.

Gordon's report made sweeping judgments and utterly false allegations, such as veterans being "targeted" in the report. The report clearly stated that an "extremist will attempt to recruit and radicalize returning veterans in order to exploit their skills and knowledge derived from military training and combat."[37] Also, "The willingness of a small percentage of military personnel to join extremist groups during the 1990s because they were disgruntled, disillusioned or suffering from the psychological effects of war is being replicated today."[38] The report never stated that veterans are being targeted by the government as Gordon's statement implies. Nevertheless, DHS and various law enforcement agencies have a legitimate concern about military personnel and war veterans who have joined extremist groups. These individuals have been known to teach other extremists the art of lethal hand-to-hand combat techniques, weapons proficiency, construction of improvised explosive devices, surveillance and countersurveillance skills, and other types of terrorist tradecraft.

Gordon's article also made misleading statements implying that the DHS views individuals opposing "restrictions to their Second Amendment rights, and those concerned about the loss of U.S. sovereignty" as "racist as well as a potential terrorism suspects."[39] Stephen Gordon's approach to journalism is absurd and nothing less than political manure meant for mudslinging.

On April 13, 2010, Alex Jones's *Info Wars*, an alternative news network marketed to right-wing extremists, posted a story titled "Secret DHS Doc Predicts Violence in Response to New Gun Restrictions." Jones is a far-right radio shock jock who pedals antigovernment conspiracy theories and right-wing extremist propaganda for profit. In response to the DHS report's leak, *Info Wars* reportedly "called the numbers listed on the document and validated its authenticity." *Info Wars* admitted to contacting the "watch captain at the Department of Homeland Security's National Infrastructure Coordinating Center, who confirmed the product number on the document as legitimate but would not comment further." *Info Wars* said that their "call to the FBI went unanswered."[40]

As usual, Alex Jones and his *Info Wars* extremist propaganda machine took Hedgecock's and Gordon's opinions about the DHS report to an entirely new level—one of conspiracy rhetoric, disinformation, mischaracterizations, and delusional paranoia.

The *Info Wars* article asserted that the "DHS wanted the document to remain secret but it was leaked, probably by 'authorized security personnel' in local law enforcement."[41] *Info Wars* further commented that "the authors of the document drag out all of the old 'rightwing' bugaboos, most notably the 1995 Oklahoma City bombing."[42] *Info Wars* believed "the tone of the document indicates that the government plans to impose restrictions on the ownership of firearms. In addition, the document warns local law enforcement that 'rightwing terrorists' will violently resist any attempt to register or confiscate guns."[43]

"The document is designed primarily to *radicalize* [emphasis added] local law enforcement and convince individual police officers that citizens opposed to violations of the Second Amendment, draconian gun legislation (including registration and ammunition tracking schemes) and illegal immigration are terrorists capable of committing acts of violence against them. It is a cynical effort to increase the tension between police and the community at large, especially members of the community that exercise the Second Amendment and oppose open border policies," *Info Wars* claimed.[44]

"In addition, the document equates opposition to the policies of Barack Obama to racism. Opposition to 'a range of issues, including immigration and citizenship, the expansion of social programs to minorities, and restrictions on firearms ownership and use' is characterized as exploiting 'racial and political prejudices.'"[45]

"Obviously, the document is part of a larger campaign by the government to circumvent legitimate political activism and characterize such activity as the behavior of a violent minority of terrorists. It is noteworthy that several issues of concern to our rulers—namely firearm possession and the effort to flood the country with lower paid workers and thus undermine the middle class—are highlighted in this until now secret and restricted document."[46]

The following day, Roger Hedgecock continued his criticism of the DHS report by hosting on his radio show Sean Smith, assistant secretary for public affairs at DHS. Smith is the principal staff advisor and assistant to the secretary and deputy secretary of homeland security for public affairs, internal communications, and all aspects of media relations and communications issues.[47] His office also coordinates the media relations units of all DHS component organizations.[48]

Smith has more than fifteen years of private-sector experience in the area of public affairs and has worked in a variety of senior communications positions both on campaigns and in the private sector. In 2008, Smith served as Pennsylvania communications director of the Obama-Biden campaign.[49] He holds a master of public administration degree from Harvard's John F. Kennedy School of Government.[50]

Given Smith's exhaustive public-relations experience and prestigious background, I had hoped that he would defend my report, support the Office of Intelligence and Analysis (I&A), and defend the department's mission space. To my great disappointment, he consistently faltered during the interview—providing inappropriate responses and lack of familiarity with the topic of discussion. Many of his answers reflected a lack of preparation, candor, and familiarity with the department's wide range of missions, specifically that of I&A and its counterradicalization responsibilities.

"So, tell me . . . tell me about this report. I mean, how long was this in the preparation? Is this a Bush Administration thing or has it been prepared since Obama got in?" Hedgecock began.[53]

"No. It was prepared initially in the previous administration. They tell me that it had been in the works for about a year," Smith responded. "Obviously, it was updated and written to be current. But it had been in the works for about a year. And it's frankly one of an ongoing series of assessments that our intelligence analysis unit produces on an ongoing basis looking at current threats, potential threats, and then they share those assessments with state and local law enforcement officials across the country."[54]

When Hedgecock asked for clarification,[55] Smith confirmed the report was indeed one in a series of assessments. Smith had no idea that he was walking into a trap.

"Has any been done on MS-13 or the Mexican Narco Wars?"[56] Hedgecock asked. He likely knew that Smith would have no idea whether an assessment had been done on this topic because it had nothing to do with the topic being discussed—the DHS right-wing extremism report.

Smith, not knowing the real answer, attempted to evade the question by responding that DHS routinely looks at the situation in Mexico and along the southern border. He cited DHS secretary Janet Napolitano's visit to a San Diego border checkpoint near Otay Mesa a few days earlier as evidence that DHS is concerned about the threat from drug cartels operating in Mexico.[57]

Hedgecock realized that his question was not completely answered and then attempted to exploit Smith's perceived lack of familiarity with the question. Hedgecock then asked Smith again about MS-13.

Surprisingly, Smith replied that he was unfamiliar with the term "MS-13."[59] I couldn't believe what I was hearing. A DHS high-ranking official had just publicly acknowledged his ignorance of one of the most notoriously dangerous gangs in America. DHS components had been deeply involved in law enforcement operations against this group, yet a departmental leader had no clue this group existed—let alone the department's role in combating it.

This admission was embarrassing for a department that is charged with enforcing illegal immigration laws, combating criminal activity by Central American gang members in the United States, and securing the homeland's southern border. How could anyone at DHS not know about Mara Salvatrucha 13 (MS-13)—a violent El Salvadoran street gang that is prevalent in many areas of the country, including metropolitan Washington, D.C., where DHS headquarters is located?

Hedgecock flippantly responded to Smith's ignorance, "Okay. That's the Salvadoran gang that has a hundred thousand members in the United States . . . according to the FBI."[60]

Smith must have been stunned by what he had just heard. His response was to agree with Hedgecock and state that the DOJ and FBI most likely were working on the issue.[61]

Likely sensing that he had gained the upper hand in the conversation, Hedgecock began to set his political trap. Hedgecock asked Smith whether Secretary Napolitano was shown the DHS right-wing report and, if so, did she endorse it?[62]

Smith responded, "She did not see this. This is something, again, that is done by the I&A—the Intelligence and Analysis Division within the Department of Homeland Security. Their job, like folks at the FBI, like folks at CIA, like folks at the National Security Agency, is to analyze intelligence that comes in. And then to sort it, to make sense of it, and to prepare in some cases instruments like this and to move it out."[63] He again concluded his statement by emphasizing that Napolitano "was not aware of this document."[64]

Hedgecock countered by asking whether the report went to state and local law enforcement—implying that Secretary Napolitano must be incompetent if she didn't review the assessment. He later asked whether the report went out without her knowing about it.[65]

Smith snickered and remarked, "I think you had it before she saw a copy of it."[66] Smith and Hedgecock both laughed briefly.

"That's not good news, by the way," Hedgecock replied.[67]

Backpedaling, Smith attempted a more serious answer, "Well, you know, she . . . look, she is briefed on these topics. She has a daily intelligence briefing that she gets every day, every morning. It's the same briefing that the president gets, but hers is tailored by DHS briefers and she was briefed on this topic, but she does not have a schedule of when these particular products go out the door to the law enforcement."[68]

Hedgecock wasted no time in taking another jab.

"Now, Mr. Smith, this thing is a broad brush. Here's the first page. 'Right-wing extremism in the United States,' I'm quoting now, 'could include groups and individuals that are dedicated to a single issue such as opposition to abortion or immigration.' Now, to people who are opposed to abortion or illegal immigration, this seems like a broad brush to label them because of their political opinion on an issue that is before Congress—both of those issues are perennially before Congress—as 'right-wing extremists.' Isn't this a broad brush?"[69]

Rather than explain the context of the definition within the paper's scope note, Smith agreed with his host, stating that parts of the assessment were poorly written.[70]

I was offended by Smith's characterization that the paper was "very poorly written." I knew great care had been taken with the wording, the phrasing, and the key judgments. The paper had numerous edits from at least four different editors and had been reviewed by several others, including managers and attorneys.

Hedgecock seemed perplexed by Smith's answer and reminded him that the assessment had been in the works for a year.[71]

Smith likely sensed another political snare, so he reverted to a defensive strategy attempting to absolve himself and the entire Public Affairs Office at DHS from having any role in drafting the report.

"Well, again, the material that was in it has been something they've been compiling and looking at. But, you know, these are reports that don't come up to the public affairs shop. They're not scrubbed by our copy editors—by any means. And I do think there was some language in this document that was unfortunate," Smith said.[72]

After this lame attempt to cover himself and those of his subordinates on public radio, Smith then contradicted himself by attempting to support the department and its counterradicalization mission.

"But look," Smith began, "the gist of the instrument in the assessments is that we are going to be vigilant as we look at violent extremists of any political persuasion or of any, you know, origin. Our job is to protect this country and to look at all threats. We don't have the luxury of picking and choosing. If there's something out there that is raising people's antennas, we're going to sound an alarm."[73]

Hedgecock was clearly not satisfied with Smith's answer. So he asked a politically charged question.

"Well, let me ask you, was there one done on left-wing extremism?" Hedgecock asked.[74]

Smith responded by indicating that one had, indeed, been done. The report entitled "Left-wing Extremism Likely to Increase Use of Cyber Attacks Over the Coming Decade," was published a few months earlier on January 26, 2009. That assessment had not been leaked.[75]

Hedgecock attempted to recover from the unexpected answer. The department was not playing partisan politics when it used the term "right-wing extremism." Hedgecock and his supporters had not anticipated this fact.

Hedgecock abruptly steered the topic away from right-wing versus left-wing extremism and tried to recover, "Well, I'd love to hear/see that one to see if it's the same sort of broad brush."[76] He then brought up another big issue—the report's statements concerning military veterans.

"This one [report] seems to think that returning veterans are going to be fodder for these right-wing extremists, even though the first page of this key finding page says there is no specific information that domestic right-wing terrorists are currently planning acts of violence," Hedgecock stated.[77]

Smith should have challenged Hedgecock on this statement, because he readily acknowledged on the air that the DHS report is talking about "domestic right-wing terrorism" and "violence." Yet Smith offered no rebuttal.

Hedgecock commented that militia membership was going down and alluded to it having been stated in the report.[78] The report did not state that the number of militias is going down. In actuality, militia membership had waned during the latter half of the 1990s and into the new millennium, but experienced a recent resurgence in 2008, 2009, and into 2010. Hedgecock then asked about veterans.[79]

Assistant Secretary Smith had a prepared response to this question, but Smith lacked the knowledge and expertise necessary to provide a thorough answer. Acknowledged subject matter experts at I&A were never consulted to provide input to the DHS media response. Smith's response initially started out well, but soon fell flat. He referenced the Oklahoma City bombing and the role played by Timothy McVeigh, a veteran.

Hedgecock quickly countered Smith with something that should have been obvious. He asked whether McVeigh could be classified a right-wing extremist. Smith said he wasn't sure whether McVeigh was.[82]

"Well, that is your example. I mean, your example is Tim McVeigh, and if he's not a right-wing extremist, then I don't know how this holds up. Plus, not to mention, there are 42 million people in this country who are veterans of the armed services," Hedgecock argued.[83]

Since he lacked a thorough understanding of the subject, Smith had nowhere to go but revert to defending the department's view of veterans.

"It's by no means that this department or this secretary diminishes the veterans who serve this country who come back and continue to serve this country proudly and honorably," Smith refuted.[84] But then he tripped over himself again with his next statement.

"But, at times, in fact the secretary was just at Walter Reed last week administering a naturalization ceremony of an Iraqi War veteran," Smith exclaimed.[85] I'm sure this statement did not appease Hedgecock or his listeners, who are vehemently anti-immigration and lament the department's handling of this issue. In fact, Hedgecock's own website harps on the issue of illegal immigration. He even had a defense fund set up for two border patrol agents who were charged with the wrongful shooting of an illegal immigrant. Smith probably had no idea with whom he was interviewing.

Refocusing his remarks, Smith again attempted to defend the department's mission to protect the country against terrorism.

"Look, Timothy McVeigh, as tragic an example as that [the bombing] was, sometimes intelligence officers are trained to look at past examples of threats that materialize and keep a close eye on those types of individuals, you know, who are driven to those kinds of actions," Smith stated.[86]

Hedgecock used Smith's statement again, making an issue of left versus right. Hedgecock stated that the Unabomber could be characterized as a left-wing extremist college professor.

Smith agreed and added additional examples of extremists such as environmental extremists and animal rights groups that had also been referenced in DHS assessments.[90]

Hedgecock then changed the subject.[91] "Look, does the secretary or the department believe that people who hold Second Amendment views consistent with the Supreme Court that it is a personal right of Americans to keep and bear arms are right-wing extremists?" he inquired.[92] Smith responded confidently. "No. And I want to point out that when she was on the border just recently in San Diego, she was asked if—and the purpose of her visit was to talk about things the U.S. can do to help stem the violence that is happening down in Mexico and to prevent a spillover into the United States side. And she was asked, does this mean you support the reauthorization of the assault weapons ban, and she said no. Because that's not something that we need to be looking at right now. We have enough tools. We have enough laws on the books right now. And we need to do what we can with the laws that are on the books."[93]

Realizing that Smith was prepared for the issue of gun control, Hedgecock switched the topic again—this time to the Tea Party movement.

Unbeknownst to me and other domestic terrorism analysts at DHS, there was a grassroots movement afoot to regain voters' confidence in the Republican Party and its platform. The movement had named itself after the Boston Tea Party. I had no idea the Tea Party had planned numerous rallies across America on the weekend my report on the rising threat from right-wing extremists was disseminated to law enforcement. It was unfortunate timing, because the paper's release gave the appearance that the DHS was concerned with conservative political activism. In reality, I had no knowledge of the Tea Party movement, nor was DHS interested in monitoring it.

Hedgecock closed the interview with a series of questions that seemed similar to an interrogation. I suspect he may have been reading from a list of questions from his listeners.

Hedgecock asked whether DHS was video recording or watching members of the Tea Party.[94]

Rather than stating emphatically, "no," the assistant secretary for public affairs provided the worst possible answer. "I can't speak to the sort of things that are law enforcement sensitive. So I can't speak to any current law enforcement operations," he said.[95] This comment was completely wrong. DHS was never interested in monitoring the Tea Party movement's rallies or other activities.

"Does the department consider the organizers of Tea Parties right-wing extremists?" Hedgecock demanded.[96]

Again, Smith provided another very weak and confusing answer: "I couldn't answer that."[97]

Hedgecock shot off another politically loaded question.

"Does the department consider people who are opposed to illegal immigration, as this footnote seems to say, right-wing extremists?"[98]

Finally, Smith gave an accurate answer. "No."[99]

"Is this report going to be withdrawn and redone?" Hedgecock asked unexpectedly.[100] I was very interested in knowing whether Smith had any "inside" information from DHS leadership about a product recall.

Smith provided a vague answer: "I think that this report, you know, we may not have seen the last of it. I'll say that."[101]

Hedgecock summarized his main assertions and recapped his main point about veterans.

"Because, in other words, when I said Unabomber and all, other than Tim McVeigh, you know, in this report there are no names. There are no names of groups. I don't really know who you're talking about. I mean, are you talking about, you know, the VFW [Veterans of Foreign Wars], or are you talking about the Ku Klux Klan? It's not really clear."[102]

Smith uttered a one-word response: "Right."[103] It was as though Smith had been verbally beaten into a stupor, seemingly agreeing with Hedgecock's opposing views.

Hedgecock concluded by indicating the report was unclear and poorly written.[104] Smith only provided a nervous laugh in response to the remark, which came across as being in agreement with Hedgecock's assessment of the report.

Sensing Smith's acknowledgement, Hedgecock inquired, "You know what I'm saying?"[105]

"Yeah, and I share some of your, you know, frustration with this document," Smith lamented.[106]

"So, is it going to be withdrawn or not? Or, do you know?" Hedgecock again asked.[107]

Not knowing the answer, Smith said, "I don't think that we're saying that at this point."[108]

Again, not satisfied with the response, Hedgecock reemphasized his point.

"Okay, so, in other words, it stands and it has been sent to all law enforcement agencies in this country—state, federal, local, and tribal."[109]

"Yes," Smith confirmed.[110]

Hedgecock's interview of Sean Smith soon concluded. I was very disappointed with what I had heard.

On the day of Hedgecock's interview with Sean Smith, the White House also made a brief statement about the report, perhaps in response to the media firestorm that ensued as a result of Hedgecock's original article.

"The president is focused not on politics but rather taking the steps necessary to protect all Americans from the threat of violence and terrorism regardless of its origins. He also believes those who serve represent the best of this country, and he will continue to ensure that our veterans receive the respect and benefits they have earned," said Nick Shapiro, a White House spokesman.[111]

During all of the media hype, I often wondered to myself, "Why did this happen?" and "What type of person would do this to the department?" and "Did I know the person responsible?" These questions haunted me for days. Then something happened that may provide an answer to these questions. A possible clue unexpectedly popped up on the Internet and, of all places, on the Oath Keepers website.

On May 11, 2009, at 2:36 p.m., an anonymous message appeared on the Oath Keepers blog forum.[112] The message was reportedly from a law enforcement officer working for the Department of Homeland Security, and he wanted to make his presence known in response to the media spectacle surrounding the leaked DHS report.

DHS has several law enforcement agencies under its organization structure, including the Federal Protective Service (FPS), U.S. Secret Service (USSS), Immigration and Customs Enforcement (ICE), and Customs and Border Protection (CBP), which includes the Border Patrol and the U.S. Coast Guard, as well as other agencies.

The anonymous message could have been sent from anybody working for any federal, state, or local government agency anywhere in the country. A gut feeling assured me that this was likely authentic—at least the DHS part of it. Nevertheless, I remain a bit skeptical that a law enforcement officer was responsible for leaking the assessment.

An unnamed individual began the anonymous message, "I am a law enforcement officer and have worked in numerous law enforcement agencies in the last many years beginning with the military. I have taken my oath to this country many times. I have also realized that we have had many 'domestic enemies' over the years."[113]

He further stated, "It was recently asked of me because of my current position, what I was going to do if the federal government begins to make illegal moves against its citizenry. Its [sic] something that all law enforcement must ask themselves. I do know the difference between a 'lawful order' and an 'unlawful order.'"[114]

"Finding this site with your videos and reading your mission statement goes along with what I've been feeling for some time. I anticipate that many states will take the appropriate action as outlined in the 10th Amendment. Until then, we wait for 'the unforgiveable line to be crossed,'" the unknown individual wrote.[115]

He concluded his secretive communication. "I'm in a more precarious position than some of the other law enforcement officers as I work for the Department of Homeland Security. That is why I must remain anonymous. Know that there are many like us that believe that the Constitution is the supreme law of the land and we'll do whatever it takes to ensure it remains intact."[116]

The clandestine message was signed, "Anonymous DHS officer."[117]

Stewart Rhodes, founder of the Oath Keepers, decided to post an immediate reply to the anonymous message from an alleged DHS law enforcement officer. His comments to the anonymous message provide insight into the group's true motivation and purposes—to infiltrate government and to intercept and release sensitive government information to the public.

He addressed his comments "To the anonymous DHS officer: Thank you sir! It is good to hear additional confirmation that there are many federal officers who do see the dangerous road we are now on, who understand how our Republic is being subverted from within the government, who remember their oath, and who do have their personal lines in the sand figured out. As word about Oath Keepers spreads, we are hearing from more and more federal officers all the time."[118]

Rhodes directed a comment to other Oath Keepers and others who visit the group's blog forum. "To our readers: Some of you may be tempted to be hard on this anonymous officer from within DHS. For example, you might think DHS itself is unconstitutional and this officer should just resign (as I slyly suggested the agents of the BATFE [sic] should do during my speech [sic] at Lexington). I advise you to hold your fire," he cautioned.[119]

Rhodes further added, "First of all, remember that DHS swallowed up many other agencies and there were many lateral transfers. For example, one of my best friends started out as a border patrol agent, then moved to U.S. Customs on the border, and then that was absorbed into I.C.E. so now he officially works for I.C.E. though he is still a customs agent. So, who can say how this man ended up in DHS?[120]

"Secondly, the restoration of our Constitutional Republic will take time and will not take place overnight. Please don't make a mistake similar to one that many Libertarian idealists make of wanting to run around condemning everyone who is in government employment (suggesting that all police and military service members should just resign). Whatever you think of any given federal agency or federal 'law enforcement' position, it is obviously good to have officers who do see there is a problem and who are willing to take a stand on some very important lines in the sand," Rhodes wrote.[121]

He counseled Oath Keepers and their supporters, "Remember, our declaration of orders we will not obey is meant to prevent the very worst from happening, so we will not have a full-blown dictatorship in this country and can right things by means of peaceful reform. That is the whole point of Oath Keepers. We are in constitutional triage. That's why our declaration does not include statements that such and such agency should not exist, or go into minutia of the many thousands of unconstitutional government laws and actions. Let's focus on the really big stuff—the stuff that could lead to another Revolution. Let's focus on making that unnecessary so we can have a peaceful restoration. This officer is letting us know he and others within DHS have lines they will not cross. That is damn good to know!"[122]

"Third, it's men like this on the inside who can and do provide information to expose what is going on. The MIAC report was leaked by a Missouri police officer who happened to be a Ron Paul supporter and was ticked about being labeled a potential terrorist. *And I have it on good information that both the DHS report that smeared veterans and the DHS Extremist Lexicon were leaked by a federal officer who was outraged at their contents* [emphasis added]. Such men deserve our thanks," Rhodes boasted.[123]

The Missouri Information Analysis Center (MIAC) is a state fusion center located in Jefferson City, Missouri. In March 2009, the MIAC disseminated an intelligence assessment to state and local law enforcement in Missouri concerning the militia movement. This assessment was also subsequently leaked to the public and media. It generated quite a bit of criticism over ill-advised statements in the report concerning supporters of third-party political candidates like Ron Paul, Chuck Baldwin, and Bob Barr, as well as comments regarding politically oriented bumper stickers.[124]

The Oath Keepers founder further proclaimed, "And I suspect we will be hearing from many more federal officers now that the elites are smearing veterans en masse as potential 'terrorists' and 'extremists' and now that just about anyone with even mildly conservative or libertarian views is likewise being added to the lists of potential enemies of the elite—er [sic], I mean the state. The more citizens they try to smear and marginalize, the more military and police will have their eyes opened."[125]

Stewart Rhodes concluded his message with the remark, "And besides, now we can add a DHS patch to our display of patches that shows that there are 'Oath Keepers among them.' That ought to get a few panties in a wad. Good fun!"[126]

The Oath Keepers had basically issued a claim of responsibility for leaking the DHS report, much like a terrorist organization would issue a media statement claiming credit for an attack. In reply, the Oath Keepers organization is not a terrorist group, but rather an incubator for antigovernment sentiment, conspiracy theories, and extremist radicalization and potential counterintelligence threat.

In fact, a few Oath Keepers members have been arrested for various criminal violations. Charles A. Dyer, a former U.S. Marine who served in Iraq, was arrested on January 12, 2010, and charged with the alleged rape of a seven-year-old girl.[127] At the time of his arrest, authorities found a stolen M-203 grenade launcher in Dyer's home in Marlowe, Oklahoma.[128] Investigators from the Bureau of Alcohol, Tobacco, Firearms, and Explosives traced the firearm's serial number back to an M-203 reported stolen from a U.S. Marines base in California.[129] Dyer, who used the online moniker of "July 4 Patriot," was a notorious militia figure who posted inflammatory antigovernment videos on YouTube calling for the violent overthrow of the U.S. government.[130]

In one video, Dyer made reference to the April 2009 DHS report on right-wing extremism, stating, "With DHS blatantly calling patriots, veterans, and constitutionalists a threat, all that I have to say is you're damn right we're a threat. We're a threat to anyone that endangers our rights and the Constitution of this republic."[131] Dyer also invites supporters and viewers of his videos to join him at his makeshift training area—"I'm sure the DHS will call it a terrorist training camp."[132]

Charles Dyer reportedly attended the Oath Keepers rally in Lexington, Massachusetts, on April 19, 2009.[133] Oath Keepers founder Stewart Rhodes allegedly admitted that he considered Dyer for a position in the group but later reconsidered.[134] At the time of Dyer's arrest, Rhodes was quick to dismiss any association Dyer had with the Oath Keepers.[135] He did this despite the fact that he had posted some of Dyer's videos on the Oath Keepers website as well as provided commentary to them.[136] Dyer's videos were removed from the Oath Keepers website soon after his arrest.[137,138,139]

Matthew Fairfield was a local leader for the Oath Keepers chapter in Cuyahoga County, Ohio. He was arraigned on April 13, 2010, on twenty-eight counts of unlawful possession of explosives and twenty-five counts of receiving stolen property.[140] Authorities searched Fairfield's home in North Olmsted on April 12, 2010, and found a crate full of explosive devices in the garage.[141] Authorities also seized detonators, detonator cord, two M-4 assault rifles, a .12-gauge pump shotgun, two semiautomatic handguns, and a .22 bolt-action rifle from a second location linked to Fairfield in Cleveland.[142]

Fairfield had been on probation for carrying a concealed weapon without a license at the Cuyahoga County Fair in Berea.[143] In February 2010, he was sentenced to two years of probation for the offense.[144] Fairfield was also a practicing sovereign citizen who was under investigation for participating in a mortgage debt elimination scheme.[145]

A third Oath Keeper was arrested after a traffic stop on April 20, 2010, in Madisonville, Tennessee.[146] Darren Huff, whose black truck was emblazoned with "Oath Keepers" decals on both door panels, was charged with traveling in interstate commerce with intent to incite a riot and transporting in interstate commerce a firearm in furtherance of civil disorder.[147] The FBI filed a criminal complaint explaining that Huff traveled to Tennessee with a pistol on his hip and an assault rifle in his truck, intent on carrying out the arrests of twenty-four federal, state, and local officials in an attempt to forestall the trial of Walter Francis Fitzpatrick, who was in custody for attempting a citizen's arrest of a grand jury foreman on April 1, 2010.[148] Fitzpatrick had unsuccessfully attempted to convince a grand jury to indict President Barack Obama on charges of treason.[149] During the incident, Fitzpatrick was charged with disorderly conduct, inciting to riot, disrupting a meeting, and resisting arrest.[150]

The FBI believed that Huff didn't want Fitzpatrick to go to trial on the aforementioned charges. As part of its case, the FBI interviewed a bank manager who said that Huff had told him on April 15, 2010, that Fitzpatrick had been arrested under false pretenses.[151] Huff reportedly admitted to being a member of the Georgia militia and allegedly stated that he, and nine or so other militia members, was headed to Madisonville, Tennessee, to "take over the city."[152] Huff also reportedly bragged to the bank manager that he would see the results of Huff's action on the news.[153]

Officers with the Tennessee State Police stopped Huff along a highway in Sweetwater, Tennessee, on April 20, 2010, for traffic violations.[154] During the traffic stop, Huff reportedly stated that he was ready to die for his rights and what he believed in and that he would not consent to a search of his truck.[155] Upon release, Huff then recorded a radio broadcast about the traffic stop, admitting that he had a loaded assault rifle and ammunition in his truck at the time of the incident.[156] As a result, the FBI made the determination that Huff had both the intent and the means to carry out his plan of action that day.[157]

The Oath Keepers appeared to be a growing problem in 2009, but I had little time to focus on their questionable activities. Congress was holding a preliminary hearing about the leaked assessment. And I&A management heard about a draft resolution being prepared by the U.S. House of Representatives mandating that all documentation related to the tasking, drafting, and coordinating of the report must be turned over for further examination.

By May 19, 2009, the Committee on Homeland Security had held a preliminary hearing concerning the DHS right-wing extremism report and considered drafting House Resolution 404 (H.R. 404).[158] Committee members ordered the draft measure reported to the U.S. House of Representatives with a favorable recommendation, as amended, by voice vote. On June 4, 2009, committee chairman Bennie G. Thompson (D-Mississippi) approved the official language of H.R. 404 and referred it to the House calendar to be ordered to be printed.[159]

The measure stated that "the Republican Members of the Committee on Homeland Security ("Committee") are pleased that the Committee reported favorably (as amended) to the full House H.R. 404, the Resolution of Inquiry. We appreciate this nearly unprecedented display of cooperation on a Resolution of Inquiry, and we commend the Majority for their support."[160]

"The Committee on Homeland Security, to whom was referred the resolution (H.R. 404) directing the Secretary of Homeland Security to transmit to the House of Representatives, not later than 14 days after the date of the adoption of this resolution, copies of documents relating to the Department of Homeland Security Intelligence Assessment titled, 'Rightwing Extremism: Current Economic and Political Climate Fueling Resurgence in Radicalization and Recruitment,' having considered the same, report favorably thereon with an amendment and recommend that the resolution as amended be agreed to."[161]

"It is critical the Committee conduct a bipartisan inquiry into the process within the Department of Homeland Security that led to the development and release of the report, as well as what steps have been taken to ensure a similar intra-departmental breakdown does not occur again. Therefore, Committee Republicans, joined by the House Republican Leadership, introduced the Resolution of Inquiry because of the seriousness of the issue and the need for answers."[162]

(1) "all source materials used in the drafting of that Intelligence Assessment;"[163]

(2) "written material reflecting when the research and writing of that Intelligence Assessment began;"[164]

(3) "a written description of the clearance process for that Intelligence Assessment and all other Office of Intelligence and Analysis-generated products that were produced for and disseminated to state, local, and tribal law enforcement agencies prior to April 20, 2009;"[165]

(4) "any written opinions or guidance produced by the Department of Homeland Security Office for Civil Rights and Civil Liberties for the Office of Intelligence and Analysis on production and dissemination of assessments to state, local, and tribal law enforcement prior to April 20, 2009;"[166]

(5) "any written opinions or guidance, produced by the Department of Homeland Security Chief Privacy Officer for the Office of Intelligence and Analysis, on production and dissemination of assessments to state, local, and tribal law enforcement prior to April 20, 2009;"[167]

(6) "a written description of the clearance process for that Intelligence Assessment and all other Office of Intelligence and Analysis-generated products produced for and disseminated to state, local, and tribal law enforcement agencies since April 20, 2009;"[168]

(7) "a written description of what role, if any, the Chief Officer for Civil Rights and Civil Liberties of the Department of Homeland Security has played in the clearance

process for Office of Intelligence and Analysis-generated products produced for and disseminated to state, local, and tribal law enforcement since April 20, 2009;"[169]

(8) "a written description of what role, if any, the Department of Homeland Security Chief Privacy Officer has served in the clearance process for Office of Intelligence and Analysis-generated products produced for and disseminated to state, local, and tribal law enforcement agencies since April 20, 2009;"[170]

(9) "a written description of what role, if any, the Under Secretary for Intelligence and Analysis of the Department has played in the clearance process for Office of Intelligence and Analysis-generated intelligence products produced for and disseminated to state, local, and tribal law enforcement agencies since April 20, 2009;"[171]

(10) "the schedule of dates, if any, Office of Intelligence and Analysis employees received or will receive privacy and civil liberties training; and"[172]

(11) "any other written information on the internal controls on the clearance process for Office of Intelligence and Analysis-generated intelligence products that have been disseminated to state, local, and tribal law enforcement since April 20, 2009."[173]

"On April 14, 2009, a copy of the DHS Office of Intelligence and Analysis (I&A) report 'Rightwing Extremism: Current Economic and Political Climate Fueling Resurgence in Radicalization and Recruitment,' was leaked to the media. The Committee believes that the report, as released, raises significant privacy and civil liberties issues for many Americans—including veterans. The Committee understands that the report was distributed on a limited basis to law enforcement and was never intended to be released publicly. H.R. 404 is a resolution of inquiry into the drafting and release process for this report and any changes to how DHS drafts, clears, and releases products generated by I&A for distribution to state, local, and tribal law enforcement."[174]

"We believe that this is the only way to fully explore how this report was created and what new procedures are in place to ensure that a similar breakdown does not happen again. We, therefore, thank the Majority for their bipartisan support in favorably reporting this critical resolution, and we look forward to working with the Majority to ensure that this resolution is considered by the full House and the Department fully complies with its provisions."[175]

Signed
Peter T. King (R-NY)
Ranking Member
Mark Souder (R-IN)
Mike Rogers (R-MI)
Charles W. Dent (R-PA)
Paul C. Broun (R-GA)
Pete Olson (R-TX)
Steve Austria (R-OH)
Lamar Smith (R-TX)
Daniel E. Lungren (R-CA)
Michael T. McCaul (R-TX)

Gus M. Bilirakis (R-FL)

Candice S. Miller (R-MI)

Anh "Joseph" Cao (R-LA)

With the passage of H.R. 404, there would likely be congressional testimony or possible congressional hearings on the subject. I could not dwell on the possibility. I had a lot of work to do. There were numerous Freedom of Information Act (FOIA) requests coming in from across the country, and letters from various senators and congressmen demanding answers. I would likely play a significant role in responding to and answering the many inquiries, as well as the eleven points raised in H.R. 404. After all, I had authored the report and retained most of the documentation related to its inception. As I had anticipated, I&A management soon requested that I assist with compiling, organizing, and presenting the necessary materials to Congress as well as help with responding to the FOIA requests and congressional letters of concern.

2

Developing Interests

On May 12, 2009, the House Appropriations Committee held a hearing at the U.S. Capitol concerning the Department of Homeland Security's (DHS) budget.[1] It had been little more than a month since the leak of the DHS right-wing extremism report. Congressman Mark Kirk (R-Illinois) abruptly shifted the discussion away from the department's budget and inquired of DHS secretary Janet Napolitano.

"I want to ask a couple of questions. One, this report—this extremist report . . . let me ask specifically, who in the Extremism and Radicalization Branch of the Homeland Environment Threat Analysis Division have you fired for this report?" Kirk demanded.

Napolitano responded, "Mr. Representative, as you know, I cannot discuss personnel matters with you, nor would it be appropriate to do that in a public committee setting . . . "

Kirk abruptly countered, "Let me interrupt you. The president just fired our commander in Afghanistan . . . a way more important person than works for you. And you can't tell us that you've taken any action whatsoever?"

Napolitano answered, "I can tell you that personnel actions are being taken, but I can also share with you that, that it's not appropriate for me to talk with you today in committee . . . These are career civil servants. Most of them have worked at the department since 9/11 . . . and they are . . . they are not . . . "

Kirk interrupted again, "So would you say the president took inappropriate action in firing a career military officer in public?"

Napolitano, visibly upset, restated, "First of all, Representative, I'm saying personnel action, appropriate personnel action has and will be taken in compliance with our nation's civil service laws. These are career civil servants."

Napolitano continued her remarks about the controversial report. Senator Kirk, seemingly somewhat satisfied with the secretary's answer, returned the committee's discussion back to the department's budget. A day earlier, at another hearing for the

House Homeland Security Subcommittee, Napolitano was asked the same question by congressman Christopher Carney (D-Pennsylvania). He wanted to know whether the person who wrote the report is "still employed." Napolitano responded, "Appropriate personnel action is being taken."

I couldn't believe what I was hearing. Congress was actually advocating that people should be fired for writing the report. This felt like an act of retaliation against me and others involved in writing it. We did nothing wrong; we were only doing our jobs.

I suspect many people were, and still are, asking themselves similar types of questions. Who wrote the DHS right-wing extremism report? What political views or values does this person embrace? Did he or she truly have an agenda as some have alleged?

Soon after the report leaked, Pat Robertson, an ultraconservative Christian media personality, speculated during an evening broadcast of the *700 Club*, "If that [sic] would have been a Republican, there would be outrage and screams for Janet Napolitano to resign immediately! . . . This [the report] is an outrage! . . . It shows that someone down in the bowels of that organization is either a convinced leftwinger [sic] or somebody whose sexual orientation is somewhat in question." His remarks were misinformed and ignorant.

My decision to write this book is twofold. First and foremost, I want to share my knowledge and expertise concerning the domestic terrorist threat. I hope to educate and warn the American people of the dangers of right-wing extremism. I also want to set the record straight concerning the DHS right-wing extremism report, dated April 7, 2009.

Hopefully, this book will serve as an accurate public accounting of the events before, during, and after the leak of this official intelligence report. It is my hope that this book will help change and ultimately reverse the negative opinions of those who listened to and believed the ill-advised media and congressional criticism. It is my opinion that some media personalities and members of Congress willfully directed and inspired others toward extremism. They did this through the creation of an imaginary enemy, which generated hysteria and paranoia among the U.S. population. Those responsible for the fabrication of this campaign of deceit used the DHS right-wing extremism report to further their own agendas. They fabricated possible reasons for why the report was written. They took things out of context and questioned the facts supporting it. I am confident that the truth will, in the end, counter and deter the potential radicalization of conservatives toward extremism, thus preventing potential criminal acts.

The DHS report was unfairly portrayed as a poorly researched, inaccurate, and politically motivated report that demonized many Americans, including conservatives, gun owners, Christians, and the Republican Party. Since I wrote the report, I know these accusations are far from the truth. DHS leadership even characterized the report as an unauthorized, improperly vetted, and far-reaching assessment written by a "rogue" element within the Office of Intelligence and Analysis. Again, these statements are a gross misrepresentation of the facts. This book sheds light on the truth by refuting media charges, dismissing public fears, resolving congressional concerns, and exposing the truth behind this misunderstood and controversial report.

Both the DHS and I were completely caught off guard when so many conservatives, media personalities, radio talk show hosts, and even members of Congress decided to identify themselves with the term "right-wing extremist." As noted in the report's scope, DHS is concerned only with violent extremists and potential terrorists, not law-abiding citizens, mainstream groups and their constitutionally protected beliefs.

I didn't expect mainstream media personalities, radio talk show hosts, politicians, and others to twist the facts, take statements out of context, and taint a government report with political motives in an attempt to erode public trust and instill fear among a large segment of the U.S. population. In my opinion, this was done in an effort to smear and erode confidence in a newly elected presidential administration. This behavior was nothing more than a series of political and social attacks designed to rally Republicans and conservatives against Democrats and liberals.

In order to understand the motive and intent of the DHS right-wing extremism report, you should know who wrote the report. My core values are built upon three areas: Family, Faith, and Scouting.

I've been a member of the Church of Jesus Christ of Latter-Day Saints (LDS) since I was five years old. A recent Gallup Poll conducted in January 2010 found Mormons to be the most conservative religious group in the United States.[2]

On April 19, 1987, I received my Patriarchal Blessing. This is a special prayer given to worthy members of the LDS Church by an ordained LDS Patriarch. It is a sacred, personal blessing from the Lord to an individual. The blessing is recorded, transcribed by the Patriarch, and then mailed to the recipient. A copy is also sent to the LDS Church headquarters in Salt Lake City, Utah, and kept on file there.

A Patriarchal Blessing serves multiple purposes. Mainly, it provides insight into a person's life. This may include blessings or promises, warnings about temptations or weaknesses, or counsel about how a person should live his life. It can strengthen a person's faith through the promises made known to him through the Spirit of God. LDS members who receive such a blessing are encouraged to study it carefully and regard it as personal scripture. It is an inspired and prophetic statement of a person's mission in life.

Due to the extremely sacred nature of a Patriarchal Blessing, church members are counseled to keep it personal and to share it (or portions of it) only with those whom the Lord's spirit reveals are ready to hear or read it. For these reasons, I do not share my Patriarchal Blessing with very many people. I do, however, want to share one thought from my Patriarchal Blessing. There is a statement that says I can be a powerful force for good. As I have reflected on my Patriarchal Blessing, I have gained a testimony of Heavenly Father's compassion, His deep sense of love for each of us, and His all-encompassing knowledge and magnificent nature. As I ponder the words of this special prayer, it gives me strength during difficult times and provides direction in times of need. It also gives me a clearer understanding of my purpose. Eerily, my Patriarchal Blessing was given to me when I was seventeen years old—eight years to the day of the Alfred P. Murrah Federal Building bombing in Oklahoma City, Oklahoma. I drew strength from it over twenty years later when faced with the greatest challenge of my career.

Another pillar of my core values is the Boy Scouts of America (BSA). I have been active in scouting since I was eleven years old. As a result, I have served in many youth leadership positions within the BSA as well as in adult leadership. I earned the Eagle Scout Award on my eighteenth birthday in 1987. I took me a little longer than most Eagle candidates, but I was also a "late bloomer." During the first three years of scouting, I participated primarily for the social aspects. I caught the scouting vision when I was fourteen years old.

While a Boy Scout, I was elected by my peers to represent our scout unit in the Order of the Arrow, a special scout program centered on service to others. As an adult, I have served as a scoutmaster, providing assistance and mentoring at least twelve boys as they earned their Eagle rank. I have also served as a merit badge counselor, assistant scoutmaster, and the committee chairman.

Looking back, I have had some rather unique scouting experiences that would later take on added significance as I developed my career as an intelligence analyst focusing on domestic right-wing extremism. In 1986, one of my merit badge counselors was a former U.S. Marine and also a member of the John Birch Society, an ultraconservative civic organization fearful of a communist infiltration into the U.S. government.

During our Citizenship in the Nation merit badge class, my merit badge counselor alluded to various antigovernment conspiracy theories. I didn't know at the time exactly what was behind his beliefs, but I didn't take him very seriously.

I distinctly remember his opening remarks to the merit badge class held in our church. "Who runs this county?" he adamantly asked.

"The president," said one scout.

"No," the instructor answered.

"Congress?" another scout guessed.

"Wrong answer," was his reply.

"The people?" I asked.

Our scout leader answered, "No. You're all wrong. God runs this country, and don't you forget it!" He would later invite two of my fellow scouts to attend a John Birch Society summer camp for youth with their parents' permission. At the time I didn't know that my scout leader was considered a "Mormon Constitutionalist"—a unique brand of right-wing extremism linked to LDS Church members and their religious beliefs concerning prophecies of Christ, America, and the Constitution.

This same adult leader also taught us what he believed was the "true" value of U.S. currency. He held a U.S. one-dollar bill in his hand and asked, "How much is this dollar worth?" We were told it was worth nothing. Not a dollar. Not even the worth of the paper and ink it was made of. He attempted to teach us that money was nothing but a "debtor's note" from the U.S. government stating that the government owed you that amount for your labor. He referred to the statement written on each bill of currency, "This note is legal tender for all debts, public and private," as proof of his claim. The term "legal" did not give any real value to the currency. He believed it was a lie and further explained that today's money has no intrinsic value because the United States Treasury went off the gold standard in 1934 and so the country declared bankruptcy in a sense. Therefore, the dollar bill he held in his hand was worth nothing, as was the money in our own pockets. I remember a fellow scout asking him, "So why do stores accept our money when we buy things with it?" I don't remember the counselor's answer to that question.

One of the requirements to earn the Citizenship in the Nation merit badge involved writing a letter to a congressman or senator about a local or national issue. Due to my earlier exposure to national events involving violent right-wing extremists, I decided to write to then-senator John Warner (R-Virginia) concerning the dangers of armed paramilitary groups.

I began my letter, dated October 14, 1986:

Terrorist activity has increased in recent years. With each passing week we hear about more bombings, the hijackings of planes, and kidnappings of political figures. I, as an American citizen, begin to wonder how much longer will it take until terrorism arrives in the United States? Personally, I feel it is already here in the form of small groups of armed men and women claiming to assist American citizens and their problems with military force. They are causing discomfort among the citizens of each community not to mention both local and federal law enforcement agencies. These particular situations are relating to the southern states as well as some western states. Why doesn't the federal government issue legislation forbidding the formation of these [secretive] societies?

I concluded my remarks with the following warning: *"What's the purpose behind allowing individuals to have their own personal militias? If terrorism does come to the United States, which I think it will shortly, it will either be started or contributed by such armed battalions."* Eight and a half years later, individuals affiliated with the modern militia movement would plan and carry out the deadliest terrorist attack in U.S. history prior to 9/11.

As a Mormon, I was naturally interested in the last days leading up to the second coming of Christ. The LDS Church embraces millennial concepts. Mormons have a deep belief, desire, and devotion to the return of Jesus Christ. They believe in the establishment of a "New Jerusalem" in the United States and that we are living in the "last days"—hence the term "Latter-Day Saints" in the church's name.

During my early teens, I remember browsing through a popular news magazine at a local drugstore. As I was skimming through the news articles, I came across a story about a police standoff involving a secretive, racist religious group in the Ozark Mountains of Arkansas. The group's name was Covenant, Sword, Arm of the Lord (CSA). As I read further, I felt drawn to the news article. At fourteen years old, I was a bit young to understand completely what was happening at a remote piece of property on Bull Shoals Lake. Nonetheless, the story struck a chord in me because it involved a religious group preparing for the last days. I was curious why they would stockpile weapons and explosives as well as engage in criminal activity in the name of Jesus Christ. I was interested in learning more about the incident and the types of people who would join such an extreme organization.

CSA was an apocalyptic religious community that was preparing for the end of the world.[3] They were interested in some of the same religious topics as I was, but they took it to the extremes. Members sold their homes, quit their jobs, and donated everything they had to a church. They even stockpiled food, weapons, and ammunition. They conducted paramilitary training activities amongst themselves and with other like-minded extremist groups.[4] I wondered what motivated a group of churchgoing people to such extremes. Why did they feel a compelling need for armed conflict? I wondered about the CSA's interpretation of the end of days and why this group felt they had an actual role to play in hastening it.

CSA was a religious extremist organization headquartered on approximately 224 acres of rugged, mountainous land in Marion County, Arkansas. It was also a paramilitary group. Its members subscribed to the "Christian Identity" religion, which professes the belief that God's chosen people comprise the white race, not Jews. They also believed that blacks and Asians were pre-Adamic species and likened them to "beasts of the field" that have no soul. The leader of CSA was James W. Ellison, who referred to himself as "the King of the Ozarks." Ellison claimed this title was bestowed upon him during a prophetic revelation.[5]

Law enforcement authorities eventually discovered that the CSA was stockpiling large quantities of weapons, explosives, incendiary devices, and ammunition and that group members had been involved in violent confrontations with law enforcement officers.[6] The most widely publicized incident occurred on June 30, 1984, when Richard Wayne Schnell, a reported CSA member, shot and killed Trooper Louis Bryant, an African-American Arkansas State Police officer, during a traffic stop near DeQueen, Arkansas.[7]

On April 16, 1985, federal law enforcement authorities obtained a search warrant for the CSA property.[8] Authorities had hoped to execute the search warrant in conjunction with the arrest of Jim Ellison. On April 20, 1985, the FBI and the Bureau of Alcohol, Tobacco and Firearms, assisted by Missouri and Arkansas state police, surrounded the compound and began negotiations with Ellison. Two days later, Ellison, along with two associates, surrendered without incident. Federal authorities also arrested members of The Order, a secret terrorist organization that has close ties to both the CSA and Aryan Nations in Hayden Lake, Idaho.[9]

Among the firearms seized were 94 long guns; 30 handguns; approximately 35 machine guns and sawed-off shotguns; and a heavy machine gun. Investigators also recovered a "live" light anti–tank weapon rocket; two improvised claymore mines; 25 improvised explosive devices; 40 improvised hand grenades; 320 blasting caps; 4,000 feet of detonating cord; 50 sticks of dynamite; 38 kinetic explosives; 3 1/2 blocks of C-4 plastic explosives; smoke grenades; black powder; safety fuse; military trip flares; smokeless powder; and several hundred thousand rounds of ammunition.[10] All arrests were made without incident, and no injuries were incurred by law enforcement, the defendants, or civilians at the compound site.

While I found this story very interesting, I was also conflicted over how these people could hoard weapons and ammunition in the name of religion and breed distrust and hostility toward the government and law enforcement. I had always thought that one's Christian faith brought comfort, joy, and peace during tumultuous times, not fear, paranoia, and hostility. I soon learned of more or equally disturbing events involving similar religious zealots within the United States.

The fugitive arrests at CSA led me to a story about a secretive, subgroup of Aryan Nations members, called The Order. Both fugitives were members of The Order, which was led by Robert Jay Mathews (aka Bob Mathews). The Order was a secretive subgroup within the neo-Nazi Aryan Nations. Order members essentially comprised a domestic terrorist organization that carried out a violent campaign of robberies, murders, and bombings that brought nearly $4 million of stolen proceeds into white supremacist coffers to fund a violent revolution. Each Order member swore a blood oath to Bob Mathews, his terrorist group, and the white race. Mathews wrote the "Oath: die Brüder Schweigen" (German for "The Silent Brotherhood"), which read:

"I as a free ARYAN man, hereby swear an unrelenting Oath upon the green graves of our sires, upon the wombs of our wives, upon the throne of God Almighty, sacred be His name . . . to join together in Holy union with those brothers in this sacred circle and do declare forthright that from this moment on I have no fear of Death, no fear of Foe, that I have a sacred duty to do whatever is necessary to deliver our people from the Jew and bring total Victory to the Aryan race. I as an Aryan Warrior swear myself to complete secrecy to the Order and total loyalty to my Comrades. Let me bear witness to you my brothers that should one of you fall in battle I will see to the welfare and well-being of your family. Let me bear witness to you my brothers, that should one of you be taken prisoner, I will do whatever is necessary to regain your freedom. And furthermore, let me bear witness to you my brothers that if I break this Oath let me be forever cursed upon the lips of our People as a coward and an Oath breaker."[11]

Mathews's oath for Order members continued, "My brothers, Let us be His BATTLE AX and weapons of war. Let us go forth by ones and by twos, by scores, by Legions, and as true Aryan men with pure hearts and strong minds face the enemies of our Faith and our Race with courage and determination. We hereby invoke the Blood Covenant, and declare that we are in a full state of War and will not lay down our swords until we have driven the enemy into the sea and reclaimed the land which was promised to our fathers of old, and through our blood and His will becomes the land of our children to be. Amen."[12]

The Order's campaign of mayhem started on October 28, 1983, when Bob Mathews robbed an adult bookstore in Spokane, Washington.[13] He also robbed a Citibank branch office in Seattle by presenting a handwritten note, walking out with $29,500.[14] Within four months of forming, the group improved upon its level of criminal sophistication and robbed a Continental armored transport truck on

March 16, 1984, as it pulled up to a Fred Meyer's department store in Seattle. Order members stole $39,000 from the armored truck.[15] The following month, Order members focused their anger of a degenerating society on an adult bookstore and X-rated cinema. They bombed the Embassy Theater in Seattle on April 22, 1984.[16] The next day, they robbed their second armored car parked outside of Bon Marche department store at the Northgate Mall in Seattle. The robbery netted the group approximately $500,000.[17]

Within a week, Order members placed another bomb consisting of three sticks of dynamite, an electric blasting cap, battery, and timer in a crawl space under the Congregation Ahavath Israel synagogue in Boise, Idaho. The resulting explosion on April 29, 1984, dissipated throughout the crawl space and did minimal damage to the building. Property damage was primarily confined to buckling of the kitchen floor. The perpetrators had waited for worshippers to leave the building prior to placing the device.[18] In May, Order members, growing increasingly paranoid that the authorities were closing in, became suspicious of a colleague, Walter West, who was also an Aryan Nations member. Suspecting he was a police informant, they reportedly picked him up at a local restaurant and drove him to an isolated location in Idaho's Kanisku National Forest. They had allegedly already dug a grave. Three Order members are suspected of murdering Walter West in the Kanisku National Forest in May 1984.[19] To this day, West's body has never been found. The case is considered closed due to a lack of solid investigative leads.

On June 18, 1984, Order members unleashed their vengeance on an outspoken Jewish talk show host, Alan Berg, gunning him down in the driveway of his Denver home using a MAC-10 submachine gun.[20] In one the greatest bank heists on record, Order members stole $3.6 million from a Brink's armored car on a highway near Ukiah, California, on July 19, 1984.[21] The group reportedly spent some of the money on weapons, military training, a ski condo, among other things, and distributed the remainder to other white supremacist groups. During their eighteen-month spree of violence and terrorism, Order members also amassed a lethal arsenal of weaponry and conducted paramilitary training activities on private land located in the forests of northern Idaho.

The Order's terroristic rampage came to an end on December 8, 1984. Federal law enforcement authorities tracked Bob Mathews and other Order members to a safe house on Whidbey Island, Washington.[22] Upon surrounding the house, several Order members surrendered to authorities. Bob Mathews, however, decided to take a stand. After a nerve-racking thirty-five-hour standoff that involved at least two fierce exchanges of gunfire between the suspect and SWAT team members, authorities attempted to end the siege by inserting tear gas into the cabin. The ensuing tear gas assault started a fire inside the safe house, which rapidly spread throughout the cabin. The safe house quickly became fully engulfed in flames. Robert Jay Mathews never emerged from the burning structure.[23]

According to white supremacists, he died a martyr's death. Mathews's remains were found among the charred rubble of the cabin the following day. Every year on December 8, white supremacists gather on Whidbey Island to remember Bob Mathews, his legacy, and his sacrifice for the white race. Many white supremacists also pay tribute to Mathews and other Order members through advocating the formation of other secretive, terrorist groups patterned after the Order.

In 1985, I learned about the murders of two U.S. Marshals on a desolate stretch of highway outside the small town of Medina, North Dakota. Members of a militant right-wing antitax movement, called Posse Comitatus, were responsible for their deaths. *Posse Comitatus* is Latin, meaning "power of the county."[24] During the 1980s, the Posse Comitatus was a loosely organized movement of antitax extremists who also held racist beliefs. The "Posse" also attracted survivalists, vigilantes, and antigovernment extremists. Some Posse Comitatus members were known to conduct paramilitary training activities.

On February 13, 1983, a Stutsman County, North Dakota, sheriff's deputy was searching for Gordon Kahl, a Posse Comitatus adherent, on an outstanding federal warrant for a probation violation. Sheriff's deputy Bradley Kapp soon located Kahl's automobile, an older-model Chrysler station wagon, at the Medina Medical Clinic in Medina, North Dakota.[25] Deputy Kapp had knowledge that members of the Posse Comitatus were meeting at the Medina Medical Clinic after hours. Kahl's parole violation stemmed from a prior arrest and conviction for tax evasion. Kapp immediately notified the Bismarck office of the U.S. Marshals Service of Kahl's whereabouts.[26]

Prior to the arrival of U.S. Marshals personnel, the deputy observed Gordon Kahl exit the medical clinic with his wife and two white males. All three men were carrying what appeared to be "Mini-14" rifles.[27] Kapp observed all four individuals exit the clinic's north parking lot and proceed to the south end of the parking lot out of his view.[28] It was apparent to the deputy that Kahl and others attending the meeting were aware of the deputy's location and possible surveillance. U.S. Marshals from Bismarck and Fargo, North Dakota, then arrived at the deputy's observation point and were briefed on the situation.[29]

Kapp and the U.S. Marshals (Robert Cheshire, James Hopson, Kenneth Muir, and Carl Wigglesworth) then observed a vehicle registered to David Broer leaving the south parking lot of the clinic with two occupants.[30] Immediately following Broer's car was the Kahl family's older-model Chrysler station wagon with four occupants.[31] It was being driven either by Kahl or a member of his family. Both vehicles proceeded north out of Medina toward the city of Woodworth, North Dakota, and were being pursued by the multiple officers. Deputy Kapp observed that another U.S. Marshals vehicle and a local police vehicle had blocked the road in front of the two vehicles being pursued. As they neared the roadblock, the two suspect vehicles went off the road and attempted to turn around in the opposite direction.[32]

As Broer's vehicle was the first to attempt to turn around, the U.S. Marshals in pursuit blocked the southbound lane at an angle with their vehicle. Upon stopping of the Broer vehicle, Deputy Marshals Cheshire and Hopson as well as the sheriff's deputy exited their vehicle on their respective sides.[33]

Kapp observed Kahl's son, Yori Von Kahl, exit the Chrysler station wagon and take his position near a telephone pole on the west side of the road. Yori Kahl was carrying what appeared to be a Mini-14 rifle.[34]

Kapp also observed Scott Faul exit the Chrysler vehicle. Faul was also reportedly carrying a Mini-14 rifle and proceeded in a northwesterly direction toward a grove of trees. Just before the shooting started, the sheriff's deputy recalls seeing Gordon Kahl exit the Broer vehicle armed with a Mini-14 rifle.[35] Kahl immediately raised his weapon and pointed it at the U.S. Marshals. Around this time, Broer was observed getting out of his vehicle but did not appear to be armed.[36]

Two other law enforcement vehicles approached the scene from the north and joined the tense standoff. The first shot fired reportedly came from Yori Kahl and appeared to hit deputy Marshal Cheshire. From that point, numerous shots rang out, which resulted in Cheshire being hit again as well as Kapp, who had observed other law enforcement officers exiting their cars after just arriving to assist in the arrest. Kapp dove for the cover of the ditch as numerous shots were being fired at the various law enforcement personnel.

After the firing had stopped, officers observed Gordon Kahl walking on the roadway in the immediate vicinity of all of the vehicles, still armed with his weapon. Kahl confronted the Medina police officer on scene and demanded the officer's revolver. The officer, fearing for his life, relinquished his weapon to Kahl, who took the gun away from the officer but spared his life.

Kapp, who had been wounded in the shootout, then observed Scott Faul assisting Yori Kahl, who appeared to have been shot, into the Medina police officer's marked patrol car. Faul and Yori Kahl then left the scene in the officer's police car.

Deputy Kapp further advised that when he had reached Medina on foot, he went immediately to the Medina Medical Clinic, where he saw Yori Kahl receiving treatment for an apparent gunshot wound. Also present were Scott Faul and Mrs. Gordon Kahl. While Deputy Kapp was being attended at the Medina clinic, Kahl entered the clinic carrying two Mini-14 rifles. Shortly thereafter, Kahl and Faul left the clinic. Joan Kahl (Gordon's wife) and her injured son, Yori, left the clinic by ambulance for Jamestown, South Dakota. The Chrysler station wagon was left in front of the clinic, where it was seized by law enforcement officers a few hours later.[37]

Gordon Kahl and Scott Faul left the clinic in the Medina police car they stole from the shooting scene. Broer and another Kahl associate left the shooting scene and proceeded directly to Streeter, North Dakota, where they were arrested. Broer's escape vehicle was also seized at the time of these arrests.[38]

After discussions with other officers at the scene who observed the bodies, autopsies, and through subsequent investigation, federal authorities determined that Muir and Cheshire were killed by multiple gunshots. Hopson was injured in the head by a gunshot. Kapp and a Medina police officer were also injured by gunfire.[39]

On June 3, 1983, federal, state, and local law enforcement authorities located fugitive Kahl at a fortified farmhouse near Smithville, Arkansas. As authorities attempted to enter the residence to arrest Kahl, he opened fire with a semiautomatic rifle, mortally wounding the Lawrence County sheriff, Gene Matthews. Despite being shot, Matthews was able to return fire, injuring Kahl. The sheriff, mortally wounded, made an immediate retreat as other law enforcement officers returned fire into the farmhouse. A two-hour gun battle ensued between Kahl and federal, state, and local law enforcement officers. Tear gas was shot into the residence, which started a fire. The fire soon spread and, within several minutes, had totally engulfed the farmhouse. The shooting stopped. After the fire was extinguished, Kahl's remains were found among the charred ruins. Matthews died at Lawrence Memorial Hospital about an hour after the initial shootout.[40]

The CSA, The Order, and Gordon Kahl incidents were my first introductions to right-wing extremism. These incidents would kindle my interest in knowing more about how these individuals radicalized to the point where they would violently resist authority as well as plot and carry out terrorist acts in the name of religion. I was also shocked to learn that both Mathews and Kahl at one point in their lives were active Mormons.

During my college experience at Brigham Young University in Provo, Utah, I would learn more about a unique brand of right-wing extremism called Mormon Constitutionalism. As previously cited in my scouting experiences, I had been exposed to the Mormon Constitutionalist mentality growing up in the LDS Church in northern Virginia. I just didn't know what it was or that it had a name. Mormon Constitutionalism was at its height during the 1950s and 1960s with prominent LDS Church leaders such as W. Cleon Skousen and Ezra Taft Benson endorsing anticommunist conspiracies, organizing constitutionally focused civic organizations like the Freemen Institute and courting the John Birch Society. I was not yet born, so I was totally unaware of this unique brand of Mormon extremism. Nevertheless, remnants of the Mormon Constitutionalist era were still evident in some members of my local congregation during the 1980s. The Mormon Constitutionalist mentality appears to be making a comeback in 2009 due largely to the rapid ascension in popularity of Mormons in the political landscape, such as national television personality Glenn Beck, Idaho gubernatorial candidate Rex Rammell, Mitt Romney, and Jon Huntsman.[41]

These three cases of right-wing extremism during the 1980s piqued my interest during my teenage years and would form the foundation for my future career in the U.S. government. They introduced me to the existence and dangers of American religious-based fanaticism. I learned that the very Christian teachings I had developed during childhood could be misinterpreted and twisted into scriptural justification for God-sanctioned violence. My emerging interest in right-wing extremist violence continued beyond my high school graduation, college education, and Mormon missionary service.

Within two days of graduating high school, I began a cross-country trip to Rexburg, Idaho. I had been accepted to Ricks College (now BYU-Idaho) and wanted to begin my college education as soon as possible. I only had a year before I would submit my papers to serve a two-year mission for the LDS Church. And I wanted to make the most of the opportunity.

Like BYU, Ricks College (now BYU-Idaho) was a private school owned and operated by the LDS Church. Within a few weeks after arriving in Idaho, I enrolled in the
summer semester. I attended college year-round and only went home for a week during
Christmas break. The rest of the time, I was busy studying and taking classes at college.

I graduated Ricks College within a year after graduating high school. I earned two
associate's degrees in one year—one in general studies with an emphasis on criminal
justice and another in law enforcement.

I then served a two-year mission for the LDS Church in Detroit, Michigan, during the late 1980s. During this experience, I served both as a trainer for new missionaries and as a District Leader (which is like a first-line supervisor in the field). My
Mormon missionary experience has had a very profound impact on my life.

Soon after arriving in Michigan, I met a missionary who was nearing the completion of his service. During our conversation, I asked him what advice he could give
to a new missionary just beginning his journey. He initially remarked, "Your mission
is million-dollar experience that you wouldn't pay a nickel to repeat." I was taken
aback by his statement. "Why would he say such a thing?" I wondered. I would learn
from personal experience that he was talking about the recurring adversities most
Mormon missionaries encounter on a daily basis. Serving a mission for the church
is a very rewarding and worthwhile endeavor. But it is also fraught with physical,
emotional, and spiritual challenges. It is a life-changing experience.

My mission service taught me self-reliance, compassion, faith, patience, and
endurance. Whether I was paired up with a difficult companion, verbally attacked
or insulted for no reason, or longing to be home, I relied on the Lord for comfort,
stability, and safety. Prayer was the lifeline that kept me from giving up, complaining, or blaming others. Personal prayer is how I've always dealt with life's difficult
situations and challenges. I listen for answers that come through the promptings of
the Holy Ghost. What I learned during my mission has also assisted me in identifying real issues, seeking solutions, and overcoming difficult circumstances. Little did
I know how important and needed my personal relationship with God and Jesus
Christ would become as I married, raised a family, and pursued a career.

Over the years, my friends and I joked about where I had been called to serve. At
the time, Detroit had been the "murder capital" of the United States. At the time, it
had one of the highest per-capita murder rates in the country. Several factors make
Michigan ripe for extremism.

First, Michigan is known for its high unemployment rate. Their economy is
closely tied to the auto industry and other manufacturing jobs linked to making
cars. For this reason, Michigan usually experiences a higher unemployment rate than
the rest of the country when the economy slows down or when manufacturing jobs
get cut. I firmly believe there is a strong correlation between high unemployment
and increases in right-wing extremist activity. When you're out of work, you may
want to place blame on something or someone—foreign outsourcing of American
jobs, failed government policy, and migrant workers are popular scapegoats for high
unemployment.

Second, Michigan continues to experience a clearly visible racial dichotomy between African-Americans and Caucasians. I was told that this racial divide has its roots in the mass migration of African-Americans to work in Detroit's auto industry during World War II. This phenomenon was very apparent on the streets of Michigan's largest city during the 1980s and into the 1990s. As a Mormon missionary proselytizing the streets of Detroit and its northern suburbs, I saw firsthand how Eight Mile Road literally served as a dividing line between "white" and "black" America. Along the border of Ferndale, Roseville, and the Detroit city limits, there was a clear and distinct separation of the races, with Caucasian families living on the north side of Eight Mile Road in Ferndale and African-American families residing on the south side in Detroit. The underlying racial tension and subtle boundaries in the form of city limits dividing the living space among whites and blacks is the likely result of the Watts riots during July 23–28, 1967. Many white families reportedly left the city around that time and moved to the outer suburbs.

With the exception of the major metropolitan areas of Detroit, Flint, and Lansing, much of the state is rural and appeals to a significant number of people seeking isolation and the chance to experience a more self-reliant lifestyle. While those characteristics in and among themselves are not particularly troubling, in many cases those same individuals may carry with them an extreme antiauthoritarian attitude due to a general lack of law enforcement presence. That attitude may be validated on a daily basis by the communications effect of the Internet and a continual outreach by extremist groups and their leadership based in other states. Moving away from the southern, more populated area of the state, the northern tier, Upper Peninsula, and "thumb" regions are more remote and isolated from the rest of the state. Michigan's harsh climate during winter months also lends itself to an emphasis on self-reliance and a survivalist mentality.

Some have also argued that Michigan's gun culture plays a role in fueling the creation of right-wing extremist groups in the state.[42] The state's relaxed attitude concerning assault rifles and the population's fixation with firearms earned it the nickname of "Militia-gun," which sounds close to the state's real name.

Like other major metropolitan areas throughout the country, Detroit has also been plagued with high crime rates, rampant drugs, prostitution, and systemic poverty. When I was there, it seemed as if at least 10 percent of homes were boarded up, burned out, or demolished. Many structures stood abandoned, left to be used as "crack houses." There were many vacant lots where houses had once stood. Some sections of the city look like a "war zone." Detroit is where I gained a real understanding of the hardships, pain, and struggles of police work. My eyes were opened to the true sacrifices of these brave men and women who work to maintain law and order.

While living in an apartment within Detroit's city limits, I witnessed and heard about many bizarre, depressing, and deplorable incidents. For example, two Mormon missionaries were shot by a teenager in Detroit about a month or so before I arrived at my mission. Both survived the attack but left their missions early. Twice, I saw the aftermath of fatal hit-and-runs. I also witnessed the annual night of arson and mayhem called Devil's Night or Hell Night.[43] Thankfully, our missionary work hours and police-imposed curfew kept us off the streets as nearly 800 arsons were set throughout Detroit on the eve of Halloween each year. On another occasion, two missionaries in my district opened a new proselytizing area near Six Mile and Woodward Avenue in the heart of Detroit. For the first two weeks living there, they were stunned by the sight of dead bodies left outside their apartment building. One was the result of armed robbery. The other, a stray bullet fired randomly.

Fortunately, I spent most of my mission in Detroit's outer suburbs and rural areas in southeast Michigan. Serving in these areas, however, also brought unique and equally strange experiences. While serving in the city of Warren, I encountered my first right-wing extremist, although I didn't know it at the time. But I soon realized that there was something odd. As my companion and I approached the side door to a single-story brick house, I noticed something I had never seen before. There was a sticker of an upside-down American flag displayed in the door's window. We knocked on the door, and an elderly man opened it. We introduced ourselves as representatives of the Church of Jesus Christ of Latter-Day Saints, and he invited us to come inside. I was carrying my scriptures, missionary lessons, and pad of paper in my right arm. So, as he greeted us, I extended my left hand. He scowled and refused to shake it. His reaction confused me. I switched the items to my left arm and tried to greet him again by extending my right hand. This time, he reached out and shook it.

As we sat down at the kitchen table, I asked him if there was something wrong with my left hand. He snapped back, "That's a Communist handshake!" I had never heard that! I told him it was also the official Boy Scout handshake. He mumbled back, "Then the Boy Scouts must be Communist." I shrugged off the comment. After talking briefly about our home states, our missionary experiences, and thoughts about Michigan, we were treated to a lengthy civics lesson replete with antigovernment conspiracy theories. After an hour or so, we finally came to the conclusion that this guy was not interested in hearing our message but had been looking for an audience for his antigovernment diatribe. We politely excused ourselves.

Later, while serving near Port Huron, we were asked to visit an inactive Mormon living in a ransacked cabin in an unincorporated area of St. Clair County. It took us a few tries to finally find the place. We had passed it once or twice and never noticed there was actually a house behind the tall weeds and brush lining the entire façade of the cabin. Inside, the place was littered with trash. It resembled an auto repair shop, but inside a living room. The middle-aged male was friendly to us but skeptical of our visit and a bit paranoid about our reason for coming to see him. I thought he might have been a little embarrassed about the empty beer bottles strewn sporadically throughout the living room and the ashtrays full of cigarette butts. Obviously, the man wasn't living the standards of the LDS Church (devout Mormons abstain from alcohol, tobacco, coffee, and tea).

I also saw small groupings of ammunition on the coffee table and fireplace mantel as well as a few stray bullets scattered on the floor. Since I grew up in a home where my dad liked to hunt, I didn't think much about it. Nevertheless, we stayed a few minutes in an attempt to assess his needs. Near the end of our visit, we shared a spiritual message with him and offered a prayer. As we stood up, I glanced over by the coffee table to see a pistol lying on the carpet. I turned around only to see a long gun hidden behind the couch. I began to feel uneasy. I nervously asked him about the rifle behind the couch. "Oh yeah, you never know when you'll need one of those," he replied. As we got into our car, I couldn't help but think how uncomfortable I felt in his house. It was a bit unnerving to know that we had innocently entered a clearly unsafe environment. I have no idea what this man thought about the government, but he was definitely paranoid about something he believed to be a threat.

A few weeks later, my companion and I visited an investigator (someone who is interested in learning about the Mormon Church) named "Chuck" who lived on Harsens Island, which is located about thirteen miles south of Marine City. Chuck was terminally ill and enjoyed the company and conversation. Through a series of visits, we learned that he was really not interested in joining the LDS Church but was looking for friendship and conversation. He welcomed discussion about religion, the afterlife, and immortality but didn't want to commit to anything. Unfortunately, Chuck also liked to drink himself into a drunken stupor. This may have been his way of dealing with his pain. Soon after being invited inside his home, we noticed Chuck was intoxicated. Since he appeared drunk, we thought it might not be good to stay there, so we decided to leave. This angered Chuck. When he realized we were leaving because of his drunken state, he jumped to the conclusion that we didn't care about him. So he decided to hasten our departure by pulling out a shotgun from the hall closet. My companion and I quickly exited the front door and briskly made our way to our car.

As we reached the car, Chuck opened the screen door, shotgun in hand, and told us to never come back. With the car doors open and one foot inside the car, my companion and I attempted to explain ourselves. Chuck put the shotgun down on the front porch and walked toward us. Thinking the danger was dissipating, I got out of the car, closed the car door, and walked toward Chuck. My companion was still standing by the driver's side door. As I neared him, Chuck bent over to his garden hose and pointed it me. I stopped in my tracks, but it was not out of the range of the hose. Chuck proceeded to spray me with water, drenching my suit coat, white shirt, and tie.

One of my final assignments was near Ann Arbor. Upon arriving into the area, I was excited to learn that a new family had recently joined the Church in a small town in southeast Michigan. I was eager to meet them. Soon, we had an appointment scheduled to teach the family the new member lessons. In the LDS Church, the "new member lessons" were a series of six instructional lessons that basically welcomed new members into the church and described their roles and responsibilities as church members. (This has since been changed.) They had also invited us over for dinner.

The family lived in an old farmhouse outside of a small town. When we arrived, the three kids were warm, cheerful, and excited to see us. The father was nice and invited us to sit down in the living room. As I sat on the couch, I noticed a three-foot-high stack of magazines almost as tall as the armrest on the couch. I thumbed through the magazine stack, and all of them were *Soldier of Fortune* magazines. I didn't take long for me to determine that the father either must be in the military or at least liked militaristic or survivalist things. The mother finished making dinner and called everyone into the kitchen. I turned around to find a wooden picnic table in the middle of the kitchen. The pantry was full of C-rations from the U.S. military. We said a prayer on the food and enjoyed a nice conversation over dinner. After finishing the meal, all of us sat down for the new member lesson and spiritual message. We had a good time together.

That Sunday, I saw the family at church. The father surprised me by wearing camouflaged pants with a white shirt and tie. He was also wearing military boots. I thought this was odd attire in a church traditionally associated with men wearing white shirts and dark ties. I approached him about it after our Sunday meetings. He said he was in the Army National Guard and felt comfortable wearing battle dress uniform pants everywhere he went.

Over the course of the three months I spent in this area, we visited this family on a weekly basis. We taught another new member lesson. Afterward, the father enjoyed explaining to us his view of politics and the world. It was a dark, paranoid worldview. He talked of a menacing and sinister plan to take over the United States. He made references to a one-world government and "New World Order." He further explained that one of the reasons he was drawn toward the Mormon Church was our emphasis on preparedness. He really liked the fact the Mormons are known for keeping a year's supply of food and other resources in case of joblessness, debilitating illness, or natural disaster. He also liked the fact that Mormons supported one another, helped other church members in need, and believed in working together to serve and better themselves and the community. He was also a staunch supporter of the Second Amendment.[44] He showed us some of his firearms, one of which resembled an AK-47–type assault rifle. I was raised around firearms, but I don't remember my dad being "proud" or "excited" about his guns. My dad's guns primarily served a single purpose—hunting animals. Of course, he had a pistol or two for home defense. But I don't recall any infatuation or fixation with assault weapons.

I eventually left the Ann Arbor area and served the remainder of my mission back in the northern suburbs of Detroit. There, another missionary and I rented a basement apartment from an elderly non-LDS woman from East Germany. I remember on several occasions she would express her fondness for Adolf Hitler. "Hitler was a good man," she would begin. "He got rid of all of the filth throughout Germany . . . the criminals and the prostitutes. He put everyone to work. There was hardly any unemployment," she rationalized. I would attempt to be polite and listen, but I could never have supported her views on Hitler. As a result, she didn't like me.

Despite finishing my missionary service in suburban Detroit, I never forgot the experiences I had serving and working in the rural areas of southeast Michigan. I returned home during the summer of 1990. I was eager to renew my enrollment in college, but I also wondered how I was going to pay for my college education.

I enrolled at George Mason University (GMU) in Fairfax, Virginia. I attended only a few semesters before I was accepted into Brigham Young University (BYU). Nevertheless, my experience at GMU has had a lasting impact. While attending GMU, I sought opportunities to finance the remainder of the college education. This led me to solicit the assistance of GMU's Career Development Center. A counselor referred me to GMU's paid internship and cooperative education programs. I compared and contrasted each program. I also began to research different careers and position descriptions. I kept looking into positions with federal law enforcement agencies but kept thinking about what I had seen in Detroit during my mission. I was at a crossroads.

For most of my life, I had wanted to become a police officer or special agent. Now I was reluctant to pursue this career. What was I going to do now? In frustration, I turned to the guidance counselor for assistance and hoped she had an answer for me. Knowing I had a deep interest and desire for a law enforcement career but wanted to mitigate the risks associated with policing, she recommended that I consider looking into an intelligence research specialist position. I found the file folder labeled "Intelligence Research Specialist/Analyst" and read through it. I realized that this was exactly what I wanted.

I later interviewed with four federal agencies looking to hire intelligence research specialist-student trainees. Three agencies offered to hire me, but only one offered me the job I was truly interested in doing—counterterrorism. Within a few months, I began working for the U.S. Army's Intelligence and Threat Analysis Center at the Washington Navy Yard in Anacostia, Maryland. I stayed in this program for three years, alternating between full-time work and full-time studies every six months. During the second part of my cooperative education experience, I transferred to BYU in Provo, Utah. I graduated BYU with a bachelor's degree in political science in 1994.

While at BYU, I watched the events at Waco unfold on television during the spring of 1993. I was saddened to learn that four Department of Alcohol, Tobacco, Firearms and Explosives (ATF) agents lost their lives along with several Branch Davidians. The tragic outcome of the Waco raid inspired me to conduct a student survey concerning the incident and its aftermath for my critical thinking class. I basically wanted to assess the student population's views of law enforcement's handling of the situation. Who was ultimately responsible for the deadly outcome? The survey results were not what I expected.

I mistakenly believed that the conservative, religious, and patriotic views embedded within Mormon culture would translate into support and favorable opinions toward ATF. The survey results were completely the opposite. Most students sided with the Branch Davidians and believed that federal law enforcement was the aggressor. The very belief system that had taught me to respect authority and support the nation's government had also influenced many others in a different direction.

Many BYU students had a distrust of the U.S. government and believed the Branch Davidians were being "persecuted" for their religious beliefs. Given the history of the LDS Church, which includes intense persecution of church members in Missouri, an extermination order issued by a governor, and the assassination of the Mormon prophet Joseph Smith, I should have anticipated that antigovernment sentiment and persecution complex might persist to this day.

So how could an extremely close-knit people of the same faith hold such diverse views on government, alternative religious groups, and law enforcement? I think a lot has to do with our family history and how and where we were raised. My family was first-generation Mormons who grew up in the eastern United States. Many of the students at BYU come from multigeneration Mormon families whose ancestors were displaced Mormon immigrant pioneers.

I also followed coverage of the Alfred P. Murrah Federal Building in Oklahoma City. From the outset, I knew it was domestic terrorism—an act likely carried out by a right-wing extremist. The date of the bombing, April 19, was too coincidental, which was the anniversary of the Branch Davidian fire two years earlier that resulted in the deaths of seventy-six Branch Davidians (including more than twenty children). The attack also occurred in the heartland of America—an unlikely place for international terrorists to strike.

On my return trip to Washington, D.C., after graduating BYU, I decided to take a more southerly route through Oklahoma City, so I could see the aftermath of the bombing site. The building had already been imploded and the debris cleaned up. As I drove down street, I caught the glimpse of a vacant lot surrounded by chain-link fencing. I initially thought it was a construction zone, but then saw the makeshift memorial of teddy bears, flowers, and handwritten notes to those that perished. I knew I was at the right place.

I parked my car across the street and walked over to the memorial. No one else was around. The immediate area seemed stopped in time. It was a solemn, empty, and spooky experience. I could feel the sadness and suffering of the victims and their families. I was ashamed that a fellow American would possess such a deep-rooted hatred of the government. I was angry that an American citizen would devise such a devious and heartless act of violence that took so many innocent lives. I felt guilty for taking a picture of the memorial. I felt as though I was somehow violating the rights of the deceased. In hindsight, I'm glad I took the photo. It serves as a constant reminder to me of the terrifying threat of homegrown extremism.

I knew very early in my life that I would serve law enforcement in some capacity. I believe God had a hand in guiding me into my career as an intelligence analyst specializing in counterterrorism. I can't help but think that my life experiences happened for a reason—a foreordained purpose. I developed an interest in studying right-wing extremism during my early teens. I am quite amazed at how many people who entered my life embraced right-wing extremist beliefs. The CSA, Order, and Gordon Kahl cases inspired an interest in learning more about right-wing extremism and domestic terrorism. Later I sought a career in the federal government, and an unexpected opportunity was opened to specialize in counterterrorism. Soon after graduating, I accepted a full-time position with the civil service, working for the U.S. Army in Washington, D.C. I couldn't wait to return to Virginia and begin my federal career, not as a student trainee, but as a full-time intelligence analyst for the U.S. government.

3

Right-Wing Extremism in the 1990s

One of the primary criticisms of the Department of Homeland Security (DHS) right-wing extremism report concerned the definition of "right-wing extremism." As a result of public and congressional backlash since the report's leak, the term has been practically removed from the DHS vocabulary. A year later, secretary Janet Napolitano was still noticeably sensitive to the term, even dismissing it during a Fox News interview in Oklahoma City at the memorial ceremony of the fifteenth anniversary of the Alfred P. Murrah Federal Building bombing.[1] "Right-wing extremism" was a phrase the secretary no longer wanted to acknowledge or say.[2]

"The question is not ideology," Napolitano told Fox News. "We've always had groups on all sides that have held beliefs that are very strong and express them very vociferously." The real issue is "the turn to violence," Napolitano explained. She expressed concern that antigovernment groups in the United States could be contemplating violent attacks.[3]

When responding to a question about the report, Napolitano reflected, "I think now, having been in the job fifteen months, the goal that we need to have is to give local law enforcement tactical, intelligence-based threat information that they can act upon—*not generalizations and not comments about ideologies* [emphasis added]." She continued on, "There is a balance there, and there is a nuance there that our department now needs to not only express but communicate with local law enforcement."[4]

At a later point during the interview, Napolitano stated that "We honor the *continued need for vigilance against the hateful ideologies that led to this attack* [emphasis added], so that we can recognize their signs in our communities and stand together to defeat them." She concluded, "I wish it were possible to stand here and say that threats from terrorism and violent extremism have gone away since then. We know that's not the case."[5]

Napolitano's statements concerning providing actionable intelligence information, "not generalizations and not comments about ideologies," appears to conflict with her later statement of the "continued need for vigilance against the hateful ideologies that led to this attack." Making such contradictory statements may be good for politics, but is not productive for intelligence decision makers and intelligence analysts.

Radical ideology is what drives and motivates extremists to commit violent acts. Beliefs provide a target by identifying a scapegoat for society's ills. Extremist ideology also introduces ideas from which criminal and violent acts are first conceived, then grow and eventually are carried out. Terrorist tactics, techniques, and procedures all emanate from a belief system. The rationale behind dehumanizing others to the point of hurting or even killing them stems from a belief. If the U.S. government and law enforcement truly desire to prevent terrorist acts, then they have a responsibility to look at the radical ideologies that nurture and breed hate, fear, paranoia, and aggression.

Whether Napolitano chooses to recognize it or not, "right-wing extremism" is an official term that has been used in academia as well as the U.S. counterterrorism, law enforcement, and security communities for the past thirty years or more.[6] It is a phrase meant to assign a general characterization to either extreme side of the political spectrum. The terms "left" and "right" have been used without much consternation. They have gone unchallenged by students, faculty, and politicians as acceptable terms to describe the political leanings of movements, groups, and individuals.

So what caused all of the fuss in Congress and at DHS? The short answer is politics. In addition, subject matter experts in both government and private sectors have had difficulty defining exactly what the term "right-wing extremism" means. Numerous definitions abound emphasizing various aspects of the terms "right wing" and "extremism." Compounding these definitional differences is the reality that radical right-wing individuals often embrace multiple and frequently simultaneous memberships in a wide range of extremist groups and affiliated ideologies. For example, Aryan Nations members embrace both neo-Nazi and Christian Identity beliefs. They have also had Klansmen and other white supremacists among their membership. Similarly, during the 1990s, the Michigan Militia had sovereign citizen and white supremacist members who were also members of the group. Extremist affiliation may evolve over a person's life. Individuals have been known to drift in and out of various extremist organizations as their contacts and beliefs change.

Traditionally, the term "right-wing extremism" has been used within the intelligence, counterterrorism, and law enforcement communities to describe fringe individuals and their radical beliefs on the extreme right of the political spectrum. DHS, however, now forbids itself from using such a generalized definition. It says it has a duty and responsibility to protect the public and also to respect the public's right to free speech and peaceful assembly. As a result, DHS must look at "extremism" through a "threat lens" that focuses on violence, criminality, and terrorist aspects of extremism.

Subject matter experts at DHS, including myself, attempted to create a uniform, standard definition of "right-wing extremism" to add clarity and consistency in our products. It was a great idea, but just as with other experts in law enforcement and academia, we had our own ideas about what constituted "right-wing extremism." This was not only a complicated task, but also a monumental and controversial undertaking. The closest we came to an official definition of "right-wing extremism" was contained within the DHS Domestic Extremism Lexicon, disseminated on March 26, 2009. The lexicon was leaked to the media in April 2009. Like the DHS right-wing extremism report that was leaked earlier in the month, the DHS extremism lexicon generated a lot controversy and public criticism. Many didn't even read it, and definitions were taken out of context. Due to public criticism, DHS officially withdrew this lexicon and has been attempting to revise it ever since. Despite a noble effort, the department has yet to reach a consensus, and the project seems to have been abandoned.

These definitions, along with the others, were officially withdrawn in the aftermath of the DHS right-wing extremism report leak in April 2009. The same definition of right-wing extremism was used in both reports. Within days of the leak, the department dropped the term "right wing" entirely from its vocabulary and would not even acknowledge it.

Prior to the DHS extremism lexicon, the FBI attempted to define right-wing extremism in its annual "Terrorism in the United States" publications from 1993 to 1999. These definitions provided the foundation for the DHS definition but could not be used in their entirety due to the different missions and authorities between I&A and the FBI. The FBI definitions varied widely from year to year, which illustrates the complexity of having to clearly define the characteristics of an ideology in a simple definition.

The FBI is a law enforcement agency and, therefore, has the means and authority to conduct criminal investigations and intelligence operations. I&A is an intelligence agency that does not have law enforcement powers. Therefore, the FBI's definitions of right-wing extremism *should* be different from the DHS definition, because it reflects the agency's law enforcement mission of investigating crime and responding to criminal acts. The following examples demonstrate how the FBI also had trouble defining what it meant by "right-wing extremism."

- "Rightwing terrorists are guided by a racist or anti-Semitic philosophy and advocate the supremacy of the white race. According to this view, all ethnic minorities are inferior in every way. Many rightwing terrorist groups also espouse antigovernment sentiments and engage in survivalist and/or paramilitary training to ensure the survival of the white race and/or the United States." (FBI, Terrorism in the United States, 1993)
- "Generally, domestic terrorist groups categorized as 'rightwing' are defined as being racist, anti-black, and anti-Semitic and are for the advancement of the

white race. In addition to advocating white supremacy and the hatred of non-white races, these groups also have engaged in acts of provocation and assault against federal and state law enforcement officials." (FBI, Terrorism in the United States, 1994)

- "Rightwing extremist groups—which generally adhere to an antigovernment or racist ideology—continued to attract supporters last year. Many of these recruits feel displaced by rapid changes in the U.S. culture and economy, or are seeking some form of personal affirmation." (FBI, Terrorism in the United States, 1995)

- "Rightwing Terrorism: The major themes espoused today by rightwing groups are conspiracies, such as the New World Order and gun control laws, apocalyptic views stemming from the approach of the millennium, and white supremacy. Many rightwing extremist groups also articulate antigovernment and/or anti-taxation and anti-abortion sentiments, and engaged in survivalist and/or paramilitary training to ensure the survival of the United States as a white, Christian nation." (FBI, Terrorism in the United States, 1996)

- "Rightwing terrorist groups often adhere to the principles of racial supremacy and embrace antigovernment, antiregulatory beliefs. Generally, extremist rightwing groups engage in activity that is protected by Constitutional guarantees of free speech and assembly. However, when individuals or groups begin to plan criminal acts, law enforcement has the predication to initiate appropriate criminal investigations." (FBI, Terrorism in the United States, 1999)

In contrast, the DHS *Office of Intelligence and Analysis*, although a member of the intelligence community, has virtually no operational capability and absolutely no law enforcement and investigative authority. It is not a law enforcement agency, so it is not required to operate within the same parameters as the FBI or any other law enforcement organization. For these reasons, DHS analysts believed right-wing extremism should not be limited to violent or criminal acts, but also include those individuals or groups that espouse, support, facilitate, or endorse violence. This perspective of extremism allows analysts to fulfill their duty to prevent terrorism before an act of violence occurs. This authority is clearly articulated in the Homeland Security Act of 2002.[7] Viewing extremism in this manner also respects the rights of peaceful, law-abiding right-wing extremists who reject violence and criminal activity. Nonviolent individuals and groups are still considered extremists as a result of their extreme positions and radical beliefs. DHS wanted to ignore reality and redefine extremism as those willing to conduct violence and criminal activity.

Right-wing extremism is also comprised of various extremist movements that favor nationalistic leanings. Right-wing extremist movements can be generally categorized into four types: the white supremacist movement; the militia movement; the sovereign citizen movement; and various single-issue movements, such as violent tax resistors, antiabortion extremists, and anti-immigration extremists. While a majority of members of these groups are law-abiding citizens, a small percentage of members advocate and conspire to commit acts of violence. Particularly concerning to federal law enforcement authorities is the potential for these movements to be infiltrated by violent extremists seeking to exploit them and their membership in order to further their private terrorist agenda.

Many factors influenced the rise in right-wing extremism in the United States during the 1990s, including high unemployment, massive government budgetary deficits, and slow economic growth. Other factors also played a role, such as the 1992 presidential election, the 1994 North American Free Trade Agreement (NAFTA), and fear related to the approach of the year 2000 (Y2K). The passage of restrictive gun laws such as the Brady Law, which established a five-day waiting period prior to purchasing a handgun,[8] and the 1994 Violent Crime Control and Law Enforcement Act, which limited the sale of various types of assault rifles,[9] were other major contributing factors leading to the creation and growth of the militia movement and other versions of antigovernment extremism. Many militia members believe that both pieces of legislation represented "a government conspiracy" to disarm the U.S. population and ultimately to abolish the Second Amendment to the U.S. Constitution.

During the 1980s, right-wing extremists were galvanized by several national issues such as increasing United Nations involvement in U.S. foreign policy, the perceived erosion of parental rights and authority through court rulings, the decline of the American family farm, and the perceived public backlash against Judeo-Christian beliefs. These issues were magnified because of the far-right's perception of a "liberal" political climate that favored expanding benefits and equal opportunities to minorities and diversity groups.

The two most important events that led to the resurgence in right-wing extremism in the 1990s were those that took place at Ruby Ridge in northern Idaho and the federal raid and siege at the Branch Davidian property in Waco, Texas. In hindsight, both law enforcement operations, although directed at domestic extremists who had violated the law, were mishandled and involved overzealous and aggressive tactical responses that led to the deaths of women and children. These were tragic events for law enforcement, the U.S. government, democracy, and the American people. In order to understand better why right-wing extremism has experienced a revival over the past two years, it is important to understand these past two events.

RUBY RIDGE INCIDENT

The actual incident at Ruby Ridge unfolded in August 1992, but the federal investigation into the alleged criminal activities of Randy Weaver began a few years earlier. Weaver and his wife embraced apocalyptic religious views. They were also fearful of the government. As a result, Randy and Vicki Weaver had gathered their belongings, sold their home, and moved their family from Iowa to a remote cabin near a mountain peak called Ruby Ridge in Boundary County, Idaho. Both Randy and Vicki were extremely devout Christians. They were fixated on the "last days," signs of the end of the world and the second coming of Jesus Christ. Due to an increasing paranoia related to the perception that the Apocalypse was approaching, Randy quit his full-time job and decided to move his family to an isolated part of Idaho to await Christ's return. Randy and his family were introduced to the Aryan Nations and began attending church services and other events at the Aryan Nations property near Hayden Lake, Idaho. A Bureau of Alcohol, Tobacco, Firearms, and Explosives (ATF) informant also attending Aryan Nations events began to take notice of Weaver and his radical beliefs. After a few years, the Weavers' income began to diminish. The ATF informant eventually approached Randy Weaver about an opportunity to make some easy money.

On October 24, 1989, the ATF informant bought two sawed-off shotguns from Randy Weaver in the parking lot of a local restaurant in Sandpoint, Idaho. The informant paid Weaver $450 for both shotguns.[10] The ATF informant later attempted to elicit Weaver's cooperation in monitoring Aryan Nations criminal activities in return for having Weaver's criminal charges concerning possession of a sawed-off shotgun reduced or dropped.[11] Weaver refused the offer because he didn't want to become a government "snitch."

In January 1991, Weaver was arraigned on the firearms charges. Due to a scheduling mix-up and conflicting dates on official paperwork mailed to Weaver, confusion resulted over his actual trial date. When Weaver failed to show up for trial due to the bureaucratic blunder, the judge issued a bench warrant for his arrest. On March 14, 1991, a federal grand jury indicted Weaver for his failure to appear in court.

As weeks and months passed without a resolution, the government appeared to have become complacent regarding the matter. Soon local media showed interest in the story. When a news helicopter flew over the Weaver cabin to get aerial footage of the property for an upcoming news story, an unidentified individual allegedly shot at the helicopter from the ground below. The incident was reported to local authorities, who soon felt pressure from national news media to do something about it. Since the case involved a fugitive from justice, local law enforcement authorities deferred the matter to the U.S. Marshals Service, who became involved in efforts to apprehend Weaver for his trial on the weapons charges as well as his failure to appear.[12]

For several months, the U.S. Marshals gathered information on Weaver in an effort to develop a viable strategy for apprehending him. The media continued to wait for government action. From their covert observations, the U.S. Marshals Service learned that Weaver had made threatening statements regarding his intent to resist violently his arrest. The Marshals decided that an undercover operation was the best way to proceed with Weaver's arrest.[13]

During the early morning hours of August 21, 1992, six U.S. Marshals traveled from Spokane, Washington, to Bonners Ferry (Idaho), switched vehicles at the sheriff's office, and proceeded to the Ruby Creek area. Wearing night-vision goggles, they abandoned their vehicle and hiked about a mile to an area near Randy Weaver's cabin. By midmorning, Weaver; his fourteen-year-old son, Sammy; and a family friend, Kevin Harris, exited the cabin for a morning stroll outside with the family dog, Striker. Sammy was armed with a .357 pistol and a .223 assault rifle. Kevin had a 30.06 rifle and Randy had a holstered pistol and shotgun. Before they left the area around the cabin, Striker began to bark and scampered into the woods. Thinking the dog was chasing wild game, Randy decided to take the logging road and ordered Sam and Kevin to follow the dog through the woods.

Hearing the bark and seeing the dog approaching their direction, the U.S. Marshals team decided to retreat, separated from each other, and attempted to outrun the dog and anyone who might have been following it. Weaver encountered a U.S. Marshal on the trail and retreated back to the cabin. Kevin Harris, Sammy, and the dog encountered two U.S. Marshals in another part of the woods. There are differing accounts as to what exactly happened next, but Weaver, Harris, and the Marshals all agree that a gunfight ensued. The government contends that Sammy shot at the U.S. Marshals upon seeing his dog gunned down by a Marshal. The Marshals in self-defense returned fire, killing Sammy Weaver. Harris fatally shot one of the Marshals during the exchange of gunfire. In the aftermath, both a U.S. Marshal and Sammy were killed.[14]

As a result of the August 21 shooting incident at the "Y" trail near the Weaver cabin, federal, state and local law enforcement authorities, including the FBI's elite Hostage Rescue Team (HRT), responded to the Ruby Ridge area. HRT members arrived at the location and assumed their positions during the late afternoon of August 22nd.[15] State and local law enforcement formed an outer perimeter of security in the general area of Ruby Ridge.

Prior to assuming their positions, HRT tactical officers received an operational briefing and were instructed by the HRT commander that their actions would be governed by modified "rules of engagement" specifically designed for this operation. The HRT commander believed the situation mandated a modification in the procedures. A law enforcement officer had been murdered, and the HRT commander did not want another officer killed. These changes to the FBI's standard rules instructed HRT snipers that they *could and should* [emphasis added] shoot all armed adult males seen outside the Weavers' cabin before a surrender announcement was made.[16]

Operating under these revised rules, an FBI sniper took position in a rocky area overlooking the cabin. During the late afternoon of August 22, the sniper fired two shots in quick succession. The first shot and wounded an adult male, later identified as Randy Weaver, as he aimed his rifle in the direction of an HRT helicopter that was hovering above the property on an observation mission. The second shot hit Harris as he was running back into the Weavers' cabin. The bullet went through Harris's body and struck an unarmed Vicki Weaver, holding her newborn child as she stood behind a curtain at the cabin's front door. She was instantly killed.[17]

Following the FBI sniper shooting incident, federal officials spent the next eight days attempting to convince Weaver and Harris to surrender. As the stand-off continued, federal, state, and local law enforcement officers performed crowd control, dealing with media and angry protestors who had gathered at the base of the mountain.[18]

With little progress in the negotiations, FBI officials eventually permitted Bo Gritz, a prominent right-wing extremist icon at the time, to intervene. Gritz, a decorated Vietnam War veteran and former Mormon temple worker, was well known for his unsuccessful run for the U.S. presidency representing the Populist Party. Gritz also gained prominence for his antigovernment speeches and self-inspired "SPIKE" (Specially Prepared Individuals for Key Events) training, which taught men and women self-reliance and paramilitary skills.[19] Gritz was successful in convincing Harris to surrender peacefully on August 30. Weaver surrendered the following day.[20] Upon surrendering, both men were taken into custody and immediately given medical attention. Soon thereafter, federal, state, and local law enforcement officials secured the area and conducted a thorough search of the cabin and surrounding property.[21]

In September 1992, the FBI conducted a thorough investigation into the events at Ruby Ridge. The investigation concluded that the U.S. Marshals "took a measured approach in developing a plan to apprehend [Randy] Weaver."[22] The FBI further concluded that "throughout the 18 month period that the marshals were responsible for apprehending Weaver, they carefully devised a plan intended to pose the least amount of risk to Weaver, his family and the marshals. At no time did we [the FBI] find that it was the intent of the marshals to force a confrontation with Weaver or his family."[23]

The FBI also noted in its investigation that the existence of a bench warrant for Randy Weaver's apprehension left the U.S. Marshals with "little choice but to proceed as it did."[24] With respect to the shooting incident at the "Y" trail near the Weaver cabin, the FBI was unable to determine conclusively who fired the first shot. Furthermore, although evidence suggested that a U.S. Marshal shot at Sammy Weaver, the FBI believed there was no indication of any wrongdoing or deliberate intention to shoot a child. "We found no proof that the shooting of the boy was anything other than an accident," the FBI investigation concluded.[25]

The FBI conducted an internal review of its conduct at Ruby Ridge and determined there were numerous problems with the agency's handling of the situation. Insufficient on-scene intelligence gathering, revisions to the FBI's rules of engagement, and command and control were among the most egregious issues cited.[26] The FBI concluded that certain sections of the revised rules not only violated the agency's standard deadly force policy, but also disregarded the U.S. Constitution and its principles of due process and presumed innocence until proven guilty. In addition, the FBI's internal investigation revealed the sniper's first shot fired at Randy Weaver was justified and met the "reasonable standard" for using deadly force. But the sniper's second shot at Kevin Harris did not meet the standard of "objective reasonableness," since there was no imminent threat to human life.[27]

In response to the Ruby Ridge incident, approximately 175 men, many of whom were affiliated with various right-wing extremist organizations, gathered on October 22, 1992, at a YMCA youth camp near Estes Park, Colorado, for a three-day conference. The event was dubbed "The Rocky Mountain Rendezvous."[28] It was organized by Pete Peters, a Christian Identity minister from Laporte, Colorado. The meeting was attended by neo-Nazis, Ku Klux Klan (KKK) members, survivalists, and other right-wing extremists and antigovernment zealots. Prominent right-wing extremist leaders such as Richard Butler (Aryan Nations), Chris Temple (Christian Identity minister), Louis Beam (Aryan Nations/KKK member), Peter Peters (Christian Identity minister), and John Trochmann (Christian Identity minister) attended. Temple and Trochmann had recently formed a group called United Citizens for Justice in an attempt to inform the public about what they believed to have happened at Ruby Ridge and to generate support for Randy Weaver.[29] Beam, a Vietnam veteran, was the conference's keynote speaker. He spoke on the concept of "leaderless resistance,"[30] a guerrilla warfare fighting tactic developed by the French Resistance during World War II, which had been successfully utilized against Nazi invaders.

The conference featured a wide range of guest speakers who presented various relevant issues to right-wing extremists, such as various antitax messages, New World Order conspiracy theories, and Christian "end times" fundamentalism. The importance of this conference did not solely come from the messages that were delivered, but more importantly, from the networking and unification that occurred. A large swath of right-wing extremists, who normally would not sit down together and discuss possible solutions to mutual issues of concern, found a common cause directed at a shared enemy—the U.S. government.

Many experts believe the Rocky Mountain Rendezvous event is the likely birthplace of the modern-day militia movement. Many of the messages delivered on October 23, 1992, focused on the government's handling of the Ruby Ridge standoff a few months earlier in Idaho. The general question posed at the conference was, "How are we [right-wing extremists] going to respond if there is another Ruby Ridge–type incident?" Larry Pratt, then president of Gun Owners of America, had an answer—the formation of private, well-armed citizen armies. He called them militias. Two years earlier, Pratt had written a book called *Armed People Victorious*. It was based on his study and analysis of "citizen defense patrols" in Guatemala and the Philippines against Communist rebels. These patrols later became known as "death squads" for their viciousness, brutality, and murderous ways. Pratt's vision would become reality within a year due to another unifying event for right-wing extremists that occurred on the brown grassy plains near Waco, Texas.

WACO INCIDENT

The history of the Branch Davidians can be traced back to Victor T. Houteff, a convert to the Seventh-Day Adventist church. Houteff started a Seventh-Day Adventist splinter group called the Shepherd's Rod, which purchased property outside of Waco, Texas. Houteff's followers relocated to the property on May 24, 1935, and established a religious commune at the property called Mount Carmel.[31]

Houteff's group later became known as the Davidians around 1942.[32] The sect's beliefs centered on Houteff's unique interpretation of the Book of Revelation, specifically concerning events of the "Last Days" and the restoration of the Davidic Kingdom.[33] After Houteff's death in 1955, a congregational split occurred, and Benjamin L. Roden organized the Branch Davidian faction.[34] With Roden's death in 1978, Roden's wife, Lois, and her son, George, assumed leadership roles in the sect.[35] David Koresh came into contact with the Branch Davidian sect in 1981 and allegedly had an intimate relationship with Lois Roden.[36] He assumed leadership of the group after successfully leading an armed revolt against George Roden in 1987.[37]

Koresh's legal name was Vernon Wayne Howell. He was born on August 17, 1959, in Houston, Texas.[38] He formally changed his name to David Koresh in 1990.[39] By 1993, approximately ninety Branch Davidians were extremely devoted to Koresh due to his charisma and ability to quote Bible verses. Many of Koresh's followers believed he was the "Lamb of God."[40]

ATF began its investigation into Koresh and the Branch Davidians when a McLennan County sheriff's deputy notified the local field office about suspicious deliveries to the Branch Davidians' property. ATF agents soon learned that numerous United Parcel Service (UPS) packages had been delivered there. According to UPS records, the packages contained materials commonly used for the unlawful manufacture of grenades.[41] The investigation also determined that Koresh had a violent past involving a shootout with a rival Davidian leader and his followers. As a result, the ATF field office in Austin, Texas, opened a formal investigation into David Koresh in June 1992.[42] The ATF had also learned that the FBI had opened a formal case on Koresh but were not actively pursuing it due to a lack of specific information related to his alleged criminal activity.[43]

The McLennan County Sheriff's Office provided ATF with a detailed account of Koresh's armed revolt against a rival Branch Davidian faction during 1987 in an alleged attempt to kill the group's leader, George Roden. Roden's family and their followers had occupied the property, called Rodenville, since 1959. Koresh ultimately seized control of the property and occupied it with his own followers. McLennan County provided an incident report to ATF, which had been written by the sheriff's department shortly after the armed confrontation. When sheriff's deputies arrived at the scene of the shootout, they saw Koresh and six of his followers firing their rifles at Roden. After the shooting ended, Roden emerged from behind a tree and was treated for a minor gunshot wound. Deputies also observed Koresh and his followers dressed in combat fatigues. They had painted their faces with black grease paint and were armed with several shotguns, .22-caliber rifles, other weapons, and more than 3,000 rounds of ammunition.[44]

During a six-month period, ATF agents gathered information from several different sources including UPS records of past deliveries to the Branch Davidian property, interviews with former cult members, firearms dealers, and reporting from state and local law enforcement officials. Investigators documented evidence of Koresh's accumulation of a large arsenal of firearms and explosives. Items listed from investigative reports included twenty-six firearms (various calibers and brand names); 100 AR-15/M-16 upper receiver units with barrels; 91 AR-15 lower receiver units (with accompanying parts and magazines); twenty 100-round drum magazines for M-16s; an M-76 grenade launcher; 200 M-31 practice rifle grenades; approximately 50 inert practice grenades; over 150 pounds of explosive chemicals including black powder, potassium nitrate, and aluminum metal powder; and one pound of igniter cord.[45]

In addition to the formidable cache of weapons, ATF learned that the Branch Davidians routinely posted "security guards" along the perimeter of the group's property. Group members were also known to conduct firearms training. Koresh preached about an impending "violent confrontation with law enforcement" and was allegedly engaging in sexual conduct with minors, as well as exerting control and influence over his followers.[46]

By fall 1992, ATF's investigation into Koresh had established sufficient evidence of federal firearms violations. Recognizing that serving warrants on such a heavily armed group posed a substantial challenge, ATF leadership organized a team of tactical planners. The planning team consisted of several experienced leaders who specialized in dynamic, high-risk entries to execute warrants, but only one of them had prior experience participating in such a large tactical operation.[47]

In January 1993, ATF started an undercover operation targeting David Koresh. ATF agents, posing as students attending classes at a local technical college, rented a small house located directly across from the Branch Davidian property in rural McLennan County—about six miles outside of Waco, Texas. One of the agents, as part of the undercover operation, met several times with Koresh and other Branch Davidian members and expressed interest in their religious beliefs. Undercover agents were able to corroborate some of the information obtained from the McLennan County Sheriff's Office and confirm reports related to Koresh's violent nature and his hatred for law enforcement.[48] As a result of the evidence gathered by the agents during the undercover operation, a federal judge granted ATF an arrest warrant for Koresh for possession of illegal firearms and explosives as well as a search warrant for the Branch Davidian property.[49]

ATF tactical planners concluded that either a siege or raid was the primary option for carrying out the warrants in the face of anticipated resistance. A siege operation would establish an armed perimeter around the property until the Branch Davidians surrendered. Given the large stockpiles of food and water, this option would likely take weeks or months to conclude. There was also the possibility of mass suicide. In contrast, a raid would end rather quickly and encompass an entry relying on the element of surprise. Attempts to lure Koresh away from the property were dismissed due to intelligence reporting indicating Koresh rarely ventured off the property. ATF tactical planners opted for a raid and began developing a tactical plan that hinged on separating the group from its weapons.[50]

In October 1992, ATF learned that the *Waco Tribune-Herald* newspaper had also initiated an investigation into Koresh. Such media interest in the Branch Davidians ultimately hampered ATF's investigation. The local newspaper reportedly began their investigation into Koresh during April 1992. By January 1993, reporters were putting the finishing touches on the newspaper's "Sinful Messiah" series, which purportedly contained "startling revelations" about the Branch Davidians, their leader, and their lifestyle. The article alluded to the group amassing weaponry.[51]

In January 1993, ATF approached representatives of the *Waco Tribune-Herald* and requested that they delay publication to ensure officer safety and preserve the integrity of the investigation. ATF tactical planners met twice with newspaper representatives during February 1993 and disclosed potential dates for the operation and training. At both meetings, the *Tribune-Herald* agreed to withhold publishing the "Sinful Messiah" articles for no more than a month.[52]

During the week preceding the planned raid, ATF agents were making final preparations for the operation, while the newspaper continued preparing its "Sinful Messiah" series for publication. ATF agents involved in the operation assembled at Fort Hood for three days of training. In addition, ATF established a command center at Texas State Technical College near Waco and finalized logistical support from local suppliers as well as state and local law enforcement. During this time, *Tribune-Herald* reporters tried to contact Koresh about the impending newspaper series to get his reaction. Their calls were ignored. Nevertheless, they anticipated a strong negative reaction, so they implemented new security procedures at the newspaper office in case of any threats.[53]

As the raid date approached, pressure began to mount as ATF planners attempted to schedule the raid ahead of the "Sinful Messiah" newspaper story. On Wednesday, February 24, 1993, ATF decided to move the raid date up from Monday, March 1, to Sunday, February 28. They were under the impression that the *Waco Tribune-Herald* planned to publish its "Sinful Messiah" series that same day. However, as the weekend approached, newspaper officials notified ATF that the series would start on Saturday morning instead of Sunday. Despite the confusion, ATF raid planners decided not to alter their plan. Too much time, money, and resources had been invested in preparing for the operation to simply postpone it and develop a new strategy. The ATF knew they could not prevent the newspaper from publishing, so raid planners expedited their plans. They decided to have the undercover agent visit Koresh on Sunday morning before the raid to assess his reaction to the newspaper story.[54]

To complicate matters further, ATF headquarters in Washington, D.C., informed raid planners on Friday afternoon that Department of the Treasury officials decided the raid should not go forward for safety reasons. By Friday evening, ATF director Stephen Higgins was able to resolve Treasury officials' concerns and received permission to proceed with the operation. Director Higgins reportedly assured Treasury officials that "those directing the raid were under express orders to cancel the operation if they learned that its secrecy had been compromised or if those in the compound had departed from their established routine in any significant way."[55]

As the weekend approached, both the *Waco Tribune-Herald* and a local television station, KWTX, were aware of the impending law enforcement operation at the Branch Davidian property. *Tribune-Herald* had received a tip as to the precise time of the raid. ATF later learned that KWTX received its information from a dispatcher with a local ambulance service providing support to the ATF operation. By Saturday evening, eleven news reporters from the *Waco Tribune-Herald* and KWTX were assigned to cover the ATF operation and were dispatched to the area surrounding the Branch Davidian property.[56]

About an hour before the raid, an ATF undercover agent walked over to the Branch Davidian property to assess whether Koresh had been angered by the newspaper article. When the agent arrived, he was asked to join a Bible study. It did not appear to him that Koresh was even aware of the "Sinful Messiah" article. Concurrent to their study session, a KWTX cameraman traveling toward the property approached a letter carrier to ask about the location of the Branch Davidian property. The letter carrier, who happened to be one of Koresh's followers, provided directions to the cameraman. During the course of their conversation, the cameraman told the letter carrier about the impending ATF raid. The letter carrier immediately contacted Koresh and warned him.[57]

The ATF undercover agent reported that he did not hear the specific warning, but noticed that Koresh was visibly upset and shaking when he returned to the Bible study. Koresh told his followers that the ATF and National Guard were coming. Upon hearing Koresh's statement, the ATF undercover agent immediately left the property. Upon reaching the undercover residence, he reported what he observed to the tactical coordinator, who in turn relayed the information to the incident commander. Not realizing the significance of the undercover agent's information, the raid commander decided to proceed with the raid.[58]

On February 28, 1993, at approximately 9:30 a.m., seventy-six ATF agents, concealed in cattle trailers, arrived at the property to serve the search and arrest warrants. Koresh had forty minutes from the time of the tip to ATF's arrival to plan and prepare a deadly ambush. ATF agents were entirely unaware that Koresh and some of his followers had armed themselves and were planning to resist violently. As the cattle trailers entered the driveway, there were no visible sign of activity inside or outside the property. When one agent remarked over the radio, "There's no one outside," a second agent responded, "That's not good."[59]

As planned, the cattle trucks stopped in front of the Branch Davidian residence. The first team to exit the cattle trailers was comprised of ATF agents armed with fire extinguishers for distracting dogs at the residence. As one agent discharged a fire extinguisher at the dogs, another opened the front gate leading to the residence. Koresh opened the front door and yelled, "What's going on?" ATF agents identified themselves, stating they had a warrant, and yelled "Freeze!" and "Get down!" Koresh immediately slammed the door before the agents could reach it.

Heavy gunfire erupted from inside the residence through the front door. It was directed at the ATF agents. The force of the gunfire reportedly bowed the front door in an outward direction. An ATF agent closest to the door was shot in the thumb before he dove into a pit near the front door. As agents returned fire, gunfire erupted from almost every front window of the residence. The Dallas and Houston tactical teams took the impact of the initial barrage of bullets as they were approaching the front of the residence. Agents retreated, scrambling for cover. One of the first shots fired at the agents hit the engine block of the lead pickup truck, disabling it.[60]

As the Dallas and Houston tactical teams attempted to get to the front of the residence, the New Orleans tactical team approached the structure's east side. Cult members reportedly threw homemade hand grenades at the agents in an attempt to slow down the assault. Seven agents from the New Orleans team approached the east wall of the residence and used a ladder to climb to the roof. Special agents Conway LeBleu, Todd McKeehan, Kenny King, and David Millen had planned to enter Koresh's bedroom on the west pitch of the roof. LeBleu and McKeehan were killed while attempting this objective. King was also shot six times before managing to roll off the roof, landing in the courtyard behind the residence. He laid there trapped during the shootout, too injured to move. King was finally rescued almost an hour and a half later, when both sides reached a cease-fire.[61]

Simultaneously, three other ATF agents were planning to enter a window on the east pitch of the roof that led to the "weapons room." As the agents reached the roof, they soon came under gunfire.[62] One of the agents managed to break the window, which allowed three other agents to enter the residence. As they entered the room, an unidentified Branch Davidian armed with an assault rifle backed out of the room and opened fire at the ATF agents through the walls. The agents returned fire but were unable to suppress the attacker's gunfire and were forced to make a hasty retreat. During the retreat, the attacker entered the room and shot an ATF agent twice in the upper thigh. Another agent returned fire and the attacker fell. The agent maintaining his position on the roof was forced to leave the location as multiple bullets blasted through the side walls and up through the roof of the residence. He narrowly escaped the attack by jumping down a ladder. The remaining three agents followed in the fourth agent's footsteps. The injured agent was shot a third time as the others attempted to drag him to a safe location. One of the agents broke his hip and severely fractured his leg from the fall down the roof.[63]

Special agents Steven D. Willis and Robert J. Williams were also killed during the ATF raid. Willis, a member of the Houston tactical team, had taken cover behind a van parked near the right front corner of the residence when he was fatally shot. Williams, a member of the New Orleans tactical team, was providing cover for other agents mounting an assault on the roof. Intense gunfire forced him to seek cover behind a large metal object on the ground to the east side of the residence, where he was shot and killed.[64]

The gunfight continued for approximately ninety minutes from the time agents arrived at the Branch Davidian property. Despite unrelenting gunfire, the ATF agents had no choice but to remain in their positions. The open, flat prairie surrounding the residence made a retreat unsafe and virtually impossible. Due to the constant and lengthy period of gunfire, ATF agents were forced to conserve their ammunition. They only returned fire when they saw individuals engaging in threatening action. Koresh and his followers, however, were not constrained. They had a seemingly limitless supply of ammunition estimated at around several hundred thousand rounds. They also had the tactical advantage of being able to hide and move within the residence. Branch Davidians were reported to have shot in the direction of the undercover house and reporters standing on the road in front of the property.

At approximately 11:00 a.m., a cease-fire was finally arranged, and the agents were permitted to leave the property.[65] The casualties were staggering—four ATF agents killed, twenty agents wounded, some severely. At least two Branch Davidians were killed by ATF agents, and several others, including Koresh, were wounded. Autopsies performed revealed that five Branch Davidians were likely killed during the initial assault. Two may have been killed by agents returning fire. A third was fatally shot in the mouth in a manner consistent with suicide. Another was shot execution-style in the back of the skull in an apparent mercy killing by another Branch Davidian, and a fifth likely died from loss of blood. Koresh was shot in the pelvis and wrist.[66]

Within hours of the shootout, ATF requested assistance from the FBI to help resolve the standoff situation. FBI headquarters dispatched hostage negotiators and other personnel to the scene. As FBI officials arrived on scene, they faced a daunting situation that included a large number of people who had barricaded themselves, refusing to surrender. The unknown number of suspects was heavily armed, possessing hundreds of weapons including fully automatic machine guns, .50-caliber rifles, and substantial supplies of ammunition, food, and water. Of greatest concern, law enforcement and civilians had already been either killed or seriously wounded during the initial operation, and those remaining inside the residence had already shown their willingness to respond violently to government authority. For these reasons, the FBI also sent the HRT to the scene.[67]

Federal law enforcement officials began negotiations with Koresh soon after the shootout started and were able to negotiate a cease-fire. The FBI assumed control over these discussions within hours of the cease-fire. Over the next fifty-one days, FBI negotiators spoke to fifty-four individuals inside the Branch Davidian residence for a total of 215 hours. Between February 28 and March 23, 1993, federal authorities were able to negotiate the successful release of thirty-five people, including twenty-one children. After debriefing the adults, federal investigators concluded that most or all of these individuals were essentially "expelled" by Koresh, who had considered them weak or troublemakers.[68]

During the entire standoff, over 700 law enforcement personnel representing numerous federal, state, and local agencies participated in the effort to conclude successfully the barricade situation. The FBI alone assigned between 250 and 300 personnel to the scene.[69]

As the siege continued, FBI officials in Washington, D.C., provided daily updates to attorney general Janet Reno and her senior advisors. After extensive and thorough review, the FBI and the U.S. military officials briefed Reno on several options for resolving the standoff. Tactical experts concluded that inserting tear gas was "the only viable, non-lethal option."[70] The agreed-upon plan called for a gradual and periodic insertion of tear gas over a forty-eight-hour period. This allowed for FBI planners to withdraw, wait, and see if people inside the residence chose to leave. The attorney general approved this operation on Saturday, April 17, and requested that it begin on Monday, April 19.[71]

On April 19, 1993, at 5:59 a.m., the FBI telephoned Branch Davidian contacts inside the residence to inform them that tear gas was going to be inserted into the structure. The FBI also wanted to assure them that law enforcement was not launching an assault. At 6:02 a.m., a tank with an attached boom approached the residence and began inserting gas into the structure. Branch Davidians inside the residence reportedly began shooting at the tank within seconds of its approach. This tear gas insertion process repeated over the course of a few hours.[72]

At 12:07 p.m., HRT officers noticed smoke coming from inside the residence. Investigators later learned that Branch Davidians started simultaneous fires at three or more separate locations within the residence. This fact was verified through multiple sources including "a team of independent arson experts; from video shot by an FBI aircraft utilizing forward-looking infrared radar technology; observations of FBI agents who saw an individual appearing to light one of the fires; and statements from survivors admitting that the Davidians set the fires."[73] Prevailing winds helped fan the flames, and the fire rapidly engulfed the residence in flames and smoke.[74]

At 12:25 p.m., FBI agents closest to the residence reported hearing what they described as "systematic gunfire" from within the burning structure. Many agents believed that the remaining Branch Davidians inside the burning structure were "killing themselves, killing each other, or both" in an attempt to avoid burning alive.[75] Hostage negotiators repeatedly broadcasted messages pleading with the residents to leave, but to no avail. Only a few heeded their calls to leave. In all, only nine adults walked out of the burning building. They received immediate medical treatment and were subsequently arrested for the murders of the ATF agents.[76]

As the structure burned, a group of HRT officers risked their lives to enter the residence through a tunnel leading to a buried bus, then to a stairway and trap door in an attempt to rescue women and children. Seeing no evidence of survivors, the agents abruptly turned around and left before they succumbed to the smoke and flame. Operational commanders on scene decided not to immediately send firefighters into the scene due to exploding ammunition and other dangerous explosions inside the residence. The HRT treated those survivors who were burned at the scene.

The injured survivors were rushed to hospitals in accordance with the previously arranged medical emergency plan.[77]

Once the fire was finally extinguished, the remains of seventy-five individuals, including twenty-five children under the age of fifteen, were recovered from the charred ruins. Official autopsies later concluded that at least seventeen individuals died of gunshot wounds, including several children. Another child was stabbed to death. In addition, five other bodies presumed to be those killed during the February 28 shootout with ATF were also discovered. All five individuals had died from gunshot wounds.

By late April, ATF firearms and explosives experts processed the fire scene and collected evidence of multiple firearms and other destructive devices that the Branch Davidians had in their possession. From this evidence, investigators concluded that "Koresh and his followers possessed 57 pistols, six revolvers, 12 shotguns, 101 rifles, more than 44 machine guns, more than 16 silencers, six flare launchers, three live grenades plus numerous components, and approximately 200,000 unused rounds of ammunition."[78] Due to the fire and explosions during the fire, experts were unable to determine with any certainty the amount of explosives that had been stored at the Branch Davidian property.[79]

A congressional panel looking into the events at Waco concluded that "the criminal conduct and aberrational behavior of David Koresh and other Branch Davidians" caused the tragedies that occurred in Waco.[80] "The ultimate responsibility for the deaths of the Davidians and the four agents lies with Koresh," the panel concluded.[81]

Congressional representatives determined that ATF's investigation of the Branch Davidians was "grossly incompetent" (despite meeting the elements of "probable cause") and "lacked the minimum professionalism expected of a major Federal law enforcement agency."[82] Congress also cited several false statements contained within the criminal affidavit related to Koresh. Congressmen believed that ATF planners "exercised extremely poor judgment" in choosing a dynamic entry approach rather than waiting to arrest Koresh when he was away from the property. Investigators had noted that Koresh rarely, if ever, left the property. Further, they believed the ATF raid plan for February 28 was "poorly conceived, utilized a high risk tactical approach when other tactics could have been successfully used, was drafted and commanded by ATF agents who were less qualified than other available agents, and used agents who were not sufficiently trained for the operation."[83] And, finally, ATF raid commanders "recklessly proceeded with the raid" despite being compromised, "thereby endangering the lives of the ATF agents."[84]

Concerning the FBI's handling of the siege, Congress concluded that the tear gas assault of April 19 should not have occurred. They believed the FBI should have continued negotiations to end the standoff "even if it had taken several more weeks."[85] The panel cited evidence that high concentrations of tear gas in enclosed spaces could significantly increase the possibility of lethal levels being reached. As a result, Congress felt the FBI failed to demonstrate "sufficient concern for the presence of young children, pregnant women, the elderly, and those with respiratory conditions."[86] Lastly, the FBI's refusal to ask for or accept assistance from other law enforcement agencies during the standoff demonstrated an institutional bias toward outside assistance.[87]

The ATF raid was captured on film for the entire world to see. KYTX cameramen were filming ATF agents as they left the cattle cars to serve the search and arrest warrants at the Branch Davidian property. *Waco Tribune-Herald* reporters also took photographs during the ATF raid. The film footage and photographs were broadcast over a variety of state, local, and national news outlets, including twenty-four-hour cable television news stations. Cable news provided continuous coverage of the event, its aftermath, and the resulting standoff. News reporters provided constant commentary and analysis about what happened and what was going on at the property. Such nationwide and continuous news coverage contributed to the large crowd of spectators and protestors outside the Branch Davidian property. Undoubtedly, public interest and the crowd of spectators during the standoff further complicated law enforcement response and ongoing operations throughout the siege.

Right-wing extremists responded to the Waco event in two major ways. First, they began to congregate at the scene of the standoff as a sign of protest to the perceived "aggressive" law enforcement tactics being used there. Many notable right-wing extremists were among the spectators and protestors who gathered near the Branch Davidian property. Timothy McVeigh was among those who came to Waco to watch the events unfold at the Branch Davidian property. He reportedly handed out antigovernment bumper stickers to the crowd. Second, they began to organize private civilian armies. Many had remembered Pratt's and Trochmann's speeches at the Rocky Mountain Rendezvous held four months earlier, citing the need for citizens to arm themselves and to organize and train their own private army. And many heeded their "call to arms" in the aftermath of the Waco incident.

THE MILITIA MOVEMENT

Within several months of the ATF raid of the Branch Davidian property in Waco, Texas, the first militia groups were formed. Among the first to organize a militia was John Trochmann, the creator of the Militia of Montana, and Norm Olson, who organized the Michigan Militia Corps. Trochmann's Militia of Montana was not a true paramilitary organization, but rather a "publisher's clearinghouse" of militia propaganda and antigovernment conspiracy materials. Trochmann made a profit from selling various "how-to" books on forming militias. He also sold survivalist manuals and antigovernment conspiracy propaganda related to fear of a United Nations–led invasion of the United States, the New World Order, "FEMA Camps" [a reference to the Federal Emergency Management Agency], among other suspected plots. For this reason, Trochmann's Militia of Montana gained the nickname "Mail Order Militia." In contrast, Olson's Michigan Militia was a true paramilitary group that was organized like a military-led organization with a hierarchal chain of command, unit structure, and ranks. More militia groups soon organized in other states.

Federal law enforcement officials define militia groups as domestic organizations with *two or more* members who (1) possess and use firearms, (2) conduct or encourage paramilitary training, and (3) espouse either violent resistance to, or the overthrow of, the federal government. All three of these factors must be present for a group to be labeled a militia.[88]

In an attempt to "save" the ideals and original intent of the U.S. Constitution, many militia members have compared themselves to the patriots of the American Revolution. They have adopted some of the symbols associated with the American Revolution, such as the "Boston Tea Party," "Minutemen," the April 19 anniversary date (Battles of Lexington and Concord in 1775), and the Gadsden Minutemen flag with its revolutionary slogan of "Don't Tread on Me." It is within this context that armed resistance against "illegitimate authority," such as the events at Ruby Ridge and Waco, are looked upon as "justifiable *defensive* actions" [emphasis added] taken to protect one's family and nation from an overreaching, zealous, and tyrannical government. In addition, some militia members further rationalize that paramilitary training, stockpiling illegal weapons, and other criminal activities are justified and necessary for self-defense and preservation. Some fringe elements of the far right further reason that defending themselves and their families against the "evil" establishment is not enough, but that preemptive, hostile action is needed.

It is extremely difficult to track the number of militia groups because many operate "underground," while others disband then reform under new group names. Likewise, the group membership may also change rapidly, leading to the formation of different factions and new leadership but without bringing in any new members. Some studies have noted that most militia members tend to be white males, between twenty and fifty-five years old.[89]

During the 1990s, federal law enforcement authorities issued a Militia Threat Typology categorizing four types of militia groups based on their level of paramilitary training, degree of radical philosophy, and possible actions.[90] Federal, state, and local law enforcement agencies were encouraged to refer to this typology and become more familiar with the types of militia groups in their area.

- Category 1 Militia—Conducts paramilitary training; bases organizational beliefs on antigovernment rhetoric; maintains primarily defensive posture; plans violent actions based upon perceived government provocation; *engages in no known criminal activity.* [emphasis added]
- Category 2 Militia—Conducts paramilitary training; bases organizational beliefs on antigovernment rhetoric; maintains primarily defensive posture; *engages in criminal activity to acquire weapons and explosives.* [emphasis added]
- Category 3 Militia—Conducts paramilitary training; *extreme* antigovernment rhetoric; *deep suspicion and paranoia; makes direct threats; plans violent action*

based upon perceived government provocation; *details response plans, surveillance and testing of explosives.* [emphasis added]

- Category 4 Militia—Conducts paramilitary training; *smaller, more isolated cells*; *openly offensive posture*; *may have splintered from another militia group*; plots *and engages in serious criminal activity, such as homicide, bombings, and other terrorist activity.* [emphasis added]

During the 1990s, several terrorist plots involved members of the militia movement. Some of them are discussed in later chapters because they involved attacking military installations in the United States. There were also several cases of militia extremists stockpiling illegal firearms and explosives.

On October 11, 1996, federal law enforcement authorities arrested six members of the West Virginia Mountaineer Militia, including the group's commander, for plotting to blow up the FBI's Criminal Justice Information Services (CJIS) facility near Bridgeport, West Virginia. The militia's commander, Floyd Looker, reportedly agreed to provide photographs of the blueprints to the FBI CJIS facility to an individual posing as a broker for an international terrorist organization plotting to bomb the building. The commander reportedly received $50,000 from the individual who was actually an undercover FBI agent. All six militia members were taken into custody for their role in the plot. Looker was convicted for his role in plotting to blow up the FBI facility.[91]

On July 27, 1996, federal law enforcement officials arrested eight militia extremists in Bellingham, Washington, who were members of the Washington State Militia. Militia members had plotted to bomb a radio tower, a bridge, and a train tunnel while a train was inside. Investigators seized two machine guns, pipe bombs, and other explosive devices from the suspects. The investigation had utilized an undercover officer who was instrumental in uncovering the militia's plans to commit the bombings.[92]

On May 2, 1997, three members of the Colorado Light Infantry militia group were arrested in Aurora, Colorado, on various firearms and explosives charges. Federal law enforcement authorities seized numerous illegal weapons including mortars, pipe bombs, machine guns, and grenades. Militia members had reportedly planned to disrupt the federal government through a campaign of pipe bombings and other violent acts.[93]

On June 12, 1997, two militia extremists were arrested for planning an armored car robbery and murdering security guards inside the vehicle. Both suspects were arrested in Jacksonville, Florida, during the final planning stages of the crime, which included stealing approximately $20 million, dismembering three guards, and killing any law enforcement officers attempting to apprehend the suspects. A subsequent investigation revealed the two men were hoping to use the armored car robbery proceeds to finance militia groups and assist them in carrying out a campaign of violent confrontations with the U.S. government.[94]

SOVEREIGN CITIZEN MOVEMENT

Following the confrontations at Ruby Ridge in 1992 and Waco in 1993, right-wing extremists in the United States had focused their efforts primarily on forming armed militia groups. However, by 1995, law enforcement and the judicial system began to recognize a new right-wing extremist phenomenon, with an emphasis on hybrid extremist groups embracing a combination of beliefs including common law justice, secessionist doctrine, and the right to maintain a well-regulated militia. Federal law enforcement refer to these groups as the sovereign citizen movement because many individuals in these groups wanted to renounce their U.S. citizenship; form their own governments, court system, or territory; and secede entirely from the United States. New groups began to emerge, referring to their bogus territories as the Republic of Texas, Christ County Kingdom of God, and Justus Township.

Sovereign citizens want to absolve themselves from their duties, responsibilities, and obligations as a U.S. citizen. Some want to secede from the United States and become totally self-sufficient, relying upon themselves as sole providers for the needs of their families and other sovereigns. Sovereign citizens adhere to a variety of political and religious ideologies, such as extreme antigovernment views, antitax, antiabortion, Christian fundamentalism, as well as racist ideology. Sovereign citizens are generally self-sufficient, but some have formed groups that have ranged in size from a few people, to several dozen members, and as large as a few hundred people.

Modern-day sovereign citizen activity in the United States originated with an ultra-right-wing movement called the Sheriff's Posse Comitatus (or plainly "Posse Comitatus"), which comes from a Latin phrase meaning "power of the county."[95] The Posse Comitatus group did not recognize federal or state law enforcement authority and resorted to the county sheriff as the "chief" law enforcement officer of the land, since he is a publicly elected official.[96]

In 1969, the first of these groups was formed in Portland, Oregon, calling itself the Sheriff's Posse Comitatus.[97] Another group, the Christian Posse Association, was organized in California later that year. By 1974, there were approximately eighty Posse-related groups throughout the country. The farm crisis of the early 1980s provided fertile ground for gaining new recruits into the Posse Comitatus movement.

At the core of the Posse belief system is the conviction that no citizen has to submit to any government authority higher than the county sheriff.[98] As a result, Posse adherents believe that they are not obligated to pay federal income taxes or Social Security payments, nor possess driver's licenses, vehicle registrations, or license plates.[99] Furthermore, Posse members believe that their unique doctrine is inspired and approved by God. Therefore, paying taxes is not only illegal, but sinful.[100] In 1983, the Posse Comitatus gained nationwide exposure during an incident in Medina, North Dakota, involving one of its members—Gordon Kahl.

The U.S. Marshals service issued a warrant for Kahl's arrest. Prior to the Medina shooting incident, Kahl had been imprisoned at Fort Leavenworth federal penitentiary for not paying federal income taxes. Upon his release, Kahl violated his probation and continued to refuse to pay his federal income taxes. In February 1983, four U.S. Marshals and two local law enforcement officers decided to confront Kahl after he left a Posse meeting. Authorities set a roadblock along a rural highway near the entrance to Kahl's residence. A shoot-out occurred, resulting in the deaths of two U.S. Marshals and the wounding of two other officers. Kahl's twenty-one-year-old son was also wounded. Kahl fled the state, resulting in a nationwide manhunt. In June 1983, federal law enforcement authorities found Kahl living in a remote location in northern Arkansas. Another shoot-out occurred, resulting in the deaths of Kahl and a county sheriff.

Over time, Posse membership declined because of faltering leadership. During the late 1980s, many Posse leaders were arrested and imprisoned. Others died of natural causes. Still others met violent deaths—like Gordon Kahl. The Posse Comitatus did not survive as an organized group. However, the Posse belief system continues to be embraced by thousands of people.

Today's sovereign citizen movement is the direct ideological descendant of the Posse Comitatus of the 1980s. Sovereign citizens are known for their campaigns of "paper terrorism"[101] and their willingness to commit acts of violence when resisting authority. Although these groups do not appear as violent as armed paramilitary groups, they are equally extreme and just as dangerous.

Sovereign citizens have their own version of law that is derived from a combination of the Magna Carta, the Bible, English common law, and various nineteenth-century state constitutions. Central to their argument is the view of a Supreme Being having embodied every person with certain inalienable rights as stated in the U.S. Declaration of Independence, the Bill of Rights, and the Bible.

The goal of the sovereign citizen movement is to defy legitimate government institutions, specifically those associated with the judicial branch and law enforcement. To assist in accomplishing this objective, they have organized a parallel judicial system to handle a variety of civil and criminal cases. Sovereign citizens use the primary tactic of issuing phony legal documents in an effort to intimidate or defraud their enemies. These documents include criminal indictments against publicly elected officials, fraudulent property liens, bad checks, counterfeit money orders, and declarations of sovereignty.

Sovereign citizens have armed themselves on occasion in an effort to defend their perceived rights of freedom and their revocation of citizenship. For example, federal authorities confronted members of a sovereign citizen group calling itself the "Montana Freemen" at a ranch in Garfield County, Montana, on March 25, 1996.[102] In the past, the Montana Freemen posted several bounties calling for the arrests and executions of various local officials. Members of this extremist group submitted numerous fraudulent money orders and property liens to local financial institutions asking for huge sums of money as payment for debts. One member submitted a $20 million money order to a small-town mayor asking him to cash it. The group was heavily armed and refused to surrender to authorities, leading to an 81-day standoff.[103] On June 13, 1996, federal authorities negotiated an end to the confrontation. In all, eighteen members were arrested and convicted of various federal crimes.[104]

Also, on December 18, 1995, federal law enforcement authorities investigated a 100-pound ammonium nitrate and fuel oil bomb placed in a thirty-gallon plastic drum behind a parked vehicle at an Internal Revenue Service (IRS) building in Reno, Nevada. A three-foot fuse had been lit but apparently burned out before reaching the explosives. An alert IRS employee discovered it while parking at the IRS building. On December 28, 1995, federal agents arrested Joseph Martin Bailie and Ellis Edward Hurst for placing the bomb at the IRS facility. Investigators believe the two men delivered the device and lit the fuse the previous evening when the building was closed after normal business hours.[105]

WHITE SUPREMACIST MOVEMENT

Another core segment of right-wing extremism is the white supremacist movement. Law enforcement officials have long believed that white supremacists constitute the most violent and dangerous component of right-wing extremism because of their willingness to act on their hatred and, in some cases, their religious justification for violence and terrorism. White supremacists believe that Caucasians, specifically Northern Europeans and their descendants, are intellectually and morally superior to other races and ethnicities. While traditional targets of white supremacists have been Jews and African-Americans, white supremacist bigotry has broadened its focus in recent years to include other ethnic groups such as Hispanics and Asians as well as alternative lifestyles such as gay and transgendered individuals.

White supremacists can be broadly grouped into four general types: neo-Nazis, members of the Ku Klux Klan (KKK), racist skinheads, and Christian Identity adherents. They each encourage and support racial separation or segregation. They share similar views on immigration, abortion, interracial marriage, multiculturalism, alternative lifestyles, and foreign outsourcing of labor from the United States.

White supremacists like to use terminology when referring to themselves in an attempt to downplay their view of racial superiority. For instance, some white supremacists like to deny they are "supremacists" and state they are only "white separatists," meaning they just believe in separation of the races. Or they will refer to themselves as a "white nationalist," stating that they are only supporting their ethnic heritage. Don't be fooled or misled into thinking these terms somehow exonerate them from being hate-based or are less menacing than the term "white supremacist" suggests.

According to some political scientists, white separatists and white supremacists are technical subsets of white nationalism.[106] A prolonged and careful examination of their propaganda and rhetoric will clearly demonstrate there is no major difference between a white nationalist, a white separatist, and a white supremacist.

Neo-Nazis can be described as groups or individuals who adhere to and promote Adolf Hitler's beliefs and use Nazi symbols and ideology. Neo-Nazis subscribe to racist as well as anti-Semitic beliefs, many based on national socialist ideals derived from Nazi Germany. They attempt to downplay or deny the Holocaust.

In February 1998, six former members of the neo-Nazi Aryan Nations were arrested in Illinois and Michigan for various weapons violations. The six men had recently formed a new white supremacist group called The New Order (TNO), named after the original "Order" terrorist group started by Bob Mathews during the 1980s. TNO members possessed firearms, bomb-making materials, hand grenades, and a pipe bomb. The group had planned to rob banks and an armored car, poison a water supply, as well as murder a prominent civil rights attorney and other perceived enemies, among other attacks.[107]

On April 14, 1999, federal agents arrested an Aryan Nations member in Cincinnati, Ohio, for planning to attack a federal building and assassinate a prominent civil rights attorney. A search of the suspect's vehicle revealed that he possessed military training manuals, bomb-making instructions, and other military-related items.[108]

The KKK is a secretive, fraternal, and religious organization of Anglo-Protestant men and women born in the United States. It is pro-Southern and known for its violent criminal activity, which has included lynching, arson, shootings, bombings, and other deplorable acts. The KKK is also known for its symbolic rituals and secretive ceremonies that include various colored robes, hoods, secret hand clasps, and code words.

On April 22, 1997, four members of the True Knights of the Ku Klux Klan were arrested in Wise County, Texas, for planning to rob drug dealers and an armored car. The suspects planned to blow up a natural gas processing and storage facility as a diversion for the armored car robbery. Federal authorities learned that KKK members had detonated at least two practice explosive devices in preparation for the planned attack on the natural gas processing facility. If they had been successful in carrying out the attack, the resulting explosion may have caused a lethal hydrogen sulfide gas release into the surrounding community, which would have resulted in a mass casualty event.[109]

Racist skinheads are primarily young white supremacists who combine their racist ideology with a skinhead ethos in which "white power" music plays a central role. Racist skinhead attire may include a shaved head or very short hair, jeans, thin suspenders, combat boots or Doc Martens, a bomber jacket (sometimes with racist symbols), and tattoos of Nazi-like emblems. Some, however, are abandoning these stereotypical identifiers. Racist skinheads are different from their antiracist and traditional skinhead counterparts, who generally do not endorse racist, nationalist, or political views as a group. Racist skinheads are also prone to criminal activity such as drug trafficking, identity theft, and home invasion robberies. They have been referred to as the "foot soldiers" of the white supremacist movement because of their willingness to promote and act upon their racist views through violence and criminal activity.

Christian Identity is a racist religious philosophy that maintains white people, not Jews, are "God's Chosen People." They believe that white people are the true descendants of the Twelve Tribes of Israel[110] and that modern-day "Jews" are a nomadic people impersonating the "House of Israel" to confuse Biblical truth as well as gain worldwide sympathy. Groups or individuals can be followers either of the "Covenant" or of the "Dual Seed-Line" doctrine. Both doctrines teach that Jews are conspiring with Satan to control world affairs and that the world is on the verge of the biblical Apocalypse. Dual Seed-Line doctrine is a particularly disturbing brand of Christian Identity that teaches that Jews are the literal offspring of Satan and that nonwhites, who are often referred to as "mud people," are not human beings. Christian Identity adherents have been linked to several violent crimes and terrorism acts during the 1990s.[111]

On July 27, 1996, a pipe bomb exploded at Centennial Olympic Park in Atlanta, Georgia, during the 1996 Summer Olympic Games. The resulting explosion killed one person and injured 112 bystanders. A second individual responding to the scene of the explosion died of a heart attack. The device had been disguised in a green military backpack with a metal plate inside to direct the blast into the crowd of people who had gathered to watch a music concert.[112] Eric Robert Rudolph was later charged with carrying out this attack.[113] He was also responsible for bombing an abortion clinic in Sandy Springs, Georgia, on January 16, 1997;[114] the bombing of the Other-Side Lounge, a gay nightclub, in Atlanta, Georgia, on February 21, 1997, that injured five patrons;[115] and the fatal bombing of another abortion clinic in Birmingham, Alabama, on January 29, 1998, which resulted in the death of an off-duty police officer and severely wounded a nurse at the clinic.[116] Both the Sandy Springs and Other-Side Lounge bombings utilized secondary devices targeting first responders and law enforcement officers. Fortunately, neither of the original explosions or secondary devices killed anyone.[117]

On October 7, 1996, three members of a Christian Identity terrorist cell were arrested for attempting to rob a U.S. Bank branch in Portland, Oregon. A fourth member of the group was later arrested in Washington. All four men belonged to a secretive terrorist group called the Phineas [*sic*] Priesthood. This group was responsible for carrying out two previous robberies as well as the bombings of a bank, abortion clinic, and newspaper office in Spokane, Washington, during the summer of 1996. Authorities seized machine guns, body armor, ski masks, and grenades from the suspects' vehicle.[118]

The Southern Poverty Law Center (SPLC) a civil rights organization based in Montgomery, Alabama, that monitors right-wing extremism, has been tracking the number of white supremacist and other hate groups in the United States for nearly three decades. They have reported a steady increase in the number of hate groups each and every year. Between 2000 and 2008, there has been a 54 percent increase, according to the SPLC.[119] The sustained increases each year can be largely attributed to an "angry backlash against non-white immigration and starting in the last year of that period, the economic meltdown and the climb to power of an African-American President," the SPLC reported.[120]

In 2009, the SPLC reported 932 active hate groups—a slight increase from 2008.[121] Among the hate groups listed by SPLC in 2009, there were 187 Klan groups, 161 neo-Nazi groups, 122 racist skinhead gangs, 37 Christian Identity organizations, and 132 other white nationalist groups in the United States.[122] During 2009, there were active white supremacist groups operating in all fifty states.[123] Texas led the nation in the number of white supremacist groups with forty-seven organizations—twenty-six chapters of the Ku Klux Klan alone.[124] New Jersey was second with thirty-five white supremacist groups with an overwhelming twenty-three racist skinhead crews.[125] California was a close third with thirty-two white supremacist groups—a combination of neo-Nazis, racist skinheads, and other white nationalists.[126] The following states rounded out the top ten states with the highest number of white supremacist groups: Tennessee (thirty-one groups); Florida (thirty groups); Missouri (twenty-five groups); Georgia (twenty-two groups); Illinois and Ohio (twenty-one groups each); Louisiana (twenty-five groups). Finally, Michigan had nineteen groups and Alabama and Virginia had eighteen groups each.[127]

RIGHT-WING EXTREMIST RETALIATION FOR RUBY RIDGE AND WACO

On April 19, 1995, a former U.S. Army veteran who was unable to find job satisfaction in his postmilitary life applied the very skills he had learned in the Armed Forces to blow up a federal building, killing 168 people and wounding hundreds of other innocents, including children. The Alfred P. Murrah Federal Building in Oklahoma City, Oklahoma, was specifically chosen for its symbolic value. This federal building housed numerous U.S. government agencies, but it was also the location of the FBI and ATF field offices involved in the Waco siege in Texas in April 1993. ATF agents from this field office participated in the raid of the Branch Davidian property outside of Waco, Texas, on February 28, 1993.

Over the ensuing two years, McVeigh had grown increasingly angry over the events at Waco. He watched the Branch Davidian compound burn to the ground, resulting in the deaths of the sect's leader, David Koresh, and seventy-eight followers including women and children.

As news spread nationally, and eventually throughout the world about the Oklahoma City bombing, many counterterrorism experts on television expressed their certainty that foreign terrorists had carried out the dastardly act of murder. I instinctively knew it was most likely an antigovernment extremist. Not only was April 19 a symbolic day for members of the militia, tax resistors, and sovereign citizen movement, it did not make sense that foreign terrorists would target a federal building that housed federal law enforcement agencies, the IRS, and the Social Security Administration in the heartland of America. During the aftermath of the Oklahoma City bombing, the media, government officials, and private sector counterterrorism officials displayed their bias when jumping to the conclusion that Muslim extremists were likely responsible for the attack. Today, there is still this same bias and lack of understanding related to domestic terrorist threats at the highest levels of the U.S. government, including congressional representatives, Homeland Security officials, and federal law enforcement authorities.

In early October 1995, unknown person(s) deliberately tampered with the westbound tracks belonging to Southern Pacific Railroad. On October 9, 1995, the Sunset Limited, a twelve-car Amtrak passenger train traveling from New Orleans to Los Angeles, derailed near Hyder, Arizona, killing one passenger and seriously injuring twelve others. At least 100 additional people received minor injuries. Federal investigators at the scene found four typed letters mentioning the ATF, "Ruby Ridge," and "Waco." The letters were signed "Sons of Gestapo." Despite receiving the anonymous claim of responsibility, investigators are unclear whether the incident was a criminal act of sabotage or terrorism. No arrests have been made in connection to this case, and the FBI continues to investigate the incident as a suspected act of terrorism.[128]

THE DECLINE OF MILITIAS

The SPLC tracked the rise of militia groups during the mid-1990s. In 1997, the SPLC noted at least 165 militia groups in the spring 1998 edition of their *Intelligence Report*, a quarterly publication sent to law enforcement and other interested organizations.[129] By 1999, there were sixty active militias operating in twenty-five states.[130]

Several factors led to a rapid decline in the number of militia groups and militia membership in general. It began with the Oklahoma City bombing. This terrorist act, and other subsequent terrorist plots linked to militia extremists, scared many away from the militia movement. Between 1995 and 1999, there were numerous arrests of militia members, including some leaders in the movement, for weapons and explosives violations as well as plotting acts of terrorism. Twenty states also passed antimilitia laws, essentially banning paramilitary training activity in their respective states. The news media demonized the militia movement in several media exposés and investigative reports. Many other militia members were simply bored with the revolution that never came. There was no foreign invasion, the New World Order conspiracy failed to materialize, and Y2K turned out to be a non-event. Still others who were more hardcore left the militia movement to join other extremist groups in the white supremacist and sovereign citizen movements. There was also a change in the presidency back to a Republican-led administration.

OTHER RIGHT-WING EXTREMISM TRENDS DURING THE 1990S

Despite the spectacular nature of some right-wing extremist attacks in the United States during the mid-1990s, federal, state, and local law enforcement were relatively effective in deterring right-wing extremist violence throughout the country. During the 1990s, law enforcement successfully prevented several violent right-wing extremist plots to attack civilian and government targets in the United States. Other factors contributing to law enforcement success in combating violent right-wing extremists are the existence of highly visible law enforcement presence and a general lack of terrorist infrastructure within the United States, which increases the difficulty of sustaining an ongoing campaign of extremist violence. Nevertheless, violent right-wing extremists were successful in carrying out dozens of small-scale violent attacks during the 1990s.

It was during the mid-1990s that horrific acts of right-wing extremist violence such as the Oklahoma City and Centennial Park bombings occurred. These attacks were intentionally designed to inflict mass casualties. Violent white supremacists, particularly those associated with the neo-Nazi and Christian Identity ideologies, were the most likely group to engage in violent action against law enforcement during this time period. Small arms and improvised explosive devices were the weapons of choice for right-wing extremists because they are widely available and easy to construct and use.

The advent of information age technologies, such as the Internet during the 1990s, gave right-wing extremists greater access to open-source information concerning weapons, tactics, and targeting. New technologies also permit encrypted communication and networking among extremists worldwide. As a result of these technological advances, active membership in organized, aboveground extremist groups started to decrease. More radical, hardcore members also began forming "underground" or clandestine groups. A terrorist phenomenon called the lone wolf (an individual acting alone to commit acts of violence) emerged as a preferred method of attack.

During the 1990s, right-wing extremists began to expand their interest in using unconventional weapons such as biological toxins to target law enforcement officers, public officials, and other perceived enemies. Nevertheless, right-wing extremist targets and tactics for biological and chemical attacks differed significantly from the pursuits of state-sponsored and international terrorist groups. Domestic right-wing extremists focused their unconventional weapons against specific targets, such as law enforcement officers, other government officials, or a building rather than attacking large populations. Further, their attack methods tended to focus on rudimentary delivery methods, such as poisoning a plate of food or contaminating doorknobs at an office building or vehicle. During the 1990s, domestic right-wing extremists limited their unconventional weapons interest to biological toxins, specifically ricin, rather than chemical agents or radiological material.

- On February 19, 1998, federal law enforcement officials arrested Aryan Nations member Larry Wayne Harris and an associate, who were suspected of possessing the deadly bacteria anthrax at a medical clinic in Henderson, Nevada.[131] Harris's arrest came at a time when most U.S. citizens associated the use of biological and chemical weapons with rogue nations such as Iran and Iraq—not domestic extremist groups. The Army's Tech Escort Unit responded to the scene and transported the suspected deadly bacteria to a testing laboratory at Aberdeen Proving Ground, Maryland. When officials learned that the substance was composed of a nonlethal anthrax vaccine and no crime had been committed, Harris was charged with a parole violation. He had previously been arrested in 1995 for possessing samples of the bubonic plague bacteria. He obtained the bubonic plague samples from a pharmaceutical supply company in Maryland. Harris used a counterfeit letterhead to order the samples, stating they were for medical test purposes.[132]

- In February 1995, two members of the Minnesota Patriots, an antigovernment militia group, were convicted of conspiring to use ricin, a highly poisonous toxin derived from the castor bean, to murder U.S. Marshals and IRS agents in Minneapolis, Minnesota. The plot involved applying a mixture containing ricin onto the doorknobs of homes and cars of several law enforcement agents. Later that year, two other Minnesota Patriots members were convicted of similar charges.[133]

- In April 1993, Canadian customs agents confiscated 130 grams of ricin from a right-wing extremist, described as a survivalist, who was crossing the Alaskan border into Canada.[134] When questioned, the suspect said he used the ricin to "kill vermin" such as coyotes and wild dogs that harmed his farm animals. At the time, he was not charged with committing a crime and was released.[135] After Canadian authorities notified the FBI, who conducted a more thorough investigation, federal law enforcement authorities executed a search warrant of his home near Mountain View, Arkansas. On December 20, 1995, federal authorities seized the ricin and arrested the suspect, charging him with possession of a poisonous substance with intent to use it as a weapon.[136]

During the 1990s, right-wing extremists exploited a variety of social issues and political themes to increase group visibility and recruit new members. Prominent among these themes were the militia movement's opposition to gun control efforts, criticism of free trade agreements (particularly those with Mexico), and highlighting perceived government infringement on civil liberties. Similarly, white supremacists continued their longstanding exploitation of social issues such as abortion, interracial crimes, and same-sex marriage. These issues contributed to the growth in the number of domestic right-wing terrorist and extremist groups in the 1990s as well as an increase in violent acts targeting government facilities, law enforcement officers, banks, and infrastructure sectors.

4

Army Counterterrorism Analyst

Another major criticism of the Department of Homeland Security (DHS) right-wing extremism report referenced the section that concerned a small percentage of "disgruntled military veterans" being targeted for recruitment into right-wing extremist groups. This is not a new phenomenon. It is a sensitive subject that some military officials have downplayed and, at times, have failed to acknowledge.

While considering passing a bill condemning the DHS right-wing extremism report, the Oklahoma Senate issued a press release on April 22, 2009, stating, "Local veterans and supporters came to the State Capitol on Wednesday to voice their criticism of a recently released report issued by the Department of Homeland Security. The report, 'Rightwing Extremism: Current Economic and Political Climate Fueling Resurgence on Radicalization and Recruitment,' suggested those who had served in Iraq and Afghanistan as well as individuals who opposed abortion and supported Second Amendment gun rights were a potential threat to national security."[1] The press release also stated, "In the most shameful manner, the report singles out returning war veterans as the most likely candidates for domestic acts of terror and opines that America's Iraq and Afghan veterans pose great danger to the security of the United States.".[2]

A week earlier, Mr. David K. Rehbein, national commander of the American Legion, had sent a letter of concern to Secretary Napolitano on April 13 about statements made in the DHS right-wing extremism report. Among his main points in the letter, Rehbein wrote, "The American Legion is well aware and horrified at the pain inflicted during the Oklahoma City bombing, but Timothy McVeigh was only one of more than 42 million veterans who have worn this nation's uniform during wartime. To continue to use McVeigh as an example of the stereotypical 'disgruntled military veteran' is as unfair as using Osama bin Laden as the sole example of Islam." He further stated that he believed the report was incomplete and politically biased.[3]

In response to the criticism, Napolitano and her advisors held a meeting with the American Legion on April 24, 2009, at DHS headquarters in Washington, D.C.[4] Among the many topics discussed was the department's commitment to hiring military veterans. A DHS press release issued after the meeting cited that "44,000 veterans are employed at the Department of Homeland Security (DHS)—veterans make up 26% of the workforce."[5] Some of DHS executive leadership includes former military, including the deputy secretary, Jane Holl Lute, and Rand Beers, senior advisor to the secretary.[6]

Unfortunately, it is a sad fact that Timothy McVeigh is one of several former military members who have used their military training and combat skills to intimidate and kill Americans due to right-wing extremist beliefs. He was mentioned in the DHS report because he is the most well known violent right-wing extremist with a military background. There are many others, such as Eric Robert Rudolph, James Burmeister, Brian Ratigan, and Verne Merrell (Spokane Bank Robbers), to name a few. Even the country's most notorious domestic terrorist organization, the Ku Klux Klan (KKK), was organized by and comprised of veterans of the Confederate Army during the immediate aftermath of the American Civil War.[7] Throughout its more than 100-year history, the KKK has undoubtedly killed thousands of people in the United States.[8] It all started with a group of six Confederate Army veterans who wanted to enact revenge against the freed slaves, the federal reconstruction efforts, and those that supported them.[9]

Rudolph, a former Army serviceman,[10] carried out a series of bombings in Georgia and Alabama in 1996 and 1997, which resulted in at least three deaths and over 100 injuries. His bombings included two abortion clinics, a bar frequented by homosexuals, and Centennial Olympic Park.

Two members of the Spokane Bank Robbers, a Christian Identity–inspired terrorist group, were former military service members.[11,12] In 1996, they carried out a violent campaign of bombings and bank robberies. Their targets included an abortion clinic, a bank, and a newspaper office in Spokane, Washington. McVeigh was included in the report for his notoriety and the level of destruction he caused. By no means is he the sole "poster boy" for disgruntled military personnel recruited by violent domestic extremists. Unfortunately, the list is rather long and quite disturbing.

I don't take lightly the subject of right-wing extremists recruiting U.S. military personnel. I was a civilian intelligence analyst for the Department of Army for eight years. During my first three years, I was a cooperative education student, working as an intelligence analyst trainee. In July 1995, I began my full-time federal career as an intelligence research specialist for the U.S. Army. I was initially assigned to the Army Intelligence Threat Analysis Center (ITAC) at the Washington Navy Yard. In 1995, I reported to the U.S. Army Counterintelligence Center (ACIC) at Fort Meade, Maryland. Army ITAC had been dissolved during the military downsizing in 1994.

I am indebted to our military members for their selfless sacrifices while serving our great country, protecting our national security, and preserving our freedoms. I really enjoyed working with the many men and women in the U.S. Army, working at the ACIC, and attending the Military Intelligence Officer's Basic Course (MIOBC) and numerous other military training courses as an Army civilian employee.

Among my many civilian duties, I was responsible for force protection issues for U.S. Army personnel and facilities throughout the world. From 1996 to 1999, I was primarily responsible for identifying and assessing terrorist threats to the U.S. Army within the continental United States (CONUS). At the time, the Army's leadership in Washington, D.C., didn't seem very interested in the topic of CONUS force protection. There had not been an attack on military personnel or facilities in the United States since Pearl Harbor.

Force protection is a term used by the U.S. military to describe preventive measures taken to mitigate hostile actions against the Department of Defense personnel, resources, facilities, and critical information.[13] Army Regulation 525-13 outlines the Army's Force Protection Program, which is built on five pillars: physical security, information operations, protective services, law enforcement, and combating terrorism.[14]

Due to the perception that no threat existed, CONUS force protection was not taken very seriously at the time. This resulted in confusion regarding mission responsibilities related to overseeing the Army's CONUS Force Protection Program. This mission bounced back and forth and in between the ACIC, Army Criminal Investigation Command (CID), and the Army's Anti-Terrorism Operations and Intelligence Cell (ATOIC) at the Pentagon for a few years. After much uncertainty, debate, and criticism, the mission was finally moved to the Army CID. An Army CID official would later acknowledge to me that they had few resources, knowledge, or expertise to deal with the CONUS force protection mission, but they did their best with such limited resources.

Before the mission transferred from the ACIC to Army CID, I was at the forefront of protecting the Army's personnel and assets in the United States. My intelligence oversight officer and I meticulously followed the Army's intelligence oversight regulations, but we also utilized the regulations to their fullest extent. After the 9/11 terrorist attacks, the Army's executive leadership began to take CONUS force protection much more seriously. Since 9/11, there have been several terrorist plots, both international and homegrown, which have targeted military personnel and facilities within the homeland. The plot to bomb Fort Dix in New Jersey and the Fort Hood shootings are some recent examples to consider.

When I assumed the CONUS force protection responsibility at the ACIC (which is, to my knowledge, the only national-level Army intelligence unit looking at the CONUS threat) in 1996, I immediately noticed that most of the domestic left-wing extremist[15] groups that had targeted the military in CONUS were now either defunct or had been dismantled through law enforcement operations. Much of the reporting from law enforcement involving threat to military personnel and facilities within CONUS mentioned militia extremists and white supremacists. I raised the issue through my chain of command and with the intelligence oversight officer. With their support, I began to monitor threats to the military from right-wing extremists who were targeting the U.S. Army for a variety of reasons.

At the time, some questioned why I was doing this, but there were legitimate reasons for doing so—white supremacists and militia extremists were targeting Army personnel and facilities for recruitment, to steal weapons and equipment, as well as plotting violent attacks. I began working closely with the Army Criminal Investigation Command (CID) and its Protective Service Unit (PSU) at Fort Belvoir in Fairfax County, Virginia. PSU is responsible for providing protective security to Army and Department of Defense (DOD) leadership during their travel in CONUS and abroad. I also reached out to my analytical counterparts at the FBI, Bureau of Alcohol, Tobacco, Firearms, and Explosives (ATF), and other federal, state, and local law enforcement agencies. I began building a rather extensive network of professional contacts. Many of these contacts have since become friends and close associates.

When monitoring threats from within the United States, I recognized that I needed to be extremely careful to ensure that all information in my possession was collected and retained in accordance with the Army's authorized intelligence activities and mission authorities—a process called intelligence oversight and outlined in Army Regulation 381-10.[16] I would apply intelligence oversight principles to everything I did at the ACIC. I did this, not only for the eight years I worked for the Army, but also later as an intelligence analyst at the DHS's Office of Intelligence and Analysis, which was also a member of the intelligence community. Intelligence oversight is a very important concept. It was central to all I did as an analyst.

The basic tenets of intelligence oversight (IO) are outlined in Presidential Executive Order 12333, "United States Intelligence Activities."[17] IO is intended to guide intelligence officers and analysts to effectively carry out their responsibilities while ensuring that their activities affecting U.S. persons are performed in a manner that protects constitutional rights and privacy while maintaining the integrity of the intelligence profession. A U.S. person is not limited to only U.S. citizens or individuals born in the United States. It also applies to permanent resident aliens residing within the United States; unincorporated associations substantially composed of U.S. citizens or permanent resident aliens; and corporations incorporated in the United States—unless directed or controlled by a foreign government. Persons or organizations in the United States are presumed to be U.S. persons unless specific information determines otherwise.[18]

The Office of Inspector General (IG) oversees the IO guidelines for the U.S. Army. Each Army intelligence unit has its own designated IO officer responsible for overseeing the intelligence collection activities of the unit. For me, that unit was the 902nd MI Group. The role of the IO officer was to make sure the unit's intelligence activities were compliant with Army Regulation 381-10 and ensure mandatory IO training was conducted for all employees each year. The IO officer is also responsible for conducting IO inspections, both planned and spontaneous, of offices under their command to ensure compliance with the IO guidelines. IO is the primary safeguard within the intelligence community to protect the civil rights and privacy of U.S. persons.

As I've stated earlier, I became very familiar with the topic of right-wing extremists targeting the U.S. military for recruitment purposes, criminal activity, and acts of violence. For many years, there have been several well-documented cases of right-wing extremists infiltrating the armed forces, recruiting military members, and/or stealing military weapons and equipment. In 1976, several active-duty Marine Corps personnel joined the Knights of the Ku Klux Klan. They were drawn to the KKK after a violent racial disturbance at Camp Pendleton, California.[19] In 1979, a renowned KKK leader recruited several active-duty servicemen from Fort Hood, Texas, into the KKK. He used them to train other white supremacists in military weapons and tactics and to provide security at KKK events.[20] Also in 1979, twenty Klansmen were discharged from the U.S. Navy after their extremist membership was discovered. Later that year, a cross was burned aboard the U.S.S. America aircraft carrier.[21]

In 1986, the White Patriots Party, a white supremacist group, recruited several members of the U.S. Marine Corps at Camp Lejeune, North Carolina, into their organization, using them as instructors for paramilitary training exercises.[22] In 1990, five U.S. Air Force (USAF) servicemen stationed at Carswell Air Force Base in Texas were discharged from the military once authorities learned they were active participants in KKK activities.[23] In 1994, five Army servicemen at Fort Benning, Georgia, were arrested for stealing military weapons, ammunition, and explosives and selling them to white supremacists.[24] Similar events involving right-wing extremists, who are also members of the U.S. military, continue to unfold each year. Again, this is not a new phenomenon. It is a topic that military officials seem to avoid or don't want to acknowledge publicly.

Right-wing extremist interest in the military encompasses a wide range of violent and nonviolent activities. Nonviolent activities involve recruitment of military personnel, exploitation of training opportunities on military installations (such as civilian marksmanship programs), and theft of military weapons and equipment. Although these actions do not pose a direct, physical threat to military personnel, it still concerns the military, the general public, and law enforcement. Recruiting, training, and acquisition of military weapons and equipment are nonviolent activities that directly impact the capability and lethality of violent criminals and potential domestic terrorists. In addition, right-wing extremist reliance on military members, particularly within the militia movement, is critical to their perceived "end times" preparation and/or their anticipated armed confrontation with law enforcement and other government officials.

Right-wing extremists are known to use a variety of methods to recruit members. They often solicit patrons at gun shows, preparedness expositions, and public shooting ranges. And, like other terrorist organizations throughout the world, right-wing extremists recruit from the prison system. For example, the Aryan Nations sponsors a prison ministry effort that continues to remain a potent source for spreading ideology and gaining converts.

White supremacists also place an emphasis on recruiting from other similar groups like racist skinheads. Many racist skinheads travel great distances to attend white supremacist events throughout the country. At these gatherings, leaders influence and nurture violent skinheads, who are viewed as "foot soldiers" for the movement. Racist skinheads have been responsible for perpetrating some of the most violent acts against minorities, including murders, shootings, and arson attacks.

Some white supremacists have attempted to recruit at high schools, colleges, and universities throughout the country. The Project Schoolyard campaign by the National Socialist Movement (NSM) is one example. Project Schoolyard involved NSM members passing out white power music CDs to high school students in various states. Also, in January 2000, the former leader of the neo-Nazi World Church of the Creator visited Northwestern University in Illinois in an attempt to form a student chapter on the campus. When visiting these institutions, white supremacists pass out flyers and place leaflets on vehicles.

Efforts to attract new members into the militia movement were largely successful during the early 1990s. Through mediums such as shortwave radio, "muster calls" in local newspapers, fax networks, and Internet bulletin boards, militia recruiting activities during the 1990s were successful at increasing membership. In colonial times, militia commanders would call other militia members to gather at a certain time and place for roll call and announcements. This was called a muster call.

The militia movement has consistently recruited members from within the law enforcement and military communities. They target law enforcement and military personnel for their training experience (particularly weapons and explosives training), their disciplined way of life, leadership skills, and access to weapons, equipment, and sensitive information. As a result, people with law enforcement and/or military experience are often promoted to significant positions in militias and are asked to teach various firearms skills and survival techniques to other members. Those knowledgeable in the subject of right-wing extremism know that many militia members during the 1990s were either serving, or had served, in the military. The exact percentage or numbers are unknown. This does not suggest that the military is involved in the premeditated harboring of extremists. Neither does it imply that the military has turned a deliberate "blind eye" to the problem of extremists infiltrating its ranks. In March 2006, the U.S. Army released the results of a confidential written survey of 17,080 soldiers. The survey results found that "3.5 percent of [soldiers] had been approached to join an extremist organization since joining the Army, while another 7.1 percent reported that they knew another soldier who was probably a member of an extremist group."[25]

Despite this effort, more needs to be done to educate military recruiters and other personnel in identifying and purging extremists from the ranks, such as educating military recruiters on how to better identify extremist tattoos during recruitment prescreening as well as a better description of the types of organizations alluded to in the revised DOD regulation.

On November 27, 2009, the DOD tightened its policy on armed forces personnel participation in hate groups. The revised policy supposedly closed a loophole in the Defense Department's Regulation 1325.6 concerning participation in dissident and protest activity.[26] The previous loophole had to do with what constituted "active participation." Active participation was interpreted by many serving in the military as active membership. As a result, some military service members rationalized that online racist activity did not represent membership. The new revised policy prohibits military service members from publication of supremacist doctrines on websites, blogs, or other forms of electronic communication using government computers.[27] The changes to the policy were reportedly spurred by the 2009 shooting attack at Fort Hood in which Major Nidal Malik Hassan killed thirteen people and wounded thirty others.[28]

White supremacists have gone to great lengths to publicize their message to U.S. military members. In 1995, the National Alliance, a prominent neo-Nazi group, purchased a billboard advertisement outside of Fort Bragg in an effort to attract active-duty service members and their dependents to the white supremacist movement.[29] In other instances, white supremacists targeted bars and nightclubs where off-duty military personnel often gathered.

White supremacists have been known to pass out business cards soliciting recruits and urging them to call racist hotlines and listen to prerecorded messages of hate. Local law enforcement agencies have reported that white supremacists especially like to target military personnel who are trained in "special forces" tactics, so they can be used to teach paramilitary and survival skills to other antigovernment members.

Militia extremists have also shown an interest in recruiting military servicemen. In 1991, a personal friend told me that he had recently attended a preparedness exposition in Salt Lake City, Utah, and witnessed the keynote speaker openly discussing the recruitment of active-duty soldiers, members of the National Guard, and military reservists into antigovernment extremist groups. When my friend asked the guest speaker to further explain his statements, the speaker stated that recruits who have law enforcement and military experience are useful for training others on topics such as gathering intelligence, weapons and explosives handling, and wilderness survival skills.

Also, during the 1990s, Jack McLamb, a former police officer in Arizona, wrote an antigovernment booklet titled *Operation Vampire Killer 2000*, which specifically targeted members of the military and law enforcement with antigovernment rhetoric and conspiracy theories.[30] McLamb also produced a regular newsletter called *Aid and Abet* that tailored the antigovernment message to fellow law enforcement officers and members of the military.[31] Through these examples, it is clear that right-wing extremists actively target the military as a viable source for new recruits.

Another disturbing and extreme example of right-wing radicals recruiting military personnel occurred during the late 1980s. In 1987, Utah law enforcement authorities were shocked to learn that white supremacists and violent criminals had infiltrated and gained control of the Utah State Guard, a volunteer force of about 400 personnel.[32] The governor of Utah created the Utah State Guard to protect state armories in the event that the Utah National Guard was mobilized and deployed overseas. Similar state guard forces had been established in other states.

Using state funds, right-wing extremists conducted paramilitary exercises in remote locations throughout Utah and Idaho. Their unauthorized training included instruction in assassination techniques, use of live ammunition and explosives, and collection of intelligence data on political groups and institutions labeled "enemies of the state." The discovery that extremists had infiltrated all levels of the Utah State Guard prompted the governor to dismantle the organization.[33] Similar circumstances of extremist infiltration have forced the governors of Texas, Virginia, and California to also dismantle or reorganize their state guard units.[34]

Intense news coverage and media discussion following the bombing of the Alfred P. Murrah building in Oklahoma City, Oklahoma, and the murder of a black couple in Fayetteville, North Carolina, increased public awareness of right-wing extremists recruiting military personnel. To the embarrassment of the military, photos of Timothy McVeigh and Terry Nichols dressed in full battle-dress uniform, standing in formation together in the First Infantry Division at Fort Riley, Kansas, were televised across America. Biographical references to McVeigh almost always focused on his Persian Gulf War veteran status. Although military leaders were quick to announce that both men no longer served in the military, these cases underscored public concern related to the extremist-military connection. While serving in the military, both McVeigh and Nichols developed an interest in guns and a shared anger at the federal government after the events at Waco.[35] Both of these issues likely attracted McVeigh and Nichols to flirt with antigovernment groups.

From his prison cell at Terre Haute, Indiana, McVeigh wrote a letter to Fox News on April 27, 2001. The letter was written five weeks prior to his scheduled execution. In his letter, McVeigh wrote, "I explain herein why I bombed the Murrah Federal Building in Oklahoma City . . . I explain so that the record is clear as to my thinking and motivations in bombing a government installation." McVeigh continued, "Foremost, the bombing was a retaliatory strike; a counter attack, for the cumulative raids (and subsequent violence and damage) that federal agents had participated in over the preceding years (including, but not limited to, Waco)."[36]

Another event occurred later that same year that shed further light on the connection between the military and right-wing extremists. On December 6, 1995, James Burmeister, Malcolm Wright, and Randy Meadows were charged with murdering a black couple in Fayetteville, North Carolina.[37] All three men were members of the Army's elite 82nd Airborne Division at Fort Bragg.[38] They were also white supremacists.

Wright was the leader of an extremist group comprised of twelve active-duty soldiers. He had a history of violence. Wright proudly displayed a spider web tattoo that he had earned for killing someone. Burmeister had often bragged to his fellow skinheads that he was going to earn his "spider web tattoo."[39] He mentioned it twice on the night of December 6.

The three men spotted their victims walking together in a store parking lot. Burmeister and Wright exited the vehicle and shot the couple in the back of their heads using a 9mm semiautomatic handgun. Meadows sped off and later met Burmeister and Wright at their rented trailer. All three men were convicted of the murders. Burmeister is serving two life sentences for being the "trigger man."

Another lesser-known example of right-wing extremists who served in the military occurred in the Pacific Northwest. Brian Ratigan, a former U.S. Army Airborne Ranger, was a member of a secretive right-wing terrorist group called the Phineas Priesthood, which is based on anti-Semitic Christian Identity beliefs.[40] Another member of the group, Vernon Jay Merrell, was also former military. He had been enlisted in the U.S. Navy.[41]

On April 1, 1996, a pipe bomb exploded outside of a newspaper office in Spokane, Washington, causing minor damage but no injuries. Literature left at the scene and a subsequent phone call to the newspaper office expressed support for the Montana Freemen and made reference to the Bible.[42]

Fifteen minutes later, two men entered a bank in Spokane and brandished firearms and explosives. After stealing approximately $72,000, the bandits left two pipe bombs on the bank counter and lit them as they left the building. The bombs exploded, causing minor damage to the bank building, but again, no injuries.[43] Literature left at the scene was identical to that found at the newspaper office. It consisted of two pages of biblical references from the books of Jeremiah, Numbers, Revelation, and Psalms. The letter was signed using a previously unknown symbol—a black cross superimposed with the letter P. Investigators would later learn this was a symbol of members of the Phineas Priesthood (named after the biblical figure, Phinehas, mentioned in the Book of Numbers). Police later recovered the suspect's getaway car, but it produced no conclusive leads.

On July 12, 1996, two masked bandits broke a window at an abortion clinic in Spokane and threw two pipe bombs into the building. The bombs exploded, causing severe structural damage to the clinic. Fortunately, there were no injuries because the health care employees were attending a conference at another location.[44] Again, biblical writing was found at the scene. This time, it was written on the inside cover of a book of matches. The quote was from Psalm 139: 13–16 found in the Bible. The scriptural passage addresses the sanctity of life, stating that God has already determined the life of the unborn.

Minutes after the clinic bombing, three masked gunmen entered the same bank in Spokane that had been robbed three months earlier and stole $32,666 in cash. The gunmen were armed with an AK-47, a shotgun, a handgun, and a 25-pound propane gas tank with a detonator. Again, authorities found a getaway car in the same parking lot as the April 1 incident, although this time, the vehicle contained an improvised explosive device consisting of several propane canisters, a timer, and a Taser. The device was constructed so that a board with nails would puncture the propane tanks, release the highly flammable gas, then a timer would fire the Taser and ignite the propane.[45]

Further investigation identified Robert Berry, Charles Barbee, and Verne Jay Merrell as the three gunmen. Ratigan was later identified as the fourth member of the extremist cell. On October 8, 1996, Berry, Barbee, and Merrell were arrested without incident in Union Gap, Washington. Federal law enforcement agents had followed the three men from Sandpoint, Idaho, to Portland, Oregon, where they aborted an attempt to rob a bank. At the time of their arrest, the men possessed two hand grenades, one handgun, a rifle, and a fully automatic AR-15. On March 13, 1997, law enforcement officials arrested Ratigan in Spokane.[46]

Upon completion of the trial, the jury was deadlocked on the bombing charges and bank robberies but ultimately convicted the four men of lesser charges of conspiracy, interstate transportation of stolen vehicles, and possession of explosive devices.[47] In the second trial, all four defendants were convicted of the bombings and bank robberies. Berry, Barbee, and Merrell were each given two life terms without parole.

When Ratigan was in court for his sentence hearing, he addressed the court and elaborated on his Christian Identity beliefs, stating that robbery is not a crime because banks charge interest (usury) and "usury is immoral in God's eyes." He continued, "abortion is violating God's commandments found in the Bible," insinuating that violence against abortion providers is not a crime. He further stated that he did not recognize the court and that the judge was a representative of the "Prince of Darkness," or Satan.[48] The judge ignored Ratigan's ramblings and sentenced him to fifty-five years.[49]

Another way the militia and white supremacist movements have shown an interest in the military involves exploiting firearms training opportunities on military installations. Many right-wing extremists sponsor or engage in some form of weapons practice and survivalist training. Most organize or build paramilitary training facilities on private property. On a few occasions, they have chosen to exploit public recreational programs and other activities sponsored at military installations.

Programs such as military-sponsored gun clubs and the Army's Civilian Marksmanship Program (CMP) have offered firearms training opportunities for militia groups in the past. Prior to the Oklahoma City bombing, congressional authorities alleged that militia groups were using the CMP under the auspices of registered gun clubs and demanded an investigation.[50] Secretary of defense William J. Perry reportedly ordered a study of potential relationships between the CMP, registered gun clubs, and proximity of militias to the base, but once again, the military found no evidence of a militia-military relationship.[51]

Another reason right-wing extremists target the military is to acquire weapons and specialized equipment. The militia movement, in particular, has created a lucrative market for military surplus stores and vendors at gun shows that sell these items. Federal law enforcement authorities are not really concerned about the legal sale of military equipment such as canned meals, camouflaged netting, and military clothing. On the other hand, military weapons, types of military ammunition such as tracer rounds, and explosives are legitimate concerns.

For over twenty years, the General Accounting Office (GAO), the investigative arm of Congress, has conducted inquiries concerning military weapons theft and has published its findings to the public.[52,53] Since 1981, GAO investigators have found poor inventory controls, inadequate storage, and deficient security at weapons depots and armories across the country. They found weapons unguarded, holes in perimeter fences, weapons left unattended on loading docks, explosives and other highly sensitive materials stored out in the open—all in violation of government regulations.[54]

Attend any gun show and you will discover military-style weapons being sold to the highest bidder. Today, there is a steady demand and a large margin of profit to be made from selling military weapons and equipment. Even the smaller parts bring a lucrative price but could have deadly consequences.

An underlying reason for the demand of military-style weapons and ammunition among right-wing extremists is that they see these weapons, communications equipment, and night-vision devices as being necessary items for survival as well as combating "the enemy." Civilian-styled firearms are generally incapable of accommodating large-capacity magazines for firing dozens of rounds of ammunition or in a rapid enough fashion needed for the war situation that many right-wing extremists envision will occur in the United States. Growing paranoia has led some right-wing extremists to acquire illegal weapons such as machine guns, grenades, mortars, mines, light antitank weapons, and armor piercing ammunition. Right-wing extremists believe these types of weapons are needed to defeat the enemy—whether it is the United Nations (UN), the U.S. government, or law enforcement personnel.

There have been several cases involving right-wing extremists plotting to burglarize National Guard armories with the intent to steal weapons or explosives. There have also been cases in which right-wing extremists planned to ambush a military convoy that was transporting weapons and equipment to a training exercise.

On July 26, 1997, a local fisherman was enjoying the outdoors in a boat on the A.B. Jewell Reservoir near Tulsa, Oklahoma. He happened to glance over the side of his boat and caught a glimpse of what appeared to be a crate of hand grenades. He immediately notified law enforcement. Police divers would later recover a huge cache of military explosives and other weapons buried under eight feet of water. Investigators traced the weapons to a gun shop owner in Tulsa.[55] Upon arresting the owner, law enforcement officials found a business card and other information that possibly linked the suspect to white supremacist groups in Arkansas and Oklahoma. It is not known why the suspect had these materials, but authorities speculated he may have been selling weapons to white supremacists.

Among the many items recovered from the reservoir and the suspect's residence were 132 M433 HE rifle grenades, a modified claymore mine, fourteen tubes of Thermex binary explosive, three half-pound blocks of TNT, a fifteen-pound shape charge, C-4 plastic explosives, and three M49-A4 60mm HE mortars. Authorities were neither able to determine the origin of the weaponry nor how the weapons were acquired. The gun shop owner was subsequently convicted of possessing the illegal weapons.[56]

Between July 1995 and March 1996, Fitzhugh MacCrae, leader of a New England militia group called the Hillsborough County Dragoons, and two other men, one of whom was an Army Reservist, stole $100,000 worth of night-vision devices from a warehouse at Fort Devens, Massachusetts. MacCrae may have been planning to steal more equipment, including weapons, from the military installation. Law enforcement authorities, however, arrested the men before further burglaries occurred. All three men were convicted of their crimes.[57]

As demonstrated from the aforementioned cases, right-wing extremists have targeted the U.S. military for training opportunities, recruitment of military personnel, and the acquisition of military weapons and equipment. During the mid-1990s, however, an interesting trend developed that continues to exist. Members of the militia movement, known for its patriotism and support for the U.S. military, began to distrust and fear the U.S. military. Various antigovernment conspiracies alleged that the U.S. military was secretly supporting a UN plan to invade the United States. The conspiracy theories purport that the U.S. military was training UN forces in house-to-house searches, massive citizen arrests, and internment camps.

Another portion of the growing mistrust and fear involves the belief that the military was increasing its involvement in domestic operations in violation of the Posse Comitatus Act of 1878. The Posse Comitatus act states that the U.S. military should not be involved in domestic law enforcement operations.[58] Furthermore, past media and congressional attention related to the military's support roles at Ruby Ridge and Waco has drawn attention to this issue to antigovernment conspiracy theories and the militia movement. In an effort to better understand the driving force behind antigovernment conspiracy theories involving the U.S. military, it is important to examine how the military obtained its role in domestic operations.

On June 18, 1878, Congress enacted the Posse Comitatus Act in response to civil rights abuses committed during the reconstruction of the Southern states after the Civil War. The law reads, "Whoever, except in cases and under circumstances expressly authorized by the Constitution or Act of Congress, willfully uses any part of the Army or the Air Force as a posse comitatus [a body of men empowered to assist a peace officer] or otherwise to execute the laws shall be fined not more than $10,000 or imprisoned not more than two years, or both."[59] Interestingly, no one has ever been convicted under the statute despite its being the law for over 130 years.[60]

It is important to note that there are several exceptions to the Posse Comitatus Act—most notably, the use of presidential authority to deploy military troops to quell domestic violence. For example, on April 29, 1992, horrific and well-orchestrated acts of violence were unleashed in Los Angeles, California, upon the acquittal of several police officers from criminal wrongdoing in the severe beating of a black motorist. Realizing the situation was beyond the capabilities of the police department and the California National Guard, the governor of California requested federal assistance to deal with the violence.[61] On May 1, 1992, the president of the United States signed an executive order authorizing the secretary of defense to use members of the armed forces to restore law and order. This order "federalized" the California National Guard and established a 3,500-member joint task force (JTF) comprised of active-duty soldiers from the 7th Infantry Division at Fort Ord, California, and Marines from Camp Pendleton, California. On May 3, 1992, the JTF convoyed into Los Angeles and restored order.[62]

The Military Cooperation with Civilian Law Enforcement Statute was enacted in 1981 to combat narcotics smuggling into the United States.[63] This legislation allowed the military to "assist" civilian law enforcement agencies in a support role to include the use of military facilities, intelligence gathering, language translation, and surveillance. The statute, however, strictly prohibits military involvement in search and seizure, arresting, or detaining suspects and using military personnel in an undercover capacity.[64]

This statute was broadened in 1986 when President Reagan signed a National Security Decision Directive. This directive formally designated drug trafficking as a national security threat. As a result, Joint Task Force-6 (JTF-6) was created in November 1989. JTF-6 was authorized to coordinate the military's growing support to law enforcement relating to antidrug operations along the U.S.–Mexican border. JTF-6 operated from Fort Bliss and other facilities in El Paso, Texas. Military personnel assigned to JTF-6 trained counterdrug agents, provided transportation support, engineered roads, built fences, and conducted surveillance along the U.S. southern border.[65]

Under the direction of President George Bush Sr., the military increased its focus on drug interdiction through the implementation of a comprehensive radar system to monitor travel along the U.S.–Mexican border and the Gulf of Mexico and the use of Airborne Warning and Control System planes in the counterdrug effort. By 1996, JTF-6 had an annual budget of $24 million dollars.[66]

At one time, JTF-6 was comprised of approximately 700 soldiers—125 conducting surveillance along the U.S. border with Mexico.[67] With increased focus in recent years on illegal immigration, terrorism, and drug smuggling, there probably has been a dramatic increase in the number of personnel working for JTF-6. In addition, the DOD antidrug budget increased from $33.6 million in 1981 to $957.5 million in 1997.[68] As the war on drugs and terrorism has escalated, the military's support to civilian law enforcement operations has also increased dramatically. In the future, strategic military plans will likely continue to emphasize military operations other than war, such as peacekeeping operations, disaster relief efforts, counterdrug interdiction, and response to weapons of mass destruction.

Since 1992, there have been multiple cases of right-wing extremists plotting to attack military units and installations in the United States. Since 1995, right-wing extremists have engaged in several plots and incidents targeting U.S. Army personnel, National Guard armories, military recruiting offices, and military installations. Further analysis of this subject suggests at least five major reasons for right-wing extremist hostility toward the military.

First, some right-wing extremists view the military as a collaborator in the training of foreign troops who will participate in an eventual overthrow of the U.S. government. Second, they believe that some U.S. military forces are actively preparing for a future role in arresting U.S. citizens, confiscating their guns, and moving them to citizen detention camps—in response to a presidential declaration of martial law. Third, since most believe in a "one-world government" or "New World Order" conspiracy theory, they rationalize the stealing of military weapons and equipment in preparation for an eventual confrontation with these sinister forces. Fourth, some right-wing extremists believe the U.S. military is increasing its role in civilian law enforcement operations deliberately. For example, military advisors are reported to have been present at both the Ruby Ridge and Waco confrontations as well as military equipment. Finally, some extremists believe the military is actively plotting to "militarize" the nation's civilian police agencies in anticipation of the military taking over civilian law enforcement agencies and becoming a united, national police force.

Many right-wing extremists view the UN as an illegal organization with no legitimate authority. In addition, many members believe the UN is conspiring to create a "one-world government" or "New World Order." In order to fulfill this sinister plan, right-wing extremists believe that the UN plans to invade the United States, overthrow the existing government, and implement a new, totalitarian form of government. Some right-wing extremists also believe that the U.S. military is currently training the foreign troops who will eventually participate in this "invasion."

Four past terrorism-related cases in particular—the Arizona Viper militia, the North American Militia, the Republic of Texas, and the Third Continental Congress splinter group—illustrate domestic terrorist targeting of military bases and personnel in the United States. I was involved in monitoring these cases from a force protection standpoint while employed as an intelligence research specialist with the U.S Army. I informed U.S. Army leadership and personnel about each of these threats. In particular, I worked closely with ATF in 1996 concerning the arrests of three militia members for plotting to attack Fort Custer Army Training Center in Battle Creek, Michigan. Also, in 1997, there was a militia plot to attack Fort Hood, Texas. I monitored this case and would later become good friends with one of the undercover officers from the Missouri State Highway Patrol.

ARIZONA VIPER MILITIA

In December 1995, both the U.S. Forest Service and Arizona Game and Fish Department contacted ATF concerning the illegal activities of a militia group using the name Viper Team. On December 21, 1995, ATF special agents met with local law enforcement officers to discuss the newly formed extremist group. Two months later, an Arizona Game and Fish officer infiltrated the group and provided substantial intelligence information.[69]

The undercover officer (UC) learned that the Viper militia was a well-organized, tight-knit group that conducted regular training exercises using firearms and explosive devices. The group subscribed to virulent antigovernment ideology and professed a willingness to use violence both as a means to further its beliefs and to defend the group. The group met on a weekly basis. ATF special agents monitored and conducted surveillance at these meetings. On one occasion, agents noticed Viper members conducting countersurveillance on them. During a meeting between representatives of several Phoenix-area militias, a Viper militia member was observed walking a dog in the area, and another member dressed as a homeless man pushing a shopping cart.[70]

In January 1996, the UC attended a Viper militia training exercise and witnessed several individuals firing fully automatic firearms and detonating several improvised explosive devices (IED). The UC described a crater approximately five feet deep and twelve feet in diameter resulting from the largest of the IED detonations. Members of the Viper militia advised the UC that the IEDs were constructed using a mixture of ammonium nitrate, nitro methane, acetone, and smokeless powder. ATF agents later identified the location of each detonation and took soil samples of the surrounding terrain, which were sent to an ATF lab for testing of explosive residue.[71]

According to court documents, several meetings between the UC and Viper members were recorded electronically. During one recording, a Viper Team member stated that the group was in the process of manufacturing fifty fragmentation grenades. The grenades were to be issued to Viper Team members. Another member discussed a possible ambush location should a Viper Team member discover that the group was being followed by law enforcement.[72]

In later meetings, the UC reported that group members professed a hatred for federal law enforcement agents and threatened violence against ATF special agents and their families. One member stated that even though she was against the murder of children, "action" would be taken against entire families of agents who acted against the militia.[73]

On May 9, 1996, federal agents recorded a meeting at a militia safe house in Phoenix, Arizona. During this meeting, group members mixed various explosive ingredients and manufactured a destructive device in the apartment. Investigators were getting concerned that they could use this knowledge of bomb making to attack government officials or facilities.[74]

On May 11–12, 1996, Viper militia members conducted a training session in a remote section of Maricopa County, Arizona. ATF special agents videotaped Viper militia members firing automatic weapons and detonating destructive devices. During the session, members told the UC that "targets" needed to be identified in case the militia needed to carry out a preemptive attack. The UC convinced group members to postpone identification of the targets until a later time.[75]

On May 15, 1996, Viper members discussed the newly enacted Anti-Terrorism Bill[76] and what it might mean to them if they were arrested. Members discussed their current involvement in a conspiracy to manufacture destructive devices and whether the devices were considered "destructive" as defined by law. One member stated that the group should begin a database of names and residences of law enforcement officials and judges. He also suggested that the group should acquire voter registration lists to assist in the endeavor.[77]

On May 19, 1996, the UC attended a meeting with the Viper Team leadership. During this meeting, potential Viper targets were discussed. According to one of the members, the group would need to focus on supplies and food sources, as well as political targets. The group then provided the UC a copy of a video made by Viper Team members on May 30, 1994. The tape featured targets the group had selected for attack in case of an "emergency." Government facilities featured on the videotape included the ATF Phoenix Field Office, the Internal Revenue Service building, the offices of the U.S. Secret Service, a Department of Justice building, and a local television station in Phoenix, Arizona. The tape also included footage of the Phoenix Police Department headquarters and an Arizona National Guard base in Maricopa County.[78]

On May 20, 1996, the UC visited the home of a Viper militia member and saw several machine guns, including a Soviet Maxim machine gun mounted on a wheeled carrier at the residence. The Viper member was also in the process of manufacturing a fully automatic SKS pistol for the UC. The UC also observed approximately 250 to 400 pounds of ammonium nitrate and a 55-gallon drum of nitro methane. The combination of these two ingredients forms a binary high explosive.[79]

On June 27, 1996, a federal grand jury indicted twelve members of the Viper militia. They were charged with conspiracy to use explosive devices to further civil disorder, unlawful possession of machine guns, and conspiracy to unlawfully make and possess unregistered destructive devices.[80]

On July 1, 1996, approximately 100 law enforcement officers served nine search warrants throughout the Phoenix metropolitan area, resulting in the arrests of multiple Viper militia members. The arrests were the culmination of a six-month ATF undercover investigation. Police seized 650 pounds of ammonium nitrate, 20 gallons of nitro methane, over 100 firearms, a suspected firearms silencer, 8,000 rounds of ammunition, hand grenades and hand grenade components, detonation cord, over 200 blasting caps, battle dress uniforms displaying the Viper militia patch, bulletproof vests, gas masks, and a vast array of militia-related documents and training materials.[81]

THE NORTH AMERICAN MILITIA

In March 1996, a group of militia members left their group to form the North American Militia (NAM). Approximately twenty members met at a coffee shop in Calhoun County, Michigan, to discuss a more "offensive" course of action. Kenneth Carter, the group's leader, told his colleagues that he had identified a possible target in their area of operation that would prove to be "a lucrative one" in the event of war. At this meeting, the group's leader issued pagers to the other members for receiving codes that would designate specific targets to attack. The group officially announced its formation on April 19, 1996—the anniversaries of both the Waco fire and the Alfred P. Murrah Federal Building bombing. At subsequent meetings, members discussed various ways to finance their activities, including narcotics trafficking, robbing drug dealers, and organizing theft rings for military weapons and equipment.[82]

On November 2, 1996, group members met to discuss ways to attack key in-frastructure targets in southwestern Michigan. Objectives included sabotaging the intersection of Interstate Highway 94 and U.S. Route 131 near Kalamazoo; taking over communications facilities in Battle Creek and Kalamazoo; destroying power facilities, fuel depots, and service stations; and stealing weapons and equipment from the National Guard. At that meeting, instruction was also given on how to conduct room-to-room searches for enemies and how to make homemade explosives.[83]

Group members also discussed a rumor that the U.S. Department of the Treasury was transporting money by rail to its headquarters in Washington, D.C. Members of the group expressed an interest in stealing some of the money on these railcars to likely finance their cause.[84]

On November 8, 1996, Ken Carter attended a hunter safety class taught at Fort Custer Army Training Center, Michigan, in order to gather intelligence on instal-lation activities. Federal authorities later learned that group members had gathered information on base facilities and military units training at Fort Custer through both overt and covert means.[85]

On November 14, 1996, NAM members again met at the local coffee shop. Carter related his observations of Fort Custer and provided a revised target list that included A-10 ground support aircraft stationed at Battle Creek Air National Guard Base. The list now included the federal building in Battle Creek, the Calhoun County jail, and a specific television station in Kalamazoo. The group continued preparing for war and held more meetings to discuss their preparations.[86]

On February 15, 1997, NAM members met to discuss their perception that the number of "foreign troops" training at Fort Custer was increasing. At a later meet-ing, a NAM member gave a briefing on the alleged training activities at Fort Custer that he observed. He stated that the installation had been extremely busy and that he had observed at least 300 soldiers, some of them "foreigners," and a large number of helicopters training at the base. NAM members also entertained the thought that Chinese military forces were at the installation.

During the course of the investigation, one NAM member expressed an interest in acquiring 200 night-vision devices available for civilian purchase through surplus sales at Fort Custer. He thought the devices could be purchased for about $200 each. Federal law enforcement authorities believed the suspect was referring to military surplus items legitimately sold by the U.S. government. Surveillance and planning continued through April 1997. On April 20, 1997 (Adolf Hitler's birthday), Carter announced to the group that they would attack designated targets on June 7, 1997. Due to ongoing preparations, the date was later changed to June 22, 1997. NAM members were arrested before they could carry out the attack.[87]

On March 18, 1998, Carter, Brad Metcalf, and Randy Graham were arrested near Battle Creek, Michigan, and were convicted of various firearms and explosives violations. Law enforcement authorities confiscated two Browning .30-caliber ma-chine guns, a Browning .50-caliber machine gun, nine semiautomatic assault rifles, a fully automatic shotgun, firearms silencers, grenade shells, a large quantity of black powder and other explosive chemicals, and stockpiles of ammunition from other members of NAM.[88]

The arrests interrupted NAM's plan to attack Fort Custer Army Training Center, the Battle Creek Air National Guard Base (adjacent to Fort Custer), and other targets. To the surprise of NAM members, there was no UN-led invasion of the United States during 1997.[89]

NAM exhibited characteristics typical of a Category IV militia group. Authorities were not able to ascertain how the group planned to enter the military installations in Battle Creek and which buildings they were planning to attack. Nevertheless, investigators had enough evidence proving that NAM members had conducted intensive intelligence gathering at both locations, including the identification of specific units training at Fort Custer and the time and location of their scheduled training activities. In addition, a federal agent investigating the group reported that NAM members had used countersurveillance techniques against law enforcement officials.[90]

During the course of the investigation, law enforcement officials learned that NAM members increasingly emphasized the importance of neutralizing Fort Custer during the beginning phase of their offensive operations. Their plan included disabling the electric, water, and gas supplies to the installation. After arresting three NAM members, authorities asked one of the suspects how he felt about the possibility of inflicting harm to others while attacking the military facilities. In response to the question, the suspect replied that "they would not take prisoners." Translated, they would shoot to kill if necessary.[91]

Federal investigators also recovered a document at the militia leader's house leading authorities to believe that NAM was receiving insider assistance. The document disclosed the types of security personnel employed at each military base, whether security personnel were armed, and if so, the type of weapons carried. The document also referenced methods of patrol and call signs. It described the existence of a pocket-sized distress button kept in the front pants pocket of security personnel at the main gate. Authorities have not identified who might have provided the information but surmise the person was most likely a former civilian guard at Fort Custer.[92]

THIRD CONTINENTAL CONGRESS SPLINTER GROUP

On July 4, 1997, Bradley Glover, 57, and Michael Dorsett, 41, were arrested at a campground in San Saba County, Texas, for possessing illegal weapons and explosives, hours before an Independence Day celebration and open house at Fort Hood. At the scene, police recovered from the suspects' vehicle explosive materials, a homemade silencer, two machine guns, five pistols, 1,600 rounds of ammunition, a police radio scanner, night-vision goggles, and body armor.[93]

The arrests followed a yearlong undercover investigation into a splinter group of the Third Continental Congress, an antigovernment extremist group with chapters throughout the country. In April 1997, two undercover officers working for the Missouri State Highway Patrol overheard a discussion outside a preparedness exposition in Independence, Missouri. Several attendees left the exposition to go outside and talk about a more violent approach toward undermining the federal government. In particular, they were concerned about the training of foreign military personnel inside the United States. They believed that these foreign troops were members of the UN and were training in preparation for an eventual UN-led invasion of the United States.[94]

As a result, the militia splinter group planned to attack military installations within the United States during the Independence Day weekend. Group members had targeted Fort Hood in Killeen, Texas, and Holloman Air Force Base in Alamogordo, New Mexico. The investigation ultimately led to the arrests of five other group members in Colorado, Kansas, Missouri, and Wisconsin. Federal law enforcement authorities confiscated fourteen pipe bombs and several machine guns from other suspects. Both Glover and Dorsett were convicted of possessing an illegal firearms silencer and converting rifles to fully automatic.[95]

This Fort Hood incident is significant because it marks the first time that a right-wing militia group attempted to carry out an attack on a military installation. For this reason alone, the plot to attack Fort Hood causes concern. The following points are important aspects to consider: (1) the suspects were in the operational phase of the attack; (2) successful implementation of the attack would have resulted in many casualties; (3) the intentions and determination of right-wing extremists to attack military targets in the United States are credible; and (4) right-wing extremists had crossed a threshold—the U.S. military became a legitimate target of their revolution.

REPUBLIC OF TEXAS

The Republic of Texas (ROT) standoff in 1997 is another example of right-wing extremists targeting suspected foreign military forces within the United States. The ROT is a multifactional extremist group comprised of tax protestors, political extremists, white collar/financial criminals, and militia extremists. ROT members believe the State of Texas is a sovereign state that was illegally annexed to the United States. They further believe that the federal government is an illegal entity within "their republic." Until his arrest, Richard Lance McLaren was the self-proclaimed "Chief Ambassador" for the ROT and had worked diligently to obtain extensive media coverage for the group.

On April 27, 1997, the Fort Davis Sheriff's Department arrested an ROT member for trespassing on a neighbor's property near the town of Fort Davis, Texas. In retaliation, three ROT members from McLaren's group entered the neighbor's residence and held two occupants hostage, claiming that the captured ROT member was a "prisoner of war." State and local law enforcement agencies responded to the scene and the Texas Department of Public Safety (DPS) assumed the lead role. Texas DPS eventually agreed to release the jailed ROT member in order to secure the safe release of the hostages. Following their comrade's release on April 28, 1997, ROT members departed the residence and returned to their armed compound.[96]

Texas DPS immediately surrounded the compound, maintained a perimeter, and began negotiations with McLaren and his associates. On May 3, 1997, McLaren and four ROT members, identified as Evelyn McLaren, Richard Otto, and Greg and Karen Paulson, were arrested without incident. However, two other ROT members, Michael Matson and Richard Keyes, fled into the mountains. Matson was ultimately shot and killed after he fired shots at several tracking dogs and a Texas DPS helicopter. Keyes remained a fugitive until a few months later, when he was arrested while hitchhiking in a Texas state park. All six ROT members were eventually convicted of possessing illegal firearms and explosive devices.[97]

Texas DPS executed a search warrant on the ROT compound. Among the many items seized were several documents that mentioned military targets in Texas. One document was titled "Roving Sand '97" (a military exercise) and was dated February 1997. A map titled "Proposed Expansion of German Air Force Aircraft Operations at Holloman AFB," and an attendance roster for the "10 DEC Roving Sands Meeting" were attached to the Roving Sand '97 document. While the Roving Sand document and the expansion map were not classified documents, they were sensitive government documents that were marked "FOR OFFICIAL USE ONLY." Investigators were unable to determine how ROT members obtained the official government documents.[98]

In addition to the documents found at the compound, law enforcement authorities learned that ROT members had conducted surveillance at both Fort Bliss and Holloman Air Force Base in Texas as part of a plan to evict foreign military personnel and equipment from the state. For several years, the German military has maintained airplanes, equipment, and personnel at both military installations. Since ROT members were known to have ties to extremists in the militia and sovereign citizen movement, it is likely that ROT members believed that foreign military forces were plotting to invade the United States.[99]

BLACK HELICOPTERS

There has been a lot of public interest concerning sightings of secretive "black helicopters" in both urban and rural parts of the United States. Right-wing extremists allege these aircraft were being used as part of a secret monitoring program designed to spy on American citizens or to disseminate chemical and biological agents to sedate the population into government compliance. In addition, many right-wing extremists believe the helicopters are part of a future UN-led New World Order invasion force that will confiscate guns from Americans and round up U.S. citizens who oppose the UN, forcing them at gunpoint into citizen detention camps.

In reality, many law enforcement agencies, and some military Special Forces units, have used very dark-colored helicopters that look "black" during training exercises or other operations in the United States. The U.S. military has applied chemical-resistant coatings to some of its helicopters in an effort to disguise the aircraft for night operations.[100] This protective coating darkens the olive green color of military helicopters until they look black. In addition, many of these helicopters and their pilots train without using their flight navigation lights.

During the mid-1990s, the U.S. Army Special Operations Command had practiced counterterrorism exercises in at least twenty-one U.S. cities.[101] "Ninja-clad commandos" rappelled from helicopters onto vacant buildings, shot automatic weapons simulated with paint ball–type ammunition, and used percussion "flash-bang" grenades during simulated hostage rescue training exercises. On a few, isolated occasions, paranoid individuals, who likely believed in New World Order conspiracies, threatened the military program, its operators, and the "black helicopters." There is no evidence these exercises had anything to do with spying, a UN-led invasion, or UN raids on U.S. citizens. I know because I provided analytical support to this military program.

As night fell on Monday, February 8, 1999, residents of Kingsville, Texas, were startled—some even scared—as several "black helicopters" with no lights flew over the town. Homeowners south of Kingsville reported walls shaking, pictures rattling, and windows vibrating as the loud thump of several helicopters flew overhead.[102]

"I didn't know what was going on," the Port Arkansas mayor said in response to questions by reporters. "They (city residents) were calling me up asking me about a bunch of black helicopters."

"It was secret," the Kingsville police chief said. "I really can't talk a lot about it."[103]

The exercise involved eight Army helicopters, flying low over the rooftops of homes before suddenly dropping off scores of tactical operators dressed in camouflage over a two-block area.

Several abandoned buildings in downtown Kingsville, Texas, were the target. They were being used by the U.S. Army Special Operations Command and Kingsville police for a hostage rescue training exercise.[104]

The exercise didn't quite go as planned. A welding torch used to cut through a fence ignited a fire inside the old police station. The fire grew rapidly and soon got out of control. The building's interior was gutted and the roof received serious structural damage. It took firefighters about twenty minutes to contain the blaze.[105]

A block from the old police station, flashbang percussion grenades exploded in an old, abandoned Exxon administrative building, shattering the windows. Police reported receiving about fifty phone calls from concerned residents during the operation.[106]

A local farmer told a news reporter that he resented the maneuvers. "I don't really like this town being turned into a war zone," he complained. "Someone could have gotten hurt."

It didn't take long for the antigovernment "conspiracy nuts" to start showing up. Early the next morning, Alex Jones and his film crew arrived in Kingsville to film the operation's aftermath. Jones operates a right-wing extremist radio show that propagates antigovernment conspiracy theories, paranoia, and lies under the guise of journalism. Jones lives in Austin, Texas, where he also operates his shoddy, sensational, conspiracy-oriented news station. Jones's conspiracy documentary of the military exercises in the Corpus Christi area was dubbed "Police State 2000."[107]

Jones narrated their arrival on a personal camcorder: "On the night of February 8, 1999, right after my radio show, I got the word that Delta Force had smashed into the first of six towns—Kingsville, Texas. We got in the car and drove through the night to the south Texas coast . . . It was incredibly surreal. Shades of *Blade Runner* [a reference to the science fiction movie]."[108]

While on scene in Kingsville, Jones snuck inside the old police station and asked his listeners, "Why are they practicing taking over police stations?"[109]

"Again, you ought to just think about that for a second . . . Why are they engaging in this behavior? . . . To condition the police as well as the general citizenry," Jones speculated.[110]

While surveying the exterior of the building, Jones found a spent shotgun shell and said, "Delta Force munitions—a solid, ceramic slug used to BLAST [emphasis added] open doors. So, the 'Jack Booted Thugs'[111] don't even have to hurt their feet anymore."[112]

Jones concluded from his investigation that the hostage rescue training exercises are "complete psychological warfare against the police, the public, and everyone else in this nation conditioning us to accept a militarized police state. It's basically terrorism."[113]

Jones's unexpected arrival put a damper on the exercises for a short time, but more training operations took place the following week. On February 16, residents woke to the sharp crack of gunfire. It was a signal marking the beginning of another exercise at the old Nueces County Courthouse. Seconds later, several black helicopters operating without lights came out of nowhere, landed, and left as quickly as they came.[114]

Soldiers clad in black were part of a training scenario to rescue an ambassador being held hostage at gunpoint. Snipers situated outside the building "took out" the role players guarding the enemy stronghold. Soldiers piling out of the helicopters faced virtually no resistance as they attempted to gain access to the target.[115]

One chopper, hovering inches above a crane at the worksite for the new federal courthouse, dropped off two other snipers. Later in the exercise, the black helicopter flew back and literally "plucked" the soldiers from the top of the crane.[116]

"It was an awesome display. Those helicopter pilots were fantastic," said a former member of the military observing the operation.[117]

Two other black helicopters landed on the courthouse roof. Still others landed at the courthouse square. A large Blackhawk helicopter also emerged from the dark night sky and settled on the ground just north of the courthouse.[118]

The training exercise was completed within minutes and ended with more cracks of gunfire and the deep, heart-thumping boom of grenade explosions as the operators made their exit.[119]

The hostage rescue training exercises concluded two days later. The stillness of the night of February 18 was abruptly interrupted with the roar of helicopter rotors accompanied by small-arms fire echoing into nearby neighborhoods. The Army's elite antiterrorist team had struck again. This time, the operation was occurring at the old Brooke Army Medical Center, another abandoned building in Corpus Christi.[120]

The tactical assault began with two MD-6 "Little Bird" helicopters flying fast and low from the southeast. Seconds later, six larger UH-60 Blackhawks flew over a nearby parade ground. Suddenly, one of the Blackhawks cut sharply into the building's light and almost seemed to vertically climb the building's façade.[121]

Sniper teams were the first to pile out of the helicopters. They surrounded the seven-story brick building. Other tactical operators had already entered it and were systematically working through rooms and hallways—flashlights blinking followed by short bursts of gunfire. Their training mission was to locate and recover classified equipment from would-be terrorists.

Suddenly, there were simultaneous flashes of bright, yellow light, followed by the loud thuds of flashbang percussion grenades. During the intermittent flashes from the explosions, commandos could be seen rappelling off the roof into rooms on adjacent floors.[122]

As the operation unfolded, cars pulled off the highway and passengers exited their vehicles onto the shoulder of the road. Television news crews stood along the road with cameras trained on the target of the attack. Residents ran out of their homes. Everyone was amazed by what they were witnessing. Explosive vibrations filled the air from the sound waves generated from the detonation of plastic explosives.[123]

"This is creepy because it could really be happening right [at] my back door," said a concerned neighbor who lived five blocks away from the site.[124]

"It scared me," she said. "It's not something you see every day, and hey, we've got live action right outside of our house."[125]

At the end of the mission, all of the choppers returned in a carefully choreographed and synchronized dance. They simultaneously landed at their predestined locations, picked up commandos along with their cargo, and lifted off without a glitch. As they disappeared into the night and headed back to the airport, the helicopters finally turned on their navigation lights.[126]

As the week wore on and more training exercises transpired, some citizens began to complain. Most, however, viewed the stealthy precision of military operations with wonderment, awe, and speculation about their purpose.

The night operations dazzled residents throughout Corpus Christi. "Those are the guys that are fighting for us," an observer commented as he raised his fist into the air.[127]

I know how they felt. Being able to witness that was truly a once in a lifetime experience. I'm grateful I had the opportunity to observe the exercises firsthand.

My time at the Army Counterintelligence Center came to a close a few months after the Corpus Christi training exercises. The ACIC's CONUS force protection program came under intense scrutiny when a former employee waged a personal campaign against the ACIC under the guise of upholding the Army's intelligence oversight (IO) regulations. He supposedly was a former Army intelligence officer that reportedly participated in the controversial infiltration of student groups during the 1960s. Perhaps he carried guilt over what he had done for the military in the 1960s. He now worked for the Army's Office of Inspector General (IG).

In 1998, he led a three-day inspection of the 902nd Military Intelligence Group, which included the ACIC. I was initially suspected of having violated the Army's IO policy. The Army IG thought the ACIC might be violating the civil rights and civil liberties of Americans but could find no violations.

We had strictly adhered to the Army's IO policy. All references to U.S. citizens and extremist groups in the news articles, court records, and other reports were "sanitized" prior to retaining them. We meticulously "blacked out" all U.S. person names, which included names of extremist groups that were actively targeting the military for extremist recruitment, weapons theft, and possible attack. No reference to U.S. persons (both individuals and groups) were included in the ACIC's finished intelligence products. When referring to extremist groups, we used generic, vague terms to describe the group and their approximate location (such as "an antigovernment militia group in a particular county and state"). The Army's IO guidelines guarded against the retention of U.S. person information. As a result, I kept the sanitized information, which only focused on extremist incidents directly targeting the military, on extremist-related arrests, bombings, threats, theft, and other criminal activities and violent acts. I meticulously organized the information according to geographic location, rather than specific groups. Every product I wrote was reviewed by the IO officer and attorney. In turn, they would give me a typed letter of review referencing the title of the product and stating it had met the Army IO guidelines. Nevertheless, in the end, the Army IG felt the ACIC's CONUS force protection–related analysis had the appearance of wrongdoing.

As they left the 902nd MI Group after the inspection, the Army IG inspection team had not found a single violation of the Army's IO rules. Despite passing the inspection, the experience demoralized me. The inspection was invasive and seemed to focus exclusively on me. All of my intelligence files (hard copy and electronic) were examined page by page. All e-mail messages were reviewed—many e-mails that I had deleted many months earlier were retrieved off of the servers. It was quite the spectacle—a truly eye-opening experience.

Despite already existing safeguards, the Army IG's scrutiny of the ACIC's CONUS force protection mission continued. The former ACIC employee-turned-inspector was able to convince the Army's Brigadier General to revise its entire antiterrorism force protection regulation—Army Regulation 525-13, Antiterrorism Force Protection: Security of Personnel, Information and Critical Resources (AR 525-13). The new changes, implemented on September 10, 1998, essentially prohibited Army intelligence organizations from collecting and retaining information pertaining to incidents within the United States, even though the only incidents of concern were related to domestic extremists targeting our own personnel, equipment, and facilities. The revised AR 525-13 delegated the Army's CONUS force protection mission and responsibility to the Army Criminal Investigation Division (Army CID) at Fort

Belvoir, Virginia. The revised regulations essentially ended the ACIC's role in the Army's CONUS force protection mission.[128] Several ACIC and 902nd employees were not happy about the changes but could do nothing about it. The Army would later reverse this policy almost three years to the day, when the 9/11 terrorist attacks occurred.[129] My analytical counterparts at the ACIC, Army CID, and the Pentagon later remarked to me that I was "a little ahead of my time." In the interim, Army CID tried its best to fulfill the mission but had few resources to devote to it during the months leading up to the September 11 terrorist attacks.

The Army Terrorism and Intelligence Operations Cell (ATOIC) at the Pentagon eventually shared the mission with Army CID. Army CID would later embed two special agents at the ATOIC to monitor CONUS force protection issues, which included domestic extremist threats to the Army. Army CID attempted to hire me but could not secure me a federal position in time. I had other job applications submitted to other federal agencies, and soon I would have three job offers.

I left my civilian career with the U.S. Army and moved on to another position with a federal law enforcement agency. Nevertheless, my experience monitoring domestic extremist threats for the military afforded me an opportunity to work with great people and network with my counterparts in federal, state, and local law enforcement. It also helped me make inroads into the intelligence and law enforcement communities. The North American Militia case, in particular, gave me the opportunity to make contact with ATF. Little did I know that ATF would soon become my new employer.

5

Developing Expertise

In October 1999, I entered a new phase of my career. A few months prior, I had been selected for an intelligence research specialist position at the Bureau of Alcohol, Tobacco, and Firearms (ATF). My background investigation was now completed, and I was asked to report to ATF's Intelligence Division at its headquarters located in Washington, D.C. At the time, ATF's Intelligence Division had only been in existence for about six years. So it was still a rather new part of ATF's organization structure.

ATF's intelligence capability was highly criticized after the 1993 Waco incident.[1] As a result, the bureau began to overhaul its intelligence operations both at headquarters and in the field. Most of ATF's intelligence capability in the early 1990s resided within its approximately 1,700 special agents in the field,[2] who gathered tactical intelligence during the course of their normal investigative responsibilities. Until March 1993, there was virtually no centralized intelligence capability at ATF.

At first, the newly created Intelligence Division had a minimal staff with an eight-hour, five-days-a-week operation.[3] There was no twenty-four-hour coverage, no weekend duty, and no extended hours to support field offices on the West Coast.

The Waco incident not only pushed the bureau into the national spotlight but also exposed its intelligence vulnerabilities. Congressional hearings examined what happened at Waco. Some of the criticism focused on ATF's failure to provide timely and accurate intelligence to its decision makers leading up to and during the failed operation. ATF's intelligence vulnerabilities had been magnified when confronted with managing a large, critical incident, such as the enforcement operation against the Branch Davidians that involved more than 100 special agents and support staff.

In October 1993, ATF had a new director, John W. Magaw, who was the director of the U.S. Secret Service until his reassignment to ATF. Director Magaw's new assignment came at the request of treasury secretary Lloyd Bentsen.[4] Magaw had vast law enforcement experience, having served nearly forty years in various positions with the Ohio State Patrol and U.S. Secret Service.[5]

Upon arriving at ATF, Magaw immediately began to implement a comprehensive strategic plan for the agency as outlined in the Government Performance and Results Act (GPRA), which was passed the previous year.[6] He also intertwined U.S. Department of Justice and Department of the Treasury recommendations on how to improve the bureau in the aftermath of Waco. These improvements were contained within two U.S. government reports published within several months of the tragedy.[7,8] Based on many of the recommendations outlined in these reports, Magaw began to build ATF's internal intelligence capability.

One of the first matters of business related to overhauling ATF intelligence involved executive staff members drafting standard operating procedures (SOP). The new procedural memo outlined ATF policies for the reporting, collection, maintenance, and dissemination of criminal law enforcement information. These SOPs are contained within ATF Order 3700.1, which was implemented within a year of Magaw's tenure. As a result, intelligence activities at ATF grew rapidly.

Magaw divided ATF's intelligence activities into two broad areas—tactical intelligence (field office level) and strategic intelligence (headquarters level). This concept was borrowed from other successful intelligence organizations within the U.S. government. Separating tactical and strategic intelligence operations allowed for better allocation of resources, oversight, and management.

Tactical intelligence (referred to as "tact-intel") can be described as pieces of information that are gathered as part of an ongoing field investigation and that are necessary for planning and conducting tactical operations (actions in the field). Tactical intelligence may include the names and aliases of criminal subjects, personal identifiers (height, weight, birth date, and Social Security number), street addresses, phone numbers, and vehicle descriptions, among other types of information.

In contrast, strategic intelligence is refined information that is national, international, or global in scope. It is generally used for policy, strategy, and planning purposes. Strategic intelligence is focused on long-term patterns, emerging trends, organization structure, leadership, tactics, and capabilities of potential adversaries. It is generally developed over a longer period of time and may include a "big picture" or view at the "30,000-foot level" concerning a particular topic or issue. Although some of my duties and responsibilities included providing tactical intelligence support, I primarily specialized in strategic intelligence—not only at ATF, but throughout my federal counterterrorism career.

Magaw understood how the importance of intelligence could help develop a better understanding of a criminal's pattern of behavior and interaction with other criminal networks. This in-depth understanding could lead an agency to improve upon its law enforcement strategies to better counteract criminal activity. He also understood the importance of exploiting publicly available and open-source information such as Internet websites, online chat rooms, and computer forums to supplement and enhance strategic intelligence.

Director Magaw soon began to "beef up" the Intelligence Division at ATF headquarters, hiring more personnel and providing 24/7 coverage to its field agents both within the United States and overseas. He created a headquarters program manager in the Intelligence Division to serve as an "intelligence coordinator" for major criminal investigations. He authorized that regulatory enforcement personnel be assigned to the Intelligence Division to provide information related to criminal violations committed by federal firearms and explosives licensees. Magaw saw the value in fusing information obtained from ATF's regulatory enforcement function with the Intelligence Division to better support and enhance ATF's law enforcement function.[9]

In the field, Magaw created intelligence groups for each ATF field division, which numbered twenty-four at the time. The number of ATF field divisions was eventually trimmed to twenty-three.

Since the field intelligence group (FIG) involved personnel and resources assigned to the field division, special agents in charge (SAC) of the field divisions insisted that the FIGs remain under their control and direct authority. The SACs probably didn't like the Intelligence Division at headquarters directing personnel and resources under their jurisdiction. Headquarters direction could send a message to agents in the field that would undermine the SAC's autonomy and authority in the field.

FIGs are comprised of a group supervisor, an intelligence officer, intelligence analyst(s), and investigative assistant(s). They are responsible for gathering, analyzing, and disseminating information from the various criminal investigations within their respective field division. The FIG sends investigative information back to headquarters for data archiving, retrieval, and further analysis. The Intelligence Division at headquarters would then conduct database searches and in-depth analysis, write products, and disseminate intelligence back to the field offices. The sharing of information back and forth creates a synergetic relationship between headquarters and the field.[10]

Within the FIG, the intelligence officer positions are assigned to special agents who are responsible for working with the intelligence research specialists and investigative assistants to gather, analyze, and disseminate tactical intelligence to field investigators as well as keep headquarters informed of their field investigations. Among their varied responsibilities, the intelligence officers monitored the surveillance and undercover logs and ensured that electronic surveillance equipment was properly used. They also oversaw the division's operational security protocols to mitigate the risk of leaks and unauthorized public disclosure of information. Magaw recommended the creation of an intelligence officer position within each special response team (SRT), which was ATF's tactical unit for serving high-risk warrants. The SRT's intelligence officer would provide time-sensitive tactical information to on-scene commanders and ATF decision makers to improve the tactical operation's success.

During major incidents or major enforcement operations, intelligence program managers at headquarters deployed to the field to assist the FIG as needed. This combined effort, called an intelligence response unit (IRU), facilitated the flow of information and actionable intelligence between on-scene commanders, decision

makers, the Intelligence Division, and other intelligence units at external law enforcement agencies.[11] The IRU concept provided ATF with the flexibility to send additional resources at a moment's notice to augment situations beyond the capability
of the FIG. Additional resources provided by the IRU ensured that information was
analyzed and disseminated in a complete, accurate, and timely fashion.[12]

Magaw also moved ATF's foreign liaison offices in Canada, Europe, and South
America under the direction of the Intelligence Division to provide the agency an
international intelligence capability.[13]

ATF also enhanced its training efforts for intelligence supervisors, intelligence officers, program managers, and analysts. They expedited this effort through leveraging
existing intelligence training programs within the intelligence and law enforcement
communities. ATF's Office of Training and Professional Development provided
crisis management training to staff at headquarters, SACs, and all supervisors and
team leaders.[14] Another ATF executive order was prepared to ensure that major enforcement operations are supervised by managers with the proper background and
training and "with the Director's office providing close oversight."[15]

Finally, ATF began developing a centralized case management system that would
allow equal access and control of information to all users.[16] This enabled special
agents, industry operations inspectors, intelligence research specialists, and investigative assistants to work collectively in a joint effort to develop intelligence, which
would then be used to its greatest potential to combat crime. Magaw's vision for
ATF intelligence was dependent on cooperation from both field and headquarters
levels. Each user of the case management system needed the ability to provide its own
information and had to be guaranteed instant and complete access to this information. The system also had to be compliant with all federal laws and regulations.[17]
Ideally, Magaw envisioned the new case management system to enable users not only
to enter and retrieve information, but also perform a wide range of queries and link
analysis. Overall, he hoped the newly developed system would enable ATF to make
better operational decisions.[18]

A few weeks after arriving at ATF, I attended John W. Magaw's retirement ceremony, which was held in a large ballroom of the Renaissance Tech World Hotel in
Washington, D.C. The hotel was located directly across from ATF headquarters at
650 Massachusetts Avenue and was the site of many ATF functions, including the
director's town hall meetings.

During Magaw's tenure at ATF, the bureau participated in several high-profile
investigations that helped regain the public's trust in the agency's ability to perform
its mission. Included among these major investigations was the Oklahoma City
bombing, the crash of TWA Flight 800, the bombing at Centennial Park during the
1996 Olympics, and the National Church Arson Task Force.[19] Magaw's legacy will
be remembered for his enthusiasm and dedication to the workforce as well as his renewed emphasis on training, science, and technology. John Magaw was instrumental
in building the ATF's K-9 training facility in Front Royal, Virginia, and the planned
move of the National Tracing Center into a newly renovated space in Martinsburg,

West Virginia, that would have expanded capabilities. He was also involved in planning the construction of two new ATF facilities, including the headquarters building in Washington, D.C., and the National Laboratory and Fire Research Center in Greenbelt, Maryland.[20]

When I arrived at ATF in October 1999, ATF's chief of intelligence, Theodore "Teddy" Royster, was also nearing retirement. He was already packing his belongings and moving out of his office. His retirement was officially only a month away, but for all intents and purposes, he was already starting his retirement. Deputy chief, supervisory special agent Mark James was in charge of managing and overseeing the day-to-day operations of the Intelligence Division.[21] Mark James was known for his strong work ethic, diligence to duty, and unwavering focus on ATF's core missions to reduce violent crime, prevent terrorism, and protect the nation.[22] His character, take-charge mentality, and leadership personified the reputation of the Intelligence Division.

Under Mark James's leadership and direction, the Intelligence Division was restructured, expanding into five branches to better manage, conduct, and provide intelligence support to the field.[23] The branches consisted of the following: Domestic Operations; Domestic Analysis; Major Case; Transnational Analysis; and Intelligence Systems.[24]

I was assigned to work in the Domestic Analysis Branch, which was comprised of intelligence analysts who supported the special agents in the Domestic Operations Branch. Analysts were paired up with special agents to work particular specialty topics called program areas. The pairing up of analysts with agents was a great idea, because it combined the analytical expertise of intelligence analysts with the experience of law enforcement officers who knew how to build a case and present it for prosecution.

Working together, analysts and agents complement each other's work. Intelligence analysts provide the agents with increased subject matter expertise regarding certain topics within ATF's jurisdiction, such as alcohol and tobacco diversion, firearms trafficking, organized crime, street gangs, and violent extremist groups. Analysts provide knowledge and experience on how to conduct a wide range of database searches, as well as how to create organization charts, link analysis, timelines, and other analytical tools that provide tactical support to ongoing criminal investigations. In contrast, the agent provides the credentials and access to open investigations and case information. Agents are also well versed in the laws under ATF's jurisdiction as well as legal proceedings and judicial processes.

This was an exciting time for my career. I could finally study, monitor, and expand my knowledge and expertise related to domestic right-wing extremist criminal activity without the restrictions and confinement of working for a military intelligence agency.

My transfer to ATF reinvigorated my interest in analyzing domestic terrorism, specifically right-wing extremism in the United States. My transition to ATF was mutually beneficial to me and the agency. I received a promotion and was able to further develop my area of expertise. The sky was the limit, and I was no longer constrained by the military's rigid domestic intelligence rules and intelligence oversight regulations. Likewise, I believe ATF benefited from my arrival, too. I had a wealth of analytical training while employed at the U.S. Army. I had attended numerous classes at the Joint Military Intelligence College at the Defense Intelligence Agency in Washington, D.C.; the U.S. Air Force Special Operations School at Hurlburt Field in Florida; and, the Military Intelligence Officer Basic Course at Fort Huachuca, Arizona. As a result, my baseline knowledge of counterterrorism and domestic right-wing extremism, coupled with my analytical training, went a long way toward giving me a head start at ATF. I also have a strong work ethic and a deep desire to contribute to my agency's mission.

Immediately upon arriving at ATF, I was given responsibility for the "violent antigovernment group" program area at ATF's Intelligence Division. ATF created the term "violent antigovernment groups" (VAG) as an umbrella category that encompassed both violent white supremacists and armed militia extremists. At the time, ATF recognized that white supremacists and militia extremists may have different causes or agendas, but they share a mutual hatred, distrust, and complete nonrecognition of the federal government. Additionally, there was a trend during the 1990s showing an increasing overlap between violent white supremacists and the militia movement.

ATF only investigates individuals embracing white supremacy, antigovernment, or militia beliefs where there is a reasonable indication that they are engaged in the violation of federal firearms and explosives laws. Some of the "tools" used by members of violent antigovernment groups are illegal firearms, explosive devices, and arson. By investigating and bringing criminal elements of violent antigovernment groups to prosecution, ATF significantly impacts extremist group activity and their respective causes.

It didn't take long for me to become immersed in the subject matter of violent right-wing extremism. Within a week after arriving, I was asked to provide instruction to newly hired special agent trainees at ATF's National Academy located at the Federal Law Enforcement Training Center (FLETC) in Glynco, Georgia. I didn't have much time to prepare the course instruction, so I immediately began preparing a PowerPoint presentation concerning the various domestic extremist groups, their radical ideology, and recent criminal incidents associated with white supremacists and militia extremists. Over the years, this block of instruction doubled in length from a two-hour presentation to four hours of classroom instruction. I faithfully taught this class on a recurring basis for over a decade. At least two different program managers told me that few classes at the ATF National Academy have experienced a similar level of consistency from the same instructor over such a length of time.

As I began teaching at the ATF Academy in October 1999, the millennium, referred to as Y2K, was fast approaching. It was only two and a half months away, and many religious zealots and right-wing extremists in the United States were stockpiling food, weapons, and ammunition in anticipation of massive civil disturbances, pending economic collapse, societal breakdown, among other "doomsday" scenarios. Some were even predicting the "end of the world."

The FBI had just released its report on Y2K, titled "Project Megiddo: A Threat Analysis for the New Millennium."[25] Soon after its release in October 1999, anti-government extremists created their own parody of the report called "An Analysis of the F.B.I.'s 'Project Megiddo.'"[26] The satirical report was sent discreetly to select law enforcement agencies, including the ATF, by a bogus extremist group called the Anti-Demonization League (a political parody concerning the Anti-Defamation League, a Jewish civil rights organization that monitored anti-Semitism and other forms of extremist threats).

The Anti-Demonization League described itself as "a loose coalition of Christian leaders formed for the purpose of countering the demonization and defamation of Christian people (especially conservative Christians) by liberal, anti-Christian, anti-Saxon and un-American groups such as the Jewish A.D.L. of the B'Nai B'rith and the Southern Poverty Law Center."[27] Their report featured a disclaimer that stated, "Since these organizations (and the bureaucratic agencies they seem to control) have been sending false, misleading information to law enforcement agencies throughout America, the 'Anti-Demonization League' has commissioned the printing and distribution of this document by Christian groups."[28]

This parody was clearly a response from right-wing extremists and so-called "conservative Christians." Such a response was a much more indirect and ambiguous rhetorical attack than that which would be directed at the DHS right-wing extremism report almost ten years later. The Anti-Demonization League's analysis of Project Megiddo did not generate much news reporting and was kept within the antigovernment extremist and law enforcement communities. Ironically, both the FBI's Project Megiddo assessment and the DHS right-wing extremism report share some very similar wording and analytical conclusions.

In Project Megiddo's executive summary, the FBI describes the purpose and intent of disseminating the report to other federal, state, and local law enforcement agencies. It was intended to "analyze the potential for extremist criminal activity in the United States by individuals or domestic extremist groups who profess an apocalyptic view of the millennium or attach special significance to the year 2000."[29] Like the DHS right-wing extremism report, it was a strategic analytical product meant for overall situational awareness. The DHS report also touched briefly on the role and influence of Christian "End Times prophecy" and apocalyptic views and how they play into a violent extremist mindset.

The Project Megiddo report begins, "The purpose behind this assessment is to provide law enforcement agencies with a clear picture of potential extremism motivated by the next millennium."[30] The FBI report did not contain operational information on domestic terrorists plotting attack as the year 2000 approached. Rather, it focused on "ideological and philosophical belief systems which attach importance, and possibly violence, to the millennium."[31] The assessment elaborated on various domestic extremist ideologies known to inspire adherents toward violence and criminal activity, such as Christian Identity, white supremacy, militias, Black Hebrew Israelites, and apocalyptic cults.

Like the DHS right-wing extremism report, the Project Megiddo assessment "verified very few indications of specific threats."[32] It further stated, "Without question, this initiative has revealed indicators of potential violent activity on the part of extremists in this country."[33]

Another interesting point brought out in the FBI assessment claimed that "certain individuals from these various perspectives [militias and white supremacists] are acquiring weapons, storing food and clothing, raising funds through fraudulent means, procuring safe houses, preparing compounds [insular communities], surveying potential targets and recruiting new converts."[34] *These conclusions are almost identical to those reached in the DHS report using an entirely different set of motivating factors.* I did not discover these parallels until I started researching material for this book. This finding gives me pause as I reflect on what transpired in the months leading up to the millennium and what occurred in the years immediately following it.

During my nearly five years at ATF, I began to notice that many of the investigations to which I was providing support dealt with violent individuals who were motivated to plan and commit criminal activity as a result of their radical and extreme beliefs. There was also many who embraced extremist belief systems, which led them to having failed relationships with close associates such as spouses, children, and their parents. The ideology of these criminals either focused on an exceedingly high level of fixation with the "end times" or the Apocalypse; raw hatred of ethnic groups or races; an obsession for firearms or explosives or an extreme antipolice attitude, including an abhorrence of ATF. Of course, some of these individuals under investigation possessed a combination of these beliefs.

About five months before I arrived at ATF, there was the first of a handful of incidents that suggested that right-wing extremists were becoming increasingly agitated about the approaching millennium and fearful of the possible ramifications of Y2K. On May 29, 1998, three heavily armed men dressed in camouflage clothing stole a water truck from a local businessman near Cortez, Colorado. Officer Dale Claxton, a local patrolman, sighted the water truck and followed it at a distance while waiting for additional law enforcement officers to arrive. Suddenly, the water truck pulled over to the side of the road, and one of the suspects jumped out carrying a fully automatic rifle. As Officer Claxton's police car approached, the suspect opened fire, shooting Officer Claxton multiple times—killing him instantly.

The three men fled the scene, eventually abandoned the water truck, and stole a flatbed pickup. They later engaged police in a running gunfight along the Colorado–Utah border. The thirty-minute shooting rampage resulted in the shootings of two other police officers. As quickly as these events transpired, the suspects then vanished into the desert, leaving law enforcement authorities baffled as to their identity and whereabouts.

Over the next several hours, 400 law enforcement officers representing agencies from four states descended upon the Four Corners area to look for the fugitives. A few days later, another police officer was shot and wounded near Bluff, Utah. When authorities arrived on scene and began to search the area, they found the body of one of the suspects—Robert Mason. He died of a self-inflicted gunshot wound to his head. The other two suspects were later identified as Jason McVean and Alan "Monte" Pilon. The manhunt continued for weeks, but neither McVean nor Pilon were found.

There are several theories concerning potential motives for stealing the water truck. Investigators believe the three men may have stolen the water truck to use it as a battering ram to rob a local bank or casino. Others believe the suspects may have been planning to use the truck to deliver a bomb to a nearby dam. Still others believe the men stole it to store water, a precious resource in desert conditions, in anticipation of widespread violence related to the turn of the millennium.

Authorities continued for months to search for the remaining two suspects. Finally, in November 1999, authorities got another break in the case. Local hunters had found a body in a remote section of Utah desert. The body was later identified as Alan Pilon, who had died from a self-inflicted gunshot wound to the head. Several months later, hunters found the remains of Jason McVean in the desert. He had also died from a single gunshot wound to the head.

There were more cases of possible millennium-related violence associated with right-wing extremists in the United States. Within six weeks of my arrival, ATF agents in the San Francisco Field Division participated in the arrests of three militia extremists who had plotted to blow up a propane storage facility in Sacramento, California. The three suspects had grown increasingly paranoid over Y2K and plotted the bombing in the hope of starting (or further destabilizing) civil order on the eve of the millennium.

During the early morning hours of Friday, December 3, 1999, Joint Terrorism Task Force officers, including FBI, ATF, and state and local law enforcement, executed simultaneous arrest warrants for Kevin Ray Patterson in Placerville, California, and Charles Dennis Kiles in Somerset, California. A third suspect, Donald Rudolph, had earlier been arrested on a domestic violence charge. Search warrants were also served at the properties of all three suspects.

Patterson, Kiles, and Rudolph had been affiliated with a local militia group called the San Joaquin Militia. Their plot reportedly began to unfold as early as 1996 at a time when many militia groups were identifying targets in their area that were susceptible to sabotage. They were looking for targets that, if destroyed, would cause a major civil disturbance that could potentially lead the U.S. government to declare martial law. The plan was reportedly part of a larger militia conspiracy to undermine and destabilize the federal government.[35]

According to witnesses, an odd assortment of right-wing extremists, illegal gun dealers, and survivalists had talked about detonating the tanks for more than a year. They discussed possibly using a fertilizer bomb similar to the one used to bomb the Alfred P. Murrah Federal Building in Oklahoma City in 1995.[36] Unknown to the suspects, the FBI had recruited an informant inside the San Joaquin Militia who had been previously arrested and charged with possession of illegal firearms. The informant was hoping to get a reduction in sentence for information he provided on possible threats and other illegal activity.[37]

The informant reported the plan to attack Suburban Propane was actually conceived in June 1998 by Patterson and Rudolph. The source also claimed that Patterson had discussed other prospective targets such as the California Aqueduct, as well as four television transmission towers in Walnut Grove, California.[38] The TV towers stood about 2,000 feet each, which is taller than the World Trade Center in New York City prior to its destruction during the September 11 terrorist attacks. The towers broadcast television signals to a seventeen-county area in the Sacramento metropolitan area. The source claimed that Patterson was seeking twenty fellow militiamen to carry out the attack on the television towers.[39]

Patterson and Kiles were also observed at a Las Vegas gun show in January 1999 talking about "blowing up" the propane storage tanks with a rocket launcher. They reportedly had approached a local gun dealer about purchasing an RPG-7 antitank missile. Allegedly, they only lacked $2,200 to purchase the item.[40]

At the same gun show, witnesses claimed that an unidentified man commented that he had heard that "militia groups were planning quite a bit of excitement" at the end of the millennium. In response to the comment, Kiles boasted, "We're going to have a big bang ourselves. We're going to take out a couple of propane tanks." Patterson reportedly grabbed Kiles's arm and pulled him away from the conversation, stating that Kiles "talked too much" and needed to keep his mouth shut.[41]

Patterson made claims to his associates that he was already making the explosives for the attack. He had also made statements to the effect that he needed three or four other men to cut through security fencing and break into the storage facility. Patterson thought that, once inside the yard, the men could fire two explosive charges from an oversize shotgun-type weapon.[42]

While conducting preliminary surveillance of potential targets in their local area, Patterson and Kiles located two propane storage tanks at Suburban Propane in Elk Grove, California. They nicknamed the propane tanks "Twin Sisters" and labeled the storage facility as "a target of opportunity." Rudolph, Patterson, and Kiles planned to carry out the attack in late 1999.

Each propane tank held approximately 12 million gallons of liquid propane. The tanks were part of the largest aboveground propane storage facility in North America. If the suspects' plans had been successful, authorities estimated the resulting explosion had the potential to kill 12,000 people within several miles of the propane facility. The potential explosion would have caused widespread fire and severe burns among the population within at least five miles of the explosion.[43]

Explosive experts later testified at Patterson's trial that he had all the materials needed to construct a thirty- to forty-pound ammonium nitrate and fuel oil explosive device. The resulting explosion from such a device is the equivalent of thirty-four pounds of TNT high explosives. The device had enough force to likely breach the steel exterior shell encasing both propane tanks in Elk Grove.[44]

During the execution of the search warrants, investigators seized detonation cord, blasting caps, grenade hulls, and various bomb-making materials including red phosphorus, black powder, and over 100 pounds of ammonium nitrate. Authorities also seized some firearms, including an AK-47 assault rifle, an Uzi semiautomatic pistol, and parts for an M-1 carbine.[45]

Patterson was described as a "restless demolitions expert"[46] who was growing increasingly paranoid and fearful of the approaching year 2000. He had stored a four-month supply of food and water in anticipation of problems associated with the millennium.[47] Furthermore, Patterson commented that he had some friends that were building bunkers in remote areas of the desert, burying cargo shipping containers, installing generators, and stockpiling weapons and ammunition in anticipation of Y2K. Patterson was known for having a particularly "dark view" of the future in which he predicted the U.S. government would ration food and gasoline, conduct mass arrests of dissidents, that martial law would be declared, and the U.S. military would forcibly confiscate firearms from U.S. citizens.[48]

Both Patterson and Kiles were convicted of threatening to use a weapon of mass destruction in 2002. Patterson was sentenced to twenty-one years in prison and five years of probation. Kiles received twenty-two years in prison and five years of probation. After a plea agreement, Rudolph was sentenced to five years in prison.[49]

The following week, on December 8, 1999, federal law enforcement authorities arrested another militia member near St. Petersburg, Florida, for plotting to bomb transmission towers and power lines to incite civil riots at the turn of the millennium. He was the leader of a militia coalition called the Southeastern States Alliance. The plot involved burglarizing a National Guard armory to obtain the necessary weapons and explosives to carry out the attack. The suspect also believed various antigovernment conspiracy theories typical of the militia movement, including that United Nations forces were planning to invade the United States in an effort to overthrow the U.S. government and implement a "New World Order"—a one-world government.[50] The subject was ultimately convicted on various firearms and conspiracy charges and was sentenced to five years in federal prison.[51]

Also, on New Year's Eve 1999, a member of the Colorado State Defense Force Reserve militia in Golden, Colorado, was arrested for leading a group of other militia extremists to a motel while he was armed with firearms and explosive devices in case civil strife erupted as a result of Y2K.[52] Of particular relevance and concern today, we are again beginning to see chatter regarding "End Times" prophecies and apocalyptic beliefs in the survivalist and extremist networks as their interest begins to emerge on the perceived relevance of the year 2012 and the end of the Mayan calendar. Like the 1990s, this type of paranoia surrounding the year 2012 will likely lead domestic extremists to once again hoard food, military equipment, weapons, and ammunition in an attempt to survive the coming Apocalypse. Unfortunately, there will be those among these extremists who will possess their weapons arsenals for the sole purpose of plotting terrorist attacks as well as hastening their own version of "Judgment Day" or bringing about the return of Jesus Christ.

Several other ATF criminal investigations focused on individuals who were violating the law as a result of their survivalist or apocalyptic beliefs. One last example of such individuals is ATF's investigation into the leader of an apocalyptic, antigovernment group called Christian American Patriot Survivalists.

On March 25, 2004, ATF agents, supported by the FBI and Pennsylvania State Police, arrested Darrell W. Sivik Sr. and George Bilunka in Crawford County, Pennsylvania, and charged them with various federal firearms violations. The arrests stemmed from an eighteen-month undercover investigation into the alleged criminal activities of an antigovernment extremist group called Christian American Patriot Survivalists or CAPS.[53]

Bilunka, the alleged leader of CAPS, was stockpiling food, weapons, and other equipment in preparation for the end of the world, which he predicted would occur in 2009.[54] Bilunka reportedly solicited the support of Sivik to help arm the group with machine guns.

Sivik, a federal firearms dealer, is a former member of the Pennsylvania Unorganized Militia and leader of a group called the Braveheart Militia.[55] He is also well known in the militia movement for operating a pirate radio broadcast advocating antigovernment conspiracy theories and Christian End Times prophecy.[56] Sivik is believed to have manufactured approximately 100 machine guns since the 1980s.

As a result of the investigation, authorities seized several automatic weapons, including a .30-caliber machine gun, several 9mm Sten-type machine guns, and two fully automatic M-16–type rifles. None of the firearms were registered. As anticipated, the arrests of Sivik and Bilunka drew criticism from other antigovernment groups throughout the region.

In a show of support, four militia supporters organized a protest outside the U.S. District Court in Erie, Pennsylvania. The militia supporters held signs denouncing gun-control legislation. Sivik eventually pled guilty to two counts of possessing an unregistered firearm. He admitted to hiding ten unregistered machine guns at a campsite near the Allegheny National Forest in Forest County, Pennsylvania. Sivik also admitted to selling machine guns to Bilunka.

The millennium came and went without any major catastrophe or economic collapse. There were a few minor issues with computers having to be upgraded or reprogrammed to recognize the date change, but nothing serious enough to disrupt the day-to-day functions of society. It will be interesting to see how today's right-wing extremists will react as we near the end of the year 2012, which has been the subject of much "end of the world" speculation and discussion as a result of various interpretations of the ancient Mayan calendar and other similar prophecies related to "doomsday."

Working at ATF afforded me opportunities to provide analytical support to sensitive law enforcement investigation and learn firsthand about the criminal activities of right-wing extremists. My knowledge and experience grew substantially during the five years I worked at ATF. I received large amounts of extremist propaganda from special agents in the field. This material was gathered either while they worked undercover inside these groups or during search warrants executed against extremist individuals. Upon receipt, I would review the written materials, watch extremist-related videotapes, or listen to audio recordings of extremist messages and sermons.

On a few occasions, I was invited to travel to ATF field offices to assist with providing tactical support to an ongoing criminal investigation. This gave me an opportunity to work closely with other intelligence analysts and special agents in the Field Intelligence Group, as well as the case agent and others involved in the investigation.

Such field experience also afforded opportunities to glimpse the complexities of large-scale law enforcement operations. Most operations involved multiple ATF field offices as well as other investigators representing a wide range of federal, state, and local law enforcement agencies. I always worked "behind the scenes" at the command post or field office. From this vantage point, I had the opportunity to review operational plans, attend the preoperational briefings, and observe the coordination and execution of simultaneous search and arrest warrants.

My first field experience involved assisting the Phoenix Field Division's Field Intelligence Group with an investigation of two white supremacists in Kimball, Nebraska. Both individuals were reportedly involved in the illegal manufacturing and possession of improvised explosive devices.[57]

Preliminary information led to a full-fledged investigation that culminated in an enforcement operation stemming from a 3 1/2-month undercover investigation by the ATF Cheyenne Field Office.[58] I was invited to travel to Cheyenne, Wyoming, to participate in the command post operation a few days prior to serving the search and arrest warrants.

The investigation focused on two members of a neo-Nazi group called the National Alliance (NA).[59] Their names were Carl "Joel" Carlson and Rex Levi Rabou.[60] The NA is a white supremacist, neo-Nazi group headquartered in Pocahontas County, West Virginia, outside the town of Marlinton. At the time, the group was led by Dr. William Pierce, author of the notorious antigovernment conspiracy novel *The Turner Diaries*, which was written in 1978 under the pseudonym Andrew McDonald.[61] It is alleged to have influenced Timothy McVeigh to devise and deliver a 5,000-pound truck bomb to the Alfred P. Murrah Federal Building in Oklahoma City, Oklahoma.[62] The massive explosion at 9:02 a.m. on April 19, 1995, resulted in the deaths of 167 people.[63] Pierce's conspiracy novel involved a similar plot targeting the FBI headquarters building in Washington, D.C., using a large truck bomb hidden in a Ryder rental truck.[64]

In April 2000, the Laramie County Sheriff's Office in Wyoming advised ATF that neo-Nazis were actively recruiting within their community.[65] ATF would later learn that the reported neo-Nazis were actually members of the NA. During the preliminary investigation, ATF learned that these NA members were allegedly also stockpiling guns and explosives as well as considering burglarizing a gun store. Further investigation revealed that Carlson was a convicted felon. Convicted felons are "prohibited persons"—which means they are not allowed to possess firearms. Allegedly, Carlson was an NA unit leader for a local group and Rex Rabou was his assistant.[66]

In May 2000, ATF successfully introduced an undercover agent to Carlson. The ATF agent posed as a leader in the National Militia.[67] The day he met Carlson, the agent was dressed in a full battle-dress uniform with a "National Militia" patch sewn on his sleeve. I was surprised to learn the agent just walked up to Carlson's residence one day and introduced himself as the commander of the National Militia. The agent was able to artfully dismiss Carlson's initial questions about how he knew Carlson's name and where he lived by simply explaining that "the militia is everywhere and knows about everyone."

Within a few days, the agent gained the trust of Carlson and Rabou. He told them that he was creating a new militia cell in Kimball, Nebraska. Both subjects expressed interest in joining the group and helping it obtain firearms and explosives in preparation for "future missions."[68]

According to court documents, the ATF undercover agent told both individuals that he was responsible for "pre-positioning supplies" in the area. He elaborated that the term "supplies" included weapons such as pipe bombs. The stated purpose of the supplies was to train fellow militia members and would be used later in "operations."[69]

Both Rabou and Carlson reportedly expressed interest in becoming members of the new militia cell. They were so enthusiastic about joining that they allegedly recruited some friends and began acquiring weapons and building pipe bombs. Rabou reportedly admitted to having prior experience in constructing pipe bombs using steel and other materials and said that he had even made a few during his high school shop class.[70]

Throughout the investigation, ATF purchased and seized five machine guns, seventy-two pipe bombs, twenty-one other improvised explosive devices, and thirty-five arrows (referred to as "exploding arrows") that were specifically designed as incendiary devices. ATF also seized large quantities of ammunition and bomb-making materials. On August 2, 2000, Joel Carlson and Rex Rabou were arrested on charges related to federal firearms and explosives violations.[71]

In April 2001, Carlson was sentenced to five years in prison and three years of supervised release. Rabou was sentenced to three years in prison and three years of supervised release.[72] It is not known whether or not Carlson or Rabou returned to the white supremacist movement.

Assisting with this investigation was an eye-opening experience for me. It was the first ATF investigation to which I provided direct analytical support. Despite not receiving a warm welcome initially from the resident agent in charge (RAC), I really enjoyed interacting with the ATF case and undercover agents—both of whom were exceptionally good at their jobs. I was surprised to learn that the Phoenix Field Intelligence Group had forgotten to notify the RAC that I was coming. The RAC was a little confused and initially upset by the sudden arrival of headquarters personnel (i.e., me). But after I explained who I was and what my purpose was for being there, we came to agreement that I was welcome to provide analytical assistance, but to stay out of his way.

Upon reviewing the operational plan and listening to the ATF undercover agent brief the other agents involved in the operation, I suddenly realized that I had really overestimated the sophistication of some white supremacists, specifically their level of operational security, which was virtually nonexistent. It was shocking that, over the course of a few weeks, an ATF agent could introduce himself without any prior contact with the subjects and gain their trust under the ruse of forming a new cell of National Militia—an audacious-sounding group name that sounded straight out of a Hollywood movie. The operational plan called for the undercover agent to pick up both subjects within an hour of each other and take them to a low-budget motel room—the only motel in town—for their militia indoctrination ceremony and to administer their "oath of office." At a predesignated point, ATF special response team (SRT) members, who were staged in an adjacent motel room, would burst through the door wearing full raid gear and arrest the unsuspecting subjects. After both arrests were carried out safely and without incident, teams of ATF agents would then execute the search warrants and process any evidence.

As the operation was wrapping up, I overheard some of the ATF agents involved in the operation discussing it. I burst out laughing when I heard what had happened at the motel. Apparently, after Joel Carlson was brought into the hotel room and as he was taking his militia "oath of office," the ATF SRT team made entry into the room. Carlson was pushed down onto the bed, promptly handcuffed, and read his Miranda rights. Carlson reportedly smiled and thanked the disguised ATF agents for their "stunt." He really thought it was a joke. Carlson was under the mistaken impression that his arrest was an elaborate hoax; some sort of "hazing" incident introducing him into the Patriot brotherhood—the militia fraternity. Only after he was whisked away into a dark-colored SUV and awaiting his co-conspirator's arrival in a C-130 military aircraft did Carlson realize that his arrest was indeed real and the beginning of his judicial proceedings related to some very serious charges.

A few years later, I had another opportunity to travel to the field to support another ATF investigation involving white supremacists. This investigation involved members of the Ku Klux Klan (KKK) who were plotting to kill the Johnston County sheriff as well as blow up the Johnston County Courthouse in Benson, North Carolina.[73] The violent plot stemmed from a domestic dispute between Charles Robert Barefoot Jr. and his ex-wife, Renee.[74] Barefoot and his former wife had gone through a bitter divorce. Knowing her husband's violent temper, membership in a violent extremist group, and love for guns, Renee Barefoot sought the judge's authorization for a protective order against her angry ex-husband.[75] Charles Barefoot apparently became enraged at the court order and plotted to seek retaliation against the judge and the sheriff who supported the court's decision.

Barefoot was the former Grand Dragon (a term for state leader) of the Church of the National Knights of the Ku Klux Klan. He had planned for his KKK group to march in the town's Annual Mule Days celebration in Benson during September 2001.[76] The Imperial Wizard (Klan term for president) of the National Knights reportedly traveled nearly 835 miles to North Carolina from the group's headquarters in Indiana to march in the parade. To Barefoot's embarrassment, the march was canceled at the last minute.[77] The town council overturned his application to participate in the Annual Mule Days parade due to safety reasons.[78] This incident led to the eventual falling out between Barefoot and the group's Imperial Wizard.[79] Barefoot ultimately left the Church of the National Knights of the KKK and formed his own group—the Church of the *Nation's* Knights of the KKK [italics added] in April 2002.[80] Barefoot became the group's self-appointed Imperial Wizard.

On July 17, 2002, during a traffic stop, local authorities arrested Barefoot for violating the protective order against his ex-wife.[81] Barefoot was charged with possession of stolen firearms and possession of explosives. Investigators later learned the subject had been plotting to bomb the Johnston County Courthouse and murder the sheriff of Johnston County.

Following Barefoot's arrest, local authorities searched his home and discovered a cache of weapons, which included handguns, rifles, an AK-47 assault rifle, and an Uzi semiautomatic pistol.[82] Investigators also found two improvised explosive devices and other bomb-making materials, including detonator cord and fuses. ATF was called to assist with processing the evidence.[83] The firearms were traced and ATF agents learned that some of the guns in Barefoot's possession were reported stolen a few months earlier.[84]

On January 1, 2003, a former member of Barefoot's KKK faction notified the North Carolina Bureau of Investigation about an alleged murder of a fellow Klansman, Lawrence Arthur Petitt,[85] during the previous year. KKK members reportedly believed Petitt was cooperating with the police and informing them about possible threats to local government officials by members of the KKK.[86] Investigators followed up on the information and found Petitt's badly decomposed body buried in a hayfield.[87] Although Barefoot did not actively participate in the murder, he let other Klan members use his van during the murder and destroyed Petitt's wallet, which had been given to him by other Klan members as evidence of the killing.[88] Barefoot was later charged as an accessory to the crime.

This experience "opened my eyes" to the potential dangers and realistic threats posed by right-wing extremists. Like other violent crime, extremist violence and domestic terrorism plots can have their origins in family conflicts, disputes with government authority, financial problems, and other forms of grievance.

During a three-month period in 2002–2003, I was temporarily assigned to work off-site at an undisclosed location in Virginia to assist with a very sensitive ATF investigation involving white gang members, some of whom were also alleged members of white supremacist groups such as the KKK. I was primarily responsible for organizing records, conducting database checks on criminal subjects, and creating a searchable electronic system of records related to the investigation for the ATF case agent. Despite working only in a part-time capacity, I provided a small contribution to the case, which was both needed and welcomed by the agents involved. This opportunity to work in the field alongside ATF agents in an undercover capacity was extremely valuable and insightful for me. It helped me gain a better appreciation and deeper understanding of the hard work, sacrifice, and dedication of those in law enforcement who operate in a covert capacity.

My analytical support to this investigation came at an especially trying time in my life. My wife was six months pregnant with our third child. There were many doctor visits, medical tests, and sleepless nights during this time. I took solace in knowing that one of the ATF agents working undercover was also going through a similar experience. His wife was pregnant with their first child. The main difference between us was the fact I could go home each night to my wife and children. He could not. His life depended on maintaining his "cover" story.

Later that year, I was invited back to help staff the multiagency command post overseeing the search and arrest warrants during the culmination of this ATF investigation. As I pulled up to the staging area during the early morning hours, I was surprised to see a few hundred law enforcement officers and support personnel assembling for the operation. Three tactical units, representing the ATF SRT, Virginia State Police, and the local Sheriff's Department, were checking their weapons and loading gear into their vehicles. I soon joined my other ATF colleagues and prepared for what would definitely be a very long day.

Similar to my time in Cheyenne a few years prior, I was able to attend the preoperation briefing and provide analytical support during the execution of the search warrants. I was primarily responsible for monitoring radio traffic from the search teams and recording the number of items seized from each scene. These items included over 100 firearms, an improvised explosives device, a small quantity of narcotics, as well as numerous other weapons and contraband. Each hour, I provided the ATF special agent in charge (SAC) with an updated printout of evidence-related statistics, which he used to brief media reporters. The SAC's hourly briefings began shortly after 9:00 a.m. and occurred hourly throughout the day. The final briefing was given to the media in time for the 5 o'clock evening news. The command post was quite the media spectacle. ATF had its mobile command center, mobile lab, and national response team (NRT) truck on-site. There were emergency personnel in an ambulance parked in the parking lot on standby. A television news helicopter landed in a different section of the parking lot. A police helicopter also made an occasional pass over the command post. Multiple television news agencies were conducting simultaneous news broadcasts. Local and national newspaper reporters huddled outside the command post, scribbling notes for their stories and waiting to interview unsuspecting task force members as they waited for the next news conference.

Inside the command post, I was busy entering information into a database from the numerous search warrant teams, updating and tracking evidence for ATF agents, the SAC, and other law enforcement press spokespersons. When I took a quick break, I glanced into the immense holding area for all of the subjects of the investigation. They were taken individually into separate rooms for lengthy interviews with investigators. When they completed their interviews, the criminal subjects were taken to an awaiting marked police cruiser and whisked away to the magistrate for further adjudication.

The experience of having to work at an undercover location also taught me the importance of operational security. The ATF agents' lives depended on it. An inadvertent disclosure to someone without a "need to know" might have serious ramifications on the integrity of the investigation and impact the safety of law enforcement officers. It taught me the importance of maintaining a low profile and being discreet about what you discuss and with whom you share information.

Throughout the country, extremist elements of the white supremacist, militia, and sovereign citizen movements view ATF as a "rogue" law enforcement agency that is undermining the Second Amendment of the U.S. Constitution. Furthermore, many right-wing extremists believe that existing gun-control laws are the first step toward a total ban on firearms ownership and possession. They believe that ATF is the primary federal agency responsible for enforcing these "unconstitutional" laws. For these reasons, violent criminals and extremists have been known to target ATF and its personnel for acts of intimidation and violence.

During my tenure at ATF, I had the opportunity to coordinate and work with the ATF Operational Security (OPSEC) Branch. I provided information concerning potential domestic extremist threats to ATF personnel and facilities and provided input to several vulnerability assessments of agency field offices performed by the ATF OPSEC Branch.

ATF faces a variety of potential adversaries and threat groups, which includes domestic or international extremists (white supremacist, militia, sovereign citizen, or other antigovernment movements, etc.). They may also include criminal elements, such as individuals or their associates that are involved in criminal proceedings for which they could face a fine or imprisonment. Another category of adversary is the "insider" or disgruntled ATF employee.

The ATF OPSEC Branch has the primary mission of protecting ATF personnel, facilities, and other assets against these potential threats. They are only concerned with potentially violent individuals or criminal groups that want to collect information about ATF to further their violent agendas or hostile antigovernment platform. They are also interested in other persons or groups who use facts and detailed information about ATF to counter ATF enforcement operations—basically, counterintelligence threats. Activities of concern to ATF include criminal, extremist, or terrorist surveillance of their facilities or personnel; observing movements and patterns of ATF personnel and equipment; using deception to obtain information through conversation or acquiring written documents through searching through trash at a facility or other surreptitious means.

When assessing potential threats from right-wing extremists, it is important to understand that extremists do *not* behave like common criminals. Numerous law enforcement officers have been killed or injured during unplanned contact with extremists. In many cases, police officers had no idea who they were dealing with until after the fact. Even those who were fortunate enough to know in advance were often caught unprepared or off guard when the situation escalated Dr. Mark Pitcavage, director of investigative research for the Anti-Defamation League (ADL), has conducted extensive research in the area of violent confrontations between right-wing extremists and law enforcement officers.[89] Developing themes originally put forward by the Justice Department's State and Local Anti-Terrorism Training (SLATT) program, he has observed that, in a number of ways, extremists frequently behave differently than traditional criminals, including when confronted by authority figures such as law enforcement officers. Pitcavage asserts that, where typical criminals are usually opportunistic and motivated by self-interest, many extremist-related criminals may be highly focused and engage in detailed planning. Traditional criminals are typically self-centered, whereas extremist criminals are often cause-oriented, putting their cause or ideological goals above their narrow self-interests. Traditional criminals are more often than not escape-oriented—they want to get away from their crimes. While this is also true for some extremist-motivated criminals, many others are far more attack-oriented, even to the point of engaging in lethal or even suicidal confrontations. Last, traditional criminals are typically undisciplined and untrained, while extremists have many opportunities for training and preparation, the nature of which may vary from movement to movement.

Extremists also have been known to plot an ambush or attempt retaliation against their "enemies," which often encompasses law enforcement, judicial personnel, and other government officials. Seeking retaliation against law enforcement officers or judicial officials is not typical of common criminal behavior (although more hardened criminals such as outlaw motorcycle gang members and organized crime have also been known to exhibit this behavior).

Pitcavage points out that when a law enforcement officer confronts an extremist, the officer is at a serious disadvantage. Extremists are unlikely to identify themselves as being affiliated with a radical group or extremist philosophy. They are usually well armed and may have already planned an escape. Many law enforcement encounters with extremists are also spontaneous, such as a traffic stop or court screening. Yet these encounters have shown a propensity for rapid and uncontrolled escalation of the situation.

As a result, Pitcavage urges law enforcement officers to rely on visual and verbal observations for their personal safety, which can alert them to potential dangers posed by possible extremists. Visual and verbal cues serve as warning signs. They are not meant as indicators of criminal activity or criminal intent. With this in mind, Pitcavage has grouped visual identifiers into three broad categories—(1) those found at a residence or other piece of property such as undeveloped land, sheds, or storage units; and (2) those associated with vehicles such as private, commercial, or recreational vehicles; and (3) personal identifiers, such as clothing, jewelry, and tattoos.

Pitcavage has grouped the majority of potential extremist identifiers at a person's residence or property into three subcategories: signs of fortification, unusual flags or banners, and warning signs directed at law enforcement or other government authority.

(1) Signs of Fortification: Foxholes, bunkers, barricades, and towers are good indicators of likely involvement or affiliation with an extremist group or ideology. Extremists have been known to place loaded firearms throughout the house. They may also booby-trap their property, as well as reinforce doors, windows, and walls to prevent easy entry.

(2) Unusual Flags or Banners: White supremacist banners, such as Ku Klux Klan or Nazi flags, are obvious. Patriotic flags, such as the Culpeper Militia flag or Gadsden Minutemen flag, have grown in popularity. These banners were first used during the Revolutionary War to symbolize freedom from oppression. Extremists may also display flags as subtle signs of protest, such as hanging the U.S. flag upside down as a "sign of distress" or using the United Nations flag for target practice.

(3) Warning Signs Directed at Law Enforcement: Antigovernment extremists in particular have developed a number of "No Trespassing" signs that are unusual because they are specifically directed at law enforcement and government officials. They are meant to intimidate and often allude to the use of deadly force against would-be trespassers.

Pitcavage has divided most potential extremist identifiers related to vehicles into five subcategories: unusual vehicle modification; bogus vehicle plates; extremist-related bumper stickers, signs, or placards; fraudulent vehicle-related documents; and extremist-related identification cards.

(1) Unusual Vehicle Modification: There are a few different ways extremists modify their vehicles. Some camouflage their vehicles to resemble the military. Others have attempted to build armored vehicles from spare parts. Still others purchase military surplus vehicles and use them at group functions.

(2) Bogus Vehicle Plates: Antigovernment extremists often create or purchase fake tags to avoid submitting themselves to an "illegitimate" government. Extremists may also place hidden messages on legitimate personalized plates to make a political statement. For example, a member of the neo-Nazi National Alliance, who was a state correctional officer during the 1990s, had a personalized license plate displayed on his vehicle that read "F ZOG" (a profane reference to the "Zionist Occupied Government").

(3) Extremist-related Bumper Stickers, Signs, or Placards: Bumper stickers are another way extremists express their views. Extremist-related bumper stickers are generally more offensive than most. Many extremist groups sell bumper stickers on their websites as a way to generate revenue.

(4) Fraudulent Vehicle-Related Documents: Many extremists do not recognize the jurisdiction of federal or state government. As a result, they may possess fraudulent driver's licenses and fake vehicle registration forms.

(5) Extremist-Related Identification: Extremists have been known to create identification cards and badges for antigovernment groups to which they belong. They may possess such items in and around their vehicles.

I've personally found Pitcavage's research to be credible, insightful, and extremely valuable. As a testament to the validity of his findings, I've incorporated much of

Pitcavage's research into the training instruction I've provided to others within the government, law enforcement, and judicial communities. I've also witnessed the truth of Pitcavage's research into officer safety issues and extremists through the ATF investigations I monitored and supported. A prime example of how Pitcavage's principles related to officer safety apply to real-world experiences can be illustrated in an ATF investigation based out of Louisville, Kentucky.

On October 14, 2001, Steve Howard Anderson, a militia member and Christian Identity adherent, was involved in a shooting incident with a sheriff's deputy in Bell County, Kentucky. Miraculously, the officer was not injured despite thirty rounds from AK-47 hitting his police vehicle in a burst of automatic gunfire. The shooting occurred after the sheriff's deputy initiated a traffic stop on Anderson for a broken taillight near Middlesboro, Kentucky. Anderson ignored the officer's orders and fled in his camouflaged Chevy S-10 pickup. Anderson had emblazoned the words "Kentucky Militia" on the truck's door panels and rear bumper.

A high-speed chase ensued with the deputy attempting to get Anderson to pull over again. Upon reaching a four-lane divided highway, Anderson attempted to elude the deputy by performing a U-turn in the highway's grass median. After circling each other a few times, Anderson slammed on the brakes, jumped out of his pickup, and fired at the sheriff's deputy with a fully automatic AK-47 assault rifle. The deputy was able to jump out of his car and seek cover behind it without being hit. Multiple bullets from Anderson's machine gun strafed the police cruiser's windshield and rearview mirror. At this point, Anderson reportedly returned to his vehicle and sped into the night. The startled deputy decided not to pursue Anderson anymore and called for assistance.

Federal, state, and local law enforcement authorities converged on the scene and began looking for the suspect. Authorities sent a bulletin to area law enforcement agencies notifying them of Anderson's involvement in the shooting and seeking his arrest. A few days later, the Kentucky State Police and local law enforcement found Anderson's abandoned truck on a country back road. Inside Anderson's vehicle, law enforcement authorities found a semiautomatic AR-15 rifle, six pipe bombs, and various types of ammunition. The firearm used in the shooting was not there.

On October 16, 2001, Kentucky State Police requested the assistance of ATF to remove improvised explosive devices hidden in the back of Anderson's pickup. ATF's special response team or SRT (special weapons and tactics team) and explosives enforcement officers searched Anderson's residence and found two more pipe bombs, twenty-four hand grenades, several rifles, numerous handguns, thousands of rounds of ammunition, and various antigovernment and racist materials.

Prior to the shooting incident in Belle County, Anderson had been operating a clandestine shortwave radio station called United Patriot Radio. His radio program, "Militia Hour," was named the number-one hate show on shortwave radio by a civil rights organization that monitors antigovernment radio programs. In previous broadcasts, Anderson was critical of the ATF and its law enforcement tactics and encouraged listeners to target federal agents for acts of intimidation and violence.

He also made threatening statements toward a local newspaper reporter who had recently released a story about Anderson, his hateful speech, and pirate radio station. During the weeks leading up to the shootout, Anderson stated that he anticipated a confrontation with law enforcement over his shortwave radio station, because he was operating without the proper permits, registration, or license. Despite an intense manhunt, Anderson had eluded capture, and there were virtually no leads concerning his whereabouts.

In an attempt to locate Anderson, ATF agents with the Louisville Field Division decided to visit the commander for the Kentucky State Militia (KSM), Charles R. Puckett, at his house.

At the time, Puckett lived in a modest home located on a beautiful piece of property in Garrard County, Kentucky, which was surrounded by dense hardwood forest with large granite rocks protruding from the forest floor. There was also a piece of the property a short distance from his house that had been cleared of trees and was graded for agricultural purposes. This area was surrounded on three sides by a stone cliff and steep, rocky terrain.

Most families would have used this area for farming, gardening, or recreational purposes. Puckett used it as a paramilitary training facility. He erected a guard shack, set up several tents, built an earthen bunker, and booby-trapped the outer perimeter with improvised explosive devices (IED) and homemade mines. At the time of their visit, ATF agents were unaware of the homemade bombs. Many were buried in the ground or hidden with the natural surroundings, and the agents had not ventured into the training area of his property.

The ATF agents, however, did notice a few things as they arrived, including the U.S. flag hanging upside down on a pole attached to his front porch. They also saw multiple rounds of ammunition loaded into pistol magazines displayed in plain view on the front seat and floor of Puckett's pickup truck. More ammunition was strewn on the floor and in ammo boxes located in Puckett's garage, where the door had been left wide open. Both Puckett and the ATF agents knew he was a convicted felon who was prohibited from possessing any firearms. But the agents did not see any illegal firearms at the time of their visit.

They asked Puckett a few questions about Steve Anderson and his possible whereabouts. Puckett reportedly acknowledged that Anderson had once been a member of the KSM, but he said Anderson was no longer a member. Puckett told the ATF agents that Anderson had allegedly been "kicked out" of the group sometime before the shooting incident due to his increasing radical views. As they departed, Puckett agreed to notify the agents if he had any contact with Anderson or received any information related to his whereabouts.

A few days later, Puckett recounted his encounter with the ATF to his fellow militia members. He reportedly remarked that he would not cooperate with the "jack booted thugs" and would not notify the authorities of Anderson's location even if he knew. He also allegedly made some threatening remarks toward ATF and the agents that visited him. This information was anonymously reported back to ATF. Based on this information and the evidence of firearms at Puckett's residence, ATF made plans to search Puckett's residence for firearms.

On November 27, 2001, ATF executed a search warrant at Charlie Puckett's residence. At Puckett's property, agents found bomb-making components for five IEDs, thousands of rounds of ammunition, two handguns, five rifles, one .50-caliber sniper rifle, and four additional IEDs described as small, booby-trap devices comprised of a .12-gauge shotgun shell, trip-wire, and a firing mechanism. Puckett was subsequently charged with felony possession of firearms and explosives.

As the search remained ongoing, ATF agents observed militia members driving in and around the vicinity of Puckett's residence. In addition, one KSM member was observed with a handheld video recorder on a road overlooking Puckett's residence and was confronted by law enforcement. A few weeks after the search warrant, an ATF agent reportedly observed a dark-colored pickup truck following him home as he left the ATF field office. When the agent attempted to confront the suspicious vehicle's occupants, the truck sped off.

On March 14, 2002, Puckett unexpectedly vanished from his home, where he had been under house arrest awaiting his trial for the firearms and explosives violations from the previous year. Before fleeing, Puckett issued a "Last Testament" through an e-mail message to other militia members and supporters. In his e-mail, Puckett denied the charges and announced his intention to become a fugitive of justice. He was later apprehended and returned to jail pending trial.

Anderson was eventually arrested over a year later. He was living in a trailer working as a handyman for a local community church in Andrews, North Carolina. He had requested free food and board from the pastor in exchange for his work at the church. Anderson was apprehended without incident on November 15, 2002, and charged with various firearms and explosives violations.

The Anderson and Puckett case clearly illustrates the potential dangers of investigating extremists and how they will attempt to intimidate, harass, and even retaliate against law enforcement officers (including those operating in a support capacity) for perceived intrusion into their lives or the lives of fellow extremists.

For about two years, I worked with the ATF OPSEC Branch on reviewing, analyzing, and assessing various threat-related letters received at the ATF director's office. When questionable correspondence came into the director's office, the executive assistant would route the letters and packages to the Intelligence Division. These "threat" letters would eventually find their way to my desk to log, review, and analyze. Most of the letters were not really threats but rather innocuous ramblings from people with psychological disorders. Nevertheless, there were a few that had a more hostile and threatening tone.

One such letter was mailed to the ATF director's office on July 4, 2002, from Fayetteville, Arkansas. It was actually a package of pseudo-legal documents with a cover letter. The letter was signed by Hollis Wayne Fincher, Commander of the Militia of Washington County (MWC). Other government agencies, including the governor of Arkansas, had received similar packages from Fincher. The documents within the package were intended to notify the governor of Arkansas about attorney general John Ashcroft's alleged public policy disclosure. Fincher claimed that Ashcroft said that gun control was a state's rights issue and not under the jurisdiction of the U.S. government. The documents declared the militia's intent to form infantry, cavalry, and artillery units as set forth in Article Eleven of the Arkansas Constitution. As commander of the MWC, Fincher claimed that Article Eleven authorizes his militia to use any firearm of any size caliber, barrel length, or magazine capacity—whether automatic or semiautomatic.

MWC members had sent other "official declarations" to state and local government officials in the past. Usually these declarations were addressed to the governor of Arkansas, but copies were also sent to other government institutions and agencies at the federal, state, and local levels. One such example is a document titled "Notice to the Governor of Arkansas," dated July 4, 2002. Prior to this notice, another document, mailed on June 12, 2000, was sent to the governor of Arkansas claiming the MWC was a tax-exempt organization. Both notices also addressed comments specifically to ATF, claiming that ATF did not have "jurisdiction" over them and that MWC members were not obligated to pay taxes to ATF for firearms they possess.

After reviewing and analyzing this packet of information, I conducted additional research and database checks on the MWC, Fincher, and his associates. I summarized this information into an internal report and forwarded it to the ATF Little Rock field office in Arkansas as a possible investigative lead. I was extremely optimistic that a preliminary case would be opened on Fincher based on the documents and the research I had conducted. It would take another three years to bring the case to fruition, but in the end, it was well worth the wait.

The information I provided sat at the ATF field office in Little Rock for almost a year. Then, in June 2003, another ATF investigation in an adjacent state reinvigorated the investigation due to a possible tie back to Fincher and the MWC.

On June 24, 2003, the Newton County Sheriff's Department in Missouri conducted a consent search of an individual's residence in Joplin for narcotics. The subject was a multiconvicted felon and was found in possession of a Sten machine gun. The individual was also in the process of manufacturing methamphetamine. Upon being interviewed, the individual stated that he had obtained the parts to build the Sten machine gun from an unidentified member of the Militia of Washington County. The suspect, however, denied being a member of the extremist group. Within two months, another ATF investigation had ties back to the MWC.

On August 1, 2003, ATF agents seized two machine guns from a member of the Militia of Washington County in Arkansas. The firearms were assembled from parts kits purchased from Inter Ordnance of America. The subject, who was later identified as an MWC member, stated that one of the firearms could not fire and the other firearm functioned as a semiautomatic. Since the individual willingly surrendered both firearms, there were no charges filed against the individual. It was only when the ATF agents left the property that they saw a sign with the name "Militia of Washington County" hanging on an outbuilding located next door. I cautiously reminded the agents they were lucky no one was shot as they left the property.

On November 8, 2006, ATF agents, assisted by state and local law enforcement officers, executed fourteen search warrants related to the investigation of Hollis Wayne Fincher in Fayetteville, Arkansas. Fincher was arrested without incident at his residence in Fayetteville, for possession of illegal firearms including a Sten submachine gun and a .30-caliber tripod-mounted machine gun. The search warrants and Fincher's arrest were the culmination of an extensive ATF investigation concerning the unlawful manufacture, possession, and transfer of machine guns. It was fulfilling to know that I had played a small part in the initial phases of this investigation.

There were many more sensitive ATF criminal investigations involving white supremacists and militia extremists during my tenure at ATF. There are too many to summarize, although some are worth noting. For example, Leo Felton, a white supremacist prison gang member, was arrested on April 11, 2001, for passing counterfeit money at a Dunkin' Donuts store in East Boston, Massachusetts.[90] Unfortunately for Felton, an off-duty police officer was standing in line directly behind him when the cashier noticed something "funny" about the $20 bill Felton handed to them.[91] Felton attempted to flee the scene but was immediately detained and arrested for the crime. ATF later became involved as a result of the discovery of explosive chemicals and other bomb-making materials at Felton's apartment. Felton had also written notes depicting an alleged plan to bomb the New England Holocaust Museum and the Leonard P. Zakim Bunker Hill Bridge in Boston, Massachusetts.[92] Felton was sentenced to twenty-one years in federal prison for his crimes.[93]

On January 4, 2002, Michael Edward Smith, a member of the neo-Nazi National Alliance, was arrested on federal firearms charges in Nashville, Tennessee.[94] The investigation stemmed from an incident where Smith was seen conducting surveillance at the Sherith Israel Congregation, a Jewish synagogue, and, from his car, pointing a high-powered rifle at people going in and out of the synagogue.[95] ATF was involved in tracing the firearm used in the crime as well as other guns seized during search warrants. Smith was sentenced to ten years for the firearms violations and three years of supervised release.[96]

On June 19, 2002, ATF agents, assisted by state and local authorities, arrested Ronald Hertzog, the self-appointed commander of the First Pennsylvania Citizens Militia, at his home in College Township, Pennsylvania.[97] Hertzog was charged with the manufacture and possession of explosive devices and illegal possession of a silencer and machine guns. Hertzog's arrest was the result of a long-term joint undercover investigation conducted by ATF and the Pennsylvania State Police. Prior to his arrest, Hertzog had been attempting to recruit new members into his organization as well as conducting paramilitary training. During a search of Hertzog's residence, investigators found three automatic assault rifles, two hand grenades, a silencer, and two 30-pound mortar shells wrapped with lead pellets, which served as shrapnel.[98] Authorities also found a collection of extremist-related literature and audiotapes concerning a wide range of antigovernment conspiracy theories. On September 18,

2002, Hertzog pled guilty to possession of an unregistered firearm/machine gun.[99] On July 2, 2003, he was sentenced to seventy months of incarceration and three years of supervised release.[100]

During February 2003, David Wayne Hull, a leader in the White Knights of the Ku Klux Klan, was arrested for federal explosives violations related to the construction and testing of an improvised explosive device.[101] Hull reportedly taught an undercover law enforcement officer (posing as an antiabortion extremist) how to make and use a pipe bomb to blow up an abortion clinic near Pittsburgh, Pennsylvania.[102] Investigating authorities seized a firearms silencer, bomb-making materials, loaded handguns, a rocket tube, military-style weapons, among other items at Hull's residence.[103] They also discovered abandoned vehicles on Hull's property with damage consistent with explosions resulting from pipe bombs.[104] Hull was sentenced to twelve years for his crimes.[105]

On July 7, 2003, Scott Allen Woodring, a member of the Michigan Militia living in Freemont, Michigan, shot two Michigan State Police emergency response team members—killing one. The standoff began when Newaygo County sheriff's deputies attempted to serve a felony arrest warrant for solicitation of a minor for sex.[106] When deputies arrived, Woodring barricaded himself in his home. The Michigan State Police emergency response team was summoned to the scene. After negotiations failed, a state police entry team entered the residence, where they were met with gunfire. Trooper Kevin M. Marshall, an eight-year veteran of the department and member of the emergency response team, was fatally shot. He was transported to a local hospital and airlifted to Grand Rapids, where he expired during surgery.[107] Woodring's house later caught fire and burned to the ground when police used pyrotechnic devices in a failed attempt to flush the suspect out of his house.[108] Authorities would later learn that Woodring had fled the scene undetected a day earlier. Acting on an informant's tip, authorities confronted Woodring on July 13 as he was sitting in a parked vehicle. Woodring exited the vehicle and pointed a rifle at the officers. He was subsequently shot and killed.[109]

Another militia suspect in Michigan would become the subject of a law enforcement investigation a few months later. On October 10, 2003, law enforcement authorities arrested Norman David Somerville in Mesick, Michigan, and charged him with unlawful possession of machine guns and attempted manufacture of marijuana.[110] Somerville is a member of the Michigan Militia Corps. He and other group members were growing increasingly agitated over the death of Scott Woodring.[111] A few months before Somerville's arrest, local law enforcement authorities were initially notified by a concerned neighbor who reported hearing automatic weapons fire in the vicinity of Somerville's forty-acre fortified compound.[112] In September 2003, an informant alerted authorities about Somerville's plan to ambush Michigan state troopers as they responded to a prestaged vehicle accident.[113] Investigators reportedly found an underground bunker, thousands of rounds of ammunition, hundreds of pounds of gunpowder, manuals on guerrilla warfare, "booby traps" and explosives, and several automatic weapons, including an antiaircraft gun.[114] At his hearing,

Somerville stated that a silent civil war was being waged in the United States between a corrupt, tyrannical government and those who want to usurp it and restore the country back to its "constitutional principles."

Within a few weeks of Somerville's arrest for plotting kill police officers in Michigan, two local police officers were shot and killed after responding to an ongoing dispute over a road-widening project outside of Abbeville, South Carolina.[115] Local law enforcement officers had responded to a complaint that highway workers were being harassed by a homeowner and his son.[116] Arthur and Steven Bixby had grown increasingly agitated over the state seizing a section of their property as part of a road-widening project.[117] The aftermath of the initial shootings on December 8, 2003, led to a twelve-hour standoff between the suspects and police.[118] During the siege, a tactical team attempted to make entry into the suspects' residence, and the suspects opened fire with high-powered rifles. A gunfight ensued, and Arthur Bixby was seriously wounded. Steven Bixby, a suspected antigovernment extremist, and his father, Arthur Bixby, were arrested and charged with killing the officers.[119]

The following week, Keith Faherty, an antigovernment extremist with "loose" affiliations to militia extremists, was arrested on December 14, 2003, and charged with possession of unregistered machine guns and manufacturing of automatic weapons.[120] He was alleged to have expressed a desire to go on a "killing spree" that would target police, nuisance neighbors, and high school students.[121] During a search of Faherty's residence, investigators seized fifteen AK-47 assault rifles (fourteen of which were fully automatic), suspected machine gun conversion parts, thirteen military-style smoke grenades, and four gas masks.[122] Faherty also booby-trapped his residence with a tear gas canister to incapacitate any would-be intruders.

Providing intelligence support to all of these ATF criminal investigations gave me valuable insights, knowledge, and experience in the types of extremist behaviors and how extremist ideology motivates individuals toward violence and criminal activity. My ATF experience also gave me the necessary analytical expertise to become a subject matter expert and gave me instant credibility with other analysts in the law enforcement and intelligence communities.

In 2003, ATF's Intelligence Division went through another office-wide restructuring. It had grown into a directorate-level organization, which meant that the Intelligence Division was no longer under the Directorate of Field Operations. It finally had an assistant director position, which gave the office the necessary power and authority to manage its own budget and hire its own personnel instead of being dependent on the assistant director for field ops. Deputy assistant director Kathleen Kiernan was the first to lead the new intelligence directorate.[123] It was called the Office of Strategic Intelligence and Information (OSII).

OSII now had a "seat at the table" during the director's morning staff meetings. In concept, this supposedly translated into more visibility, responsibility, and influence. Despite having been elevated to the directorate level, OSII still continued to function as a division.

OSII provides and oversees analytical tradecraft training for both headquarters and field personnel. It also funds and operates the bureau's state-of-the-art case management information system—the National Field Office Case Information System (N-FOCIS). The N-FOCIS system consists of two companion computer applications called N-FORCE (criminal investigations) and N-SPECT (industry operations). N-FOCIS eliminates the need for hard copy and duplicate forms. All criminal- and inspection-related reporting is totally automated and operates within a secure electronic environment. This system maintains a central repository of information that allows both analysts and agents to fully exploit investigative information for analytical purposes.

OSII also facilitates interagency partnerships through intelligence liaison officers. Liaison officers are assigned to a variety of federal agencies including the FBI, DHS, INTERPOL, the National Drug Intelligence Center, and the Financial Crimes Enforcement Network, among other organizations. Through these outreach efforts, ATF is able to leverage, as well as contribute to, the law enforcement and intelligence communities as part of their information-sharing efforts.

In September 2003, I received an unexpected phone call from an analytical counterpart who had left his federal position at the Defense Intelligence Agency (DIA) for a contractor's position at the newly created Department of Homeland Security (DHS). He was working in a brand-new DHS organization called the Directorate of Information Analysis and Infrastructure Protection (IA/IP). He told me that DHS was looking for analysts who were knowledgeable about domestic terrorism issues, specifically domestic non-Islamic extremists (e.g., white supremacists, militia extremists, etc.). He explained that this type of specialized knowledge was hard to find, especially within the U.S. government, and that he immediately thought of me as the perfect candidate for the job.

At the time, DHS IA/IP was given "spot hire authority," which meant they could bypass the normal hiring process to expedite specific personnel with specialized knowledge and experience. There currently wasn't a vacancy announcement, but my contact said he could send over a conditional offer in writing. I was honored that DHS would offer me a job. But I was comfortable and content working for ATF and politely declined the offer. Little did I know that I would seriously reconsider employment opportunities at IA/IP within eight months.

Working for ATF began to take a different direction with the arrival of a new deputy assistant director in March 2004. With the departure of assistant director Kathleen Kiernan, a new deputy assistant director assumed responsibility for the relatively new OSII Directorate. She served as the "acting director" for about a year. Much like other past changes to midlevel management, new leaders bring new ideas, which often results in organizational restructuring. The acting director requested and assumed responsibility for preparing and delivering the director's morning briefing. This had previously been the responsibility of the Field Operations Directorate. This newly assigned responsibility would eventually consume me and four other analysts and ultimately would take us away from our primary assignments.

With the renewed emphasis on the director's morning briefing came additional roles and responsibilities for the intelligence analysts and their supervisors. Multiple rotating-duty analyst positions were created. Initially, this was a rotating responsibility for all analysts. Each and every analyst was expected to help with researching, writing, and preparing the director's morning briefing. I didn't mind the "team" approach with everyone sharing the burden of the new responsibility.

Within a few weeks, ATF leadership began to notice a difference in the quality, appearance, timeliness, and efficiency of the briefing. The briefing seemed better and more comprehensive when certain analysts were working on it. As a result, a decision was made to retain those analysts who were best at researching, writing, and preparing the briefing as well as delivering it to the director.

By June, five analysts were permanently assigned to this task; I was one of them. The other analysts were allowed to return to their respective areas of responsibility and conduct business as usual. Unfortunately, I could no longer devote the necessary time and attention to my area of responsibility. Participating on the director's "dream team" was a full-time job. This assignment took me away from my primary area of responsibility—monitoring violent antigovernment groups. For this reason, I eventually left ATF.

I immediately called my DHS point of contact and inquired if the position was still available. He said the position was still open. I applied, was selected, and within two months I reported to my new assignment at the DHS.

6

Life at DHS

"We finally have your domestic terrorism analyst!" Karen Mohr proudly proclaimed to retired general Patrick M. Hughes, assistant undersecretary for information analysis (IA), near the end of the morning threat briefing. "I know you've been expecting him for a long time."

"Well . . . where is he?" Hughes inquired. I raised my hand in response, but he couldn't see me.

"He's over there, standing along the back wall," Mohr said, pointing across the room toward where I was standing.

The room was filled with people. Those standing in front me stepped aside to allow General Hughes a straight, unobstructed view to the back wall. Hughes, grabbing the edge of his glasses with one hand and squinting with both eyes, looked at me in an attempt to catch a glimpse of his new arrival.

"Daryl Johnson, reporting for duty, sir. I recently transferred from ATF," I reluctantly stated. I wasn't used to this sort of introduction to an executive-level decision maker. Plus, receiving special attention in front of my peers was a bit overwhelming.

"Well, it's about time you got here," Hughes emphatically stated. "There's a lot of work to do and we really needed someone with your knowledge and expertise. Welcome aboard!"

This was only my second day in the office. I had just joined my Department of Homeland Security (DHS) colleagues in the Information Analysis and Infrastructure Protection Directorate (IAIP) after spending nearly five years as an intelligence analyst at the Bureau of Alcohol, Tobacco, Firearms, and Explosives (ATF). At the time, IAIP was a combined effort of IA and infrastructure protection (IP). In 2005, IAIP bifurcated into two distinct agencies within DHS. The infrastructure analysis agency moved to another building entirely, while the intelligence office remained at Building 19.

It was my first time attending the morning threat briefing at DHS. This briefing at IAIP, however, differed significantly from the one at ATF in that it was open to everyone in the office who wanted to attend. In fact, everyone was strongly encouraged to attend. The threat briefing was held each weekday morning at 7:00 a.m. sharp. The briefing was given to General Hughes (retired) and his staff to update them on any overnight developments occurring throughout the world that were relevant to homeland security.

At the time, there was no conference room big enough in Building 19 to accommodate the large crowd of employees numbering between fifty and seventy-five people each day. For this reason, the briefing was held in the secretary's conference room in Building 3. Since seating was limited around the large oak table situated in the middle of the room, most attendees would stand shoulder to shoulder toward the back of the room or congregate near the doors. A line of padded chairs positioned arm to arm were aligned against both walls that paralleled the table.

General Hughes, his principal deputy, office-level staff, and division chiefs were seated at the table. Immediate supervisors, analysts, and administrative staff were required to stand. All would listen intently to the classified portion of the briefing each day. Some IAIP leaders had advance copies of the briefing slides and would turn the pages in unison as each slide was presented.

The length of the morning briefing was generally between thirty minutes and an hour, depending on how many items needed to be presented. The actual presentation usually consisted of about thirty to fifty slides. Briefers would take about a minute per slide on average.

At the conclusion, Hughes often would ask questions and offer comments about the various topics addressed during the briefing. He would then make various administrative announcements and open the floor for questions from the workforce. It was a very informal, hands-on experience, which was different than I'd ever experienced before.

In contrast, the ATF director's morning briefing was very formal. It was held in the director's suite—a rather ornate setting for an intelligence analyst. The director's suite consisted of a large conference room, administrative receiving area, and the director's office.

The ATF director, his deputy, the chief of intelligence, and the briefer (an intelligence analyst) were the only people permitted to attend the director's morning brief. The briefing was given while sitting down on a couch and plush chairs. Very few questions were asked, and administrative remarks were rarely made.

As General Hughes finished his remarks that day, he offered to answer any questions as he had done at other morning meetings. It was during this question and answer period that my division director introduced me to Hughes and IAIP's management team. Indeed, it was quite the introduction. Everyone's eyes and ears were focused on me. It was an awkward and humbling experience, but it felt good to know that I was needed and appreciated.

After the meeting, Mohr, my new division director, asked me to accompany her back to Building 19, where she escorted me and a group of other new arrivals around the office. She gave us a personal tour of IAIP's work space. Mohr kept introducing us to all the other division directors, branch chiefs, and fellow analysts who had not attended the morning briefing. We were also introduced to almost every support office in the building. As we were taking the tour, Mohr would always take a moment to introduce me as "the new domestic terrorism analyst from ATF."

DHS was created within eighteen months of the devastating terrorist attacks on September 11, 2001. The horrific attacks on the World Trade Center and Pentagon resulted in 2,995 deaths, over $100 billion in property damage, and nearly $2 trillion in combined loss to the U.S. economy.[1] The idea of creating a homeland security agency, however, was actually conceived and proposed six months prior to the 9/11 terrorist attacks.[2]

On March 21, 2001, congressman Mac Thornberry (R-Texas) proposed a bill (H.R. 1158) to merge the Federal Emergency Management Agency (FEMA), U.S. Customs, U.S. Border Patrol, and several infrastructure protection offices into a National Homeland Security Agency responsible for protecting the United States' borders and its critical resources.[3] Despite a noble effort, the bill did not pass.

Before the department's creation, various "homeland security"–related missions and activities were spread out among forty different federal agencies. There were also over 2,000 separate congressional appropriations related to homeland security prior to the agency's establishment.[4] These issues, combined with the 9/11 terrorist attacks, necessitated the creation of a single government entity.

On September 20, 2001, just eleven days after the deadliest terrorist attacks on American soil, President George W. Bush announced to the American people, during a joint session of Congress, his intent to create an Office of Homeland Security (OHS).[5] This newly created office would be responsible for coordinating a national strategy to safeguard the country against terrorism and respond to any future attacks. President Bush later signed Executive Order 13228 on October 8, 2001, which officially authorized the establishment of OHS. On that day, he also appointed then-governor Tom Ridge (R-Pennsylvania) as the director of this new office.[6]

E.O. 13228 created two organizations within the White House to discuss and further establish specific homeland security policy.[7] OHS was responsible for developing and implementing a national-level strategy to better coordinate federal, state, and local counterterrorism efforts in an effort to secure the country from terrorist threats and respond to future attacks.[8] This mission is still carried out by the Office of Intelligence and Analysis (I&A).

A Homeland Security Council (HSC) was also created. This body was responsible for advising the president on all homeland security matters. The HSC was comprised of cabinet members responsible for homeland security–related activities and fulfilled a role similar to that of the National Security Council (NSC).[9]

A month after the 9/11 terrorist attacks, senator Joseph Lieberman (D-Connecticut) submitted another bill (S. 1534) that was similar to H.R. 1158 in that it proposed the creation of a cabinet-level department for homeland security.[10] This initiative proposed a dramatic increase in the size of the homeland security office, which at the time numbered only a few dozen people. Although hearings were later held on S. 1534, it met a similar fate as its predecessor, and no further action was taken.[11]

A third attempt was made on June 2, 2002.[12] On this day, President Bush again addressed the nation and proposed the creation of a cabinet-level department responsible for protecting the United States. The president outlined four essential mission areas that corresponded to the four suggested divisions within the proposed department.

On June 6, 2002, in response to the president's speech, the White House released a document further explaining the concept of a Department of Homeland Security and provided a proposed organizational chart, a list of major government departments and agencies that would comprise the new department. It also included congressional committees responsible for overseeing homeland security activities and proposed appropriations for the upcoming fiscal year 2003 budget allocating money for the creation of the new department.[13]

Although the president of the United States can propose legislation, Congress alone has the authority to pass legislation for the creation of a new cabinet-level department. On June 18, 2002, Congress received the drafted text of the Homeland Security Act of 2002 from the president, which proposed the creation of a Department of Homeland Security, along with an outline of its major mission priorities.[14] This proposal was very similar to language used in documents released from the White House on June 6.[15]

On June 24, 2002, congressman Dick Armey (R-Texas) introduced the president's proposal to the U.S. House of Representatives.[16] It was called H.R. 5005. This congressional action again authorized the creation of a Department of Homeland Security. After amendments in committee, the bill passed the House on July 26, 2002.[17] On November 19, 2002, the U.S. Senate passed the bill.[18] President Bush finally signed the bill into law, officially known as the Homeland Security Act (HSA) of 2002, on November 25, 2002.[19]

Generally speaking, HSA 2002 formally established the Department of Homeland Security, its secretary position, and its suboffices and corresponding leadership positions within the department. It established a departmental mission and provided appropriate definitions for this mission. HSA 2002 also brought together twenty-two government agencies from throughout the U.S. government under one umbrella.[20] As of this writing, HSA 2002 remains the primary legal authority for the department. Each DHS organization has an applicable section of the HSA 2002 that explains its respective roles, responsibilities, and functions.[21]

DHS headquarters is currently located at the Nebraska Avenue Complex (NAC) in the northwest section of Washington, D.C. It has resided there since its creation in 2003. DHS headquarters will remain at the NAC until at least 2013. Currently, the department is in the process of constructing a new $4 billion headquarters complex at the former site of St. Elizabeth's psychiatric hospital in the southeast section of the District of Columbia.[22]

There were plenty of jokes circulating around the office about the new DHS headquarters being relocated to a "nut house." The new headquarters complex will accommodate the twenty-two DHS components, including U.S. Coast Guard, Customs and Border Protection, Transportation Safety Administration, and other agencies. The first anticipated occupation at the new DHS site will be the U.S. Coast Guard headquarters in 2012.[23]

The Department of Homeland Security's current headquarters at the NAC sits on property that previously included a 250-acre estate called the Grasslands.[24] In the early nineteenth century, Nathan Loughborough owned the Grasslands estate.[25] His son, Hamilton Loughborough, later inherited the property during the time leading up to the American Civil War.[26]

For most of the Civil War, the Grasslands property was located in Union-controlled territory. Its southwest property line bordered Fort Gaines.[27] Hamilton Loughborough, a Washington attorney, is characterized as an unrepentant Southern sympathizer. Two of his sisters were arrested for attempting to smuggle fine dresses to friends in Virginia.[28] His son, Henry, joined the Confederate Army and was among general Jubal Early's 15,000 soldiers when they marched on northwest Washington in July of 1864.[29] According to his wife's diary, Henry took this opportunity (so close to home) to sneak away from his unit one night and join his father and other family members for dinner at the Grasslands. He reportedly returned to his company just in time as they left marching westward away from the district.[30] Also, around this time, some historians speculate that Early's troops may have occupied Fort Gaines for a short time. Earlier that year, General Ulysses S. Grant had summoned most troops in the Washington area to bolster his army on its march to Richmond, Virginia.[31] As a result of Grant's order, the entire area was left virtually defenseless, including Fort Gaines, which is believed to have been abandoned (or very lightly defended) at the time of Early's march on Washington.

Another very interesting story involving the DHS headquarters property occurred around the time of the Lincoln assassination. On April 15, 1865, John Wilkes Booth shot and killed president Abraham Lincoln at Ford's Theatre in Washington, D.C., and fled on foot.[32] That same day, Lewis Payne stabbed secretary of state William Seward in a failed assassination attempt.[33] George Atzerodt had also planned to kill vice president Andrew Johnson, but backed out at the last minute.[34] Within hours of Lincoln's assassination, authorities reportedly sealed off major routes throughout the city in order to thwart the assassins from escape.

Booth is believed to have fled the city over a bridge spanning the Anacostia River in southeast Washington near today's Washington Navy Yard.[35] Authorities captured Payne in D.C. soon after the attacks.[36] Atzerodt, however, spent the night at a hotel a few blocks away from Ford's Theatre.[37] The next morning, Atzerodt reportedly walked to Georgetown (a neighborhood in Washington, D.C.), sold his pistol, had breakfast, and took a stagecoach northwest along Rockville Pike.[38] As he neared Tenleytown, Atzerodt noticed federal troops searching for potential suspects. He exited the coach in the area of the Grasslands estate, fled north on foot, hitched a ride, and made his escape to Germantown.[39]

Authorities suspected that John Wilkes Booth may have fled to the Loughborough mansion house and may have been hiding in the basement.[40] After all, the Loughborough family had been sympathetic toward the Confederacy and would be a likely location for a safe house. Booth was not there.

At the conclusion of the Civil War, Henry Loughborough sold the estate to William C. Whitney, secretary of the navy, who had been appointed by president Grover Cleveland.[41] Whitney used the Grasslands property as a country home and was known to rent it during weekends to family and friends, including President Cleveland.[42]

The Grasslands estate was eventually sold again, but this time it was subdivided into several lots. Today, the Japanese Embassy, the Switzerland ambassador's residence, and American University Park are all located on remnants of the Loughborough property.[43] DHS headquarters and NBC News Channel 4 also reside near the historic Grasslands mansion.

Until 2005, the U.S. Navy owned and operated the NAC as a communications, intelligence, and interpretation facility. The Navy purchased the property for $1 million in 1942 and began constructing many of the red brick structures that exist there today. Prior to the Navy's ownership, the Mount Vernon Seminary for Women owned and operated the property.[44] The seminary's chapel still resides at the NAC and serves as the primary location for town halls and other meetings. The chapel's steeple was removed when the military took over the facility. Like other large DHS organizations at the NAC, IAIP used the chapel for special speaking engagements, as well as town hall meetings for its workforce.

The NAC is comprised of a thirty-eight-acre campus and has about thirty-two buildings on site. As previously noted, many of the buildings are old brick structures built by the Navy during and after World War II.[45] All buildings at the NAC have a numerical designation.

IAIP, later renamed the Office of Intelligence and Analysis (I&A), occupies NAC Building 19. The gym and cafeteria, both located across the street from Building 19, are housed in Buildings 12 and 13 respectively. For years, there were no signs on the campus that directed employees and visitors around the maze of brick buildings. Finally, in 2009, signs were installed on the façade or near the entrance to all NAC buildings.

Since the buildings were over sixty years old, few of them had been hardwired for twenty-first-century technology. Neither did they have the necessary infrastructure to support this technology. Few buildings had been constructed with central heating and air conditioning. In 2003, climate control for some buildings was carried out "the old-fashioned way" by opening windows or having a fan circulate the hot air. Heat for some buildings was controlled with a single switch located in the basement maintenance room.

Between October and April, the heat was turned on in Building 19. If the heat needed to be turned off prematurely, it required that the facilities manager be notified. He would then assign a building maintenance worker to turn the heat on or off. Such a simple task could take hours, even days, to schedule. Meanwhile, the employees suffered as the furnace continued to blast hot air into the building, even when the outside temperature was near 70 degrees. As a result, DHS has invested millions of dollars in facility upgrades in an attempt to improve working conditions at various buildings throughout the NAC.

My coworker, who was one of the first DHS employees to arrive at the NAC, shared a story about a computer that overheated and caught on fire in the DHS Operations Center in 2003. The small fire was manually extinguished, doors and windows were opened to rid the room of smoke, and work continued uninterrupted. Large, mobile electric generators (the size of a tractor-trailer truck) were later brought in to supply much-needed power for the computers, printers, copiers, and other office equipment.

For these reasons, DHS employees created a number of nicknames for the NAC, such as "Nacatraz," due to its lack of respectable accommodations and appalling working conditions. It was like working at a maximum-security federal penitentiary like Alcatraz.

Still other DHS employees drew comparisons between the NAC's architecture and that found in Nazi concentration camps or a nineteenth-century prison. Some I&A employees referred to Building 19 as "Cell Block 19." One employee was brazen enough to record such a reference in their actual contact information found on the DHS global e-mail directory. This individual, who happened to be a first-line supervisor on I&A's management team, listed their physical location as "Cellblock 19W-1-020."

Like other DHS component agencies, IAIP derives much of its legal authority from the Homeland Security Act of 2002 (HSA 2002). HSA 2002, Title II, Subtitle A, specifies the responsibilities of the undersecretary of IAIP.[46] Among the first responsibilities listed are "(1) To access, receive, and analyze law enforcement information, intelligence information, and other information from agencies of the Federal government, State and local government agencies (including law enforcement agencies), and private sector entities, and to integrate such information in order to—(A) identify and assess the nature and scope of *terrorist threats* to the homeland; (B) detect and identify *threats of terrorism* against the United States; and, (C) understand such *threats* in light of actual and potential vulnerabilities of the homeland . . . (3) To integrate relevant information, analyses, and vulnerability assessments (whether such information, analyses, or assessments are provided or produced by the Department or others) in order to identify priorities *for protective and support measures* by the Department, other agencies of the Federal government, State or local government agencies and authorities, the private sector, and other entities [emphasis added]."[47]

The DHS counterterrorism mission is not limited to organized terrorist organizations. There is no mention of the terms *international* or *transnational* when referring to the word "terrorism" or "terrorist threat" in HSA 2002. As a result, I&A attorneys have interpreted the term "terrorism" as referring both to foreign and domestic threats.

DHS began officially functioning as a new department on January 24, 2003.[48] On this day, the Honorable Thomas J. "Tom" Ridge was sworn in as the first secretary of homeland security. Ridge had been serving as the director of the Office of Homeland Security at the White House since October 2001.[49] Prior to this, Ridge was twice elected governor of Pennsylvania.[50] In 1982, he was elected to serve as congressman for Pennsylvania in the U.S. House of Representatives and served six consecutive terms.[51] Ridge was the first Vietnam combat veteran elected to the U.S. House.[52]

Soon after the creation of DHS, the president signed Executive Order 13354 on August 27, 2004, establishing the National Counterterrorism Center (NCTC).[53] NCTC was given the same basic mission as the new Office of Information Analysis and Infrastructure Protection at DHS. NCTC's mission states that it will *"lead our nation's effort to combat terrorism at home and abroad by analyzing the threat, sharing that information with our partners, and integrating all instruments of national power to ensure unity of effort."*[54] This is a much simpler, yet very similar, regurgitation of IAIP's mission. NCTC's mission authorities come not only from E.O. 13354, but also the Intelligence Reform and Prevention of Terrorism Act of 2004 signed into law on December 17, 2004.[55]

NCTC is a hybrid organization comprised of over 500 analysts and agents representing about sixteen departments and government agencies.[56] In August 2004, IAIP was a very new organization and was at a disadvantage when compared to NCTC. IAIP had not yet developed a comprehensive and cohesive operational capability, neither within the homeland nor abroad. Congress did not grant IAIP an inherent collection capability in the traditional sense of having human sources, signal intelligence, or other covert means of gathering information. Congress objected to the MI-5 model of domestic intelligence agency due to possible civil rights and privacy concerns. Plus, the creation of such an agency was perceived as an encroachment upon the FBI and its domestic law enforcement and intelligence mission. It barely had any resources or personnel to manage its day-to-day operations. Therefore, IAIP had no written policies and procedures to govern its operations. In contrast, NCTC already had existing capabilities within the various government agencies represented. As a result, NCTC was able to establish itself more quickly and efficiently through using already-existing resources and assets. It had both a strategic and operational advantage over IAIP.

Several other presidential executive orders related to DHS, its organization structure, and its mission were also given during 2002 and 2003. Secretary Ridge served as DHS secretary until February 1, 2005.[57] He was nearing the end of his tenure upon my arrival at DHS.

Mr. Paul Redman was the first assistant secretary for information analysis in IAIP. He only served in that position between March and June 2003. Mr. William Parrish replaced Redman as the "acting" assistant secretary from July to November 2003 until a permanent replacement was found. Lieutenant general Patrick M. Hughes assumed the position on November 17, 2003.[58]

During his tenure at DHS, Hughes began initial operations of the DHS intelligence support system.[59] Hughes departed DHS on March 15, 2005.[60] He had only served as IA's assistant secretary for less than two years. Thus, a pattern of leadership rotation began to emerge. The high turnover in I&A leadership would later have a role in how the agency dealt with the leak of the right-wing extremist report and resulting political fallout.

In the fall of 2003, Hughes reportedly realized that DHS needed to develop expertise and knowledge of domestic terrorist threats. In September 2003, I received a phone call from a colleague who used to work for the Department of Defense (DOD). He was now working as a contractor for IAIP. At the time, I was entering my fifth year as an intelligence research specialist at ATF. My role was to monitor the criminal activities of violent right-wing extremists within the United States.

I credit Hughes for convincing me to transfer to DHS. He had a reputation of being a strategic thinker and visionary. He knew there were other terrorist threats emanating from within the United States. He recognized that there was an information gap at DHS regarding domestic extremist threats. This "gap" needed to be filled, and I felt that I was the person to fill it. General Hughes and his staff obviously believed there was a dire need for such analytical expertise.

In August 2004, I received a second offer to join IAIP. Things had changed within the intelligence office at ATF. I had been assigned additional responsibilities that took me away from my full-time criminal investigations duties in support of agents in the field. I had been asked to arrive at work by 5:00 a.m. to assist in preparing the ATF director's morning briefing. This initially began as a rotational assignment but soon grew into a full-time responsibility. As a result of this change, I decided that, this time, I would accept the DHS offer.

On my first day at DHS, I attended the mandatory orientation training. After gaining a familiarization with the department and filling out all the paperwork, I arrived at Building 19, my designated workplace, the following day.

For nearly three years, IAIP's workspace at Building 19 was only partially refurbished. In 2004, employees occupied only the third and fourth floors of the building. The entire basement, first, and second floors were completely uninhabitable. It resembled a building under demolition. The carpets were stained with mildew. Huge holes were knocked into the walls. Entire sections of wall had sheetrock missing. Many ceiling tiles had been removed or broken, exposing the mesh of wiring and steel framework above the ceiling. Broken office furniture littered many rooms and hallways. Asbestos was later found in the walls and ceiling of Building 19's basement.[61]

As you can imagine, this was a terrible environment in which to work. Building 19's lack of clean workspace, poor ventilation, and lack of modern infrastructure contributed to other problems, such as overcrowding on the building's third and fourth floors, lack of adequate conference room space, power outages, recurring sick leave, temperature fluctuations, and computers crashing. It's hard to believe that these deplorable working conditions existed until 2006.

My new work environment was rustic, yet vibrant with youthful ideas. Creative thinking was encouraged and new views considered. I really believed there that this fledging organization held promise. This spirit of entrepreneurship and mutual cooperation is one of the reasons that DHS was attractive to me.

Unfortunately, there was no desk waiting for me at IAIP. Like most of the other IAIP employees, I was required to share a desk with two or three other people at a time. Sometimes we would have to occupy the desk simultaneously, but most of the time, we used the desk while other people were out of the office. This practice was called hot bunking. Few enjoyed it.

Each morning, I checked with the administrative assistant to see what desk was available. This varied daily (sometimes hourly), depending on the number of employees who were out of the office for various reasons. Many times, during a phone conversation or work project, I was told to move to a different desk, because another person had returned. Many employees, including myself, often complained about such work accommodations, or lack thereof. It was to no avail. I considered it a miracle that any work got done on time under such deplorable working conditions.

When my complaints about hot bunking finally motivated my division's executive assistant into action, he took me downstairs to an unoccupied part of the building and loosened a piece of office furniture from an old desk that was in disrepair. This piece of office furniture was probably used for stacking papers. It was about sixteen inches wide and about five feet long. This "portion of desk" was barely wide enough to place a piece of paper on it and left no room to rest an elbow or arm for writing. We hauled this piece of furniture up four flights of stairs, because the elevator didn't work, and placed it in an empty space between two windows.

"There's your new desk," the executive assistant replied, with a smile on his face.

The next day, he had a phone line installed through the ceiling tiles, and a new phone was placed on my desk. There was little to no working room at my "desk," but at least I had something resembling one. I was also grateful to have a separate phone line instead of having to share with multiple people.

In August 2004, there was only one other analyst working domestic terrorism issues for IAIP. He was a contractor and had very little knowledge (and basically no experience) in this area. He willingly admitted that his background and expertise focused on transnational Muslim extremism. But it was better than working the subject alone, and he was eager to learn. He was not comfortable with the topics of white supremacists, violent antigovernment groups, animal rights extremists, ecoterrorists, anarchists, etc.

Since there were few homegrown Muslim extremist groups at the time, I asked him to research and analyze the animal rights and environmental extremist movements. He began to immerse himself in information concerning both topical areas—specifically the criminal activities, tactics, and capabilities of the Earth Liberation Front (ELF) and Animal Liberation Front (ALF). He did his best to learn and was a quick study.

I was excited to have someone with whom to share my knowledge and expertise as well as to mentor into a domestic terrorism analyst. Unfortunately, his time at IAIP was drawing to an end. He was a member of the Pennsylvania National Guard and was unexpectedly deployed to Iraq soon after my arrival. Once again, I was the only analyst looking at domestic terrorist threats.

In January 2005, I was getting ready to leave on a business trip to the Federal Law Enforcement Training Center (FLETC) in Glynco, Georgia, when another analyst came running down the hall and stopped at my supervisor's desk. She had an urgent tasking from Secretary Ridge. It was a request to provide threat input to a draft DHS strategic policy document for fiscal years 2006 through 2011.

The analyst said she was almost finished drafting the terrorist threat portion of the document when she realized there was nothing that addressed domestic terrorist threats. My supervisor called me over to his desk.

"Daryl, could you write something up for this tasking to the secretary?" he asked. I replied "Sure, what is it?"

"It's some sort of budget document for Secretary Ridge. It's looking at potential threats three to five years out, so money and resources could be appropriately allocated in anticipation of such threats," he said.

The project analyst added, "I've been working on it and noticed there was nothing that mentioned domestic terrorism threats. I thought it would be a good idea to include something about those threats. It doesn't have to be long, just a few paragraphs—no longer than a page or two."

"I'd be happy to write something up for you. When do you need it?" I asked.

"Well, that's the problem. It's due to the secretary by the end of the week. Can you have something for me tomorrow or Thursday at the latest?" the project analyst pleaded.

Unfortunately, I was leaving for FLETC the following morning, and my supervisor knew it. He took the pressure off me and said, "Don't worry about it. We'll get your protégé to write something in your absence." My colleague agreed he would write something up, and everyone seemed content with this plan of action.

The following week, I returned to the office and began reading my e-mail. Since the tasking seemed like an important one, I was eager to review the input my colleague provided to it. I skipped down several, more recent e-mails and found the message regarding our input to the secretary's tasking. It had an attachment, and I wasted no time in opening it.

After a quick review of the document's contents, I immediately realized that the input only discussed the threat from animal rights extremists and ecoterrorists. There was no mention of the threat from right-wing extremists, such as white supremacists and violent antigovernment groups. I began to draft a response to forward to my supervisor about the oversight but heard his voice talking to someone.

I immediately walked over to him and explained what I had read and recommended that I write up an addendum to address the other domestic terrorist threats inadvertently omitted.

"Daryl, don't sweat it," my supervisor said. He further reassured me, "It's an internal DHS document used for budget purposes only. It is not a real threat assessment. There's no need to rewrite it."

Being new, I may have overreacted to the situation. My supervisor's words, however, would come back later to haunt us. I was about to get my first dose of how Washington politics can sting an individual's career. Politics, unfortunately, saturates work at DHS. Congress apparently had its hands in everything IAIP did. I later learned that the department answers to eighty-six congressional committees and subcommittees—an astonishing number that I firmly believe stymies the department's ability to get anything done in a timely, responsive manner.[62]

A few weeks after that conversation with my supervisor, it happened. After eating dinner at home, I turned on the television to watch the *ABC Evening News.*

"The Homeland Security Department is focusing on possible terror threats from radical environmental and animal rights activists without also examining risks that might be posed by right-wing extremists, House Democrats said Tuesday," the report began.[63] I grabbed the television remote and turned up the volume.

"A recent internal Homeland Security document lists the Animal Liberation Front and the Earth Liberation Front with a few Islamic groups that could potentially support al-Qaeda as domestic terror threats," the reporter continued.[64] "The document does not address threats posed by white supremacists, violent militiamen, antiabortion bombers, and other extremists."

Peter Jennings had just briefed a short news segment about the budget document I was attempting to amend. A national-level news network had broadcast a story about something in which I had been indirectly involved. It wasn't a positive story, though. I wondered what impact, if any, this would have on my work the following day. I couldn't wait to go to work the next day and tell my supervisor what I had just heard.

When I arrived at the office the next morning, I immediately began searching the Internet for a transcript of the news broadcast to share with my supervisor. There were short articles in the *New York Times* and the *Washington Post.* These news stories were excerpts from a more lengthy and detailed article featured in the *Congressional Quarterly.*

The *Congressional Quarterly* article was titled "Animal Rights Groups and Ecology Militants Make DHS Terrorist List, Rightwing Vigilantes Omitted." It was written by a guy named Justin Rood.

The article began, "The Department of Homeland Security (DHS) does not list rightwing domestic terrorists and terrorist groups on a document that appears to be an internal list of threats to the nation's security."[65]

Rood further reported, "According to the list—part of a draft planning document obtained by the *Congressional Quarterly* magazine—between now and 2011, DHS expects to contend primarily with adversaries such as al-Qaeda and other foreign entities affiliated with the Islamic Jihad movement, as well as domestic radical Islamist groups. It also lists leftwing domestic groups, such as the Animal Liberation Front (ALF) and the Earth Liberation Front (ELF), as terrorist threats, but it does not mention anti-government groups, white supremacists and other radical rightwing movements, which have staged numerous terrorist attacks that have killed scores of Americans."[66]

Rood's article concludes, "Domestic terror experts were surprised the department did not include rightwing groups on their list of adversaries."

A journalist had a copy of an internal DHS document—the very document I was concerned about a week earlier. This type of behavior was something unfamiliar to me.

An editorial written for the *New York Times* revisited the topic over a month later. "A draft planning document from Homeland Security obtained by *Congressional Quarterly*, includes a survey of domestic threats notable for an over focus on extremist groups on the political left—miscreants committing crimes in the name of the environment or animal rights."[67]

"Glaringly omitted are the militia fanatics, white supremacists and other violent groups at the other end of the spectrum—antigovernment groups like Aryan Nations and anti-abortion extremists with a proven appetite for murderous violence," it lamented.[68]

The *New York Times* editorial concluded, "The average wary American should have two words to say in reaction: Timothy McVeigh."[69]

The media organizations were not properly informed. IAIP monitored all domestic threats—including those from right-wing extremists. DHS policy prohibited employees from speaking to, or interacting with, the media. DHS guidelines specifically required its employees to refer all media inquiries immediately to the DHS Office of Public Affairs or other designated spokesperson.[70]

The *Congressional Quarterly* story ultimately inspired congressman Bennie G. Thompson (D-Mississippi), who served at the time as the ranking member for the House Committee on Homeland Security, to make a public statement, conduct an internal inquiry, and hold a public hearing. Thompson's hearing produced a congressional mandate issued on the tenth anniversary of the Oklahoma City bombing titled "Ten Years after the Oklahoma City Bombing, the Department of Homeland Security Must Do More to Fight Rightwing Domestic Terrorists."[71]

"According to a recent public report, a U.S. Department of Homeland Security (DHS) five-year budget planning document failed to mention rightwing domestic terrorist groups in its list of terrorist threats facing the United States, even though the document listed leftwing domestic groups such as environmental terrorists," the memo began.[72]

"Democratic Members of the House Committee on Homeland Security are very concerned that this oversight demonstrates DHS administrators are not adequately considering rightwing domestic terrorist groups that are focused on attacking America in order to further their political beliefs."[73]

"As the bombing of the Alfred P. Murrah Building in Oklahoma City ten years ago demonstrated, rightwing domestic terrorists are capable of harming America in ways similar to al-Qaeda. Indeed, white supremacists, violent militiamen, anti-abortion bombers, and other rightwing hate groups have shown a remarkable ability to resist law enforcement authorities. In 2003, for example, the American radical right staged a 'comeback,' with the number of skinhead groups doubling from the prior year."[74]

"The Department has a key role in fighting domestic terrorism, especially with respect to its duties to conduct threat analysis and protect critical infrastructures. As DHS implements its new plan to focus on risk as a means of allocating scarce anti-terrorism resources, it must consider the threat that rightwing domestic terrorists pose to critical infrastructure and America as a whole."[75]

"If DHS' long-term planning documents do not consider these and other risks posed by rightwing domestic terrorists, then lower-level agents working to fight these groups may not be receiving enough budgetary, policy, or administrative support from their superiors. This means possible threats to our homeland could go undetected."[76]

"According to a 2004 issue paper written by the Council on Foreign Relations and the Markle Foundation, the FBI also distinguishes three primary categories of domestic terrorism: leftwing, rightwing, and special interest. Leftwing groups generally are opposed to capitalism, while rightwing groups are opposed to taxation, the Federal government, and international organizations, or motivated by racial or religious hatred."[77]

"Congress established DHS after the 9/11 terror attacks 'to prevent terrorist attacks within the United States.' In the Homeland Security Act of 2002, DHS is specifically required to: identify and assess the nature and scope of terrorist threats to the homeland; detect and identify threats of terrorism against the United States; and understand such threats in light of actual and potential vulnerabilities of the homeland. These requirements necessarily include preventing terror attacks posed by domestic groups as well as traditional foreign groups such as al-Qaeda."[78]

"Regarding domestic terror threats, IAIP officials stated that they analyze the information to determine whether domestic groups possess the 'capability and intent' to conduct a 'catastrophic' attack on U.S. critical infrastructure or resources. However, nothing in the Homeland Security Act limits IAIP analysis to 'catastrophic attacks' or critical infrastructure or resources. It is unclear why the Department has chosen this limited interpretation of its statutory responsibility to identify and assess 'the nature and scope of terrorist threats to the homeland.'"[79]

"This report provides some of the framework for this analysis, but it is only a first step in the process. As 9/11 showed us, America's security can only be assured if our intelligence and law enforcement agencies do a better job evaluating threats, including thinking of risks that are 'outside the box,' and break down bureaucratic barriers to information sharing and action. There may be rightwing terrorists here in America that want to create just as spectacular a disaster as the 9/11 attacks, and we cannot fail to meet this threat."[80]

Thompson's memo then listed seven recommendations for improving DHS analysis of domestic right-wing terrorist threats.

"First and foremost, DHS must return to its overall statutory mandate to determine 'the nature and scope of terrorist threats to the homeland' by including in its long-term planning a genuine consideration of the risks posed by rightwing domestic terrorists. Without this planning, the intelligence analysts and agents on the frontline may not get the budgetary and administrative support they need from above."[81]

Second, "Congress or DHS should establish an advisory council of groups with experience monitoring rightwing domestic terrorists. There are several organizations, such as the Southern Poverty Law Center, the Simon Wiesenthal Center, the Anti-Defamation League, the National Association for the Advancement of Colored People, the National Coalition of Anti-Violence Programs, the National Abortion Federation, and others with long-standing experience in monitoring rightwing domestic terrorist groups and assessing their danger. Congress or DHS should establish an advisory council of these groups in order to ensure that the Department has as much information as possible about the risks rightwing domestic terrorists pose."[82]

Third, "DHS must redefine its definition of 'critical infrastructure' to include those 'soft targets' most at risk of attack by rightwing domestic terrorists. Just as al-Qaeda may want to destroy prominent symbols of America authority and inflict mass casualties, as on 9/11, and leftwing domestic environmental terrorist groups may attack what they perceive as anti-environmental structures, such as dams, rightwing domestic terrorists may strike at what best communicates their message of hate."[83]

Among other recommendations are that DHS and the FBI should work together to create and maintain a comprehensive list of domestic terror groups or individuals.[84] DHS must think "outside the box" about the types of attacks rightwing domestic terrorists may conduct.[85] The FBI and DHS should work closely to set government-wide standards for focusing on right-wing domestic terrorists and sharing information on these risks.[86] Additionally, while DHS should not interfere with ongoing FBI investigations, the Department should have access to the relevant data it needs to make a determination of the risks to America posed by rightwing domestic terrorists.[87] This congressional report was signed by Bennie G. Thompson, Ranking Member of the House Committee on Homeland Security as well as representatives Donna Christensen, Peter DeFazio, Eleanor Holmes Norton, among other members of Thompson's committee.

Despite Representative Thompson's misunderstanding that DHS was already looking at right-wing extremist threats, I couldn't have asked for a better endorsement. At the time, I was the only analyst working domestic non-Islamic terrorism issues. Thompson's mandate gave me the justification needed to propose the creation of a domestic terrorism analytical unit at IAIP. After all, I was recruited and ultimately hired at DHS to perform this very mission—to lead a team of analysts to monitor, assess, and warn about terrorist threats originating from within the country.

At the time of this incident, General Hughes had already left IAIP. My former division director, Karen Mohr, was serving as the acting assistant secretary (Hughes's vacated position). My new supervisors sought approval for assigning three contractors to help me with the mission. Within several weeks, I was asked to lead a team of three contractors. I identified the necessary analytical program areas, and we divided these accounts between the four of us. Within a few months, we were drafting the first finished intelligence products dealing with domestic terrorism issues. It took a little poking and prodding to IAIP's leadership, but we were finally able to disseminate a few products to our primary customers—state and local law enforcement. Our products were well received and instantaneously garnered positive feedback from the law enforcement community. Nevertheless, such success did not come without challenges and setbacks.

As the newly assembled Domestic Terrorism Analytical Section (DTAS) embarked on our first project, I encountered our first stumbling block. One of the contractor analysts had drafted a very well-written paper concerning the history, origins, and criminal activities of the ALF and ELF. When I proofread the document for the first time, I thought I had a rising, brilliant domestic terrorism analyst. My hopes nearly came to tears after I received a phone call from my counterpart at the FBI's Domestic Terrorism Analysis Unit (DTAU). DTAS analysts regularly met with their counterparts at FBI. And we always coordinated draft papers through FBI DTAU. I&A management had always sought permission or approval (I referred to it as getting a "mother may I") from FBI headquarters prior to releasing domestic extremism–related reports. It was as if I&A had no confidence in itself as an organization.

A few days earlier, I had sent the draft paper over to FBI headquarters for coordination and comment. I was surprised to learn from my counterpart that large portions of text in the document had been literally cut and pasted from a couple of FBI assessments concerning the same topic. The analyst had plagiarized most of the document. As I checked the source citations used in the document, it became apparent that the analyst had cut and pasted major portions of text. I apologized to the FBI and sought advice from my supervisor. We broached the topic with the analyst and his explanation made sense, but nonetheless it was inexcusable. The analyst was a retired police officer. He had not received the required training as an intelligence analyst and was used to "cutting and pasting" information into police reports he had written in the past. Since he was not a federal employee, we could not take any administrative action. He was eventually reassigned to another position in our division and eventually moved on to a different agency.

Prior to his departure, the analyst made a good-faith effort to draft another assessment. This time, it was his original work and addressed a topic that we felt the private sector was interested in. The paper addressed nonconventional criminal tradecraft used by animal rights and environmental extremists to harass and intimidate private organizations and corporations into meeting the demands of the ALF and ELF. The assessment was reviewed, edited, and coordinated with the appropriate offices and agencies. It was officially disseminated to private-sector industries dealing with this type of threat, as well as state and local law enforcement.

It didn't take long for a second leak to occur. It had been almost a year to the day since the 2005 leak, but fortunately this one did not generate as much media coverage. It was the second leak of DHS domestic terrorism–related information within a year, but it was the first involving the new domestic terrorism team that had been assembled under my lead.

On Friday, April 14, 2006, *TPM Muckraker* ran a story for their "Talking Points Memo" series titled "Exclusive: DHS Warns Companies of 'Evil' Terrorist Flyer Distribution."[88] It was written by Justin Rood, the same writer who wrote the previous article in 2005 criticizing DHS for not monitoring right-wing terrorist activity.[89]

That afternoon, a law enforcement contact at the Montana All Threats Analysis Center (a state fusion center in Montana) notified me of the unauthorized disclosure as I was driving home for the weekend. The leaked document was titled "Preventing Animal Rights Extremist and Eco-Terrorist Attack: Fundamentals of Corporate Security." It had been written by an inexperienced contract analyst on my team. Again, the entire assessment was posted on the Internet and linked to the news article. I was frustrated that this discomforting situation had happened again.

The article was written to smear DHS and embarrass IAIP leadership. It was yet another attempt to humiliate the department's effort to monitor domestic extremist activity in the United States. The article insinuated that DHS was wasting its time and valuable resources looking at "leftwing extremists" who were only attacking property and not killing anyone.

"You gotta see it to believe it," the article began.[90]

It went on to say, "In a bulletin issued yesterday, the Homeland Security Department warns U.S. businesses of the threats they face from animal rights group and 'eco-terrorists.' Such radical extremist groups may use several tactics—each devastating in its own way—including: organizing protests; flyer distribution; inundating computers with e-mails; tying up phone lines to prevent legitimate calls; and sending continuous faxes in order to drain the ink supply from company fax machines."[91]

"That's right. If the ink runs out of your fax machine, that means the terrorists have won," the author wrote.[92]

Rood criticized, "To be fair, these groups have engaged in vandalism and arson, which DHS also warns of. But, c'mon. E-mail inundation is something a $40 billion security agency needs to worry about?"[93]

He continued, "The real outrage in this is that on the very day some DHS yahoo spent time and government money producing this bulletin, a jury was convicting a white supremacist on five counts of trying to obtain a chemical weapon and stolen explosives. The man's dream was to explode a briefcase 'dirty' bomb inside the U.S. Capitol."[94]

"Needless to say, I'm told DHS has yet to send out a warning on wackos like him: white supremacists, militias, anti-abortion groups or other violent far-right groups that have actually killed people. It's the vicious leftwing flyer brigades that pose the greatest danger," Rood wrote.[95]

Obviously, Rood had a valid point. He felt that other potential adversaries, such as those on the far right of the political spectrum, posed a more dangerous threat—and they do, from a purely murderous point of view. What he did not realize or understand is that IAIP was monitoring other domestic threats as well. We had published articles and other products about white supremacists, militia extremists, and sovereign citizens too. Rood was either completely unaware of these other products or he deliberately failed to mention them because it detracted from his criticism.

Whether or not he intended it, Rood's article was picked up and read by animal rights and environment activists. They ultimately posted his article on *Portland Indy Media*, an alternative news source and message board affiliated with *Indy Media* and frequently used by animal rights extremists, eco-militants, and anarchist extremists for communication.

"Oh man, we are so . . . bad! the world best beware of us animal rights and environmental terrorists. Fliers, protests, and faxes! Oh my god!" one person commented to the *Portland Indy Media* posting about the DHS assessment.[96]

"Haha, while you were not looking!" another user wrote. "Does this mean that the great SUV BURN is still on? Great to have our village guardians setting by a warm fire, looking at a window where a bad deed was once done—in the hope of catching the miscreant next time."[97]

The ALF later added both DHS assessments to an index on their website. The ALF index was titled "Gangs at War against Animal Rights Advocates."[98]

Upset that another sensitive IAIP document had been leaked to the public and posted on the Internet, I decided to write an e-mail message to IAIP leadership explaining my frustration and outlining my concerns about both unauthorized disclosures. I sent the e-mail message on Monday, April 17, 2006, to my immediate supervisor, division director, IAIP attorneys, and the agency's production management team.

"This unauthorized disclosure was the likely result of Mr. Justin Rood, an independent media correspondent and former writer for the *Congressional Quarterly*," I wrote.

"Mr. Rood now serves as a reporter/blogger for *TPMMuckraker.com*, a news blog dedicated to reporting on public corruption and abuses of the public trust. He also serves as a security correspondent for the *Government Executive* magazine," I added.

I went on to say that "as a result of Mr. Rood's article, an extremist affiliated website picked up on the story and posted the DHS assessment on its website for all anarchists, animal rights extremists and eco-terrorists to read and comment on."

I reminded IAIP leadership that Rood had been responsible for launching another "smear campaign" against DHS in April 2005. His original article was first featured in *Congressional Quarterly* and soon made its way into the mainstream media with other negative articles featured in the Associated Press, the *Washington Post, New York Times, LA Times,* and MSNBC. As a result, congressman Bennie Thompson called a hearing, largely based on Rood's allegations and the *Congressional Quarterly* article.

This led to the congressional hearings and a mandate for DHS to focus more on the threat from domestic right-wing terrorists. I was concerned that this latest leak would lead to similar actions.

"What are DHS/I&A going to do about this security breach?" I asked. "He [Justin Rood] blatantly ignored the security warning and document-handling instructions clearly printed on the front page of this assessment. Someone should look into the possibility of recourse against this individual."

Fortunately, nothing significant was released within the context of the assessment. No personal identifying information or investigative, case-related information was released into the public domain as a direct result of Rood's gross negligence. Nevertheless, it was disturbing to see a sensitive intelligence document meant solely for law enforcement displayed in its entirety on the Internet for anyone to see, including the very extremists we were writing about.

At a minimum, I thought DHS would orchestrate a media strategy to refute Rood's allegations. I thought DHS investigators would eventually confront him about his blatant act of unauthorized disclosure and attempt to identify the person who released the document to him. As demonstrated from his past news reporting about IAIP, Rood demonstrated that he could not remain objective and clearly held a grudge against DHS.

By Thursday, April 20, 2006, my e-mail made its way to the DHS Internal Security Division. I received a response to my e-mail message from the chief of the Internal Security and Investigations Division (ISID).

ISID had the authority to conduct investigations pursuant to section 40 of the United States Code Title 1315, law enforcement authority for the secretary of homeland security concerning the protection of public property. In the past, this office had conferred with the FBI on cases involving the leak of classified information either to unauthorized persons or to the media. The main criteria for an investigation by this division, in conjunction with the FBI, would be a prosecutable offense. Generally speaking, the assistant United States attorney will only consider a case for prosecution if it involves the unauthorized disclosure of classified information. This incident did not involve such a scenario.

That being said, DHS Management Directive 11042.1 addresses the loss, compromise, or suspected compromise of incidents involving unclassified "For Official Use Only" (FOUO) information and permits the local security official to conduct an inquiry at the request of the originator. Accordingly, IAIP may request that their security officer look into the matter.

"I would strongly recommend that Justin Rood not be contacted as it will only serve to heighten his interest in the assessment. Moreover, it is unlikely that he will reveal the source of the document," the DHS ISID official said.

"In my opinion, as we expand our distribution of FOUO to our state, local, and tribal partners, such leaks will become more prevalent. My division will continue to look at all cases where classified information is intentionally compromised," he concluded.

His words were discomforting, but fortuitous. From a civil or criminal prosecutorial standpoint, nothing could be done about the leaks. We had to accept the fact that leaks do and will continue to occur at IAIP. As a result, we had to take extra care to ensure that our finished intelligence documents were written in such a way that sensitive information would not compromise an ongoing criminal investigation or sensitive law enforcement activity. This was something I took very seriously.

Both leaks had brought their own share of headaches, frustration, and learning experiences. I capitalized on both opportunities to build and enhance IAIP's domestic terrorism analytical capabilities. Within another year, I found myself leading a team of four contracted analysts, with plans in place to hire three additional analysts who would be actual federal employees. My supervisor was grooming me to becoming a branch chief in the near future, and he would often joke that I would have my own "division" someday at IAIP.

I definitely wanted this program to grow, but I also realized that I needed to be extremely judicious about the type of analysts we were going to hire. I wanted to better serve the law enforcement community and earn the respect of IAIP's leadership. I needed to hire the best-qualified domestic terrorism analysts. I wanted individuals that already had well-established contacts in the law enforcement and intelligence communities. They had to have strong writing skills and possess in-depth knowledge about the various types of domestic extremist groups, their radical ideologies, and terrorist tradecraft. I wanted to establish a "dream team" of domestic terrorism analysts. This was my vision. I set my goals high and, with time, I eventually achieved them through much patience, persistence, and perseverance.

7

Team Leader

On February 15, 2005, the Honorable Michael Chertoff, former assistant attorney general, was confirmed and sworn in as the second secretary of the Department of Homeland Security (DHS).[1] Like many at the Office of Intelligence and Analysis (I&A), I attended his reception and inaugural speech to the department's workforce held in the Nebraska Avenue Complex (NAC) gym soon after his swearing-in ceremony.

I was disappointed to see secretary Tom Ridge leave, because he was such a likable person. Politics and bureaucratic infighting, however, had reportedly taken its toll on Ridge, and it was time for him to move on in his career. Nevertheless, with a new secretary, a fresh perspective and new ideas emerged throughout the department. Chertoff served in the secretary position until January 2009.[2]

Among his significant accomplishments at DHS, Chertoff completed a systematic evaluation of the department, its agencies, operations, and policies shortly after becoming secretary. This evaluation is referred to as the second stage review (2SR).[3] The department needed organizational realignment and reprioritization, which included Information Analysis and Infrastructure Protection's (IAIP) position within the department.

On July 15, 2005, Chertoff announced 2SR's findings, which included a reorganization of the department.[4] The reorganization was finalized and implemented on October 1, 2005.[5] Of particular interest to IAIP, 2SR split the organization into separate agencies.

The Office of Information Analysis (IA) was renamed the Office of Intelligence and Analysis (I&A), and its assistant secretary position was elevated to the undersecretary level.[6] This meant that I&A had a direct line to the secretary of homeland security instead of sharing the responsibility with its sister organization, the Office of Infrastructure Protection (IP). Similarly, IP became a separate entity within DHS with its own undersecretary position.[7]

While Chertoff was actively planning 2SR, IAIP was busy building a team of analysts to monitor and assess threats from domestic non-Islamic extremists. Timing was everything. My immediate supervisor had recently left for another contracting job. His replacement, a true leader by the name of Chris Stevens, arrived to work full of enthusiasm and a strong desire to affect positive change. He had a vision for the branch and was eager to elevate the work performance of his subordinates. Stevens quickly took charge, laid out his expectations, and began meeting with each analyst individually. When he met with me, I explained that I had arrived at IAIP a year earlier under the impression that I was going to lead a team of analysts. I was now alone, struggling to keep up with the vast amount of work. I had recently lost the only support network I had at IAIP—a contract analyst unfamiliar with the subject matter who recently deployed to Iraq.

"We're going to get you some help," Mr. Stevens said.

He couldn't believe there was only one analyst working domestic extremist issues at DHS. I was surprised to learn that he was familiar with the types of domestic terrorist threats that existed in America. He had read a number of books on the topic and had a handle on some of the domestic terrorism–related terminology.

From his prior work at the FBI, Chris Stevens knew that the domestic terrorist threat was often underestimated. He knew these types of extremists possessed an extreme hatred for the U.S. government, minority communities, and many other targets. He vowed to elevate my visibility within the agency and immediately began looking for ways to reallocate a limited number of resources under his supervision. Within a few weeks, I had a list of eligible contractors, along with their résumés.

"Take some time, review these résumés, and let me know if there's anyone qualified to help you out," he said.

I knew there was little chance that any of the contractors had previous experience working domestic terrorism issues. I was hopeful, however, that some might have law-enforcement backgrounds. I was looking for someone with at least some familiarity with the subject matter, as well as the customers we were serving.

It didn't take long for me to find a few possible fits for my team. I proposed selecting a retired police detective from Connecticut; a young Army serviceman who had been recently discharged; and two young civilian analysts from the Army. It was the best I could do. I was willing to mentor and train them, if they were willing to work alongside me.

By March 2005, all four contractors had arrived and were eager to work. Chris Stevens named our team the Domestic Terrorism Analysis Section (DTAS).

The contractors came from a variety of backgrounds and levels of experience—none with any knowledge or understanding of domestic extremism in the United States. Each of them required a lot of mentoring and guidance. Their work required close supervision to ensure accuracy.

I was grateful and indebted to Mr. Stevens for his understanding and unwavering support. The creation of DTAS clearly illustrated that IAIP finally followed through with its promise and commitment to establish a domestic counterterrorism analytical capability within the organization. I believe IAIP matured as an agency by expanding its analytical effort to include domestic terrorist threats within the United States.

It is important to note that, in the beginning, DTAS was not only responsible for monitoring, analyzing, and assessing right-wing, left-wing, and single-issue-extremism-related threats, but also that of domestic Islamic extremists, street gangs, and other criminal organizations that may or may not have a terrorism nexus. We were literally the "dumping ground" for anything believed to be a threat within the homeland.

Despite adding four analysts, I soon found myself back where I started—overwhelmed with work and with few resources to complete it. I had to lower my expectations and broaden my knowledge and perspective. I originally planned to have one analyst assigned to each of the broad domestic terrorism categories—right-wing extremism, left-wing extremism, and single-issue extremism. Then I learned my team would be responsible for looking at homegrown Muslim extremism. I thought I might have had enough resources to begin a systematic approach to analyzing these threats. Only then did I learn that we would also be responsible for handling any requests related to street gangs, such as Mara Salvatrucha 13 (MS-13), outlaw motorcycle gangs, drug trafficking organizations, and other forms of organized crime.

It didn't take long to start feeling like we needed even more analysts! Fortunately, I had analytical counterparts in the law enforcement community who could help us learn more about these nontraditional threats. In hindsight, I was glad that we didn't receive too many requests for information related to these topics, because none of us had any in-depth knowledge or experience working these areas.

Although DTAS was comprised of a small team of analysts, we had to examine a rather broad spectrum of threats. It required everyone not only to get smart on a primary account, but to also work secondary areas of emphasis and cross-train to help each other. I was honored to have this opportunity to mentor and lead other analysts. I was proud of the work we accomplished.

The remainder of IAIP's analytic workforce was well established and fully staffed. They were working terrorist threats from abroad (like al-Qaeda), threats to critical infrastructure, terrorist weapons and tactics, and human smuggling.

In August 2005, Mr. Charles E. "Charlie" Allen was appointed the undersecretary for intelligence and analysis and replaced acting assistant secretary Karen Mohr. Allen's arrival at DHS coincided with the creation of the new undersecretary position inspired by 2SR. He also inherited a brand-new agency—the newly named Office of Intelligence and Analysis (I&A).

Allen's superb reputation in the intelligence community preceded his arrival and instantly elevated I&A's standing within the intelligence community.

Allen chose Dr. Mary Connell as his deputy undersecretary for intelligence and analysis (DUSI). Like Mohr, Connell was detailed from the CIA on a two-year assignment at

I&A, with the possibility of a third-year extension. Supposedly, Connell made it known soon after her arrival that subordinate managers were to refer to her as "Doctor" Connell. As a result, Connell was loathed by many of I&A's managers.

Connell "ruled" I&A with her uncompromising, hard-nosed management style. She was known for her meticulous edits and shrewd, yet annoying, comments. Analysts learned to tolerate her finicky revisions, petty comments, and contempt for "factoids"—a term used by Connell that referred either to "too much information" or "too many facts." They learned to despise this word, as it appeared on many of the papers she edited. Connell personally reviewed every draft paper published at I&A. No paper was ever disseminated without her absolute approval. If approval was not received in writing, papers would languish on her desk until they were revised, rejected, or finally approved. Sometimes this would take multiple rewrites, but usually, if an analyst's paper didn't make the cut the third time through, it was "killed."

Connell definitely adhered to the "publish or perish" approach to intelligence analysis. In other words, I&A's very existence depended on how many reports and assessments it produced to its stakeholders and customer base. Analysts were rated quantitatively on how many products, briefings, and other analytic projects they completed each year.

Allen probably knew of Connell's difficult personality and reputation and may have used Connell's apparent weaknesses to his social advantage. Everyone could focus their frustration, scorn, and growing resentment at Connell while Allen, the person with the real power and authority to make decisions, escaped the direct fire of employee criticism.

Allen's management style and personality was a drastic contrast to Connell's. At times, Allen came across as a grandfather-like figure. Yet he could be stern and inflexible when he wanted to be. I remember that, during his first month as undersecretary, Allen made his rounds throughout I&A's work space. He paused at nearly every occupied cubicle to shake the person's hand and thank them for their service to the country. This made a very favorable impression upon me. He almost always had something positive to say to everyone he happened to meet in the hallways as he traversed from one meeting to another. He was known to arrive very early and work late into the night. Allen reportedly slept overnight at the NAC on many occasions in an effort to complete his many daily tasks.

At his town hall meetings, Allen came across as friendly, warm, and open-minded. He enjoyed reporting back to the workforce concerning I&A's contributions to the intelligence community. His speeches were filled with numerous accolades about the office gathered from his many engagements and personal conversations with well-known figureheads such as chiefs of police, agency directors, ambassadors, and politicians.

Among his most visible accomplishments at I&A, he took pride in the planning and completion of I&A's building renovations. He frequently referenced the building improvements during his town hall meetings. He took great pride in renovating the men's bathroom ventilation system. I readily admit this was a prolonged problem in need of repair, but there were other, more pressing and serious problems related to office processes, information access, and computer system upgrades that were left unaddressed.

One of Allen's first items of business was to visit representative Bennie Thompson, chairman of the Homeland Security Subcommittee in the U.S. House of Representatives. Earlier in the year, Thompson had issued a mandate to DHS to do more to combat right-wing terrorist threats. In anticipation of the November 8 meeting with Thompson, I was asked to provide background information in the form of a talking-points memo to Allen about I&A's efforts to combat domestic terrorist threats. The talking points were meant to assist Allen in resolving any of Thompson's remaining concerns concerning the April 19 congressional report. I don't know whether Allen bothered to read Thompson's report. Nonetheless, I tried to inform I&A management about it as opportunities presented themselves.

After spending two years at DHS, it seemed to me that many DHS employees were only concerned with foreign terrorist threats to the homeland. The threat was always viewed through an international or transnational lens. In fact, DHS leadership and many of its employees even often misused the term "domestic terrorism," altering it to mean terrorist attacks on U.S. soil. In reality, the term has always meant violence from terrorist groups or individuals based and operating entirely within the United States or its territories *without foreign direction*.

Despite efforts to educate and remind DHS leadership and coworkers regarding the proper use of this term, many continued to misuse it to mean international terrorist threats inside the United States. After all, many rationalized the use because DHS was established as a result of the 9/11 terrorist attacks that were carried out by Muslim extremists from abroad, who were affiliated with a foreign terrorist group. Therefore, all references to "domestic terrorism" in the Homeland Security Act of 2002 and other departmental related legislation, such as the various presidential directives, must have meant foreign-directed terrorist acts on U.S. soil (according to the ill-informed). This misinterpretation of the term "domestic terrorism" continued to gain popularity throughout the department to my dismay. Further, the United States Code's definition of "domestic terrorism" doesn't offer much clarity either. In fact, 18 USC, Section 2331, Item 5, may be the primary source of the problem. The department's deep misunderstanding of domestic terrorism was clearly illustrated as recently as 2010, when an antitax zealot chose to end his tax grievance with a suicide attack on an IRS processing center.

On February 18, 2010, Andrew Joseph Stack III, who had a longstanding dispute with the IRS over the federal income tax, packed his single-engine Piper Dakota aircraft with a fifty-five-gallon drum of gasoline.[8] He was on a mission. No one anticipated that he would fly his personal aircraft from the Georgetown Municipal Airport in Austin, Texas, into a seven-story office building housing an IRS processing center just a short distance away.[9] Soon after takeoff, Stack, without hesitation, slammed his small plane into the Echelon office building, causing a massive explosion. It was early afternoon, and the building was full of federal employees. An IRS employee and Joe Stack were killed instantly from the impact.[10] Thirteen other IRS employees were injured.[11] As smoke billowed from the stricken building and shards of glass and other debris rained to the ground, those watching the scene unfold could not help but draw comparisons to the 9/11 terrorist attacks on the World Trade Center in New York City. But this attack, although similar, was on a much smaller scale. Stack left behind a lengthy "manifesto" on the Internet for all to read. He was highly critical of the IRS and taxation, which was the overriding theme among other grievances.

There was little doubt this was an act of domestic terrorism. Joe Stack had retaliated for losing his personal battle with the IRS.[12] And his manifesto made it clear that he wanted to influence government policy concerning the nation's tax system. He didn't choose to fly his plane into just any federal building. He chose the IRS—a legitimate target in Stack's perverted worldview.

To my shock and discouragement, Homeland Security Secretary Janet Napolitano commented that Joe Stack's attack on the IRS processing center was *not* an act of domestic terrorism during a radio interview on WAMU's *Diane Rehm Show*.[13]

"He had his own personal issues and personal motives and was carrying out a personal agenda," Napolitano reportedly said.[14]

"To our belief, he was a lone wolf. He used a terrorist tactic, but an individual who uses a terrorist tactic doesn't necessarily mean they are part of an organized group attempting an attack on the United States," Napolitano stated.[15] The term "lone wolf" describes violent lone offenders who generally subscribe to extremist or terrorist causes without necessarily belonging to a group. It is used exclusively within the counterterrorism community to describe a certain type of terrorist.

Napolitano's statement was not only misinformed, it was ignorant. Napolitano never consulted domestic terrorism subject matter experts within her department. And it was the first time that DHS had ever preempted the FBI in making a public announcement concerning whether a particular incident in the United States was terrorism or not. The FBI, as the lead agency for investigating acts of terrorism in the United States, had always made the determination based on the result of their thorough criminal investigation.

A week after Napolitano's ill-advised statement, the 111th Congress passed House Resolution 1127, dated March 2, 2010, expressing their concern about the suicide plane attack on the IRS.[16] Their statement totally contradicted Napolitano's view of the incident.

"Whereas all federal employees, and those from the Internal Revenue Service in particular, have experienced a terrible tragedy in the suicide plane attack on February 10, 2010," the resolution began.[17]

"Whereas Vernon Hunter [deceased IRS employee], who lost his life the *terror attack* [emphasis added], had 48 years of public service," it read.[18]

"Now therefore be it resolved, that the House of Representatives—strongly condemns the *terror attack* [emphasis added] perpetrated deliberately against federal employees . . . rejects any statement or act that deliberately fans the flames of hatred or expresses sympathy for those who would attack public servants of our Nation," it concluded.[19]

The latter half of this pronouncement is a likely reference to representative Steve King's (R-Iowa) comments to an independent journalist during the Conservative Political Action Conference in Washington, D.C., during the immediate aftermath of Stack's attack.

"I think if we would've abolished the IRS back when I first advocated it, he wouldn't have a target for his airplane," King said.[20] "And I'm still for abolishing the IRS."[21]

"It's sad the incident in Texas happened," King rationalized.[22] "But by the same token, it's an agency that is unnecessary, and when the day comes when that is over and we abolish the IRS, it's going to be a happy day for America."[23]

Surprisingly, the FBI, despite having opened a domestic terrorism investigation into the incident, has not publicly acknowledged whether or not Joe Stack's deliberate act met the criteria for domestic terrorism. Perhaps the FBI did this to save Napolitano further embarrassment. This incident, and Napolitano's comments about it, typifies the DHS's apparent lack of understanding and bias toward ideologically motivated violence of the non-Islamic variety.

It was very apparent that the entire DHS approach to countering terrorism was heavily focused on the threat from Muslim extremists at the detriment of the domestic non-Islamic extremist threat in this country. Mirroring the intelligence community's counterterrorism analytical efforts, I&A devoted much of its resources to analyzing and assessing the threat from al-Qaeda, its affiliates, and homegrown Muslim extremism. Within my branch alone in 2008, domestic terrorism analysts (non-Muslim threats) were initially outnumbered at least ten to one—despite the hundreds of analysts throughout the intelligence community already focused on the Muslim extremist threat. Traditional domestic extremists, such as white supremacists, militia extremists, sovereign citizens, animal rights extremists, ecoterrorists, and the like, were not part of the DHS vocabulary.

This myopic view of terrorism stems from several inherent issues within the department. First, the vast majority of the workforce at DHS headquarters came from the Department of Defense (DOD), military services, and intelligence communities (IC), while only a small percentage of employees came from the law enforcement community. An overemphasis on military and IC experience hampers the department's ability to understand the law enforcement community, as well as the diverse set of issues and concerns from the nation's police agencies. Furthermore, members of the IC are intimately familiar with Presidential Executive Order 12333, which limits the ability of the intelligence community to monitor and collect information related to domestic threats within the United States. Similarly, the Posse Comitatus Act prohibits the U.S. military (including the DOD) from looking at threats involving U.S. persons.

As a result of these legal restrictions, much of the DHS workforce simply takes a narrow-minded approach to the homeland mission—attempting to replicate what they knew from their previous work experience within the IC and military environment. Furthermore, the task of monitoring and assessing domestic terrorist threats has traditionally rested with federal law enforcement agencies—primarily the FBI. Agencies such as the Bureau of Alcohol, Tobacco, Firearms and Explosives (ATF), U.S. Secret Service (USSS), and U.S. Marshals Service (USMS) also investigate the criminal activities of domestic extremists and assist the FBI with their domestic terrorism investigations.

Another problem was the lack of continuity in leadership—especially within I&A. Between 2004 and 2009, the department had three secretaries. I&A's executive leadership is comprised of an undersecretary and deputy undersecretary and their respective support staff. There is also a deputy assistant secretary position for the Analysis and Production Directorate, which is the core function of I&A. Since 2003, various people have rotated in and out of these positions. In 2005, the undersecretary for I&A became a politically appointed position. Therefore, it is generally expected to change with each presidential administration. When the undersecretary leaves, their designated deputy either serves in an acting capacity until a new undersecretary is appointed or departs soon after the undersecretary's departure.

Despite having had only two presidential elections during 2003–2010, the undersecretary of intelligence and analysis position has changed six times (including those serving in an acting capacity). There was also a seventh person nominated, Phil Mudd, but his name was later withdrawn amid a national controversy surrounding the alleged CIA-enhanced interrogation program. Over this same seven-year period, I&A initiated six major office restructurings. My immediate supervisor and second-line supervisor changed five times each.

I&A was always in a state of transition. Change of leadership is a major contributor to this systemic problem. But other factors influence this predicament. When faced with a challenge, I&A often resorts to restructuring by changing the organization's focus to better understand, refine, and clarify its mission. Very rarely had I&A leadership showed a willingness to assert itself within the department and toward its primary competitors (CIA, FBI, etc.) to defend its "turf" or set boundaries regarding mission space. As a result, the organization is constantly attempting to establish itself within the IC and law enforcement community, forever hoping for recognition.

A major contributor to this mass exodus and endless migration at I&A is what some analysts refer to as threat fatigue. The term "threat fatigue" describes a very real condition resulting from the many, long work hours spent analyzing and assessing the credibility of terrorist threats—including false alarms—coupled with persistent, yet constant and evolving trends in terrorist tactics and tradecraft.

Undersecretary Allen once mentioned this term at an office town hall meeting, but expressed his disapproval if any I&A analysts succumbed to such a condition. Many people use other terms to describe this circumstance, such as "burnout," "being stressed out," or "overworked." Threat fatigue has very real emotional, psychological, and physical side effects. I've experienced this firsthand—a lack of sleep; restless nights; lower immunity to disease and sickness; and the persistently high levels of stress that can lead to other serious medical conditions such as hypertension, anxiety, as well as stress/panic attacks. I witnessed these conditions among many of my coworkers at I&A.

With such a high turnover in the workforce, you're expected to "pick up the slack" and take on additional duties and responsibilities for extended periods of time. The work only increases as I&A managers constantly think of new ways to satisfy stakeholders' demands. They rarely decline external requests, fearing it will lead to unsatisfied customers, which often translates to congressional inquiry and scrutiny.

I recall a fellow analyst's remarks soon after arriving at DHS. He said that I&A can be compared to "an airplane attempting to be assembled in midflight soaring high above the earth, while its engineers and workers constantly shift their duties in an attempt to build the aircraft's fuselage traveling 500 miles per hour at 30,000 feet." Others commented that they felt a "huge weight taken off of their shoulders" when they left the organization.

It is no secret that about 60 percent of I&A's workforce is comprised of contractors.[24] Of the approximately 800 I&A employees, only about 150 are actually intelligence analysts. Many of the analysts are contractors from companies such as General Dynamics, Booz Allen & Hamilton, and CENTRA. Analysts are the heart and mind of any intelligence agency. Among I&A's analytical workforce, there has been a disproportionately high number of GS-13, GS-14, and GS-15 personnel—the highest pay grades in the U.S. government's general schedule (GS) pay system. Very few entry-level analysts are being mentored and groomed for I&A's future. I&A is caught in a predicament. In order to meet demand, it must recruit and hire seasoned analysts who can "hit the ground running" and who will require less supervision and training. However, this leaves the organization "top heavy" with a disproportionate number of analysts in the higher-paid positions and very few being nurtured for the agency's future. Furthermore, I&A's ability to offer newly hired analysts a promotion or promise of higher pay is a major incentive for people to apply to I&A positions. The higher pay grade is an enticement for recruiting seasoned analysts from other agencies who otherwise would not leave their respective agencies to work at DHS.

The department's widespread bias against, and lack of understanding about, the topic of domestic non-Islamic terrorism can be further illustrated through a couple of interactions I had with I&A's executive-level management.

In January 2007, Chris Stevens (my branch chief) and I met with Mr. Jack Tomarchio, principal deputy assistant secretary for I&A, at his office on the third floor of Building 19. At the time, Tomarchio had just been assigned to serve as principal deputy undersecretary for operations at I&A. He was the primary senior official in charge of establishing the intelligence office's partnership with state and local governments to build a domestic intelligence sharing network.[25]

At a manager's meeting, Tomarchio had expressed interest in learning more about current domestic extremist activity in the United States. Chris Stevens scheduled a meeting between me and Tomarchio and also came along to observe the discussion and take notes. Stevens was curious to see if Tomarchio would have any tasks or action items for our branch as a result of the meeting.

Mr. Stevens knocked on Tomarchio's door, which was already open.

"Come in, gentlemen! Sit down and make yourselves comfortable," Tomarchio greeted us.

Jack, as he preferred to be called, was a nicely dressed and well-mannered man.

Upon entering Tomarchio's office, Chris Stevens and I took turns shaking Jack's hand. We then sat down in separate chairs in front of Tomarchio's desk.

"Mr. Tomarchio, I'd like to introduce you to our lead subject matter expert on domestic terrorism, Daryl Johnson," Mr. Stevens said.

"Good to meet you, Daryl," Tomarchio began. "So, tell me about these domestic terrorists. What have they been up to?"

In an attempt to better understand his question, I asked "What types of extremists are you interested in discussing? There are several different kinds of domestic extremists."

Tomarchio replied, "Well, I'm from Pennsylvania, so let's start there. What types of extremists do we have in Pennsylvania?"

"Currently, there is an Aryan Nations faction in Potter County, as well as racist skinheads affiliated with Hammerskin Nation in Harrisburg, Philadelphia, and northeastern Pennsylvania. There are also militia extremists and sovereign citizens active in various parts of the state," I responded.

Tomarchio replied, "Those guys aren't really a threat, are they? I mean, they're just a bunch of beer-drinking bubbas living in the backwoods and hills of Pennsylvania. Do they really pose a dangerous threat?"

"They certainly do," I said.

"They're not really interested in causing the same magnitude of attack as al-Qaeda, but they're still capable of killing people," I continued. "And, unlike al-Qaeda, they are a very real concern to many law enforcement officers who encounter violent white supremacists and antigovernment extremists on a fairly regular basis."

I explained to Tomarchio that there was a much greater chance of our state and local law enforcement officers facing a threat from white supremacists, sovereign citizens, or other antigovernment extremists than an al-Qaeda operative in the heartland of the United States—especially outside of major metropolitan areas. Tomarchio seemed to be satisfied with the explanation. We continued our discussion for another ten minutes.

At the conclusion of our visit, Tomarchio asked if I was interested in joining him during an upcoming visit to Pennsylvania's State Capitol building in Harrisburg. He was scheduled to meet with the governor's staff, Pennsylvania state police, and their state's emergency management office to discuss plans for establishing a DHS-sponsored state fusion center—a joint effort between DHS and state and local agencies. I agreed to accompany him to Harrisburg.

I had mixed feelings as I left that meeting. On one hand, I was excited about the possibility of going to a State Capitol building to meet with a governor's staff. Nevertheless, I was a little concerned over the stereotypical remark Tomarchio had made concerning domestic right-wing extremists. Again, I&A leadership had shown its misunderstanding about the potential dangers and relevant threat from domestic extremists.

On April 6, 2007, I met Tomarchio at the State Capitol in Harrisburg and presented a briefing on the newly created Homeland Environment Threat Analysis Division, as well as the extremism and radicalization mission at I&A.

Tomarchio later resigned from the department in August 2008 and returned to the private sector.[26] A few months prior to his departure, a major FBI domestic terrorism investigation concluded with the arrests of four militia members in Tomarchio's home state of Pennsylvania. The FBI investigation involved a plot to kill government officials (including discussions about assassinating presidential candidates).

On June 7, 2008, FBI agents, assisted by state and local law enforcement authorities, seized a substantial amount of firearms and explosives from members of the Pennsylvania Unorganized Militia. Among the many weapons were sixteen improvised explosive devices (bean can grenades), bomb-making components, explosive chemicals, and multiple firearms from the suspects, including AK-47 assault rifles, a .50-caliber rifle, an SKS assault rifle equipped with a grenade launcher, and thousands of rounds of ammunition.[27,28] One suspect also possessed a flamethrower, homemade cannon, and "lightning machine," which had been fabricated from metal-coiled mattress frames.[29,30]

Another incident that illustrated I&A management's misunderstanding of domestic terrorism involved a statement from a division director during a production meeting I attended. The meeting concerned the development of a domestic terrorism incident database. At the start of the meeting, the division director remarked while chuckling, "I don't know why we're having this meeting. We're prohibited from looking at the criminal acts and violent activity of U.S. citizens." The attorney in the room corrected this misinformed impression that we were wasting our time.

A third incident, which included an odd discussion about domestic terrorism and involved DHS leadership, occurred a few weeks later.

It was May 2, 2007, at 9:00 a.m. and Charlie Allen, undersecretary for intelligence and analysis at DHS, was appearing on C-SPAN as part of its *Washington Journal Program*. As I walked past a television suspended from the ceiling in Building 19, I caught a glimpse of Charlie Allen's face on the television screen. I noticed in the bottom corner of the television screen that the topic of today's C-SPAN program was "Potential Terrorist Activity in the U.S." I raised the volume on the television just in time to catch the first question from the show's host.

"How many of these groups are within the United States? And are you just looking at Islamic groups? Or what other groups do you look at?" the host asked.[31]

Allen responded, "What we're looking at . . . no, we're looking at a variety of groups. We're looking at Islamic extremism in the United States . . . looking at bottoms up . . . the FBI is doing a great job in doing, what I would call, extraordinary investigative intelligence to disrupt extremists. But we're looking at more broadly, why people become radicalized? What would cause them to cross that red line from being radical, to creating violence—to engaging in violence. *We look at white supremacists. We look at black separatists. We look at those who are concerned about our environment and are willing to commit violence there. So we look broadly at extremism in the United States* [emphasis added]."[32]

Four minutes into the program, the first call was received. "Our first call for Mr. Allen comes from Fairfax, Virginia, on our line for Democrats. Good morning," the program host said.[33]

The first caller was an elderly woman. She immediately asked, "Good morning. I'd like to know, why is it?—and, notice that I say 'Zionist' not 'Jewish'—when anybody tries follow up on the Zionist connection, they immediately shut down and cut off?"[34]

She continued her conspiratorial views: "We know that these people were standing on top of their cars, cheering and waving while the buildings are falling . . . we know they were ushered out of the country rapidly so that they couldn't be questioned . . . we know that they were in casing buildings, so that they could set up explosives to bring our buildings down."[35]

Without batting an eye, Allen calmly sipped a cup of coffee, looked down at the table in front of him, and patiently waited to respond.

The caller concluded her remarks by stating, "Believe me, if we have another attack and you don't follow down that Zionist connection, you will have lost!"[36]

Allen forthrightly refuted the absurd comments: "Well, the attacks of 9/11 were perpetrated by Osama Bin Laden, and by [Ayman al-] Zawahiri—the number two. They were directed, coordinated by the central leadership. And they used Khalid Shaq Mohammed. We're happy that he's in prison down in Guantanamo Bay. It was a murderous act by al-Qaeda central leadership. And this was not an issue of Zionism."[37]

Allen's answer was succinct and to the point.

The program host turned to Mr. Allen and asked, "How do economics play into whether or not a person becomes part of a radical group?"[38]

"I think that's a factor," Allen began. "Particularly for the 'footsoldiers,' the people who feel really dispossessed. We find in some of the extremists that some of these people are well educated, they are middle class."

Allen continued, "If you looked at some of the extremists in the United Kingdom, those that are convicted in the 2004 plot that was very well covered by the *New York Times* yesterday . . . these are people who have become self-segregated, alienated from society. They may be first- or second-generation immigrants to society. And unlike the people that came over and were very pleased with living in the West, these have become somewhat alienated and self-segregated."[39]

The host received another caller from "Baltimore, Maryland."[40]

"Hi. Good morning," said the caller.[41]

"Good morning," the host replied.[42]

The caller introduced himself by saying, "I'm an African-American Muslim and I heard at the beginning of this show that you categorize this as not a war against Islam, but a war against what you consider to be a radical form of Islam."[43]

He continued, "The host actually asked the question I was going ask about other radical groups and other religions."[44]

"I guess my issue is that there have been many extremist groups of other religious. The Ku Klux Klan is the one that always comes to mind with the illuminated crosses. They went to church every Sunday. But they terrorized the South and different parts of the country for years. And, even today, we had David Koresh. We had Timothy McVeigh. All of these people were Christians—the abortion bombers. But we don't . . . when we talk about them in the press and when official administrators discuss them, they never discuss radical Christians."[45]

The host turned her attention to Allen and rephrased the caller's point: "Are these radical groups taken as seriously as Islamic radical groups?"[46]

"Absolutely," Allen responded. "We take all extremist groups willing to commit violence—any white supremacist group in this country is an issue. And I will leave that to the bureau, because it does investigative work on groups that are willing to commit violence or planning violence."[47]

Allen restated his answer: "But, yes . . . we take these just as seriously and I appreciate the call from your audience. But we also look, as I said earlier, at people, environmentalists, who engage in violence. Also, people, animal rights groups who engage in violence. White supremacist groups are very much a focus. We have analysts in my office working on this right now."[48]

As I watched the program unfold, I was glad to hear Allen acknowledge that his organization was keeping a watchful eye on white supremacists, black separatists, animal rights extremists, and ecoterrorists. I&A management had publicly acknowledged this important work conducted by members of my team.

I also chuckled at the notion of Charlie Allen's having to respond to the various absurd conspiracy theories conveyed by some of the program's call-in guests.

Allen's strongest statement about domestic terrorism came in response to a caller who was a self-proclaimed African-American Muslim. I wondered if Allen would have given us the same level of publicity if that call would not have been made. While Mr. Allen acknowledged the work of I&A's domestic terrorism analysts, he may have also been paying us "lip service" so as not to give the impression that I&A was engaging in any sort of racial or religious profiling.

A particularly important piece of congressional legislation related to I&A's countering radicalization mission was formally proposed on July 5, 2007.[49] The U.S. House of Representatives, 110th Congress, had issued its conference report titled "Implementing Recommendations of the 9/11 Commission Act of 2007."[50] Section 2402 of this document outlines I&A's radicalization mission. The section was named "Sense of the Congress Regarding the Prevention of Radicalization Leading to Ideologically-Based Violence."[51]

In its report, Congress cited that the threat of radicalization leading to ideologically based violence "transcends borders and has been identified as a potential threat within the United States."[52] They said that radicalization had been identified as a precursor.[53] Countering the threat of violent extremists, both domestic and international, was identified as a critical element of the U.S. plan in the fight against terrorism.[54] Furthermore, Congress learned that law enforcement agencies throughout the country had identified radicalization as an emerging threat. They cited that, in recent years, law enforcement authorities had identified cases of extremists operating inside the United States, a phenomenon known as "homegrown extremism." Such extremists had the intent either to provide support for, or directly commit, terrorist attacks within the United States.[55]

Congress noted in its report that radicalization could not be prevented solely through law enforcement and intelligence measures, but analysis of the radicalization process was also needed.[56]

Most of the language and emphasis in this congressional report was focused on Muslim extremist radicalization and the threat from a transnational network of extremists.

Nevertheless, congressional representatives recognized that there were many other non-Islamic influences that had been identified as contributing to the spread of radicalization and acts of ideologically based violence.

"Among these is the appeal of *leftwing* and *rightwing hate groups* [emphasis added], and other hate groups, including groups operating in prisons," Congress said.

The report further stated that "other factors must be examined and countered as well in order to protect the homeland from *violent extremists of every kind* [emphasis added]."[57]

For these reasons, Congress recommended that the secretary of homeland security, in consultation with other relevant federal agencies, should make a priority of countering domestic radicalization that leads to ideologically based violence.[58] They then outlined several steps that DHS should take to research, analyze, and counter this growing problem.

First, they recommended the use of intelligence analysts and other experts to better understand the process of radicalization *from sympathizer to activist to terrorist* [emphasis added], including the recruitment of employees with diverse worldviews, skills, languages, cultural backgrounds, and expertise.[59] They also recommended consulting with outside experts to ensure that the lexicon (glossary of terms) used in public statements by department spokespersons and intelligence products was precise and appropriate and would not aid extremists by offending religious, ethnic, and minority communities.[60]

Congress specifically identified prison radicalization and postsentence reintegration of inmates as distinct and unique issues of concern.[61] They advised that the department look into these issues in concert with the attorney general and state and local corrections officials.[62]

Next, Congress requested that DHS pursue broader avenues of dialogue with minority communities throughout the country, including the American Muslim community, to foster mutual respect, understanding, and trust.[63]

DHS was also admonished to work with state, local, and community leaders to educate government officials about the threat of radicalization that leads to ideologically based violence and the necessity of taking preventive action at the local level.[64]

Finally, DHS was advised to facilitate the sharing of best practices from other countries and communities to encourage outreach to minority communities and develop partnerships among and between all religious faiths and ethnic groups.[65]

These 2007 recommendations from Congress concerning the implementation of the 9/11 Act gave I&A the approval and guidance it needed to embark on its new radicalization mission which, at the time, was a unique mission for I&A within the intelligence community. In anticipation of assuming this new mission, I&A implemented an office-wide restructuring, which created the Homeland Environment and Threat Analysis Division (HETA) and brought resources from both the current and strategic analytical divisions together under one division director. Two other analytical focused divisions also emerged—one emphasized border security as well as the effects of weapons of mass of destruction and the other stressed critical infrastructure threat analysis.

In addition to these three analytical divisions, four other divisions provided support to the analytical workforce. These divisions include the Production Management Division (PM), Information Management Division (IM), Collection Requirements Division (CR), and the Intelligence Watch and Warning Division (IWW).

PM was responsible for implementing the production process at I&A. They developed the product lines and I&A style guide for writing and conducted final editing, review, and formal release of all I&A finished intelligence products. They also ensured that all internal vetting and external coordination procedures were completed prior to the dissemination of a product.

IM basically was in charge of upgrading, installing, maintaining, and managing I&A's computer systems. They are the information technology (IT) folks.

IWW was responsible for keeping the undersecretary for intelligence updated on current events and recent developments of interest to DHS, particularly I&A leadership. They prepared a daily briefing, which was disseminated to the I&A workforce, and provided input to the secretary of homeland security's daily briefing.

Lastly, CR developed, coordinated, and managed the information needs of I&A and its state and local partners. They also oversaw I&A's open-source collection effort. Unlike other national-level intelligence agencies, I&A has no traditional collection capability. They rely heavily on the reporting of other intelligence agencies that have collection capabilities, such as Human Intelligence and Signals Intelligence. Congress has only authorized an open-source collection capability for I&A because our legislators were likely sensitive to Americans' stigma to having a "domestic spy agency" and the potential civil rights liabilities and privacy concerns that come from such an organization.

As I&A was about to embark on its office-wide restructuring, there was a lot of anxiety among the workforce. Analysts wondered if they were physically moving to another area of the building. Some had concerns about changing supervisors and having to readjust to different management styles. Others worried that they would be assigned new analytical topics.

With tension rising and anticipation mounting in the workforce, I returned to the office from lunch with some of my work colleagues. We were discussing the planned reorganization as we entered the third floor of Building 19. Dr. Connell was coming down the hallway in our direction. We suddenly lowered our conversation to a whisper and respectfully waved at Connell as she walked by us.

Connell looked up from the paper she was reading. She turned her head, looked directly at me, and said, "Your job is secure!"

She then went back to reading and kept walking down the hall.

I was perplexed by her statement.

I later learned that her comment meant that the domestic terrorism mission was going to survive the office restructuring, which meant I had the support of I&A's executive leadership team! My enthusiasm, however, would be short-lived.

From January 2007 to May 2009, I was reassigned from the Strategic Analysis Division to HETA's Extremism and Radicalization Branch (ERB). I was the senior analyst for the domestic extremism analytical team. We had been working for the Strategic Analysis Division before being moved over to HETA. We were responsible for identifying and assessing potentially violent *non-Islamic* extremist threats within the United States.

From its inception in January 2007, HETA's mission has been to "produce actionable intelligence and assessments to include forecasts, using all sources of information, on the threat posed to homeland security by domestic and transnational terrorist and extremist groups, cells, or individuals with a presence in or connection to the Homeland."[66]

ERB had the mission to "identify, monitor, and analyze the entire spectrum of extremist groups/individuals, their ideologies, and radical activities in the Homeland in an effort to better understand the radicalization process, detect extremist-related criminal activities, and assess the potential threat identified radicalization activities and influences pose to the United States. Improve understanding of how extremist political, cultural, religious, or other influences may impact various ethnic communities within our borders. Collaborate, support, and facilitate the sharing of information between Departmental components, State & Local Fusion Centers, the Intelligence and Law Enforcement Communities, and others in an effort to nurture a network of partnerships. Continually refine our analytical tradecraft to better discern, assess, prevent, and/or respond to threats to the Homeland."[67]

ERB's focus on Muslim extremist radicalization was pretty well staffed with nearly thirty analysts in 2008, although several of them soon left for their new assignments at various fusion centers. At the time, there were only three domestic terrorism analysts. To make matters worse, HETA leadership decided to organize the branch according to four geographic regions, rather than organize by subject matter. This model was taken from a tactical intelligence unit one would find at a federal law enforcement agency or military organization, not an agency focused on strategic intelligence like I&A.

As a result of circumstances beyond my control, HETA's management decided to dismantle DTAS as a unit, and its analysts were reassigned to one of the geographic teams. My hopes for a smooth transition were quickly dashed.

This was an excruciating setback for me and the team because we could not specialize in certain areas necessary for developing subject matter expertise. Instead, we had to focus on multiple issues that transcended geographical boundaries, making it extremely difficult to track various extremist movements, identify emerging trends, as well as assess national threats. The younger, less experienced analysts also had a difficult time mastering the wide range of extremist movements and their numerous activities.

It was a difficult time for me during the office-wide restructuring. I had attempted to convince new division managers of the value of structuring the new branch according to subject matter, rather than geographic regions. I even wrote a proposal outlining the negative impact of geographic versus topical breakdown. My new management listened to my arguments, but ultimately held to their decision for a geographical construct. Leadership's reasoning at the time was based purely on the need to provide better support to the growing number of fusion centers throughout the country. They rationalized a regional approach made the best sense and would enable ERB analysts to network with their state and local counterparts as well as better serve their needs.

Five months after the reorganization, it was obvious to many of the analysts that management had made the wrong decision.

External requests for information from law enforcement agencies, which included I&A's own field representatives, were not being routed to the geographic teams. Rather, they went directly to subject matter experts because they were the individuals with the most knowledge, understanding, and experience.

Subordinate analysts were also relying on the subject matter experts, who were scattered among the various geographic teams, because they had the answers to often complex questions. In addition, ERB was working on several state radicalization assessments at the time. These assessments were not being researched, analyzed, and written according to what geographic region they corresponded. Instead, various parts of the assessments were being assigned to and written by those analysts who had expertise. For example, an assessment for Illinois/Indiana was assigned to the Western Team, although the state resided in Central Team's region. Similarly, the Missouri assessment was assigned to the Central Team, although the state was located in Midwest Team's region. Exacerbating this problem was the fact that not enough analysts had been assigned to fully staff the Midwest Team. As a result, the Northeast Team ended up covering both regions. Three other regionally focused papers were being worked on by analysts outside of that geographic region.

Lastly, a national-level assessment was on the production schedule that contradicted the regional geographic approach entirely.

Subject matter experts had been writing a vast majority of the content of the many state assessments (which were divided into topic-specific sections) for all of the state radicalization assessments. The geographic team approach had yet to add any significant value to the state radicalization assessment project. Many subordinate analysts were also struggling to learn their newly assigned accounts. Section leads were either too busy writing assessments themselves, or too busy responding to other requests for information, to effectively mentor their subordinates. Thus, many of the junior analysts sought guidance from the subject matter expert rather than their team lead.

On May 3, 2007, I wrote an internal informal proposal for my division management discussing the negative aspects of the regional approach.

"The current organization structure of the U.S. Extremism & Radicalization Branch is not functioning as intended," I wrote. "An emphasis on geographic areas of the Homeland has yet to add any significant value to the state radicalization assessment project or the branch mission."

Using my past experience working for the U.S. Army and ATF, I outlined several reasons why ERB's geographic approach was more conducive to organizations with an "operational" mission, such as a law enforcement agency or military unit.

The Office of Intelligence and Analysis is not—and was never designed to be—an operations-focused organization. I&A was given no collection authority. Thus it has virtually no ability to collect information (i.e., via confidential informants, undercover officers, wiretaps, and other traditional intelligence collection methods).

I&A did not oversee any field-related operations. The organization has facilitated the assignment of liaison officers and senior intelligence analysts to the state fusion centers, but their numbers are small and they have multiple responsibilities related to the daily operations of the fusion centers. In 2010, I&A had fifty-five such field representatives with plans to increase the total of field representatives to all seventy-two fusion centers by the end of the year.[68] These representatives primarily serve as "liaison officers," but they are also cross-trained as report officers who collect information from state and local law enforcement and share the information with DHS headquarters.

In November 2007, I wrote a second informal paper that outlined the benefits of reconstituting the domestic terrorism unit, formerly known as DTAS. My new first-line supervisor was supportive of this effort.

"With respect to domestic terrorism analysis, the current organizational structure of the Extremism & Radicalization Branch is not functioning as intended," I wrote. "An overemphasis on geographic regions instead of subject-specific accounts has marginalized the importance of having subject matter experts, impeded junior analyst growth and hindered the development of analysts into future subject matter experts."

Instead of leading and mentoring domestic terrorism analysts as I had been promised, I was doing the work of an average analyst confined to a geographical area. I also had to backfill another analyst's vacancy for a second geographical region because no one else in the branch was knowledgeable enough to understand the domestic extremism issues for that area. This left very little time to devote to mentoring young analysts, training them in a wide range of domestic terrorism topics and attempting to analyze national trends.

I further explained that, to their detriment, junior domestic terrorism analysts were forced prematurely to diversify their accounts beyond their current skill level and ability. Analysts originally assigned to monitor a specific extremist ideology were now required to analyze the entire spectrum of extremist groups and ideologies (encompassing hundreds of different extremist groups and ideologies) for a geographic region. They were overwhelmed and confused. They didn't know to whom they should report. They were not comfortable working for the other team leads who knew virtually nothing about domestic non-Islamic terrorism and had little interest in learning about it.

"Due to the large number of extremist groups/ideologies present in a region, analysts are having difficulty understanding the breadth, scope, and area of operation regarding these groups and movements which often conduct activities on a national scale," I wrote. "For this reason, analysts are not capable of providing in-depth analysis on a particular group or ideology nor identify significant developments within national movements."

"Domestic terrorism analysts have voiced concern and confusion over who has ultimate responsibility for overseeing their work and reviewing the reports they produce," I said. "Mentoring opportunities and group discussions among the domestic terrorism analysts are limited due to lack of physical proximity. The current seating arrangement also inhibits the development of group identity and collaboration among the domestic terrorism analysts."

Another problem was that regional team leads were occasionally assigning tasks beyond the scope of expected duties and responsibilities of a domestic terrorism analyst, such as coordinating entire state assessments with production management. In contrast, the other senior intelligence analysts were arbitrarily assigning other analysts with no background or expertise in domestic terrorism to write on a variety of subjects related to this topic. This led to factual inaccuracies, improper characterizations of extremist groups and ideologies, and failure to coordinate products with the appropriate subject matter expert(s). These problems led to a few isolated intelligence oversight violations. As a result, the Office of General Counsel had to closely scrutinize and ultimately rescind a few I&A products dealing with black separatists, an antiabortion group, and homegrown Muslim extremist groups.[69,70,71]

Domestic terrorism analysts currently employed or seeking employment within I&A expected to work with other domestic terrorism analysts—together as one team—under the direction of someone who is well versed in the subject. Assigning new analysts to regional teams under the direction of senior intelligence analysts with little knowledge and experience related to domestic terrorism likely proves frustrating and confusing to new analysts, and will thus create a negative work experience.

In the past, I had worked with former division chiefs and branch chiefs (both the Information Analysis Strategic Division and Threat Analysis Division) toward the creation of a domestic terrorism team. Unforeseen circumstances, such as the recent division realignment in 2008, stymied this effort. My proposal ended with the recommendation to reorganize the domestic terrorism analytical section within the ERB and place all domestic terrorism analysts sitting together as a team.

I mentioned several advantages to doing this. First, it ensured that domestic terrorism–related products complied with I&A's intelligence oversight guidelines, ensuring they are written in a clear and concise manner, thus avoiding or diffusing potential concerns raised by the Office of General Counsel. It created a better atmosphere for mentoring and leading other domestic terrorism analysts, thus creating future subject matter experts. It improved production for domestic terrorism–focused reports by going through a centralized vetting process for such products, which would provide greater insight and analysis to the product. It better served the law enforcement community and other stakeholders by providing an analytical capability more closely aligned to those found in such agencies. It improved morale among the domestic terrorism analysts. Division management agreed with my proposal, and the Domestic Terrorism Analysis Team was reformed.

Since my team continued to be grossly understaffed and I was the only subject matter expert, I was interested to read the 9/11 Act recommendations concerning the recruitment of employees with diverse worldviews, skills, languages, cultural backgrounds, and expertise.[72] I wasted no time in reaching out to my law enforcement contacts and other domestic terrorism experts in the private sector to see if they knew anyone who was looking to relocate to Washington, D.C.

Prior to HETA's creation, I had been given four full-time employee positions (a term used to describe a position or billet for a federal employee) by division management to begin building a bona fide team of domestic terrorism analysts. I worked closely with my supervisor and initiated the hiring process for four analysts (actual federal employees, instead of contractors), so the organization wouldn't be left without a domestic terrorism analytical capability when contracts ran out or changed each fiscal year.

In the summer of 2006, two junior analysts arrived within a few months of applying because they were already working for different agencies within DHS. One transferred from U.S. Customs and Border Protection (CBP) and had intimate knowledge of the illegal immigration issue, which is a "hot issue" for right-wing extremist radicalization. The other analyst came from the Federal Protective Service (FPS), a departmental component dealing with securing and guarding federal buildings throughout the country. The FPS analyst had unique knowledge and expertise pertaining to various extremist-related activities directed at federal buildings, such as property crimes, sovereign citizen attempts to circumvent security using fraudulent identification, and numerous extremist threats directed at these facilities.

The final two analysts, who were both considered subject matter experts in the private sector, took nearly two years to finally report for duty. This prolonged period to "report to duty" resulted from a combination of problems, such as I&A's lack of internal hiring authority, poorly developed personnel procedures, the DHS security background investigation, which was extremely backlogged, and other unanticipated administrative issues such as the office restructuring.

During the adjudication process for granting a security clearance for one of the subject matter experts, the DHS Office of Security came to the mistaken conclusion that this particular applicant had been involved in domestic terrorist organizations. He was sent a four-page letter stating why the department was rejecting his clearance due to derogatory information related to his involvement in subversive organizations that were against the U.S. government. To the contrary, this individual had attended various white supremacist– and militia extremist–related activities in a professional work capacity—unique experience that made him a subject matter expert on the belief systems and activities of such groups. His clandestine work experience had been approved and closely monitored by his supervisors. He had to report back to them each time he attended such activities. I had forewarned the background investigator about this applicant's unique work experience, but somehow it got lost in translation as the investigator prepared his final write-up. Fortunately, the DHS Office of Security reversed its decision once they received the applicant's thorough explanation and written verification from his former supervisor.

The other applicant brought unique skills and qualifications not only related to domestic extremism, but also computer technology, open-source research, and other interesting analytical techniques. His conversion to government service from the private sector proved invaluable to our efforts at DHS and the intelligence community writ large.

In August 2008, our team received an intern from American University who assisted us on various projects. One such project was the Domestic Terrorism/Ideologically Based Violence (DTx) incident database that I proposed and helped create. The initial operating capability for DTx was declared on June 21, 2007.

In October 2008, a contractor joined the team. He had specialized in domestic extremism–related issues at the Orlando Fusion Center, the South Carolina Law Enforcement Division, and other organizations. The contractor's hiring was a result of a junior analyst leaving I&A and returning to FPS due to her growing frustrations with I&A and its time-consuming production process. She was growing increasingly frustrated with the fast-paced "publish or perish" mentality at I&A.

Despite the many setbacks, I&A now had a fully functioning, well-qualified team of domestic terrorism experts.

As part of fulfilling its statutory duty, I&A receives, analyzes, and disseminates information that potentially relates to acts, organizations, or individuals associated with domestic terrorism and ideologically based violence. In order to better segregate and analyze such data, my team created DTx. This database provided I&A with a centralized repository for subject matter experts to gather, manage, and track data related to domestic terrorism and ideologically based violence incidents. It served as a resource for I&A analysts engaged in strategic analysis and provided real-time responses to Homeland Security officials' requests for information on domestic terrorism.

The DTx system was a web-based data repository accompanied by a database of incidents related to domestic terrorism and ideologically inspired criminal activity. Users were able to examine data as categorized by the responsible group, activity, or target, and also perform comprehensive searches based on date, location, ideology, and a variety of other filters. Domestic terrorism analysts within HETA served as the subject matter experts responsible for adding, deleting, analyzing, and editing data within DTx. Users who have search and view capabilities were limited to I&A analysts in HETA, Borders and CBRNE (a term for chemical, biological, radiological, nuclear, and explosives threats), and the Homeland Infrastructure Threat and Risk Analysis Center (HITRAC). DTx-derived information was shared with other DHS components such as Immigration and Customs Enforcement, the Federal Protective Service, U.S. Secret Service, and Customs and Border Protection, but these components never possessed DTx user accounts.

All data entered into DTx was related to incidents that have occurred or are suspected to have occurred (i.e. anonymous claims of responsibility). A majority of this data consisted of publicly available information including but not limited to press reports, broadcast media, and the Internet. Other data sources included widely distributed federal, state, and local law enforcement and intelligence information considered "For Official Use Only"—a category of unclassified information meant for official government use, not for public disclosure.

As a threshold matter, any information entered into DTx had to relate to either a target familiar or common to domestic terrorism or extremism (federal buildings, abortion clinics, animal testing laboratories, etc.) or a person who subscribed to terrorist or extremist ideology and who is mentioned in the media, police report, or some other DTx source material. For the latter, this meant that a person who subscribed to a terrorist or extremist ideology alone would not be entered into DTx. It is when that ideology is *coupled with a criminal act* that information in DTx becomes relevant, which is why the person in question must appear in a police report, news report, or other similar bulletin describing extremist violence or criminal act that has taken place or is claimed to have taken place.

In addition to this threshold requirement, a new record had to satisfy several layers of legal, policy, oversight, and substantive controls prior to being created in DTx. These controls were implemented directly into the DTx "new record" interface.

DTx was designed for internal I&A use only; however, I&A analysts occasionally responded to external requests for information and shared appropriate search results with federal, state, and local government entities with homeland security responsibilities.

Throughout its duration, DTx increased the productivity of analysts who utilized the system by reducing the amount of time needed to search for needed information. It also improved I&A's overall production by ensuring products were accurate, complete, and properly sourced. Finally, the database had a positive impact on I&A's mission as a result of improved response times and comprehensive search results in response to information requests.

The domestic terrorism unit within the ERB focused on a wide range of domestic extremist threats, including right-wing extremists, left-wing extremists, and single-issue extremists. Domestic counterterrorism experts at the FBI, academia, and nongovernment organizations, such as Rand Corporation and STRATFOR, use these terms to broadly categorize domestic extremists according to their political leanings or devoted cause. Each of these broad categories can be further subcategorized according to an extremist's favored ideology or cause. Much like our analytical counterparts at the FBI, academia, and private sector, DHS analysts used these broad terms to group various extremists.

Internally, I&A defined the term "extremist group" as "an organization that promotes, supports or executes violence against people or destruction of property to attempt to cause societal change."[73] I&A further defined the term "radicalization" as "the process of adopting an extremist belief system leading to an individual's willingness to facilitate, support, or use violence to cause societal change."[74] Our team was concerned *only* with those movements, groups, and individuals that use their distorted political or social positions to encourage, support, direct, or conduct acts of violence or criminal activity. This is the analytical framework under which we were working during 2007–2009.

Right-wing extremists are generally described as those radical movements, groups, or individuals that are either primarily hate oriented or who are mainly antigovernment—rejecting federal authority in favor of state or local authority. This term also may refer to right-wing extremist movements that are dedicated to a single issue, such as opposition to abortion or immigration. This is not about law-abiding groups or mainstream organizations—although many misinterpreted it that way when criticizing the DHS report. The report only referenced those groups and individuals who encourage, support, direct, or conduct acts of violence or criminal activity. Right-wing extremists are broadly divided into subgroupings, such as white supremacists, sovereign citizens or Freemen, and antigovernment militias. White supremacists can be further divided into specific types of radical ideologies, such as Ku Klux Klan affiliates, neo-Nazis, racist skinheads, Christian Identity adherents, and so on. Similarly, antigovernment militias are generally viewed as being either aboveground groups or underground organizations. Sovereign citizens, such as the Montana Freemen, are their own unique movement and usually do not have additional subcategories.

Left-wing extremists are generally described as those radical movements, groups, or individuals that embrace anticapitalist, Communist, or Socialist doctrines and seek to bring about change through violent revolution rather than through established political processes. The term also refers to left-wing, single-issue extremist movements that are dedicated to causes such as environmentalism, opposition to war, and the rights of animals. Although they have left-wing leanings at their core, animal rights, environmental, and antiwar extremists are better labeled "single-issue extremists" since they focus primarily on a single cause or issue. Unlike the 1960s and 1970s, there are few, true left-wing extremist organizations operating in the United States.

Single-issue extremists can be generally described as those radical movements, groups, or individuals who focus primarily on a single issue or cause—such as animal rights, environmental, or antiabortion extremism—and often employ criminal acts. Group members, however, have been known to associate with more than one issue. For example, environmental extremists have been known to be simultaneously involved in animal rights extremist movements. Antiwar extremists have also been known to participate in environmental extremism. Single-issue extremists can favor either left-wing or right-wing positions—spanning both sides of the political spectrum. But they stick to their particular issue, whether it's violent opposition toward abortion, taxation, or immigration or fervent support for animal rights, the environment, or violent opposition toward the wars in Iraq and Afghanistan.

The intelligence community (IC) had a mechanism for nominating and designating foreign terrorist organizations.[75] They have an official U.S. government list of international terrorist groups.[76] However, there was no similar mechanism in the intelligence or law enforcement communities for nominating or designating domestic terrorist or violent extremist groups operating in the United States. In the absence of a formal or statutory definition, I&A's application of the label "extremist" was based upon analytic judgment of a group's actions, ideology, and most importantly, its assessed willingness to support or conduct violence in furthering its ideology.

I&A was the only federal agency looking at the topics of "domestic extremist radicalization" within the United States. There were, however, several federal government agencies and nongovernment organizations looking at extremism and radicalization from an international perspective. Similarly, the FBI was monitoring the criminal activities of domestic terrorists in the U.S., but not their radicalization activities. As a result, the daunting responsibility of determining which ideologies, groups, and individuals met the DHS criteria to be considered "extremist" resided in the knowledge, experience, and analytical judgment of I&A subject matter experts.

The primary factor used to differentiate homeland extremist groups from criminal groups (such as street gangs, outlaw motorcycle gangs, and other organized crime groups) is the assessed intent of the group or individual. I&A designated extremist groups in the United States based upon analytic judgment of a group's actions, ideology, and most importantly, its assessed willingness to support or conduct violence in furthering its ideology. I&A designates criminal groups as those groups that engage in activities that are primarily motivated by financial gain. I&A occasionally performed analysis of criminal groups when authorized to do so by statute, presidential directive, and in support of lawful activities of DHS components.

I&A analysts routinely collaborated with their federal, state, and local law enforcement counterparts and private sector partners in an effort to determine which ideologies, groups, and individuals should be considered "extremist." They would then analyze the capability and intent of these "extremists" in an effort to assess any potential threat(s). Any criminal threat–related information was then given to the appropriate law enforcement agency for further inquiry and appropriate action.

It is important to note that the FBI is the lead federal agency for investigating terrorism—not extremist radicalization. As a result, the FBI has the lead in determining which acts are considered "terrorism" and which groups are considered "terrorists." There must, however, be suspected or known criminal activity for the FBI to become involved. Although constrained in a different way, I&A was not limited to having a criminal predicate like the FBI. In contrast, I&A had the authority to monitor and assess extremists who have the potential to become violent. This was not always an easy undertaking. I&A's role complemented the FBI's counterterrorism mission through analyzing extremist ideologies that inspire and motivate extremist groups and individuals toward violence and terrorism. The FBI responds to terrorist incidents and investigates threats and known or suspected criminal activity. In a sense, I&A is the watchdog that warns of potential danger, and the FBI is the law enforcement entity that takes appropriate action. Further, those FBI analytical and operational units that monitored domestic terrorism and violent extremists within the U.S. were not part of the intelligence community, like I&A.

To my knowledge, former DHS secretaries Ridge and Chertoff never once expressed an interest in domestic terrorism. They were mostly concerned with international terrorist threats from Muslim extremist groups. In five years, I never received a single request from the secretary. From my perspective, this single-minded focus on international terrorist threats was not limited to the secretary and staff. It was pervasive throughout much of the department's workforce. Between 2004 and 2009, virtually no one in DHS leadership had expressed an interest in or attempted to understand the potential threat from domestic non-Islamic extremists.

By February 2008, HETA and ERB were a year old. Like other divisions in I&A, many analysts in our division and branch had come and gone. Several left for I&A field positions at the state fusion centers. Others transferred to the National Counterterrorism Center or other agencies within the intelligence community. I&A's radicalization mission was now well entrenched in the department. It was often referenced in the remarks and speeches of DHS leadership. The work of ERB's domestic terrorism unit was also cited alongside of the threat posed from homegrown Muslim extremism.

On February 6, 2008, Undersecretary Allen delivered testimony to the U.S. House of Representatives, Subcommittee on Intelligence, Information Sharing and Terrorism Risk Assessment.[77] His remarks were titled "Homeland Security Intelligence at a Crossroads: The Office of Intelligence and Analysis Vision for 2008."[78] Among his many comments, Allen gave an endorsement of HETA, its radicalization focus and support to both of ERB sections—those that monitored radicalized Islamic groups as well as those responsible for looking at domestic groups.

"My office is dedicated to assessing the threat of radicalization and extremism," Allen stated. "Our top priority is radicalized Islam (Sunni and Shia groups); however, we also look at radicalized domestic groups; to include white supremacists, black separatists, and fringe environmentalists."[79]

Again, I couldn't help but notice Allen's emphasis on *his* radicalization mission priorities—radicalized Islamic groups. His statements lend additional support to my inclination that domestic terrorism was Allen's "alibi" to any accusation that I&A was profiling American Muslims.

Allen then made an important distinction by clarifying I&A's work from that of the FBI: "We do not monitor known extremists and their activities; instead, we are interested in the radicalization process—why and how people are attracted to radical beliefs and cross the line into violence."[80]

"We are using nontraditional intelligence and working closely with our state and local partners to leverage their insights and expertise to build a baseline of radicalization that leads to ideologically based violence in their localities," he continued. "From this baseline, we plan to develop an integrated framework for tracking a radical or extremist group's risk for terrorism and assisting policymakers in developing strategies to deter and prevent it."[81]

Nontraditional intelligence likely refers to I&A's dependence on open-source intelligence (OSINT), the perspectives of nongovernment organizations, DHS component reporting, as well as state and local law enforcement reporting. These are nontraditional sources of information for the intelligence community in Washington, D.C. Each intelligence agency, except I&A, has their own internal collection capability (e.g., Human Intelligence or HUMINT; Signals Intelligence or SIGINT; Measurements and Signature Intelligence or MASINT; and Imagery Intelligence or IMINT; among other categories of intelligence collection management).

"Our key intelligence sources are the data that our components gather in their daily operations. DHS intelligence never before has pursued such an effort—one that is important to support the department, our state and local partners, and the intelligence community," Allen testified.[82]

HETA's other branches also received some publicity in Undersecretary Allen's testimony.

Allen stated, "As a complement to our efforts to look at threats inside the homeland, such as radicalization, we further are collaborating with our DHS operating components to focus on a third analytic element, potential threats from particular groups entering the United States—groups that could be exploited by terrorists or other 'bad people' to enter the homeland legally or to bring in CBRN [an acronym for chemical, biological, radiological, and nuclear threats] or other materials. We further focus on travel-related issues of interest to the department, such as visa categories and the Visa Waiver Program."[83]

With the hiring of two subject matter experts and the unexpected arrival of a fourth seasoned domestic terrorism analyst (including me), my vision of having a top-notch domestic terrorism unit comparable to the FBI was beginning to take shape. I&A was finally in a position to better serve their state and local law enforcement customers by writing timely, in-depth intelligence reports on a variety of domestic terrorism–related topics. Our analytical judgments complemented each other, making the analysis that much stronger. I had a team of subject matter experts that could not only oversee the work of junior analysts on the team, but also assist other analysts with their questions and work assignments related to domestic extremist activity in the United States. We possessed the ability to increase both the quality and quantity of our work.

Each of us brought a well-established network of law enforcement, intelligence, and nongovernment contacts. These contacts facilitated increased sharing of domestic terrorism–related information with DHS, and increased the number of requests for information, training opportunities, and other forms of law enforcement support. Our work greatly enhanced I&A's state and local outreach efforts and helped establish I&A relevance among the law enforcement community. Our greatest challenge and crowning achievement would come within a few months of the domestic terrorism unit's reestablishment.

I&A had a national conference on the horizon. State fusion centers were eager to engage I&A on the topic of domestic terrorism. Such conferences provided marketing and networking opportunities for I&A and allowed the organization to convince its stakeholders of the agency's importance and relevance. It was finally our turn to facilitate I&A's relationship with state and local law enforcement and fusion centers.

8

Gaining Recognition

It was 3:30 p.m., and I was preparing to leave the office after another productive day at the Office of Intelligence and Analysis (I&A). The Fourth of July weekend was fast approaching, and I was looking forward to the three-day weekend. I turned off the computer systems, gathered my things, and quickly packed them into my backpack. A coworker and I were walking toward the door to the second-floor stairway when someone shouted my name.

"Daryl Johnson! Just where do you think you're going?" I recognized the voice as coming from the branch chief for the Strategic Analysis Group—a unit within the Homeland Environment and Threat Analysis Division (HETA) responsible for alternative, forward-leaning analysis such as the Homeland Security Threat Assessment (HSTA), among other projects.

"Hi, Steve. What do you need?" I hurriedly asked, because I was hoping to beat some of the traffic during the evening rush hour.

"Can you stay a few more minutes? It's important," he said. He had a worried look on his face, and I could tell this was an urgent matter. Steve had never done this before, so I didn't mind sticking around to help him with whatever was troubling him.

"Sure. What's going on?" I curiously asked.

"It's Mary," he gasped. "I just got out of a meeting with Dr. Connell. She didn't like our recommendations for the upcoming HS-SLIC conference."

HS-SLIC, the Homeland Security State and Local Intelligence Community of Interest, began as a pilot program between the department and six states. Two years later, it had grown into the first nationwide network of intelligence analysts focused on homeland security.[1] The initial pilot program lasted from March to September 2006 and involved the states of Arizona, California, Florida, Illinois, New York, and Virginia.[2] Its purpose was to facilitate information sharing between Department of

Homeland Security (DHS) headquarters, specifically I&A, and the state and local fusion centers.

HS-SLIC primarily consisted of a secure portal accessible from any computer that had the correct encryption code on it. By 2008, the pilot program had expanded to fusion centers in forty-five states, the District of Columbia, and seven federal agencies.[3] Intelligence analysts at I&A interacted with their law enforcement counterparts at these various agencies and shared information, analyzing it in an attempt to prevent or respond to current, emerging, and future threats to the country.[4]

Each week, HS-SLIC members would meet virtually via a secure Internet portal to discuss analytic topics, emergent threats, and other homeland-security-related topics.[5] Annually, DHS hosts a national HS-SLIC analytic conference and regional conferences. Each year, the program also hosted a conference at the classified level to discuss important analytic topics and threat trends, such as border security and threats to critical infrastructure.[6] In July 2008, HS-SLIC was just two years old, and its second annual conference was just a few months away in September.

"So, what are you planning to do now?" I asked Steve.

With a smile on his face, he replied, "Well . . . Mr. Johnson, it's your turn to shine."

"What do you mean by that?" I asked. I knew what he meant. Connell must have asked for a domestic terrorism conference, but I wanted it confirmed.

"Mary wants us to organize a domestic terrorism conference," Steve sighed. "The bad news is that we only have a few days to plan it."

"What?" I asked.

"You heard right. She wants a draft agenda by Monday morning," Steve reported. "That only gives us this afternoon and tomorrow to get it right before the three-day weekend."

I returned to my desk, threw down my backpack, and grabbed a pad of paper and a pen. Fortunately, the other subject matter experts on my team were still in the office. This would make brainstorming ideas a lot easier. I knew that with the help of my teammates, we could put together a good program within a few hours.

Steve found a conference room, and a few of his analysts joined us for the discussion. Remarkably, it took less than two hours to consolidate our ideas into a cohesive conference agenda. We fine-tuned it the next morning and immediately started making phone calls to see if our list of guest speakers and panelists were available the week of the conference in September. Just about everything fell into place as planned.

We had decided on inviting an amazing keynote speaker. One of the other analysts knew him from his previous job and had a well-established relationship. The proposed keynote speaker was Tom Martinez, a former member of a white supremacist terrorist group called The Order during the 1980s.[7] Upon learning that Order members were plotting criminal and terrorist-related activity, Martinez called the FBI and became a federal witness to testify against the other Order members.[8] Since 1985, he has been in the federal witness protection program after receiving death threats for what he had done.[9]

We thought Martinez would be an excellent keynote speaker. His experiences of being recruited and indoctrinated into the white supremacist movement would provide unique insights to those attending the conference. Plus his involvement in the outer periphery of a real domestic terrorist organization would prove especially interesting for exchanging thoughts and ideas concerning the radicalization process of domestic extremists as well as the forces and factors that lead individuals toward violence.

Like all of the other guest speakers and panelists, Martinez was available. He was very eager and excited to assist with the conference. He commented that he "felt honored" to do whatever he could to help state and local law enforcement gain a better understanding of the dangers and threats posed by white supremacists operating in this country. Like any other high-profile speaker, the request for Martinez to speak was arranged through a professional speaker's bureau. Martinez was employed by Keppler Associates. A call placed to Keppler Associates revealed that the cost associated with Mr. Martinez's appearance was $3,000, which included travel expenses (including airfare and rental car) and lodging fee. As a favor to us, Martinez agreed to extend his services to include a special appearance at an exclusive lunch hour being planned for fusion center directors in attendance as well as a second guest appearance during a munch and mingle social hour for everyone in attendance, planned for later that evening. Both extracurricular activities were offered as part of Martinez's speaking package at no extra charge to the government.

By this time, we had less than two months before the week of the conference. Steve and his staff quickly put together a proposal for Martinez's appearance and submitted a budget request. There was enough money in the conference budget to afford a few thousand dollars for the keynote speaker's travel expenses and presentation fee. The proposal was approved by Dr. Connell and Undersecretary Allen and forwarded to the DHS Budget Office for final authorization.

To our dismay, the DHS Budget Office rejected the request initially on the grounds that our proposal had not been properly bid. The DHS Budget Office said that we needed to allow for the fair competition of other keynote speakers. Steve thought we could get around this dilemma through a short-suspense clause [an exception for short notice] since the conference was less than two months away. There wasn't enough time to find other, comparable speakers, assess their willingness and availability, and then open it up for bidding. Tom Martinez was a one-of-a-kind keynote speaker.

We immediately submitted an exemption to the DHS Budget Office and explained that there were few guest speakers with his credentials, and none of them had gone through the experience of becoming radicalized into a terrorist organization. Martinez's unique background was a necessary component of the conference theme and was clearly unmatched by anyone else.

The DHS Budget Office took several weeks to get back to us. We were now less than two weeks away from the start of the conference. I&A leadership and their staff were cautiously optimistic that our counterarguments to the budget office were convincing enough to be approved. Martinez was left hanging for nearly a month. As time gradually ticked away, he was growing increasingly concerned that airfare would greatly exceed his original offer. So we were forced to gamble on how the DHS Budget Office would rule. We advised him to purchase his airline tickets and make his hotel reservations.

As we began our final preparations for the conference, we received the upsetting news that the budget office had once again declined our request. Steve, the other participants in the conference planning team, and I couldn't believe it.

When challenged as to why they wouldn't approve Tom Martinez as the conference keynote speaker, the DHS Budget Office reportedly said, "It doesn't pass the *Washington Post* test." In other words, the DHS wanted to avoid the appearance of any impropriety of having a former "domestic terrorist" address a group of law enforcement officers. They appeared to have never considered the fact that Tom Martinez was a government witness who led authorities to the terrorist group. And that he received several death threats for helping the police.

We were depending on Martinez's remarks to get the conference started on the right tempo. This was an extremely frustrating and disappointing development. We were left scrambling for a replacement speaker.

Upon hearing the news, Allen sent us an e-mail message. His only comment was "I'm in disbelief."[10]

To make matters worse, Martinez ended up with a $500 airfare that was nonrefundable. He had to absorb that cost at his own expense. What a disaster!

"What a stupid outcome. It's not a logical or rational decision," I thought to myself. At the time, I was still naïve to the political charades and congressional shenanigans at DHS. The Homeland Security State and Local Intelligence Conference 2008 National Analytic Conference was held from September 16–18, 2008, at the U.S. Naval War College in Newport, Rhode Island. Roughly 150 participants from 40-plus state, local, and federal agencies and Canada met to gain a better understanding of the extent and impact of non-Islamic domestic extremists within their regions.[11]

The conference opened with a series of overview presentations to help set the stage for the panels and workshop discussions that were the primary focus of the conference. Instead of Martinez as the keynote speaker, an analyst from I&A's own domestic terrorism team provided a case study of a white supremacist apprehended in Massachusetts for targeting Jewish facilities. His comprehensive briefing concerning the criminal activities and radicalization of Leo Felton was very well received.[12]

The associate general counsel for intelligence at DHS then provided a broad-based analysis of the balance between civil liberties and domestic terrorism analysis. This presentation was followed by a classified threat briefing presented by the I&A research director. It discussed various threats involving demographic and travel security, borders, weapons of mass destruction, health security, critical infrastructure, and demographic and radicalization threats.[13]

The main focus of the conference was a series of workshops that divided violent domestic extremism into three areas: single-issue extremists; white supremacists; and violent antigovernment groups. Each workshop began with an expert panel discussion. This was followed by HS-SLIC regional breakout sessions in which participants discussed the various groups, their sizes and current levels of activity, and potential future actions on a state-by-state and regional basis. The workshops concluded with a wrap-up session that reported the key findings from each of the regions.[14]

The conference concluded with a breakout session on "Gaps and the Way Ahead" for the analytical community.[15]

The key conclusions from this conference were that domestic non-Islamic extremists remain a cause for concern across the spectrum—single-issue groups such as animal rights extremists and ecoterrorists, white supremacist groups like Hammerskin Nation and Aryan Brotherhood, and violent antigovernment groups such as the various militia and sovereign citizen extremist movements.[16]

Not surprisingly, there were key regional differences across the spectrum of the various groups, and details of these differences were presented in the body of a conference report. However, there were some interesting commonalities. For example, within the single-issue groups, the consensus of the workshop participants was that there is a high degree of mobility between the members, with individuals gravitating to different groups and in geographically dispersed locations. They agreed that single-issue groups were the most active, but only a few adherents would conduct violence against people. Another consensus finding was that white supremacists are the most violent and capable of violent attacks of all the groups. Finally, the participants concluded that the violent antigovernment groups had declined significantly since the mid- to late 1990s, with the exception of groups in Michigan and California. The focus of existing groups appears to be anti–federal authority and tax avoidance. The attendees agreed that the level of violent activity of these groups is generally low and that the most likely to act would be a violent lone offender. An important caveat regarding this assessment was the potential impact of the election, which could raise a number of potential trigger issues for these groups—immigration, race, tax increases, gun laws, and so on.[17]

The conference attendees also agreed that their communities of interest should take advantage of the HS-SLIC web portal to improve information sharing, and they identified the domestic extremism lexicon as a first step to employ this collaborative tool.[18]

To encourage and facilitate information sharing, an ad-hoc presentation on the use of the HS-SLIC portal was provided on the final day of the conference. Participants were briefed on a number of the information-sharing and collaborative tools, such as secure messaging, web portals, and discussion forums.[20]

A final conference report was issued to I&A executive leadership in December 2008.[21] Among the report's key findings, it stated, "An amalgamation of conference participants identified a 50-50 prospect that within the next six months (through March 2009) one of the violent domestic extremist groups would carry out a high-profile attack—referred to by participants as 'an attention-getting event' on a national scale—precipitated by the Presidential transition, worries about severe economic losses, or other uncertainties."[22]

It went on to relate that "Participants were most concerned about single-issue extremist groups . . . which already engage in the highest levels of violent activity, but they also are attentive to the response of white supremacist groups to the Presidential transition. Violent antigovernment groups . . . were perceived to constitute a lesser threat because they generally react violently only if they believe their constitutional rights have been violated or they have been attacked by the Government."[23]

"The perception of the domestic extremist threat varies among the regions, among the states within regions, and even among jurisdictions within the states. Participants in the Central Working Group assigned the greatest probability of a high-profile attack occurring in their region over the next six months (into March 2009), whereas the Western and Southeastern Working Groups believe the odds of such an attack in their regions are better than even. The Northeast region participants consider the threat in their region to be more limited," it said.[24]

The report's recommendations concluded that "Information sharing among federal, state, and local agencies and departments is key to successful anticipation, identification, and tracking of threats from domestic extremist groups. Participants agreed that information sharing can be enhanced by greater use of Homeland Security State and Local Intelligence Community (HS-SLIC) and training that focuses on requirements to ensure that collaboration works."[25]

It continued, "Conference participants identified a number of events and factors that could result in a violent, high-profile attack. These 'triggers' could result in spontaneous responses or be used by leaders as a convenience to rally members. The triggers vary widely among extremist groups and include the following:"[26]

- "A worsening economy that could increase anger among already disaffected groups that blame the U.S. Government and other groups for their economic condition or insecurity."[27]
- "The immigration issue which, however addressed, will likely exacerbate tensions in southern border communities and other areas where large immigrant populations reside."[28]
- "Government legislation or enforcement, or activities by other groups perceived to threaten individual rights."
- "Activities related to exploitation or development of natural resources or to genetic research."[29]

Looking back over the conference findings, there was an overwhelming support for what would later serve as the foundation for the DHS right-wing extremism report. A severe and prolonged economic downturn, an unprecedented presidential election, and the continued fermentation of polarizing national issues, such as illegal immigration, were major themes addressed in the report. They were also issues brought to light as a result of the working groups and panel discussions at the 2008 HS-SLIC conference.

Upon the conclusion of the conference, we arrived back at DHS headquarters mentally, emotionally, and physically exhausted. To say the least, planning the content and logistics for 150-plus people over a four-day period, which included their travel days, was extremely stressful.

We had little downtime after the conference adjourned. Connell had been anticipating our return to the office. While we were away, she had spent her time carefully crafting a rigorous production plan for a relatively new I&A product line—the Homeland Security Reference Aid (HSRA). She wanted to capitalize on the conference's success and produce several HSRAs on domestic extremism–related topics. We had already produced three of these products prior to the conference. Each of these HSRAs had been very well received by state and local law enforcement and fusion centers. Our reference aids on the National Socialist Movement (neo-Nazi group), Volksfront (another neo-Nazi group), and the Hammerskin Nation (racist skinhead group) were major topics of discussion during one of the breakout sessions.

Connell wanted at least a dozen more of these products, and she wanted them finished by the end of the year. I met with the other members of my team, and we compiled a list of likely topics for these HSRAs. Among the identified topics were a couple of racist skinhead organizations, a couple of Ku Klux Klan factions, two national sovereign citizen movements, several neo-Nazi groups, a couple of militia extremist groups, and three single-issue movements: the Animal Liberation Front, Earth Liberation Front, and Army of God (a violent antiabortion group). In order to keep track of all of the reference aids, I found a whiteboard with easel and created a matrix for tracking the status of each product. We had a lot of work ahead of us and a short deadline to meet. I wanted to make sure that each product was written in a timely fashion, routed through the various editors, and coordinated properly. It was quite the visual aid, and it generated considerable discussion and jeers from those who passed our work space. We were now getting a lot of attention from the organization's leadership as well as its customer base. It was finally our opportunity to "shine" and capitalize on our growing popularity.

We had come a long way since the day I arrived. I remember when, in 2005, I attempted to distribute our first domestic terrorism product. The *Domestic Terrorism Newsletter* consisted of four pages of incident and case summaries of extremist-related events within the United States. The article summaries were often accompanied by pictures and analytical comments. It resembled a mini-newspaper focused entirely on domestic extremism.

It took me requesting a face-to-face meeting between myself, the division director, and the acting assistant secretary, Karen Mohr, to finally convince Information Analysis and Infrastructure Protection (IAIP) leadership to approve release of the *Domestic Terrorism Newsletter*. It was I&A's first domestic extremism–related product. Positive feedback started pouring in.

"This is just the type of product that I find helpful in fulfilling my homeland security mission. It is timely, concise and relevant. I can both read and comprehend its content in less than 30 minutes. The analysis after each article is right to the point regarding the relevancy of that particular article's content to what we at the state and local level are trying to achieve. Keep up the good work!" said one law enforcement analyst.[30]

"I make a point to save all the newsletters that I receive from your office. I am with an Intelligence Unit in the Pennsylvania State Police and the information contained within these newsletters is very pertinent to my duties," said another.[31]

"Given the current trend of fixation on the international terrorist threat, it is good to see that someone is still paying attention to the known and potential domestic threats as well. Thank you for including us on your mailing list," stated a state law enforcement officer.[32]

Even a DHS component agency weighed in with their thoughts of the product, stating, "The Federal Protective Service has a mission to provide law enforcement and security services to over 8,000 buildings and properties in the Homeland. This type of info is essential to FPS's ability to manage the threat from domestic terrorists and criminals. It appears that there must have been some delay in planning, production and dissemination of this info as much of the content is dated. This information needs to be distributed in a more timely manner to be effective for the officers, agents and other users in the field. Kudos to the compilers of this data. Great format. Sharp product."[33] It is important to note that the time delay had nothing to do with the work of my team, rather a persistent problem with I&A's production process.

"I receive a great deal of e-mails related to Homeland Security. I read your publication and find it very informative," read another response.[34]

Overall, sixteen customer feedback forms were submitted within a week. This had been one of the best responses to any of I&A's products. Besides providing comments similar to those previously cited, all of the feedback forms stated that the product was relevant to their needs. There were no negative responses to the survey regarding this product.[35]

I&A leadership's initial reluctance to publish the newsletter likely resulted from their lack of familiarity with the topic and possible lack of knowledge concerning stakeholders' needs. This was a viable topic of concern for law enforcement officers and criminal analysts across the country.

Connell later criticized this product as being too remedial and lacking thought-provoking analysis. She changed its title and format a couple of times, attempting to make it appear more scholarly. It had been intentionally designed to be concise and simple. It was tailored to a specific customer set—the police officer and criminal intelligence analyst working for the various state and local police agencies.

Connell also criticized the product for not being timely enough. Some of the articles were a month or two old by the time the newsletter was disseminated.

Part of the problem with timeliness related to the product sitting on a decision maker's desk for several weeks before it was reviewed, edited, and finally approved for release.

Soon after her arrival at I&A, Connell summoned my branch chief and me about the *Domestic Terrorism Newsletter*. "Are you the author of this piece?" Connell asked, holding a copy of a recent draft version of the newsletter.

"Yes, ma'am," I said.

"Well, the information is old and stale," she replied. "It needs to be updated immediately."

"Okay. I'll get it back to you within a week," I agreed.

"No, that's too long," she responded. "You are a subject matter expert, correct?"

"Yes, I am," I said.

"Then you'll have it back to me by Monday?" Connell asked.

"Yes, ma'am," I agreed.

It was Thursday morning, and I don't even know if I had enough material to update the entire newsletter. Fortunately, half of the articles were considered current enough to meet Connell's expectation. I only had to rewrite two pages of the newsletter.

By Monday, Connell was given an updated version of the newsletter. She looked it over, signed the cover sheet, and told me it was ready for release. She had promised an expeditious review the second time around. The updated version of the *Domestic Terrorism Newsletter* was disseminated later that day.

During August 2008, an anonymous person posted to the Internet all previous versions of the *Domestic Terrorism Newsletter* (along with its many title changes). The person had obviously submitted a Freedom of Information Act (FOIA) request to the department asking for all previous editions of the newsletter. I knew this because they had posted each of them (in their entirety) on an Internet blog.

Initially, I was upset that once again something had leaked and found its way onto the Internet. But, as I read the blog, I had to chuckle at this individual's sense of humor. He was poking fun at a product I had personally written. But this time, he was commenting on the fact that it had evolved and changed its title numerous times. This was not another attack on my team, but a reflection of Connell's inconsistent guidance and wavering on whether there was any intrinsic value in the product. She didn't approve of its basic, simplistic approach. No one wanted to read a scholarly dissertation on a series of extremist-related events.

"Hi, and welcome to another installment of Friday FOIA Fun," the blog began. "This week, it isn't just any old Friday FOIA Fun, however—it's a very special *homegrown extremist edition*, wherein we are reminded that there are, in fact, *white* people out there who would like to kill us all, and—even more surprisingly—that the government is still concerned about these sad, pathetic, and above all *pale* terrorists."

The blog article continued, "All of this, of course, is brought to us through the modern wonders of the Freedom of Information Act. Remember. When you positively, absolutely, have to know within three to six months, use the Act that some out of several researchers agree occasionally produces the goods: the *Freedom of Information* Act!"[36]

"All hyperbole aside, though, the anal-retentive but inestimably well-meaning folks at the Department of Homeland Security recently released what they claim are every issue of the short-lived *Domestic Terrorism Newsletter*—seven issues in all," the writer stated.

The sarcasm went on, "In addition to erratically redacting some, but not all, of the classification markings, they also redacted the issue and/or volume numbers, so we just have to *trust* that they're telling the truth when they say this was it." The individual's post pointed out that the FOIA results were provided as really "horrible photocopies" that had been scanned and turned into an Adobe PDF files. They said that the files were provided for their readers' "viewing and reading pleasure."[37]

The blog owner correctly described the newsletter as an irregularly published product first issued in 2005. It was an unclassified, largely open-source publication provided to law enforcement throughout the country, which reported on noteworthy news items concerning domestic terrorists and terrorist acts. They properly assessed that rather than concentrating on militant Islamic extremists, the product's emphasis was on more secular "ne'er-do-wells—eco-terrorists, white-supremacists, right-wing anti-government nuts, and so on."[38]

They accurately described the newsletter's table of contents, which "broke up its coverage into a couple of sections, which rarely stayed the same from issue to issue."[39]

"One could argue that this was adaptability in the face of changing real-world conditions; one could also argue that DHS struggled to determine the scope and focus of the publication, and constantly experimented with the contents," he wrote.[40] This demonstrated that even an outsider could see the internal struggle with the product.

"The last issue of the *Domestic Terrorism Newsletter* was in the second quarter of 2007, published in or after April, 2007," the blog said. "By that point, it was just two pages, covered seven items, and had almost as much analysis and commentary as it did excerpts from news articles."[41]

It further stated, "The writing was on the wall, but by the next issue the 'Newsletter' had become the 'Domestic Terrorism Digest,' and before the year was out, it would make the complete transition to an intelligence report, dropping the two-column format of the *Newsletter* in favor of a more conventional report format."[42]

The blog entry concluded, "I *do* also have all the issues to date of the *Domestic Terrorism Digest*, and will be making those available next week. Now, though, here are the seven issues of the *Domestic Terrorism Newsletter*, just in time for Earth Day."[43]

Production of the *Domestic Terrorism Newsletter* came to a screeching halt in September 2007. The product received several makeovers in Dr. Connell's attempt to make it conform to her expectations. Several attempts were made to revive the newsletter, but Dr. Connell made sure it would not survive. We were, however, able to get one final issue published in March 2009. It would be the very last edition of the newsletter.

Despite having a good track record of consistent positive customer feedback, Dr. Connell "killed" the product because it did not conform to her expectations of quality and in-depth analysis. Ironically, the acronym for *Domestic Extremism Digest* is D.E.D. which is one letter away from "dead."

The numerous changes over the life cycle of the *Domestic Terrorism Newsletter* illustrated the intense level of scrutiny our work received. Over the nearly six years I worked at I&A, it did not appear that other analytical sections received the same nitpicky review and political attention as our products received. It was extremely frustrating to see our products constantly barraged with a litany of questions and seemingly unfair critique while others dealing with border security, infrastructure protection, and international terrorist threats seemingly passed through the review process with very few unreasonable comments or attention to political sensitivities.

Another product that received a large degree of both internal and external scrutiny was the Domestic Extremism Lexicon. In late January 2009, I was approached by an analyst working in the Strategic Analysis Group (SAG) of HETA. This is the same unit that helped us organize, plan, and carry out a successful conference in Newport, Rhode Island, just a few months earlier. We had worked with SAG on a few other joint projects in the past, including the HSTA for 2008 and 2009 and an assessment called "Leftwing Extremists Likely to Increase Use of Cyber Attacks Over the Coming Decade," released on January 26, 2009.

The SAG analyst was wondering if I thought an extremism glossary of terms would be helpful to state and local law enforcement. It would be extremely useful to consolidate and standardize terminology currently being used in DHS products as well as state and local reports. Over the years, a litany of terms had been thrown around in various law enforcement and intelligence products used to describe a variety of domestic terrorism– and extremist-related topics. I agreed that it was a worthwhile endeavor, and we immediately set forth on identifying and consolidating a list of terms and their associated definitions. Further, Congress had asked I&A to develop a lexicon as a part of its radicalization mission.

Our work on this project initially began as a working group between the author, his supervisor, two other subject matter experts, and me. We quickly came up with an extensive list of words related to the project and began to define each of these terms. This proved more difficult than I had originally expected. Nevertheless, through considerable discussion and debate, we finally came to an agreement on what we meant by each term.

As the document's scope indicates, the product provides definitions for key terms and phrases that often appeared in DHS analytical products that address domestic (non-Islamic) extremism. This lexicon was intended to promote the usage of a commonality of terms in order to better facilitate information sharing and knowledge transfer among DHS intelligence analysts and state and local homeland security and law enforcement officials. Since everyone knew we were defining terms associated with extremist groups and ideologies clearly linked to violence, we didn't feel the need to insert the word "violent" for each and every definition. We thought it was better to clarify this up-front in the document's scope note. Again, this document was written for a state and local law enforcement audience and not the general public. Despite the numerous leaks we experienced over the years, we certainly didn't think that congressional representatives, the news media, and the general public would take these definitions out of context and portray them as attacks against their mainstream belief systems. I never thought these same people would use these very terms and definitions to attack DHS and to further their own political agendas. In the wake of the unauthorized disclosure of the DHS right-wing extremism report, the Domestic Extremism Lexicon product was soon described on the airwaves of American television stations, newspapers, and radio stations.

"Another controversial report and more damage control at the Department of Homeland Security," Lou Dobbs of CNN reported on May 5, 2009. "The same department that issued a report suggesting returning war veterans were susceptible to extremist groups is also issuing what it calls the 'Domestic Extremism Lexicon.'"[44] Dobbs went on to describe the document and discussed various definitions related to his political causes and took them out of context, portraying them as describing the legitimate and law-abiding activities of U.S. citizens.[45]

To the contrary, the lexicon product never intended to portray mainstream Americans as extremists. It described those ideologies that were known to motivate citizens toward more radical views that were known to spawn criminal activity and violence.

"A DHS spokesperson today told us that the dictionary was not authorized," Dobbs reported.[46] "That it was recalled shortly after it was let out and state and local law enforcement officials have been told to ignore it."[47]

Dobbs then interviewed representative Peter King (R-NY), ranking member of the Homeland Security Committee, about the lexicon. Dobbs asked King for his reaction to the document.

"Lou, actually, it's very distressing," King said.[48] "The Department of Homeland Security is supposed to be defending us against another attack from Islamic terrorism. That's the reason this department was created."[49] In reality, this statement is conjecture on the part of Representative King. According to the Homeland Security Act of 2002, DHS was stood up to protect the United States from all terrorist threats. Islamic terrorism is not singled out in this piece of legislation that became law.

"To me, it's missing its purpose. You went through all of those different definitions of different types of extremists. Nowhere in that dictionary do you see the term 'Islamic extremist.'"[50]

"The department was set up primarily, let's face it, to protect us from another terrorist attack from Islamic terrorists, and yet they talk about everything but that."[51]

"This is really wrong, and the fact that it's happened twice now shows there is a department really out of control with a tremendous lack of discipline," King said.[52]

Dobbs responded, "This document could have been produced by someone in China under Mao Tse-Tung or it could've been produced in the Nixon administration."[53]

"This is the kind of egregiously offensive product coming from the agency . . . . I can't even pronounce it. I can't even string the words together that make up this agency."[54] Dobbs then asked King what was going with this "agency" [the one that produced the lexicon].

"This, I believe, is a unit that's gotten out of control," King stated. "By the way, the civil rights unit within the Department of Homeland Security had been opposed to a number of these findings they made and yet this unit was still able to get this report released."[55]

"This seems to be a rogue element in the department, at least I hope it is. I hope this does not reflect the thinking of the department," said King.[56] "We have to be very, very careful about having the federal government getting involved in thought control."[57]

"I really don't want the federal government to be determining whether or not a person who feels certain ways about the environment or about animals or about certain religious issues should be considered an extremist," King stated.[58] "That to me is the type of thought control, mind control that is very dangerous," King said.[59]

"I think the department should be set up to target specific terrorist groups affiliated with overseas groups who intend to bring about violence to our country," King remarked.[60]

Dobbs said, "The idea that this department has again committed what looks to be like . . . it's beyond political correctness. To me, it appears to be absolutely agenda driven and with the complicit, if not acquiescent, approval of Janet Napolitano."[61]

Dobbs then suggested to King that Napolitano should be held accountable for the work of an obviously poorly managed, misguided agency.[62]

"Lou, you're absolutely right," King responded. "She called me two weeks ago to say they made a mistake on the first report. Now, we have the second report. I mean, this is back to back."[63] King said this was a very serious matter—a department with real power, making these types of mistakes or intentional policy decisions.[64]

"This is dangerous to the country," King concluded.[65]

Dobbs ended his interview with King by discussing Napolitano's failure to use the word "terrorist" when it came to referencing Osama bin Laden or al-Qaeda, only to use the terrorist label when talking about those that oppose illegal immigration or returning war veterans.[66]

Dobbs's coverage of the lexicon story was politically motivated, biased, and a shoddy piece of journalism. King clearly misspoke when he said the Department of Homeland Security should only be looking at threats from Islamic terrorists.

His statement goes against wording in the Homeland Security Act of 2002, which does not limit the department's role to preventing terrorism from overseas threats. DHS attorneys agree that the department can look at domestic terrorists that are non-Islamic.

King's remarks epitomized the narrow-minded and biased thought process concerning DHS's monitoring of terrorism. He neither understood the statutory authority of the department nor the context of the Domestic Extremism Lexicon. It was never designed to include Islamic terrorism, as Representative King pointed out, because it focused solely on domestic extremist threats that are rooted in uniquely American extremist ideology.

It is interesting to note that both Dobbs and King portrayed the lexicon as being released after the DHS right-wing extremism report. They made it sound as if Napolitano ignored the criticism about the right-wing report and sent out a second controversial report to spite her critics. In reality, the Domestic Extremism Lexicon was disseminated on March 26, 2009. This is about two weeks before the release of the department's right-wing extremism report. It appears to me that Dobbs and King had no real interest in discussing the merits of the lexicon, but were motivated politically to use the product as a means to embarrass Napolitano and Obama too.

Contrary to what an alleged DHS press spokesperson said to Dobbs, the Domestic Extremism Lexicon was an official, authorized DHS product. It was posted to the I&A homepage on the Homeland Security Data Network and other classified systems, and was also sent out via e-mail broadcast to numerous addressees who had previously requested DHS products. The lexicon was subsequently recalled a month and a half later because of media and congressional criticism. In order for a product to be "recalled," I&A's Production Management Division must send an administrative recall notice to all original recipients of the document and remove it from the various computer systems. Administrative recall notices are usually a result of some form of erroneous information contained within a document. Every previous document recall at I&A was always rewritten in a more precise format and immediately redistributed back to the customers. Furthermore, no I&A product had ever been withdrawn as a result of media exposure, political motivations, or public outcry. Yet this was the case with the Domestic Extremism Lexicon.

Soon after the administrative recall, the author (SAG analyst) arranged a series of meetings with domestic terrorism subject matter experts, I&A attorneys, the DHS Office of Civil Rights and Civil Liberties (CRCL), Privacy Office, and the DHS Lexicon Office. The DHS Lexicon Office was not involved in the initial vetting of the glossary. Several meetings between representatives of these offices took place during the summer of 2009. All definitions and terms in the lexicon were reviewed and, if required, redefined to everyone's satisfaction. Changes to the lexicon were finalized during the first week of September. We believed the glossary of terms was ready once again to be redistributed to I&A stakeholders who had been anticipating the updated version.

Our hopes gradually turned to frustration as the lexicon continued to languish for another three months as the Office of General Counsel (I&A attorneys), Privacy Office, and CRCL continued their methodical and deliberate discussions over the terms and definitions. The process had greatly reduced the number of terms and definitions in the original lexicon. The glossary had been trimmed from eight pages of terms and definitions to a miniscule few pages. In December 2009, a finalized rewrite of the lexicon was forwarded to I&A leadership for review and approval.

It was pointed out to I&A leadership that the lexicon product was an attempt to arrive at a common understanding of what these terms mean. The Domestic Extremism Lexicon was viewed as a positive step forward in improving the overall quality of I&A intelligence products. It was anticipated that these definitions would be used by state and local fusion center personnel who had requested that DHS define these terms. It was also noted that the FBI did not have a common glossary of domestic extremism–related terms.

Past concerns were raised about the lack of a lexicon. Similar terms had been used inconsistently between the different offices of I&A. On multiple occasions, there was little context within a sentence or product to inform the reader why certain terms were selected or appropriate. In January 2010, I&A leadership supported and approved the revised Domestic Extremism Lexicon for release to state and local law enforcement. The DHS Lexicon Office, however, continued to delay and stall its release for fear of generating more negative publicity for the department. They were unwilling to take the risk. Once the author and domestic terrorism subject matter experts saw no hope for the product's release, they moved on to other projects and tasks.

Despite challenges regarding the production of domestic extremism–related reports at DHS, my team enjoyed many successes. Besides a handful of Homeland Security Reference Aids and the *Domestic Terrorism Newsletter*, I&A's domestic terrorism team contributed to many other products written by external law enforcement and intelligence agencies. On multiple occasions, our analytical counterparts at various fusion centers would coordinate and collaborate on topics related to domestic extremist activity in their respective jurisdictions.

We also received numerous invitations to provide training for, or to speak on, a variety of domestic terrorism topics to federal, state, and local law enforcement meetings, working groups, and conferences. In 2008, we presented briefings and conducted trainings at nearly thirty events, including several at the Bureau of Alcohol, Tobacco, Firearms, and Explosives (ATF) National Academy, the FBI Academy, multiple visits to state fusion centers, and at various law enforcement–sponsored conferences. During the first quarter of 2009, we conducted eighteen presentations to similar audiences. We received numerous accolades for providing this type of support, which was both relevant and desperately needed in the field. At the time, few federal agencies were providing tailored domestic counterterrorism training specific to geographic regions for state and local law enforcement.

"Thanks for your support, despite all that is going on at [DHS] headquarters, as far as the field is concerned you guys are the ONLY ones providing intelligence with value added," reported a field representative.[67]

Another said, "I participated in the HS-SLIC Domestic Terrorism Conference in Rhode Island. Feedback from the various fusion center participants was very positive. Daryl Johnson and his team proved to be experts in the domestic terrorism field and the fusion center has expressed interest in potential future collaboration on domestic terrorism products."[68]

"I wanted you to know that during my recent HS-SLIC Advisory Board meeting with Dr. Connell and others, I was able to highlight the good work that Daryl Johnson and his group have been doing," said a fusion center director.[69]

The director of another state fusion center commented, "I really do appreciate your and your group's efforts at DHS and have continued to tell both Charlie and Mary that when I get a chance. You guys are a bright light in DHS's efforts."[70]

"We continue to receive GREAT verbal feedback on I&A's domestic terrorism briefings. Even more encouraging, the subscription rate was directly benefited by this tour— as we received approximately twice as many requests to join the state fusion center network in the last week as any other week previously," wrote a fusion center analyst.[71]

Another analyst at a state fusion center reported that "DHS I&A received some very positive feedback from the National Guard regarding I&A's assessment of a white supremacist group's attempt to penetrate their armory security. It was concise, on point and very informative. Keep up the good work. You guys are filling a huge intelligence gap for us."[72]

We also provided analytical support to state and local law enforcement by addressing their questions and concerns related to domestic extremist activity in their geographic area. This was not our primary area of focus, but it evolved as more and more contacts in the field learned of our existence and subject matter expertise.

In addition to providing information regarding the formation of new extremist groups and their activities, we would occasionally receive requests to assist ongoing criminal investigations. This was not a routine responsibility of I&A analysts, but given the domestic terrorism team's unique knowledge, experience, and preestablished relationships of trust with law enforcement, we would receive occasional inquiries from state and local police agencies.

I&A is prohibited from conducting law enforcement investigations, but we certainly provided analytical support to those conducting the investigations. This type of assistance fell outside the traditional I&A methods of support, only because most analysts did not have an extensive network of law enforcement contacts and well-established trusted relationships like we did.

During autumn 2008, I was invited to participate and asked to lead a pilot working group looking at white supremacist, sovereign citizen, and militia extremist activity in Missouri and Illinois. The working group consisted of analysts from DHS, FBI, the Missouri State Highway Patrol, Illinois State Police, Chicago Police Department, Kansas City Terrorism Early Warning Group, and St. Louis Terrorism

Early Warning Group. Our goal was to identify which types of domestic extremist groups were active in each state, their activities, and whether or not there were any linkages between extremist groups in the respective states.

During a few three-day trips to cities in Illinois and Missouri, I learned extremely valuable information concerning white supremacist, sovereign citizen, and militia extremist activity in both states. The militia movement was actively recruiting in Missouri. Neo-Nazi group membership was believed to be growing in Illinois, and their activities had increased in the state. White supremacists in both Missouri and Illinois were using the nomination of a liberal African-American presidential candidate to aid their recruitment and to further their various racist causes. These same extremists in both states were also using the illegal immigration issue for similar outcomes. Of particular note, citizens in Missouri were increasingly purchasing and stockpiling weapons and ammunition, not because there was rampant crime, but out of fear of more restrictive gun laws being imposed by a new presidential administration and other changes in national political leadership. Issues fueling this trend were increasing citizen concerns about ammunition shortages and perceived government corruption. This was confirmed through state and local law enforcement officials in Missouri, and by the ATF in Kansas City. During discussions with multiple federal firearms licensees (gun dealers) in Missouri, ATF learned of this surge in firearms and ammunition purchases. At DHS, we were also aware of this emerging trend through monitoring chatter on various extremist websites, forums, and message boards.

With the election of Barack Obama in November 2008, there were going to be administrative changes. At I&A, many hoped this change would finally facilitate Connell's long-anticipated departure, but amazingly there were still rumors circulating that she was going to be the next undersecretary for I&A or serve as the acting undersecretary indefinitely. Anticipating a likely change in administration, Chertoff appointed Mr. Roger P. Mackin as the principal deputy undersecretary for I&A on September 10, 2009.[73] I often wondered if Chertoff knew Connell's reputation in I&A and decided to bring in Mackin, an outsider, to fill the void in leadership.

Roger Mackin would ultimately become the acting undersecretary for I&A with Allen's resignation on January 20, 2009. Among his first actions as acting undersecretary, Mackin announced the departure of Connell.

"With the scheduled return of Dr. Mary Connell to her parent agency, I wish to say farewell and to announce the reassignment of the former HITRAC Director as the new Acting Deputy Assistant Secretary of Intelligence, effective January 21, 2009," Mackin stated in his e-mail broadcast to the entire I&A workforce.[74]

"Dr. Connell joined I&A three years ago to help Under Secretary Charles Allen create a new I&A organization and to establish the tradecraft of Homeland Security Intelligence," he wrote.[75]

At a follow-up town hall meeting held on January 28, 2009, the audience broke out in loud applause when Mackin announced there were going to be changes to Connell's analytical production processes.

Prior to his arrival at I&A, Mackin worked for four years in the private sector assisting with the development of the state fusion center network.[76] He had served as the director of intelligence at the Office of National Drug Control Policy.[77] In March 2003, he was also appointed counternarcotics officer and U.S. interdiction coordinator at DHS.[78]

According to the department's press release dated September 10, 2008, Mackin's "service to the nation began in the United States Air Force where he earned two bronze stars for special operations assignments in Vietnam. He advanced to the rank of Lieutenant Colonel in the Air Force reserves upon conclusion of his active duty service, at which time he launched a career as an operations, paramilitary and counter-intelligence officer in the Central Intelligence Agency that lasted nearly 30 years."[79]

Mackin's law enforcement background was refreshing to see. All previous assistant secretaries and undersecretaries, including the acting ones, came from the intelligence community. Mackin was the first to have a law enforcement background. Under his leadership, I&A's production process was changed. Release authority for finished intelligence products was delegated down to the division level to assist in relieving the "logjam" of products that had accumulated on Connell's desk for the past six months.

Mackin created a motto for the office and had the words "Developing the Right Information to the Right People at the Right Time" inscribed on the wall of Building 19's main stairway. Ironically, these words are not only reminiscent of his brief legacy at I&A but will also forever link Mackin to the DHS right-wing extremism report.

On January 21, 2009, DHS welcomed its third secretary, Janet Napolitano, who was sworn into office that day. She served as governor of Arizona from 2003 to 2009.[80] Prior to serving as governor, Napolitano was the attorney general of Arizona from 1999 to 2002.[81] In 1993, she was appointed as the United States attorney for the District of Arizona.[82] As U.S. attorney, Napolitano assisted with the investigation of Michael Fortier of Kingman, Arizona, and his associations with Oklahoma bombing suspect Timothy McVeigh.[83] In 1996, she was also involved in the investigation and subsequent prosecution of twelve members of the Viper militia for firearms and explosives violations in Phoenix, Arizona.[84] Members of the Viper militia were suspected of having conducted surveillance on several federal buildings and military installations with the intent of attacking them at an unspecified time in the future. Given Napolitano's background and experience dealing with these cases in Arizona, I assumed she would be an advocate of I&A's domestic extremism analytical efforts—particularly those relating to violent right-wing extremists. McVeigh and Viper militia members are examples of right-wing extremist threats.

Janet Napolitano, Secretary
of Homeland Security. Photo
courtesy of DHS.

Charles E. Allen, Former Undersecretary
for Intelligence and Analysis. Photo
courtesy of DHS.

Bart R. Johnson, Principal Deputy
Undersecretary for Intelligence and
Analysis. Photo courtesy of DHS.

Caryn A. Wagner, Undersecretary
for Intelligence and Analysis. Photo
courtesy of DHS.

ATF special response team members prepare to enter fugitive white supremacist Steve Anderson's home near Somerset, Kentucky. Photo courtesy of ATF.

Hidden bunker located on the property of Kentucky militia leader Charlie Puckett. Photo courtesy of ATF.

The Alabama Free Militia possessed an arsenal of weaponry including dozens of rifle grenades. Photo courtesy of ATF.

Automatic weapons seized from the Christian American Patriot Survivalists in Crawford County, Pennsylvania. Photo courtesy of ATF.

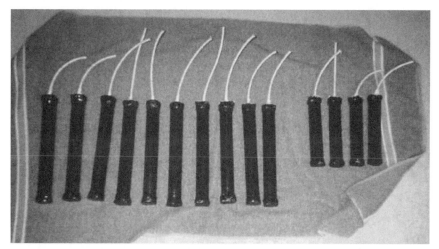

Two National Alliance members in Kimball, Nebraska, manufactured nearly 100 improvised explosive devices, among other lethal weapons, for an ATF undercover agent. Photo courtesy of ATF.

Ronald Struve, a rightwing extremist in Spokane, Washington, was charged with possessing numerous illegal firearms he was likely selling to other like-minded individuals. Photo courtesy of ATF.

Right-wing extremist Ronald Struve also possessed multiple pounds of high explosives and military ordnance capable of killing a lot of people. Photo courtesy of ATF.

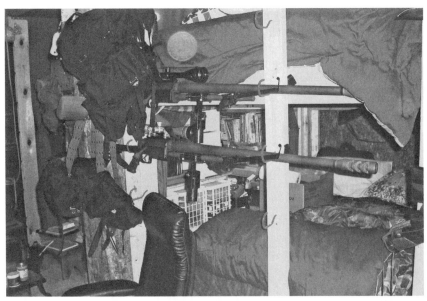

Two Armalite .50-caliber sniper rifles were among an arsenal of weapons found in a right-wing extremist's underground bunker in the Midwest during 2007. Photo courtesy of ATF.

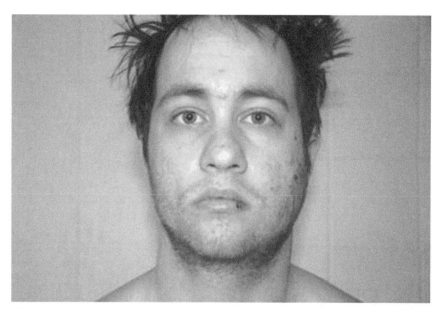

White supremacist Richard Poplawski killed three Pittsburgh Police Officers on April 4, 2009, fearing they were going to take his guns away. Photo Courtesy of Allegheny County Prosecutor's Office.

Bloody scene where a Pittsburgh police officer died from multiple gunshots from Poplawski's high-powered rifle. Photo courtesy of Allegheny County Prosecutor's Office.

A BearCat armored vehicle sustains multiple hits during a gun battle with deranged white supremacist Richard Poplawski. Photo courtesy of Pittsburgh Police Department.

Militia sympathizer Joshua Cartwright lies mortally wounded next to his pickup truck after a high-speed chase. Cartwright had previously killed two Okaloosa County sheriff's deputies over fears of losing his gun rights. Photo courtesy of FDLE.

Cartwright's tattoo on his left forearm reads "Don't Tread On Me, Liberty or Death"—a phrase often associated with right-wing extremist views. Photo courtesty of FDLE.

Sovereign citizens Jerry and Joseph Kane lay mortally wounded after killing two West Memphis Police officers on May 28, 2010. Two other officers were shot during the ensuing gun battle. Photo courtesy of West Memphis Police Department.

The Echelon building is engulfed in flames soon after Joe Stack slammed his small plane into the IRS processing center in Austin. Photo courtesy of the Austin Police Department.

Immediate aftermath of Joe Stack's attack on the Internal Revenue Service processing center in Austin, Texas, on February 18, 2010, using a small aircraft packed with 50-gallon drums of gasoline. Photo courtesy of the Austin Police Department.

9

Gathering Storm

On a clear, cold day in the Midwest, several hundred people gathered in downtown Springfield, Illinois. A large U.S. flag was draped down the four-story façade of an old brick building. People were cheering as they held cardboard political signs in the air that read "Obama '08."[1]

Within the shadow of the State Capitol, Senator Barack Obama (D-Illinois) was about to make an important announcement. He was planning to publicly announce his candidacy for president of the United States. Obama was entering the primary race for the Democratic nomination, which was over eighteen months away.[2]

"Today, another son of Illinois will take his first step on his journey to Washington," Senator Dick Durban (D-Illinois) began his opening remarks.[3] Durban was making a reference not only to Obama, but also to president Abraham Lincoln, who was from Springfield, Illinois.[4]

Obama, his wife, and their two daughters slowly made their way to the stage. Obama waved his hand high in the air, then stooped low to shake the hands of dozens of people lining the perimeter fencing surrounding the grandstand. The Obama family finally reached the steps to the stage. As they approached the podium, Barack and Michelle continued waving to the crowd, exchanging greetings and occasionally bending over to shake the hands of supporters below them who were lined up along the front of the stage. The crowd was excited. Those gathered for the announcement continued to sustain their applause and loud cheering. Political placards were interspersed throughout the crowd, with supporters waving the signs above their heads.[5]

"Hello, Springfield!" Obama shouted. "I know it's a little chilly . . . but I'm fired up!"[6]

"You didn't come here for me. You came here because you believe in what this country can be," Obama remarked.[7] "In the face of war, you believe there can be peace. In the face of despair, you believe there can be hope."[8]

195

In a firm, resounding voice, Obama stated, "In the face of the politics that shut you out . . . That's told you to settle . . . That's divided us for too long . . . You believe that we can be 'one people,' reaching out for what's possible, building that more perfect union. That's the journey we're on today," he said.[9]

He continued, "It was here, in Springfield, where North, South, East, and West come together, that I was reminded of the essential decency of the American people—where I came to believe that through this decency, we can build a more hopeful America."[10]

"And that is why, in the shadow of the Old State Capitol, where Lincoln once called on a divided house to stand together, where common hopes and common dreams still live, I stand before you today to announce my candidacy for president of the United States of America,"[11] Barack Obama declared. The crowd immediately erupted into loud applause and deafening cheers.

Just a month earlier, a similar announcement was made back in Washington, D.C. It preempted the boisterous campaign speeches and political posturing that would soon be given on the State Capitol lawn in Springfield, Illinois.

It wasn't such a grand presentation. No crowds had gathered. No political signs were made. No flags hung, nor loud chanting heard. It came as a routine phone call.

The soft, persistent ringtone of the secure telephone sitting on my desk gave no indication of the importance and level of sensitivity of the message I was about to receive. I was busy working at my desk at the Department of Homeland Security (DHS) on the second floor of Building 19. On about the third ring, I stopped what I was doing and picked up the phone's receiver.

"Hello, DHS," I answered. This was my standard greeting. We are taught in the intelligence community to remain anonymous when answering the phone in case someone was attempting to elicit information, such as the media.

"Daryl, this is Mike at the U.S. Capitol Police," said the voice on the other end of the call. I had met Mike a year earlier during one of our many visits to federal law enforcement agencies around Washington, D.C. Such routine visits were often scheduled not only to introduce domestic terrorism team members to their analytical counterparts and law enforcement partners, but also to facilitate information sharing.

We made regular visits to the FBI, Bureau of Alcohol, Tobacco, Firearms and Explosives (ATF), and U.S. Park Police every few months. We met with other law enforcement organizations on an annual or semiannual basis, such as the Federal Protective Service, U.S. Secret Service, U.S. Marshals, and U.S. Capitol Police, among a host of other agencies. It was part of our duties and responsibilities to conduct liaison activities and to continue fostering collaborative working relationships with external government entities.

"Hi, Mike, what can I do for you?" I asked.

"Have you ever heard of Barack Obama?" Mike inquired.

"No. I can't say I have," I responded. I had no idea who this person was, and I was beginning to wonder why Mike was asking.

"Well, he's a Democratic senator from Chicago, he is African American and he's thinking about running for president," Mike stated.

"Daryl, have you seen any extremist chatter concerning Barack Obama running for president?" Mike asked.

"No, we haven't yet. But, then again, we haven't been looking either," I stated.

Mike then proposed the very question to which I was attempting to formulate an answer. "What do you think is going to happen when the Ku Klux Klan, neo-Nazis and other white supremacists get wind of this?"

I shuddered at the thought.

"It will be the perfect recruiting tool for right-wing extremists. His campaign will most certainly lead to a huge increase in white supremacist activity. There will surely be threats," I somberly assessed.

"We need you to scour the Internet for any hints of white supremacist interest in Obama," Mike requested. "And if you see anything, please send it to us immediately."

"You got it," I promised.

After hanging up the phone, I immediately walked over to the open-source intelligence (OSINT) branch at the Office of Intelligence and Analysis (I&A) to speak with one of the analysts devoted full-time to reviewing domestic extremist websites and public forums for any hints of violent rhetoric or criminal activity.

The OSINT branch was an extremely valuable resource for I&A, especially my team. As I've said before, Congress never authorized I&A to have a covert collection capability. Thus, unlike many of the other members of the intelligence community, I&A could not hire informants or use undercover operations against terrorists or any other clandestine collection mechanisms. I&A is totally reliant upon other intelligence agencies within the U.S. government and law enforcement organizations for this type of information. In this regard, the organization more closely resembles a consumer of intelligence rather than an intelligence producer.

In 2008, the Office of the Director of National Intelligence recognized I&A's OSINT collection capability.[12] This capability is exclusively overt in nature, meaning that it can only observe publicly available information on the Internet. As a result, the OSINT branch was forbidden to join private e-mail lists, password-protected websites, or Internet chat.

Despite such constraints, we used the OSINT branch to its fullest capability. We gave them a list of white supremacist, militia extremist, and sovereign citizen websites to monitor. We also had other websites identified that were related both to anarchist and single-issue extremists. Since we had only one analyst devoted full-time to the project, we had to prioritize what extremist movements and activities justified monitoring. The OSINT branch would look for chatter about the formation of new extremist groups and any hints of criminal activity, such as teaching or soliciting criminal tradecraft, threats against law enforcement, or government officials, along with references to recent arrests.

Since it involved potential threats to a current senator and presidential hopeful, the U.S. Capitol Police request met I&A's criteria for the type of activity we were authorized to monitor. I relayed the information from Capitol Police to the open-source officer. He immediately added the request to his already-lengthy list of priorities.

After a few days, the open source officer reported back to me. No threats to Obama had been found. There wasn't even a mention in extremist chatter about Obama's announcement in Springfield.

Since nothing had been found, my team and I decided to lower our level of interest in this subject from a primary to a secondary requirement. We needed to refocus our limited efforts on other priorities, such as the growth of the white supremacist and militia movements.

I reported our negative findings back to the Capitol Police. We agreed, however, to continue looking for any threat-related information concerning Obama that might surface at a later time.

One of the more difficult tasks I had to face as an analyst related to finding quantitative data concerning growth and declines within the various domestic extremist movements inside the United States.

Historically, there have been statistical problems with determining the number of extremists within the United States. It is a daunting task to have to keep up with the number of new groups, as well as those that are waning in popularity or have since become defunct. It is virtually impossible to know the exact number of extremists in a particular movement at any given moment.

Extremist membership ebb and flow is very fluid as people join one group, only to leave for another soon thereafter. Many individuals hold multiple memberships. Extremist groups themselves often experience rapid change as new leaders take the group in new directions, which can cause organizational restructuring or new group names. Others experience factional infighting that results in organizational splits or causes the whole group to fold entirely. Displaced members then join other like-minded organizations or may yet leave the movement for good. In addition, many people may sympathize or support a particular extremist cause, but for whatever reason never join an organized group. As a result, they remain "off the radar," so to speak.

A retired ATF agent once told me that trying to count the number of extremists in a particular movement is an impossible task. He likened it to having to ask someone to count the number of fans for any particular sports team.

First, you must determine what constitutes a "fan." Is it someone who wears a sports jersey of their favorite team? Or is it someone who buys season tickets to all the home games? What about those individuals who travel with the team on the road when they play away games? What about those fair-weather fans that seemingly "jump on the bandwagon" during a winning season and act as if they've liked the sports team all along? Finally, should we consider those who abandon the team and stop watching the games during a difficult season?

Intelligence analysts and subject matter experts struggle with these same types of questions when attempting to determine who meets the threshold of being an "extremist" and how many extremists exist in a particular movement from year to year.

Organizations like the Southern Poverty Law Center (SPLC) and the Anti-Defamation League (ADL) spend a lot of time monitoring right-wing extremists. There are also other nongovernment organizations that monitor both single-issue and left-wing extremists. These organizations attempt to determine objective estimates of the number of white supremacist, militia, and sovereign citizen groups in the United States. It is a cumbersome task that becomes much more difficult when attempting to provide reasonably accurate estimates at the movement level.

The SPLC is a Montgomery, Alabama-based civil rights organization that is engaged in monitoring right-wing extremist groups, including white supremacists and militias. The SPLC *Intelligence Report* publication is one of the most comprehensive and well-respected sources for credible and timely intelligence on the tactics, activities, and goals of right-wing extremist organizations within the United States.[13]

The ADL is headquartered in New York City, New York, and has several regional offices located in major cities around the country. ADL has provided timely and accurate intelligence and conducts ongoing monitoring of the activities of right-wing extremist organizations, including white supremacist groups and militias. It operates a nationwide network of experts on right-wing extremism who issue regular intelligence reports and provide specialized testimony in court cases, as well as training thousands of law enforcement and correctional staff each year.[14] It also has experts on left-wing extremists and domestic Muslim extremists.

Since nongovernment organizations like SPLC and ADL do not have the same legal constraints and oversight regulations as government agencies, law enforcement officers often use them as resources when they need information about a particular extremist group or individual as part of their ongoing criminal investigations or public safety mission. Both the SPLC and ADL have also occasionally provided expert consultation during court proceedings involving the alleged criminal activities of white supremacists, militia extremists, and sovereign citizens.[15,16] Furthermore, ADL and SPLC have provided expert testimony during congressional hearings on topics related to extremism.[17,18] For these reasons, law enforcement agencies, including the FBI, often cite the work of the SPLC and ADL in their intelligence assessments and police reports. This does not mean that law enforcement is working hand-in-hand with the SPLC or ADL to investigate individuals or groups. In fact, quite the opposite is true. Law enforcement's relationship with these organizations is a "one-way street"—meaning information is shared with law enforcement without any obligation or expectations.

Due to their unique work related to protecting human rights, SPLC and ADL have a much broader threshold for the types of extremist individuals and groups upon which they monitor and report. Both organizations are concerned with the whole range of problems that extremist movements can cause to communities, not simply the criminal problems. They can collect and retain information gathered through their own research on any group or individual they deem to be adversarial. They are not bound by the legal standards of "reasonable suspicion" or "probable cause" because their investigations are not limited to criminal subjects. Law enforcement understands that SPLC and ADL have different views on who may be an "extremist." As a result, officers, agents, and analysts do not use information that is not directly germane to their law enforcement duties to protect the public or conduct criminal investigations. As a result, certain "hate groups" as determined by SPLC or ADL may not necessarily be a law enforcement or national security concern because, although they may be hate groups, they may not be engaging in criminal activity.

Much like the FBI and other federal, state, and local law enforcement agencies, my team used relevant SPLC and ADL information in our analysis. We would also cite various SPLC and ADL articles, reports, and projects in our intelligence reports. I have maintained long-standing relationships with both the ADL and SPLC and have found both organizations to be professional, credible, and useful sources.

Compounding the problem with estimating the number of extremists is the fact that many extremist groups are not known to have formal membership rosters and still others do not have membership requirements. Exacerbating this dilemma are the many extremist group spokespersons that exaggerate membership numbers for publicity purposes. A prime example of this is the famous 10,000 members of the Michigan Militia figure that was given to news reporters researching the militia movement soon after the Oklahoma City bombing.[19] This number was repeatedly quoted in numerous news articles since the mid-1990s without any further questioning or substantive proof that this number was even accurate. And, like sports teams, extremist movements are known to have hard-core followers (called true believers), adherents who are unaffiliated with any particular extremist group, and still an unknown number of strong sympathizers at any given moment in time.

The SPLC is well known for its annual "Year in Hate" review, which is reported in the spring edition of their quarterly magazine, *Intelligence Report*.[20] As a result of many of the aforementioned problems, the SPLC has chosen to emphasize its annual count on the number of extremist groups rather than attempting to count membership totals. Group numbers are extremely useful and provide some measure of objective statistics.

First, the number of extremist groups has been known to rise and fall rapidly due to various political and economic climates, changing social conditions, as well as organizational infighting and restructuring. The ADL's "Racist Skinhead Project" provides a good illustration of this point.

In 2009, the ADL reported the findings of their in depth-study titled "Racist Skinhead Project."[21] The ADL's Racist Skinhead Project involved identifying and tracking racist skinhead groups and related criminal activity in the United States.[22] Despite a lot of hard work and valiant effort on the part of the ADL working jointly with several law enforcement officers throughout the country on the project, the ADL readily admits it can only provide a rough estimate of the actual number of racist skinheads in the United States.[23] Over a five-year period, for example, the ADL monitored the activity of various racist skinhead "groups" in the metropolitan Phoenix area. They reported seeing a variety of groups appearing and disappearing within relatively short periods of time. The ADL noted, however, that despite this fluctuation in the number of groups that were forming and disbanding, the number of individuals belonging to these groups did not fade or simply disappear, but generally increased. Racist skinheads' allegiance to the overarching white supremacist cause remained steady. Their devotion to a greater cause outweighed their loyalty to any particular group.

Because of circumstances such as these, the ADL often counsels not to rely on "group-counting" along as a measure of the strength or weakness of an extremist movement. One group may have a hundred members, while another might have only eight—yet they would still be "groups" on a list. Moreover, often an increase in group numbers may actually represent a weakness in the movement, as when a once-large extremist group fractures into several squabbling factions and offshoots due to infighting. Any analyst must use all potential measurements, including criminal activity levels, organized events, Internet social networking activities, and more in order to come up with any reasonably reliable estimates.

Another problem facing those who want to quantify the number of extremist groups or membership is the fact that not all groups are equal. Some are hardly more than a website, list server, or forum. Still others exist in the real world and have memberships that number in the thousands. SPLC attempts to factor this into their annual group totals by counting different chapters within an extremist group as individual groups. Nonetheless, the fact that one group may not be equivalent to another in terms of membership numbers can be somewhat distorting.

Third, some extremist movements like the Animal Liberation Front (ALF), Earth Liberation Front (ELF), and the antiabortion extremist movement do not form groups. They rely on their ideology to motivate adherents to action. Still other extremist movements, like sovereign citizens, operate as a loose-knit network of adherents with movement spokespersons and traveling salesmen to indoctrinate others into their causes. When new tactics emerge, such as the "common law courts" in the sovereign citizen movement during the 1990s, it can mistakenly look as if there has been explosive growth in the number of "groups." In reality, it was likely the same number of sovereign citizen extremists practicing their tactics in a more organized manner. When sovereign citizens stopped forming their common law courts by the year 2000, it looked as if the movement disappeared entirely. This was far from the truth. The sovereign citizen movement did not experience a sudden drop in membership as some thought, but rather had adopted a new tactic called redemption. This new sovereign citizen tactic emphasized an individual's sovereignty, rather than forming a sovereign citizen group like a common law court.

Lastly, an increase in the number of groups within a movement does not necessarily mean an increase in membership. This phenomenon can best be exemplified with the fading of various "old-school" racist groups since 2003.

During the 1980s and 1990s, large neo-Nazi and Ku Klux Klan organizations dominated the white supremacist movement. By 2002, many of these groups found themselves losing power and influence within the movement either due to civil litigation, law enforcement operations, or the death of a charismatic leader from natural causes. This led to organizational infighting among several large white supremacist groups such as the Aryan Nations (Hayden Lake, Idaho), the National Alliance (Marlinton, West Virginia), and the World Church of the Creator (Peoria, Illinois).

Due to a combination of ideological differences, losing an $8 million lawsuit, and the death of its leader, Aryan Nations split into five factions over the course of several years. Former Aryan Nations leaders started new groups such as the Church of True Israel (Noxon, Montana), the Church of the Sons of Yahweh (Calhoun, Alabama), the Tabernacle of the Phineas Priesthood (Lexington, South Carolina), and two groups in Idaho and Alabama that still used the name Aryan Nations.

A similar thing happened in 2002, with the death of William Pierce, the leader of the National Alliance. NA, which was one of the largest neo-Nazi groups in America at the time, experienced several offshoots as key leaders left to form their own neo-Nazi groups, including White Revolution, National Vanguard, and the North American Front. NA membership decreased dramatically during this time. However, on paper, it looked as if the neo-Nazi movement was growing with the formation of seven new groups.

The World Church of the Creator (WCOTC) lost a copyright infringement lawsuit, and its leader was arrested for plotting to murder the judge who had been overseeing the case. With their leader incarcerated, the group remains in a state of disarray and is still searching for a new successor. Many WCOTC members are still adhering to the group's ideology but have no spokesperson or group headquarters to provide strategic goals and objectives.

It is equally futile to attempt to measure extremist movement growth by tracking extremist-related criminal activity. Monitoring and recording such incidents can be quite useful but has limitations and flaws. For example, extremist-related criminal acts are often underreported, and many incidents are never reported in the media. Delays between carrying out the criminal acts, and when someone is arrested for the crime or is convicted of it, can range from a few months to several years. As a result, criminal activity, in and of itself, cannot be used exclusively to track changes in movement strength, group numbers, or membership totals. Furthermore, this method cannot be used to monitor growth and declines related to extremist movements or groups with a low association with criminal activity, such as many militia groups.

With all of this in mind, my team took an all-source analytical approach to our research, which meant that we gathered data from a variety of sources, including intelligence, law enforcement, and other government reporting. We also gathered data from nongovernment organizations, publicly available news sources, and Internet websites. This way, we could remain updated on many different issues from an assortment of sources. Hopefully, having multiple sources of information would help substantiate data and bolster any analytical hypotheses.

Our research on the DHS right-wing extremism report began as early as February 2007 when then-Senator Obama announced he was running for president. Between April 2007 and March 2008, we were gathering data on a variety of factors that would later paint a clearer picture that a renaissance in right-wing extremism activity was currently under way. The first indication was the posting of a few hundred paramilitary training and militia propaganda videos on the Internet.

In March 2007, Mark Koernke, a prominent militia figure in Michigan, was released from prison.[24,25] He had served nearly six years for assaulting a police officer.[26] In 2001, Koernke fled the scene of a bank robbery in Dexter, Michigan, and led police on a fifty-mile high-speed chase. He was convicted of assault with a deadly weapon, resisting and obstructing an officer, and fleeing a police officer.[27]

During the 1990s, Koernke was known on the antigovernment lecture circuit for his trainings on the "New World Order" and other antigovernment conspiracy theories. He also operated an hourlong shortwave radio program called "The Intelligence Report." Past news reporting about Koernke described him as a person "whose talk is so violent, they're shunned by even the most far-right citizens' militias."[28]

Within six weeks of Koernke's parole, his son, Edward (twenty-seven years old at the time), is believed to have started posting militia-oriented recruitment and paramilitary training videos on YouTube.[29] Edward is believed to have used the Internet moniker Liberty Tree Radio.[30] Ironically, Edward also created his Liberty Tree Radio YouTube channel on April 19, 2007[31]—a symbolic date for militia extremists. April 19 is the anniversary date for the Battle of Lexington and Concord (American Revolutionary War).[32] It also marks the anniversary of the end of the Branch Davidian siege in Waco, Texas and is the date of the Oklahoma City bombing.[33] For these reasons, this day takes on added significance to right-wing extremists.

The majority of militia training and recruitment videos began appearing online soon after Koernke's parole. Topics presented in the online videos included field medical training, fire and maneuver exercises, field craft, and how to operate various weapons. Propaganda pieces posted to Liberty Tree Radio's YouTube channel included aspirations to attack the United Nations and the federal government as well as depictions of the lynching of judges and other government officials.[34]

The posting of militia recruitment and paramilitary training videos on the Internet was concerning, and it corresponded with the beginnings of a resurgence in militia extremist activity in the United States.

It is no coincidence that new militia groups began forming around this time. Militia-related training announcements also began to increase. The announcements were calling for renewed paramilitary training activity and field training exercises (also called FTXs) to be held in various locations across the country.

Of very real concern to us, access to the knowledge of bomb making, weapons training, and tactics was becoming increasingly available online—unlike during the last surge of right-wing extremism in the 1990s. Access to this type of information would likely increase the competence and size of existing militia extremist groups and facilitate the growth of both existing and new groups. The existence of bomb-making instructions (including entire how-to explosives manuals) on the Internet could bolster militia groups' capabilities to harm or even kill perceived enemies.

Numerous other militia websites followed Liberty Tree Radio's lead and began posting their own paramilitary training videos. These videos often served as supplemental aids to militia FTXs, which take a great amount of energy to organize and carry out. These training videos had an advantage over FTXs in that they allowed individual militia members to gain knowledge of paramilitary training without having to actually attend an organized field event.[35]

According to several militia websites in 2007, the tactics and methods demonstrated in the paramilitary videos posted by other militia groups was instructive in building the competence of newer, fledgling groups by giving them inspiration and providing examples by which they could organize their own groups and implement FTXs.[36]

In the past, militia extremists have been known to use paramilitary training to prepare for encounters with law enforcement.[37] As a result, we were concerned that the dissemination of paramilitary training through online videos may increase the threat of violent confrontation during future encounters with law enforcement.

Other past incidents involving militia extremists plotting violent acts against law enforcement further amplified our concerns. Ironically, two of these incidents occurred in Michigan, in the same general area where the Koernkes operated.

In October 2003, Norman David Somerville, who was associated with the militia movement, was arrested on charges stemming from a plot to ambush police officers and emergency responders using a vehicle-mounted machine gun, antiaircraft gun, and numerous other weapons.[38]

Earlier that same year, Scott Allen Woodring shot and killed a Michigan State Police tactical officer as police were attempting to serve a search warrant at Woodring's residence on July 7, 2003.[39] Woodring had been a former chaplain in the Michigan Militia during the 1990s.[40] He was a practicing sovereign citizen at the time of the shooting.

Two years earlier, Steven Howard Anderson, a former militia member in Kentucky, opened fire on a police officer during a traffic stop.[41] Anderson had evaded capture for over a year. Subsequent police search of his home revealed several illegal weapons, two homemade bombs, and twenty-five fragmentation grenades.[42]

In March 2009, our team noticed that the number of militia training videos had made substantial gains in volume within the preceding two years.[43] In fact, by April 2009, we had identified over 262 paramilitary training videos posted by militia extremists.[44]

The posting of paramilitary training videos online was a significant development. These online videos were indicative of an emerging trend—increased militia extremist activity and proliferation of new militia groups. The possibility of third-party file sharing of these paramilitary training videos was also taken into consideration.

The broad, online dissemination of paramilitary training videos may have affected the recent resurgence of militia extremist activity in the United States. We assessed that the increase in online distribution of video training material—compared to the lack of such videos during the 1990s—would likely increase the propagation of paramilitary knowledge among militia extremists. We were concerned that the dissemination of paramilitary training videos could magnify the threat to law enforcement personnel by spreading intimate knowledge of combat expertise to individuals adhering to an extreme antigovernment ideology.

In early 2008, my team attempted to draft an intelligence report on the topic of militia training videos, but branch editors continually subjected it to editorial criticism and other comments suggesting this was not a Homeland Security concern. This draft report was never disseminated. Nevertheless, we found other uses for the data gathered from this project. Despite the setback, we continued to work with our state and local law enforcement contacts to evaluate the effects and possible increased threats associated with the increased posting of online paramilitary training videos.

I documented the formation of forty-five new antigovernment militia groups over a six-month period between October 2007 and March 2008. This was a highly unusual development, because before 2007, the militia movement group numbers had slowly been declining. This was the largest increase within fifteen years, and it occurred within a six-month time period. By July 2010, the number of known militia groups had exploded to at least 215 groups. According to the SPLC, the count included 330 militia groups in 2010.[45]

Another quantitative data set we considered were the numerous online threats against Obama that soon flooded the Internet. Two incidents leading up to the 2008 presidential election offer some insights into this emergent trend. On the night of June 2, 2008, Obama clinched the Democratic Party's nomination for the presidential election.[46] Within a few months, threats were aimed at killing Obama.

The Democratic National Convention was held during August 25–28, 2008, in Denver, Colorado. The night before the convention, two men driving a pickup truck were pulled over by local police for driving erratically.[47] Local law enforcement discovered the driver was operating a motor vehicle on a suspended license. The driver, Tharin Robert Gartrell, also had a small quantity of methamphetamine in his pants pocket. A search of the truck yielded a Ruger .22 bolt-action rifle with threaded barrel and scope mounted on it and a Remington .270 rifle, 40 rounds of ammunition, along with a bulletproof vest. A trace of both rifles' serial numbers indicated that the Ruger .22 rifle had been stolen in Kansas in 2005. Authorities also discovered what appeared to be a mobile meth lab in the backseat of the pick-up truck.[48]

During their investigation, authorities learned the vehicle was owned by Shawn Adolf, Gartrell's cousin, and later determined Adolf had several outstanding felony arrest warrants.[49] Investigators eventually discovered that Adolf was reportedly staying at the Denver Tech Center Hyatt Hotel in Aurora. When they arrived at the Hyatt hotel, they found a third individual, identified as Nathan Dwain Johnson, and a female subject in the room.[50] After receiving consent to search the hotel room, they discovered more methamphetamine in Johnson's pants pocket. While conducting a follow-up investigation, Johnson told the police that Adolf was staying at another hotel in the Glendale area.[51] As police attempted to contact Adolf at the Glendale hotel, Adolf broke a back window of their sixth-floor hotel room and jumped onto a roof of the hotel located a few levels below the window. Police converged on Adolf's whereabouts, and he was ultimately arrested. Investigators found more methamphetamine in Adolf's room.[52]

During an interview of an unnamed female, she stated that she had witnessed Adolf, Johnson, and Gartrell speaking negatively about Obama.[53] She further stated that she believed that Adolf, Johnson, and Gartrell were all "racists" and possibly associated with white supremacist groups.[54] She said that all three individuals were commenting on how Obama was a "nigger" and further stated they "could not believe how close he (Obama) was to becoming president," and that no "nigger" should ever live in the White House.[55] The female also stated that Adolf believed that Obama had a room on the third floor of the hotel they were staying in.[56] A thorough investigation determined there was no developed plot to kill Obama and no direct links to organized hate groups.[57] Two subjects were charged with possession of methamphetamine and a third charged with federal gun violations.[58]

The other threat case involving discussions to kill Barack Obama concerned two white supremacists who had met on a message board belonging to the neo-Nazi skinhead group Supreme White Alliance.[59]

On October 22, 2008, Daniel Cowart and Paul Schlesselman were taken into custody for plotting to rob a residence in Bells, Tennessee.[60] Cowart and Schlesselman had met on the Internet through a mutual friend. Both individuals claimed to have very strong beliefs and views regarding "White Power" and "Skinhead" causes.[61] Soon after meeting, they began discussing going on a "killing spree" that included killing eighty-eight people and beheading fourteen African-Americans.[62]

The numbers 88 and 14 have significance in the white supremacist movement. The number 88 stands for the "88 Precepts"—a white supremacist creed encompassing eighty-eight principles for living their lives. The "88 Precepts" is also an essay written by a notorious Order member (white supremacist terrorist cell), David Lane, while incarcerated in a federal penitentiary. Lane later died in prison on May 28, 2007.[63]

According to a criminal affidavit, Cowart and Schlesselman discussed robbing and burglarizing a federal firearms licensee to gather weapons and ammunition to be "more equipped" for their killing spree.[64] Schlesselman was later found in possession of an illegal sawed-off shotgun, which he said was modified to make it "easier to maneuver" during the "killing spree."[65] The two suspects further stated that their final act of violence would be an assassination attempt on presidential candidate Barack Obama.[66] They had even gone as far as decorating their car with neo-Nazi slogans like "14/88," "Sieg Heil," "Honk if you love Hitler," "WWHD (What Would Hitler Do)," and a swastika.

In between these two incidents (which were characterized by investigators as "talk" rather than actual plotting), Bill White, leader of the American National Socialist Workers Party based in Roanoke, Virginia, was making an appeal for donations on his website for a special issue of his group's *National Socialist* magazine.[67]

White posted on his website an image of the proposed magazine cover. The cover featured a picture of Barack Obama waving to a crowd of supporters that was taken at his February 2007 rally in Springfield, Illinois.[68] A circular symbol resembling the crosshairs of a sniper rifle scope was superimposed over Obama's head. A headline in huge red print stated "Kill This NIGGER!"[69]

White was hoping to debut this special edition of his magazine just in time for the presidential election in November 2008. Fortunately, he did not receive enough money to print the magazine in its entirety, but he was able to release a mini-version of it anyway.

There were many other threats to Obama leading up to the 2008 presidential election. Many of these threats were made on the Internet from blog posts, chat rooms, and online forums. Unfortunately, many were untraceable and lacked firm information upon which investigators could follow up. Whenever we stumbled across a threat to Obama, we always referred it to both the Secret Service and U.S. Capitol Police. Some of the online threats we discovered included the following:

On February 15, 2008, an anonymous person posted on a blog, "The KKK or someone WILL assassinate Obama! If we get a NIGGER President all you NIG-GERs will think you've won and that the WHITE people will have to bow to you. OBAMA WILL DIE, KKK FOREVER!"[70]

On April 22, 2008, an anonymous individual posted a threat to Barack Obama to the SPLC's *Hatewatch* blog: "ATTENTION, IF OBAMA BECOMES PRESED-ANT [sic] I WILL KILL HIM MYSELF MAKE NO MISTAKE ABOUT IT."[71]

On January 31, 2009, an anonymous individual using the moniker "Heil Hitler" posted another threat to the SPLC's *Hatewatch* blog: "I WILL KILL OBAMA NIGGA. HEIL HITLER!!!! DEATH TO JEWSSSSSSS AND NIGGAS!!!"[72]

Some months earlier, during an interview with Fox News–Chicago in May 2007, Railton Loy, Grand Wizard of the National Knights of the Ku Klux Klan based in Osceola, Indiana, made one of the first known references to assassinating Barack Obama.

"I'm not going to have to worry about him, because somebody else down south is going to take him out," said Loy. "If that man is elected president, he'll be shot sure as hell. The hate would be so deep down south."[73]

Again, these were just a few examples of the types of threats presidential candidate Obama was receiving during his campaign in 2007 and 2008. He continued receiving similar threats in 2009 and 2010.

My team also observed a dramatic increase in the number of Stormfront members. Stormfront is the oldest and largest white supremacist site on the Internet.[74] This became yet another data point indicating a rise in right-wing extremism.

During 2008, Stormfront added 20,469 new users, which was within the expected range of new memberships for previous years.[75] However, within the first three months of 2009, Stormfront eclipsed this number by adding 32,359 new users.[76] Total Stormfront membership nearly doubled in two years, growing from 99,548 members (noted in January 2007) to 164,991 members by April 2009 (the month of the report's release).[77] Furthermore, Stormfront added over 2,000 new members in just a single day on November 5, 2008—the day immediately following the 2008 presidential election.[78]

Another source that pointed to a rise in right-wing extremism was the comprehensive listing of hate-oriented websites published every year.

Since 1996, Raymond A. Franklin has published an annual listing of hate-oriented websites, forums, list servers, and other forms of new electronic media.[79,80,81] Franklin's publication, called the Hate Directory, has grown into a 175-page document, making it the most complete listing available of hate-oriented Internet use.[82] Its ever-expanding list of hate websites now encompasses bias-oriented video games, Internet service providers, newsgroups, mailing lists, and web rings.[83]

Franklin himself determines which Internet sites to include in the Hate Directory. His decision is based on whether a group or individual "advocates violence against, separation from, defamation of, deception about, or hostility toward others based upon race, religion, ethnicity, gender or sexual orientation."[84] The Hate Directory is updated throughout the year and is distributed to law enforcement communities and civil rights organizations throughout the world.[85]

Since the Hate Directory encompassed all forms of hate-oriented use of the Internet, I used it to analyze the specific number of white supremacist–affiliated sites, particularly those associated with the KKK and neo-Nazi groups.

A review of KKK websites listed in the Hate Directory between 2006 and 2010 shows a noticeable increase in 2007 and again in 2009. Both of these years correlate to significant events related to Obama's political campaign for president.

In February 2007, Obama announced his intent to run for president. This announcement coincided with a 7.5 percent increase in the number of KKK-related Internet sites.[86] This only includes websites linked to active KKK groups operating within the United States.

Similarly, in 2009, when Obama was sworn in as the forty-fourth president of the United States, there was a 6.25 percent increase in the number of KKK sites online.[87]

It is also interesting to note that twelve KKK groups experienced an expanding web presence during 2007.[88] A review of those new KKK websites revealed that some groups formed new chapters in various states as well as constructed new websites specifically focused on their women and children auxiliaries.

Validating all of the data we collected, the SPLC released its 2008 hate group numbers in March 2009. The SPLC's annual "Year in Hate" report was released just a few weeks ahead of the DHS right-wing extremism report.

In its 2009 "Year in Hate" document, the SPLC reported that the number of active hate groups had increased during 2008 from 888 groups to 926—a rise of more than 4 percent in one year.[89] The same report noted a 50 percent increase in the number of hate groups since 2000.[90]

Although DHS did not consider some of the groups listed in the Southern Poverty Law Center's report as violent extremist groups, the SPLC's group count gave support to what we were seeing through our open-source collection efforts and law enforcement reporting.

Experts who monitor domestic terrorism know that extremist movements, groups, and individuals are influenced by controversial, often polarizing, national issues. Historically, right-wing extremists have taken strong stances on the issues of gun control, the right to life (abortion debate), same-sex marriage, and multiculturalism, among a host of other national issues. The debate surrounding the topic of illegal immigration appears to have trumped all other national issues for right-wing extremists today.[91,92,93] For the white supremacist movement, this is not a new or emerging issue.

Historians have noted a strong correlation between large migrations of foreigners to the United States and increased acts of violence against immigrants. For example, riots and violence erupted in Philadelphia in the mid-1800s following a large influx of Irish Catholic immigrants.[94] The KKK peaked in the 1920s with approximately five million members, at the time lessening its focus on African-Americans and shifting its attention to Catholic and Jewish immigrants.[95] In Texas, during the 1980s, a Klan group systematically harassed and attacked Vietnamese fishermen in an effort to put them out of business and drive them from the town.[96]

In 2008, my team published an intelligence assessment highlighting the trend of white supremacist groups accelerating the level of their proselytizing and protest activity to focus on the anti-immigration debate.[97] We noted that KKK factions and neo-Nazi groups have engaged in a noticeable increase in activity such as cross burnings, racist Internet postings, leafleting campaigns, rallies, unity and social gatherings, and violent video games as they exploit community fears and frustration over what they describe as an "immigration explosion." The research for this project provided more data that supported a rise in right-wing extremist activity.

Historically, white supremacist rallies attracted around fifteen to twenty participants. During 2006 and 2007, however, several rallies that focused on anti-immigration had at least fifty participants, and one even attracted approximately 200 demonstrators, according to media reporting.[98,99,100,101,102,103,104]

In addition, we observed an expansion of the locations where white supremacists have sponsored anti-immigration protests. Our review of open-source information revealed that during the previous five years, the majority of anti-immigration demonstrations by white supremacists occurred in states on the U.S.–Mexican border, such as California and Texas. During the same period, right-wing extremists hosted anti-immigration protests in at least twenty-eight states, indicating that the immigration debate had spread beyond the border states to other areas of the country.

White supremacists and other right-wing extremist organizations were playing upon societal frustration related to the immigration debate to recruit new members. Of particular concern, several new Klan groups had emerged and were expanding into other areas of the country.

An Imperial Wizard of the North Carolina–based Cleveland Knights of the Ku Klux Klan stated that his group was gaining members because people who would not normally consider joining were signing up out of frustration over illegal immigration, according to an online media interview.[105] The Empire Knights of the Ku Klux Klan, established in Florida in 2005, had expanded to eighteen states by January 2007.[106] KKK-affiliated groups were also spreading to areas of the country that historically had not experienced much Klan activity. For example, the Brotherhood of Klans group claimed to have established chapters in areas of Iowa that have had a large influx of Mexican immigrants.[107]

White supremacist groups appeared to be recruiting the more extremist members of community and mainstream groups who are energized to take stands against illegal immigration. According to media reports at the time, law enforcement officials expressed concern that some anti-immigration extremists might be susceptible to recruitment by more hard-core racist groups such as the KKK and inclined toward violence.[108] Media reports indicated several incidents of white supremacists attending events in 2007 organized by mainstream anti-immigration groups.[109]

On September 16, 2007, nine racist skinheads attempted to join a protest hosted by a mainstream, anti–illegal immigration group in Simi Valley, California.[110]

On August 25, 2007, members of an identified neo-Nazi group planned to attend an event put on by a mainstream, anti–illegal immigration group in Crystal Lake, Illinois.[111]

And on July 21, 2007, members of a different identified neo-Nazi group attended a rally in Maryland hosted by a mainstream anti–illegal immigration group.[112]

An internal survey of extremist right-wing websites during 2007 and 2008 indicated that white supremacists are using the Internet heavily in their campaign against immigration. The Internet provides a multifaceted venue for radicalization and recruitment that has long been exploited by many types of extremists. White supremacists began using the Internet to recruit in the mid-1990s, according to the ADL, and thousands of racist blogs, forums, and websites now exist.[113] Many are incorporating anti-immigration rhetoric created by the owners of websites and comments posted by website users.

We had also noticed that immigration was a prevalent topic on Stormfront. As of January 2008, hundreds of member-generated posts contained the word "Mexican" in disparaging messages. User-generated posts with derogatory terms for Hispanics occurred even more frequently.[114]

A review of the National Alliance website, belonging to one of the largest neo-Nazi groups in the country, noted numerous articles in its immigration section, including "20 Questions for Congress about Immigration," "The End of the World as We Know It," and "Whose Country Is It, Anyway?"[115]

KKK groups were also turning their websites' attention to the hot topic of illegal immigration. The largest Klan group in the United States had several articles and political cartoons related to immigration on its website.

Right-wing extremists were using the Internet to promote racist music and video games critical of immigrants; they posted video clips from anti-immigration rallies as well as cartoons, pictures, and songs with anti-immigration messages.[116] Music, video games, and websites are especially successful propaganda tools for recruiting youths into the white supremacist movement.[117,118]

A white supremacist band based in North Carolina attracted a following, in part, through anti-immigration songs such as "Our Land, Not Your Land."[119] This song is the background music to at least one anti-immigration video available on YouTube.[120] Furthermore, the band's CD, unlike the majority of white power music, is available through a mainstream music download company, thus providing the band with credibility and exposure.[121]

A white supremacist addressed the immigration issue by creating the interactive game *Border Patrol*. The object of this free video game is to shoot racist caricatures of Mexicans as they attempt to cross the U.S. border.[122]

Since at least 2003, white supremacists and other extremist anti-immigration groups were reportedly targeting minority individuals, especially Hispanics, for violent attacks. They were not concerned about whether their victims were in the

United States legally. A review of crime statistics for the United States indicated that the number of hate crimes against Hispanics has risen especially rapidly in areas experiencing a significant influx of immigrants from Mexico and Central and South American countries. According to FBI data, hate crimes nationwide against Hispanics rose by 35 percent from 2003 to 2006, the last year for which comparable data has been compiled.[123] A report from the Los Angeles Human Relations Commission indicates that hate crimes against Hispanics in Los Angeles County doubled from 2003 to 2007.[124] And, in November 2011, the FBI released its annual report on hate crimes in the United States for 2010.

"Hate crimes motivated by the offender's bias toward a particular ethnicity/national origin were directed at 1,222 victims," the FBI report read.[125] It is important to note, however, that this particular category of victims is separate and distinct from those based on race, religion, or sexual orientation.

"Of these victims, 66.6 percent were targeted because of an anti-Hispanic bias," it read.[126] The remaining 33.4 percent of incidents reported under this category covered all other types of ethnic and national groups combined.

This growing trend of anti-Hispanic hate crime is exemplified in the 2010 murder of Juan Varela, a second-generation Latino-American, who was gunned down by his neighbor Gary Thomas Kelly. Kelly reportedly shouted to Varela, "Hurry up and go back to Mexico, or you're going to die," moments before he killed him.[127]

Law enforcement data passed to my team had taught us that affiliation with an organized white supremacist group is not necessarily a prerequisite for carrying out violent racially motivated attacks. In contrast, many racially motivated attacks involved individuals who espoused a white supremacist ideology with no particular group affiliation. We learned that such attacks by white supremacists were generally spontaneous—often targets of opportunity. Typically, multiple white supremacists are involved in unprovoked attacks on a minority victim. Only rarely have organized groups openly called for assaults or attacks; smaller white supremacist or militia groups, which more closely resemble a leaderless resistance concept, are more likely to plot an attack in advance.

Right-wing extremists had already planned and committed numerous violent attacks against Hispanics in several states. Open-source reporting indicated that members of Aryan Nations and the Imperial Klans of America were arrested for allegedly assaulting Hispanics during 2007.[128,129,130] In addition, two unaffiliated racist skinheads attacked and tortured a Hispanic teenager in Texas in 2006.[131] Around this time, a few right-wing extremist radio shows had also endorsed violence against political figures who support amnesty for illegal immigrants.[132,133]

Furthermore, law enforcement authorities had previously disrupted plots that could have resulted in multiple deaths and incited acts of retaliation or a broader immigration backlash.

In November 2005, a former White Knights of the Ku Klux Klan member was sentenced to fourteen years in prison after he constructed five pipe bombs for an attack against a bus carrying Mexican farm workers.[134,135]

Also, a member of the Central Wyoming Militia was arrested in February 2007 after communicating his plans to travel to the Mexican border to kill immigrants crossing into the United States.[136]

In April 2007, federal law enforcement authorities arrested six members of the Alabama Free Militia for various firearms and explosives violations. The federal investigation reportedly stemmed from a plot in which militia members allegedly discussed and conducted reconnaissance for a machine gun attack on Hispanics.[137,138]

Over the past several years, right-wing extremists have continued to use the immigration debate as a rallying point and recruitment focus because it remains an issue to the U.S. public. Mounting frustration over a perceived lack of government action concerning illegal immigration has the potential to facilitate individuals or small groups toward violence in the future. If violent acts occur, they will likely be isolated, small-scale attacks directed at specific immigration-related targets, such as a Hispanic community center or foreign consulate of Latin American countries.

I made use of multiple sources to form the judgment that right-wing extremism was on the rise in the United States. And I applied this same principle to determine that a small percentage of military personnel were being targeted for recruitment by right-wing extremists. Not only was this statement based on my experience while employed in the U.S. Army as an intelligence analyst that worked CONUS force protection issues, but there were other reliable sources of information that came to this same conclusion.

In November 2007 the National Socialist Movement (NSM) Commander sent an e-mail to the group's Yahoo! mailing list claiming, "NSM Colorado is now being led by a man just back from the war in Afghanistan. *As our Military vets come home from the fight, they are forming up new NSM Chapters* [emphasis added]."[139]

In September 2008, an unidentified KKK member named "Eric" posted a message on a message board maintained by White Revolution that exhorted neo-Nazis to *"recruit Veterans, they have been 'down that road' that many of you have not . . . They can be a valuable asset to any militia group."*[140]

A subsequent posting to the White Revolution forum by an individual named "JoeMayhem" of the Southern California Militia asserted that they soon *"will be looking to expand to others with military experience, and then forward."*[141]

In March 2009, the World Knights of the Ku Klux Klan announced on its website that they were creating a new unit within their organization called the Military Division. The announcement read, "This is the Klavalier (military) Division of the World Knights of the Ku Klux Klan, to be accepted into this very elite division, you must meet all the requirements below before being accepted or even an application be considered with the Klavalier division of the World Knights of the Ku Klux Klan."[142] Membership requirements included being a member of the World Knights as well as having "some military knowledge or skills or willingness to learn. If klaiming [sic] in military or ever been in any military branch you must show proof of these klaims [sic]."[143] Other membership requirements included being physically fit, able to follow orders from higher-ranking officers, able to fire and clean a firearm, and able to learn survival skills.[144]

Another example included remarks by a member of the NSM. "Party members will have ranks and uniforms . . . Most of our members have military backgrounds and other things I can't go into right now."[145]

In addition to the many statements concerning recruiting veterans into white supremacist organizations, there were also examples of current or former military personnel who embraced white supremacy and plotted to carry out acts of violence during the months leading up to the release of the DHS right-wing extremism report.

The March 24, 2009, issue of the *Marine Corps News* cited an incident in which a Marine was charged in connection with a plot to kill President Obama. He possessed a large cache of white supremacist material.[146]

On April 4, 2009, an individual reportedly influenced by racist ideology shot four police officers (killing three) in Pittsburgh, Pennsylvania. The suspect had recently been discharged from the U.S. Marine Corps for assaulting a drill instructor.[147]

White supremacists are not the only right-wing extremists who target members of the military for recruitment. Militia members are also known to recruit military personnel and war veterans. In fact, the militia movement perhaps may recruit more military members and war veterans than any other type of right-wing extremist group. This makes sense given the militia movement's adherence to a military-type organization (squad, battalion, division, etc.) and rank structure (sergeant, lieutenant, major, commander, etc.). Some recent examples include various statements made on various militia-focused Internet forums.

The most popular of militia-oriented public forums is "A Well Regulated Militia" or AWRM. AWRM has a section of its website devoted to military members (including veterans). The forum is called the Veteran's Forum.[148]

During the 2008 Memorial Day weekend, a person using the Internet moniker "Arty" posted an interesting message in AWRM's Veteran's Forum. The message was titled "Attention All Vets!"[149]

"We all took an oath to support and defend the Constitution of the United States against all enemies foreign and domestic," a person using the name Arty says. "As we all know, our country is so damn far from the Constitutional principles outlined. How to fix this from a vet's angle?"[150]

He further states, "Join veteran's groups, such as American Legion, V.F.W., DAV, etc. . . . The American Legion's Preamble reaffirms that oath to the Constitution."[151]

"Without all the talk of NWO, elite, etc. . . . begin serious discussions one on one with the folks there. Recruit the younger vets of more recent wars, such as Desert Storm, Somalia, Global War on Terror, and so on. Get them involved in discussions of how our country has strayed. Folks from all walks of life can relate to government's increasing control in our lives" he says.[152]

"Once you have generated some interest, begin to move towards getting folks to work at the state level (the state politicians really listen to veteran's groups) to pressure politicians to return to Constitutional principles."[153]

"Once the vet groups are thinking in the right lines, if the political solution fails, we would have a potential recruitment base for the militia."[154]

A sovereign citizen group called the Republic of Florida used an American Legion hall in Rockledge, Florida, to elect their own governor and organize their own "common law" court.[155] Imagine the audacity of these sovereign citizens who used a facility built for the social activities of war veterans to plot and organize extremist group meetings and to discuss how to undermine the U.S. government through the establishment of a shadow government. It is also really disturbing to think that the American Legion actually sanctioned this type of behavior by allowing a group of eighty sovereign citizens to gather at their meeting hall in Rockledge.[156]

There were many other statements by militia forum members that caught my interest.

On July 15, 2009, another AWRM member posted an announcement concerning his newly created militia group, "The 47 WOLFPACK is already a militia MC [i.e., motorcycle club]—all ex-military."[157]

On July 30, 2008, [Au: Should this be 2009? Chronology is lost here.] another AWRM member using the moniker SRT Lone Wolf posted a message about a newly formed militia group. He describes his group, stating, "We are a small unit (calling ourselves a SFG) that is located in northern central NJ. Although we have two members as far away as MD, we are always seeking new members and would love to have you aboard the team. Right now all of us are vets and one of us is currently U.S. Army reserve."[158]

On January 19, 2009, a member of a militia forum using the online screen name "Wolf Pack Medic" sent out an invitation to other militia members to join his group in an upcoming Field Training Exercise (FTx) in Maryland. In his message, he states, "All of our instructors are ex active military, and PMCs and two special operations guys. This is our first official FTX so please come out and join us."[159]

Indications of militia recruitment of veterans came from other websites besides the AWRM forum.

As part of its public debut, the Idaho Citizens Constitutional Militia's commanding officer posted a recruitment announcement on the group's website, stating, "Those former members of the military, I will expect your assistance in establishing, modeling, and enforcing these standards for those who have never served in the armed forces."

He goes on to say, "I seek to recruit only those who are seriously minded about forging a formidable civil defense force and will accept nothing less than the same excellence required of our members of the armed forces."[160]

On January 29, 2009, a new Kentucky militia group calling itself the 105th Blue Guard placed the following recruitment message on its public website: "We need you! The N. KY. Militia is currently recruiting enlisted personnel and appointing officers. If you are 17-65, we can use you just e-mail us. We need leaders. If you have military exp. or law enforcement, the 105th is the place for you."[161]

Other sources of information pertaining to right-wing extremist recruitment of military personnel included official law enforcement reporting.

A primary law enforcement source was an FBI Assessment, dated 7 July 2008, titled "White Supremacist Recruitment of Military Personnel Since 9/11."[162] This assessment, which can be found on the Internet, cites numerous examples of military servicemen currently affiliating with white supremacist groups, as well as espousing the racist tenets of white supremacy. It also indicated that white supremacists intend to recruit military personnel—including those returning from the wars in Afghanistan and Iraq.[163]

The FBI assessment identified 203 individuals with confirmed or claimed military service active in the white supremacist movement.[164] These 203 individuals had reportedly affiliated with a variety of neo-Nazi groups, racist skinheads, and KKK organizations. It is important to note that this number only reflects those individuals who are the subject of an FBI case. In addition, this number does not include military personnel affiliating with other right-wing extremist groups, such as antigovernment militias or sovereign citizen groups.

Open-source, FBI, and other law enforcement reporting for 2007 through 2009 indicated that white supremacists with military experience frequently have higher profiles in the white supremacist movement—including serving in leadership positions.

The current NSM state leader for Oregon was formerly enlisted with the Oregon Army National Guard.[165]

FBI's Montana Joint Terrorism Task Force (JTTF) reported in January 2006 that the leader of the NSM chapter in Butte, Montana, claimed to have served in Iraq with the U.S. Marine Corps.[166]

According to corroborated source reporting from FBI, a U.S. Marine Corps officer expressed interest in starting a new unit in California for the NSM upon his return from Iraq.[167]

Another source of law enforcement reporting came from the U.S. Army's Anti-Terrorism Intelligence and Operations Cell (ATOIC) at the Pentagon. The message was likely written by an Army Criminal Investigation Command desk officer assigned to the ATOIC.

In an unclassified message sent to federal, state, and local law enforcement on January 22, 2009, the ATOIC message reads, "Recent Internet postings continue to indicate that members of extremist groups are joining the military, possibly in order to gain expertise in weapons and bomb making training."[168]

The message further states that "Some reports indicate these individuals are enlisting easily due to the Department of Defense's struggle to maintain recruitment in the time of an unpopular war. Additionally, neo-Nazi groups are encouraging members with clean records and no tattoos to infiltrate the military to receive training to benefit the group."[169]

"Currently, 46 members of a white supremacist social network site identify themselves as active military personnel," it read.[170]

The ATOIC message also commented that the presence of white nationalist extremists in the military had recently gained federal authorities' attention. The ATOIC remarked that "extremist groups and street gangs continue to recruit those in the military and former military members due to knowledge of weapons and lack of a criminal history."[171]

"This information is provided for your situational awareness," the message concludes.[172]

Three PowerPoint presentations obtained from U.S. Army trainings were used as background material for this judgment. They were downloaded from military-related websites. The titles of the presentations include: *Tactics, Techniques, and Practices: 'Keeping Us Ready & Relevant—Soldiers First'—Extremism* (NATO website); *Extremist Organizations* (2nd Battalion, 46th Infantry Regiment); and *Criminal Street Gangs in the "Military"* (Kenneth F. Kelly, a retired chief investigator and security threat group advisor for the United States Army in Europe). These presentations were used as training tools for military personnel and commanders at all levels to educate military personnel on the issue of gang members and extremists in the military.

The fact that white supremacists and militia extremists are known to recruit military personnel and war veterans was also reported by the SPLC and ADL on more than one occasion prior to 2009.

In an article titled "Evidence of Extremist Infiltration of the Military Grows," released in August 2008, the SPLC reported that the founder of the White Military Men website identified himself in his New Saxon account as "Lance Corporal Burton" of the 2nd Battalion Fox Company Pit 2097, from Florida, according to a master's thesis by graduate student Matthew Kennard. Under his "About Me" section, Burton wrote: "Love to shoot my M16A2 service rifle effectively at the Hachies (Iraqis)," and "Love to watch things blow up (Hachies House)."[173]

The SPLC article also noted in the same article that a Blood and Honour member—who claimed to be an active-duty soldier taking part in combat operations in Iraq—identified himself to Kennard as Jacob Berg. "There are actually a lot more 'skinheads,' 'nazis,' white supremacists now [in the military] than there has been in a long time," Berg wrote in an e-mail exchange with Kennard.[174]

"Us racists are actually getting into the military a lot now because if we don't everyone who already is [in the military] will take pity on killing sand niggers," Berg said. "Yes I have killed women, yes I have killed children and yes I have killed older people. But the biggest reason I'm so proud of my kills is because by killing a brown many white people will live to see a new dawn."[175]

I felt assured that the unique combination of social, political, and environmental factors in the United States such as the 2008 presidential election, economic downturn and resulting recession, a prolonged housing crisis with increased home foreclosures, the unresolved illegal immigration debate, and returning military veterans suffering from posttraumatic stress disorder and a stagnant economy would definitely feed into a likely resurgence. There were also rumors circulating on the Internet about the year 2012. The lunatic fringe was already speculating an impending societal collapse, the Apocalypse or other "end of the world" event looming in the not too distant future. This reminded me of the same fearful and paranoid rhetoric that preceded the Y2K hype that gave birth to so many preparedness expos and extremist stockpiling activities.

It was around this time of rebuilding the domestic terrorism team that I was asked to present a briefing to the DHS Radicalization and Extremism Working Group (REWG). The REWG was stood up to facilitate discussion about radicalization, to educate and share information with representatives from other departmental agencies. The working group was chaired by the director of the DHS Office of Civil Rights and Civil Liberties (CRCL). At the time, CRCL was a collaborative body that was interested in working with other organizations like I&A to develop strategies, seek guidance, and foster outreach efforts with various ethnic and religious communities such as the Muslim, Jewish, and Christian sects. A few of my colleagues had previously been invited to give presentations on a variety of extremist- and radicalization-related topics. All of them, however, had focused on either foreign adversarial influence inside the United States or abroad. No one had ever educated the working group on purely domestic extremism and radicalization issues.

On Tuesday, March 14, 2008, I was invited to present a briefing on the topic of domestic animal rights extremism and ecoterrorism for the REWG. The briefing was held at the Nebraska Avenue Complex, Building 1. I discussed the types of ecoterrorist and animal rights extremist causes, their operational capabilities, recruitment tactics, and radicalization influences. I also highlighted the recent arrests of multiple members of the ALF and ELF during 2007–2008 as part of Operation Backfire. The briefing was well received and stimulated considerable discussion among REWG members. As a result, I was invited back the following month to give another briefing. This time, the REWG wanted to know more about white supremacist and militia extremist activities and radicalization.

On Tuesday, April 22, 2008, I presented the briefing on domestic right-wing extremist groups. I elaborated on the three primary types of right-wing extremists (white supremacists, militia extremists, and sovereign citizens), their affinity for firearms and explosives, and the right-wing extremist phenomena of insular communities (fortified or remote compounds) in the United States. I also discussed right-wing extremist recruitment tactics and radicalization influences. I concluded my presentation with a single slide depicting the convergence of potentially volatile factors that may indicate a future rise in right-wing extremism in the country. Again, the briefing was very well received and stimulated considerable discussion among REWG members.

Based largely on REWG feedback and direction from my division director, I requested a subordinate analyst to begin compiling the research we had gathered concerning the previously identified social, political, and environmental factors and their potential impact on increasing right-wing extremist activity. We named the project "The Gathering Storm." This would later become the DHS right-wing extremism report.

Our research on this subject continued from May 2008 through the end of that year. It was not a primary area of emphasis but considered more of an ancillary duty. As we found more data that either validated or refuted the hypothesis, we would save it in the project folder. Also, during this time period, we incorporated this hypothesis into various federal, state, and local law enforcement training sessions, conferences, and seminars. One such event involved my participation in a domestic extremism working group in the Midwest.

During August 5–8, 2008, I traveled to Springfield, Illinois, to meet with analytical counterparts from the Illinois State Police, Missouri State Highway Patrol, FBI, Chicago Police Department, and other law enforcement agencies in Missouri and Illinois. The meeting's purpose was to form a working group to take an in-depth look at domestic extremist activity occurring in both states to see if there were any interstate activities of concern or transient extremist networks. Over a three-day period, we held various meetings in a conference room at the Statewide Terrorism Intelligence Center.

The Missouri-Illinois Domestic Extremism Working Group came up with several key findings. As of 2008–2009, National Socialists, KKK, and Christian Identity adherents were present and active in both states, but not known to be engaging in any ideologically based criminal activity. White supremacists in Chicago, however, had engaged in recent criminal activity. Nevertheless, the region had a rich history of white supremacist criminal and terrorist-related activity.

Militia members were present and organizing in Missouri, but not Illinois. Militia members in Missouri and Illinois had been convicted of various firearms and explosives violations in the past. Militia members in both states have also been known to threaten law enforcement and government officials. In addition, militia members in Missouri had been convicted of plotting terrorist-related activity during the late 1990s. We observed that new militia groups had recently formed in Missouri and later in Illinois during the course of this project.

Sovereign citizens had engaged in recent white-collar criminal activity in Missouri and posed a potential threat to law enforcement officers. Some sovereign citizen groups in Missouri had organized and were actively recruiting. In contrast, sovereign citizens in Illinois were more loosely organized and did not appear to have very many followers.

At the time the working group convened, there were reported increases in firearms purchases throughout Missouri. People were stockpiling weapons and ammunition. Fear of more restrictive gun laws, change in national political leadership, ammunition shortages, and perceived government corruption were believed to be driving this trend. In contrast, Illinois had not experienced this type of activity.

Similar to other areas of the country, white supremacists in Missouri and Illinois were using the issue of illegal immigration to recruit new members and to further their cause. Both states had experienced anti-immigration rallies that involved the participation of white supremacists and antigovernment extremists. Similarly, white supremacists in Missouri and Illinois were also reportedly using the nomination of a liberal African-American presidential candidate for recruitment purposes. These observations were based on Internet chatter from known extremists in both states as well as reports of white supremacist literature distribution, extremist rallies, and other extremist-related events.

We held subsequent meetings in Jefferson City, Missouri, in September and Chicago, Illinois, the following month. At these meetings, working group members reported their findings, shared information, and contributed to the group's ongoing discussion. As each working group session adjourned, assignments were made to each member of the working group with the intent to report back to the group at the next scheduled meeting. Our goal was to produce a multiagency, collaborative product addressing the various observations we had made at previous meetings. I volunteered to compile the raw material into a finished intelligence assessment.

Due to other work-related demands and projects, it took several weeks to produce a final draft. Finally, in January 2009, I presented the final draft to the working group members for review, revision, and interagency coordination. Unfortunately, some of the information had to be pulled out due to ongoing investigative activity. Decision makers at the various agencies then began to weigh in on the product, and the document began to be held up in legal review. The information slowly started to get out of date. Ultimately, a legal conflict developed over the types of information law enforcement could collect, retain, and disseminate versus the type of information the intelligence community was authorized to handle related to U.S. person information. Since I&A is a member of the intelligence community, the organization decided to withdraw its agency seal from the document because there was too much U.S. person data contained within the draft report. Other agencies followed suit due to ongoing sensitive investigative activities. The report was never published.

Another event occurred in the weeks following the presidential election. On November 24, 2008, my team had one of our regular meetings with the FBI's Domestic Terrorism Analytical Unit (DTAU). The meeting was held at FBI headquarters in Washington, D.C. Among several items of business was a discussion about the recent election of Barack Obama as the forty-fourth president of the United States as well as the economic recession. We had met with DTAU analysts about a month earlier and had discussed the same subject. However, this time it was more meaningful because the election results were in and Barack Obama had indeed been elected president of the United States. It was no longer conjecture. At this meeting, we discussed the possibility of writing a joint product between the FBI and DHS concerning the economic and political climate fueling a rise in right-wing extremist recruitment and radicalization. I was hesitant to pursue a joint product with the FBI because my team had already invested so much time and effort into researching the "Gathering Storm" project. We concluded the meeting with no formal agreement to write a joint product and without any arrangements to pursue this joint endeavor.

Soon after our meeting with the FBI, I directed a fellow team member to begin writing a draft report on this topic in early December 2008. As the draft was being written, we continued to monitor various sources of reporting for additional data regarding social, political, and environmental factors impacting right-wing extremist growth in the United States between January and March 2009.

With the presidential inauguration underway, change was in the air once again at I&A. Along with changes in new presidential administrations, there comes an adjustment at most agencies within the federal government. Departmental executives, who are often political appointees, leave and new leadership takes their place.

Within I&A, many were hopeful that this change would finally facilitate Connell's long-anticipated departure. Amazingly, as Allen submitted his resignation, there were still rumors circulating that Connell was going to be the next undersecretary for I&A or that she would serve as the acting undersecretary for an indefinite period of time. Anticipating a likely change in presidential administration, Secretary Chertoff had already appointed Roger P. Mackin as the principal deputy undersecretary for I&A on September 10, 2009—almost two months prior to Election Day.

Mackin ultimately became the acting undersecretary for I&A when Allen submitted his resignation on January 20, 2009. Among his first actions as acting undersecretary, Mackin announced the departure of Connell.

Under Mackin's leadership, I&A's production process was changed. In an e-mail broadcast to the entire I&A workforce in January 2009, Mackin delegated release authority for finished intelligence products to division directors. This was done in an effort to relieve the "logjam" of products that had accumulated on Connell's desk for the past several months.

10

Four Questions

I arrived in Missouri Monday afternoon, March 9, 2009, and took a shuttle from the airport to my hotel room in downtown Kansas City. By evening, the cloudy, warm day had given way to a ferocious thunderstorm that rolled in from the west, unleashing a torrential downpour of rain, fierce lightning, and blustery winds. It made for a miserable walk to the Power and Light district for my evening dinner. Overnight, I had a hard time sleeping due to the constant clap of thunder and intermittent flashes of lightning. By early morning the storm had ceased. The sun was shining and inviting. It gave no hint to the drastic changes that had occurred outside overnight.

Little did I realize at the time that this wrath of nature was symbolic of another fierce storm waiting on the horizon. Much like the "Gathering Storm" project I had been involved with over the past year and a half, this storm was also a metaphoric one—a political storm that would have a chilling effect on the entire fusion center program. The "political storm" awaiting us was created from the ashes of a heated nationwide election that took control away from the Republican Party, who had conceded multiple congressional seats, as well as the White House, to the Democrats. Much like the storm that overtook Kansas City that March evening, this storm would bring "chilling" relations between the Democrats and Republicans.

The Missouri Information Analysis Center, otherwise known as the MIAC, had disseminated a report on the modern-day militia movement in February 2009.[1] It was one of many reports produced by the Missouri fusion center in a given year on a variety of law enforcement subjects. Further, this particular MIAC report was one of dozens produced by the nationwide fusion center network concerning domestic extremist activity in the United States. Under the leadership of Van Godsey, the MIAC had a reputation of being "one of the best fusion centers" in operation. For many, this report would not be a reflection of the MIAC's standard of excellence.

I quickly showered, put on my suit coat, and headed out the door for the three-block walk to the venue site at the Marriott Hotel and Convention Center located on Twelfth Street in downtown Kansas City. I was in town to attend the 2009 National Fusion Center Conference. Several Office of Intelligence and Analysis (I&A) employees had been invited to represent the office at the conference as well as take turns staffing a brand new forty-foot-long exhibit depicting the work of I&A.

Close to 1,000 representatives from various federal, state, and local government agencies attended the third annual National Fusion Center Conference, which was held on March 10–12, 2009.[2] Most attendees were involved with DHS or its state fusion center program. Many others, however, were representatives from various law enforcement and government agencies around the country as well as the media.

The 9/11 Act of 2007 recommended the establishment of a fusion center network.[3] Fusion centers are multiagency facilities staffed by representatives from state agencies or major urban governments. Fusion centers were recommended as the best way for federal, state, local, and tribal governments to share information and intelligence about a wide range of threats including terrorism, criminal activity, and other hazards such as natural and man-made disasters. Fusion centers were also strongly encouraged to share relevant threat-related information with the owners and operators of critical infrastructure within their respective geographic areas.[4]

Since its beginnings in 2007, the state fusion center program has created some seventy centers across the country, with the Department of Homeland Security (DHS) providing personnel, financial, and technical support.[5] DHS has directed more than $327 million in funding to the fusion center program.[6]

The National Fusion Center Conference offers its stakeholders an opportunity to learn more about best practices, new trends, intelligence tools, technologies, and processes that can enhance and assist their information sharing and intelligence collaboration efforts across all three levels of government.[7]

The 2009 fusion center conference also had an emphasis on the fusion center program's policies and practices involving privacy, civil rights, and civil liberties.[8] The inclusion of these initiatives resulted from mounting criticism of state fusion centers from the American Civil Liberties Union (ACLU) and other human rights watchdog groups. Civil rights organizations wanted to make sure fusion centers were paying diligent attention and fostering a climate of respect for civil rights and liberties. It is important to note that the federal government, through the DHS Office for Civil Rights and Civil Liberties, the DHS Privacy Office, and the Department of Justice's Bureau of Justice Assistance, provides training, technical assistance, and guidance to ensure that the privacy and civil liberties policies established by fusion centers are consistent with federal guidelines.[9]

The National Fusion Center Coordination Group (NFCCG) is responsible for planning, organizing, and carrying out the national fusion center conference each year.[10] The NFCCG had developed an agenda for its 2009 conference that focused on "strengthening the integrated national network of state and major urban area fusion centers that share information and intelligence with the federal government and each other."[11]

Prior to arriving at the conference in Kansas City, DHS secretary Janet Napolitano stopped by the MIAC in Jefferson City and joined Missouri governor Jay Nixon during a tour of the facility to observe its operations.[12] Godsey, the MIAC director, led Napolitano and Nixon on their tour of the fusion center.

In August 2008, Godsey and I spent time together during my trip to Jefferson City to participate in the Midwest domestic extremism working group. At the time, he gave me a similar tour of the MIAC facility. It was the first time I had met him, and I found him to be a very personable, likable, and compassionate man.

Godsey and I shared a similar belief that the threat of domestic terrorism was on the rise. We discussed the current political and economic climate that was fueling much of this rise in white supremacist, sovereign citizen, and militia activity throughout the country. Both of us expressed concern over where our nation was headed with this threat—a likely mass-casualty-producing terrorism attack. We agreed that our nation's leaders in Washington did not appear to be taking this threat very seriously.

The MIAC is co-located with the State Emergency Management Agency's Emergency Operations Center at the Missouri National Guard's Ike Skelton Training Center in Jefferson City.[13]

Napolitano and Nixon were briefed on-site concerning national security matters before taking a tour of a mobile command center positioned on-site as well as observing the technological capabilities of the Emergency Operations Center.[14] Napolitano and Governor Nixon then traveled to Kansas City, where they each gave separate addresses to the federal, state, and local officials that had assembled that afternoon during the opening day.[15]

During her remarks, Napolitano commented that "Fusion centers, like the one in Jefferson City, are the centerpieces of intelligence-sharing efforts to thwart terrorism and other dangerous risks to communities."[16]

"The reason we have Homeland Security, and the reason we have fusion centers, is we did not have the capacity to connect the dots on various bits of information prior to 9/11," Napolitano said.[17]

"Fusion centers are not domestic spy agencies and not designed to invade the privacy of citizens," Napolitano said.[18]

Governor Nixon echoed Napolitano's statements during his remarks by stating "the fusion center in Jefferson City has already paid dividends, resulting in arrests and cold cases that have been resolved."[19]

"We're not out there snooping on anybody," Nixon said.[20] "This isn't about snooping. Fusion centers take existing law enforcement resources and analyze information."[21]

During their remarks, Napolitano and Nixon spoke very highly of the MIAC, complimenting the work of its employees and specifically mentioning the outstanding leadership of Van Godsey.

As part of the 2009 conference agenda, the NFCCG had incorporated a break-out session titled "Integrating the Privacy and Civil Liberties Framework into Your Fusion Center's Operations."[22]

One particularly sarcastic media representative made a particularly interesting observation during the privacy and civil liberties session. In her blog article titled "Copfest 2009! National Fusion Center Conference Mobs Downtown,"[23] the reporter wrote, "Civil liberties might have been a priority of the conference's coordinators, but not of the attendees, judging by lots of empty seats."[24]

The reporter was attempting to make the assumption that the topic of civil rights and civil liberties was not a priority for state fusion centers judging by the number of attendees at the breakout session. She was, however, completely unaware of the likely reason why so few had attended this discussion. It had nothing to do with the subject matter, but may have been a result of the guest speaker, Mike German, policy counsel on national security, immigration, and privacy for the American Civil Liberties Union (ACLU).[25]

German is a former FBI agent and whistle-blower with sixteen years of law enforcement experience.[26] During his esteemed FBI career, he had experience working in an undercover capacity to infiltrate white supremacist and militia groups in California and Washington during the 1990s.[27] In 2005, German publicly criticized the FBI for mishandling a Florida terror investigation and accused other agents of falsifying documents in the case in an effort to cover repeated missteps.[28] He was reportedly retaliated against for complaining about the problems at FBI.[29]

I first met German in 2005 soon after arriving at DHS. I had heard about his story in the news. Due to his undercover work, I decided to reach out to him to get his insights into a particular subject related to the white supremacist movement. My research had uncovered a possible new trend emerging within the white supremacist movement, and DHS leadership was interested in getting more clarity on the issue.

I located German's personal e-mail address from a list server to which we both subscribed and immediately contacted him. We met on two occasions, and he provided me with some very helpful insights into my questions concerning the topic. I was grateful for his willingness to meet with me and share information.

German had reportedly fallen out of favor with those in law enforcement as a result of the way he handled his whistle-blowing activities.[30] German reported his concerns to Congress in 2004.[31] Being a former law enforcement officer that "defected," German's employment with the ACLU likely contributed to the low attendance at the civil rights breakout session.

German reportedly commented during the privacy and civil rights session that when he was an agent, he felt that the rules that guarded citizens' privacy made him more effective.[32]

"Every investigation opened on an innocent person or group is a waste of security resources," he said.[33]

German reportedly referenced a few ACLU reports about fusion centers that found, among other things, "a troubling lack of transparency existed in the fusion center model."[34]

German also identified a possible issue with the fusion center program concerning the collection of information by one agency for one purpose that is kept by another for intelligence purposes.

"This is the kind of stuff that overshadows the good work being done and leads conspiracy theorists to believe that fusion centers are really just tools for a domestic spying program," German said.[35] His opinion on the subject of the national fusion center program likely did not sit well with those in attendance. I suspect Mike German, along with the ACLU's notorious reputation for litigation, has probably fueled the DHS's reluctance to pursue and ultimately fulfill its congressionally mandated domestic counterterrorism mission.

I spent most of the conference manning I&A's booth with my colleagues. I was able to attend a few of the breakout sessions but spent a lot of time at the booth.

During the week, I was also able to network with some of my law enforcement contacts in Missouri. One evening, I was given a tour of the Kansas City Police Department's (KCPD) training academy by a trusted contact within the KCPD. On another occasion, I met with a couple of Bureau of Alcohol, Tobacco, Firearms and Explosives (ATF) agents and had lunch at a well-known Kansas City barbecue restaurant.

At lunch, the agents told me about a recent surge in firearms purchases throughout Missouri. Federal firearms licensees (FFLs) had informed ATF that many firearms purchasers were making comments that the reason why they were buying guns and hoarding ammunition was a direct result of the election of Barack Obama. Many purchasers stated that they were "concerned about a possible gun ban, ammunition shortages or imposition of stricter gun control laws."[36] Reporting about a rise in gun purchases, firearms, and ammunition hoarding (as well as fears of a gun ban) had also been corroborated through open-source as well as other law enforcement reporting.[37,38,39,40,41] The topics of firearms and ammunition purchases, as well as weapons stockpiling, were already being discussed as early as October 2008 in various militia forums on the Internet.

"I have been trying to stockpile gear for a long time. As we near the election and what looks like the probable election of a gun grabber, I'm wondering how folks would be/are prioritizing items," said one user.[42] "So how are you folks prioritizing with possible impending bans?"[43]

"The dark times have begun, and a very harsh winter approaches [a reference to the 2008 presidential election]," remarked another.

"Ammo and mags [short for ammunition magazines]. Mags will go up several times in price as opposed to guns which will probably only double. Not that we plan on being affected by it much since we plan on shooting the bastards [an alleged reference to government officials] by then. But for any last minute stuff, NOW is the time to buy before Joe Idiot gun owner runs out and drives up prices/creates shortages for crap he probably doesn't even have the balls to use," said a third user.[44]

A fourth stated, "The prioritization of supplies in general has been much on my mind as of late."[45]

"When I went to the gun show this past weekend, I was amazed at how many people were there. I have NEVER seen that gun show THAT packed! People were wheeling carts full of ammo out the door to their cars. People know, something bad is going to happen. We militia types aren't the only ones aware of this," pointed out another.[46]

Alex Jones's *Info Wars* site was also reporting on the trend under the heading "Obama's Gun Ban List Is Out." An *Info Wars* reporter wrote, "Gun-ban list proposed. Slipping below the radar (or under the short-term memory cap), the Democrats have already leaked a gun-ban list."[47]

"It serves as a framework for the new list the Bradys [reference to supporters of the Brady law] plan to introduce shortly. I have an outline of the Bradys' current plans and targets of opportunity. It's horrific," the writer stated. "They're going after the courts, regulatory agencies, firearms dealers and statutes in an all-out effort to restrict we the people. They've made little mention of criminals."

The *Info Wars* article continued, "Now more than ever, attention to the entire Bill of Rights is critical. Gun bans will impact our freedoms under search and seizure, due process, confiscated property, states' rights, free speech, right to assemble and more, in addition to the Second Amendment."[48]

"Note that Obama's pick for this office, Eric Holder, wrote a brief in the Heller case supporting the position that you have no right to have a working firearm in your own home," the article stated. "In plain English this means that ANY firearm ever obtained by federal officers or the military is not suitable for the public."[49]

The article concluded, "The last part is particularly clever, stating that a firearm doesn't have a sporting purpose just because it can be used for sporting purpose—is that devious or what? And of course, 'sporting purpose' is a rights infringement with no constitutional or historical support whatsoever, invented by domestic enemies of the right to keep and bear arms to further their cause of disarming the innocent."[50]

Another message circulated on several Yahoo! Groups—some of which have been known to cater to white supremacists, sovereign citizens, and militia extremists.

"I just watched about a ten minute piece on CNN about the Obama Administration and his Attorney General nominee, moving to gut Second Amendment rights and how, in effect, Obama has proven to be the best gun salesperson in years because many gun stores now have so many orders in place gun manufacturers will need up to eleven months to make the guns sold!" the e-mail stated.[51]

On Monday, March 16, 2009, I returned to the office in Washington, D.C. The time I had spent at the 2009 National Fusion Center Conference was very productive. I had to write up an after-action summary of the conference, document everything I had learned from my various discussions with my law enforcement counterparts, and brief my subordinate team members on the trip. Finally, I had to begin the arduous task of reading through all of the e-mail that had accumulated during my absence.

After getting caught up on most everything, I learned that another task from Secretary Napolitano had made its way through I&A's executive secretary's office to my desk. The secretary's tasking concerned more questions about domestic extremist activity in the United States.

Within weeks of her appointment, Napolitano began asking questions about the domestic extremist threat within the United States. She was the first secretary at DHS to express an interest in the topic of domestic terrorism—the non-Islamic variety. Her questions stemmed from a briefing item presented in January 2009 concerning a recently released DHS assessment on left-wing extremists and their likely use of cyber attacks within the next ten years. This report was released on January 26, 2009, just a few weeks after Napolitano's arrival at DHS.

Each weekday morning, I&A's briefing team presents the secretary's morning briefing, which highlights current events of interest to DHS, classified intelligence reporting, and new products being disseminated by I&A. The secretary has never reviewed or approved I&A products for release. Nevertheless, the briefing team was responsible for keeping the secretary updated on what topics were being drafted into finished intelligence reports, who was the intended audience of these reports, and when the reports were being released just in case there was any media publicity.

As a result of the left-wing cyber-attack capabilities assessment being briefed soon upon her arrival at DHS, Napolitano began asking follow-up questions related to domestic extremist activity and potential domestic threats.

In early February 2009, Napolitano's first round of questions dealt generally with how DHS, specifically I&A, defined the term "extremist," what mechanisms existed for determining which groups were considered extremists, and whether a list of extremist groups existed.[52]

These were difficult questions to answer because there was no widely accepted or official U.S. government definition of extremist and extremism. In addition, there were no approved mechanisms within the law enforcement and intelligence communities to determine which groups were considered "extremists." Furthermore, there was no official government list of extremist groups. Nevertheless, the intelligence community (IC) did have a mechanism for nominating and designating foreign terrorist organizations and did have an official U.S. government list of international terrorist groups. There was no similar list in the IC or law enforcement community for nominating or designating domestic terrorist or violent extremist groups operating in the United States.

At the time, no government agency at any level was formally charged with determining which U.S. groups met the threshold to be considered an "extremist group." I&A was the only federal government agency looking at the topics of "extremism and radicalization" within the United States. However, there were several federal government agencies and nongovernment organizations looking at extremism and radicalization from an international perspective. As a result, the daunting responsibility of determining which ideologies, groups, and individuals met the DHS criteria to be considered "extremist" resided in the knowledge, experience, and analytical judgment of I&A's subject matter experts. This determination was primarily focused on various extremist groups and radical belief systems that endorsed violence and related criminal activity and have been known to motivate others toward acts of violence and terrorism.

I&A's analysts routinely collaborated with their federal, state, and local law enforcement counterparts and private sector partners in an effort to determine which ideologies, groups, and individuals should be considered "extremist." They then analyzed the capability and intent of these "extremists" in an effort to assess any potential threat(s). Any criminal threat–related information was then given to the appropriate law enforcement agency for further inquiry and appropriate action.

By the end of my first week back at the office, I received a second tasking from Napolitano. It had been routed through I&A's executive secretary's office, logged, and assigned to me for action late on a Friday afternoon.

On Monday, March 23, 2009, I read the tasking and saw that Napolitano had four more questions concerning domestic extremist activity in the United States. This time, Napolitano wanted to know the answer to the following questions:

1. "Are we seeing an increase in domestic extremist activity?"[53]
2. "If such an increase exists, is it related to the ethnic background of the new President and his diversified cabinet?"[54]
3. "What's the possibility of it escalating to violence?"[55]; and
4. "What are we going to do about it?"[56]

Since I was relatively new to answering questions directly given from the secretary of Homeland Security, I immediately consulted with my first-line supervisor and division director concerning how to proceed with answering Napolitano's questions as well as the type of format I should use to respond to the tasking.

My division director thought I should answer questions 1, 2, and 3. She thought the FBI was better suited to respond to question 4 since it dealt with operational and response issues.

After my meeting with the division director, I walked over to the FBI representatives' offices on the other side of Building 19. The FBI had two special agents and an analyst assigned to I&A as the FBI liaison team. They agreed to work with us on the secretary's tasking by answering the fourth question. The final draft was due in three days on Thursday, March 26, 2009.

I was able to complete a draft white paper for the secretary's tasking that same day. I submitted it to my immediate supervisor for review. After consulting with the division director, my supervisor came back to me and suggested that I change the format to a question-and-answer format. Within a few hours, my division director requested that I place the questions and answers into a formal memorandum similar to the one I had used to respond to the first series of questions from Napolitano. I completed the memorandum before I left for the day.

For the first time since my arrival at DHS, the secretary was asking questions about domestic extremism, and my team was responsible for responding to these questions. The spotlight was clearly beginning to shine on us. This was a complete departure from the international terrorist focus of past DHS secretaries. I never fathomed the enormous impact that these four questions would have on my career, and indirectly in my personal life.

Napolitano's interest in this topic may have also stemmed from her past experience dealing with violent right-wing extremists in her home state of Arizona. Soon after Janet Napolitano's name was announced as President Obama's nominee for DHS secretary, I remember remarking to other analysts on my team, "Finally, we have a secretary that is familiar with the domestic terrorist threat!" I thought we had an ally.

When I received the second round of questions from Napolitano, I was excited, yet nervous. I now knew that the secretary's interest in domestic terrorism was not a passing thought, but a genuine concern. I knew this opportunity would likely bring increased visibility to me and my team, our branch, and ultimately to the division. It had the potential to translate into an increased emphasis on this often-overlooked mission and possibly bring more resources. I also realized it meant working harder, longer and being subjected to increased scrutiny from the lawyers, editors, and management. This meant that each of us would have to set aside our personal interests for the greater good of the organization.

As I began working on this latest request from Napolitano, another event that would later impact this project was unfolding back in Missouri. On March 25, 2009, the Missouri State Highway Patrol (MSHP) retracted a controversial report on militia activity.[57]

The controversy surrounded a report titled "The Modern Militia Movement" prepared by Godsey's Missouri fusion center in February 2009.[58] The document was released to federal, state, and local law enforcement agencies in an effort to share information on militia extremists.

The eight-page report was labeled "unclassified" but contained sensitive law enforcement information not meant for public disclosure. Critics of the report noticed a number of editing and design errors, including a misspelling of Obama's name.[59]

The report contained no sources, and some sentences appeared to have been lifted from a 2005 Southern Poverty Law Center report on right-wing domestic terrorism. It linked people who supported third-party candidates and opposed abortion, immigration, and gun control with the possibility that they were members of militias.[60]

Initially, the MIAC attempted to pacify critics by releasing a statement reaffirming its "regard for the Constitutions of the United States and Missouri" and expressed regret that "any citizens or groups were unintentionally offended by the content of the document."[61]

Department of Public Safety (DPS) director John M. Britt retracted the portions of the report that noted third-party and Republican presidential candidates by name. Governor Jay Nixon, a Democrat elected in 2008, publicly defended the report.[62]

Conservatives, including members of the Republican Party, criticized the MIAC report for "lumping people with conservative political persuasions in with domestic terrorists and potentially opening them to harassment from law enforcement."[63] They felt that the earlier statements did not go far enough to apologize.[64]

The controversy was aired on national cable news programs, conservative radio programs, and politically oriented blogs on the Internet.[65]

By Wednesday afternoon, March 25, 2009, public and political criticism continued to mount. As a result, Colonel James F. Keathley, superintendent of the MSHP, felt it necessary to hold a press conference and released a public statement to the media and general public stating that the MIAC report "did not meet the patrol's standard for quality and would not have been released if it had been seen by top officials."[66] His statement also said that he would change how such reports are reviewed before being distributed to law enforcement agencies in Missouri.[67]

Keathley's announcement followed a press conference in which lieutenant governor Peter Kinder suggested "putting the director of public safety on administrative leave and investigating how the report was produced."[68]

"For that reason," Keathley wrote, "I have ordered the MIAC to permanently cease distribution of the militia report."[69]

Keathley's memo stated that the MIAC report was compiled by an employee of the MIAC and reviewed only by the center's director before being distributed to law enforcement agencies across the state.[70]

"In the future," Keathley wrote, "reports from the center will be reviewed by leaders of the Highway Patrol and the Department of Public Safety. The patrol will also open an investigation into the origin of the militia report."[71]

Lieutenant Governor Kinder began to politicize the MIAC report stating, "The report 'slanders' opponents of abortion and critics of illegal immigration."[72]

"Under the guidance of the present director, who apparently must think it is Nixon's secret service, the Department of Public Safety has taken on the new and sinister role of political profiling," Kinder said.[73]

"Also troubling," Kinder remarked, "the report makes no mention of Islamic terrorists or those who might subscribe to ideologies associated with liberals, such as environmental radicals."[74]

This statement was utterly ludicrous. The MIAC report was clearly focused on the modern-day militia movement, not Islamic terrorists. It was not meant to cover all types of terrorist threats. Rather, it was a strategic assessment of a single type of domestic extremist threat—the militia movement. It was absurd to expect such a document to talk about Islamic terrorists, since no Islamic terrorists had ever been known to affiliate with militia groups in the United States.

"Let's be very clear. There are extremists and ultra extremists in every group mentioned above," he said, referring to antiabortion and border security activists. "But not just in these groups."[75]

Kinder also commented that the director of public safety for Missouri, John M. Britt, "should be suspended and that the state legislature should investigate how the report was prepared."[76] This was an indication that he was attempting to politicize the MIAC report.

Since the controversial report was written and reviewed at the state fusion center level, Van Godsey, the MIAC director, became the scapegoat. He fell victim to the public criticism and resulting political firestorm.[77]

Keathley blamed Godsey because he "signed off" on the report. As a result, Keathley believed Godsey was ultimately responsible for the report's content.[78]

On Monday, June 8, 2009, Keathley announced the appointment of Lieutenant David A. Hall as the new MIAC director, replacing Godsey,[79] who had led the MIAC since former governor Matt Blunt created it in 2005. He was reassigned to MSHP's Division of Drug and Crime Control.[80]

In the aftermath of the controversy, Keathley also implemented new production policies and procedures that required future MIAC reports to be reviewed and approved by the MSHP superintendent and DPS director John Britt.[81]

"The release of a report of militia groups last month by the Missouri Information Analysis Center (MIAC) has led me to take a hard look at the manner in which the Missouri State Highway Patrol oversees the dissemination of law enforcement information by the MIAC," Keathley stated.[82] "My review of the procedures used by the MIAC in the three years since its inception indicates that the mechanism in place for oversight of reports needs improvement."[83]

· Keathley went on to say, "Until two weeks ago, the process for release of reports from the MIAC to law enforcement officers around the state required no review by leaders of the Missouri State Highway Patrol or the Department of Public Safety."[84]

"That process has been unchanged since the MIAC began issuing these reports in June 2007," Keathley said.[85]

"Law enforcement officers require intelligence of the highest quality and the report in question does not meet that standard," Keathley said.[86] "For that reason . . . I am creating a new process for oversight of reports drafted by the MIAC that will require leadership of the Missouri State Highway Patrol and the Department of Public Safety to review the content of these reports before they are shared with law enforcement."[87]

Until the leak occurred, leaders in the MSHP and DPS would have had no valid reason to know about, let alone review, a single MIAC report. They likely had no formalized analytical training or experience and were generally not monitoring the day-to-day criminal or extremist activities occurring in their jurisdiction. They may not have possessed any formalized training or experience as editors. As a result, there was no valid reason why the MIAC would have vetted products through its senior leadership.

Why would Keathley want to subject himself to such a tedious, minuscule task of reviewing analytical reports or, at least, agree to do so in a letter? Most likely, he was trying to protect his career. It would have made more sense for Keathley to hire a professional editor/reviewer for the MIAC and offer legal assistance from the MSHP headquarters. Neither was done. Hence, the MIAC was not well served by Keathley's solution to the problem. As I would later learn, an executive-level review process does not increase the quality of analysis nor improve language in reports.

Such procedures only serve to "politicize" intelligence reports and protect the careers of indecisive decision makers. Furthermore, it undermines the analytical integrity of the report as well as the organization responsible for disseminating it. These processes also stymie the intelligence process by inserting multiple layers of review and placing politicians in the role of "editor in chief." In turn, products are no longer written as they were intended. Reports fortunate enough to make it out the door are often sanitized to the point that they lose their intelligence value due to lack of specificity and timeliness. Still, many other draft reports are "killed" (i.e., never disseminated) for political reasons and are never released to those who truly need the information. The executive-level review process is primarily meant to eliminate risk (they like to call it "risk mitigation") to an organization's existence and secure the careers of its leaders.

Keathley concluded his letter by stating, "In the future, high-level review of these reports prior to issuance will ensure not only that law enforcement officers get better quality intelligence, but also that certain subsets of Missourians will not be singled out inappropriately in these reports for particular associations."[88]

One can assume Keathley's remarks are directed at the media accusations about extremist ties to third-party candidates and extremist bumper stickers. A careful review of the MIAC report, however, points out an important distinction between what was portrayed by the media and Keathley's letter and what was actually written in the report. Words were taken out of context for political reasons to attack opposition leaders as well as the fusion center program in general.

The MIAC report states, "*Militia members* most commonly associate with 3rd-party political groups. It is not uncommon for *militia members* to display Constitutional Party, Campaign for Liberty, or Libertarian material. *These members* [i.e. militia extremists] are usually supporters of former Presidential Candidates: Ron Paul, Chuck Baldwin, and Bob Barr [emphasis added]."[89]

These statements are accurate. Consider any number of the many militia paramilitary training videos posted on YouTube during 2008 and 2009. Many of the videos end with political endorsements for Ron Paul. Similarly, many white supremacist, sovereign citizen, and militia-related websites, along with their propaganda, had political endorsements for Ron Paul, among others who would be considered third-party candidates. This did not mean that Ron Paul is an "extremist" or that his party is a supporter of extremism; rather, right-wing extremists tended to be attracted to Ron Paul and supported his candidacy.

Now, compare the MIAC report's actual wording to what is portrayed in an official statement by the Missouri Libertarian Party. In an official press release dated March 15, 2009, Mike Ferguson, Missouri Liberty Party spokesperson, titled his remarks "Missouri Liberty Party Condemns Missouri Highway Patrol Training Document as Political Profiling."

Ferguson stated, "An internal document designed for law enforcement education purposes inaccurately and dangerously implies that among the indicators of possible involvement in extremist, militant militia activity is support for the Libertarian Party."[90]

"The memo claims that membership in, among other groups, the Libertarian Party and/or the display of what it calls 'political paraphernalia' in support of the party or its 2008 presidential nominee (former U.S. Congressman Bob Barr) could be an indicator that someone is involved in a 'militant militia,'" Ferguson wrote.[91]

Both of these statements are inaccurate. The MIAC was not engaged in "political profiling" as the title of Ferguson's press release insinuated. Furthermore, the MIAC report did not make the claims alleged by the Missouri Liberty Party.

The report did not state that members of third parties are extremists as the Missouri Liberty Party mistakenly asserts. It did not say that Libertarian Party membership or the display of propaganda supporting the party is an indicator of militia involvement. Rather, the report stated that militia extremists "most commonly associate with 3rd-party political groups."[92]

There is a very distinct difference between stating that militia extremists commonly associate with third-party political groups and display third-party propaganda and the erroneous assumption that all third-party members are suspected of involvement in militia groups. Keathley and other state leaders should have publicly refuted these claims as erroneous, taken out of context, and completely off-base.

In addition, in reference to bumper stickers, the report stated, "Militia members commonly display pictures, cartoons, bumper stickers that contain antigovernment rhetoric. Most of this material will depict the IRS, FBI, ATF, CIA, UN, and law enforcement in a derogatory manor. Additionally, racial, anti-immigration and anti-abortion material may be displayed by militia members."[93]

Similarly, the *Kansas City Star* newspaper erroneously reported that the MIAC's militia report suggested that "domestic militias often subscribe to radical ideologies rooted in Christian views," among a list of other national issues.[94]

The report was actually talking about Christian Identity, which the document describes as religious "adherents [that] believe that whites of European descent can be traced back to the 'Lost Tribes of Israel.' Many consider Jews to be the satanic offspring of Eve and the Serpent while non-whites are 'mud people' created before Adam and Eve."[95] Christian Identity is a racist religious philosophy that maintains non-Jewish whites are "God's Chosen People" and the true descendants of the Twelve Tribes of Israel. Groups or individuals can be followers either of the Covenant or Dual Seed-Line doctrine; all believe that Jews are conspiring with

Satan to control world affairs and that the world is on the verge of the biblical Apocalypse. Dual Seed-Line adherents believe Jews are the literal offspring of Satan and that nonwhites are not human beings. Christian Identity adherents have been known to commit multiple acts of violence, such as the 1996 Centennial Olympic Park bombing in Atlanta, Georgia, and the bombings of an abortion clinic, a newspaper office, and a government building in Spokane, Washington, during 1996.[96,97]

With this in mind, all of the criticism over the MIAC report's supposed reference to "Christians" was absolutely ludicrous. The only reference to the Christian religion or the word "Christian" in the entire MIAC report was the definition of "Christian Identity"—a purely racist belief system.

In hindsight, the MIAC report did need some improvement. There were spelling errors, lack of source citations, and it could have used better placement of maps and other graphics. Also, some of the sentence structure could have been better clarified. Nevertheless, grammatical and editorial types of errors were the only valid issues with the MIAC report. The real issues, a need for more resources and better training for fusion centers, largely went unnoticed in the resulting media and political criticism.

The critics, including some media representatives, took things completely out of context and jumped to conclusions without giving the fusion center, highway patrol, and Department of Public Safety the benefit of the doubt. They never asked for clarification.

The MIAC, along with many other state fusion centers, lacked the necessary resources, such as editors and legal counsel, which may have prevented some of the mischaracterizations related to the *Modern Day Militia Movement* report. Furthermore, at the time of the MIAC leak, no standardized analytical tradecraft training had been offered to the fusion center program. Therefore, fusion center managers, analysts, and administrative support personnel had to rely on their own agency resources and funding for any writing, briefing presentation, or public speaking training courses. Unfortunately, most fusion centers at the time were too short-staffed, overwhelmed with their work, and lacked information and guidance on available training opportunities for their personnel.

To make matters worse, the fusion center program lost a great ambassador and leader in Van Godsey. Law enforcement throughout Missouri largely supported the product and its findings. Nevertheless, there were those who were offended by some of the report's poorly worded language. Individuals' careers were essentially ruined. The MIAC's domestic terrorism analysis capability was practically shut down due to the state leadership's inability to formulate effective counterarguments as part of its press strategy. The MIAC's integrity was called into question, and many lost faith in the state's leaders as a result of the political maneuvering, infighting, and backbiting that ensued.

Keathley's new production review procedures placed a virtual stranglehold on domestic extremism reporting and timely intelligence dissemination. The topic had become too politically charged. With the Republican losses during the 2008 election, domestic extremism reporting had become too volatile and a highly politicized issue. Risk-averse decision makers decided to cave in to the political pressure.

The leak of the MIAC report was a prelude of things to come. The same type of risk-averse tactics used against the Missouri fusion center and its employees as a result of public criticism of its militia report would soon be used at I&A, but on a much larger scale. Dirty, and often politically motivated, tricks such as taking information out of context, bashing political opponents, and blaming others rather than accepting personal responsibility are now very familiar to me. And, like the MIAC, the personal lives of public servants would be unjustly disrupted, scapegoats blamed, and careers forever changed.

Back in Washington, D.C., I had just completed the draft memorandum responding to Napolitano's four questions concerning whether we were seeing a rise in domestic extremism activity throughout the country.[98] I&A's executive secretary office was responsible for managing the task. They had requested a final draft due to DHS components for coordination by Wednesday, March 25, 2009, at 12:00 p.m. This was just 2 1/2 business days from the time I started working on the task.

I was required to work under an extremely short production schedule for this tasking. The time from receipt of the original tasking (20 March 2009) to product dissemination (8 April 2009) was thirteen business days. My team, however, had been conducting research since April 2008 with the intent of eventually writing a similar assessment. The division director used the secretary's tasking to hasten the drafting and dissemination of this assessment.

On Monday, March 23, 2009, my division director again changed the format of my response to the secretary. She decided that the tasking was best served by drafting a Homeland Security Intelligence Assessment. This would not only provide Napolitano with the answers she was seeking, but also inform state and local law enforcement about the rise in right-wing extremism activity throughout the country, along with the potential threat this posed. An assessment format would ensure the widest dissemination possible and provide a valuable tip to law enforcement about a growing national problem.

During March 23–24, 2009, I continued drafting the assessment. Fortunately, I had a partially written preliminary draft from which to work. So I was still on target to meet the upcoming deadline. By Tuesday afternoon, March 24, I forwarded the completed draft assessment to my immediate supervisor, division editor, and division director for their review, comments, and suggested revisions.

The draft assessment was titled "Domestic Issues Affecting Rightwing Extremist Radicalization." It was eight pages long and contained many of the same themes as the officially released assessment disseminated on April 7, 2009. It contained twenty-three source citations—much of which were considered publicly available information.

On the morning of Wednesday, March 25, I incorporated division-level revisions and included edits and feedback from I&A's Office of General Counsel (OGC), I&A's intelligence oversight (IO) officer, and the DHS Policy Office. After making all of the recommended changes, I submitted the document for a second review by the division editor and division director.

Once it was approved, I forwarded the final draft back to the Executive Secretary's Office at I&A for further coordination with various other department-level offices, including DHS component agencies, the Office of Civil Rights and Civil Liberties (CRCL), Office of Management, and the DHS Operations Office and other departmental organizations.

"I&A has attempted to incorporate all comments and edits received," read the Executive Secretary's Office e-mail message to the various DHS offices coordinating on the report.[99] "Please review and provide final clearance NLT 1800 hrs today, 25 March 2009. Thank you."

Concurrent with the internal DHS coordination, I forwarded the draft assessment to the FBI's Office of Intelligence for external coordination and review. FBI returned minor comments and edits back to me the following day.

The DHS Privacy Office provided a response that morning. They had no comment since the assessment did not name a single living individual or group. They were primarily concerned with protecting privacy information and would only provide comments if there were names of groups or individuals or other types of personal identifying information. I intentionally did not include such information in this assessment to avoid any legal, privacy, or civil rights concerns.

By 6:00 p.m. that evening, the Executive Secretary's Office sent out the following message to those still reviewing the report: "Your clearance was due by 1800 hrs today; we have received zero responses. If we do not receive your response by 0900 tomorrow, we will consider your silence as concurrence. Thank you."[100]

"CRCL's comments on the edited version of this document. The edit is contained in the document, and also copied in the body of this email for BlackBerry users," a CRCL representative responded within thirty minutes.[101] "These comments have been cleared at CRCL. Please circulate to the other clearing offices. Thanks."

Among CRCL's edits was an attempted rewrite of the right-wing extremism definition. CRCL's revised definition read, "In the absence of a formal definition, rightwing extremism in the U.S. may include those groups and movements involved in criminal, violent or illegal activity, which employ a distorted version of center-right political positions as a justification for criminal activity, violence or terrorism. This term may also refer to violent rightwing extremist groups dedicated to a single issue or belief, such as opposition toward abortion or immigration, or violently asserting racial, ethnic or religious supremacy."[102]

I did not agree with the proposed CRCL definition. It was too restrictive. Extremism should not be limited to those groups or individuals solely involved in criminal, illegal, or violent activity. CRCL's definition was more accurately describing ideologically motivated violence, which is the definition of "terrorism." Extremism has a much broader definition, because it is the phase that precedes terrorism. Extremism involves ideologies that facilitate individuals and groups toward violence and terrorism. It is the gestational stage for creating terrorists. Any definition needs to account for those who encourage, support, or direct others toward violence and criminal activity, but do not necessarily engage in it themselves. DHS has the mission to prevent terrorism, and one of the ways to do that is to analyze and assess potential threats (i.e., extremists) before they conduct a violent or criminal act.

Despite formal notification and a deadline, no other DHS offices submitted feedback to the I&A Executive Secretary's Office concerning the draft report.

After incorporating CRCL's feedback on the morning of March 26, I made a few other revisions and submitted a revised draft to my division director for review. I notified the division director of CRCL's concern related to the definition. Since we were running out of time, my division director requested a one-week extension to finish the office-level review process and to resolve the remaining concern with CRCL over the definition of right-wing extremism. The Executive Secretary's Office granted the extension and requested that the final version of the assessment be submitted no later than Friday, April 3, 2009.

The extension made sense because as of 9:30 a.m. on Thursday, March 26, the Executive Secretary's Office had yet to hear back from any other department concerning their review of the report.

"Report was distro'd [yesterday] and the only comments received have been from CRCL, which you are aware of," the Executive Secretary's Office said in an e-mail updating me on the status of the review process.[103]

"Do you anticipate the FBI having significant edits?" the e-mail read.[104] "If not, I would like to start pushing this through the Leadership for review and approval."[105]

I provided an update to the executive secretary concerning the FBI's input and continued working on incorporating CRCL's edits.

By Thursday afternoon, I had addressed all of CRCL's initial recommended changes. The only remaining unresolved issue was the definition of right-wing extremism.

CRCL insisted on using a very narrow interpretation of "extremism" that focused exclusively on those who commit acts of violence and criminal activity. I countered their point with the fact that many extremists have been known to endorse, support, and facilitate violence through rhetoric, propaganda, and fund-raising activities. They also provided safe haven to violent criminal and domestic terrorists but stopped short of actually participating in violent or illegal acts. This explanation, however, did not appease any of their concerns.

At 5:26 p.m. on Thursday evening, the executive secretary and I proposed the following definition of right-wing extremism to CRCL, which built upon their changes to the existing definition: "In the absence of a formal definition, rightwing extremism in the U.S. may include those groups and movements that *encourage, support, direct or conduct violent or illegal activity* [emphasis added], which employ hatred or a distorted version of center-right political positions as a justification for those activities. This term may also refer to violent rightwing extremist groups dedicated to a single issue or belief, such as opposition toward abortion or immigration, or violently asserting racial, ethnic or religious supremacy."[106]

At first, it appeared as though CRCL was willing to concede these points (the fact that extremists could encourage, support, direct, and conduct violent or illegal activity) and incorporate them into a new definition. Nevertheless, by 6:45 p.m., CRCL had reverted back to its original, hard-line stance that extremists only come in the violent variety.

"We [CRCL] believe that we shouldn't generate a document that, if it were relied upon publicly, could make it easier for extremists to recruit to their cause," a CRCL representative states in response to our e-mail sent to them at 5:26 p.m.[107] "It could be so used because the existing definition is susceptible to the interpretation that DHS thinks groups bear government scrutiny based on the content of the ideas."[108]

"Characterizing extremist groups by the most innocuous portion of their ideology could do more to legitimize and strengthen radical groups than anything they themselves might do," he said.[109] "A failure to distinguish between protected political speech and the actual extremist groups in our communications may give the impression that DHS is engaged in ideologically-based monitoring of groups."[110]

CRCL then proposed another narrow definition of right-wing extremism: "In the absence of a formal definition, rightwing extremism in the U.S. may include those groups and movements *involved in criminal, violent or illegal activity* [emphasis added], which employ a distorted version of center-right political positions as a justification for criminal activity, violence or terrorism. This term may also refer to violent rightwing extremist groups dedicated to a single issue or belief, such as opposition toward abortion or immigration, or violently asserting racial, ethnic or religious supremacy."[111]

Since CRCL's proposed definition was far too restrictive, I decided to consult I&A's Office of General Counsel (OGC) for arbitration. Along with my question concerning the definition of right-wing extremism, I submitted a revised draft of the report, which had incorporated the other CRCL suggested revisions, for second review by OGC. I did not hear back from OGC until four days later.

On Monday, March 30, 2009, I received a response from an attorney at I&A OGC concerning the definition of right-wing extremism.

"I have spoken with Daryl and exchanged emails with [another domestic terrorism subject matter expert at I&A]," said the attorney.[112] "Based on that exchange, I have no legal objection to continuing to use the original definition in the product."[113]

"This definition is worded consistent with the other definitions in the glossary and makes clear that there are two broad categories of rightwing extremism," the attorney said.[114]

The attorney further stated that they did not agree with revising the definition of right-wing extremism for the following reasons.

"It [the revised definition] inserts an assumption which is incorrect ('in the absence of a formal definition') because this is a formal definition by virtue of inclusion in the DHS glossary product," the attorney argued.[115]

"Not all rightwing extremists encourage, support, direct, or conduct violent or illegal activity. Therefore, it is inaccurate to make such an assertion in the definition," the attorney further stated.[116]

"Characterizing a position as 'distorted' sounds like an opinion rather than a statement of fact," the attorney wrote.[117] "Additionally, the reader would need to understand what constitutes a non-distorted view of 'center-right political positions' in order to understand the definition."[118]

"After much thought, I am not convinced that the existing definition needs changing," the attorney concluded.[119]

As a result of the attorney's feedback, we continued to stick with the original, broad definition. OGC and division leadership and I believed that violence and criminal activity are the paramount public safety and national security concerns emanating from extremism, but not necessarily a prerequisite to becoming an extremist.

Despite this legal ruling, my division editor, division director, and CRCL continued to exchange several e-mail messages and phone calls discussing the pros and cons of various renditions of the right-wing extremism definition between March 27 and April 7. The primary area of disagreement continued to center on whether violence and criminal activity were necessary criteria for groups or individuals to be considered "extremist."

As the definition debate raged on, I was busy making numerous corrections to the draft assessment resulting from both senior editors' reviews. These editors existed at the office level and were in addition to the branch- and division-level editors who had already reviewed the report several times each. In total, there were twenty-eight rewrites of the report over a two-week period. I had written twenty-eight distinct versions of the report since March 25.

By Friday, April 3, 2009, a final, polished version of the report was submitted to the Executive Secretary's Office. On Monday, April 6, 2009, a copy of the report was placed into Secretary Napolitano's briefing book.

On Tuesday morning, April 7, 2009, I&A's briefing team presented a summary of the report. At this point, the definition of right-wing extremism was still being debated between CRCL, my division editor, and division director. It was obvious that CRCL was not content with the legal advice we had received from I&A's OGC a week earlier. As we were nearing the final stages of preparing the report for release, a senior official at CRCL continued to debate the merits of using a narrow interpretation of the right-wing extremism definition.

"The fundamental problem which we are having difficulty addressing is that many groups rally around any given issue, and many people hold extreme views, but only a few people and groups merit government scrutiny," the senior-level CRCL official wrote.[120] "Moreover, the Constitutional standard is that the scrutiny is warranted only because of the likelihood of illegal or violent activity, not due to the extreme nature of the viewpoints held by the individual."[121]

"This predicate must be present before the government uses a viewpoint as justification for surveillance, monitoring, or other investigation," he argued.[122] This CRCL official may not have been aware that I&A is not a law enforcement agency. I&A does not conduct surveillance or investigative activities, so using this argument was a bit of a stretch.

"We know it is not your intent, but despite some edits the reader may still be left with the impression that 'extremism' is defined by one's position on particular political issues or the fact that particular beliefs are strongly held, and that an opinion such as opposition to abortion or favoring immigration enforcement is sufficient to get a group labeled as 'rightwing extremist' and subjected to government scrutiny," he concluded.[123]

In a last-ditch effort to convince us to use the narrow CRCL definition, the senior-level CRCL official again submitted a similar definition to those that had been overruled by OGC on March 30.

"Here is another attempt to compromise on the footnote definition," the senior CRCL official wrote.[124] "Rightwing extremism in the United States can be broadly divided into those groups and movements that are primarily hate-oriented (based on hatred of particular religious, racial or ethnic groups), and those that are mainly anti-government, rejecting federal authority in favor of state or local authority, or rejecting government authority entirely. It may include groups and individuals that are dedicated to a single issue, such as opposition to abortion or immigration. *These groups are subject to law enforcement scrutiny only when they have been involved in violent and/or illegal activities in furtherance of their ideology or there is reasonable suspicion that they will be in the future* [emphasis added]."

We again voiced our position that "extremism" was not limited to those who solely carry out violence and criminal activity. CRCL was stubborn and unwilling to listen to the I&A attorneys, I&A leadership, or subject matter experts. They had their mind made up and appeared closed to reaching a compromise.

"We are obviously not going to agree on this . . . ," the senior CRCL concluded his message.[125] Out of frustration, he reminded I&A that they "cannot say that CRCL concurred with the product without that sentence at the end of the definition."

"The sentence is not perfect, but at least it provided some context and differentiated between ideology and ideology that has a nexus to illegal activity," he argued.[126]

"The very simple fix that we have been advocating for a few weeks now is to create a definition that focuses primarily on proclivity to violence or illegal activity and secondarily on ideological orientation," he wrote.[127] "Otherwise there is simply no predicate justifying the inquiry into First Amendment-protected activities."[128]

We had heard enough. It was time to make a decision. The secretary had already been briefed on the report earlier that morning and was told it would be disseminated to law enforcement by the end of the day. As evening approached, my division director had to finally make a decision regarding the matter.

Taking into account OGC's and my reservations about CRCL's wording, she decided to respectfully decline CRCL's recommendations regarding the definition of right-wing extremism. CRCL had made no concessions and totally disregarded input from I&A attorneys and subject matter experts. By 5:30 p.m., my division director authorized the final release of the Homeland Security Assessment titled "Rightwing Extremism: Current Economic and Political Climate Fueling Resurgence in Radicalization and Recruitment" to the law enforcement community. We were confident with the existing definition coupled with the wording contained within the report's scope note properly placed the definition into the context of terrorism and violent activity.

Two days after the report was disseminated, on Thursday, April 9, 2009, I accompanied my immediate supervisor and division director to a meeting with Secretary Napolitano, which was held in Building 5 at the Nebraska Avenue Complex. We were joined by members of the FBI's Domestic Terrorism Analytical Unit, FBI liaison officers to DHS, and representatives from the National Counterterrorism Center.

I began the meeting with a brief summary of the right-wing extremism report and its key findings. I personally handed Napolitano a copy of the report during our meeting with FBI and watched her thumb through its pages. I don't know if she ever read the entire report, but she was definitely aware of it both before and after its release. Napolitano nodded her head in agreement as I explained the various points discussed in the report. At the time, she appeared to have no objections to the report or its findings.

My summary was immediately followed by the FBI, who provided a forty-five-minute briefing on the agency's domestic terrorism operational activities and other criminal investigations associated with right-wing extremists in the United States. This addressed Napolitano's question about what was being done about the rise in extremism in the United States.

Reflecting back on the day of the report's release, as I left the office that day, I was exhausted as a result of the many long days I had worked on the secretary's task. I did, however, feel a sense of accomplishment and was looking forward to the anticipated positive feedback from those who received the report.

During my evening commute home, I received an unexpected e-mail from one of my colleagues working Muslim extremism issues in the division's Extremism and Radicalization Branch.

"Nice work guys—this looks awesome," his e-mail read.[129]

Soon thereafter, I received a similar compliment from my immediate supervisor in another e-mail. I quickly responded with a text message of my own.

"Thanks guys. I'm glad all the hard work and perseverance finally paid off with the product's release," I said. "I think this one will reap great feedback benefiting the entire office. Hopefully, the Secretary will be impressed."[130]

The next morning, I arrived back at the office eager to start my day. The secretary's task, which had consumed much of my time and effort over the past few weeks, was finally completed. I was excited to get back to my normal routine of monitoring extremist activity in the United States and responding to state and local law enforcement requests for information.

As I did every morning, I immediately opened Microsoft Outlook and began reviewing all of the e-mail messages that had accumulated since I'd left the office the previous day. There were a lot of e-mail messages to read because many had remained unopened due to my focus on the secretary's tasking.

As I was nearly finished reading my e-mail, a new message came into my inbox from I&A's Production Management Division at 8:10 a.m. The subject line read, "Feedback: Rightwing Extremism Report IA-0257-09 Feedback."[131]

"Mr. Johnson," the message began. "Please see the below feedback from [name deleted] Intelligence Operations Specialist/DHS Representative, FBI CT Watch, regarding the subject product."[132]

I remember thinking "Well . . . that's unusual" in response to the e-mail. I&A typically did not receive feedback from its own employees about products written by their coworkers. In fact, I don't recall a single instance where an I&A employee had previously submitted formal feedback to I&A's Production Management Division concerning a report written by the agency, which made this an extremely rare occurrence. I scrolled down the message to read what this person had to say.

"HETA [a reference to the Homeland Environment and Threat Analysis Division at I&A]," the message began. "After reading your IA-0257-09 report re Rightwing Extremism, I feel compelled to ask for clarification and provide some feedback, if I may. I will try to address my concerns in order of their appearance in the report."[133]

The message continued, "On p.2, the footnote reads: 'Rightwing extremism in the United States can be broadly divided into those groups, movements, and adherents that are primarily hate-oriented (based on hatred of particular religious, racial or ethnic groups), and those that are mainly antigovernment, rejecting federal authority in favor of state or local authority, or rejecting government authority entirely. It may include groups and individuals that are dedicated to a single issue, such as opposition to abortion or immigration.'"[134]

The person then asked, "Is the implication here that people that oppose abortion or immigration on purely religious or constitutional basis fall into the realm of extremists?"[135]

He then listed several other questions and concerns.

"On p. 3, paragraph 4 reads: A recent example of the potential violence associated with a rise in rightwing extremism may be found in the shooting deaths of three police officers in Pittsburgh, Pennsylvania, on 4 April 2009. The alleged gunman's reaction reportedly was influenced by his racist ideology and belief in antigovernment conspiracy theories related to gun confiscations, citizen detention camps, and a Jewish-controlled 'one world government.'"

He then inquired, "On whose account are you basing that his [Poplawski] 'reaction was reportedly influenced by his racist ideology . . . '?"[136]

"There are reports that Richard Poplawski, the shooter, had been dishonorably discharged from the USMC, and that he had a protective order against him. Both of these incidents would have made him ineligible to (legally) purchase guns. My point is that—yes—he subscribed to extremist views, but that his reaction was most likely influenced by fear of being arrested for illegally possessing weapons, and not because his 'racist ideology . . . '" he stated.[137]

"The footnote reads: A prominent civil rights organization reported in 2006 that 'large numbers of potentially violent neo-Nazis, skinheads, and other white supremacists are now learning the art of warfare in the [U.S.] armed forces,'" he said.[138]

"You are referring to the Southern Poverty Law Center's Intelligence Project titled 'A Few Bad Men,' dated July 7, 2006. This report was debunked by Under Secretary of Defense David S. Chu on a letter sent to the SPLC. Said report was heavily based on a (subsequently discredited) single-source," he said.[139]

"Moreover, the SPLC and the Anti-Defamation League, both left-leaning organizations with amnesty agendas, were used as sources for the recent, embarrassing Missouri Intelligence Analysis Center report 'The Modern Militia Movement,' on which Police were instructed to look for Americans who were concerned about unemployment, taxes, illegal immigration, gangs, border security, abortion, high costs of living, gun restrictions, FEMA, the IRS, The Federal Reserve, and the North American Union/SPP/North American Community," he asserted.[140]

"The MIAC report also said potential domestic terrorists might like gun shows, short wave radios, combat movies, movies with white male heroes, Tom Clancy novels, and Presidential Candidates Ron Paul, Bob Barr, and Chuck Baldwin!" he remarked.[141]

"As you may well know, Colonel James F. Keathley, Superintendent of the Missouri State Highway Patrol, retracted the report two weeks ago after complaints from moderate and conservative groups," he said.[142]

"Overall, I found your report to be very informative and containing good analysis. I, however, object to some of the premises set forth and to the sources (or lack thereof) of some of your statements, as presented above," he commented.[143] "One more thing; you have perked my interest . . . has HETA published a report on left-wing extremism that I could read to learn about *that* subject?"[144]

He concluded his feedback with the statement, "Keep up the good work."[145]

From reading between the lines of his comments, it became abundantly clear to me that this individual harbored a grudge against the MIAC, SPLC, and ADL—three reputable organizations with which I maintained a close working relationship.

I immediately walked over to the division editor's office.

"Did you see the recent feedback we received concerning the right-wing extremist report?" I asked.

"No, not yet," the editor replied.

"It came from an I&A employee and it's not very positive," I said. "I plan to respond to it as quickly as I can, and I would like you to review my response."

"Okay," the editor answered. "Please forward the e-mail message, so I can take a look at the feedback."

After sending the feedback message to the editor, I began writing a response to the person's questions in an attempt to address his concerns. I coordinated my response with the division editor and then sent an e-mail back to the Production Management Division to be shared with the individual providing the feedback. Due to other work-related obligations I encountered throughout the day, my response was sent late in the afternoon.

My e-mail began, "Here is HETA's response to these questions. Please pass this along to the requestor. Thanks."[146]

There were four questions that needed to be answered.

The first question read, "Is the implication here that people that oppose abortion or immigration on purely religious or constitutional basis fall into the realm of extremists?"[147]

"DHS/I&A is not concerned about peaceful, law-abiding groups of any persuasion. As framed by the context of the assessment, I&A addresses groups and individuals who embrace extremist positions on various political and social issues as well as endorse, support or use violence and illegal activity to further their political positions," I responded.[148]

The second question read, "On whose account are you basing that his (Richard Poplawski) 'reaction was reportedly influenced by his racist ideology . . . '?"[149]

In response, I said, "There has been multiple media reporting, based on investigations by reporters (and confirmed by I&A research), that indicate Poplawski held racist and extreme antigovernment beliefs—including that the federal government could potentially institute a 'gun ban.'"[150]

"Dozens of incidents similar to Poplawski's involving deadly confrontations between extremists and law enforcement officers indicate that Poplawski most likely reacted as a result of his paranoid extremist and conspiracy oriented beliefs," I continued. "According to his Internet postings, Poplawski self-identified as a skinhead, used racist terms to describe various minorities and believes 'Zionists' (i.e., Jews) are controlling/influencing the federal government, mainstream media, banking system, etc. As a result, it is reasonable to assess that he believes any gun control laws or gun confiscations are therefore orchestrated by Jews and that police officers are acting at the behest of this Jewish 'conspiracy'; this anti-Semitism on his part also likely influenced his actions."[151]

The third question pertained to the Southern Poverty Law Center's Intelligence Project titled "A Few Bad Men," dated July 7, 2006.[152]

The individual's feedback stated, "This report was debunked by Under Secretary of Defense David S. Chu on a letter sent to the SPLC. Said report was heavily based on a (subsequently discredited) single-source."[153]

Nevertheless, this individual was clearly unaware that the SPLC provided a rebuttal to Under Secretary of Defense Chu, dated 12 October 2006.[154] SPLC also sent another letter to the new secretary of defense, dated 26 November 2008, reaffirming their previous concern.[155]

I continued, "With respect to monitoring extremist activity in the U.S., based on analytical experiences we judge both organizations as being objective and thorough in their research and analysis and regard them to be reputable and credible sources of information. Both organizations have been commended numerous times by Federal, state and local law enforcement agencies, and experts from both organizations have provided expert testimony for the government in cases relating to extremism."[156]

"Furthermore, FBI recently wrote an assessment ('White Supremacist Recruitment of Military Personnel since 9/11,' dated 7 July 2008) about this same concern," I answered.[157]

The last question asked, "Has HETA published a report on leftwing extremism that I could read to learn about *that* subject?"[158]

"HETA has published an assessment in January 2009 on leftwing extremism and their potential to conduct cyber attacks," I said.[159]

"Groups adhering to a leftwing ideology, however, are not very active today and currently do not show any indication of becoming violent," I commented.[160] "Nevertheless, HETA has published several articles and assessments on single-issue groups whose ideology is generally defined as 'on the left'—including but not limited to animal rights extremists, eco-terrorists, and black supremacists."[161]

I was satisfied with the answers I provided to this person. Nevertheless, I was still very concerned about the individual's motivation behind submitting the feedback, which was pretty much a negative response with political overtones. Since he worked off-site and had not frequented my work environment at Building 19, I was aware of this person but hardly knew him.

I later learned that this same individual had approached a member of I&A's counterintelligence team on more than one occasion to give him a "heads-up" when he was planning to participate in "Tea Party" protests in Washington, D.C. I mention this only because DHS was criticized for possibly "spying" on the Tea Party protests, which was not true. At the time I was writing the DHS right-wing extremism report, I was totally unaware of the Tea Party's existence. As with any organization, there are extremist elements within it. Judging by his comments to the counterintelligence officer, it appears that this individual may have been part of the "fringe" element.

This individual allegedly remarked to the counterintelligence officer, "In case you see my face in any protest photos, I want you to know that I am merely exercising my First Amendment rights!"

11

Aftermath

Monday, April 13, 2009, began as an inviting spring day. I took the day off to help the local Boy Scout unit finish delivering hundreds of bags of mulch as part of their annual fund-raiser. The scouts had the day off too due to the school system's spring break.

It had been a few days since the release of the right-wing extremism report. In between making mulch deliveries, I was listening to the radio. The upbeat tempo of the music from a local classic rock station kept me motivated and focused on the work at hand. As the time neared the top of the hour, the station's regularly scheduled music programming was briefly interrupted for a news brief. As I was about to press the button, I heard something that immediately caught my attention. I raised the volume to hear more.

"An unclassified report from the Department of Homeland Security warns that the economic crisis and the election of president Barack Obama will reinvigorate white supremacist and antigovernment militia groups," the lead news story began.[1] "But critics say the report shows that people with conservative opinions are being singled out by the Obama administration."[2]

"What the heck?" I remember thinking to myself. I couldn't believe that another Department of Homeland Security (DHS) report had been leaked. Leaks were becoming all too frequent at the DHS. It appeared as though these leaks were deliberate attempts to undermine the integrity of the department as well as shape negative public opinion toward DHS.

"The economic downturn and the election of the first African-American president present unique drivers for right-wing radicalization and recruitment," a news correspondent stated.[3] "The report also says that right-wing militias may try to recruit returning veterans from the wars in Afghanistan and Iraq."[4]

Soon my DHS-issued cell phone was abuzz. A flurry of e-mail messages from work began streaming onto my BlackBerry. Most of the e-mail messages concerned the leak of the right-wing extremism report.

The first e-mail message came in at 8:37 a.m. from the DHS National Operations Center (NOC) duty officer: "The NOC has been inundated this morning with telephone calls from citizens about the release of this document—'Rightwing Extremism: Current Economic and Political Climate Fueling Resurgence in Radicalization and Recruitment'—via the internet. It is unknown as to when this document was leaked; however, the calls are still coming in."[5]

"Here's the document that we are receiving calls about," read another.

"It may be one of those days . . . ," responded a third.

None of us were aware at the time that a well-known television evangelist, Pat Robertson, had directed his listeners on Monday's *700 Club* broadcast to call the DHS Operations Center.

"This is an outrage!" Robertson said. "Ladies and gentlemen, I want you to do something about it . . . I want you to call a number. This is the Department of Homeland Security . . . Get on the phone and call them!"[6]

The telephone numbers to the DHS National Operations Center (NOC) and National Infrastructure Coordinating Center (NICC) were also printed on the last page of the report. These numbers were included in a standard contact statement placed at the end of all of I&A's reports. The contact numbers were not unique to the right-wing extremism assessment. Rather, they were a reminder to recipients of all DHS intelligence products to report suspicious activity. These numbers were never intended to serve some sinister purpose, as some have alleged.

"So, it's out. And there is a blog entry regarding the definition of all things!" my division director wrote in her e-mail dated Monday, April 13, 2009, at 10:10 a.m.

I began to contemplate what work would be like the following day. It would surely be chaotic. The report I had written just a few days earlier was now being scrutinized on national news. I had no idea that media interest would grow and that my report would become the subject of scorn and ridicule aimed at the new presidential administration.

"The report, which was first disclosed to the public by nationally syndicated radio host Roger Hedgecock, makes clear that the Homeland Security Department does not have 'specific information that domestic rightwing terrorists are currently planning acts of violence,'" read a *Washington Times* article on Tuesday morning.[7] "It warns that fringe organizations are gaining recruits, but it provides no numbers."[8]

"So, if you disagree with Obama on amnesty for illegals or stand up for the Second Amendment, you are branded a 'rightwing extremist' by the Department of Homeland Security and become the subject of scrutiny by some 850,000 local and state law enforcement personnel," Roger Hedgecock wrote in his article for the *World Net Daily* news.[9]

"This is the second time that intelligence reports worrying about rightwing extremism have been made public," a reporter for *Security Management* wrote.[10]

"In March, a leaked report from the Missouri Information Analysis Center, a state fusion center, listed the characteristics of violent militia members, which included support for presidential candidate Ron Paul. The state retracted the report after it was leaked."[11]

Fox News reported, "The summary contains few proper names, has no footnotes of any significance, lists very few sources, and is drafted with a prejudice against anyone who criticizes the role of the federal government in our lives today. It lumps together in its definition of 'rightwing extremism' hate groups, anti-government groups, and single issue groups 'such as opposition to abortion or immigration.'"[12]

The Fox News correspondent said, "My guess is that the sentiments revealed in the report I read are the tip of an iceberg that the DHS would prefer to keep submerged until it needs to reveal it. This iceberg is the heavy hand of government; a government with large and awful eyes, in whose heart there is no love for freedom, and on whose face there is no smile."[13]

By Tuesday afternoon, April 14, 2009, every major television news network was carrying the story—CNN, MSNBC, Fox News, CBS, ABC, and many local television affiliates. Portions of the DHS report were displayed on national television for all to see. My words were being analyzed and examined to death. Some reporters were taking things out of context, misinterpreting my statements and spinning them for political purposes. Others were becoming emotional over highly charged media speculation concerning alleged motives and intent behind the report.

As I arrived at the office that morning, I could already feel the tension in the air. My division director greeted me within minutes, took me inside her office at Building 19, and briefed me on the situation at DHS headquarters.

I was told that I&A's executive-level management (above my division director) was not happy about the situation and wanted full disclosure over how the report was generated, who reviewed it, and who was responsible for signing off on it.

"Daryl, be really careful," my division director counseled. "They're looking for 'scapegoats,' and I don't want you to do anything that would jeopardize your career or that of your teammates." Her warning sent a chill down my spine. I couldn't believe that I&A leadership were internalizing the problem. My team had a proven track record. We were high performers and well respected by state and local law enforcement and fusion center representatives. I couldn't believe I&A management was deliberately attempting to place blame on its employees—the intelligence analysts. Despite my initial confusion over management's decision to internalize the problem, I soon realized that my division director's counsel was good advice. It was best to keep a low profile during this tumultuous time.

By midmorning, my immediate supervisor and I were summoned to Roger Mackin's office by an office assistant. Mackin, who was acting undersecretary of I&A at the time, had received a phone call from Capitol Hill. He wanted us by his side as he returned the call.

As we entered Mackin's office, he immediately wanted to know—who reviewed the right-wing extremism report? He also wanted answers about any concerns raised by the DHS Office of Civil Rights and Civil Liberties (CRCL). It was obvious that Congress had been tipped by an insider about our prior disagreement with CRCL over the report's definition. That information had not been made public at the time.

We advised Mackin that all existing office procedures had been followed. Everyone responsible for "signing off" on the report, according to the newly revised I&A production guidelines, had reviewed the report and provided their input. Mackin himself, along with the acting deputy assistant secretary of intelligence (DASI) for analysis and production, had announced an overhaul of the production, vetting, and dissemination procedures during a town hall meeting just two months earlier.[14]

It was reassuring to Mackin that we had followed his revised office procedures. He nodded his head in agreement as we told him about the steps we had followed in coordinating and vetting the right-wing extremism report. He was relieved to hear that we had also documented the coordination and vetting process, which supported the fact that we had clearly followed existing office procedures.

The list of approving officials included my immediate supervisor, division director, multiple editors, the Office of General Counsel, the intelligence oversight officer, the production management director, among others. At the time, CRCL was not part of I&A's production process. They had only recently begun providing consultation to I&A as a courtesy. I&A was not obligated to have CRCL review its products nor was I&A mandated to follow any of CRCL's recommendations.

Mackin and the DASI had recently instituted new guidelines related to I&A's production procedures in January 2009.[15]

In an e-mail broadcast sent to all I&A employees on Friday, January 30, 2009, I&A's Production Management Division stated, "Attached is a copy of the new I&A Production Process that was briefed to you this week. We will be putting this new process into action starting Monday."[16]

In a memo titled "Changes to Office of Intelligence and Analysis Production Process," the acting DASI stated, "A&P leadership has decided to make some changes to I&A's finished intelligence production process, effective immediately."[17]

"These changes are intended to make it easier to, in Acting Undersecretary Mackin's words, 'Get the right information to the right people at the right time,'" she wrote.[18]

"These changes, which are intended to speed the analytic production and editorial process, will place new empowerment as well as responsibilities in the hands of both analytic and production personnel," she said.[19] "The Production Branch (PB) has been briefing the analytic divisions on these new procedures, and will continue to work with all concerned to make this transition to a leaner and more agile clearance process as painless as possible."[20]

As outlined in the new office procedures, the most significant change was the delegation of final approval and release authority from the DASI to the division directors.

Under a section titled "Final Approval and Release," the revised production procedures memo read, "Once division approval is received, the final draft and completed abstract (required for both recordkeeping purposes and dissemination guidance) are sent to the Production Branch (PB) by the Branch Chief or Branch Designee for final editing and release."[21]

As we waited for Roger Mackin to return the phone call to Capitol Hill, we told him that the only unresolved concern was with CRCL and their issue related to the definition of right-wing extremism. CRCL thought the definition was too broad and wanted to limit it only to violent groups and individuals.

We advised Mackin that over a two-week period, we had attempted to reach a compromise with various versions of the definition. Despite our repeated attempts to reword the definition, we were still unable to persuade CRCL to incorporate aspects of the definition recommended by subject matter experts. CRCL remained inflexible. Ultimately, the Office of General Counsel was consulted, and they decided we should use the original definition, since it was already preapproved, having been used in another, previously released report. Mackin appeared satisfied with our answers.

He then picked up the phone and called Capitol Hill to relay the information we had just shared with him. At the conclusion of the phone call, Mackin thanked us for our time and said he appreciated our quick and thorough responses. We left his office feeling good about what we had shared with the acting undersecretary of intelligence. Nevertheless, we suspected it was just the beginning. There was plenty more work to do to help our division director and other managers resolve concerns from DHS leadership, Congress, and the media.

By Wednesday, April 15, 2009, Napolitano issued an official press statement regarding the report. Her remarks were titled, "Statement by U.S. Department of Homeland Security Secretary Janet Napolitano on the Threat of Rightwing Extremism."[22]

The department's press release began, "The primary mission of this department is to prevent terrorist attacks on our nation. The document on rightwing extremism sent last week by this department's Office of Intelligence and Analysis is one in an ongoing series of assessments to provide situational awareness to state, local, and tribal law enforcement agencies on the phenomenon and trends of violent radicalization in the United States. I was briefed on the general topic, which is one that struck a nerve as someone personally involved in the Timothy McVeigh prosecution."[23]

"Let me be very clear: we monitor the risks of violent extremism taking root here in the United States. We don't have the luxury of focusing our efforts on one group; we must protect the country from terrorism whether foreign or homegrown, and regardless of the ideology that motivates its violence," it read.[24]

"We are on the lookout for criminal and terrorist activity but we do not—nor will we ever—monitor ideology or political beliefs. We take seriously our responsibility to protect the civil rights and liberties of the American people, including subjecting our activities to rigorous oversight from numerous internal and external sources," the press release continued.[25]

To address the veteran concern, Napolitano wrote, "I am aware of the letter from *American Legion* National Commander Rehbein, and my staff has already contacted him to set up a meeting next week once I return from travel. I will tell him face-to-face that we honor veterans at DHS and employ thousands across the Department, up to and including the Deputy Secretary."[26]

"As the department responsible for protecting the homeland, DHS will continue to work with its state and local partners to prevent and protect against the potential threat to the United States associated with any rise," her statement concluded.[27]

Despite Napolitano's official press release, conservative criticism about the report continued to mount. By Wednesday, most news outlets were carrying Napolitano's remarks, but it did little to quell the outrage. The airwaves continued to be "lit up" with news of the new DHS "warning."

"There's a disturbing new trend we can report to you this morning. Two new reports out document an alarming rise in the number of 'hate groups' in the United States," reported the host of the *Early Show* on CBS.[28]

"A new warning out from Homeland Security, the U.S. is ripe for terror recruiting by extremists. No, we're not talking al-Qaeda. We're talking U.S. war veterans," said Fox News correspondent Megyn Kelly.[29] "That's who the Department of Homeland Security said we need to be aware of in a new report that has some military groups and others outraged."[30]

"Dramatic warning here at home to tell you about, the Department of Homeland Security tonight telling law enforcement agencies that homegrown right-wing extremist groups are growing," said CNN correspondent Anderson Cooper.[31] "They're gaining strength, according to the report, by exploiting fears about President Obama's race as well as fears about the economy."[32]

Most news programs were providing daily updates concerning the report, the department's response, and the growing controversy stemming primarily from conservative outrage.

Wolf Blitzer reported on his nationally syndicated *Situation Room* show on CNN, "Conservative outrage over a 'red flag' from the Homeland Security Department warning of a potential threat from right-wing extremists. The response to that so intense that now the Homeland Security Secretary herself is trying to quell the anger."[33]

During his evening broadcast, Shepard Smith stated, "Right-wing extremists could be using the troubled economy to incite violence and recruit new members—that's according to the Department of Homeland Security."[34]

MSNBC's Keith Olbermann remarked on the *Countdown*, "In its latest threat assessment, the Department of Homeland Security warns of a possible increase in violence from right-wing extremists. Extremists [are] being defined as 'those who are hate-oriented and single issue.'"[35]

While most news stories were objective in their remarks about the report, other, more incendiary news personalities launched an attack against the report and its perceived motive and intent.

Rush Limbaugh on his morning talk radio show remarked, "This is an effort to criminalize political dissents—standard, ordinary, everyday political dissent . . . We are not the extremists. 'They' are the extremists," he said.[36]

"If the Bush Administration had done this to 'left-wing' extremists, it would be all over the press as an obvious trampling of First Amendment rights of folks," said Roger Hedgecock, another conservative radio talk show host.[37]

"The Department of Homeland Security tonight warning of a new terrorist threat facing America," Lou Dobbs began his story on CNN. "The threat comes from what it calls 'right-wing extremists' in this country."

Dobbs continued, "The report says people who are opposed to restricting Second Amendment rights to bear arms or who are concerned about illegal immigration and border security could well fall under the Department of Homeland Security definition of an 'extremist.'"[38]

The report was all over the news. The DHS was scrambling to get a clear, concise message out. But the story was growing by the day and increasingly out of control.

It appeared as though numerous news outlets were broadcasting negative stories about the DHS report. This perception, however, was being fueled by Fox News, which was being shown on almost every television screen at DHS headquarters. In reality, only a few television news programs had taken a negative slant on the report itself.

As the political pressure mounted, Napolitano was forced to interrupt her official travel to the southern border to give an impromptu press conference. Her earlier press release had done very little to appease the anger.

"We do not exist to infringe, impede, or invade anybody's constitutional rights of free speech, of free assembly, or anything else like that," Napolitano began her remarks.[39] "We exist to protect the country against the [threat to] the Homeland consistent with the Constitution. And, so, in there is where that product was created and what it was designed to do."[40]

A few days later, Napolitano took another opportunity to address the critics during an interview with CNN correspondent John King on the fourteenth anniversary of the Oklahoma City bombing.

When asked a question about language in the report describing the recruitment of military veterans, Napolitano responded, "The report is not saying that veterans are extremists—far from it. What it is saying is returning veterans are targets of right-wing extremist groups that are trying to recruit those who commit violent acts within the country. We want to do all we can to prevent that."[41]

Later in the same interview, Napolitano stated, "At the Department of Homeland Security, we were stood up because of a terrorist act—9/11. But that came on the heels of Oklahoma City, which was a domestically caused terrorist act."

She continued, "So, one of our missions that Congress has given us and what we do is try to keep everybody informed—what are the kinds of things that could lead to an act of violence, but in this case, where are groups recruiting."[42]

In response to a question concerning the definition of right-wing extremist, Napolitano answered, "I regret that in the politicization of everything that happens in Washington, D.C., some took offense."[43]

"But when you read the report, what it was saying is 'Look, we have a threat of terrorism within our own shores and one of the groups being targeted to see if they align with that [extremist view] are some of our veterans," Napolitano said.[44] "Let's make sure we prevent that.'"[45]

King asked if Napolitano regrets anything that was written in the report. Napolitano responded, "In retrospect, anything can be written differently to prevent politicization."[46]

"But I think any fair reading of the report says this is very consistent with other reports that have been issued before," she stated.[47] "They [DHS reports] were issued before Obama was president [and] they're being issued now. They are meant to give people what is called 'situational awareness' and they're certainly not meant to give offense—far from it."[48]

"The last thing the Department of Homeland Security is about is infringing on anybody's constitutionally protected rights," Napolitano stressed.[49] "On the other hand, at the very edge of the debate, are extremist groups that have committed violent crimes. They've committed bombings and the like."[50]

Napolitano concluded, "That's where you cross from constitutionally protected free speech, freedom of assembly, all the rights we cherish into Homeland Security and law enforcement. When that right is not being exercised, it's being abused."[51]

A day earlier, the White House reportedly had distanced itself from the report. When asked for comment on the report and its contents, White House spokesman Nick Shapiro said, "The president is focused not on politics but rather taking the steps necessary to protect all Americans from the threat of violence and terrorism regardless of its origins. He also believes those who serve represent the best of this country, and he will continue to ensure that our veterans receive the respect and benefits they have earned."[52]

In hindsight, most of the criticism about the DHS right-wing extremism report focused on the definition and statements concerning "disgruntled" military veterans. As a result, two of the largest military veterans' organizations in the country weighed in on the controversy.

David K. Rehbein, national commander of the American Legion, sent a letter to Napolitano on April 13, 2009, criticizing the report's statements concerning returning military veterans.

"First, I want to assure you that the American Legion has long shared your concern about white supremacist and anti-government groups," Rehbein wrote.[53]

"In 1923, when the Ku Klux Klan still yielded unspeakable influence in this country, the American Legion passed Resolution 407," he explained.[54] "It resolved, in part, ' . . . we consider any individual, group of individuals or organizations, which creates, or fosters racial, religious or class strife among our people, or which takes into their own hands the enforcement of law, determination of guilt, or infliction of punishment, to be un-American, a menace to our liberties, and destructive to our fundamental law.'"[55]

"The best that I can say about your recent report is that it is incomplete." Rehbein stated.[56]

"The American Legion is well aware and horrified at the pain inflicted during the Oklahoma City bombing, but Timothy McVeigh was only one of more than 42 million veterans who have worn this nation's uniform during wartime," Rehbein argued.[57]

"To continue to use McVeigh as an example of the stereotypical "disgruntled military veteran" is as unfair as using Osama bin Laden as the sole example of Islam."[58]

"In spite of this incomplete, and, I fear, politically-biased report, the American Legion and the Department of Homeland Security share many common and crucial interests, such as the Citizen Corps and disaster preparedness," Rehbein said.[59]

He concluded his letter by stating, "I would be happy to meet with you at a time of mutual convenience to discuss issues such as border security and the war on terrorism. I think it is important for all of us to remember that Americans are not the enemy. The terrorists are."[60]

The following day, Wednesday, April 15, the leader of the nation's largest combat veterans' organization, the Veterans of Foreign Wars (VFW), released a statement stating that a leaked government document that mentions disgruntled military veterans as potential security threats should have been worded differently, but he took no issue with the document's purpose, which was to assess possible threats to the safety and security of the United States.[61]

"A government that does not assess internal and external security threats would be negligent of a critical public responsibility," said Glen M. Gardner Jr., national commander of the 2.2 million-member VFW and its auxiliaries.[62]

"The report proves that DHS is doing its job, and that's to protect America and Americans," said Gardner, a Vietnam veteran of the U.S. Marine Corps from Round Rock, Texas.[63]

"The report should have been worded differently, but it made no blanket accusation that every soldier was capable of being a traitor like Benedict Arnold, or every veteran could be a lone wolf, homegrown terrorist like Timothy McVeigh. It was just an assessment about possibilities that could take place," said Gardner.[64]

The following week, local veterans and their supporters assembled at the State Capitol in Oklahoma City, Oklahoma, to voice their criticism of the recently released DHS report They were upset at the suggestion that those who had served in Iraq and Afghanistan, as well as individuals who opposed abortion and supported Second Amendment gun rights, were labeled a potential threat to national security.[65]

"The report's opening sentence states that there is no evidence of impending attack but then proceeds to offer assessment without fact that veterans make up a fertile recruiting ground for domestic terror groups," said state senator Steve Russell (R-Oklahoma).

"In the most shameful manner, the report singles out returning war veterans as the most likely candidates for domestic acts of terror and opines that America's Iraq and Afghan veterans pose great danger to the security of the United States," he asserted.[66]

Russell served in both Iraq and Afghanistan. He now chaired an organization called Vets for Victory.[67] Russell reportedly said he was "stunned by the Homeland Security report."[68]

In response to the report, Russell drafted a Senate Resolution that was approved on April 22. The resolution was critical of the current administration's perceived "mischaracterization of our wartime service."[69]

"I say administration because the report includes opinion from both the Departments of Homeland Security and Justice," Russell said.[70] "My resolution also takes issue with the blatant political and ideological profiling of tens of millions of average Americans who treasure legal citizenship, sound fiscal spending, a culture of life and the right of an individual to bear arms."[71]

"In one fell swoop, this 'assessment' crosses the line between considering political dissent and expression, to that of violating civil liberties by being unduly singled out as a profiled threat to society at large," Russell explained.[72]

"Taken at face value, this report from our Department of Homeland Security would qualify the vast majority of Oklahomans as threats to our national security," Russell assessed.

"If upholding traditional American values such as the sanctity of life, the right to bear arms and defending your country is extremist, then I stand so accused," he concluded.[73]

Russell's Senate Resolution 42 also stated that the "Oklahoma State Senate supports America's military veterans, who have risked their lives preserving the nation instead of attacking it, and believes that the traditional American values under attack by the Obama Administration should be respected and revered by the federal government."[74]

On Friday, April 24, 2009, Napolitano and her senior-level advisor, Rand Beers, held a meeting with representatives from the American Legion, including commander David Rehbein, in an attempt to resolve concerns over the veteran issue.[75]

"Whether it's providing support for first responders, helping to secure our borders, enforcing smart and tough immigration laws or boosting preparedness for natural disasters, the veterans who make up our workforce play a prominent and critical role in accomplishing DHS' mission," a DHS press release said concerning the meeting with the American Legion.[76] Forty-four thousand veterans are employed at the DHS, comprising 26 percent of the department's workforce.[77]

"Secretary Napolitano helped men and women [who] have bravely and honorably served our country become American citizens," it read.[78] "They put themselves on the frontlines to protect a country that wasn't even their own."[79]

The DHS press release concluded, "It is their service and the service of so many other veterans, including those that work each day at DHS, that is the true example of commitment to our country and not political games or folly."[80]

The American Legion and its representatives were treated with more respect and dignity by the department's leadership than the DHS employees who were directly involved in the drafting, vetting, and release of the right-wing extremism report.

So it was extremely surprising, and very disturbing, to later learn that local American Legion chapters at various locations throughout the country were fostering the growth of radical right-wing extremists such as militia groups,[81,82] Oath Keepers,[83] sovereign citizens,[84] and other antigovernment groups.[85] This was done with the apparent knowledge and support of local American Legion chapter leaders within months of their organization criticizing the DHS for merely pointing out that extremist groups would likely target returning veterans for recruitment. The American Legion was literally permitting right-wing extremist groups to use their facilities for meetings, elections, and other events. Obviously, given the high level of media coverage on the subjects of sovereign citizens, militias, and Oath Keepers, local American Legion leaders must surely know that these groups embrace antigovernment conspiracy theories and anti-American views. Such extremist groups along with their radical views also appear to be at odds with the aforementioned American Legion Resolution 407.

The American Legion was allowing these radical right-wing extremist groups to meet at their facilities where they spew hatred for Obama and undermine the U.S. government, its laws, and institutions through holding elections to form their own de facto governments. It seems apparent to me that the American Legion was either actively participating in these subversive activities or tacitly supporting them by providing a place for antigovernment extremists to gather, recruit, and conduct their radicalization activities.[86]

It is surely hypocritical to accuse DHS of portraying U.S. war veterans as potential terrorists, yet encourage and permit these very radical ideologies to flourish and grow within a veterans organization. It is a very serious situation deserving more attention. It also appears that some right-wing extremists were actually targeting the American Legion for recruitment as a deliberate strategy.

On Tuesday, April 14, my division director had asked that I accompany her to an executive-level meeting held in Building 5. The meeting was chaired by deputy secretary Jane Holl Lute and Beers. The meeting concerned the department's internal review processes and what, if any, changes were needed. Various DHS headquarters decision makers were also in attendance, including leaders from CRCL and privacy and policy offices. There was some obvious tension between my division director and I and the CRCL representatives since we had attempted to reach a compromise on the definition of right-wing extremism a few weeks earlier. At the meeting CRCL representatives took full advantage of the fact they had dissented on the definition to absolve themselves of any responsibility and to further their agenda. They made no acknowledgement of their concurrence on other parts of the report that had drawn much criticism, such as the perceived mischaracterization of military veterans, conservatives, gun owners, and opponents of illegal immigration.

Lute, herself a former member of the military, was calm and collected as she directed the meeting's agenda. Her main concern focused on instituting an interim review process to ensure future reports were given proper political consideration. Lute was determined to see that the department did not encounter another media fiasco concerning its intelligence reports.

Beers then laid out his proposal to create the "G6" review process. Beers, a former Marine Corps officer during Vietnam, had been serving as counselor to Secretary Napolitano since January 21, 2009.[87] Before his appointment, he was the co-leader of the Department of Homeland Security Transition Team for the incoming Obama administration.[88]

Lute then sought input from those in attendance. For the most part, my division director and I sat silently. We had nothing to say. The decision appeared to have already been made, and any dissension from us would have only furthered CRCL's contention that "we" were the problem.

The meeting adjourned, and everyone left for the evening. It was the first and last time I was ever involved in any leadership meetings or discussions related to the report and its aftermath—even as a passive observer.

Concurrent to the media publicity and conservative outcry came multiple letters from U.S. congressional representatives. The congressional letters proved to be yet another attack on the department, its analysts, and its mission.

"I am writing regarding an April 2009 report generated by the Department's Office of Intelligence and Analysis (I&A) entitled, 'Rightwing Extremism: Current Economic and Political Climate Fueling Resurgence in Radicalization and Recruitment,'" began a letter from congressman Bennie Thompson (D-Mississippi).[89] "This report seems to raise significant issues involving the privacy and civil liberties of many Americans—including war veterans."[90]

I was a little surprised and perplexed that Thompson would send such a letter to the DHS about a report on right-wing extremism. In 2005, Thompson held congressional hearings on the tenth anniversary of the Oklahoma City bombing and issued a mandate to DHS requesting that the department "do more to fight rightwing domestic terrorists."[91] The DHS report he was now openly criticizing was doing exactly what Thompson had mandated to DHS just four years earlier.

"This report appears to have blurred the line between violent belief, which is constitutionally protected, and violent action, which is not," Thompson said.[92] "I am disappointed and surprised that the Department would allow this report to be disseminated to its state, local and tribal partners in its present form."[93]

"As you know, the Committee's Subcommittee on Intelligence, Information Sharing and Terrorism Risk Assessment recently held a hearing on fusion centers and associated privacy and civil liberties issues . . . . Given this positive collaboration, I am dumbfounded that I&A released this report," Thompson wrote.[94]

Thompson further stated, "I am particularly struck by the report's conclusion which states that I&A 'will be working with its state and local partners over the next several months to ascertain with greater specificity the rise in rightwing extremist activity in the United States, with a particular emphasis on the political, economic and social factors that drive rightwing extremist radicalization.'"[95]

"I would like more information about what types of activities I&A intends to undertake in the next few months in this regard," Thompson requested.[96]

"Additionally, please provide a written description of your clearance process for I&A generated intelligence products that are to be disseminated to state, local and tribal law enforcement," Thompson inquired.[97] "In general terms, I would like information on what role, if any, the Chief Privacy Officer and the Officer for Civil Rights and Civil Liberties play in the preparation and clearance process for such products. I would also like information on what role, if any, they played with respect to this particular report."⁹⁸

Thompson's letter not only opened my eyes to the double standard and hypocrisy surrounding Washington politics, it also validated my suspicion that CRCL itself was "playing politics" by leaking information to congressional representatives about what had occurred relative to the definition issue prior to the release of the right-wing extremism report.

With both Mackin's call from Capitol Hill and Thompson's letter, it appears that CRCL may have added "fuel to the fire" by contacting congressional representatives. Thompson's letter was dated April 14, 2009—the same day the media firestorm erupted. Yet the media had not picked up on the fact that there had been some dissension within the department over the definition of right-wing extremism. This was reported days later as the controversy dragged into a second week.

In addition to writing multiple talking points for I&A leadership in preparation for their congressional testimony about the report, my team and I had to compile information and assist with providing responses for over forty Freedom of Information Act (FOIA) requests that were submitted in the days after the leak. This proved to be an excruciating experience with which few analysts are prepared to deal. We had to balance the right to public disclosure with the merits of safeguarding sensitive law enforcement information, ongoing criminal investigations, and covert investigative techniques used by sworn law enforcement officers to acquire information contained in the report.

As the media controversy, public criticism, and congressional scrutiny continued into another week, I felt obligated to assess the situation within I&A and weigh the potential impacts on the team's mission and possible consequences. I was already keeping my team members updated on what I was hearing from the division director and others who were involved in office decisions. I also needed to give them my personal assessment of the situation. I had a "gut feeling" on what was probably going to transpire. My division director had already given me a "heads-up" that I&A management had decided to abandon support for its employees out of their need for self-preservation. I&A managers involved in revising the production process were certainly not going to admit to their role in changing office procedures. They had their own careers to protect. It was easier to blame the analysts.

Thus, I began thinking about my options. Being an optimist, I was hoping the situation would improve, that the mission would survive and my team would remain intact. That said, I was also smart enough to realize the gravity of the situation and the possible repercussions resulting from self-serving decision makers. As a result, I felt compelled to share my concerns and possible plans with my team in an honest attempt to look after them and to prepare them for a probable worst-case scenario.

I quietly summoned my entire team into a vacant office one morning and closed the door. I gave them a quick update on recent developments related to the leak of the right-wing extremism report and resulting aftermath. I then gave them some advice.

"I don't know how this situation is going to play out. It's not looking good," I said. "As a result, each of you needs to think about the possibility that this mission won't survive and that our team might be dissolved."

"You need to think about looking for another job," I said, looking at each team member. I didn't want to scare them into thinking they were going to be fired, although some congressmen and media personalities were calling for my resignation. Nevertheless, I knew that the federal hiring process was a long, involved procedure, and I wanted to give my team members a fair shot at getting out, if the situation continued to deteriorate inside the agency.

As the media frenzy and FOIA requests were starting to wind down, the congressional hearings concerning the right-wing extremism report were about to begin.

On Wednesday, May 6, 2009, U.S. Representative Peter T. King (R-New York), ranking member of the Committee on Homeland Security, along with Republican leader John Boehner (R-Ohio), Republican whip Eric Cantor (R-Virginia), Republican conference chairman Mike Pence (R-Indiana), and other Republican members of the House Committee on Homeland Security introduced a Resolution of Inquiry, House Resolution 404 (H.S. 404), asking Napolitano to release information used in compiling the so-called 'Rightwing Extremism' report."[99]

"We need to get to the bottom of how this report was developed, and what kind of approval process occurred before it was sent out as gospel to police departments across the country," King said.[100] "We have made repeated requests that the Committee holds a bipartisan oversight hearing, but unfortunately those requests have been ignored."[101]

"We are left with no other alternative but to demand answers from the Secretary of Homeland Security herself," King stated.[102]

"The report that came out of DHS was offensive, and unfortunately Secretary Napolitano still has a lot of explaining to do," added Boehner.[103] "She has not explained how this report came about, why she signed off on it, or why she defended it, rather than immediately apologizing to the current and former members of America's Armed Forces."[104]

Boehner concluded his statement, "I'd like to thank Ranking Member King for leading the effort to get this matter resolved."[105]

King's Resolution of Inquiry directed Napolitano to submit to the House of Representatives within fourteen days after the date of adoption all documents related to the right-wing extremism assessment.[106]

"We need thoughtful, bipartisan oversight of the Department of Homeland Security," King said.[107] "The American people need to know how exactly the Department reached the conclusion that veterans returning from Iraq and Afghanistan might be recruited by extremists."

"What's more, how did a report go forward ignoring the input of the Office of Civil Rights and Civil Liberties at DHS?" King questioned.[108] "It is absolutely crucial that one hand knows what the other hand is doing. It doesn't seem like that's what happened here."[109]

Two congressional hearings were held that raised questions to Napolitano regarding the DHS right-wing extremism report. The first was held in the House Appropriations Committee, Homeland Security Subcommittee on Tuesday, May 12, 2009. The second was held the following day.

On Wednesday, May 13, 2009, the Homeland Security Committee in the U.S. House of Representatives held a hearing on the Department of Homeland Security's Fiscal Year 2010 Budget Request.

Also, on May 13, 2009, senators Tom Coburn (R-Oklahoma) and John Ensign (R-Nevada), members of the U.S. Senate Homeland Security and Government Affairs Committee, sent a letter to Napolitano concerning the right-wing extremism report.

"As members of the Senate Homeland Security and Government Affairs Committee, we would like to receive more information about the mission and operations of the Department of Homeland Security's (DHS) Office of Intelligence and Analysis (I&A)," the letter began.[110]

"Many of our colleagues have recently shared our concerns with you about the report on rightwing extremism. This and other reports issued by the little known Homeland Environment Threat Analysis Division (HETA) within I&A raise troubling questions about its mission and purpose in the intelligence operations of DHS."[111]

"We believe in a robust intelligence infrastructure. However, the I&A reports and analysis we have seen serve little real intelligence purpose except to blur our constitutional protections. It is imperative that reports issued by the federal government be backed by factual and relevant data and intelligence."[112] The Coburn and Ensign letter then lists twelve items requested to gain a better understanding about the workings of I&A. The list included items such as the official production and vetting process for intelligence reports; the total budget of I&A for each year since its inception; the total budget for HETA each year since its creation; all relevant documents explaining the core mission and goals of I&A and HETA; explanations of the primary function and responsibility of I&A and HETA; organization charts; and a list of accomplishments and successes of the office since its inception.[113]

There were also a few items related to the right-wing extremism report, including copies of all unclassified sources used in the report; the definition of right-wing extremism that was offered by CRCL; details related to future reports and analysis that HETA may release over the next twelve months; a copy of all reports issued by HETA over the past eighteen months; and changes to the production process *since* [emphasis added] the issuance of the right-wing extremism report.[114]

On Tuesday, May 19, 2009, Thompson issued a statement providing an update concerning House Resolution 404.

"When this DHS-produced assessment first surfaced in April, like many Americans, I had issues with its content," Thompson stated.[115] "Certainly, its definition of 'rightwing extremism,' which did not clarify that extremist violence was the Department's true focus, raised considerable concern."[116]

"So did the suggestion that returning war veterans posed a potential threat to the homeland," Thompson continued.[117] "That's why, on April 14, 2009, I wrote the first letter from Congress to Secretary Napolitano about this assessment."[118]

"In it, I asked for, among other things, information on the Department's clearance process for this and other assessments," Thompson said.[119] "I particularly wanted to know why the report focused on veterans. On April 25, 2009, the Department responded to my concerns in writing."[120]

"In her letter, Secretary Napolitano explained that DHS 'does not focus on in-dividuals or groups solely based on their First Amendment-protected associations, beliefs, or speech,'" Thompson remarked.[121] "She explained that the Office of Intel-ligence and Analysis directorate within the Department targets terrorism and other violent criminal behavior that threatens the nation."[122]

"The Secretary explained that the Department's review found that since the De-partment was established in 2003, there had never before been a robust clearance process for I&A intelligence products," Thompson said.[123]

"The clearance process that was in place, moreover, was insufficient. Specifically, she told the Committee that the assessment was disseminated by I&A without the agreement of the Office of Civil Rights and Civil Liberties," he stated.[124] "It is my understanding that a new clearance process is being established that takes into con-sideration the very concerns that this Committee has expressed."[125]

"The Committee will look to the new I&A leadership to utilize the new clearance process going forward," Thompson continued.[126] "Certainly, Bart Johnson, the new Deputy Undersecretary for Intelligence and Analysis, is uniquely skilled to take the lead on reforming the DHS assessment process, given his extensive experience as a former Colonel with the New York State Police."[127]

"His twenty-three years as a New York State Trooper and most recently the DNI's Director for Homeland Security and Law Enforcement Support and Outreach, qualify him to fix I&A's broken process," said Thompson. "He knows what intel-ligence the nation's first preventers need and he knows how to deliver it to state and locals."[128]

"Let the record reflect that in addition to providing a written response to my letter, Secretary Napolitano also sent representatives to brief both Majority and Minority staff on April 23, 2009," the congressman wrote.[129] "I understand the Department also provided briefings to a number of other Committees."[130]

"We appreciate the frankness of the briefers who presented to the Committee," Representative Thompson stated.[131] "They provided a clear description of what hap-pened, what didn't happen, and what will be happening to make things right."[132]

I have no idea what was briefed to the House Homeland Security Committee. I was neither consulted about these testimonies, nor was I given an opportunity to review the official version of events as recounted by I&A leadership. I certainly hope they gave a true accounting of what occurred and accurately described everyone's level of involvement.

Thompson also stated, "Additionally, let the record also reflect that on May 8, 2009, the Department provided the Committee with source material used by I&A to develop the extremism assessment."[133]

"When this assessment surfaced, DHS had a lot to answer for. In my view, the Secretary has provided those answers and has been extremely forthcoming," Congressman Thompson explained.[134] "More broadly, I look forward to continuing to work with the Secretary and the new I&A leadership team to help this struggling directorate turn into a vital information sharing partner with state, local and tribal law enforcement."[135]

An afterthought amidst the chaos was a frivolous lawsuit filed by the Thomas Moore Law Center based in Ann Arbor, Michigan. I had absolutely no involvement in this suit nor any insight into how I&A or DHS responded to it. Nevertheless, on April 19, 2009, the law center announced that it had filed a federal lawsuit against Homeland Security secretary Janet Napolitano.[136]

"The non-profit law firm said the U.S. Department of Homeland Security's 'rightwing extremism policy,' reflected in an Intelligence Assessment publicized last week, violates the civil liberties of combat veterans as well as American citizens by targeting them for disfavored treatment on account of their political beliefs," read a news account of the lawsuit.[137]

"The lawsuit was filed in the U.S. District Court for the Eastern District of Michigan on behalf of conservative radio talk show host, Michael Savage, Gregg Cunningham (president of the pro-life organization Center for Bio-Ethical Reform, Inc.), and Iraqi War Marine veteran Kevin Murray, according to the Thomas Moore Web site," the news article stated.[138]

"The Law Center claims that Napolitano's department violated the First and Fifth Amendment rights of these the plaintiffs by attempting to chill their free speech, expressive association, and equal protection rights," it read.[139]

"The lawsuit further claims that the Department of Homeland Security encourages law enforcement officers throughout the nation to target and report citizens to federal officials as suspicious rightwing extremists and potential terrorists because of their political beliefs," the article concluded.[140]

As result of the political controversy and public outcry surrounding the leaked DHS report, acting undersecretary for I&A, Roger Mackin, who for all intents and purposes was "in charge" at I&A, was essentially forced to step down.[141] On April 24, 2009, a news report announced that Mackin had abruptly transferred to another position in the intelligence community.[142] Another had mistakenly reported Mackin had been "fired."[143]

Few outside of I&A knew that other I&A managers played a role in advising Mackin on various office-wide decisions, including changing I&A's production process. There have been absolutely no consequences for these individuals who continue to make poor choices and ill-advised decisions at I&A at the expense of the organization, its employees, and stakeholders. In fact, the DASI, who was primarily responsible for advising Mackin on changing I&A's production procedures, received a pay raise of over $13,000 within six months after the leak of the DHS right-wing extremism report.[144] As of this writing, she continues to function in a high-level managerial position at I&A.

"The head of the Homeland Security agency responsible for a controversial report that suggested veterans were being recruited to commit terrorist acts in the U.S. is being replaced by a former FBI and CIA official," the *Washington Times* newspaper reported on April 24, 2009.[145]

A day earlier, Napolitano had announced that the White House intended to select Phillip Mudd as its nominee for the new undersecretary for intelligence and analysis.

"Mr. Mudd is a 24-year career FBI official, who currently serves as the associate executive assistant director of the Bureau's national security branch," the *Washington Times* reported in the same article.[146]

Concurrent to Mudd's nomination, Napolitano also stated that she was appointing Mr. Bart R. Johnson as the new principal deputy undersecretary at I&A.[147] Johnson was currently serving as the director of homeland security and law enforcement at the Office of the Director of National Intelligence at the time of his selection for the principal deputy undersecretary position.[148]

Although the newspapers didn't say as much, Mackin's premature departure from I&A on April 23, 2009, was almost certainly a direct result of the congressional and public backlash surrounding the DHS report. Mackin was reassigned to lead the cyber security section at the Office of the Director of National Intelligence.[149]

A DHS press spokesman described Mackin's reassignment as being planned for weeks and predating the intelligence assessment controversy. Insiders believe that Mackin was the first "scapegoat" blamed as a result of the right-wing extremism report controversy.

At the time of the report's release on April 7, 2009, there was no indication that Mackin was moving to a new position. In fact, there were rumors throughout the office that Mackin may have been in contention for being the next undersecretary position. Further, Phil Mudd's nomination had not yet proceeded to the formal confirmation hearing phase.

As a result of Mackin's untimely departure, Johnson, recently appointed as I&A's principal deputy undersecretary in March 2009, assumed Mackin's role as acting undersecretary for I&A—the fifth in as many years.[150]

Mudd's confirmation, however, would be held up indefinitely due to Republican-led criticism of Mudd's reported involvement in the controversial CIA interrogation program for terrorism suspects.[151] As public and congressional criticism mounted, Mudd eventually withdrew his name from consideration on June 5, 2009.[152] He probably thought it would be a futile effort to continue pursuing the position in light of the growing criticism. He also likely wanted to spare I&A further congressional and public ridicule that had resulted from the leaked DHS right-wing extremism report. It took nearly four months to find another nominee for I&A's undersecretary position.

That same day, Johnson sent out an impromptu request to meet with each division and respective personnel to inform them that Mudd had decided to withdraw his name from consideration for the Undersecretary position. Johnson soon made his way to the HETA division work space to meet with HETA personnel. I was standing among the fifty-plus HETA employees that had gathered around my team's work space for Johnson's unexpected announcement. Few, if any, of us knew what he was going to say.

After his brief remarks about Mudd, Johnson caught a glimpse of a sign hanging on one of the computer monitors that read "HETA."

Bart Johnson immediately asked, as he pointed to the sign on the monitor, "This is the division that wrote the right-wing extremism report. So who wrote it?"

I was standing a few feet away from Johnson. In response to his question, I raised my hand. He looked in my direction and literally took a step back away from me.

He said something like, "If you told me that you wrote that assessment based on the facts as you knew it, and that the information was taken out of context and spun for political purposes, I would back you up in a heartbeat. But, that's not what happened."

"Actually, that is what happened, sir," I replied. "I would be happy to meet with you in your office to explain exactly what occurred."

He replied, "I'll have to take a rain check on that. As you can see, I'm extremely busy, but I'll get back to you."

He never did.

Within days of Mudd's unexpected withdrawal, Johnson and his leadership team implemented an office-wide restructuring. This reorganization affected about 800 federal employees and government contractors at I&A. This was likely done in an attempt to appease congressional concerns related to the DHS right-wing extremism report.

I&A's reorganization was likely caused by the unauthorized leak of a law enforcement–sensitive report, an event beyond the organization's control and most likely motivated by an organization's fear for its very existence.

The acting DASI told me in a hallway of Building 19 within days after the leak that the organization's literal existence was "hanging in the balance" and that I&A could not afford another "screwup."

At a town hall meeting to discuss the impending office reorganization, I&A's chief of staff, who later left for another job soon after the office restructuring, made a comment to the effect, "Some of you are going to be happy about these changes, and many of you are not."

"We're all going to have to deal with it," he said. "It all depends on whether you look at it as a glass half empty or a glass half full."

As part of the office-wide restructuring, many basic office units, called branches, were moved from one division to another. Others were merged with each other or dissolved altogether. Many employees commented to me that they inferred from the chief of staff's remarks that they either needed to accept the organizational changes or find another job. There was no room for discussion or debate.

Personally, it was extremely frustrating seeing the lives of hundreds of my coworkers being unnecessarily disrupted as a result of conservative media personalities, politicians, and others taking things out of context, politicizing my report, and misinterpreting its findings.

I wanted people to understand that the report was not politically motivated. It was an honest attempt to warn and inform law enforcement of a growing threat within our country. After all, I personify the conservative mindset. I represent the very constituency that lashed out at the report. I'm married with children, an Eagle Scout, gun owner, and Mormon.

Some criticized that the points raised in the report were obvious and didn't say anything. Yet to my knowledge, I&A was the first to connect the dots and write about this unique convergence of socioeconomic and political factors influencing a rise in extremism in this country.

I was also distraught at my inability to speak up for myself, the agency I worked for, or the genesis behind the report. The DHS Public Affairs Office had a difficult time managing the department's response. They appeared disorganized, unprepared, and ill-equipped to handle the situation. This exacerbated my sense of helplessness over the entire situation.

I was basically isolated from decision makers and immediately cut out of the loop. I&A leadership quickly took control of the situation from an organizational perspective and barely consulted us about anything.

Within days of the leak, I&A management canceled all domestic terrorism training for state and local law enforcement. Commitments for briefings presentations were put on hold indefinitely and went unheeded. Simultaneously, I&A management halted all work related to domestic extremism. The subject had become too politically charged. As a result, my team and I were left floundering day-to-day without any meaningful work to do. I&A management thought it was best to operate this way—at least for the near term. It was a matter of organizational preservation.

12

Validation

In the months following the 2008 presidential election, there was a flurry of violent incidents attributed to right-wing extremists. These incidents had yet to evolve into a trend.

In December 2008, a police bomb technician and a detective were killed in Woodburn, Oregon, when a bomb exploded inside a police command post.[1] The bomb, which was initially thought to have been a hoax, was placed outside a bank building in an attempt to distract police from a planned robbery attempt of another bank in the same town. Bruce and Joshua Turnidge, a father and son team, were later charged and convicted of the murders of both police officers.[2] During their trial, the Turnidges were described as antigovernment zealots who were fearful of an impending economic collapse, gun bans, and confiscations.[3] Both received death sentences for the murders.[4]

In January 2009, a self-proclaimed neo-Nazi went on a shooting spree in Brockton, Massachusetts, killing two, raping a third, and wounding two others.[5] The shooter, Keith Luke, had reportedly "devised an 'evil plan' fueled by racism to kill as many non-whites and Jews as he could before taking his own life."[6] Despite assaulting five people, Luke's plan to attack a Jewish synagogue was thwarted when police intercepted his vehicle. This led to a shootout that temporarily distracted Luke, who eventually wrecked his van into two other vehicles.[7] Luke was arrested and imprisoned for his violent acts.

Both of these incidents, along with a few others that were less violent, weighed heavily on my mind as I wrote the Department of Homeland Security (DHS) right-wing extremism report. I knew these incidents were the manifestation of a new violent phase of right-wing extremism—the beginning of a resurgent wave of violence that would soon engulf the nation.

Saturday, April 4, 2009, started off as a relaxing weekend for me. The right-wing extremism report was mostly completed after the office-level editing and review process was finished. I was waiting a final resolution of the definition issue with the Office of Civil Rights and Civil Liberties (CRCL) at DHS. My division director was optimistic that the report would be ready for release later in the week.

Two hundred forty-five miles away to the west, a different scene was unfolding in Pittsburgh, Pennsylvania. It would come to represent the very thing about which I was most concerned. The growing animosity and the increasing paranoia were now being manifested in violent acts. I knew the ensuing violence would be a direct result of the election of a black president, his new administration, and a faltering economy. Mainstream America, the media, and our legislators were completely unaware of the approaching threat. The underlying hatred and paranoia had permeated various radical American subcultures. It was reaching a boiling point.

A self-proclaimed white supremacist was about to carry out one of the most violent right-wing extremist incidents directed at law enforcement since the Oklahoma City bombing. For me, this incident would come to represent "the shot heard around the nation." It may have been a defining moment, one that would signify the beginning of a new armed revolt—a symbolic revolution in the minds and hearts of our nation's radicalized conservative citizenry. It clearly demonstrated that violent right-wing extremism was once again alive and growing.

A domestic dispute between a mother and her twenty-two-year-old son escalated at 1016 Fairfield Street, a two-story brick ranch-style house located on a hilly suburban street.[8,9] Richard Andrew Poplawski had, once again, arrived at his mother's home after a long night of drinking. Intoxicated, he popped a Xanax pill and passed out on his mother's living room couch in the Stanton Heights neighborhood of Pittsburgh.[10,11]

Margaret Poplawski, Richard's mother, woke up that morning to discover that one of her son's dogs had urinated on the kitchen floor.[12] Having a dog inside the house was apparently a sore subject in the Poplawski household. This was not the first time the dog had made a mess inside the house.

Margaret, a youthful-looking, heavy-set woman, went over to the living room couch and shook her son, telling him to wake up. She was angry about the situation and tired of her son's laziness. An argument ensued. Fed up with her son's disrespect and defiant attitude, Margaret Poplawski had finally reached a breaking point. She picked up the phone and dialed 911. Margaret wanted the police to intervene and assist her with evicting her son from the house.[13]

Richard, however, overheard his mother's phone call and didn't like the fact that she had called police.[14]

Poplawski had an obsession with guns. He took photos of himself holding his weapons in various poses.[15] At this time, he already owned at least three long guns and two handguns—and a crate of over 1,000 rounds of various types of ammunition.[16,17] Poplawski regularly practiced his firearms proficiency at a family-owned cabin in Clarion County, Pennsylvania, outside of Pittsburgh.[18] The cabin had neither running water nor electricity.[19] There was a makeshift firing range at the hunting cabin that featured a kitchen sink, a steel door, a metal wheelbarrow, and other objects riddled with bullet holes.[20] Poplawski also had a stash of emergency essentials inside the cabin (and at his mother's house) in case of civil disorder, which Poplawski eagerly anticipated.[21]

Poplawski believed in the false notion that the U.S. government was secretly plotting to restrict firearms ownership and possible "gun bans," thus curtailing a citizen's constitutional "right to bear arms." Poplawski obtained some of his ideas from his personal library, which included books such as *Give Me Liberty: A Handbook for American Revolutionaries* and *Ethics of Homicide.*[22]

Poplawski likely rationalized that police might choose to remove his firearms as a result of the mounting tension between him and his mother. A worse scenario would be if his mother accused him of an act of domestic violence; then he would face the very real possibility of being prohibited from possessing firearms as a result of federal law, if convicted.

After hearing his mother's 911 call, Poplawski walked over to his bedroom and began putting on a bulletproof vest. It was an old police surplus vest with the letters "P-O."[23] The letters "L-I-C-E" had been removed from the vest which used to read "P-O-L-I-C-E." It now had just the first two letters of Poplawski's last name. "PO" was a nickname Richard Poplawski had received from his friends.[24] He then strapped on a gun holster, put on his Pittsburgh Penguins hockey jersey, and grabbed his guns.[25]

Poplawski later commented that he was "suiting up" for his "intended battle" with police.[26]

Margaret, seeing her son openly arming himself for war, asked him, "You're really not going to do this?"[27]

Richard said nothing to his mother, but acknowledged thinking, "Come on with it!"[28]

Eight minutes after the 911 call, Pittsburgh police officers Stephen Mayhle and Paul Sciullo arrived at the Poplawski residence. They got out of their respective cars and walked up the sidewalk to the front door. They had no idea that an armed gunman lay in waiting inside the house. The Allegheny County dispatcher received confirmation that the two officers had arrived on scene at 7:11 a.m.

Margaret Poplawski greeted the officers but reportedly didn't inform officers that her son was armed and looking for a confrontation. She opened the door, admitting Sciullo inside, and reportedly told him, "Come and take his ass."[29]

As Sciullo entered the residence, Poplawski rounded the corner of his bedroom door, armed with a .12-gauge shotgun.[30] Without warning, Poplawski aimed the shotgun at Sciullo and opened fire.[31]

Both officers had virtually no time to react. From six feet away, Poplawski unloaded a high-velocity round from his shotgun.[32] Sciullo had no time to seek cover. His body absorbed the impact from the shotgun blast, sending him stumbling backward onto the floor. He was killed instantly, with his lifeless body resting at the front door.[33]

Immediately upon seeing her son gun down Sciullo, Margaret Poplawski screamed, "What the hell have you done?"[34] She later recalled instinctively running down the hallway and down into the basement to escape the ensuing bloodbath.[35]

Standing outside the doorway, Mayhle heard the gunshot and saw his partner fall back from the impact. He radioed his dispatcher and shouted for help.[36] Poplawski retreated into the kitchen, where he awaited Mayhle's reaction.[37]

Mayhle removed his .40-caliber Glock semiautomatic pistol from his holster and entered the residence.[38] Within seconds, Poplawski engaged Mayhle in a shootout. Multiple shots were exchanged between Poplawski and Mayhle as they ran from room to room.[39] During the gunfight, Poplawski randomly fired five more rounds from his shotgun, then ran out of ammunition.[40] Mayhle managed to fire eight rounds, hitting Poplawski twice—once in the chest and another in his leg.[41,42] Poplawski appeared unfazed by his injuries, but Mayhle had no idea that Poplawski was wearing a bulletproof vest.

Filled with rage and running out of ammunition, Poplawski recklessly began firing his .357 Magnum pistol; the bullets ripping through walls separating him and Mayhle.[43,44] Poplawski then ran to his bedroom to grab his AK-47 assault rifle as he continued wildly shooting. Mayhle was seriously injured during the volley of shots from Poplawski. In an effort to escape the hail of bullets, Mayhle ran out of the house to seek cover.

A neighbor, who was awakened by the shots, rushed to a window and saw Mayhle sprawled on the ground near the sidewalk leading to the front porch of the Poplawski residence.[45] He watched in horror as Poplawski emerged from the house, aimed an AK-47 assault rifle at the injured officer, and fired three times into the defenseless officer at close range.[46]

Mayhle was shot five times—twice in the head and three times in the back.[47] He died of his wounds. The same neighbor saw Poplawski return inside the residence.[48]

A third officer, Eric Kelly, soon arrived on scene. Kelly, who was familiar with the Stanton Heights neighborhood, lived down the street from the Poplawski residence with his wife and two young daughters. At his home, Kelly's wife heard the gun shots, but didn't realize her husband would soon be under attack and fighting for his life just a few blocks away.[49]

As Kelly exited his police vehicle, Poplawski reportedly opened fire again with the AK-47, hitting the officer multiple times.[50] A neighbor saw Kelly stumble out of the vehicle while shooting in the direction of the house.[51] Despite being shot multiple times, Kelly managed to crawl behind his police cruiser to seek cover.[52] The Allegheny County 911 center began receiving calls of "shots fired" at 1016 Fairfield Street from neighbors.

Another neighbor later reported seeing Poplawski stand over Sciullo and shoot the deceased officer in the neck just to make sure he was dead.[53]

"He could have been playing possum," a neighbor testified that Poplawski told him.[54]

At 7:17 a.m., a fourth officer arrived at the Poplawski residence after receiving a call of "shots fired."[55] As he pulled up to the front of Poplawski's residence, the officer caught a glimpse of Kelly lying on the ground next to his police SUV.[56] He also observed Sciullo lying on the front porch and Mayhle dead on the front lawn. None of the officers were moving.

Hearing the approach of a fellow officer's police cruiser, Kelly attempted to raise his arm either in a call for help or as a warning sign of the impending danger.[57] The arriving officer rushed to Kelly's aid. He immediately noticed that Kelly had been severely wounded. The officer noticed that Kelly's police SUV was riddled with bullet holes.[58]

As the officer attempted to render first aid to Kelly, who lay mortally wounded, more gunfire erupted from the Poplawski residence. Bullets hit Kelly's police SUV, sending shrapnel into the assisting officer's hand.[59] The officer returned fire into the residence, and the shooting stopped.[60]

By this time, numerous Pittsburgh police officers began arriving on scene, including members of the special response team (also known as SWAT) who took positions around the Poplawski residence.[61] Emergency medical services also arrived and were able to transport Kelly, who had been shot seven times, to a local hospital, where he later died from his injuries.[62]

"I shot three cops," Poplawski boldly proclaimed during a phone call to a friend during the subsequent standoff with police.[63] "I got shot. I'm probably going to bleed to death, or go to jail for the rest of my life."[64]

Poplawski exchanged intermittent gunfire with police for nearly three hours after the initial gun battles with Officers Sciullo, Mayhle, and Kelly.[65] An armored SWAT vehicle (called a BearCat) used during the standoff received multiple gunshots from Poplawski's AK-47. Investigators found bullet holes in the front driver and passenger sides, the driver side portal, the engine access panel, and passenger side brush guard of the armored BearCat vehicle.[66] Other bullets were found to have struck cement sidewalks, paved streets, and neighboring homes.[67]

Three hours into his standoff with police, Poplawski called 911 and said he was ready to surrender.

"I'm lying in a pool of blood, and I can't really move," Poplawski told the dispatcher.[68] "I'm not shooting any more cops because my weapons are out of ammunition and they're under the table. I'm done taking innocent police officers' lives."[69]

A tactical team entered the Poplawski residence and took him into custody at 10:45 a.m. Poplawski was transported to a local hospital to treat the wounds in his leg.

"You should have killed my son," Margaret reportedly told police as she exited the home. She screamed, "He's a cop killer!"[70]

During a subsequent search of the house, investigators observed numerous articles of ballistic evidence and firearms in plain view throughout the Poplawski residence.[71]

During her interview after the shootings, Margaret Poplawski reportedly stated that her son had enlisted in the U.S. Marine Corps (USMC) a few years prior but had been dishonorably discharged for assaulting his drill sergeant during basic training.[72] She further reported that since Richard's discharge from the USMC, he had been stockpiling firearms and ammunition in anticipation of an impending cataclysmic economic collapse.[73] Poplawski allegedly believed that the police would no longer be able to protect society after an economic collapse.[74] His mother also stated that he only "liked police when they were not curtailing his constitutional rights, which he was determined to protect."[75]

Investigators would later learn that Poplawski was a self-proclaimed white supremacist who frequented white supremacist websites on the Internet, such as Stormfront.org, one of the oldest and largest white supremacist online forums.[76] Poplawski posted several messages on Stormfront that were intertwined with conspiracy theories involving an impending economic collapse at the hands of "Zionist occupiers," the alleged harm associated with race mixing, as well as his fear of an erosion of constitutional rights, such as gun bans and confiscations at the behest of the new presidential administration.[77]

During subsequent police interviews while in custody, Poplawski "blamed the government and the politicians."[78] "He said it was the people at the top who were causing all of his problems," an officer said.[79]

"My mother was extremely stupid to call police knowing I had guns at the ready in the house," Poplawski told an investigator from his hospital room.[80]

Allegheny County prosecutors would later testify that Margaret Poplawski had a moral duty to notify police that her son had armed himself, but no legal obligation.[81]

"All of you cops are fuckers," Poplawski reportedly stated while at the hospital soon after being taken into custody.[82] "I should have killed more of you."[83]

"Niggers like you are the reason people like me shoot people like you," Poplawski shouted to police as he was handcuffed to his hospital bed.[84]

Poplawski eventually surrendered and was charged with three counts of criminal homicide and nine counts of attempted homicide.[85]

Pittsburgh police chief Nathan Harper stated that, at least twice before, his officers had responded to the Poplawski residence on domestic disputes.[86]

At first, investigators were unclear as to why Poplawski had shot at the officers. Although Poplawski had no known membership in extremist organizations, reports from public sources provide some context for his actions, including ideological interests that featured a convergence of racism, antigovernment conspiracy theories, and a growing paranoia over an economic collapse, gun bans, and gun confiscations. Poplawski's friends had also commented that he was upset about having recently lost his job.

Growing suspicion, anxiety, and paranoia likely attributed to extremist beliefs and conspiracy theories, compounded by Poplawski's financial uncertainty, produced conditions in which he reacted violently to perceived symbols of authority and government oppression. Poplawski's antigovernment and conspiratorial beliefs certainly contributed to creating a potentially dangerous environment for law enforcement officers and the surrounding community.

The fatal shooting of three Pittsburgh police officers occurred the weekend before the DHS right-wing extremism report was released. On Monday morning, I added the Pittsburgh shooting incident to the right-wing extremism report as a recent example of the type of violence I had anticipated from the resurgence of right-wing extremism. I was hopeful that other law enforcement officers would take note of the root causes of the Pittsburgh shooting. And, coupled with the DHS right-wing extremism report that served as a warning of an emerging violent extremism trend, I was cautiously optimistic that future right-wing extremist threats could be detected and avoided.

Within a few days after the Poplawski shooting, I found myself at the center of a highly charged political firestorm. It was during this tumultuous time of public outcry and congressional scrutiny that two more law enforcement officers were gunned down at the hands of yet another right-wing extremist. No one in Washington, D.C., seemed to pay attention to what happened in Okaloosa County, Florida. There was virtually no national news coverage. Few knew we were witnessing the emergence of a new trend in right-wing extremism.

On Saturday afternoon, April 25, 2009, two sheriff's deputies went to a public gun range in Okaloosa County, Florida, to confront Joshua Cartwright about another domestic abuse report from Cartwright's wife, Elizabeth, who was being treated for injuries at a local hospital.[87,88]

At 12:45 p.m., deputies Warren "Skip" York and Burton Lopez arrived in separate vehicles at the Shoal River Sporting Clays shooting range near Crestview.[89] They immediately spotted Cartwright standing next to his pickup truck in the gravel parking lot. He had just finished shooting at the range.

As they exited their patrol cars, both deputies confronted Cartwright and explained why they were there.[90] When they attempted to put him in handcuffs, Cartwright reportedly became uncooperative and agitated.[91] The situation rapidly escalated.

In an attempt to subdue Cartwright, York fired his Taser, hitting Cartwright above the waist. Cartwright immediately fell to the ground, but because of his large size, he was not fully affected by the five-second jolt of electricity. After being hit with the Taser, Cartwright mustered enough strength to pull a concealed handgun that was holstered around his ankle and began firing at the two deputies.

Lopez was immediately hit in the shoulder. After striking Lopez, Cartwright fired backward over his head in the direction of Deputy York, who scrambled to seek cover behind his patrol vehicle. Cartwright got up off the ground and exchanged gunfire with Lopez, striking him in the head.[92]

After the initial exchange of gunfire with Lopez, Cartwright attempted to flee the scene.[93] Witnesses reported seeing York approach the passenger side of Cartwright's truck, open the door, and attempt to jump inside in an effort to apprehend Cartwright. A scuffle ensued, and Cartwright fired several more rounds from his handgun, striking York multiple times.[94] York stumbled backward and fell to the ground next to the pickup truck. Cartwright fled the scene.

A high-speed pursuit ensued that eventually ended near Defuniak Springs. Cartwright's truck hit a pair of spike strips used to flatten car tires. Due to the high rate of speed, Cartwright lost control of the truck, and it skidded off the road onto a grassy embankment and flipped onto its hood.[95]

As police converged on the accident scene, Cartwright emerged from the truck shooting and began shooting at responding officers. Approximately sixty rounds were exchanged between Cartwright and the police officers involved in the vehicle pursuit.[96] Cartwright was struck multiple times during the shootout. He retreated to the back side of his truck, sat on the ground, and reportedly turned the gun on himself. He shot himself twice in the head.[97]

According to the resulting investigation, authorities learned from Cartwright's friends that he had expressed interest in joining a militia group. He had a fixation with weapons and firearms training. He was enlisted in the Florida National Guard and held a full-time job at Sprint but had recently been fired.[98] Just hours before the shooting rampage, Cartwright had the phrase "Don't tread on me / Liberty or death" (a popular militia slogan) tattooed on his arm.[99]

Cartwright's wife told investigators that her husband had grown increasingly fearful of the U.S. government and believed it was "conspiring" against him.[100] She also stated that he had been severely disturbed that Barack Obama had been elected president and was concerned about a potential gun ban.[101]

As two more law enforcement officers lay dead in a dusty parking lot in the panhandle of Florida—the sixth and seventh officers killed by right-wing extremists since the 2008 presidential election—Congress was on a "hunt" for people to fire over the issuance of the DHS right-wing extremism report. This was a notably prescient report that correctly predicted an upsurge in right-wing extremism recruitment and violent radicalization activity in the days just before an actual resurgence in right-wing extremism violence was manifested in a rapid series of incidents that occurred during the summer of 2009. The shooting deaths of seven law enforcement officers within a six-month period was evidence of this resurgence.

Around the time of the Okaloosa County shootings, Bart Johnson, I&A's newly appointed principal deputy undersecretary, was busy preparing his speech to I&A's workforce. He was carefully crafting his message. His remarks would focus on the organization's "way forward" in light of the recent events that surrounded the right-wing extremism report. He had not made any effort to speak to those responsible for researching and writing the report—my team. If he had taken time to meet with us, he would have known about the increasing number of right-wing extremist incidents that were "piling up" that gave credence to the report. Bart Johnson could have cited these incidents to defend his organization, its mission, and its workforce.

On Monday, May 18, 2009, Bart Johnson made his debut at a town hall meeting held at the Nebraska Avenue Complex chapel. Everyone in attendance likely knew that Johnson was going to talk about the DHS right-wing extremism report and the ensuing controversy. It had been all over the news for three weeks. The negative responses from Fox News and Congress weighed heavily on the workforce. There were rumors of organizational changes resulting from the controversy—a possible office-wide restructuring. Reorganization was I&A's answer whenever criticized by Congress, perhaps because it seemed to be a very easy way to show Capitol Hill that you were addressing their concerns.

As I was nearing the chapel entrance, I noticed my division director and branch chief standing outside the chapel's double doors. As I walked by my supervisors, the division director pulled me aside to tell me that Johnson was planning to talk about the right-wing extremism report at the town hall meeting. I immediately noticed the worried look on both of their faces.

My division director then explained that Johnson had a staff meeting immediately before the town hall, where he berated her in front of other I&A managers. I was shocked.

"Bart's view of the report is not good," she said. "Don't be shocked when he says negative things about it."

Until then, I had been somewhat hopeful that Johnson would understand the purpose and intent of the right-wing extremism report. I had grossly underestimated the gravity of the situation and how it was being handled within I&A.

A bit stunned and confused, I entered the chapel, which had been packed to capacity with nearly five hundred people. Johnson began his speech with a warm welcome to I&A's workforce. Johnson then presented an overview of his vast law enforcement experience—highlighting the various assignments and leadership positions he held during the past thirty years. As I had anticipated, he appeared very qualified for the position in which he was now serving.

A few minutes passed. I glanced over to my left to see the acting deputy assistant secretary of intelligence (DASI) standing a few feet away. She had ascended rapidly up the ranks of I&A's leadership. She had arrived at I&A soon after I did. And, like me, she was a GS-14 senior intelligence analyst. In 2007, she was appointed director of the Homeland Infrastructure Threat and Risk Analysis Center (HITRAC), a newly created unit that blended the vulnerability and risk assessment work of the Infrastructure Protection Directorate (IP) with potential threats assessed by I&A. To my knowledge, she had very little managerial experience, so this appointment was very surprising.

In January 2009, she was promoted to serve as the acting DASI under Mackin. I found this appointment utterly astounding. In less than five years, someone who appeared to have little managerial experience or formal leadership training could be promoted from a GS-14 to the senior executive service level.

She knew what Johnson was about to say. I had no knowledge at the time that she was secretly plotting my demise.

A few weeks earlier, the acting DASI had canceled all domestic terrorism briefing presentations and training sessions given by my team. She did this under the auspices of an audit and review of the briefing material. Twelve briefing presentations scheduled from April through August 2009 (which had already been approved and committed to) were canceled. I thought this was a temporary situation but soon learned that our training opportunities were being forever terminated.

By canceling the briefings, the acting DASI was sending a message that there would be no more domestic terrorism training for various state fusion centers, U.S. attorney offices, and other law enforcement agencies.

Soon thereafter, the acting DASI halted all draft responses to state and local law enforcement dealing with domestic extremism–related topics. She also put a stop to all draft reports on similar subjects making their way through the editing and coordination process. These drastic measures would prove to be the beginning of the end of our domestic terrorism team at DHS I&A.

I was nervous and felt alone as I anxiously awaited Johnson's town hall remarks. I now knew for sure he was going to talk about the report. I knew his comments would not be supportive, either.

I then heard Bart Johnson make reference to "the recent distraction" that had "demoralized" the office. This was it. I listened intently, trying not to show any emotion.

"The right-wing extremism report written by an analyst in HETA did not complete the proper vetting process," Johnson said. "It was an unauthorized report."

"What is he talking about?" I remember thinking.

"The analysis within the report was weak and lacked any supporting evidence," Johnson remarked.

"Am I being set up?" I wondered.

"It had no value to our stakeholders and should not have gone out in its present form," Johnson said.

I couldn't believe what I was hearing. Bart Johnson was reciting the same erroneous points I had heard on Fox News just a month earlier.

"Where was he getting his information?" I questioned. His facts about the report were completely untrue. And he was broadcasting this erroneous accounting of events to the entire workforce.

"This will not happen again on my watch," Johnson said, at the end of his remarks. His comment reminded me of the Oath Keepers motto, "Not on Our Watch!"[102]

I knew Bart Johnson's statements about the report were not accurate reflections of what really occurred. I was angry that my senior-level leadership would choose to publicly humiliate subordinates in front of their peers.

As the meeting adjourned, I walked over to the acting DASI, who was only a few feet away from where I stood, and pulled her aside to inquire whether Johnson's remarks were directed at me or my division director. I needed to know whether I should anticipate any disciplinary action.

She didn't look at me, but responded under her breath, "It's your division director."

From then on, I&A town hall meetings took on a new meaning for me and my fellow domestic terrorism team members. We were always on guard about possible comments directed at our division or team. The next several town halls revolved around organizational changes that resulted from the leak and its ensuing aftermath.

After the town hall meeting, I met with my division director to talk about what had just transpired. I wanted her perspectives on the organizational changes that were surely to come. The division director remained hopeful that Mudd, the congressional nominee for the undersecretary position, would have a different perspective about the report and our future than Johnson. We were scheduled to meet with Mudd the next day, and he would surely give us an indication of where things were heading.

As I made preparations for our meeting with Mudd, Johnson was busy making plans of his own. He was overseeing a total overhaul of how I&A would coordinate its future reports—especially those that dealt with domestic terrorism–related topics. A new, much more meticulous review process was in the making. Six offices, instead of the usual two or three, would now be responsible for giving final approval to release any of I&A's intelligence reports. Joining the new review process were the Office of Civil Rights and Civil Liberties, the DHS Policy Office, the DHS Privacy Office, and the DHS chief operations officer. They joined I&A's Office of General Counsel and intelligence oversight officer to form the "Gang of Six" or G6—a new nickname created by the I&A analysts who were directly subjected to the setbacks resulting from this latest change in production procedures.

In his letter to congressional representatives, dated on May 21, 2009, Johnson wrote, "The Department will not target, for information gathering or enforcement purposes, individuals or groups based on their political beliefs . . . Unfortunately, the rightwing extremism report should have been better written and was not properly approved by senior management prior to its release."[103]

"With that in mind, we have implemented new processes to allow for more meticulous review of intelligence products produced by I&A," Johnson said.[104] "In particular, we have instituted more comprehensive internal controls to safeguard the high standards we have set for ourselves."[105]

Johnson stated, "These internal controls merit further refinement to ensure the timely release of critical and mission essential products and information."[106]

"Accordingly, we are now in the process of developing a rigorous permanent framework to ensure I&A can both provide timely intelligence and analysis products to our state and local partners and robustly safeguard privacy and civil liberty," he said.[107] "The new framework will take into full consideration the operational requirements of our law enforcement partners, ensuring they have the flexibility they need to protect their communities."[108]

Bart Johnson's office-wide reorganization would formally dissolve HETA (the division responsible for writing and releasing the right-wing extremism report), relieve its division director of any leadership role, and create a new system of checks and balances relating to the review of future I&A intelligence reports. By design, Johnson's new review process would ultimately become the perfect quagmire to stymie any and all reports pertaining to extremism and radicalization, especially those that addressed domestic non-Islamic extremism.

On Tuesday, May 19, 2009, I accompanied my immediate supervisor and HETA division director to a government building on Vermont Avenue in downtown Washington, D.C.

We prepared much of the day for our meeting with Mudd, who had recently been nominated as I&A's next undersecretary for intelligence by Obama. A senior-level I&A official told me weeks earlier that Mudd was supportive of continuing the domestic extremism and radicalization mission. My division director, immediate supervisor, and

I believed Mudd would counterbalance Johnson and the acting DASI as far as maintaining this important, now controversial, mission.

The primary purpose of our visit was to provide Mudd with an informal "orientation briefing" on radicalization and homegrown extremism. We were advised that, since Mudd was not officially confirmed, our briefing was for informational and familiarization purposes only.

As I walked up to the building's entrance and reached to open one of the glass doors, it was locked. I then noticed a sign on the door that read "Closed at 5:00 p.m." I looked at the time, noting that it was 4:52 p.m.

"Why were the doors locked already?" I wondered.

I relayed this information to my division director and branch chief, who were making their way down the sidewalk. They also checked their watches to see if we had mistakenly arrived too late. We were nearly ten minutes early.

I then realized that we had been "stood up."

As I turned around and glanced back at the street to see if our ride was still available, I noticed the division director for production management and other I&A managers standing at the curb waiting for the DHS shuttle to return them to the Nebraska Avenut Complex.

I called out to my division director, who was walking away in the opposite direction, and pointed to our colleagues standing at the street just a few yards away.

We approached our colleagues to inquire if we were late or, perhaps, had the wrong time. Production management's director explained that the briefings had ended early.

We then learned that the acting DASI had unilaterally decided to brief Mudd about the radicalization and homegrown extremism mission—the very topic we were supposed to discuss. No one had bothered to tell us.

In doing so, the acting DASI had also eliminated our only opportunity to give a true accounting of events surrounding the right-wing extremism report to an incoming senior-level agency official. This was a cunning and dirty little trick.

The acting DASI was not in a position to speak about the agency's radicalization mission. She knew very little about the topics of radicalization and homegrown extremism given her short tenure in the position. Nevertheless, she arbitrarily decided to brief the topic herself without any expert consultation or prior knowledge of these often misunderstood and complex matters.

During the drive back to the Nebraska Avenue Complex, I told my division director and branch chief that I believed the acting DASI had done this deliberately. I suggested that she may have even used this same tactic to brief Johnson soon after his arrival concerning the events surrounding the right-wing extremism report.

The acting DASI had a motive to fabricate this different version of events—to absolve herself of any contributing role to the situation by changing the production guidelines and review process a few months before the report was written and released. I question whether the acting DASI had divulged this most important piece of information to Johnson, DHS leadership, or congressional representatives.

In the weeks after the leak, I&A received 215 pieces of feedback concerning the right-wing extremism report.[109] The feedback consisted primarily of e-mails, not formal feedback forms. One hundred eighty-nine submissions were from individuals considered "non-consumers" of Homeland Intelligence products.[110] This is an important factor to weigh when analyzing the feedback. Submissions from nonconsumers came primarily from angry citizens and military servicemen. The majority of these nonconsumer submissions were negative comments criticizing the product and characterizing it as "politically motivated, a violation of civil liberties or portraying veterans in a negative way."[111]

In addition to the e-mails received, over 1,500 phone call complaints were logged by the DHS I&A Office of Public Affairs.[112] Again, all of these complaints were from nonconsumers of Homeland Security intelligence reports.

Despite the fact that an overwhelming majority of feedback came from nonconsumers, I&A's Production Management Division still included all of this information and compiled it into a report that focused exclusively on analyzing customer feedback.[113] The document was inappropriately titled "An Analysis of Complaints."[114]

"The vast majority of individuals who submitted feedback on this product were not traditional customers of DHS I&A information and reporting," the document said.[115] So I question why such feedback was included in this document.

"Customers of DHS I&A Intelligence products were largely split over the quality of analysis," the document began.[116]

"Active-duty and retired military largely viewed the Assessment as politically biased and a negative portrayal of soldiers returning from Iraq and Afghanistan," it stated.[117] "Non-Customer submissions focused strongly on potential violations of civil liberties and perceived political bias at DHS, reflected in the Assessment."[118]

Feedback from traditional stakeholders was scant—twenty-six feedback forms were submitted by state and local law enforcement agencies and other I&A customers.[119] This number of responses is typical of the amount of feedback generated from other I&A reports. Most reports released by I&A receive fewer than twenty formal feedback forms.[120]

Due to the unique circumstances leading to such a large amount of atypical feedback, I felt it was necessary to qualify the type of feedback into two categories: traditional customers and noncustomers. I felt that the Production Management Division had unfairly saturated their statistics with negative feedback submissions that emanated primarily from noncustomers who shouldn't have received a copy of the report due to the law enforcement nature of the report. Production Management was also including all of the feedback from the general public as well. Of course, they were also not the intended audience for this report. For these reasons, I decided to send an e-mail to the Production Management Division requesting that they weigh such factors when they conducted their review of the feedback submissions.

"Having reviewed I&A-Production Branch's 'Analysis of Complaints' pertaining to I&A's recent Rightwing Extremism assessment, I would expect that the response will be more positive or neutral from state and local law enforcement than the traditional national security community," I wrote.[121]

"Negative feedback has always been a strong consideration for sensitive Homeland Security and law enforcement issues, but judgments should be limited primarily to the intended customers instead of general readership—given the political nature of this disclosure," I said.[122]

"I strongly believe that I&A has successfully created a trusted Information Sharing Environment (ISE) through the domestic terrorism team's established support of state and local law enforcement, which is traditionally ignored by the national security elements of the intelligence community," I wrote.[123]

I continued, "Given that the traditional national security and intelligence community—including the military—were not the intended customers, please consider that their feedback should be judged appropriately due to the political interpretation resulting from the unauthorized disclosure of an official homeland security document containing sensitive law enforcement information."[124]

"My recommendation would be that I&A reconsider the original use of the 'law enforcement sensitive' caveat for dissemination of our assessments when analyzing feedback—given the over-sensitive response by our non-law enforcement customers, guidance from I&A's Intelligence Oversight officer pertaining to the dissemination of domestic law enforcement information to the intelligence community, and the potential unauthorized disclosure of future 'For Official Use Only' products," I concluded.[125]

Production Management honored my request to divide the feedback into different categories. Nonetheless, they still included feedback from the general public and military members in their analysis, which I felt unfairly depicted the right-wing extremism report in a negative light. They did, however, separate these complaints into their own distinct sections with accompanying graphic depictions of feedback results.

Surprisingly, I&A had not received any negative feedback regarding the right-wing extremism report from a law enforcement agency in the weeks following its release. That changed when Bart Johnson took charge.

The Major Cities Chiefs Association letter, dated May 18, 2009, coincided with House Resolution 404, which dealt with a formal congressional inquiry into the DHS right-wing extremism report.[126]

"It has come to the attention of the Major Cities Chiefs Association that HR 404 will come to the Full Committee for a vote tomorrow," the letter began.[127] "The Major Cities Chiefs agrees that the document that was the underlying cause of this resolution was poorly researched and produced, deeply flawed and an embarrassment to the Department of Homeland Security."[128]

"It certainly did not represent MCC's values and standards of professional conduct," the letter read.[129] "All of that being said, subsequent positive remedial steps have been taken by DHS to address the situation."[130]

"First, the document has been retracted, and the Department has apologized to veteran's organizations. Second, new pre-release review procedures are in place. Third, the Department has provided a full briefing to Committee staff regarding the circumstances surrounding the bulletin," the letter stated.[131]

"Most importantly, Secretary Janet Napolitano has appointed one of state and local law enforcements' own, Col. Bart Johnson (NYSP, Ret.) as Deputy Under Secretary of Intelligence and Analysis," the letter said.[132] "The Secretary and new Deputy Under Secretary have pledged to refocus the efforts of I&A so that it better addresses the needs of state-local-tribal governments."

"Our experience with Col. Johnson as Chair of the Criminal Intelligence Coordinating Committee is that he is a man of highest integrity, and very respectful of privacy and civil liberties concerns," the Major Cities Chiefs remarked.[133] I found it interesting that this letter openly acknowledged the association's past dealings with Johnson. The Major Cities Chiefs waited almost a month and a half to write their letter of concern. They also used the letter as an opportunity to applaud Johnson, who had nothing to do with I&A at the time of the right-wing extremism report's genesis and release. So given Johnson's recent appointment to I&A, his obvious disdain for the right-wing extremism report, and past affiliation with the Major Cities Chiefs Association, it was very apparent to me the true motives behind the Major Cities Chiefs letter. It was yet another opportunity for Johnson to slam me, my team, and the division director.

"Based on the above and the fact that most if not all of the underlying documents requested by the Committee are being provided, the Major Cities Chiefs Association sees little value in continuing debate on this particular bulletin," the letter stated.[134] "We are confident that necessary change has been implemented, and we believe this new leadership should be given the opportunity to deliver the type and quality of work product the Department and this nation can be proud of."[135]

The letter echoed many of the same points raised in Johnson's town hall meeting. It also set the stage for his plans for organization changes and new review processes.

Johnson's town hall speech and the corresponding letter from the Major Cities Chiefs was followed by a string of more violent incidents that would gain national-level attention—not only from the media, but also law enforcement and national security agencies. A majority of these violent incidents were perpetrated by the very domestic extremists about whom the DHS report had warned. These incidents appear to have had no bearing on Johnson's decision making or opinion of the right-wing extremism report.

On May 27, 2009, a nationwide manhunt was under way for a man charged with making threats to President Obama in St. George, Utah. The U.S. Secret Service had filed an affidavit reporting that Daniel James Murray, who owned eight registered firearms, allegedly told a bank employee in Utah that he "was on a mission to kill the president" after withdrawing $13,000 from his bank account.[136] According to investigators, Murray blamed Obama for "a banking system he says has failed and caused worldwide chaos."[137] Murray was eventually arrested on June 5, 2009, at a casino in Las Vegas, Nevada.[138]

Four days later, an antigovernment extremist entered the lobby of the Reformation Lutheran Church in Wichita, Kansas, on May 31, 2009, at the start of Sunday services. He was armed with a pistol and was on a "mission from God." The perpetrator, Scott P. Roeder, was looking for a late-term abortion provider, Dr. George Tiller, who attended church there. After loitering for a moment in the men's restroom, Roeder emerged to find Tiller, a church usher, standing in the hallway handing out Sunday programs and talking with some of his fellow church members.[139] Roeder reportedly walked up to Tiller from behind and shot him in the head at point-blank range. As he escaped to his car parked across the street, Roeder pointed the gun at other church members, who were attempting to stop him. Roeder was apprehended three hours later during a traffic stop near Merriam, Kansas.

Investigators learned that Roeder was well known in the antiabortion extremist movement. During the late 1990s, Roeder submitted a letter and other articles to a radical antiabortion publication called "Prayer & Action," operated by a known member of the Army of God, a violent antiabortion group based in Norfolk, Virginia.

On June 1, 2009, Michael Bray, a member of the Army of God and a convicted arsonist, posted a letter to Roeder on a well-known pro-life website.[140]

"You have acted in righteousness and mercy," Bray wrote. "Who among those who believe the Truth can deny the obvious good use of you made by the Lord of Hosts as you sought to deliver the innocents from the knife of a baby murderer?"[141]

Bray continued, "But how pleasing it is to know that He makes effective use of the deeds of those who obey Him."[142]

"The congregation of Reformation Lutheran church [in] which George Tiller was serving [as] an usher at the time of his termination was properly indicted by your actions," he stated.[143] "Tiller's blood is on their heads for tolerating his murders and refusing to correct him."[144]

Concerning the Reformation Lutheran Church in Wichita, Bray commented, "Such a 'church' is no church, but a Synagogue of Satan."[145]

According to law enforcement sources, Roeder was also a known affiliate of the sovereign citizen movement including the Montana Freemen and the U.S. Constitutional Rangers. In April 1996, the sheriff of Shawnee County, Kansas, stated that Roeder was reportedly a member of the Montana Freemen.[146]

In April 1996, a traffic stop on Roeder's vehicle revealed a fraudulent, "sovereign citizen" license plate.[147] In addition, a search of the vehicle's trunk revealed a small cache of bomb-making components.[148] He was sentenced for multiple parole violations in June 1996, but was released with time served.[149] In early March 1999, the explosives charges were dropped.[150]

On June 4, 2009, Bart Johnson held another town hall meeting to address Mudd's unexpected announcement concerning his withdrawal from consideration for the undersecretary position amid fears that he would face congressional scrutiny over his alleged involvement in the CIA torture memo scandal involving enhanced interrogation techniques on terrorist detainees at Guantanamo Bay, Cuba.[151]

A few days earlier, the acting DASI had held her own "mini-town hall" to informally announce the dissolution of HETA, the reassignment of its division director, and the temporary merger between the remnants of HETA and the Critical Infrastructure Threat Analysis (CITA) Division.

This interdivisional restructuring was the beginning stage of a much larger, office-wide reorganization that would take place a few months later. This mini-reorganization of sorts was a temporary stopgap measure until a more permanent solution could be implemented.

HETA's personnel and office space merged with CITA under the banner of a new office called the Domestic Threat Analysis Division or DTAD. DTAD was led by the former deputy director of HITRAC. The DTAD director was known for his controlling and often confrontational management style. He had an alliance, and what appeared to be a personal friendship, with the acting DASI. As a result, I knew this new office arrangement was not going to be a good situation for me and my team.

Johnson's second town hall meeting began with his remarks about the recent shootings in Wichita, Kansas (of Dr. Tiller) and Little Rock, Arkansas. On June 2, 2009, a homegrown Muslim extremist fatally shot a military serviceman outside an Army recruiting office in Little Rock.[152]

Although both incidents involved a lone gunman who was motivated by radical ideology, it was no surprise that Johnson chose to focus his remarks more on the Little Rock incident than the Wichita shooting. He commented on how the Little Rock shooting was evidence of a rising threat from homegrown Muslim extremists. He practically ignored the assassination of Dr. George Tiller at his place of worship in Wichita, Kansas.

The real shocking comment from Johnson concerned the manner in which he referred to shooting death of Tiller. Bart Johnson referred to this incident as "the murder of that *abortionist* [emphasis added]."

The term "abortionist" is a derogatory term used by conservative Christian anti-abortion opponents as well as right-wing extremists to dehumanize, publicly humiliate, and belittle women's health care providers.

After the second town hall meeting in as many weeks had adjourned, a colleague of mine strolled over to the Nebraska Avenue Complex cafeteria for an early lunch. He was standing in line to pay for his meal when a former I&A employee working at another office at DHS headquarters approached him in line and started a conversation.

As they were both standing in line chatting, the topic of the DHS right-wing extremism report and the resulting media controversy came up.

"That paper is completely illegal!" the former I&A employee adamantly declared.

"Those responsible for writing it should be 'shut down' and *imprisoned* [emphasis added]," he said.

Surprised at the vehement response to his question about the right-wing extremism report, my colleague responded, "Wow! That's kind of harsh, isn't it?"

Rather than answer the question, the former I&A employee who had made the vehement remarks changed the subject. He had no idea that the person he was talking to worked for me and would later share the conversation with fellow team members, including me.

On Monday morning, June 8, 2009, two fellow team members and I met with the newly appointed DTAD director and his deputy to discuss the content of a domestic terrorism PowerPoint presentation related to sovereign citizens. During the meeting, the DTAD director made two concerning comments, which illustrated a clear misunderstanding of I&A's mission authorities and intelligence oversight guidance.

The DTAD director alleged that Executive Order 12333 "prohibited" I&A from collecting information on U.S. citizens. He also alleged that my team had produced an "illegal" product. We immediately challenged this assertion. We explained that all domestic extremism–related reports were coordinated and reviewed by the Office of General Counsel and intelligence oversight officer. We also cited the very legal authorities beyond I&A's Intelligence Oversight Guidelines Memo (dated April 2008) that gave us the ability to collect, retain, and disseminate information on certain U.S. persons who affiliated with violent domestic extremism ideologies and extremist groups. These authorities included the 2002 Homeland Security Act, the 2002 USA PATRIOT Act, and Homeland Security Presidential Directive 5.

We also offered to brief the DTAD director and his deputy on various domestic extremist–related topics to help increase their knowledge and understanding of the subject matter. This invitation went unheeded. The DTAD director made no attempt to gain a better understanding of the root causes of domestic terrorism. His demeanor projected a desire to closely monitor our activities.

As we struggled to maintain I&A's domestic terrorism emphasis, more violent incidents attributed to right-wing extremism continued to unfold.

Shortly before 1:00 p.m. on Wednesday, June 10, 2009, a lone gunman armed with a rifle entered the U.S. Holocaust Memorial Museum in Washington, D.C., and immediately opened fire on guards manning the front entrance of the museum.[153] The gunman shot one guard and was wounded by return gunfire from two other security officers.[154]

The mortally wounded security guard and the shooter were transported by D.C. Fire and Emergency Medical Services Department personnel to an area hospital, where the security guard was pronounced dead and the suspect was admitted in critical condition.[155] The guard was later identified as thirty-nine-year-old Stephen Tyrone Johns of Temple Hills, Maryland.[156]

James Von Brunn, the shooter, had connections with the white supremacist extremist movement and embraced an anti-Semitic ideology, which included the false belief that the Holocaust never occurred. It is clear that Von Brunn's extremist beliefs served as the primary motivation for his attack on the National Holocaust Museum in Washington, D.C. He reportedly launched the attack soon after he discovered that his Social Security check had been cut in half.[157] In his conspiratorial world view, the Jews controlled the governments as well as financial institutions. He blamed "the Jews" for canceling his Social Security.

On that day, fellow team members and I worked late into the evening. As we were shutting off our computers and packing our things to leave the office, the DTAD division director arrived at my desk around 7:00 p.m. He wanted to discuss the Holocaust Memorial shooting incident.

The DTAD director appeared visibly irritated, and his demeanor appeared hostile. The reason for his visit resulted from a series of news articles I had forwarded to I&A field representatives concerning the shooting earlier that day. Many of the news articles cited the DHS right-wing extremism report, noting that the Holocaust Memorial shooting and the Tiller murder served as evidence that the report had been vindicated. I made no mention in my e-mails about my personal opinion. I was merely forwarding the news articles to keep our field representatives informed about what had occurred.

Prior to the DTAD director arriving at my desk, I received a phone call from the acting DASI at about 6:30 p.m. Her voice was abrupt and stern.

"You need to stop sending those e-mails to the field," she snapped. "What is the point of sending the e-mails? What are you hoping to accomplish?"

I told her that I was merely keeping the field representatives informed about the situation unfolding outside of the Holocaust museum, including the resulting aftermath.

"I'm afraid you're going to wake a sleeping bear," she said. I took this to mean that I was somehow instigating the field representatives to get angry at headquarters about how they handled the whole situation related to the right-wing extremism report. I never intended to do such a thing. I was merely keeping the field representatives apprised of what was going on.

Despite the lack of rationale behind the acting DASI's wild accusations, I nevertheless agreed to stop forwarding news articles.

As I attempted to greet the DTAD director as he approached my desk, he reiterated some of the same concerns raised earlier by his mentor and friend, the acting DASI.

"Stop sending those e-mails!" he abruptly stated.

I responded that I'd already agreed to stop sending them.

He immediately responded, "How do you know that your paper [i.e., the DHS right-wing extremism report] didn't incite the shooter?"

I couldn't believe what I had just heard.

"Are you kidding?" one of my analysts responded to the director's accusation.

For the next ten minutes, all three of us proceeded to refute the DTAD director's statement concerning whether the report had incited Von Brunn to attack the Holocaust Memorial museum. At times, the discussion grew heated.

Von Brunn had, in fact, been involved in the white supremacist movement for decades. In 1981, Von Brunn was arrested for storming the Federal Reserve armed with a handgun and other weapons while threatening government employees.[158] He conducted the raid in a desperate attempt to "arrest" the Federal Reserve chairman.[159] Von Brunn was convicted and sent to prison for his actions against the Federal Reserve.[160] For these reasons, it was incomprehensible for the DTAD director to assume that the DHS right-wing extremism report had anything to do with the Holocaust Memorial museum shooting. Furthermore, there was no evidence gathered during the criminal investigation that indicated that Von Brunn was angry about the DHS report.

During our conversation on the evening of the Holocaust Memorial museum shooting, the DTAD director again seemed confused about I&A's legal authorities, intelligence oversight, and counterterrorism mission. After the initial argument subsided, the tone of the discussion became more constructive and productive. The entire conversation lasted about forty-five minutes. I left work that day exhausted and emotionally spent. I had weathered yet another personal attack from my leadership.

Two days later, Shawna Forde, a leader of the Minutemen American Defense group, was one of three individuals arrested on Friday, June 12, 2009, by sheriff's detectives in Pima County, Arizona, for the murder of a Mexican-American man and his nine-year-old daughter.[161] According to law enforcement authorities, Forde and her two accomplices, Jason Eugene Bush and Albert Robert Gaxiola, broke into the home of Raul Flores and his family in Arivaca, Arizona, on May 30, 2009, apparently in the commission of a robbery.[162] The invaders reportedly shot all three members of the Flores family who were present at the time, killing the father and daughter and leaving the mother wounded.[163] While Bush was the suspected gunman in the shootings, authorities learned that Forde was the mastermind behind the home invasion robbery.[164]

In May 2009, Forde was listed as the national executive director of Minutemen American Defense on the group's website.[165] The San Diego Minutemen website also reported that Forde accomplice Bush was the group's operations director at the time of the murders.[166]

The Minuteman American Defense website and blog reportedly contained numerous photos of Forde and friends at Minutemen and "Tea Party" events, including an April 15 event in Phoenix where Forde is seen holding her favorite protest sign that read "Stop the Obama-Nation of America."[167] The group's website also included derogatory descriptions of minorities such as depicting immigrants as violent criminals, drug addicts, and "subhuman Mexicans."[168]

On July 12, 2009, a Chambers County, Texas, sheriff's deputy was shot and killed after responding to a domestic dispute between a local resident and utility worker attempting to shut off his meter.[169] The suspect, Gilbert Ortez Jr., had just retired from his job as a Texas Parks and Wildlife game warden and was a decorated Iraq war veteran.[170] His pension reportedly was not enough to live on, so he was looking for supplemental work, which he was having trouble finding.

After the initial confrontation with the sheriff's deputy, Ortez barricaded himself inside his mobile home.[171] A nine-hour standoff ensued. After receiving no contact from Ortez inside the trailer, law enforcement officers entered the residence to find Ortez dead from a self-inflicted gunshot wound.[172]

While conducting a search of Ortez's mobile home, investigators found over 110 improvised explosive devices and components, firearms, ammunition, and silencers.[173] Law enforcement agents also found several firearms and drawings containing swastikas and other Nazi themes.[174] Investigators were unable to determine whether Ortez had connections to white supremacist groups. Nevertheless, it appeared that he had an affinity for white supremacist symbolism.[175] This incident was yet another example of the type of resurgence in right-wing extremism the DHS report had warned about.

The summer of 2009 was not only stressful due to the large number of violent right-wing extremist attacks we were tracking and providing responses to state and local fusion centers, but the DTAD director kept the pressure on us practically every day. He made it increasingly difficult for us to work. Our briefing presentations had been canceled. All reports had been pulled from the production process. Each and every state and local response was placed on hold for an indefinite period of time.

The DTAS director also made us uncomfortable through making his negative opinions known to us.

On July 30, 2009, I met with the DTAD director and his deputy concerning another draft domestic terrorism PowerPoint presentation, which had been edited numerous times during the past month.

The deputy director and I were chatting about various things for about five minutes when the DTAD director finally arrived. The director shut the door behind him and immediately inquired, "So, who is this guy you have working for you?"

I explained that he was a domestic terrorism subject matter expert that I recruited from the Mid-Atlantic Great Lakes Organized Crime Law Enforcement Network (MAGLOCLEN).

The DTAD director replied, "Well, you need to tell him that he needs to go back to the private sector . . . . He rubs me wrong . . . I get a bad vibe from him."

I responded to the DTAD director's criticism by stating that I believed the analyst had a very deep understanding of domestic terrorism and a wealth of knowledge of extremist groups, their radical ideology, and their activity.

I further stated that "I did not hire him for his personality, but for his expertise."

"There's no doubt that he knows his stuff," the director countered. "But I don't think he's ready to play in the 'big leagues.'"

Our conversation concerning this individual ended with the DTAD director inquiring whether I was going to relay this message back to the analyst or should he [the DTAD director]. I agreed to broach the topic with the analyst. We then went on to discuss the PowerPoint slides.

The DTAD director had made it clear that he wanted us gone. I was taken aback with the director's rude approach when discussing private personnel matters. The following month, the unprofessional behavior continued.

The DTAD director continued his outright assault against I&A's domestic terrorism program by next attacking a critical component of our work—the Domestic Terrorism/Ideologically Motivated Violence (DTx) incident database. He was systematically taking apart the mission and doing away with analytical tools, reports, and briefings that we needed to effectively do our work.

On August 13, 2009, the DTAD director called a meeting to discuss the future of the DTx incident database. The DHS Privacy Office as well as I&A's Office of General Counsel, an intelligence oversight officer, and an information technology (IT) specialist attended the meeting. Each of these offices expressed their full involvement, support, and approval of the DTx database. Their points were irrelevant to the DTAD director. His mind was already made up. He was "pulling the plug" on DTx.

As his points were being challenged and the merits of the DTx system substantiated by those in attendance, the DTAD director abruptly excused himself from the meeting and turned it over to his deputy to adjourn it. The next day, the DTAD director recapped his salient points from the meeting in an e-mail addressed to those who had attended.

"Please review and make sure I am characterizing your position and the other areas correctly as I intend to take these opinions to Bart [Johnson], so he understands the status of the database and where each office stands," the DTAD director wrote.[176]

"First, the current database is authorized because we have an approved Privacy Assessment," he said.[177]

However, he then wrote, "The Privacy Office should be aware of this Assessment but may have a different opinion on the topic based on new management. The CRCL Office did not review or coordinate this Privacy Assessment. Front office does not have visibility of the database."[178]

"Second, I&A OGC have no problem with the database from a legal perspective. We have the legal authority to have, operate and maintain a DT database," the director continued.[179]

"Third, I&A Office of Intelligence Oversight has no problem with the database from an Executive Order 12333 perspective as the database's operational construct and the SOPs [Standards of Performance] in place are compliant with the executive order," he wrote.[180] "Spot and annual inspections confirm compliance."[181]

He continued, "My analysis of the database and my assessment of the challenges we may face by potential critics revolve around several points."

"First, the lexicon used to parse the reports is not approved by the department," he argued.[182] Thus, "the definitions of the groups and subsequently the reports ingested into the database could be challenged."[183]

This argument had no validity. Incidents were divided according to group types for ease of sorting and searching. We did not use the Domestic Extremism Lexicon as a guide to organizing the database. In fact, DTx was created two years before the Domestic Extremism Lexicon was written.

"Second, the sources of information are inconsistent," he reasoned.[184] "These are not federal reports, but are a compilation of state and local court documents, law enforcement reports, and media."[185]

The DTAD director had attempted to argue the merit of using federal reporting exclusively because they were properly vetted according to intelligence community standards. Nevertheless, there is an obvious benefit to using an all-source approach, which ensured that we captured all relevant incidents and not those limited to federal reporting only. I found it utterly hypocritical that the DTAD director would raise this issue when DHS regularly relied on (and even provided funding to develop) similar incident databases that captured domestic and international terrorism incidents, such as the University of Maryland's Global Terrorism Database.[186] The Global Terrorism Database is maintained and operated by the National Consortium for the Study of Terrorism and Responses to Terrorism (START), which includes DHS as one of its many sponsors.[187] START's database, however, was not as detailed and inclusive as DTx when it came to capturing domestic terrorism incidents.

"Third, the database relies on human analytic judgment to parse the material into database fields," he stated.[188] "The analyst's experience determines where a report is filed in the database."[189]

The human analytical review process was a necessary step to determine which incidents met the criteria to be entered into the database and which did not. This ensured that all legal and intelligence oversight requirements were being followed.

"Finally, the database is incomplete because of the informal process used to receive reporting."[190]

This last point really had no relevance because the database was always expanding as more incidents were discovered and reported. In a sense, any incident database would be incomplete.

Bart Johnson, along with input from the DTAD director, apparently made the decision to shut down the DTx database solely because he did not want to risk another potential political liability. The plug was pulled on DTx later that month, another step in Johnson's plan to shut down the domestic terrorism team and its mission.

On August 25, 2009, the DTAD director called a branch meeting to discuss his performance expectations and other work-related items of business.

As he entered the room, the first thing out of the DTAD director's mouth was the phrase, "Those f---ing fusion center reps!"

"They need to get their heads out of their asses!" he screamed. "They remind me of the incompetence of my nineteen-year-old son."

Apparently these statements were in response to him having to answer several questions about I&A's lack of response to several state and local support requests (SLSR) concerning domestic extremism. By September 2009, Johnson had finished planning the office-wide reorganization. I&A's organizational restructuring was fully implemented. HETA was now officially closed.

"The Homeland Security Department is expected to tell House lawmakers today that it has realigned its intelligence office, which came under heavy criticism this year for warning in a report that veterans returning from Iraq and Afghanistan could be recruited and radicalized by rightwing extremists to carry out violent acts," read an article in the *Government Executive* magazine.[191]

"Changes to the department's Office of Intelligence and Analysis will be the focus of a hearing called by House Homeland Security Intelligence Subcommittee Chairwoman Jane Harman (D-California) who also wants to know how the unit's broad goals outlined this year are being implemented," the article stated.[192]

The article continued, "[Bart] Johnson and other department officials were called to testify late Wednesday in a closed hearing before the House Intelligence Subcommittee."[193]

"Through the realignment, the focus of the intelligence office will be on serving state and local intelligence groups, commonly referred to as fusion centers," a department spokesman said.[194]

Harman said she wanted "to ensure that the intelligence office is not duplicating the work of other intelligence agencies."[195]

"I&A is not a mini-CIA," Jane Harman said during the interview.[196]

"The department's inspector general concluded in a report issued in December that Homeland Security had made improvements in supporting fusion centers, but several problems remained, such as providing them with adequate and timely information and helping them to navigate the department's complex bureaucracy," the article said.[197]

Harman said she believed that "the department is heading in the right direction with its changes to the intelligence office."[198]

Harman also said she wanted to learn more about "the department's plan for ensuring timely dissemination of information to fusion centers, especially when it comes to dealing with material that is overly classified."[199]

The article also stated that Harman "wants to know how the department is facilitating information sharing from the bottom up, or from fusion centers to the federal government."[200]

A DHS inspector general's report, which had been quoted in the article, said "the department had fallen short in deploying intelligence analysts to the fusion centers."

"To that end, the department will announce that it plans to provide each of the nation's 72 fusion centers with at least one analyst by October 2010," the Homeland Security spokesman said.[201]

Deploying intelligence analysts and liaison officers to all state and local fusion centers will definitely assist with the sharing of information between I&A and law enforcement. Nevertheless, Johnson's plan to "shut down" an analytical unit that was providing essential intelligence in support of such efforts did more to damage information sharing between the two entities than improve it. Johnson's actions "gutted" his own organization of one of its most effective information-sharing units—the domestic terrorism team—at a time when their work was needed the most.

13

Correcting the Record

In January 2009, the acting deputy assistant secretary of intelligence (DASI), in her newly appointed position, changed the agency's production process. She made the decision to remove herself from the review and approval process for finished intelligence reports at the Office of Intelligence and Analysis (I&A). She delegated this responsibility to the division directors in an effort to get rid of a production "choke point." Never before had division directors been responsible for approving and releasing reports at I&A. This was the responsibility of Mary Connell.

The acting DASI's modification to the production process proved to be a major contributing factor regarding how the report was coordinated, staffed, and released. So when the media began reporting that the assessment was "unauthorized" and not properly vetted, I began to suspect that Department of Homeland Security (DHS) leadership was attempting to cover up the truth by misrepresenting the facts about the assessment. By doing so, DHS leadership absolved the acting DASI of accountability for her decision to change the production procedures. The false allegation of an "unauthorized report" also insinuated that I somehow circumvented established procedures, undermined the chain of command, and secretly released the report to thousands of law enforcement agencies around the country without the prior knowledge and consent of DHS leadership.

When she changed the production procedures, the acting DASI did not include the Office of Civil Rights and Civil Liberties (CRCL) in the coordination and vetting process of draft I&A reports. Further, the acting DASI was the person who actually "shut down" my team's training sessions to law enforcement and "killed" all domestic extremism–related production at I&A.

There was a lot at stake for the acting DASI, who had applied for the deputy undersecretary for analysis (DUSA) position, which was a promotion and included a hefty pay raise. Admitting that she changed the production procedures might have affected her chance to be selected for the permanent DUSI position. Since she was already serving the senior executive service (SES), there was a $13,000 bonus waiting for her at the end of fiscal year. She did not get the permanent DUSA position later that year. Bart Johnson selected a well-seasoned CIA manager named Dawn Scalici. Prior to assuming her position at DHS, Scalici served as the director for production and strategic planning at the Central Intelligence Agency's (CIA) Office of Iraq Analysis.[1] At the CIA, she was responsible for current and strategic analysis on Iraq and oversaw advance planning, analytic tradecraft, and community collaboration.[2] Scalici, however, was not a permanent employee of I&A. She remained a CIA official on a two-year assignment to I&A.

On August 21, 2009, before Scalici's arrival, the acting DASI held a town hall meeting for managers, analysts, and support staff of the Analysis and Production Directorate. Since I knew there would be organizational changes, I came prepared to take notes.

"Odd leaders took us in odd directions at odds with our leadership," she began. This was a veiled reference to the former HETA division director and others involved in staffing, approving, and releasing the DHS right-wing extremism report. These remarks, however, more accurately described the acting DASI and Johnson—two "odd leaders" that unnecessarily took the agency in "odd directions" and "at odds" with the truth.

I looked around the room and saw a few people shake their heads in dismay at the acting DASI's statement. The bizarre opening statement was indicative of the acting DASI's strange persona—a disheveled woman who had a quirky, nervous laugh that often accompanied her statements in large meetings, as if she was somewhat unsure of herself. She followed up her statement about various oddities at I&A with an even more disturbing remark.

"Politics plays a role in what we do," she said with emphasis. The room was silent. I couldn't believe what I was hearing. She had just admitted to playing politics in her role as a DHS intelligence official. More worrisome, she admitted to supporting political agendas when reviewing intelligence. This statement, which shows a lack of integrity, is also an act of defiance that goes against the very principles spelled out in the intelligence community's (IC) analytic standards as directed by the Office of the Director of National Intelligence (ODNI). IC analytical standards specifically state that intelligence analysis must be "independent of political considerations."[3]

The acting DASI then followed up this statement by commenting, "We will begin to 'flag' inappropriate comments in your papers."

"There will be no end to the scrutiny of our tradecraft standards," she further stated.

Politics has no place in the U.S. intelligence community. The acting DASI said to me in April 2009 that I&A's very existence was "hanging in the balance." She rationalized that I&A leadership had to take drastic measures for the organization's ultimate preservation.

The acting DASI went on to say that the DHS transition team (a body of political appointees assigned to DHS after the 2008 presidential election) had reached the following assumptions about I&A: "It's too big. It is not responsive to state and local law enforcement. And it is replicating the intelligence community." This observation echoed Senator Harman's (D-California) view of I&A as reported in the media after a congressional hearing in February 2008.

The acting DASI concluded her remarks that day by stating, "If you don't like where you are, now is the time to move where you want to be . . . . Some will be asked to move . . . . We haven't tried to hide anything." She then opened the floor to field questions from the workforce.

One employee asked if the reorganization was going to affect those representing I&A at other agencies—a position referred to as "detailee."

"There are details that are required and details that are desired," the acting DASI responded. "We need to evaluate whether we need to be there or find a new home."

Another employee asked a question about I&A's interaction with the twenty-two DHS components and information-sharing efforts between the DHS components and I&A.

"We need to do more with the components," the acting DASI responded. "They are ready to be 'folded' into us and join our production process."

This statement was divorced from reality. For years, I&A had struggled with the problem of information sharing and collaboration with the DHS components. I don't believe they were ready to be "folded into us" and willing to "join our production process." By 2009, a few DHS components began to share information with I&A, but the majority chose to keep the information to themselves. After all, these agencies had their own intelligence offices fully staffed with agents, intelligence analysts, and reports officers. They had no reason to interact with I&A. Some thought this would bring an added layer of bureaucracy into their work, which would have a negative impact on their ability to produce timely intelligence. Furthermore, many agency administrators did not want "headquarters" (I&A is a headquarters element) getting involved in their business and telling them what to do. Certainly, these agency heads were also fearful of politics getting involved in their very important work. We were not afforded such a luxury at I&A.

At the end of September 2009, a new name surfaced as a potential candidate for the vacant undersecretary position previously held by Allen; it had been held up in committee for several weeks. Mudd had withdrawn his name due to his alleged involvement in the Guantanamo Bay enhanced interrogation technique program— often referred to as the "torture memo scandal" by the media.

I&A employees and managers had been anxiously awaiting the confirmation of Caryn Wagner, who became the successor to Charlie Allen in early 2010. To no surprise, Wagner did not have any acknowledged law enforcement experience. As most of her predecessors, she had spent most of her career within the intelligence community and at the Department of Defense.

Employee morale at the time of Wagner's confirmation hearings was at an all-time low. Morale had actually been high for a few months in early 2009, but that all ended in April. Not only did the leak and its aftermath have a profound impact on the office, but management's mishandling of the situation made a very stressful situation many times worse.

On Tuesday, December 1, 2009, the U.S. Senate's Select Committee on Intelligence held the first of two confirmation hearings related to Wagner's nomination for the position of the DHS undersecretary for intelligence and analysis.

I was interested in knowing whether the report (and the leak) would be mentioned during the confirmation hearings and, more importantly, how Wagner would respond. Neither I&A management nor DHS leadership expressed much interest concerning identifying the source of the right-wing extremist paper leak. To my surprise, both issues came up, but I was not surprised by Wagner's scripted responses.

Senator Sheldon Whitehouse (D-Rhode Island) began the hearing with an interesting question about political leaks in Washington.

"Leaking is politics in Washington. It's the way people expand their turf and make their moves," Whitehouse said.[4] "So a tolerance for it has developed that I think, frankly, needs to be adjusted."[5]

He continued, "I would like to hear both of you put yourselves on record on the subject of leaks, how seriously you will take their investigations, whether you'll engage in them yourselves. And how you consider that a problem."[6]

"Senator, I share your concern about leaks and also your perspective on why they happen," Wagner responded.[7] "I do take them seriously."[8]

"If I am confirmed and I have reason to believe that anyone in my organization is leaking, I will deal with that as a matter of management accountability," she said.[9] "If it rises to a level that it requires a crime's report be submitted, I would certainly support doing that."[10]

"So I share your concern and I'll take every action that I can to ensure that leaks do not come from I&A if I'm confirmed," she concluded.[11]

No one in DHS leadership seemed interested in identifying the person responsible for causing such public and congressional fervor. A DHS press spokesperson told me that an investigation "was not worth pursuing" because the report was not a classified document and, therefore, not subject to any criminal penalties. I acknowledged such a dilemma, but countered that DHS leadership could certainly have taken administrative action if it turned out that a DHS employee had indeed leaked it. My point went unanswered.

"Thank you . . . I assume I can hear you say that you'll provide your full cooperation to such investigations?" Whitehouse inquired.

"Yes," Wagner replied.

Sometime later, Senator Ron Wyden (D-Oregon) began to question Wagner about various inappropriate intelligence reports released by I&A.

"Ms. Wagner, it seems to me that there are some very serious problems that are now facing the Department of Homeland Security's intelligence unit," Wyden began.[12]

Wyden continued, "Let me start by reading a brief excerpt from a report that the committee approved unanimously earlier this year. And I quote here, 'The committee has raised a number of concerns with reports issued by the Department of Homeland Security, Office of Intelligence and Analysis, that inappropriately analyzed the legitimate activities of U.S. persons. These reports raised fundamental questions about the mission of the Office of Intelligence and Analysis and often used certain questionable open-source information as a basis of their conclusions.'"[13]

"Now, the committee is not talking here about one instance. They are talking about a pattern," he said.[14] "And this report was approved unanimously by the entire committee."[15]

"So, my first question is—if you're approved, what specific steps would you take to make sure that the office stops this inappropriate analysis of the legitimate activities of law-abiding Americans?" Wyden asked.[16]

Besides the DHS right-wing extremism report, there were other I&A reports that had drawn criticism from both Congress and the American Civil Liberties Union. Possible examples included an intelligence assessment on the Nation of Islam and various raw intelligence reports on the activities of seemingly law-abiding America Muslims. It could be argued that such reports were "inappropriate" or lacked good judgment as far as social and political sensitivities related to these groups. In contrast, the DHS right-wing extremism report did not violate the privacy, civil rights, or legitimate activities of law-abiding Americans. In fact, it didn't name a single living person or group in the entire document. Thus, if Wyden meant to include the DHS right-wing extremism report in his remarks about inappropriate analysis, he was seriously misinformed.

"Senator Wyden, I am aware of some of the troubling reports that had been released from I&A in the past," Wagner responded.[17] "And, if I am confirmed, I intend to attack that several different ways."[18]

"There are a couple of issues that are reflected in those reports," she said.[19] "One is basically poor tradecraft—lack of analytic rigor. The other is the problem with the failure to take into proper account privacy, civil rights, civil liberties, and First Amendment–protected speech."[20]

She stated further, "The problem with the definitions in one particular product was [that] it did not draw a sufficient distinction between beliefs and actions."[21] This statement was clearly referring to the DHS right-wing extremism report.

"So I would put in place a very strict tradecraft training program to include mentoring for the analysts," she counseled.[22] Ironically, there was no emphasis on analytical tradecraft training at I&A during the nearly five years leading up to the release of the DHS right-wing extremism report. Only after the politicization of the report did I&A finally decide to develop and implement an analytical tradecraft training course that was in line with the intelligence community standards. In fact, prior to 2009, Connell refused to abide by the intelligence community standards of analytical tradecraft, because she felt that I&A had a unique customer in state and local law enforcement and, therefore, a need for a unique style of writing that she called "Homeland Security intelligence."

Wagner continued, "I would also ensure that there is training for everyone on the guidelines that we are to follow that flow from E.O.[i.e., Executive Order] 12333 and have been coordinated with the Justice Department to make sure that all of those concerns vis-à-vis privacy, civil rights, and civil liberties are built into the reports early on."[23] It is obvious that Wagner had no idea that all of these reports were subjected to intelligence oversight review and coordination with the Justice Department (i.e., the FBI) prior to release. All I&A analysts had also received mandatory E.O. [i.e., Executive Order] 12333 training each year. Most were well aware of I&A's intelligence oversight guidelines, including me—the author of one of the "inappropriate" analytical reports referenced by Wyden. Wagner concluded, "Finally, as sort of an insurance measure, I would make sure that there is in place a very thorough vetting process for review before those reports are actually released."[24] Such a thorough, comprehensive vetting process had existed at I&A during Allen's tenure but was abandoned at the behest of the acting DASI in an effort to streamline the timely release of more intelligence reports.

Wyden followed up his initial questions by asking, "Do you believe that it is ever appropriate for your office to analyze the legitimate activities of law-abiding Americans?"[25]

"No, Senator, I do not," Wagner emphatically responded.[26]

On Thursday, December 3, 2009, Wagner's second confirmation hearing was held before the U.S. Senate Homeland Security and Government Affairs Subcommittee chaired by Senator Joe Lieberman (D-Connecticut). Unlike the initial hearing, Wagner was subjected to some very pointed questions about the DHS right-wing extremism report by Senator Susan M. Collins (R-Maine).

"Earlier this year, I&A produced a report on right-wing extremism in the United States that was widely panned," Collins began.[27] "It was considered to be poorly written and inadequately sourced that needlessly offended a number of veterans' organizations such that Secretary Napolitano had to make apologies for the department."[28]

Collins continued, "It's also of concern to me to learn when we looked into this that the Office of Civil Rights and Civil Liberties had not concurred with the release of the report, and yet it was released."[29]

"The Office of General Counsel had not reviewed the report and yet it had been released," Collins said.[30] This was not an accurate statement. The report had been reviewed by the Office of General Counsel at I&A. It is also important to note that there was not a requirement to have CRCL concur with any I&A report in order for it to be released. Coordination with CRCL was merely a courtesy at the time the DHS right-wing extremism report was written.

"My first question is, have you read this report?" Collins inquired.[31]

"Yes, Senator Collins, I have," Wagner answered.[32]

"What is your judgment of the quality of the analysis in the report?" Collins again asked.[33]

"I believe that the report shows some serious shortcomings in tradecraft and in concern for privacy, civil rights, and civil liberties," Wagner replied.

Wagner's response concerning serious shortcomings related to privacy, civil rights, and civil liberties is misleading. No personal identifiable information on U.S. persons was included in the report. Similarly, there were no violations of U.S. persons' civil rights or civil liberties in it. Ms. Wagner's statements implied that HETA analysts were not concerned with privacy, civil rights, civil liberties, and First Amendment–protected speech and, therefore, "failed" to safeguard or protect these rights. This is far from the truth. We were well versed in I&A's intelligence oversight policy derived from E.O. 12333. There were no privacy, civil rights, or civil liberties violations associated with this report. In addition, there was no violation of any U.S. person's First Amendment right of free speech, nor was any implied—the scope note of the paper clearly stated that the subjects of the report were *violent extremists*. The DHS Privacy Office reviewed the DHS right-wing extremism report and acknowledged that the report did not concern them because no names appeared within its pages. Nonetheless, I agree with Wagner's testimony that portions of the right-wing extremism report could have been written better; its analytical tradecraft could have been written more clearly. However, as stated earlier, the absence of applying the intelligence community's analytical tradecraft practices was a systemic issue across I&A, and not limited to either the right-wing extremism report or the radicalization mission in general.

"Do you believe that the department and I&A, in particular, has now adopted a sufficient process to help ensure the quality of future reports and prevent poorly sourced and poorly written reports such as this one from being released in the future?" Collins inquired.

"I know that they have taken steps to put in place a process for vetting, reviewing, and releasing reports to ensure that the tradecraft is rigorous and that the appropriate concerns for privacy, civil rights, and civil liberties have been accommodated in the reports," Wagner replied.[34] "If confirmed, I will certainly review that process to make sure it's adequate."[35]

Bart Johnson's G6 review process was certainly not adequate. It selectively subjected certain I&A reports, namely those that dealt with domestic non-Islamic extremism, to an endless cycle of revisions. This process had placed a stranglehold on DHS domestic terrorism reports to the detriment of the safety of law enforcement officers and the well-being of large minority groups in the United States.

Wagner rambled on, "And I intend to focus a great deal—along with Dawn Scalici, who's the new deputy undersecretary for analysis . . . has worked at the National Counterterrorism Center, to ensure that that we are inculcating the analysts with the appropriate tradecraft, providing them mentoring, taking advantage of the Analytic Ombudsman at the DNI, and everything we need to do to raise the level of tradecraft in I&A . . . ."[36]

Collins interrupted Wagner, "Thank you."[37]

Following multiple confusing or false statements by DHS leaders under oath, and misleading questions by congressional representatives during hearings, I decided to approach newly appointed deputy undersecretary for analysis (DUSA) Dawn Scalici with my concerns. Since Scalici was new to I&A, and in my direct chain of command, I hoped she might be objective and sensitive to my issues concerning how the department, and I&A leadership specifically, had mishandled the situation. My concerns were addressed in writing. I gave Scalici two memorandums that outlined all the issues and my concerns. The first memo was given to Scalici shortly after her arrival at I&A. The other one was handed to her as I was leaving DHS for another federal job.

A few days prior to Scalici's arrival, I had received a copy of the ODNI's evaluation of the DHS right-wing extremism report. I remember hearing something about a congressional request to the ODNI's office to review the report, but no one bothered to share the final evaluation with me until I asked about it.

In response to a congressional request, the ODNI's office submitted their evaluation of the DHS right-wing extremism report on August 6, 2009. It concluded there were significant shortcomings in the analytical tradecraft employed in the report.

It is important to note that the ODNI reviewer made no attempt to contact me or the other I&A analysts who were involved in the research, drafting, and review phases. I did not receive a copy of the ODNI evaluation until fifteen weeks after the evaluation's release on November 25, 2009. It was released to me only after my persistent requests.

The ODNI evaluation began with a statement about how DHS "withdrew" its right-wing extremism assessment. To the contrary, DHS never issued a formal recall of this document. Rather, the report was removed from DHS websites for internal review but had never been withdrawn or recalled, which requires a formal notice from the Production Management Division to delete or destroy all existing copies. As was standard procedure, the DHS right-wing extremism report was disseminated via an e-mail broadcast and posted to DHS websites. Although the report was eventually removed from DHS websites, it has never been officially rescinded in writing as required by the production management office.

The ODNI evaluation did not take into account the origins, time frame, or intended audience for this assessment. It did not note the original tasking by Napolitano to I&A, which dealt with "intelligence and operational plans to intercept and disrupt domestic terror actors." This request is not within I&A's mission authorities. As a result, this portion of the tasking was given to the FBI to answer regarding operational concerns. HETA division management broadly interpreted the original tasking to encompass an overview of the forces and factors fueling radicalization of violent extremists in the United States. HETA analysts were directed to focus on this aspect of the secretary's tasking.

I was required to work under an extremely short production schedule for this tasking. The time frame from receipt of the original tasking (March 20, 2009) to product dissemination (April 7, 2009) was thirteen business days. Analysts, however, had been conducting research on their own since April 2008 with the intent to eventually write a similar assessment. The HETA division director used the secretary's tasking to hasten the drafting and dissemination of this assessment.

The DHS right-wing extremism report was an authorized and fully vetted intelligence report that was disseminated through official channels. Nevertheless, I&A executive leadership and department-level management have mischaracterized the assessment and incorrectly stated the facts concerning the drafting and dissemination of this product. DHS media spokespersons used the term "unauthorized" when referring to the report, which insinuated that an analyst or production employee sent it out in a way that circumvented the systems in place. This is completely inaccurate. Furthermore, at the time of the report's release, CRCL was not part of I&A's formal vetting process.

I followed all existing steps in I&A's production process as outlined in internal memos and communications from I&A leadership. The report was also formally disseminated to DHS stakeholders through I&A's Production Management Division.

Over a two-and-a-half-week time frame, there were twenty-eight rewrites of the draft assessment amidst conflicting guidance from the HETA division director, the Executive Secretary's Office, and I&A editors related to format, focus, and analytical framing. The report's format also evolved from informal talking points, to a question/answer format, to a formal memorandum/letter with accompanying appendix, and finally a decision to produce a finished intelligence assessment.

The report was vetted through multiple layers of editing, which included several reviews and extensive rewrites at the branch level, division level, and at the office level. No objections or concerns were raised pertaining to the report's nonconformance to the intelligence community's analytic standards.

The report was coordinated through every mandatory office as outlined in I&A's production process, including I&A's Office of General Counsel (two attorneys), the intelligence oversight officer, as well as the FBI. Although not required, the report was also coordinated with the CRCL and the DHS Privacy Office, among others.

The DHS Privacy Office raised no objections because the report did not contain any personal identifiable information (PII) such as names of individuals or groups, addresses, phone numbers, or other types of PII.

CRCL had several suggested edits and made several comments about various issues of concern to them. It is important to note that CRCL raised no concerns about the section pertaining to disgruntled military veterans, which was a major point of contention with the public, special interest groups, and Congress. I addressed all CRCL concerns, responded to their comments, and incorporated their edits—all except one concerning the definition of right-wing extremism, which was located in the footnote on page two of the report.

HETA management, CRCL representatives, and I attempted to resolve the definition issue by drafting several rewrites. CRCL briefly reached a consensus with I&A on the revised definition, but then CRCL reverted back to its narrow definition.

Since no compromise was reached after several days, HETA referred the matter to I&A Office of General Counsel (OGC). An OGC attorney intervened and advised HETA to revert back to the original definition that CRCL objected to—the primary reason being that any revised definitions would conflict with an already-approved definition of right-wing extremism that was included in the DHS Domestic Extremism Lexicon product. This glossary of extremist terminology had been formally disseminated a week earlier on March 26, 2009. The attorney advised against having two different definitions, which would confuse DHS stakeholders. As a result of OGC's recommendation, HETA officials, including myself, decided to go back to the original broad definition.

At the time of the report's release, I&A analysts were not trained in the intelligence community standards (ICD 203) of analytical tradecraft and effective writing, nor were these standards consistently applied by the editors and reviewers of I&A reports. I&A's former deputy assistant secretary for intelligence and analysis (DUSI), Mary Connell, had instituted a distinct standard of writing and analysis, which did not mandate strict adherence to the ICD 203 standards.

Further, the former DASI believed that I&A's unique customers (federal, state, local, and tribal law enforcement) required an approach to writing that differed from the IC writing style. I&A has since responded to the criticism of this assessment by instituting a rigorous analytical tradecraft training program for all I&A analysts to ensure the IC standards are followed. This training program, however, did not exist prior to the dissemination of the DHS right-wing extremism report.

Public and congressional criticism of the report also cited a lack of source as references. For unknown reasons, I&A Production Management has always removed endnotes (source citations) from finished intelligence reports prior to dissemination. Most intelligence agencies include source citations in their finished intelligence reports. I&A reports, however, do not contain source citations when they are released.

Many sources used for the background information guiding the report and its preparation were not disclosed due to law enforcement sensitivities. These sensitivities relate to the protection of sources and methods that would negatively affect ongoing criminal investigations.

I was asked to produce the assessment at the Unclassified/For Official Use Only classification level. As a result, we utilized as many open-source materials as possible, such as newspaper and magazine articles, Internet chatter, and nongovernment organization reporting. Such publicly available material was supportive of the law enforcement–sensitive information and was used wherever possible to minimize the risk of inadvertent disclosure of law enforcement sources and methods to others who had no need to know.

Due to well-established prior relationships with the nongovernment organizations cited in the report (such as the Southern Poverty Law Center and Anti-Defamation League), I assessed this reporting to be credible and reliable. In addition, representatives from these organizations have testified as expert witnesses at the local, state, and federal level during criminal proceedings. Other federal agencies (including, but not limited to, the FBI) have also cited the same organizations as credible sources in various finished intelligence reports. If I&A editors had asked for a source summary statement, this information would have been noted in the strengths and limitations of the underlying sources. I collected and submitted a substantial amount of law enforcement–sensitive materials that included details of arrests, law enforcement reports of investigation, as well as specific examples of "Internet chatter" that was referenced in general terms within the report.

I was also concerned about potential leaks because I knew other finished intelligence reports dealing with domestic terrorism issues had been leaked to extremists and the media. For this reason, I decided to "sanitize" the report as much as possible to prevent any potential damage to sensitive law enforcement sources and methods resulting from an inadvertent disclosure of the report. HETA management and I anticipated and discussed the likelihood of a leak prior to dissemination. This law enforcement–sensitive data included information obtained from undercover operations by sworn law enforcement officers; law enforcement use of undercover identities on the Internet; and I&A's monitoring of publicly available extremist message boards, websites, and forums for potential threats and possible criminal activity, any of which (if disclosed) could jeopardize ongoing collection and enforcement efforts.

The media's comparison between the left-wing assessment on cyber attacks and the DHS right-wing extremism report is problematic. The right-wing report was intended as a broad overview dealing with multiple, interrelated themes. The other report dealt with the left-wing extremist capability to conduct cyber attacks. Furthermore, the left-wing extremist paper was allowed to develop over a lengthy time period (approximately one year), and the editing process was not constrained. Both papers, although produced by different analysts in HETA, went through the same editorial process and vetting chains, thus showing a systematic problem with inconsistent standards being applied at the division and office levels.

Scalici hinted at a new, laborious review process in a *Homeland Security Today* article published in January 2011 titled "DHS Fusion Center: Tough Tightrope."

"At DHS, I&A safeguards are built in," Scalici said.[38] "All intelligence reports are reviewed by civil liberties experts."[39]

"We're working to build processes in place that integrate a similar review process into all state reports, as well," Scalici was quoted as saying.[40]

Scalici's comment about "safeguards" was disingenuous, since many safeguards were already in place at I&A before the leak. The only thing that changed after the leak is that CRCL inserted itself into the intelligence process and was able to secure veto authority over any I&A reports it deemed inappropriate from a political standpoint.

After enduring ten months of the G6 review process, I decided to write a memorandum for record to Scalici that again raised issues concerning how DHS had handled the situation. I personally handed the memo to her on March 29, 2010, during a closed-door meeting between my immediate supervisor, Scalici, and me.

"Since the leak of the DHS Rightwing Extremism report, I&A leadership has implemented new policies and procedures that have made a significant adverse impact on the Department's mission, specifically related to detecting, identifying and warning about domestic non-Islamic extremist threats," I wrote.

"The most prevalent hurdle is the Group of Six (G6) review process," I said. "The major 'choke point' within the G6 review process is the DHS Office of Civil Rights and Civil Liberties (CRCL)."

The G6 review process negatively impacted I&A's intelligence analysis, because some of the recommended changes to reports seemed to use standards that were in direct conflict with the IC analytic standards. G6 reviews adversely affect an analyst's objectivity and political neutrality. The apparent purpose and intent of the G6 review process is to "screen" reports for objectionable words, phrases, or topics that are "politically sensitive" or perceived as "offensive" to certain groups of people. In other words, it involves a "risk-averse" approach to intelligence analysis.

The G6 review process also impacts the timeliness and relevance of I&A reports through a seemingly endless cycle of edits, revisions, and comments that can last for several days or weeks. Some offices—particularly CRCL—have even sent conflicting opinions about certain topics or reports, which further delays timely dissemination. Specific to reports dealing with domestic extremists, the G6 applied an additional level of scrutiny that resulted in multiple cycles of review and constant correcting. As a result, I&A stakeholders' needs are not being adequately met or thoroughly addressed.

The G6 review process has called into question the reliability of credible sources of intelligence, such as various open-source intelligence as well as information from reputable nongovernment organizations (e.g., the Southern Poverty Law Center and Anti-Defamation League) without providing adequate reasons for these objections. Further, G6 objections related to the use of properly vetted open-source information impacts the reliability of reports by withholding information from I&A stakeholders based solely on a risk-averse process.

I&A's internal editing and review process also hampered the department's radicalization mission, particularly related to domestic non-Islamic extremists. Multiple state and local support responses, briefings, and other reports were sanitized to the point of irrelevance, redirected to less risky topics, or stopped entirely. I firmly believe that reports dealing with domestic non-Islamic extremist topics are subjected to a higher level of scrutiny than other reports that may deal with U.S. persons.

For example, a PowerPoint presentation on domestic terrorism had been subjected to numerous G6 reviews and revisions on each slide, endnotes, and briefing notes. Such revisions had been ongoing since June 2009. The presentation had still not been approved when I left DHS in April 2010. However, other presentations within the same division that addressed different topics were approved without G6 review or the same level of division scrutiny. Such an example clearly illustrated a collaborative effort by CRCL and I&A management to stymie analysis in this area.

As previously noted, numerous domestic terrorism training and briefing requests from external agencies and organizations had been canceled, declined, or postponed indefinitely—but briefing requests related to transnational terrorism or critical infrastructure were encouraged and allowed without these same standards being applied.

Editors also constantly questioned the analytical statements and judgments of subject matter experts, rather than limiting their comments to grammatical and substantive edits. Editors made some sarcastic remarks attempting to minimize the importance of domestic terrorism analysis, such as questioning whether the Earth Liberation Front committed terrorist acts or second-guessing the classification of animal releases, sabotage, and arson attacks by radical animal rights and environmental extremist causes as acts of domestic terrorism. Editors edit; analysts analyze.

The leak and its aftermath has had a significant adverse impact on I&A's workforce, the analytical integrity of the organization, and its radicalization mission. The manner in which I&A leadership chose to respond to the leak had a significant negative impact on the organization as a whole.

After the leak and per Napolitano's request, HETA analysts initially revised the DHS right-wing extremism report into a version titled "Resurgence of Violent White Supremacist and Antigovernment Groups." To my knowledge, this revised report was never officially released. Therefore, the original report was not replaced or redone in a more useful or more precise fashion as Secretary Napolitano said in her congressional testimony. It basically had the same judgments and analysis as the previous report. The main difference in the second report was that the term "right-wing" was removed and some of the poor wording (such as "disgruntled military veteran") was changed for clarity.

In contrast, much effort was directed at revising the DHS Domestic Extremism Lexicon after it was formally recalled in April 2009. After more than a year of revisions, coordination, and review, the DHS Domestic Extremism Lexicon had still not been released. DHS leadership appears to still be uncomfortable with defining the terms "extremism" and "radicalization."

Anonymous DHS officials have been quoted in the media as characterizing those responsible for writing and releasing the report as having "taken on a 'maverick' attitude."[41] This statement is blatantly false. Similarly, Napolitano's statement that the office acted "without authorization" as noted in her congressional testimonies on May 12 and May 13, 2009, was incorrect.[42,43] The assessment was written in response to information needs of I&A customers and in compliance with statutory and policy limitations. HETA, the office that produced the report, has always complied with all production-related requirements within the department and I&A. In addition, HETA had also made every attempt to coordinate reports with required offices both internally and externally. Such characteristics are directly opposite of the "maverick" label.

In the aftermath of the right-wing extremism report's leak, DHS and I&A leadership deliberately chose to blame its employees for the alleged errors and mistakes in the report, rather than confronting and refuting the falsehoods, mischaracterizations, and contextual fabrication from the media, Congress, and special-interest groups. This directly undermined the organization's analytical integrity for reasons mentioned above and further eroded employee morale. To make matters worse, the new division director attempted to retaliate against other domestic terrorism analysts and me during our annual performance appraisals. Fortunately, this totally unnecessary situation was resolved through the formal grievance process. The continued departure of numerous I&A employees including several analysts, senior analysts, the branch chief, and the senior intelligence officer in 2010 also attested to the low morale and distrust in I&A's workforce.

My initial meeting with Scalici occurred in her office on Wednesday, February 17, 2010. I was joined by a coworker and the chief of I&A's Customer Assurance and Analytic Tradecraft Office.

Scalici began the meeting with an acknowledgment of I&A management's mishandling of the situation related to the right-wing extremism report leak and resulting aftermath. She noted that she had not been employed at I&A during the time but wanted to give me an opportunity to discuss my concerns with her as well as elicit my ideas on "where we should go from here."

I expressed my sincere appreciation to Scalici for finally having a meeting to hear my side of the story, but I mentioned how deeply frustrated I was over how long it had taken to have it. I also brought up how long it took to get a copy of the ODNI review of the report and identified some of the reasons I felt delayed in receiving a copy of it.

I specifically raised the issue of I&A leadership's continued misrepresentation of facts including statements by Wagner during recent congressional testimony in response to Senator Collins. I also cited other examples of mischaracterizations of the report by I&A and DHS leadership soon after it was leaked.

In response to my concerns, Scalici requested that I provide her with a list of "falsehoods" as well as supporting documentation in order to ensure that the record would be corrected. I compiled a complete list and gave it to Scalici upon my departure from I&A.

I brought up the recurring frustrations with the G6 review process—specifically CRCL's conflicting feedback and the endless stream of comments and trivial concerns during the coordination process. I also mentioned my frustration with division management and division editors selectively stalling domestic non-Islamic terrorism analysis and cited the numerous state and local support responses, the domestic terrorism overview briefing, and briefing notes to Napolitano.

Scalici responded that she had wondered why she had not seen any domestic non-Islamic terrorism focused reports in a while and made a note of it. She agreed to address this issue at an upcoming planning meeting.

Scalici confirmed there was an upcoming meeting on Friday, February 19, 2010, to discuss I&A's mission authorities related to analyzing homegrown violent extremism and domestic non-Islamic terrorism. It was her hope to develop a production plan for 2010.

Near the end of the meeting, Scalici talked about improving the analytic tradecraft for I&A and thanked us for our input and ideas in this area. She briefly referenced the new analytic tradecraft training effort under way at I&A and encouraged us to attend the training.

Two days after my meeting with Scalici, I attended the 2010 production meeting. It was aptly titled "Domestic Terrorism Production Plan: The Way Ahead." The meeting was also attended by Scalici, the acting Domestic Terrorism Analysis Division) director, my immediate supervisor, production management officials, and representatives from the various G6 offices. Scalici chaired the meeting and advertised it as a way to discuss development of a domestic terrorism production plan for 2010.

"DHS I&A will conduct tailored analysis and produce assessments of violent domestic terrorist groups," Scalici said. "We will partner with the FBI, Directorate of Intelligence, and other federal partners to prepare classified and unclassified Homeland Security Assessments and Homeland Security Reference Aids for our state and local customers. This production will focus on two analytic lines and will focus primarily on three organizations."

Despite Scalici's attempt to develop a domestic terrorism production plan for the following year, the acting division director for the newly created Domestic Terrorism Analysis Division (DTAD)—an ironic title for a new division that did virtually no domestic terrorism analysis—deliberately chose to limit I&A analysis only to violent environmental extremists, violent anarchist extremists, and violent skinheads at the expense of other, more lethal forms of domestic extremism, such as neo-Nazi groups, sovereign citizens, and militia extremists.

When questioned about the logic behind imposing these boundaries, analysts were told that the aforementioned "groups" (environmentalists, anarchists, and skinheads) had attacked infrastructure in the past (identified as being a clear DHS mission and implying that domestic terrorist acts against other targets are not a DHS mission unless linked directly to infrastructure threats). The acting DTAD director also rationalized that all three forms of domestic extremism were "transnational in nature," which mitigates intelligence oversight, civil rights, and civil liberties concerns and had no history of infiltrating law enforcement, thus limiting the potential for future leaks. His response had nothing to do with the level of threat or violent capability of domestic extremist groups. When challenged, the DTAD director decided to add violent militia extremists to the list but limited DHS monitoring efforts related to militias to illegal weapons possession and explosives stockpiling only.

Prior to my departure from DHS, I requested an independent review of all talking points, notes, and testimony from I&A leadership regarding the report to ensure the accuracy of their statements to further correct the record. I specifically asked Scalici to request copies of all talking points, notes, and prepared written statements from the acting DASI (former HITRAC director), I&A OGC, Bart Johnson (acting undersecretary for I&A) and the acting DTAD division director (formerly the deputy HITRAC director). I singled out these individuals because each either personally appeared before Congress or may have provided input to congressional testimony concerning the DHS right-wing extremism report.

As of this writing, there have been no updates concerning my request, so I am left to assume it never took place. I did not have a final meeting with management like the other departing I&A employees had experienced. No attempt was made to retain a known subject matter expert. It was certainly not a professional way to treat a federal employee with nearly twenty years of civil service.

I appreciated Scalici's attempts to understand what had occurred and how it had affected the agency. She had made an effort to hear my concerns, start a fresh relationship, and forge a new path. She also apologized on behalf of I&A management for taking so long to meet with me about what had happened ten months earlier. Unfortunately, these meetings came nearly 300 days too late and did not involve those responsible for misrepresenting the facts and retaliating against employees for no good reason. In addition, I knew Scalici was a detailee on a two-year assignment. She was not a permanent employee at I&A. Other high-level DHS officials, including I&A managers, have taken advantage of similar situations in the past by stalling or ignoring requests, guidance, and other good ideas from detailees serving in leadership positions within the department. I knew this situation would likely be no different.

Despite another round of anticipated change for I&A in 2010, it assuredly did not bring renewed job satisfaction for me or many others. I had grown weary of the constant change. I never anticipated that my career at DHS would change so abruptly. This experience (the DHS right-wing extremism report and resulting aftermath) was a significant, life-changing event for me. My career ambition was stymied—practically shut down and shoved aside. All I had worked for over the past twenty years seemed to disappear before my very eyes. The personal lives of my coworkers and I were unnecessarily disrupted. I lost faith in DHS leadership and questioned the integrity of the organization.

Soon after my departure, I&A restructured for the second time in less than a year. Despite these changes, many critical elements related to organizational success remain absent, incomplete, or severely lacking. This includes reliable computer systems; missing or severely hampered legal authorities related to human capital and intelligence collection; no formal policies and procedures related to crucial office operations, such as human capital and budget; high turnover in leadership and staff; and a continual lack of bold, determined, and committed leaders.

I've finally come to the realization that constant change does not benefit an organization or lead to its maturation. Rather, it undermines loyalty, destroys morale, and, in the end, demoralizes a large portion of the workforce. I had endured nearly six years of recurring change at work. I'd seen hundreds of people transition through I&A since 2004. I knew my time to leave had finally come.

14

Retrospective

Monday, April 19, 2010—the fifteenth anniversary of the bombing of the Alfred P. Murrah Federal Building in Oklahoma City was being observed. Janet Napolitano was busy delivering a speech to a group of survivors, their families, friends, and first responders. Everyone had gathered at the bombing site in downtown Oklahoma City for the annual memorial ceremony.

Nearly 1,350 miles away in Washington, D.C., at Department of Homeland Security (DHS) headquarters, I was busy preparing my farewell notice to the many work-related friends, colleagues, and law enforcement contacts I'd made over the years. I'd never anticipated leaving—especially under these circumstances. Things had been going so well before the leak. I thought I would serve the rest of my federal career at the department.

It's ironic that Napolitano was using the Oklahoma City bombing anniversary to promise the nation that her department would remain vigilant in the face of domestic terrorist threats. Meanwhile, back in D.C., DHS eviscerated its team of analysts who were looking at such threats, and their senior domestic terrorism analyst was formally announcing his impending departure. Many other analysts that had worked domestic terrorism issues at DHS had already left for other employment opportunities throughout the U.S. government. Napolitano had no idea that her department's entire domestic terrorism analytical unit had been systematically dismantled and was now essentially "blind" from its ability to assess and warn of domestic non-Islamic threats.

In November 2009, Bart Johnson and others in Office of Intelligence and Analysis (I&A) management made a decision to abruptly do away with the domestic terrorism team. Johnson gutted the domestic terrorism team and reassigned us to various geographical teams to work Muslim extremism topics in the United States.

Months earlier, Johnson, the acting deputy assistant secretary of intelligence (DASI) and the Domestic Threat Analysis Division (DTAD) director oversaw the cancellation of all reports on militia extremists, ecoterrorists, white supremacists, sovereign citizens, antiabortion extremists, and other forms of non-Islamic threats. They also suspended all law enforcement training on such threats. Under Johnson's direction, previously approved domestic terrorism training was hastily abandoned, leaving state and local agencies scrambling to find replacement speakers on short notice. Many were unable to find alternate speakers.

Johnson and his leadership team blocked multiple briefings for state and local officials on extremist groups, such as the sovereign citizen movement—a growing domestic terrorism threat. One such training had been scheduled for law enforcement officials in Missouri in February 2010, three months before a member of the sovereign citizen movement and his son murdered two policemen in neighboring Arkansas. We will never know whether such training might have saved those officers' lives.

In response to the angry outcries from state fusion centers and local law enforcement officers who were left in precarious situations, all I could say was "Sorry, they [Bart Johnson, the acting DASI, and acting DTAD director] won't let us do anything for you anymore."

It was troubling and embarrassing how I&A managers handled the whole situation in the days and months after the leak of the right-wing extremism report. It was a disgraceful and unnecessary overreaction to what should have been a manageable situation—something all too familiar within the intelligence community (i.e., leaks).

Announcing my departure was a very poignant time for me. I was glad to be removing myself from a manufactured toxic work environment. I realized that things were not going to change at I&A. After all, I had given the agency and its management almost a year to rectify the situation, but nothing improved. It progressively got worse.

It was clear to me that I was no longer wanted at the agency. In November 2009, the acting DTAD director attempted to retaliate against me and two other domestic terrorism analysts for our involvement in writing the right-wing extremism report.[1] For no valid reason, the DTAD director downgraded our annual performance appraisals and attached a memorandum for record criticizing our lack of analytical tradecraft and professionalism. The acting DTAD director was so callously indifferent to his actions that he didn't even try to personalize the memorandums we had each received. All memos were worded exactly the same with our names being the only difference. There were no facts to support his baseless accusation. When challenged in three separate formal grievances, the DTAD director had nothing to back up his claim—just his "opinion." When it came down to it, he was unable to justify his actions in front of an arbitrary board. Needless to say, the acting DTAD directly lost his case and had to reinstate my performance appraisal to its original rating of "outstanding"—which meant I had exceeded all performance measures.

Unbeknownst to the acting DTAD director, I had meticulously documented my year's accomplishments, which far exceeded each of the goals set by I&A management. The other analysts who had also filed formal grievances both won their cases and had their original performance rating restored. It was a bittersweet victory for each of us. We received our just reward for a lot of hard work, but it came at tremendous cost and personal toll. The acting DTAD director's actions had only solidified my resolve to leave the organization.

As I packed up a few remaining items and placed them into a moving box, a cable news television program was replaying portions of Napolitano's speech at the Oklahoma City memorial ceremonial earlier that day. Napolitano was shown touring the Oklahoma City National Memorial Museum with then–Oklahoma governor Brad Henry, Oklahoma City police chief Bill Citty, and fire chief Keith Bryant prior to giving her speech at the memorial site.[2]

"Good morning," Napolitano began her remarks.[3] "I am humbled to be here today to mark this solemn anniversary, and to honor the 168 lives taken from us, now 15 years ago in an unspeakable act of terrorism."[4]

"We honor the survivors, their friends, and family members, whose continued sense of hope, and strength of spirit, inspires us all," she said.[5]

Napolitano continued, "We honor the first responders who risked their lives rushing into the Murrah Building in acts of selflessness reminiscent of those we've seen since . . . in the response to 9/11, after the Fort Hood shooting . . . and in daily acts of heroism that often don't make the evening news."[6]

"We honor the continued need for vigilance against the hateful ideologies that led to this attack, so that we can recognize their signs in our communities and stand together to defeat them," Napolitano said.[7]

"I wish it were possible to stand here and say that threats from terrorism and violent extremism have gone away since then," she stated. "We know that's not the case."[8]

"Indeed, in the 15 years since this attack, the reality of terrorism has come home to us again," Napolitano said.[9] "And our adversaries continue to look for ways to exploit our openness and take innocent lives."[10]

"Nor have we shed the reality of domestic violent extremism," she stated.[11]

"Today, our first priority remains protecting against, and preventing, another terrorist attack on America. And we have learned from this tragedy by continuing to implement and refine the security standards and procedures developed since 1995," Napolitano remarked.[12]

"Our nation has faced down violent extremism before. We've witnessed terrorism, at home and abroad, and could witness it again someday," she concluded.[13]

The bells tolled at 9:02 a.m.—the exact time the bomb went off. Those in attendance then observed 168 seconds of silence, one second for each victim killed in the blast that day.[14]

In her speech that day, Napolitano also spoke about the threat from international terrorists and briefly touched on her recent actions to better protect federal buildings from attack.[15]

"This week, the DHS-led Interagency Security Committee announced new security standards for all federal buildings and facilities," Napolitano said.[16] "And our Federal Protective Service announced the broad deployment of a new risk assessment tool to help their inspectors keep more than 9,000 facilities secure."[17]

"Last week, however, the Government Accountability Office once again released a report exposing gaping vulnerabilities at federal buildings protected by private security guards managed by the Federal Protective Service," she said.[18]

The fifteenth anniversary of the Oklahoma City bombing coincided with recent concerns among government officials and terrorism experts that antigovernment sentiment was increasing with a sizable portion of the American population leaning toward the fringe and, perhaps, toward violent action. One week earlier, DHS and the FBI released an intelligence bulletin warning about the sovereign citizen movement, which I wrote. The bulletin concerned the latest incarnation of the evolving domestic terrorist threat.[19] It warned of a new sovereign citizen group calling itself the Guardians of the Free Republics (GFR). GFR had issued a proclamation requesting the governors of several U.S. states to step down from their positions or be forcibly removed.[20]

In March 2010, the Southern Poverty Law Center (SPLC) released its report titled "Rage on the Right," which documented that white supremacists and antigovernment extremist groups had ballooned since the election of President Obama. Mark Potok, editor of SPLC's *Intelligence Report* magazine, wrote in his press release that "the fifteenth anniversary of Oklahoma City should remind Americans that the same sentiments that led to McVeigh's terrorist act have arisen again today."[21]

"The anniversary comes as the nation witnesses a dramatic resurgence of militias and other Patriot groups," Potok warned,[22] "a comeback driven by widespread populist anger at racial changes in the population, soaring public debt and the terrible economy, the bailouts of bankers and other elites, and an array of initiatives by the Obama administration that are seen as 'socialist' or even 'fascist.'"[23]

The *New York Times* op-ed page on April 19, 2010, echoed a similar warning from former president Bill Clinton, who was president at the time of the Oklahoma City bombing.

"In the current climate, with so many threats against the president, members of Congress, and other public servants, we owe it to the victims of Oklahoma City, and those who survived and responded so bravely, not to cross it [the line over to violent political speech] again," Clinton said.[24]

Remarks from Potok and Clinton that day brought me strength and solace as I prepared to leave my nearly-twenty-year career in domestic counterterrorism behind. I viewed Napolitano's remarks as a mere publicity stunt. I remembered her act of political cowardice in April 2009 when she backtracked from the analysis contained within the right-wing extremism report. As I packed, I noted that she was sending out a contradictory message in her remarks on national television.

During an interview with Fox News on April 19, 2010, Napolitano responded to a reporter's question concerning the current state of domestic extremism in the United States.

"*The question is not ideology* [emphasis added]," Napolitano said.[25] "We've always had groups on all sides that have held beliefs that are very strong and express them very vociferously . . . . Instead, the issue is 'the turn to violence.'"[26]

Hours earlier, Napolitano had mentioned "the *continued need for vigilance against the hateful ideologies* [emphasis added] that led to this attack" in her remarks at the Oklahoma City bombing memorial.[27] The statements contradict each other—confirmation of a true politician.

During her Fox News interview, Napolitano was merely parroting the opinions of the DHS Office of Civil Rights and Civil Liberties (CRCL).

In her contradicting statements that day, Napolitano failed to realize the importance of monitoring extremist ideologies that motivate extremists toward acts of violence. Monitoring a person's behavior becomes all the more clear when coupled with an understanding of extremist ideology. Analysts and agents who are attempting to identify potential threats and prevent acts of violence should avoid looking exclusively at suspicious behaviors. It is too time consuming and yields an inordinate number of "false" positives. In fact, there are more innocent people being subjected to highly intrusive privacy and civil rights procedures under the ruse of "suspicious behavior" than if authorities focused on extremist belief systems.

Every day, at airports throughout the country, Americans are being subjected to invasive screening procedures that are intended to detect explosives, weapons, and possible would-be terrorists. Yet not a single bomb has ever been smuggled aboard a domestic U.S. flight by a terrorist. Many amateur photographers and young students working on their hobbies or school projects have been accosted by security personnel and had their photos removed. Few, if any, terrorists in the United States have been arrested in the act of conducting photography as part of their preoperational surveillance.

In other words, it seems pointless to be looking for "all types of suspicious behaviors"—they're everywhere! Something "suspicious" to one person might be totally acceptable behavior to another. What appears to be "nervous" behavior more often than not has a legitimate explanation, such as a medical condition.

To counter and prevent terrorism, the types of behavior law enforcement should focus on involve those who *join* extremist groups, *embrace* extremist belief systems, or *espouse* violence and criminal activity derived from such ideologies. Unlike the types of suspicious activity reporting advocated by the DHS "If You See Something, Say Something" campaign, these behaviors actually have a proven track record for recognizing those who have the greatest potential for carrying out acts of terrorism or higher propensity toward violence and criminal activity. And, unlike other forms of suspicious behavior, they are less likely to intrude on the everyday lives of ordinary citizens. Given the limited law enforcement and counterterrorism resources, it makes more sense to identify those extremist groups, movements, and radical ideologies that spur others to act violently than to closely monitor the behaviors of everyone who either acts, looks, or exhibits "suspicious" behavior. Further, extremist ideologies more often than not have long, identifiable histories of motivating individuals to violence and criminal activity that is easily visible and clearly articulated, which provides the necessary justification for law enforcement and intelligence monitoring or investigative efforts.

Napolitano's remarks on the fifteenth anniversary of the Oklahoma City bombing came nearly a year after the DHS right-wing extremism report was publicly maligned on national television and in the halls of the U.S. Capitol. The chronology of right-wing extremist attacks and arrests that ensued shortly thereafter apparently did nothing to change Napolitano's views of the report.

During the same Fox News interview, Napolitano could be seen bristling at the term "right wing." She said it was a term she no longer wanted to use.[28] Funny, she didn't bristle at this term when the FBI and I briefed her about it in April 2009.

When the Fox News correspondent read some of the less-controversial statements from the report, Napolitano agreed that "the threat posed by lone wolves and small terror cells is more pronounced than in past years" and that "the current economic and political climate has some similarities to the 1990s," which precipitated the Alfred P. Murrah Federal Building bombing.[29]

Napolitano also partially agreed with the line that reads "the economic downturn and the election of the first African-American president present unique drivers for rightwing radicalization and recruitment."[30]

Nonetheless, Napolitano stated that the 2009 report was "not written in a fashion that was usable by local law enforcement."[31]

"I think now, having been in the job fifteen months, the goal that we need to have is to give local law enforcement tactical, intelligence-based threat information that they can act upon—*not generalizations and not comments about ideologies* [emphasis added]," Napolitano said in reference to the DHS report.[32]

This statement is misinformed. I&A has a strategic intelligence (i.e., "big picture" or national) mission. The agency is not (and has never been) tactical in nature. Further, I&A has very little collection or operational capability. The agency is incapable of generating a single piece of tactical intelligence of any significance for law enforcement. That is why the right-wing extremism report was written in such a broad fashion. It was meant to convey an important message to law enforcement about a change in the threat environment within the United States. It was never intended to provide police with "actionable intelligence."

For these reasons, Napolitano's speech at the Oklahoma City bombing memorial was disingenuous. It portrayed a message that DHS was vigilant to threats from right-wing terrorists. In reality, this was completely opposite of what was happening at DHS headquarters—the department's domestic terrorism analytical unit had been systematically dissolved and of its subject matter experts essentially "gagged" from saying anything.

Later that year, Napolitano reportedly referred to the right-wing extremism report as "ancient history" during a luncheon hosted by the *Christian Science Monitor*.[33] When pressed to answer whether the report had been "vindicated" in the past eighteen months since it came out, Napolitano responded that "it was time move on."[34]

Napolitano seemed uninterested in acknowledging the long list of incidents that followed the very types of threats mentioned in the report, including the slaying of three Pittsburgh police officers, the murder of Dr. George Tiller, the Holocaust Memorial shooting, the surge in presidential threat cases, the arrest of an ex-Marine with ties to right-wing movements who possessed a grenade launcher and many other incidents which clearly validated the report's analysis.[35]

"The kind and quality of the products we put out for law enforcement now are so much more operational," Napolitano explained.[36]

She further said, "What we needed to do in our department was really think through what is it that a standard local fusion center needs. How do we inform them about trends? About tactics? How do we get information back from them?"[37]

"And so that report to me is almost ancient history, and I'll put it there," Napolitano concluded.[38]

In reality, most I&A reports have not changed since April 2009. On the tenth anniversary of the 9/11 terrorist attacks, the Center for Investigative Reporting (CIR) released an assessment of I&A's intelligence reports. It was characterized as "intelligence spam and too generic."[39]

An article featured in *Newsweek* magazine in September 2011, which was based on CIR's findings, stated, "A year after Sept. 11 [2001], the Homeland intelligence and analysis office was created to keep state and local law enforcement informed about domestic terror threats."[40]

"The operation, intended to bring together the many limbs of the intelligence monster, has become feared for something else: spam," the article read.[41]

According to their examination, CIR concluded that "despite a clear mandate from Congress and hundreds of millions spent on personnel and technology, the office [I&A] has fallen far short of its mission and done little to improve the accuracy and quality of the nation's intelligence data."[42]

The CIR concluded that despite publishing more than 21,000 reports [averaging close to 300 a month in recent years], much of the agency's reports are outdated, irrelevant, or too vague.[43] Many I&A intelligence reports were also found to be nothing more than "regurgitated news."[44]

A former midlevel DHS official told CIR that "they [I&A] produce almost nothing you can't find on Google."[45]

Mandatory "analytical tradecraft training" designed to improve the agency's analysis was instituted soon after the right-wing extremism report controversy. But, as of this writing, no widespread changes to I&A's unique writing style have yet taken effect.

Despite Napolitano's insinuation that I&A had done nothing "significant" to assist state and local law enforcement with their operations to combat right-wing extremist threats, multiple success stories were related to the work of my team.

On September 25, 2008, two tactical officers with the Illinois State Police were shot during a drug raid in Carbondale, Illinois.[46] The suspect, William Patrich, who shot at officers, was killed as SWAT officers returned fire.[47] DHS subject matter experts assisted with making a connection between the deceased suspect and a known sovereign citizen group and white supremacist groups. Patrich's known ties to right-wing extremist groups have not been publicly disclosed until now.

"Daryl and his team's intelligence input have significantly expanded the joint law enforcement investigation, which of course is still ongoing," lauded an Illinois State Police senior advisor to a high-ranking DHS official.[48]

In January 2009, an analyst on my team assisted the Florida Fusion Center (FFC) in Tallahassee concerning a potentially violent white supremacist that was believed to be in the state.[49] I&A analysts used variations of the subject's user ID and photos gathered from extremist websites, thus enabling the FFC to find the true identity of the subject. This information was then used to discover where he lived. The information was ultimately forwarded to the Tampa Bay Regional Domestic Security Task Force for further investigation.[50]

Regarding information we had provided a National Guard unit concerned with white supremacists infiltrating the military, the National Guard unit stated, "it was concise, on point and very informative. Keep up the good work; you guys are filling a huge Intel gap for us."[51]

"Daryl Johnson and the domestic terrorism unit provided great support regarding context on an upcoming antigovernment extremist event in Charlotte," read one weekly activity report submitted in November 2008. "With Daryl's information, I was able to notify Charlotte PD as well as leverage analytical support from the North Carolina Information Sharing and Analysis Center (ISAAC)."[52]

In October 2008, an I&A field representative wrote, "Daryl Johnson passed along an outstanding brief on animal rights extremist groups that we use to begin educating focus group members . . . comprised of police and security professionals of colleges, businesses and facilities concerned about threats to animal research/testing."[53]

"Thanks to Daryl Johnson and the domestic terrorism team for their support in regards to material and briefs on radicalization in America and domestic terrorism reports," read another field report from March 2009. "I am using this material to prepare briefs for the fusion center's Terrorism Liaison Officer (TLO) class in April."[54]

And another said, "Thanks to Daryl Johnson for passing information concerning possible white supremacist threat to police officers in New Jersey. New Jersey law enforcement officers said the report was very timely and actionable."[55]

"Met with a newly-assigned detective to metro police department's intelligence unit who is charged with investigating white supremacist activities in the metro area. Follow-up communications with the domestic terrorism team have resulted in plan to jointly assess current active membership/concentrations of a racist skinhead group and the Aryan Brotherhood in the area," read another field report.[56]

Of course, Napolitano never bothered to inquire about our previous work or if there was any positive feedback from law enforcement concerning our support.

Despite having our work stopped and deliberately blocked by I&A management and CRCL, I was still able to assist law enforcement officers with gathering useful information and, in one case, taking a dangerous and illegal weapon off the street.

In November 2009, Daniel Wayne Moreschi, a neo-Nazi white supremacist, was arrested in Ashe County, North Carolina, and charged with three felony counts of breaking and entering and larceny.[57] Moreschi was a suspect in a recent string of burglaries in the Laurel Springs and Jefferson areas.[58]

Ashe County sheriff deputies stated that during a search of Moreschi's residence, they discovered white supremacist literature and indications that Moreschi may be affiliated with the Aryan Brotherhood.[59]

On December 1, 2009, I provided additional information about Moreschi to Bureau of Alcohol, Firearms, Tobacco, and Explosives (ATF) agents in North Carolina. Based on this information, ATF agents decided to follow up on this information and interview Moreschi. A week later, the ATF notified me that they had seized a sawed-off shotgun from Moreschi and were able to charge him with a felony firearms offense.

"If you'd never sent this to me, we probably would not have known about this guy, since he lives in a county our agents don't frequent too often," said an ATF agent.[60]

Prior to the report's leak, I had been monitoring YouTube for militia videos in May 2008 when I noticed that the Hutaree militia had recently posted some paramilitary training videos. Over a period of a few months, I monitored their online activities and assessed they were growing increasingly agitated and paranoid. I recognized a disturbing pattern of behavior seen with other domestic extremist groups that begin plotting attacks, such as the Covenant, Sword, Arm of the Lord. I passed this information along with my observations to the Michigan Intelligence Operations Center (MIOC) in early August 2008.

In September 2008, I was approached by an analyst working at the MIOC during the 2008 HS-SLIC conference held in Newport, Rhode Island. She pulled me aside during one of the breaks and introduced herself. She said she wanted to know more about the Hutaree militia. She said the FBI was also interested. I told her that I had previously sent information about the group to the MIOC through I&A's field representative. We exchanged a few e-mails about the Hutaree during late September 2009, then nothing more.

In March 2010, several members of the Hutaree militia were arrested for plotting to kill police officers. The conspiracy charges were later dropped against the Hutaree Militia members, but two were ultimately convicted of weapons violations. Although we had nothing to do with the criminal investigation related to the Hutaree, I am confident that the information I provided the MIOC in August 2008 and later in September 2008 was instrumental in bringing law enforcement attention to a very dangerous and potentially violent militia group that had radicalized right before my eyes. And, though the terrorist plotting aspect of the case was later dismissed, I am confident a threat was mitigated.

There are many other examples of positive things we did for law enforcement, and there are many more would-be success stories that never came to fruition due to the high level of scrutiny and canceled work.

One such example involved a sovereign citizen training I was scheduled to present to law enforcement officers at a conference held at the Lake of the Ozarks, Missouri. This was one of many law enforcement trainings that were canceled as a result of the congressional backlash to the right-wing extremism report. In May 2010, two

West Memphis police officers were killed during a traffic stop involving sovereign citizens. Two other officers were wounded in an ensuing shootout with the suspects in a Wal-Mart parking lot, leaving both suspects dead. Other sovereign citizen–related shootings occurred in Odessa, Texas (September 2010),[61] and Page, Arizona (June 2011).[62] That these trainings were canceled for no other reason than politics means that many law enforcement officers were left untrained about this menacing and growing threat.

Sitting on the bench, so to speak, while the opposition was running amok was an extremely frustrating and discouraging experience. A close law enforcement contact summed up my aggravation.

"You know, Daryl, it's amazing how virtually every agency in the country has weighed in on sovereign citizens after the West Memphis shootings," he said.[63] "Where were they when the movement was obviously showing signs of emerging again?"[64]

"I still take great satisfaction in the fact your team was virtually the only one raising the flag when we [state and local law enforcement] could see it coming," he continued.[65] "Of course, you paid dearly for it."[66]

"It's ironic your former employer cannot even put out a strategic product on any DT [domestic terrorism] trend now," he ended.[67] "What a joke they [DHS] have made of this effort."[68]

In early 2009, I had also proposed a project that involved taking a survey of over 100 incarcerated domestic terrorists in an attempt to ascertain the forces and factors that affected their "radicalization" to the point of carrying out or plotting violent acts. This survey would have been sent to various federal law enforcement officers responsible for investigating these violent offenders through my established network. Case agents from the ATF and FBI would have completed the survey to the best of their ability based on information, notes, and case files they had initiated during their investigations of these dangerous individuals. Survey results would then be put into a computer database for archives, research, and analysis. A key component of the survey involved the role of mental illness (whether or not the individuals had a family history, signs of, or official medical diagnosis) in an individual's decision to pursue violent criminal activity.

I was planning to write several reports based on the findings of this survey—one of which might have provided helpful insights into mental illness and the extent of its role in acts of domestic terrorism. Immediately after the assassination attempt on representative Gabrielle "Gabby" Giffords (D-Arizona) on January 8, 2011,[69] I wondered if this survey and subsequent analysis could have shed more light on the influence of inflammatory political rhetoric, extremist propaganda, and divisive, hotly contested political issues on mentally ill individuals who take violent action.

Furthermore, at the time of the leak, we had four reports in draft concerning the resurgence of the militia movement. They were both canceled due to I&A leadership's reaction to the controversy. These reports would have alerted law enforcement throughout the country to a growing threat. In 2010, nine Hutaree militia members were arrested in Michigan for plotting to kill law enforcement officers.[70] In 2011, five members of the Alaska Peacemakers Militia were arrested for plotting to kill law enforcement officers and kidnap a judge.[71] Also, in November 2011, four militia members in Georgia were arrested for plotting to buy explosives and make a deadly toxin in a bizarre plan to attack government officials. Again, if released, these reports on the militia movement could have provided situational awareness and perspective about a resurging problem. I have no doubt there will be other criminal cases and domestic terrorist plots involving militia members in the near future, but prominent political figures, the public, and media dismissed the MIAC report and the DHS right-wing extremism assessment as politically motivated attacks against conservatives. This was clearly not the case.

In March 2009, my unit wrote a formal response to the Wisconsin Fusion Center concerning antiabortion extremist activity in their state. The paper was reviewed by I&A attorneys, intelligence oversight, and senior-level editors. Since this preceded the April 2009 right-wing report, the I&A attorneys and intelligence oversight office were approving release of I&A reports. CRCL had yet to become involved in the review process.

I&A's Office of General Counsel (OGC) and the intelligence oversight officer approved the antiabortion extremist paper for release with some modifications and a request for limited distribution only to the agency that requested the information (i.e., the Wisconsin Fusion Center). The paper was officially released to just the fusion center a few days after the right-wing extremism report was released. I&A's field representative reviewed the information my team had provided. He then prepared a threat assessment concerning a local demonstration by pro- and antiabortion groups.[72] Only two copies of the assessment were distributed—one to the fusion center director and another to a local police department.[73]

Nevertheless, once the controversy erupted over the right-wing report, the antiabortion extremism paper was immediately rescinded by CRCL, who had just been given authorization to review and "veto" any objectionable papers written by I&A. CRCL characterized the antiabortion extremist paper as improper in an internal DHS memo.[74] Although the field representative's assessment was technically an intelligence oversight violation, CRCL admitted that due to the limited distribution of the field representative's assessment it was "unlikely to have any impact on civil rights or civil liberties."[75] CRCL made sure that all copies of the assessment, along with its supporting documentation, were subsequently destroyed or deleted.[76] The I&A field representative was also required to attend intelligence oversight and privacy training, which emphasized I&A's authorities and the requirement to follow I&A's intelligence oversight procedures at all times to ensure constitutionally protected activities are not violated.[77]

A year and a half later, Ralph W. Lang, an antiabortion extremist, was arrested in Madison, Wisconsin, after he accidently discharged a .38-caliber pistol in his hotel room on May 26, 2011.[78] When police responded, they found antiabortion extremist literature, the .38-caliber pistol and ammunition, and a map of the United States with dots denoting the locations of reproductive health care facilities.[79] Upon his arrest, Lang reportedly stated that he was planning to "lay out abortionists because they are killing babies."[80] Lang also admitted to planning to go to a Planned Parenthood clinic in Madison to shoot an abortion provider in the head.[81]

During 2007–2009, the vast majority of intelligence oversight violations at I&A (except for the antiabortion extremism response to Wisconsin) included reports written about Muslim extremists.[82] Other I&A analysts not on my team wrote these reports.

I find it hypocritical that I&A would first admit that the antiabortion extremist assessment was an "intelligence oversight" violation. They downplayed multiple, more egregious intelligence oversight violations concerning other I&A reports related exclusively to monitoring the activities of Muslim Americans. I&A leadership dismissed one such gross violation as "unintentional" and "inadvertent" violations of the intelligence oversight rules.[83] Another incident involving a Muslim American was admittedly a violation of I&A's interim intelligence oversight guidelines, but, once again, it was downplayed as having "no evidence of any lasting impact on civil liberties and privacy rights, nor . . . any impact on national security or U.S. relations with other nations."[84] A third violation was defended "as within its [I&A] authority."[85] A fourth was recalled due to not properly labeling a Muslim extremist group a U.S. person but immediately corrected and rereleased.[86] None of the analysts who wrote these reports were required to take intelligence oversight training.

One would suppose that CRCL would heavily scrutinize these documents that focused on Muslim Americans, since a core CRCL mission is to conduct departmental outreach to Muslim Americans, but they did the opposite. They downplayed the violations. It appears CRCL chose not to weigh in on these reports, which practically ignored all of the intelligence oversight violations concerning Muslim Americans. But they selectively scrutinized the only domestic non-Islamic report mentioned in the intelligence oversight violations covering a two-year period.

The only logical explanation for CRCL's blatant bias is the level of public and congressional backlash related to the right-wing extremism report. There appears to be no other reason. CRCL's decision to single this out demonstrates its clear political bias.

In March 2010, senator Jim Sensenbrenner (R-Wisconsin) submitted a request—nearly a year after the antiabortion extremism assessment was scrutinized—inquiring whether there was a report on antiabortion extremist activity in Wisconsin.[87] If so, Sensenbrenner wanted a copy of it.[88]

Prior to the right-wing extremism report's leak, it was quite unusual for Congress to request copies of I&A reports. Perhaps Sensenbrenner was on a "fishing expedition" with the intent to bash I&A again for producing another controversial domestic extremist report. I&A released the two-page report my team provided the field representative along with the assessment, which was subsequently rescinded to Senator Sensenbrenner. I never heard anything more about it.

CRCL and the DHS privacy office took their disdain for I&A's domestic terrorism analysis even further. When developing DHS's privacy training for state and local fusion centers, they made a negative example of the right-wing extremism report. I had heard through the law enforcement officers' "grapevine" that representatives from the DHS privacy office were making ill advised, and even blatantly false, statements to state and local law enforcement officers about the right-wing extremism report. In June 2011, a close contact in the law enforcement community sent me a disturbing message about one such training session held by a DHS privacy officer.

"I had Suspicious Activity Reporting (SAR) training today," the message began.[89]

"The 'Privacy' instructor [name deleted] started her block with an exercise that went like this," she said.[90] "We all stood with our eyes closed and she asked questions."[91]

Her message went on to say, "We were told to sit down when we agreed. She asked who was Pro-Life, who supported the 2nd Amendment, etc. Of course by the 3rd question, we were all down. She then said that there was actually a report describing all of us as 'domestic extremists.' I knew immediately she was referring to the DHS rightwing extremism report (although most no-one else did), so I asked."[92]

"Initially, the privacy instructor would not confirm what she was referring to," the officer reported. "She [DHS privacy instructor] went on to add that "we could be 'data based' for our beliefs."[93]

"By this time, I just blew my top and told her I took great exception to her characterization of the report and mentioned that her own agency had defended it for several days until the political heat became too great," the law enforcement officer said.[94] "She eventually admitted she was talking about your report."[95]

"I'm telling you, Daryl, this crap has to stop!" he said.[96] "Of course my evaluation of her presentation was not good. I don't even know to whom to complain. The heck with it, I'm writing to 'Madam Secretary.'"[97]

In August 2010, Jane Holl Lute, deputy secretary at DHS, reportedly submitted a request to I&A concerning domestic extremist threats to the proposed 9/11 mosque in New York City.[98] Lute allegedly requested a list of possible domestic extremist groups that might threaten the mosque.[99] I&A management reportedly became conflicted whether they should respond to the deputy secretary's request and if so, what their response should be.[100]

I&A management probably knew that the most likely threat to the mosque comes from right-wing extremists, specifically white supremacists. However, CRCL had constrained I&A from writing about such extremists and had ingrained within I&A a strict interpretation that groups needed to be clearly engaged in criminal activity or violence to pass their litmus test.

I&A also had another problem related to this request. Their subject matter expertise in the area of domestic non-Islamic extremism had dwindled significantly to a single analyst. There was no doubt that this directly impacted the organization's ability to provide a thorough and timely response to the deputy secretary's request.

For these reasons, I&A management simply ignored Lute's request and chose not to provide a response.[101] Surprisingly, Lute reportedly never followed up as to why a response was never provided.[102] This story was corroborated during multiple conversations I had with DHS employees.

Since the 9/11 terrorist attacks in 2001, there have been several incidents in which mosques within the United States have been attacked by arson, bombing, and/or vandalism. Each of these attacks can be attributed to relatively new phenomena derived from an intense hatred and fear of Muslims called Islamophobia.[103]

Perhaps, if this request from Lute had been handled by I&A instead of dismissed outright, they might have forewarned law enforcement about this ongoing threat. This incident was preceded by another equally disturbing action from CRCL.

In June 2010, Dawn Scalici reportedly asked the sole remaining domestic terrorism analyst at the agency to compile a sampling of domestic extremism–related reports that were officially released by I&A over the past few years.[104] Several examples were provided to Scalici, including multiple Homeland Security reference aids on various white supremacist and sovereign citizen groups.[105] These reports, along with several others concerning transnational and homegrown Muslim extremism, were compiled into a read-book for Lute.[106] The read-book was then submitted for G6 review.[107]

During the G6 review process, CRCL representatives reportedly removed all products relating to domestic non-Islamic extremism, leaving only those reports pertaining to Muslim extremism.[108]

When I&A management confronted CRCL about doing this, CRCL supposedly remarked that, since these products were produced prior to the implementation of the G6 review process (which had been instituted after the leak), they were not "official" or "approved" and, therefore, CRCL believed they were illegitimate.[109]

This action, if true, is utterly astounding. It is very disturbing that CRCL now wielded so much power that they could rewrite their version of DHS history. It is equally upsetting that CRCL could essentially ignore the fact that all of these products had gone through all of the necessary steps for release. It's as though CRCL refuses to recognize that I&A (or DHS) at one time had a robust domestic terrorism analytical effort. They purposefully removed any indication of its mere existence in a formal tasking from Lute.[110]

There have been no finished intelligence reports from DHS or the FBI addressing the threat to Muslim Americans from right-wing extremists or other criminals in the United States spurred by Islamophobia. This is particularly distressing since the nation has experienced more attacks against mosques in America than successful terrorist attacks perpetrated by Muslim extremists since the 9/11 terrorist attacks.[111] To put things into perspective, the Hutaree militia, an extremist Christian militia in Michigan accused in 2011 of plotting to kill police officers and planting bombs at their funerals, had an arsenal of weapons larger than all of the combined Muslim plotters charged in the United States since the 9/11 attacks.

The mounting anti-Islamic sentiment, paranoia, and fear that swept the United States and Europe in the wake of the 9/11 terrorist attacks came to the forefront of worldwide news networks on July 22, 2011. Anders Behring Breivik, a right-wing extremist living in Norway, carried out terrorist attacks targeting Norwegian government offices in Oslo and a youth camp for the political opposition's party on the island of Utoya.[112] Breivik was arrested and charged with killing more than eighty people (many of whom were young adults)—a massive loss of life from two seemingly effortless terrorist attacks carried out with easily obtainable explosives and common firearms.[113] Among Breivik's many causes was an extreme hatred of Muslims and fear of an Islamic conquest of Europe.[114]

"The killings in Norway could easily happen here," I told the *New York Times*.[115]

"This attack in Norway should be a wake-up for our decision makers," I said during an *NBC Nightly News* interview.[116]

"We could have a similar attack here, and that's my greatest fear," I said.[117] "We could have a Timothy McVeigh type carry out a mass shooting event or a vehicle bomb attack that resulted in mass casualties."[118]

Six weeks earlier, in an interview with the SPLC, I warned, "My greatest fear is that a domestic extremist in this country will be emboldened to the point of carrying out a mass-casualty-producing attack because they perceive no one is being vigilant about the threat from within our country from our own radicalized citizenry."[119]

Such a mass-casualty-producing attack in the United States has yet to transpire. Nevertheless, the political climate in this country, coupled with the heated rhetoric and the resurgence in right-wing extremism, has symbolically saturated the American landscape with a highly flammable fuel. All that's lacking is a spark.

For the past few years, the intelligence community has remained in the top ten places to work in the federal government. However, a 2010 internal survey placed I&A near the bottom of all government workplaces.[120] Similar survey results for I&A were reported during 2005–2009. A majority of I&A employees said "they were not satisfied with their jobs or the organization."[121] According to the 2010 survey, I&A employees reported they would not recommend their organization as a good place to work.[122] More than 60 percent of the agency's employees said they were planning to take other jobs within a year.[123] The collective opinions of over 100 intelligence analysts illustrated that I&A could, indeed, sink to a new low.

A primary cause of this negative opinion of I&A was clear. Management had compromised the analytical integrity of the office through their mishandling of the right-wing extremism report situation. Withdrawing support of the report, coupled with the misrepresentation of facts and ensuing retaliation against those who wrote it, had sent a clear message to other analysts in the office—when faced with adversity or controversy, analysts should not expect support from their leadership.

For these reasons, I decided I could no longer live in silence. I felt compelled to refute the lies, the cover-up, and the disinformation. For weeks, I wrestled with the idea of going public with my story. It was a difficult decision because I didn't know how I would be portrayed in the media. Given the subject matter, I was also concerned for my family's safety. I wondered how this might impact my federal career. Through much prayer and consultation, I finally came to the decision that going public was the right thing to do. I wanted to set the record straight, so no one could manipulate the situation for political gain. I was also well aware that some right-wing extremists, such as Charles Dyer, the Oath Keeper, had used my report as a recruiting tool for the militia movement due largely to how the DHS report was portrayed by dishonest news personalities and power-hungry politicians.

On June 7, 2011, the *Washington Post* broke my story to the public. The SPLC followed suit the next day by publishing my interview with them in their *Intelligence Report* magazine. Several other news outlets picked up the story and incorporated various aspects of it into other news items related to the right-wing extremist threat.

On June 9, 2011, the DHS Office of Public Affairs responded to my interviews with the *Washington Post* and SPLC with an article of their own published in *Homeland Security Today* magazine, which is the DHS propaganda arm. The department's weak rebuttal lacked specifics and featured several half-truths intermingled with lots of "smoke and mirrors."

I wasn't surprised to see that they had once again attempted to distort the truth, deflect blame, and avoid responsibility for what they had done.

The department's response glossed over the distinction between domestic non-Islamic extremism and homegrown Muslim extremism. They mingled both subjects under the umbrella of "domestic terrorism." The *Homeland Security Today* correspondent who wrote the story was not sophisticated enough to catch this distinction. Moreover, state and local law enforcement officials, as well as state fusion center officials in the *Washington Post* story, had voiced their dissatisfaction with receiving only reports that addressed the general problem of radicalization, without regard to who was doing what. In short, almost all of the DHS response was predictable political spin.

DHS officials and others (who remained anonymous) who were interviewed by *Homeland Security Today* said my claims were not true. Yet no one would go on the record to bolster such claims. Anonymity lessens credibility.

According to *Homeland Security Today*, numerous federal and other unnamed officials familiar with the matter said the DHS right-wing extremism report was the most "poorly constructed analytical product in DHS history."[124]

The article further stated that DHS records obtained by *Homeland Security Today* under the Freedom of Information Act in June 2009 indicated that "the report was wrongly disseminated to law enforcement agencies because of problems with it that were identified by DHS's Office of Civil Rights and Civil Liberties."[125]

The *Homeland Security Today* article also mentioned that "descriptions of the withheld Office of Civil Rights and Civil Liberties documents indicated someone did not comply with the procedures for releasing the assessment to the law enforcement community despite the office's concerns."[126]

Both statements are misleading. At the time, there was no DHS policy, regulation, or written guidance concerning mandatory coordination of intelligence reports with the Office of Civil Rights and Civil Liberties. CRCL did raise concerns, but the only remaining concern was the definition of right-wing extremism. After a lengthy period of deliberation, I&A attorneys overruled CRCL on the wording of this definition. This disagreement between CRCL and I&A attorneys was explained in the SPLC interview.

Homeland Security Today quoted a senior DHS official who stated, "I&A has federal intelligence analysts assigned to issues covering a wide range of violent extremist groups, including non-Islamic domestic terrorism threats such as violent militia movements and violent sovereign citizen movements"[127]

Nevertheless, the official never stated how many DHS analysts were working on the topic of non-Islamic domestic terrorism. At the time of the article, there were now only two analysts monitoring domestic non-Islamic extremism at I&A—a newly hired junior analyst straight out of college with no analytical experience and few, if any, law enforcement contacts, and a government contractor whose assignment to DHS was subject to change at a moment's notice.

DHS authorities were quick to announce that since January 2010, I&A had provided several non-Islamic domestic terrorism briefings. They cited participation in round-table discussions at multiple fusion centers in more than ten states.[128]

The DHS official commented that "I&A has also conducted violent domestic extremism presentations for the National Monuments and Icons and Critical Manufacturing sectors of critical infrastructure in Washington, D.C."[129]

The DHS official failed to mention that such briefing presentations had only resumed within the past few months after a prolonged absence. All briefing presentations on this subject were abruptly canceled in April 2009 and through much of 2010. Unlike the briefings given prior to April 2009, the new briefings were thoroughly reviewed by CRCL, heavily re-edited, and carefully scripted to avoid any politically incorrect statements and lacked specificity and substance. These new briefings were generic, sanitized briefings of national trends and tactics with little specificity and virtually no reference to groups and individuals who may present a terrorist threat.

DHS officials claimed that since April 2009, I&A had released ten products that specifically mention non-Islamic homegrown violent extremists and fifty products that discuss the general terrorist threat to the homeland or terrorist tactics, techniques, and procedures, regardless of motivation or ideology, to state, local, and tribal partners. The article then cites several joint intelligence bulletins between DHS and the FBI discussing incidents such as the Austin plane crash into the IRS, the 2010 Pentagon shooting, the shooting of Congresswoman Giffords, and the arrest of a white supremacist charged with placing a bomb along a Martin Luther King Day parade route.[130]

Again, these statements are misleading. In reality, the ten reports about non-Islamic homegrown violent extremists were actually written by the FBI. The FBI shares these reports with DHS as a courtesy. DHS only provides edits and comment. These are not unique DHS intelligence reports and do not contain substantive analysis. They are basically regurgitated news reporting meant to provide situational awareness. The FBI obliges the DHS by placing the DHS logo on these reports. The other types of reports mentioned by DHS are focused on terrorist tactics and tradecraft. Again, this statement is deceptive. These reports are not exclusively focused on domestic non-Islamic extremists. They contain generic references to both domestic and international extremists and do not contain much analysis.

It is interesting to compare the number of DHS reports released over this same time period concerning Muslim extremism and Islamic terrorism. In 2011, I&A produced over 300 raw intelligence cables about Muslim extremists. There were only a few related to domestic non-Islamic extremists in 2009, none in 2010, and just three reports during 2011. The 2011 reports were likely meant to appease recent media scrutiny.

DHS also produced over 100 finished intelligence reports related to al-Qaeda, its affiliates, and other Muslim extremism–related topics during 2010–2011. Yet DHS and unnamed fusion center officials claim that they do not "see any lessening in the amount" of intelligence collected on domestic non-Islamic extremists.[131]

In the *Homeland Security Today* article, the unnamed DHS official commented that I&A's information-sharing efforts have prevented acts of terrorism across the country, including the recent arrest of a white supremacist that attempted to attack Spokane, Washington, in January 2011.[132]

This statement is simply not true. An alert Federal Protective Service (FPS) officer reportedly discovered the suspicious backpack containing the explosive device. FPS is a law enforcement agency with the DHS that has very little interaction with DHS/I&A. So DHS/I&A did not prevent this attack; a vigilant law enforcement officer did. Furthermore, since I&A has no operational capability, it is not in a position to really "prevent" any act of terrorism. All I&A can do is alert law enforcement to possible terrorist threats and emerging trends. Thus, this appears to be an exaggerated example of I&A's accomplishments.

A week after going public, House Homeland Security chairman Peter King (R-New York) held the second of two hearings on Islamic radicalization in the United States. King believed that U.S. prisons were becoming "an assembly line for radicalization" of Muslims.[133] The second hearing focused on the manufactured threat of "PrIslam," as lawmakers and news reporters began referring to it.

According to the *American Prospect*, a magazine that published an article about King's PrIslam hearing, "one could indeed imagine that bloated U.S. prisons—warehouses for human misery that house more than two million people—might turn into hotbeds for Islamic radicalization. But it hasn't turned out that way."[134]

Professor Bert Useem, from Purdue University, testified before King's committee and pointed out that terrorists tend to be middle class and educated, which is why they're preoccupied with politics and current events.[135]

"Prisoners tend to be less educated and commit crimes for personal gain rather than ideology," Useem said.[136]

According to the Congressional Research Service, since the 9/11 terrorist attacks, only one plot has involved Muslims who became radicalized in prison.[137]

Karen Greenberg, director of New York University's (NYU) Center for Law and Security, told the *American Prospect* magazine that her research indicated that antigovernment terrorists who commit crimes similar to Islamic extremists face fewer charges and serve lighter sentences.[138]

"The right-wing guys, for lack of a better term, get lower sentences. There are fewer stings in progress against them," Greenberg said.[139] "If explosives are involved, they get charged for explosives instead of weapons of mass destruction, as they might be in a jihadist terrorism case."[140]

In reality, there is a much greater prison radicalization problem involving white supremacists than Muslim extremists. For the white supremacist movement, prison radicalization serves as a force multiplier that allows it to boost membership and expand its influence both within and outside of prison walls. Members of white supremacist prison gangs are obliged to carry out the activities and goals of the "prison gang" within correctional institutions. They then perpetrate acts of violence within our communities upon their release. And, in the case of white supremacist prison gangs, they also spread racist, anti-Semitic, and other extremist messages to susceptible members of American society.

The Creativity Movement, a white supremacist organization (formerly known as the World Church of the Creator), has successfully recruited from among the prison population. The Creativity Movement, unlike other white supremacist organizations outside the prison system, allows inmates to join the organization while still incarcerated. Several members of the Creativity Movement have carried out murderous shootings, firebombings, and other terrorism acts in the United States.

The anti-Semitic Christian Identity movement also claims to have infiltrated the prison system to recruit and indoctrinate inmates by posing as representatives of legitimate fundamentalist Christian denominations. A leader in the Christian Identity movement said that after receiving approval from prison officials and gaining access to the inmate population, he introduced his white supremacist and racist ideology under the guise of "religion."

Prison authorities have identified dozens of white supremacist prison gangs operating inside correctional institutions throughout the country. Correctional officers have labeled these gangs as "security threat groups" due to their propensity for violence and widespread criminality, which poses a threat to correctional officers and prison staff.

White supremacist prison gangs, such as the Aryan Brotherhood, Aryan Brotherhood of Texas, and the Aryan Circle, constitute a radicalization threat. Despite King's personal bias toward Muslim extremism and narrow interpretation of prison radicalization, white supremacist prison gang members meet the U.S. government's definition of radicalization, which includes the process of adopting an extremist belief system that involves a willingness to use violence for societal change. The majority of white supremacist prison gang recruitment occurs within the correctional institution, although members of Aryan prison gangs often continue to recruit outside of prison walls. In addition, members express violent racist rhetoric upon release and have been known to carry out acts of violence in the name of the white supremacist ideology.

White supremacist prison gangs are heavily involved in narcotics production and trafficking in our communities. Gang members have made numerous threats against law enforcement and have been found in possession of identifying information on several federal, state, and local law enforcement officers. Additionally, white supremacist prison gang members have been involved in weapons stockpiling and possession of explosive devices once released from prison.

These organizations sympathize with white inmates and view them as soldiers of the white supremacist cause. Some white supremacist organizations have even established prison outreach programs to provide inmates with "prisoner support" and racist publications filled with white supremacist propaganda intended to fuel extremism and attract them to other, more hard-core white supremacist causes.

For example, members of the Soldiers of the Aryan Culture, one of the most active white supremacist prison gangs in Utah, were implicated in an unrealized plot to use a pipe bomb to attack Jewish athletes at the 2002 Winter Olympics in Salt Lake City.[141]

In addition, a member of a white supremacist prison gang, who had been "radicalized" in prison, was arrested on April 19, 2001, for plotting to bomb the Northeast Holocaust Memorial Museum in Boston, Massachusetts (and other property perceived to be associated with Jews), in order to incite a "racial holy war."[142]

Of course, Peter King dismissed the topic of neo-Nazis plotting terrorist attacks and white supremacist prison radicalization as mere criminal matters that should be handled by agencies within the Department of Justice. He failed to acknowledge that non-Muslims are capable of committing horrendous acts of ideologically motivated violence in the name of a cause other than a perverted interpretation of Islam. Other congressional representatives who subscribe to King's thought process play "Russian roulette" with the country's safety and security.

As I read about King's radicalization hearings in the news, I reflected on a question that has haunted me since the leak occurred—who would do such a thing? Did the person responsible for leaking the DHS right-wing extremism report know that it would cause such malice between Americans and political controversy among our politicians and government leaders?

There is no way to really know for certain who leaked the 2009 DHS right-wing extremism report. An Oath Keeper, who chose not identify himself, claimed responsibility for the leak.

Tracking the release of the report was an impossible thing to do. I&A had no security protocols in place to number, encrypt, or electronically monitor its reports once released. The report had been sent to more than seventy state fusion centers and hundreds of federal, state, and local law enforcement agencies. These organizations, in turn, forwarded the report to many more law enforcement officers, private-sector security personnel, and other emergency responders.

I had met DHS employees who supported the "Birther" movement (people who believe president Barack Obama is not a U.S. citizen) and the "Truther" movement (people who believe the 9/11 terrorist attacks were not carried out by al-Qaeda operatives). There had also been recent cases of law enforcement and correctional officers belonging to neo-Nazi groups, the Ku Klux Klan, and the sovereign citizen movement.

There is, however, one individual who stands out from the other possible suspects. His code name was "Beowulf." A number of curious circumstances point to his possible role in leaking the DHS report.

Dr. Bruce D. Tefft was a DHS contractor who worked for Community Research Associates (CRA Inc.) at the time the report was leaked.[143] CRA Inc. described itself as "the foremost contractor to the U.S. Department of Homeland Security, Office of Grants and Training." According to the executive profile on Bloomberg's *Businessweek*, Roger Mackin, former acting undersecretary for intelligence and analysis at the time of the right-wing extremism report controversy, has been the chief executive officer of CRA Inc. since 2005.[144] Surprisingly, Mackin made no mention of his brief stint as acting undersecretary for I&A in his executive profile. Given the fact CRA Inc. is a very small company, it is possible that Tefft and Mackin knew each other.

In February 2008, Tefft participated as a panelist and guest speaker at the America's Truth Forum—an Islamophobic symposium organized to "expose the threat of Islamist terrorism in Dallas, Texas."[145]

Tefft joined Robert Spencer, director of Jihad Watch; Roger Hedgecock, a conservative talk radio show personality; and other speakers on the panel. Norway mass murderer Anders Behring Breivek reportedly idolized Robert Spencer, quoting Spencer's anti-Muslim remarks over fifty times in his manifesto.[146] Hedgecock was credited for breaking the story on the leak and incited conservative attacks against the DHS right-wing extremism report. Both Spencer and Hedgecock have positioned themselves as voices of the far right in America—Spencer for his anti-Muslim views[147] and Hedgecock for his vehemently anti–illegal immigration stance.[148] This was certainly interesting company for a former CIA chief of station and founding member of the CIA's Counterterrorism Center in 1985.[149]

Tefft was also named as a codefendant, along with the New York Police Department, in a lawsuit related to workplace harassment, which resulted from Tefft's inappropriate remarks concerning an exaggerated threat from radical Islam that were attached to various e-mail messages sent from Tefft's multiple list servers.[150] A blog affiliated with America's Truth Forum featured an appeal for "Dr. Bruce Tefft's Defense Fund."[151]

Tefft, while participating as a panelist at a jihad and global terrorism seminar held at the University of Toronto in September 2004, reportedly remarked, "Islamic terrorism is based on Islam as revealed through the Qu'ran."[152]

He further stated, "To pretend that Islam has nothing to do with September 11 is to willfully ignore the obvious and to forever misinterpret events."[153]

"There is no difference between Islam and Islamic fundamentalism, which is a totalitarian construct," Tefft said.[154]

Tefft went on to say, "Of the 6,000 or more mosques in North America, 80 percent are radical in orientation and devoted to spreading an intolerant Wahabi strain of Islam."[155]

Despite these improper statements, Tefft was known within the law enforcement and intelligence communities for his open-source information list servers on Yahoo!

I was first introduced to Tefft's list servers soon after leaving the DHS in April 2010. Since I was completely unaware of Tefft and his e-mail groups, I had no idea what he had been saying and doing during the 2009 time frame. In 2010, law enforcement officials alerted me to several disturbing messages they had received from Tefft around the time of the leak of the DHS right-wing extremism report. According to law enforcement sources, Tefft often used an alias, the online screen name "Beowulf," when posting messages and replying to subscribers' questions.

Tefft also openly admitted to operating "an international open source (OSINT) collection network which reviews more than 1,600 articles and messages per day from law enforcement, intelligence, military, academic and media sources and disseminates approximately 10% of these to 15,000 readers"—a likely reference to his OSINT e-mail list.[156]

Law enforcement concerns about Tefft related to the many disparaging remarks he made against the SPLC. In addition, his sources often came from questionable media sites and ultraconservative commentaries. He regularly circulated stories gathered from such "far right" sources as the *Free Republic, Canada Free Press, Publius Forum,* the *Red State,* and *Liberty Papers*.[157] Many of Tefft's postings carried a common theme—a growing disdain for president Barack Obama and a hatred for secretary Janet Napolitano and DHS.

One law enforcement source familiar with working domestic terrorism issues told me that Tefft had commented on a few of his past articles, appearing to express sympathy toward and openly support well-known antigovernment extremist causes, such as the sovereign citizen movement. In fact, Tefft operated an e-mail group called "Indigenous-Sovereign."[158] He was also known to speak favorably of right-wing extremist personalities, like former Phoenix police officer Jack McLamb and sheriff Richard Mack.

Over several days, I read dozens of articles written by Tefft, which were posted on his open-source list servers. Many of the titles concerned me, such as "Southern Poverty Law Center Is a Non-Credible, Anti-Conservative Hate Group."

At the end of the article, Tefft, using his Beowulf alias, remarked, "Let me add to that, that I've personally dealt with the SPLF [*sic*] and have found them to be completely disinterested in putting out accurate information."[159]

He further stated, "Their [SPLC] attitude is if it hurts people they don't like, they don't care whether it's true or not. So, I would take ANYTHING the SPLF [*sic*] had to say about ANY GROUP with an hourglass full of sand."[160]

On April 10, 2009, an unknown individual made similar, disparaging remarks about the civil rights organization during the first known web postings in the God-LikeProductions web forum concerning the leaked DHS report. These comments were very similar to ones made by "Beowulf."

Tefft had expressed familiarity with the terms "Mecha," "La Raza," and "La Voz de Atzlan." These names, which are used to describe various Mexican nationalist movements, also appear in the same anonymous postings that referenced the DHS report.

My interest was piqued as I began searching through Beowulf's archive of messages. I was looking specifically for any postings around the time of the right-wing extremism report's leak on April 9, 2009. I noted that many unfavorable articles about the report were posted on Tefft's e-mail groups. His messages about the report included various degrading titles such as "The Founders Were 'Domestic Terrorists' According to Obama's DHS"; "Obama's Intel Services More Worried About Right Wing Terror Than Islamists?"; "Department of Hopeless Speculation"; "Open Notice to DHS" [which contains the message "F U DHS"]; "Demonizing Veterans, DHS Déjà vu"; and "Do Liberals Now Make the DHS List of Potential Domestic Terrorists[161]"?

During 2011, other articles posted by Tefft (i.e., Beowulf) included titles such as "Napolitano, Muslim Brotherhood Affiliates Met Secretly"; "Obama Is Advancing Islam's Interests Not Ours"; and "Obama, Egypt and History of the Muslim Brotherhood."[162] These articles are clearly attempting to link Napolitano and Obama to an imaginary sinister collusion with Muslims.

In one article titled "Professional 'Anti-Hate' Group Goes to Bed with Reds," Tefft remarks, "Unfortunately, no 'news.' SPLC has long been known as a communist front."[163]

During 2007–2009, Tefft reportedly had access to law enforcement–sensitive information through various mailing lists to which he surreptitiously subscribed. I'm sure he touted his DHS contracting work, along with his NYPD training activities, to justify his access. In reality, Tefft had no valid reason to receive sensitive law enforcement information related to terrorism. On more than one occasion, Tefft had been removed from law enforcement lists for disclosing sensitive law enforcement information to unvetted users of his Yahoo! Groups. The most recent incident occurred in February 2011, when he was promptly removed from an unidentified law enforcement list for pushing out information not authorized outside of official law enforcement channels.[164]

Law enforcement and intelligence officials also noted that Tefft had circulated past DHS intelligence reports (including the daily DHS open source) on his Yahoo! lists. However, no one recalled whether Tefft ever circulated the DHS right-wing extremist report on his lists.

At a minimum, Tefft's unauthorized circulation of sensitive law enforcement reporting to nonvetted subscribers on his Yahoo! Group lists constitutes a breach in government information handling procedures. At worst, he willingly disclosed this information to hundreds, if not thousands, of people with no established "need to know." He certainly had the means, the motive, the access, and right contacts (i.e., Roger Hedgecock).

The leak and its aftermath should have been handled differently. The DHS Public Affairs Office should have challenged the false assertions and mischaracterizations of the report from various conservative commentators. They certainly should not have made up a story of the report being "unauthorized" or released by a rogue, maverick team of analysts. This false and futile attempt to calm the criticism only led to the development of mistrust in DHS leadership.

Napolitano should have stood her ground and had faith in her department's ability to analyze and warn of potential domestic terrorist threats. Should she have backed her department's analysis instead of distancing herself from it, she might have been vindicated within weeks, as right-wing extremist attacks occurred. Instead, she caved in to the political pressure. Napolitano then misrepresented the facts while under oath.[165,166]

Certainly, Bart Johnson, the acting DASI and DTAD director, did a horrible job of managing the crisis from within I&A. Johnson not only failed to inform department leadership of what really happened, but he also took no interest in learning the truth and stopped very valuable work at a critical time of heightened threat activity.

Seeing no improvement in sight, I took a position at another agency. Despite the promotion, the shortened commute, and better quality of life, I felt somewhat unfulfilled and empty. I was not going to miss the high-stress environment, the constant scrutiny of my work, and the numerous letdowns and cancellations of business trips, briefing presentations, and training. But I was frustrated to leave the type of work I truly loved. Yes, it was my decision to leave the agency, but I&A management had created such a difficult work environment that I felt I could not continue pursuing my subject matter expertise. I eventually filled this void by forming my own consulting firm exclusively focused on monitoring domestic non-Islamic extremism in the United States and educating others on this purely homegrown threat.

In November 2011, Bart Johnson announced his departure from I&A. He had accepted a new position as executive director of the International Association Chiefs of Police (IACP). In his farewell notice to I&A employees, Johnson remarked, "On September 11, 2001, I watched from the sidelines as terrorists attacked our cities and killed thousands of our fellow citizens, including two of my good friends."[167]

"The grief was worsened by the terrible frustration that despite all my training, my oath to serve and protect, my desire to do something, I was not equipped to honor their sacrifice and ensure that such a horrible tragedy never happened again," he wrote.[168]

As I read these words, I couldn't help but think of the very oath of office I had made on four separate occasions to "support and defend the Constitution of the United States against all enemies, foreign and domestic." I was confident that I had fulfilled my obligations to this oath, but how many others at DHS took a much more narrow interpretation of "domestic enemies" who threaten the Constitution. Through his actions during the entire DHS right-wing extremism controversy, Bart Johnson certainly demonstrated that he had a limited view of "domestic enemies," which was basically Muslim inclusive.

At DHS, I felt I was performing an important work—analyzing and assessing domestic extremist threats—for the protection of our country. However, in 2009, it appeared that Congress and a large portion of the American population no longer wanted DHS to perform this vital work. It brings no solace to know that the Department of Homeland Security no longer has a group of subject matter experts looking at the threat from right-wing extremists. It is disturbing to know that DHS leadership attempted to cover up the truth by manufacturing a story of an unauthorized report written by a rogue group of intelligence analysts. It is unnerving to know that many DHS leaders, including Napolitano, continue to misuse the term "domestic terrorism" to mean the threat from homegrown Muslim extremists, despite knowing the difference between the two threats. And when there actually were legitimate acts of domestic terrorism, Napolitano utterly refused to recognize them.

It is also worrying that DHS media spokespersons and unnamed DHS officials persist in misleading the American public into thinking the department is being vigilant toward non-Islamic terrorist threats in the homeland. If this were the case, then I would think that DHS would be shocked to know that domestic non-Islamic extremists have received DHS funding for equipment and DHS training for their paramilitary training activities. Surprisingly, DHS had inadvertently given $5,000 in federal grant funding to a militia group in Oregon to purchase radio equipment.[169] In November 2010, an unsuspecting local law enforcement officer gave an official DHS training class on "radicalization" to approximately thirty members of a militia group in Zanesville, Ohio.[170] Despite notification of DHS officials, nothing appears to have been done about either case. From these examples, it doesn't appear that the Department of Homeland Security is too concerned with the threat of right-wing extremism despite a period of heightened violent activity.

As the 2012 presidential election approaches, nothing that led to the most recent right-wing resurgence has changed. Over the past four years, the economy remains sluggish, with the unemployment rate hovering around 10 percent nationally. Obama, his administration, and his policies (some controversial) remain. Controversial and divisive political issues such as illegal immigration are left unaddressed, unresolved. And despite numerous threats against congressional representatives, an actual assassination attempt of a U.S. congresswoman, and calls for a "cease and desist," heated political rhetoric continues to fan the flames of political defiance, disruption, and discord—even death threats. No one in power appears to have heard nor heeded the warning call. Nevertheless, right-wing-inspired extremist attacks and terrorist plots continue. This growing list of violent plans and actual acts of domestic terrorism testify to the significance and importance of the DHS right-wing extremism report.

Fear of the unknown, continued economic uncertainty, increased hatred toward political parties and their causes, along with a hotly contested presidential race has set the stage, once again, for an interesting year. And, I fear, if the flames of discontent are persistently stoked, an uncontrollable inferno will rage to the point where it consumes us as a nation in one horrific act of senseless violence. Only then will some unfortunately recognize that history has repeated itself—hearkening back to some of America's darkest days.

History has already borne witness to the prescient analysis of the DHS right-wing extremism report. History will also bear witness to whether dismantling the DHS domestic terrorism team, halting all domestic extremism analytical work at DHS, and government leaders turning a "blind eye" toward the right-wing extremist threat from within was ultimately a wise thing to do.

Notes

CHAPTER 1

1. http://www.godlikeproductions.com/forum1/message769206/pg1, dated April 11, 2009.
2. Ibid.
3. Ibid.
4. Ibid.
5. Aztlan is a mythical location allegedly belonging to an ancient, indigenous people who lived in the geographical area known as Mexico, the American Southwest, and Pacific Northwest. Radical Mexican separatists today want to secede eight southwestern U.S. states back to Mexico, including Arizona, California, Colorado, Nevada, New Mexico, Oregon, Texas, Utah, and a portion of Washington State. They believe Aztlan will ultimately be repatriated and given back to this purported indigenous people.
6. Mecha is an acronym for "Movimiento Estudiantil Chicano de Aztlan" or "Chicano Student Movement of Aztlan." It is a radical, separatist student organization that encourages anti-American activities and acts of civil disobedience. The Mecha movement romanticizes the myth of Aztlan and encourages Latinos to get involved in promoting their ancestry and indigenous consciousness to further the cause of establishing Aztlan.
7. http://oath-keepers.blogspot.com/2009/03/welcome-to-oath-keepers_02.html, viewed May 8, 2009.
8. Ibid.
9. "Rightwing Extremism: Current Economic and Political Climate Fueling Resurgence in Radicalization and Recruitment," U.S. Department of Homeland Security, Office of Intelligence and Analysis, April 7, 2009.
10. La Raza is a broad term used to describe those whose ancestry is indigenous to the area of modern-day Mexico. It's also used to describe the unification and camaraderie among various Mexican separatist causes.
11. http://oath-keepers.blogspot.com/2009/03/welcome-to-oath-keepers_02.html, viewed May 8, 2009.

12. United States Code, Chapter 33, Title *5, §3331.*

13. "Constitution's Link to the Oath of Office," Office of Personnel Management, Constitution Initiative, viewed August 8, 2010.

14. Ibid.

15. Ibid.

16. Ibid.

17. Ibid.

18. Ibid.

19. Ibid.

20. http://www.oath-keepers.blogspot.com, viewed May 8, 2009.

21. "Interview with Sean Smith, Assistant Secretary for Public Affairs at DHS," Roger Hedgecock Radio, April 14, 2009.

22. Ibid.

23. "Judgment Day in Mystery Babylon?" *World Net Daily*, September 13, 2001.

24. "Rathergage II: Certification of Live Birth a Clear Forgery," *World Net Daily*, November 25, 2008.

25. "What's Obama Hiding from Us?" *World Net Daily*, October 17, 2008.

26. Hedgecock, Roger. "Disagree with Obama? Gov't Has Eyes on You," *World Net Daily*, April 13, 2009.

27. "Rightwing Extremism."

28. Ibid.

29. Hedgecock, Roger, "Disagree with Obama?"

30. Ibid.

31. "Rightwing Extremism."

32. Hedgecock. "Disagree with Obama?"

33. Ibid.

34. Gordon, Stephen. "Homeland Security Document Targets Most Conservatives and Libertarians in the Country," *The Liberty Papers*, April 12, 2009.

35. Ibid.

36. Ibid.

37. "Rightwing Extremism."

38. Gordon. "Homeland Security Document."

39. Ibid.

40. "Secret DHS Doc Predicts Violence in Response to Gun Restrictions," *Info Wars*, April 13, 2009.

41. Ibid.

42. Ibid.

43. Ibid.

44. Ibid.

45. Ibid.

46. Ibid.

47. "Assistant Secretary for Public Affairs: Sean Smith," DHS Official Website, June 1, 2009.

48. Ibid.

49. Ibid.

50. Ibid.

51. Interview with Sean Smith, Assistant Secretary for Public Affairs at DHS, *Roger Hedgecock Show*, April 14, 2010.

52. Ibid.
53. Ibid.
54. Ibid.
55. Ibid.
56. Ibid.
57. Ibid.
58. Ibid.
59. Ibid.
60. Ibid.
61. Ibid.
62. Ibid.
63. Ibid.
64. Ibid.
65. Ibid.
66. Ibid.
67. Ibid.
68. Ibid.
69. Ibid.
70. Ibid.
71. Ibid.
72. Ibid.
73. Ibid.
74. Ibid.
75. Ibid.
76. Ibid.
77. Ibid.
78. Ibid.
79. Ibid.
80. Ibid.
81. Ibid.
82. Ibid.
83. Ibid.
84. Ibid.
85. Ibid.
86. Ibid.
87. Ibid.
88. Ibid.
89. Ibid.
90. Ibid.
91. Ibid.
92. Ibid.
93. Ibid.
94. Ibid.
95. Ibid.
96. Ibid.
97. Ibid.
98. Ibid.

99. Ibid.

100. Ibid.

101. Ibid.

102. Ibid.

103. Ibid.

104. Ibid.

105. Ibid.

106. Ibid.

107. Ibid.

108. Ibid.

109. Ibid.

110. Ibid.

111. "Federal Agency Warns of Radicals on Right," *Washington Times*, April 14, 2009.

112. "Oath Keepers on the Inside: Testimonial from Officer within the Department of Homeland Security," Oath Keepers Blog Spot, May 11, 2009.

113. Ibid.

114. Ibid.

115. Ibid.

116. Ibid.

117. Ibid.

118. Ibid.

119. Ibid..

120. Ibid.

121. Ibid.

122. Ibid.

123. Ibid.

124. "'Fusion Centers Expand Criteria to Identify Militia Members," *Fox News*, March 23, 2009.

125. "Oath Keepers on the Inside."

126. Ibid.

127. "A Patriot Hero Goes Down," Mother Jones, Januray 22, 2010.

128. Ibid.

129. "Ex-Marine's Arrest Spurs Serious Threats," *News 9*, January 21, 2010.

130. "A 'Patriot' Hero Goes Down."

131. Ibid.

132. Ibid.

133. "Oath Keeper Chief Denies Accused Rapist Was Member," SPLC, *Hatewatch* Blog, January 22, 2010.

134. "After Dyer's Rape Arrest, Oath Keepers Disavow Any Association with Onetime Key Figure," Crooks and Liars, January 21, 2010.

135. "Oath Keeper Chief."

136. "A 'Patriot' Hero Goes Down."

137. Ibid.

138. "July4Patriot at Broken Arrow, OK Tea Party," Oath-Keepers.blogspot.com, July 9, 2009.

139. Rhodes, Stewart. Post Concerning Upcoming Tea Party Rally in Broken Arrow, Oklahoma, Oath-Keepers.blogspot.com, June 29, 2009.

140. "North Olmsted Man Had Live Bombs in His Garage on Louis Drive, Authorities Say," *Cleveland Plain Dealer*, April 15, 2010.

141. Ibid.

142. "Man Charged with Having Explosives Seemed Paranoid, Landlord Says," *Cleveland Plain Dealer*, April 20, 2010.

143. "North Olmsted Man."

144. Ibid.

145. "Anti-Government Sovereign Citizens on the Rise in Ohio," *WKYC*, November 25, 2010.

146. "Georgia Man Accused of Traveling to Tennessee for Armed Takeover of Courthouse," *WBIR*, May 4, 2010.

147. Ibid.

148. Ibid.

149. Ibid.

150. Ibid.

151. Ibid.

152. Ibid.

153. Ibid.

154. Ibid.

155. Ibid.

156. Ibid.

157. Ibid.

158. Report 111-134, U.S. House of Representatives, 111th Congress, 1st Session, June 4, 2009.

159. Ibid.

160. Ibid.

161. Ibid.

162. Ibid.

163. Ibid.

164. Ibid.

165. Ibid.

166. Ibid.

167. Ibid.

168. Ibid.

169. Ibid.

170. Ibid.

171. Ibid.

172. Ibid.

173. Ibid.

174. Ibid.

175. Ibid.

CHAPTER 2

1. House Committee on Appropriations, Subcommittee on Homeland Security, Hearing on the Department of Homeland Security, Witness: Secretary of Homeland Security Janet Napolitano, May 12, 2009.

2. Newport, Frank. "Mormons Most Conservative Religious Group in the U.S.," Gallup Poll, January 11, 2010.

3. "The Covenant, the Sword, the Arm of the Lord," Federal Bureau of Investigation-Kansas City Field Office, Memorandum, July 2, 1982.

4. Ibid.

5. "The Covenant, the Sword, the Arm of the Lord," Federal Bureau of Investigation-Little Rock Field Office Memorandum, September 7, 1984.

6. Ibid.

7. Ibid.

8. "The Covenant, the Sword, the Arm of the Lord," Federal Bureau of Investigation, Briefing Paper, May 20, 1985.

9. Ibid.

10. Ibid.

11. Mathews, Robert Jay. "Oath—Die Bruder Sweigen," 1983.

12. Ibid.

13. US v. Gary Lee Yarborough, et al., U.S. Court of Appeals for the Ninth Circuit, July 6, 1988.

14. "Chronology of Neo-Nazi Crimes," *United Press International*, December 30, 1985.

15. US v. Gary Lee Yarborough.

16. "Domestic News," *United Press International*, September 30, 1984.

17. "Aryan Group, Jail Gangs Linked," *Washington Post*, December 18, 1984.

18. "National News Briefs," *United Press International*, April 30, 1984.

19. US v. Gary Lee Yarborough.

20. Ibid.

21. Ibid.

22. Ibid.

23. Ibid.

24. "3 Killed in Arkansas Fight Believed to Involve Fugitive," *New York Times*, June 4, 1983.

25. U.S. v. Scott Faul, et al. United States Court of Appeals for the Eighth Circuit, May 14, 1984.

26. Ibid.

27. Ibid.

28. Ibid.

29. Ibid.

30. Ibid.

31. Ibid.

32. Ibid.

33. Ibid.

34. Ibid.

35. Ibid.

36. Ibid.

37. Ibid.

38. Ibid.

39. Ibid.

40. "3 Killed in Arkansas Fight Believed to Involve Fugitive," *New York Times*, June 4, 1983.

41. "LDS Church Issues Statement on Rex Rammell," *Rexburg Standard Journal*, December 24, 2009.

42. Jacobs, Samuel P. "Why Militias Love Michigan," *Daily Beast*, March 31, 2010.

43. http://en.wikipedia.org/wiki/Devil's_Night, accessed July 13, 2010.

44. Second Amendment to the United States Constitution reads "A well regulated Militia, being necessary to the security of a free State, the right of the people to keep and bear Arms, shall not be infringed."

CHAPTER 3

1. "The Issue Is 'Turn to Violence,'" Fox News, April 20, 2010.

2. Ibid.

3. Ibid.

4. Ibid.

5. Ibid.

6. FBI, "Terrorism in the United States," Annual Reports, 1986–2005. Various academic and professional journals dealing with the subjects of terrorism and counterterrorism.

7. Homeland Security Act of 2002, Public Law 107-296, 107th Congress, November 25, 2002.

8. The Brady Handgun Violence Prevention Act, 103rd United States Congress, Public Law 103-159, November 30, 1993.

9. Violent Crime Control and Law Enforcement Act of 1994, 103rd United States Congress, Public Law Number 103-322, September 13, 1994.

10. "Report of the Ruby Ridge Task Force," U.S. Department of Justice, June 10, 1994.

11. Ibid.

12. Ibid.

13. Ibid.

14. Ibid.

15. Ruby Ridge Task Force Report—Allegations of Improper Government Conduct, U.S. Department of Justice, June 10, 1994.

16. Ibid.

17. Ibid.

18. Ibid.

19. "Intelligence Files: Bo Gritz," Southern Poverty Law Center, 2009.

20. Ruby Ridge Task Force Report.

21. Ibid.

22. Ibid.

23. Ibid.

24. Ibid.

25. Ibid.

26. Ibid.

27. Ibid.

28. "Patriot Timeline," Southern Poverty Law Center, Intelligence Report, Summer 2001.

29. Junas, Daniel. "Rise of Citizen Militias: Angry White Guys with Guns," *Covert Action Quarterly*, April 24, 1995.

30. http://www.louisbeam.com/estes.html, viewed June 15, 2010.

31. http://www.shepherds-rod.org/photo/page1.html, viewed June 14, 2010.

32. "A Chronology History of the Branch Davidians," Apologetics Index, viewed June 14, 2010.

33. "The Shepherd's Rod: Volume 1," Victor T. Houteff, 1930.

34. "A Chronology History of the Branch Davidians."

35. Ibid.

36. "Mr. Retardo: The Making of a Messiah—David Koresh's Twisted Road to Waco," *Dallas Observer*, July 27, 1995.

37. "ATF Investigation of Vernon Wayne Howell also known as David Koresh," U.S. Department of Treasury, September 30, 1993.

38. Ibid.

39. Ibid.

40. Ibid.

41. Ibid.

42. Ibid.

43. Ibid.

44. Ibid.

45. Ibid.

46. Ibid.

47. Ibid.

48. Ibid.

49. "Investigation into the Activities of Federal Law Enforcement Agencies toward the Branch Davidians," Committee on Government Reform and Oversight, Committee on the Judiciary, U.S. Congress, August 2, 1996.

50. "AFT Investigation of Vernon Wayne Howell."

51. Ibid.

52. Ibid.

53. Ibid.

54. Ibid.

55. Ibid.

56. Ibid.

57. Ibid.

58. Ibid.

59. Ibid.

60. Ibid.

61. Ibid.

62. Ibid.

63. Ibid.

64. Ibid.

65. Ibid.

66. Ibid.

67. Report to the Deputy Attorney General on the Events at Waco, Texas (February 28 to April 19, 1993), U.S. Department of Justice, October 8, 1993.

68. Ibid.

69. Ibid.

70. Ibid.

71. Ibid.

72. Ibid.

73. Ibid.

74. Ibid.

75. Ibid.

76. Ibid.

77. Ibid.

78. "ATF Investigation of Vernon Wayne Howell."

79. Ibid.

80. "Investigation into the Activities of Federal Law Enforcement Agencies toward the Branch Davidians," Committee on Government Reform and Oversight, Committee on the Judiciary, U.S. Congress, August 2, 1996.

81. Ibid.

82. Ibid.

83. Ibid.

84. Ibid.

85. Ibid.

86. Ibid.

87. Ibid.

88. "Project Megiddo: A Threat Analysis for the New Millennium," Federal Bureau of Investigation-DTAU, October 1999, p. 22.

89. Duffy, James E. and Brantley, Alan C. "Militias: Initiating Contact," Federal Bureau of Investigation, Critical Incident and Response Unit, 1997.

90. Duffy, James E. and Cooper, Gregory. "Militia Threat Typology," Federal Bureau of Investigation, Critical Incident and Response Unit, 1997.

91. "Terrorism in the United States—1996," Federal Bureau of Investigation, 1997, p. 7.

92. Ibid.

93. "Terrorism in the United States—1997," Federal Bureau of Investigation, 1998, p. 6.

94. Ibid.

95. "Background Information: Sheriff's Posse Comitatus," Federal Bureau of Investigation, 1987.

96. Ibid.

97. Ibid.

98. Ibid.

99. Ibid.

100. Ezekiel, Chapter 18 and Chapter 22, Bible, King James Version.

101. The phrase "paper terrorism" refers to the sovereign citizen tactic of using fraudulent legal documents and filings, as well as misuse of legitimate documents, against perceived enemies to intimidate, harass, and coerce them.

102. "Terrorism in the United States—1996," p. 7.

103. Ibid.

104. Lackey, Thomas. "Montana Freemen Leaders Receive Long Prison Sentences," *Seattle Times*, March 17, 1999.

105. "Terrorism in the United States—1995," Federal Bureau of Investigation, 1996, p. 6–7.

106. Various books, websites, and journal articles.

107. "Terrorism in the United States—1998," Federal Bureau of Investigation, 1999, p. 5.

108. "Terrorism in the United States—1999," Federal Bureau of Investigation, 2000, p. 7.

109. "Terrorism in the United States—1997," p. 4.

110. "The Twelve Tribes of Israel" is a term used to refer to the descendants of Abraham through his son Jacob (later named Israel) and his twelve sons as mentioned in the Bible (see Genesis 35:23–26).

111. "Christian Identity," Anti-Defamation League, 2005.

112. "Terrorism in the United States—1996," p. 4.

113. U.S. v. Eric Robert Rudolph, U.S. District Court—Northern District of Georgia, November 15, 2000.

114. Ibid.

115. Ibid.

116. "Terrorism in the United States—1998," p. 3.

117. Ibid.

118. "Terrorism in the United States—1996," p. 4–5, 8.

119. "Rage on the Right," Southern Poverty Law Center, Intelligence Report, Issue 137, Spring 2010.

120. Ibid.

121. Ibid.

122. "Active Hate Groups in the United States in 2009," Southern Poverty Law Center, Intelligence Report, Issue 137, Spring 2010.

123. Ibid.

124. Ibid.

125. Ibid.

126. Ibid.

127. Ibid.

128. "Terrorism in the United States—1995," p. 3.

129. "Active Patriot Groups in 1997," Southern Poverty Law Center, Intelligence Report, Issue 90, Spring 1998.

130. "Active Patriot Groups on the Internet in 1999," Southern Poverty Law Center, Intelligence Report, Issue 98, Spring 2000.

131. "Two Charged with Making Biological Weapons," *CNN*, February 19, 1998.

132. Ibid.

133. "Terrorism in the United States—1998," Federal Bureau of Investigation, Counterterrorism Division, 1999, p. 14.

134. "Chronology of Incidents Involving Ricin," James Martin Center for Nonproliferation Studies, February 3, 2004.

135. Ibid.

136. Ibid.

CHAPTER 4

1. "Veterans and Supporters Call for Apology from Homeland Security over Report on 'Rightwing Extremists,'" Oklahoma State Senate, April 22, 2009.

2. Ibid.

3. Rehbein, David K. "Letter to Secretary Janet Napolitano," American Legion, April 13, 2009.

4. Weigel, David. "Napolitano's Meeting with Veterans," *Washington Independent*, April 24, 2009.

5. Ibid.

6. Ibid.

7. http://en.wikipedia.org/wiki/Ku_Klux_Klan, accessed July 5, 2010.

8. Foner, Eric, and Garraty, John A. *The Reader's Companion to American History*, Houghton Mifflin, 1991.

9. http://en.wikipedia.org/wiki/Ku_Klux_Klan, accessed July 5, 2010.

10. US vs. Eric Robert Rudolph, Plea Agreement, U.S. District Court-Northern District of Alabama, April 4, 2005.

11. "Fourth Bombing Suspect Arrested," *Eugene Register*, March 14, 1997.

12. "Spokane Area Suspect Also a Nuclear Worker in the Northwest," *Associated Press*, October 29, 1996.

13. The DOD Dictionary and the Joint Acronyms and Abbreviations master data base are managed by the Joint Doctrine Division, J-7, Joint Staff. All approved joint definitions are contained in Joint Publication 1-02, *DOD Dictionary of Military and Associated Terms*, as amended through April 2010.

14. AR 525-13, "Anti-Terrorism," January 4, 2002.

15. Left-wing extremist: A movement of groups or individuals that embraces anticapitalist, Communist, or Socialist doctrines and seeks to bring about change through violent revolution rather than through established political processes. The term also refers to left-wing, single-issue extremist movements that are dedicated to causes such as environmentalism, opposition to war, and the rights of animals.

16. AR 381-10, "U.S. Army Intelligence Activities," May 3, 2007.

17. Executive Order 12333, "United States Intelligence Activities," President of the United States, December 4, 1981.

18. Ibid.

19. "California Marine Base KKK," *NBC Evening News*, December 3, 1976.

20. "Question and Answer on Fayetteville Murder and Hate and the Military," Anti-Defamation League, December 12, 1995.

21. Wilayto, Phil. "Fighting the Klan in the Military," *Southern Changes*, Vol. 2, Number 4, 1980, p. 8–11.

22. Landy, Jonathan S. "Army Brass Rattled by Ties of Soldiers to White Supremacists," *Christian Science Monitor*, December 15, 1995.

23. "KKK Ties?" *Orlando Sentinel*, February 16, 1990.

24. "Going Under: An Infiltrator of Hate Groups Remembers," Southern Poverty Law Center, Intelligence Report, Summer 2009, Issue Number 134.

25. "Report: Militias May Seek Elite Soldiers," *New York Times*, March 22, 1996.

26. Department of Defense Instruction, Number 1325.06, U.S. Department of Defense, November 27, 2009.

27. "DoD Tightens Rules on Extremist Groups," *Air Force Print News Today*, June 14, 2010.

28. "Army Honors Dead, Searches for Motive in Fort Hood Shootings," CNN, November 7, 2009.

29. Holthouse, David. "A Few Bad Men," Southern Poverty Law Center, July 7, 2006.

30. "Operation Vampire Killer 2000," Jack McLamb, 1992.

31. http://www.jackmclamb.org, viewed 10 June 2010.

32. Carter, Mike. "State Guard Reorganizes As 'Wackos' Infiltrate," *Salt Lake Tribune*, November 23, 1987.

33. Ibid.

34. Kelderman, Eric. "State Defense Forces Grow, Project New Image," *Stateline*, December 31, 2003.

35. McVeigh, Timothy. "Letter to Fox News," April 26, 2001.

36. Ibid.

37. Kovaleski, Serge F. "Soldiers in White Supremacist Uniforms; 2 Murder Suspects from Ft. Bragg Were Part of Fringe Culture," *Washington Post*, December 11, 1995.

38. Ibid.

39. "Surprise Witness at Burmeister Trial," *WRAL*, February 13, 1997.

40. "Fourth Bombing Suspect Arrested," *Eugene Register-Guard*, March 14, 1997.

41. "Bomb Suspect Was Nuclear Plant Worker," *Seattle Post-Intelligencer*, October 29, 1996.

42. "Three with White Supremacist Ties Charged with Robberies, Bombings," *Associated Press*, October 10, 1996.

43. "Trial Begins in Spokane Bank Robbery Spree," *The Oregonian*, March 3, 1997.

44. Ibid.

45. "Pre-Incident Indicators of Terrorist Incidents: The Identification of Behavioral, Geographic and Temporal Patterns of Preparatory Conduct," University of Arkansas, May 2006.

46. US vs. Brian Edward Ratigan, United States District Court, Case No. 2:97CROOO66-001, 1996.

47. "Spokane Valley Bomber Receives 2 Consecutive Life Terms," *The Oregonian*, October 31, 1997.

48. "Bomber Sounds Warning before 55-Year Sentence," *Spokesman Review*, December 3, 1997.

49. Ibid.

50. Ensign, Tod. "The Militia Military Connection," *Covert Action Quarterly*, Fall 1996.

51. Ibid.

52. "Small Arms Parts: Poor Controls Invite Widespread Theft," General Accounting Office, August 28, 1999.

53. "Internet Sales: Undercover Purchases on eBay and Craigslist Reveal a Market for Sensitive and Stolen U.S. Military Items," General Accounting Office, April 10, 2008.

54. "Inventory Management: Vulnerability of Sensitive Defense Material to Theft," General Accounting Office, September 1997.

55. Barber, Brian. "Federal Agents Raid Gun Shop, Find Weapons," *Tulsa World*, August 5, 1997.

56. Ibid.

57. "Neo-Militia News Archive (October-November 1996)," Anti-Defamation League, 1996.

58. U.S. Federal Code, Title 18, Section 1385.

59. Ibid.

60. Young, Steven E., *Posse Comitatus Act of 1878: A Documentary History*, 2003. CRS 6, p. 366.

61. "Guard Receives Heroes' Welcome," *Los Angeles Times*, May 14, 1992.

62. "The Troops: Elite U.S. Forces Sent in to Perform a Rare Role," *New York Times*, May 2, 1992.

63. U.S. Federal Code, Title 10, Sections 371–380.

64. Ibid.

65. "History of Joint Task Force North," NORTHCOM Website, viewed 10 June 2010.

66. Thevenot, Chad. "The Militarization of the Anti-Drug Effort," National Drug Strategy Network, July 1997.

67. Ibid.

68. Ibid.

69. Bauer, Gary, et al., "Viper Militia," ATF, Criminal Affidavit, July 1996.

70. Ibid.

71. Ibid.

72. Ibid.

73. Ibid.

74. Ibid.

75. Ibid.

76. "Anti-Terrorism and Effective Death Penalty Act of 1996," Public Law 104-132, April 24, 1996.

77. Bauer et al., "Viper Militia."

78. Ibid.

79. Ibid.

80. Ibid.

81. "Authorities Seize Guns, Explosives from Militia," *Austin American-Statesman*, July 3, 1996.

82. U.S. vs. Bradford Metcalf, U.S. District Court-Western District of Michigan, Southern Division, March 17, 1998.

83. Ibid.

84. Ibid.

85. Ibid.

86. Ibid.

87. Ibid.

88. Ibid.

89. Ibid.

90. Ibid.

91. Ibid.

92. Ibid.

93. "FBI: Militia Group Planned to Attack Military Bases," *Associated Press*, July 23, 1997.

94. "Private War of Bradley Glover," Anti-Defamation League, September 4, 1997.

95. "Arrests Linked to Militia Plot on U.S. Bases," *Cleveland Plain Dealer*, July 23, 1997.

96. "Republic of Texas; Richard Lance McLaren," Memorandum to Pentagon, Federal Bureau of Investigation, September 8, 1997.

97. Ibid.

98. Ibid.

99. Ibid.

100. http://en.wikipedia.org/wiki/Black_helicopter, accessed July 3, 2010.

101. "Coastal Towns Terrorized by Military Exercises," *Associated Press*, February 15, 1999.

102. Ibid.

103. Ibid.

104. Ibid.

105. Ibid.

106. Ibid.

107. "Police State 2000: Delta Force Hits Kingsville," Alex Jones, *Info Wars*, 1999.

108. Ibid.

109. Ibid.

110. Ibid.

111. Some strong proponents of the Second Amendment use the term "Jack Booted Thugs" to describe federal law enforcement agents, specifically ATF and FBI. This is a derogatory term generally used by individuals with extreme anti–law enforcement views and utter contempt for federal authority.

112. "Police State 2000."

113. Ibid.

114. "Army Special Forces Storm Old Courthouse in Mock Hostage Training Exercise," *Associated Press*, February 18, 1999.

115. Ibid.

116. Ibid.

117. Ibid.

118. Ibid.

119. Ibid.

120. "Army's Delta Force Stages Fake Assault at BAMC's Old Site," *San Antonio Express-News*, February 19, 1999.

121. Ibid.

122. Ibid.

123. Ibid.

124. Ibid.

125. Ibid.

126. Ibid.

127. Ibid.

128. Army Regulation 525-13, Antiterrorism Force Protection: Security of Personnel, Information and Critical Resources, dated 10 September 1998.

129. Pratt, Ginger P. "The 902d Military Intelligence Group and Homeland Security, *Military Intelligence Professional Bulletin*, July-September 2002.

CHAPTER 5

1. "Investigation of Vernon Wayne Howell, Also Known as David Koresh," Report, U.S. Department of Treasury, September 30, 1993.

2. "Use of Force: ATF Policy, Training and Review Process," U.S. General Accounting Office, March 1996, p. 2.

3. "The Aftermath of Waco: Changes in Federal Law Enforcement," 104th U.S. Congress, Hearings before the Senate Judiciary Committee, November 1, 1995.

4. "Director Magaw Ends Tenure at ATF," ATF Press Release, October 28, 1999.2

5. Ibid.

6. Ibid.

7. "Investigation of Vernon Wayne Howell."

8. "Report to the Attorney General on the Events at Waco, Texas," U.S. Department of Justice, October 8, 1993.

9. "The Aftermath of Waco."

10. Ibid.

11. Ibid.

12. Ibid.

13. Ibid.

14. Ibid.

15. Ibid.

16. Ibid.

17. Ibid.

18. Ibid.

19. "Director Magaw Ends Tenure at ATF," ATF Press Release, October 28, 1999.

20. Ibid.

21. "Mark James, Vice Chancellor of Administrative Services," Metro Community College Website, Biography, viewed July 21, 2010.

22. "ATF Strategic Plan, Fiscal Years 2010–2016," U.S. Department of Justice, 2009.

23. "ATF Accountability Report—FY1999," U.S. Department of Treasury, May 2001, p. 35–37.

24. Ibid.

25. "Project Megiddo: A Threat Analysis for the New Millennium," FBI, Domestic Terrorism Analysis Unit, October 1999.

26. "An Analysis of the F.B.I.'s 'Project Megiddo,'" Anti-Demonization League, December 1999.

27. Ibid.

28. Ibid.

29. "Project Megiddo: A Threat Analysis."

30. Ibid.

31. Ibid.

32. Ibid.

33. Ibid.

34. Ibid.

35. "The Sacramento Division: A Brief History," Federal Bureau of Investigation, Sacramento Field Division website, viewed June 10, 2010.

36. "Twin Threats," *LP Gas Magazine*, April 1, 2001.

37. Ibid.

38. Ibid.

39. Ibid.

40. Ibid.

41. Ibid.

42. Ibid.

43. "The Sacramento Division: A Brief History."

44. "Twin Threats."

45. Ibid.

46. Ibid.

47. "Informant Told FBI of Alleged Y2K Plot," *Los Angeles Times*, December 20, 1999.

48. "Twin Threats."

49. "The Sacramento Division: A Brief History."

50. "Terrorism in the United States—1999," Federal Bureau of Investigation, p. 9.

51. "False Patriots," Southern Poverty Law Center, Intelligence Report, Summer 2001, Issue 102.

52. Abbott, Karen. "Golden Militia Figure Convicted of Selling Illegal Explosives," *Denver Rocky Mountain News*, January 11, 2001.

53. "Pennsylvania Man Pleads Guilty to Weapons Charges," *Associated Press*, August 18, 2004.

54. Ibid.

55. Ibid.

56. "Crawford Man Charged By ATF," *Erie Times News*, March 26, 2004.

57. "White Supremacy Ties by Local Man Indicated," *Wyoming Tribune-Eagle*, August 5, 2000.

58. "Phony 'National Militia' Netted Two Pipe-Bomb Suspects," *Denver Rocky Mountain News*, August 5, 2000.

59. "White Supremacy Ties by Local Man Indicated."

60. Ibid.

61. "Q&A on *The Turner Diaries*," Anti-Defamation League, May 16, 1996.

62. "Extremism in America: *The Turner Diaries*," Anti-Defamation League, 2005.

63. "Summary of Reported Injuries Due to the Oklahoma City Bombing," Oklahoma State Department of Health, December 1998.

64. McDonald, Andrew. *The Turner Diaries*, Barricade Books, 1996.

65. "Phony 'National Militia'."

66. Ibid.

67. Ibid.

68. Ibid.

69. Ibid.

70. Ibid.

71. "White Supremacy Ties by Local Man."

72. "Man Sentenced to 35 Months in Prison for Pipe Bombs," *Associated Press*, April 20, 2001.

73. "Alleged White Supremacist Arrested for Possible Bomb Plot," WRAL, July 19, 2002.

74. "Southern Gothic: NC Klan Case Expose Seedy Underworld," Southern Poverty Law Center, Intelligence Report, Issue Number 126, Summer 2007.

75. Ibid.

76. Ibid.

77. Ibid.

78. "Arrest in Bomb Plot Spotlights KKK," *Raleigh News and Observer*, July 22, 2002.

79. Ibid.

80. "Leader of Splinter Group Called 'Hothead' by National KKK Leader," *Associated Press*, July 24, 2002.

81. "Southern Gothic: NC Klan Case."

82. "Alleged White Supremacist Arrested."

83. Ibid.

84. "Southern Gothic: NC Klan Case."

85. Ibid.

86. Ibid.

87. Ibid.

88. Ibid.

89. Pitcavage, Mark. "Officer Safety and Extremists: An Overview for Law Enforcement Officers," Anti-Defamation League, 1999.

90. "The Strange Story of Leo Felton," *New York Times*, May 27, 2003.

91. Ibid.

92. "The Strange Story of Leo Felton."

93. Ibid.

94. U.S. v. Michael Edward Smith, United States Court of Appeals for the Sixth Circuit, U.S. Department of Justice, November 18, 2005.

95. Ibid.

96. Ibid.

97. "Militia Man's Home Had Guns, Grenades," *Pittsburgh Post-Gazette*, July 5, 2002.

98. Ibid.

99. U.S. v. Ronald W. Hertzog, United States Court of Appeals-3rd Circuit of Pennsylvania, March 29, 2005.

100. Ibid.

101. U.S. v. David Wayne Hull, U.S. Court of Appeals for the Third District, October 30, 2009.

102. "Klan Sect Leader Sentenced for Pipe Bomb," Associated Press, February 25, 2005.

103. U.S. v. David Wayne Hull."

104. Ibid.

105. Ibid.

106. "State Trooper Killed In Standoff In Newaygo County", Michigan State Police, Press Release, July 7, 2003.

107. Ibid.

108. Ibid.

109. "Fugitive Shot Dead by Police," WLAJ, July 14, 2003.

110. U.S. v. Norman David Somerville, United States District Court-Western District of Michigan, October 16, 2003.

111. Ibid.

112. Ibid.

113. Ibid.

114. Ibid.

115. "An Outsider's Murder Trial Shakes Southern Town," *New York Times*, February 15, 2007.

116. Ibid.

117. Ibid.

118. "Abbeville Standoff Suspect to Face Death Penalty," WYFF, August 3, 2004.

119. "Father, Son Charged with Murder in Abbeville Standoff Deaths," WYFF, December 9, 2003.

120. "Man Pleads Guilty to Federal Gun Charge, Said He Wanted to Go On 'Killing Spree,'" *Associated Press*, March 17, 2004.

121. "Man Pleads Guilty to Federal Gun Charge."

122. Ibid.

123. "Biography: Dr. Kathleen Kiernan," Kiernan Group Website, accessed July 21, 2010.

CHAPTER 6

1. "How Much Did the September 11th Terrorist Attacks Cost America?" Institute for the Analysis of Global Security, 2004.

2. Brief Documentary History of the Department of Homeland Security (2001–2008), U.S. Department of Homeland Security-History Office, Written by History Associates Incorporated, 2008.

3. Ibid.
4. Ibid.
5. Ibid.
6. Ibid.
7. Ibid.
8. Ibid.
9. Ibid.
10. Ibid.
11. Ibid.
12. Ibid.
13. Ibid.
14. Ibid.
15. Ibid.
16. Ibid.
17. Ibid.
18. Ibid.
19. Ibid.
20. Ibid.
21. Ibid.
22. "Coast Guard Headquarters Gets Full Speed Ahead," *Federal News Radio*, January 8, 2010.
23. Ibid.
24. "If This Land Could Talk," *Legal Times*, April 7, 2003.
25. "A Mansion's History of Insecurity," *Washington Post*, July 3, 2003.
26. Ibid.
27. Ibid.
28. "If This Land Could Talk."
29. "A Mansion's History of Insecurity."
30. Ibid.
31. Ibid.
32. Ibid.
33. Ibid.
34. Ibid.
35. Ibid.
36. "If This Land Could Talk."
37. Ibid.
38. Ibid.
39. Ibid.
40. Ibid.
41. Ibid.
42. Ibid.
43. "A Mansion's History of Insecurity."
44. Goode, James M. *Capital Losses: A Cultural History of Washington's Destroyed Buildings.* Smithsonian Institution Press. 1979.
45. Ibid.
46. Public Law 108-296, Homeland Security Act of 2002, 107th Congress, November 25, 2002.

47. Ibid.

48. "DHS Senior Leadership: The First Five Years (2003–2008)," U.S. Department of Homeland Security-History Office, Written by History Associates Incorporated, 2008.

49. Ibid.

50. Tom Ridge Biography, Information Warfare Site, viewed February 17, 2010.

51. Ibid.

52. Ibid.

53. Executive Order 13354, National Counterterrorism Center, August 27, 2004.

54. "About the National Counterterrorism Center," National Counterterrorism Center website, viewed February 17, 2010.

55. Ibid.

56. Ibid.

57. "DHS Senior Leadership: The First Five Years (2003–2008)," U.S. Department of Homeland Security-History Office, Written by History Associates Incorporated, 2008.

58. Biographic Sketch: Lieutenant General Patrick M. Hughes, *Strategic Roost*, viewed January 3, 2011.

59. Ibid.

60. Ibid.

61. "Homeland Security Office creates 'Intelligence Spam,' Insiders Claim," *Center for Investigative Research*, September 5, 2011.

62. O'Keefe, Ed. "Eye Opener: Too Much Oversight at DHS?" *Washington Post*, July 20, 2009.

63. "Democrats: HSD Omits Rightwing Threats," *Associated Press*, April 20, 2005.

64. Ibid.

65. Rood, Justin. "Animal Rights Groups and Ecology Militants Make DHS Terrorist List, Rightwing Vigilantes Omitted," *Congressional Quarterly*, March 25, 2005.

66. Ibid.

67. "Homeland Eyes Right and Left," *New York Times*, May 27, 2005.

68. Ibid.

69. Ibid.

70. Public Affairs Guidance and Designated Spokespeople, DHS Management Directive, January 24, 2003.

71. "Ten Years After the Oklahoma City Bombing, the Department of Homeland Security Must Do More to Fight Rightwing Domestic Terrorists," Bennie G. Thompson, House Committee on Homeland Security, April 19, 2005.

72. Ibid.

73. Ibid.

74. Ibid.

75. Ibid.

76. Ibid.

77. Ibid.

78. Ibid.

79. Ibid.

80. Ibid.

81. Ibid.

82. Ibid.

83. Ibid.

84. Ibid.

85. Ibid.

86. Ibid.

87. Ibid.

88. "Exclusive: DHS Warns Companies of Evil Terrorist Flyer Distribution," *TPM Muckraker*, April 14, 2006.

89. Ibid.

90. Ibid.

91. Ibid.

92. Ibid.

93. Ibid.

94. Ibid.

95. Ibid.

96. "DHS Memo: Prevent Attacks by Animal Rights and Eco-Terrorists," *Portland Indy Media*, April 15, 2006.

97. Ibid.

98. "Gangs at War against Animal Rights Advocates," Animal Liberation Front.com, viewed January 29, 2011.

CHAPTER 7

1. "Michael Chertoff: DHS Secretary from 2005–2009," U.S. Department of Homeland Security, January 20, 2009.

2. Ibid.

3. Brief Documentary History of the Department of Homeland Security (2001–2008), U.S. Department of Homeland Security-History Office, Written by History Associates Incorporated, 2008.

4. Ibid.

5. Ibid.

6. Ibid.

7. Ibid.

8. "Man Crashes Plane into Texas I.R.S. Office," *New York Times*, February 18, 2010.

9. Ibid.

10. Ibid.

11. Ibid.

12. "Pilot Crashes into Texas Building in Apparent Anti-IRS Suicide," *Fox News*, February 18, 2010.

13. "Napolitano Says Suicide Plane Crash Wasn't Related to Domestic Terrorism," *Washington Post*, March 10, 2010.

14. Ibid.

15. Ibid.

16. House Resolution 1127, 111th Congress, U.S. House of Representatives, March 2, 2010.

17. Ibid.

18. Ibid.

19. Ibid.

20. "GOP Rep. Steve King Justifies Suicide Attack on IRS Building," YouTube, February 19, 2010.

21. Ibid.

22. Ibid.

23. Ibid.

24. "DHS Use of Intel Contractors Discussed at Hearing," *Homeland Security Today*, June 26, 2009.

25. "Biography: Jack Tomarchio," *CM Equity*, viewed January 30, 2011.

26. Ibid.

27. Search Warrant: Marvin Hall, U.S. District Court-Western District of Pennsylvania, June 6, 2008.

28. Search Warrant: Morgan Jones, U.S. District Court-Western District of Pennsylvania, June 6, 2008.

29. Search Warrant: Marvin Hall."

30. Search Warrant: Morgan Jones."

31. "Potential Terrorist Activity in the U.S.," C-SPAN, *Washington Journal*, May 2, 2007.

32. Ibid.

33. Ibid.

34. Ibid.

35. Ibid.

36. Ibid.

37. Ibid.

38. Ibid.

39. Ibid.

40. Ibid.

41. Ibid.

42. Ibid.

43. Ibid.

44. Ibid.

45. Ibid.

46. Ibid.

47. Ibid.

48. Ibid.

49. Implementing Recommendations of the 9/11 Commission Act of 2007, United States House of Representatives, 110th Congress, Conference Report 110-259, July 5, 2007, p. 282.

50. Implementing Recommendations of the 9/11 Commission Act of 2007, United States House of Representatives, 110th Congress, Conference Report 110-259, July 5, 2007.

51. Ibid., p. 282.

52. Ibid.

53. Ibid., p. 283.

54. Ibid.

55. Ibid.

56. Ibid.

57. Ibid.

58. Ibid.

59. Ibid.

60. Ibid.

61. Ibid.

62. Ibid.

63. Ibid.

64. Ibid.

65. Ibid.

66. "HETA Overview," I&A, PowerPoint presentation, 2007.

67. Ibid.

68. "Office of Intelligence and Analysis: Vision and Goals," Testimony of Undersecretary of I&A Caryn Wagner, U.S. House of Representatives, House Committee on Homeland Security, May 12, 2010.

69. Letter from Acting General Counsel at DHS to the General Counsel of the Intelligence Oversight Board, April 2009.

70. Intelligence Oversight Inquiry Into the Production and Dissemination of Office of Intelligence and Analysis Intelligence Note, Memorandum from Undersecretary for Intelligence and Analysis to DHS Acting General Counsel, March 28. 2008.

71. Letter from Acting General Counsel at DHS to the General Counsel of the Intelligence Oversight Board, November 24, 2008.

72. Implementing Recommendations of the 9/11 Commission Act of 2007, United States House of Representatives, 110th Congress, Conference Report 110-259, July 5, 2007, p. 283.

73. "HETA Overview," I&A PowerPoint Presentation, 2007.

74. Ibid.

75. The Interagency Intelligence Committee on Terrorism (IICT)-led National Intelligence Priorities Framework (NIPF) Counterterrorism (CT) Priorities and U.S. Department of State Foreign Terrorist Organizations (FTO) processes.

76. Ibid.

77. "Homeland Security Intelligence at a Crossroads: The Office of Intelligence and Analysis Vision for 2008," U.S. House of Representatives-110th U.S. Congress, Hearing Before the Subcommittee on Intelligence, Information Sharing and Terrorism Risk Assessment, February 26, 2008.

78. Ibid.

79. Ibid.

80. Ibid.

81. Ibid.

82. Ibid.

83. Ibid.

CHAPTER 8

1. "The Homeland Security State and Local Community of Interest," DHS Press Release, September 18, 2008.

2. Ibid.

3. Ibid.

4. Ibid.

5. Ibid.

6. Ibid.

7. "Tom Martinez: Former Hate Group Member," Keppler Associates, viewed February 12, 2011.

8. Ibid.

9. Ibid.

10. E-mail Response from Charlie Allen, September 1, 2008.

11. "2008 HS-SLIC National Conference Report," Office of Intelligence and Analysis, December 11, 2008.

12. Ibid.

13. Ibid.

14. Ibid.

15. Ibid.

16. Ibid.

17. Ibid.

18. Ibid.

19. Ibid.

20. Ibid.

21. Ibid.

22. Ibid.

23. Ibid.

24. Ibid.

25. Ibid.

26. Ibid.

27. Ibid.

28. Ibid.

29. Ibid.

30. Consolidated Customer Feedback Survey Results-Domestic Terrorism Newsletter, I&A Production Management Division, August 10, 2005.

31. Ibid.

32. Ibid.

33. Ibid.

34. Ibid.

35. Ibid.

36. "Friday FOIA Fun: Homegrown Extremist Edition," Entropic Memes, *Slugsite* blog, April 18, 2008.

37. Ibid.

38. Ibid.

39. Ibid.

40. Ibid.

41. Ibid.

42. Ibid.

43. Ibid.

44. "U.S. Department of Homeland Security Extremism Lexicon," Lou Dobbs Commentary, CNN, May 5, 2009.

45. Ibid.

46. Ibid.

47. Ibid.

48. Ibid.

49. Ibid.

50. Ibid.

51. Ibid.

52. Ibid.

53. "U.S. Department of Homeland Security Extremism Lexicon," Lou Dobbs Commentary, CNN, May 5, 2009.

54. Ibid.

55. Ibid.

56. Ibid.

57. Ibid.

58. Ibid.

59. Ibid.

60. Ibid.

61. Ibid.

62. Ibid.

63. Ibid.

64. Ibid.

65. Ibid.

66. Ibid.

67. Select excerpts from consolidated feedback from state fusion centers, various authors, 2008–2009.

68. Ibid.

69. Ibid.

70. Ibid.

71. Ibid.

72. Ibid.

73. "Appointment of Roger Mackin as Principal Deputy Undersecretary for the Office of Intelligence and Analysis," DHS Press Release, September 10, 2008.

74. "Departure of Dr. Mary Connell and Reassignment of the Acting DASI," Office-Wide Broadcast Announcement, January 20, 2009.

75. Ibid.

76. "Appointment of Roger Mackin."

77. Ibid.

78. Ibid.

79. Ibid.

80. "Janet Napolitano," *Encyclopedia Britannica*, viewed February 13, 2011.

81. Ibid.

82. Ibid.

83. "Napolitano Appointed Homeland Security Director," KTAR, December 1, 2008.

84. "Two Viper Militia Members Enter Felony Guilty Pleas," Reuters, December 20, 1996.

CHAPTER 9

1. Barack Obama Presidential Candidacy Speech."

2. Ibid.

3. Ibid.

4. www.nps.gov/liho/index.htm, viewed February 23, 2011.

5. Barack Obama Presidential Candidacy Speech.

6. Ibid.

7. Ibid.

8. Ibid.

9. Ibid.

10. "Obama Declares He's Running for President," *CNN*, February 10, 2007.

11. Barack Obama Presidential Candidacy Speech.

12. "United States Intelligence Activities," Presidential Executive Order 12333 (as amended), July 2008, p. 24.

13. http://splcenter.org, viewed February 20, 2011.

14. www.adl.org, viewed February 20, 2011.

15. Jordan Gruver v. Imperial Klans of America, Commonwealth of Kentucky-46th Judicial District, Meade Circuit Court, February 22, 2007.

16. Personal Restraint Petition of Kurtis Monschke, Washington Court of Appeals, Division II, September 30, 2008.

17. "ADL to Congress: There Is a 'Virus of Hate' on the Internet," Anti-Defamation League, Press Release, May 20, 1999.

18. "Anti-Bias Group Warns Congress of Military Extremists," *New York Times*, July 29, 2009.

19. "Militia Movement: Inside the Michigan Militia," WWMT-NewsChannel3, February 11, 2010.

20. "The Year in Hate," Southern Poverty Law Center, *Intelligence Report*, 2000–2010.

21. www.adl.org/racist_skinheads, viewed February 20, 2011.

22. Ibid.

23. "Statistical Problems Related to the Number of Extremists in the U.S.," E-mail Message-Militia Watchdog Mailing List, April 24, 2006.

24. "A Look at the Michigan Militia, Then and Now," *Ann Arbor.com*, March 25, 2010.

25. Michigan State Department of Corrections, Offender Tracking Information System, URL: http://www.state.mi.us/mdoc/asp/otis2profile.asp?mdocNumber=295350, accessed 20 April, 2009.

26. "A Look at the Michigan Militia."

27. Ibid.

28. Ibid.

29. www.youtube.com/user/libertytreeradio, viewed May 1, 2007.

30. "Officials See Rise in Militia Groups Across U.S.," *Associated Press*, August 12, 2009.

31. User Profile, www.youtube.com/user/libertytreeradio, viewed May 15, 2009.

32. http://www.tourlexington.us/Patriots%27%20Day.html, viewed February 24, 2011.

33. "April 19th: An Ominous Anniversary," *KTAR*, April 19, 2010.

34. www.youtube.com/user/libertytreeradio, viewed May 1, 2007.

35. Ibid.

36. Various forum posts and video comments by presumed militia members.

37. "DC Politics Fueling a New Wave of Militias," *Salt Lake Tribune*, September 5, 1994.

38. "Norman David Somerville Sentenced to Prison for Unlawfully Possessing Machine Guns," ATF Press Release, March 26, 2004.

39. "State Trooper Killed in Standoff in Neweygo County," Michigan State Police, Press Release, July 7, 2003.

40. "Scott Woodring-Personal Friend," American Patriots Friends Network, Message Board, July 9, 2003.

41. "Fugitive who shot at cops pleads guilty," *Cincinnati Inquirer*, June 1, 2003.

42. Ibid.

43. 3 I&A analysis of online video distribution.

44. Ibid.

45. "Active 'Patriot' Groups in the United States-2010," Southern Poverty Law Center, Intelligence Report, Issue Number 141, Spring 2011.

46. "Obama Clinches Democratic Nomination," *ABC News*, June 3, 2008.

47. U.S. v. Shawn R. Adolf, United States District Court-District of Colorado, Criminal Complaint, August 26, 2008.

48. Ibid.

49. Ibid.

50. Ibid.

51. Ibid.

52. Ibid.

53. Ibid.

54. Ibid.

55. Ibid.

56. Ibid.

57. Ibid.

58. Ibid.

59. "Alleged Plotter against Obama Was Member of Supreme White Alliance," Southern Poverty Law Center-*Hatewatch* blog, October 28, 2008.

60. U.S. vs. Daniel Cowart and Paul Schlesselman, United States District Court-Western District of Tennessee, October 24, 2008.

61. Ibid.

62. Ibid.

63. "David Lane, White Supremacist Terrorist and Ideologue, Dies in Prison," Anti-Defamation League, May 30, 2007.

64. U.S. vs. Daniel Cowart and Paul Schlesselman.

65. Ibid.

66. Ibid.

67. "Neo-Nazi Magazine to Feature Obama Assassination Cover," Southern Poverty Law Center-*Hatewatch* blog, September 12, 2008.

68. www.overthrow.com, viewed September 30, 2008.

69. Neo-Nazi Magazine.

70. http://strider333.blogster.com/kkk_threatens_obama, viewed February 15, 2008.

71. "Comment: Racist Attacks on Obama Growing More Heated," SPLC-*Hatewatch* blog, April 22, 2008.

72. "Comment: Neo-Nazi Magazine to Feature Obama Assassination Cover." SPLC-*Hatewatch* blog, January 31, 2009.

73. "KKK Imperial Wizard Warns of Death Threat against Barack Obama," Fox News-Chicago, May 23, 2007.

74. Historical analysis of Stormfront statistics from 2004 to 2009, www.stormfront.org, viewed April 7, 2009.

75. Ibid.

76. Ibid.

77. Ibid.

78. "Report: U.S. Is Ripe for Recruiting by Extremists," *Associated Press*, April 13, 2009.

79. Franklin, Raymond A., Hate Directory: 2007, July 15, 2007.

80. Franklin, Raymond A., Hate Directory: 2008, January 15, 2008.

81. Franklin, Raymond A., Hate Directory: 2009, February 15, 2009.

82. "Biography: Raymond A. Franklin," www.d1067424.mydomainwebhost.com/ray-franklin, viewed February 20, 2011.

83. Ibid.

84. Franklin, Raymond A., Hate Directory: 2009.

85. "Biography: Raymond A. Franklin."

86. Analysis of the Number of Ku Klux Klan Affiliated Websites from 2006 to 2010 derived from the Hate Directory listings for 2006, 2007, 2008, 2009, and 2010.

87. Ibid.

88. Ibid.

89. "The Year in Hate," Southern Poverty Law Center, *Intelligence Report*, Spring 2009, Issue 133, p. 48–65.

90. Ibid.

91. "Extremists Declare 'Open Season' on Immigrants: Hispanics Target of Incitement and Violence Overview," Anti-Defamation League, May 23, 2006.

92. "Immigration Fervor Fuels Racist Extremism," Southern Poverty Law Center, May 17, 2006.

93. "Ku Klux Klan Rebounds," Anti-Defamation League, 2007.

94. *American Extremists*, John George and Laird Wilcox, Prometheus Books, 1996.

95. Ibid.

96. Ibid.

97. "Immigration Debate: Rallying Rightwing Extremists," DHS Office of Intelligence and Analysis, Intelligence Assessment, September 15, 2008.

98. "Ku Klux Klan Rebounds."

99. Southern Law Enforcement Bulletin, Anti-Defamation League, August 2006.

100. Southwest Law Enforcement Bulletin, Anti-Defamation League, May 2006.

101. "KKK Comes to Tupelo; Residents Unite in Prayer," *Daily Journal*, October 21, 2007.

102. "Local Law Agencies Want Feds to Help Pay Nazi Protest Costs," *Action News 3*, September 16, 2007.

103. "Part II: On the Campaign Heil," *Columbia City Paper*, May 15, 2007.

104. *Midwest Law Enforcement Bulletin*, Anti-Defamation League, October 2006.

105. "KKK Growing in the Carolinas, with a New Target," WCNC, May 2, 2007.

106. "Ku Klux Klan Rebounds."

107. Ibid.

108. "Feds Watching Anti-Immigrant Extremists," *USA Today*, May 20, 2007.

109. Ibid.

110. "Protesters Target Simi Church," *Ventura County Star*, September 17, 2007.

111. E-mail to the National Socialist Movement Distribution List, August 21, 2007.

112. E-mail to the National Alliance, July 24, 2007.

113. "Poisoning the Web: Hatred Online," Anti-Defamation League, June 9, 2008.

114. http://www.stormfront.org, January 29, 2008.

115. www.natall.com, January 29, 2008.

116. www.youtube.com, January 31, 2008.

117. Fleischer, Tzvi, "Sounds of Hate," AIJAC Report, August 2000.

118. "Education and Extremism," Southern Poverty Law Center, Summer 2004.

119. "Better Dead Than Red," CD-Baby.com, January 29, 2008.

120. "Anti-Immigration Activism," YouTube.com, January 31, 2008.

121. "A Better Land," iTunes, January 30, 2008.

122. "Racist Games," *Resist.com*, January 30, 2008.

123. Hate Crime Statistics, Federal Bureau of Investigation, December 20, 2007.

124. "Hate Crime Report, 2005," Los Angeles Human Relations Commission, December 2006.

125. Hate Crime Statistics, 2010, Uniform Crime Report, FBI, November 14, 2011.

126. Ibid.

127. "Surge in Hate Crimes against Latinos: Two Thirds of Attacks Target Hispanics," UK Daily Mail, November 15, 2011.

128. "West Police Targeting White Supremacists in 'Hate Crime,'" *Waco Tribune*, August 16, 2007.

129. "Suing the KKK," *ABC News*, July 26, 2007.

130. "3 Men Accused of Picking Fights to Intimidate Minorities," *Deseret News*, April 17, 2007.

131. "Moving On, and Trying to Shed 'Victim' Label Teen Testifying in D.C. for Stricter Hate Crime Laws after Brutal Attack," *Houston Chronicle*, April 17, 2007.

132. "Extremists Advocate Murder of Immigrants, Politicians," Southern Poverty Law Center, March 30, 2007.

133. Tom Metzger Press Release, June 26, 2007.

134. "Former Klansman Admits Plot to Bomb Migrants," Southern Poverty Law Center, *Intelligence Report*, Fall 2005.

135. "Ex Klansman Gets Maximum Sentence," CNN, November 20, 2005.

136. "Four Charged with Gun Violations," *Casper Tribune*, April 18, 2007.

137. "Agent: Men Planned to Attack Mexicans," *al.com*, May 2, 2007.

138. "Defense Lawyer: Alabama Militia Raids 'Much Ado About Nothing,'" *Huntsville Times*, April 27, 2007.

139. National Socialist Movement Yahoo! Group posting on "NSMworld," November 2007.

140. Posting by "Fallschirmjager173" from "Carroll County, New Hampshire," to the "White Revolution" forum in September 2008.

141. Posting by "JoeMayhem" of the Southern California Militia to the White Revolution Forum in Autumn 2008.

142. www.worldknights.org/Klavalier_Division.html, viewed March 30, 2009.

143. Ibid.

144. Ibid.

145. http://unitedglobalistmovement.blogspot.com/, April 23, 2009.

146. "Marine Duo Accused of Threatening President Obama," *Marine Corps News*, March 24, 2009.

147. "Poplawski's Teen Trouble Deepens into Alienation, Anger," *Pittsburgh Tribune-Review*, April 8, 2009.

148. www.awrm.org, viewed February 23, 2011.

149. "Attention All Vets!," www.arwm.org, May 28, 2008.

150. Ibid.

151. Ibid.

152. Ibid.

153. Ibid.

154. Ibid.

155. "Growing Sovereign Citizen Movement In Central Florida," WFLV, February 24, 2011.

156. Ibid.

157. www.awrm.org/forums, July 15, 2009.

158. www.awrm.org/forums, July 30, 2008.

159. www.awrm.org, viewed January 30, 2009.

160. www.idahomilitia1.com/index.html, viewed February 20, 2009.

161. http://nkymilitia.weebly.com/index.html, viewed 29 January 2009.

162. "White Supremacist Recruitment of Military Personnel Since 9/11," Federal Bureau of Investigation, July 7, 2008.

163. Ibid.

164. Ibid.

165. "Neo-Nazi Flyers Distributed in S. Oregon," *Associated Press*, April 23, 2009.

166. "White Supremacist Recruitment," p. 10.

167. Ibid.

168. "Extremists in the Military," Anti-Terrorism Intelligence and Operations Cell, January 22, 2009.

169. Ibid.

170. Ibid.

171. Ibid.

172. Ibid.

173. "Evidence of Extremist Infiltration of the Military Grows," Southern Poverty Law Center, August 27, 2008.

174. Ibid.

175. Ibid.

CHAPTER 10

1. "The Modern Day Militia Movement," Missouri Information Analysis Center, February 20, 2009.

2. "DHS Secretary Napolitano, Missouri Governor Nixon Address Annual National Fusion Center Conference," DHS Press Release, March 11, 2009.

3. Ibid.

4. Ibid.

5. Ibid.

6. Ibid.

7. Ibid.

8. Ibid.

9. Ibid.

10. Ibid.

11. Ibid.

12. Ibid.

13. Ibid.

14. Ibid.

15. Ibid.

16. "Homeland Security Chief Checks Out Jefferson City Fusion Center," *Associated Press*, March 12, 2009.

17. Ibid.

18. Ibid.

19. Ibid.

20. Ibid.

21. Ibid.

22. "2009 National Fusion Center," NFCCG, Conference Agenda, March 10–12, 2009.

23. "Copfest 2009! National Fusion Center Conference Mobs Downtown," Nadia Pflaum, March 11, 2009.

24. Ibid.

25. "Intelligence Expert and Former FBI Agent Joins ACLU as National Security Counsel," American Civil Liberties Union, Press Release, October 5, 2006.

26. German, Michael. *Thinking like a Terrorist: Insights from a Former FBI Agent*. Potomac Books, January 2007.

27. Ibid.

28. "Report Finds Cover-Up in an FBI Terror Case," *New York Times*, December 4, 2005.

29. Ibid.

30. Ibid.

31. "FBI Whistleblower: White Supremacists Are Major Domestic Terrorist Threat," National Public Radio, June 13, 2005.

32. "Copfest 2009."

33. Ibid.

34. Ibid.

35. Ibid.

36. Conversation with ATF agents, Kansas City Field Division, March 13, 2009.

37. "Stocking Up Priorities? Uppers, Mags, Ammo, Reloading?" AWRM Forum, October 14, 2008.

38. "Gun Sales Rise on Fears of Obama Victory," *Hal Turner Show*, October 29, 2008.

39. "All Private Guns Will Be Confiscated by September 2009, US Tells Russia," AWRM Forum, March 20, 2009.

40. "Obama's Gun Ban List Is Out," *Info Wars*, March 13, 2009.

41. "Can You Survive Economic Crisis?" *World Net Daily*, March 8, 2009.

42. "Stocking Up Priorities?"

43. Ibid.

44. Ibid.

45. Ibid.

46. Ibid.

47. "Obama's Gun Ban List Is Out."

48. Ibid.

49. Ibid.

50. Ibid.

51. "This Will Anger Many," Peter Mancus, Various Yahoo! News Groups, January 31, 2009.

52. I&A EXSEC Tasking, Tracking Number SBS-005-09, "Follow-Up to Leftwing Extremists/Cyber Attacks Product," February 10, 2009.

53. I&A EXSEC Tasking, Tracking Number SBS-047-09, "Domestic Terrorism Plan," March 20, 2009.

54. Ibid.

55. Ibid.

56. Ibid.

57. Letter Concerning the MIAC Militia Report, Col. James F. Keathley-Superintendent of MSHP, Department of Public Safety, March 25, 2009.

58. "The Modern Militia Movement," Missouri Information Analysis Center Strategic Report, February 20, 2009.

59. Letter Concerning the MIAC Militia Report.

60. "MIAC Director Reassigned Over Report," *News Leader*, June 11, 2009.

61. "Highway Patrol Chief Retracts Militia Report; Will Change Review Process for MIAC Reports," *Kansas City Star*, March 26, 2009.

62. Ibid.

63. Ibid.

64. Ibid.

65. Ibid.

66. Ibid.

67. Ibid.

68. Ibid.

69. Ibid.

70. Letter Concerning the MIAC Militia Report.

71. Ibid.

72. Ibid.

73. Ibid.

74. Ibid.

75. Ibid.

76. Ibid.

77. "MIAC Director Reassigned Over Report," *News Leader*, June 11, 2009.

78. Ibid.

79. Ibid.

80. Ibid.

81. Ibid.

82. Letter Concerning the MIAC Militia Report.

83. Ibid.

84. Ibid.

85. Ibid.

86. Ibid.

87. Ibid.

88. Ibid.

89. "The Modern Militia Movement."

90. "LP Missouri Condemns Missouri Highway Patrol Training Document As Political Profiling," Mike Ferguson-Missouri Liberty Party Spokesperson, Press Release, March 15, 2009.

91. Ibid.

92. "The Modern Militia Movement."

93. Ibid.

94. Ibid.

95. Ibid.

96. "Terrorism in the United States—1996," Federal Bureau of Investigation, 1997.

97. "Ex-Fugitive Says Brother Bombed Spokane City Hall," *The Columbian*, March 16, 1998.

98. I&A EXSEC Tasking, Tracking Number SBS-047-09, "Domestic Terrorism Plan," March 20, 2009.

99. "{Request Clearance}Task # 0903-20-1552: S1 TASKER (SBS 047-09)—Domestic Terrorism Plan," I&A Executive Secretary's Office e-mail, March 25, 2009, at 2:38 p.m.

100. "{Request Clearance}Task # 0903-20-1552: S1 TASKER (SBS 047-09)—Domestic Terrorism Plan," I&A Executive Secretary's Office e-mail, March 25, 2009, at 6:10 p.m.

101. "{Request Clearance}Task # 0903-20-1552: S1 TASKER (SBS 047-09)—Domestic Terrorism Plan," I&A Executive Secretary's Office e-mail, March 25, 2009, at 6:42 p.m.

102. Ibid.

103. "{Request Clearance}Task # 0903-20-1552: S1 TASKER (SBS 047-09)—Domestic Terrorism Plan," I&A Executive Secretary's Office e-mail, March 26, 2009, at 9:43 a.m.

104. Ibid.

105. Ibid.

106. "{Request Clearance}Task # 0903-20-1552: S1 TASKER (SBS 047-09)—Domestic Terrorism Plan," I&A Executive Secretary's Office e-mail, March 26, 2009, at 6:45 p.m.

107. Ibid.

108. Ibid.

109. Ibid.

110. Ibid.

111. Ibid.

112. "Review of Product for Resubmission," I&A OGC E-mail, March 30, 2009, at 6:09 p.m.

113. Ibid.

114. Ibid.

115. Ibid.

116. Ibid.

117. Ibid.

118. Ibid.

119. Ibid.

120. "Revised Rightwing Extremism Definition," Office of Civil Rights and Civil Liberties E-mail, April 7, 2009, at 2:44 p.m.

121. Ibid.

122. Ibid.

123. Ibid.

124. Ibid.

125. "Revised Rightwing Extremism Definition," Office of Civil Rights and Civil Liberties E-mail , April 7, 2009, at 6:27 p.m.

126. Ibid.

127. Ibid.

128. Ibid.

129. "RE: Homeland Security Assessment: "Rightwing Extremism: Current Economic and Political Climate Fueling Resurgence in Radicalization and Recruitment," dated 7 April 2009," E-mail Message, April 7, 2009, at 6:18 p.m.

130. "RE: Homeland Security Assessment: "Rightwing Extremism: Current Economic and Political Climate Fueling Resurgence in Radicalization and Recruitment," dated 7 April 2009," E-mail Message, April 7, 2009, at 6:25 p.m.

131. "Feedback: Rightwing Extremism Report IA-0257-09 Feedback," E-mail Message, April 8, 2009, at 8:10 a.m.

132. Ibid.

133. "Feedback: Rightwing Extremism Report IA-0257-09 Feedback," E-mail Message, April 8, 2009, 05:22 a.m.

134. Ibid.

135. Ibid.

136. Ibid.

137. Ibid.

138. Ibid.

139. Ibid.

140. Ibid.

141. Ibid.

142. Ibid.

143. Ibid.

144. Ibid.

145. Ibid.

146. "RE: Feedback: Rightwing Extremism Report IA-0257-09 Feedback," E-mail Message, April 8, 2009, at 3:12 p.m.

147. Ibid.

148. Ibid.

149. Ibid.

150. Ibid.

151. Ibid.

152. Ibid.

153. Ibid.

154. Letter Addressed to David S.C. Chu-Under Secretary of Defense, Southern Poverty Law Center, October 12, 2006.

155. "Extremists Continue to Infiltrate the Military," Letter Addressed to Robert Gates-Secretary of Defense, Southern Poverty Law Center, November 26, 2008.

156. "RE: Feedback: Rightwing Extremism Report IA-0257-09," 3:12 p.m.

157. Ibid.

158. Ibid.

159. Ibid.

160. Ibid.

161. Ibid.

CHAPTER 11

1. "DHS Report Worries about Rise of Right-Wing Extremism," *Security Management,* April 13, 2009.

2. Ibid.

3. Ibid.

4. Ibid.

5. "Homeland Security Assessment: "Rightwing Extremism: Current Economic and Political Climate Fueling Resurgence in Radicalization and Recruitment," dated 7 April 2009," DHS e-mail thread, April 13, 2009.

6. "DHS Rightwing Extremist Report," *700 Club,* April 15, 2009.

7. "Federal Agency Warns of Radicals on the Right," *Washington Times,* April 14, 2009.

8. Ibid.

9. Ibid.

10. Ibid.

11. Ibid.

12. "Six Things You Should Know about the DHS Report on Rightwing Extremism," Fox News-Judge Andrew Napolitano, April 15, 2009.

13. Ibid.

14. "Changes to Office of Intelligence and Analysis Production Process," Memorandum for record, DHS Office of Intelligence and Analysis, January 30, 2009.

15. "New I&A Production Process," E-mail Broadcast from I&A Production Management Directorate, January 30, 2009, at 1:55 p.m.

16. Ibid.

17. "Changes to Office of Intelligence and Analysis."

18. Ibid.

19. Ibid.

20. Ibid.

21. Ibid.

22. "Statement by U.S. Department of Homeland Security Secretary Janet Napolitano on the Threat of Right-Wing Extremism," DHS Press Release, April 15, 2009.

23. Ibid.

24. Ibid.

25. Ibid.

26. Ibid.

27. Ibid.

28. "DHS Report: Rising Tide of Hatred," CBS-*The Early Show*, April 15, 2009.

29. "Homeland Security Warns of Possible Right-Wing Extremism," Fox News, April 15, 2009.

30. Ibid.

31. "DHS Warning: Recession Radicals," CNN, *Anderson Cooper Show*, April 14, 2009.

32. Ibid.

33. "DHS Warning Over Rightwing Extremists Outrages Conservatives," CNN, *Situation Room*, April 15, 2009.

34. "DHS: Rightwing Extremists May Use Economy to Incite Violence," Fox News, Shepherd Smith, April 15, 2009.

35. "Not In Their Right Minds," MSBNC, *Keith Olbermann's Countdown*, April 15, 2009.

36. Ibid.

37. Ibid.

38. "Rightwing Extremists?" CNN, *Lou Dobbs*, April 15, 2009.

39. "DHS Warning Over Rightwing Extremists Outrages Conservatives," CNN-*Situation Room*, April 15, 2009.

40. Ibid.

41. "Janet Napolitano Defends Rightwing Extremism Report," CNN, John King, April 19, 2009.

42. Ibid.

43. Ibid.

44. Ibid.

45. Ibid.

46. Ibid.

47. Ibid.

48. Ibid.

49. Ibid.

50. Ibid.

51. Ibid.

52. "Federal Agency Warns of Radicals."

53. Letter Addressed to Secretary Janet Napolitano, National Commander-American Legion, April 13, 2009.

54. Ibid.

55. Ibid.

56. Ibid.

57. Ibid.

58. Ibid.

59. Ibid.

60. Ibid.

61. "DHS Report Was a Threat Assessment, Not Accusation," Veterans of Foreign Wars, April 15, 2009.

62. Ibid.

63. Ibid.

64. Ibid.

65. "Veterans and Supporters Call for Apology from Homeland Security over Report on 'Rightwing Extremists,'" Oklahoma State Senate, Press Release April 22, 2009.

66. Ibid.

67. Ibid.

68. Ibid.

69. Ibid.

70. Ibid.

71. Ibid.

72. Ibid.

73. "Senator Proposes Resolution Opposing Obama Administration's on 'Rightwing' Extremists as Possible National Security Threats," Oklahoma State Senate, Press Release, April 16, 2009.

74. Ibid.

75. "Napolitano's Meeting with Veterans," *Washington Independent*, April 24, 2009.

76. Ibid.

77. Ibid.

78. Ibid.

79. Ibid.

80. Ibid.

81. "Blue Guard Riders," This Blue Marble Forum, August 13, 2009.

82. "Hannibal Militia Adopts New Name," *The Post-Standard*, January 11, 2011.

83. "Oath Keepers Tyler Texas Group," *Patriot Action Network*, January 4, 2010.

84. "Action 9 Exposes Growing Sovereign Citizen Movement in Florida," *Action 9 News*, February 24, 2011.

85. "New Jersey Patriots," *Patriot Action Network*, October 12, 2010.

86. "Attention All Vets!" A Well Regulated Militia-Veterans Forum, May 28, 2008.

87. "Rand Beers, Undersecretary National Protection and Programs Directorate," U.S. Department of Homeland Security, Press Release, viewed March 4, 2010.

88. Ibid.

89. Letter from Bennie Thompson to Secretary Janet Napolitano, April 14, 2009.

90. Ibid.

91. "10 Years After the Oklahoma City Bombing, the Department of Homeland Security Must Do More to Fight Rightwing Domestic Terrorists," U.S. House of Representatives, Committee on Homeland Security, April 19, 2005.

92. Letter from Bennie Thompson to Secretary Janet Napolitano, April 14, 2009.

93. Ibid.

94. Ibid.

95. Ibid.

96. Ibid.

97. Ibid.

98. Ibid.

99. "King, Republican Leaders Want Answers on DHS Rightwing Extremism Report," House Committee on Homeland Security, Press Release, May 6, 2009.

100. Ibid.

101. Ibid.

102. Ibid.

103. Ibid.

104. Ibid.

105. Ibid.

106. Ibid.

107. Ibid.

108. Ibid.

109. Ibid.

110. Letter to Homeland Security Secretary Janet Napolitano, United States Senate Homeland Security and Government Affairs Committee, Signed Tom Coburn and John Ensign, May 13, 2009.

111. Ibid.

112. Ibid.

113. Ibid.

114. Ibid.

115. "Statement of Chairman Bennie G. Thompson: Markup of House Resolution 404," U.S. House of Representatives, Homeland Security Committee, May 19, 2009.

116. Ibid.

117. Ibid.

118. Ibid.

119. Ibid.

120. Ibid.

121. Ibid.

122. Ibid.

123. Ibid.

124. Ibid.

125. Ibid.

126. Ibid.

127. Ibid.

128. Ibid.

129. Ibid.

130. Ibid.

131. Ibid.

132. Ibid.

133. Ibid.

134. Ibid.

135. Ibid.

136. "Ann Arbor-Based Law Center Sues Homeland Security Over 'Rightwing Extremism' Issue," *Ann Arbor News*, April 19, 2009.

137. Ibid.

138. Ibid.

139. Ibid.

140. Ibid.

141. "DHS Picks New Chief for Intelligence Office," *Washington Times*, April 24, 2009.

142. Ibid.

143. Statement by Fox Reporter Brian Kilmeade, *Fox and Friends*, Fox News, April 24, 2009.

144. "Federal Employee Salaries: 2009 and 2010," *Asbury Park Press*, Data Universe, viewed March 30, 2011.

145. "DHS Picks New Chief for Intelligence Office," *Washington Times*, April 24, 2009.

146. Ibid.

147. Ibid.

148. Ibid.

149. Ibid.

150. "Testimony of Acting Undersecretary Bart R. Johnson, Office of Intelligence and Analysis: FY2010 Budget Request," House Committee on Homeland Security, Subcommittee on Intelligence, June 24, 2009.

151. "Nominee for Homeland Security Intelligence Chief Withdraws," *Los Angeles Times*, June 6, 2009.

152. Ibid.

CHAPTER 12

1. "Bruce and Joshua Turnidge Get Death Penalty in Woodburn Bank Bombing," *The Oregonian*, December 22, 2010.

2. Ibid.

3. Ibid.

4. Ibid.

5. "Killing 'Non-White People' Was Motive in Brockton Shooting Spree, Police Say," *Boston Globe*, January 22, 2009.

6. Ibid.

7. Ibid.

8. "Affidavit Outlines Shootings That Left Three Pittsburgh Police Officers Dead," *Pittsburgh Post-Gazette*, April 6. 2009.

9. Poplawski Crime Scene Photos, Pittsburgh Police Department, April 4, 2009.

10. "Poplawski's Statement, Police Reports Detail Stanton Heights Shootout," *Pittsburgh Tribune-Review*, April 8, 2009.

11. "Suspect Admired Officers' Bravery, Jury Could Get Case Today," *Pittsburgh Tribune-Review*, June 25, 2011.

12. Police Criminal Complaint: Commonwealth of Pennsylvania versus Richard Andrew Poplawski, Pittsburgh Magistrate Court, April 4, 2009.

13. Ibid.

14. "Suspect Admired Officers' Bravery."

15. "Poplawski Browsed Web Just Before Shooting," *Pittsburgh Tribune-Review*, June 24, 2011.

16. Poplawski Crime Scene Photos.

17. "Poplawski Trial: Day 3," *Pittsburgh Tribune-Review*, June 22, 2011.

18. Poplawski Criminal Investigation Photos, Pennsylvania State Police, April 5, 2009.

19. "Poplawski Browsed Web."

20. "Poplawski Trial: Day 4," *Pittsburgh Tribune-Review*, June 30, 2011.

21. Ibid.

22. "Poplawski Trial: Day 3."

23. "Suspect Admired Officers' Bravery."

24. Ibid.

25. Ibid.

26. Ibid.

27. Ibid.

28. Ibid.

29. Police Criminal Complaint.

30. Ibid.

31. "Poplawski Trial: Day 5," *Pittsburgh Tribune-Review*, June 24, 2011.

32. Police Criminal Complaint.

33. "Shootings of Police Admitted In Phone Calls to Friend, 911," *Pittsburgh Tribune-Review*, June 22, 2011.

34. Police Criminal Complaint.

35. Ibid.

36. "Suspect Admired Officers' Bravery."

37. Ibid.

38. "Poplawski Trial: Day 3."

39. "Suspect Admired Officers' Bravery."

40. "Poplawski Trial: Day 4."

41. "Suspect Admired Officers' Bravery."

42. "Poplawski Trial: Day 3."

43. "Suspect Admired Officers' Bravery."

44. "Poplawski Trial: Day 3."

45. "Affidavit Outlines Shootings That Left Three Pittsburgh Police Officers Dead," *Pittsburgh Post-Gazette*, April 6, 2009.

46. Ibid.

47. "Shootings of Police Admitted."

48. "Affidavit Outlines Shootings."

49. "Stories about Slain Officers Bring Convicted Killer to Tears," *Pittsburgh Tribune-Review*, June 28, 2011.

50. Police Criminal Complaint.
51. "Suspect Admired Officers' Bravery."
52. Police Criminal Complaint.
53. "Shootings of Police Admitted.
54. Ibid.
55. Police Criminal Complaint.
56. Ibid.
57. Ibid.
58. Ibid.
59. Police Criminal Complaint.
60. Ibid.
61. Ibid.
62. Ibid.
63. "Shootings of Police Admitted.
64. Ibid.
65. Police Criminal Complaint.
66. Ibid.
67. Ibid.
68. "Shootings of Police Admitted."
69. Ibid.
70. Ibid.
71. Police Criminal Complaint.
72. Ibid.
73. Ibid.
74. Ibid.
75. Ibid.
76. "Poplawski's Web Postings Warned of 'Enemies,'" *Pittsburgh Post-Gazette*, April 7, 2009.
77. Ibid.
78. "Suspect Admired Officers' Bravery."
79. Ibid.
80. "Poplawski Trial: Day 5."
81. "Poplawski Trial: Day 6," *Pittsburgh Tribune-Review*, June 25, 2011.
82. "Suspect Admired Officers' Bravery."
83. Ibid.
84. "Poplawski Trial: Day 5."
85. Police Criminal Complaint.
86. "Gunman Kills 3 Officers in Pittsburgh," *New York Times*, April 4, 2009.
87. Offense Report #004640, Okaloosa County Sheriff's Office, April 25, 2009.
88. Officer Involved Shooting: Joshua Cartwright—PE-27-0044, Investigative Summary, Pensacola Regional Operations Center, September 26, 2009.
89. "Officer Involved Shooting Death: Joshua Cartwright," Memo, Florida Department of Law Enforcement, October 8, 2009.
90. Officer Involved Shooting: Joshua Cartwright.
91. Ibid.
92. Ibid.
93. Ibid.
94. Ibid.
95. Ibid.

96. "Two Okaloosa Deputies Dead, Shooter Stopped and Killed in Walton," *Defuniak Herald*, May 5, 2009.

97. Officer Involved Shooting: Joshua Cartwright.

98. Ibid.

99. Ibid.

100. Offense Report #004640.

101. Ibid.

102. Oath Keepers Motto, http://www.oathkeepers.blogspot.com, viewed May 21, 2011.

103. Letter to Senators Tom Coburn and John Ensign from Janet Napolitano, Department of Homeland Security, May 21, 2009.

104. Ibid.

105. Ibid.

106. Ibid.

107. Ibid.

108. Ibid.

109. "Analysis of Complaints Submitted in Response to DHS I&A Assessment on Rightwing Extremism from April 7, 2009," I&A, Production Management Division, April 17, 2009.

110. Ibid.

111. Ibid.

112. Ibid.

113. Ibid.

114. Ibid.

115. Ibid.

116. Ibid.

117. Ibid.

118. Ibid.

119. Ibid.

120. Personal observations of I&A Production Management Spreadsheets and other forms of data collection concerning consumer feedback, 2005–2009.

121. "RE: Production Branch's Analysis of Complaints," I&A E-mail Message, dated April 20, 2009, 11:15 a.m.

122. Ibid.

123. Ibid.

124. Ibid.

125. Ibid.

126. "Statement of Major Cities Chiefs of Police Regarding House Resolution 404," Major Cities Chiefs of Police, May 18, 2009.

127. Ibid.

128. Ibid.

129. Ibid.

130. Ibid.

131. Ibid.

132. Ibid.

133. Ibid.

134. Ibid.

135. Ibid.

136. "Man Charged for Alleged Obama Death Threat," *CBS News*, June 5, 2009.

137. Ibid.

138. "Man Accused of Threatening Obama Arrested," *Associated Press*, June 6, 2009.

139. "Suspect in Shooting Death of Abortion Provider George Tiller May Be Charged Today," *Wichita Eagle*, June 1, 2009.

140. Letter from Michael Bray to Scott Roeder, June 1, 2009.

141. Ibid.

142. Ibid.

143. Ibid.

144. Ibid.

145. Ibid.

146. "The Suspect at a Glance," *Washington Post*, June 2, 2009.

147. Ibid.

148. Ibid.

149. Ibid.

150. Ibid.

151. "The Case of the Disappearing Nominee," *Newsweek*, June 4, 2009.

152. "Gunman Kills Soldier outside Recruiting Station," *New York Times*, June 1, 2009.

153. "Fatal Shooting at Holocaust Museum," Metropolitan Police Department, Press Release, June 10, 2009.

154. Ibid.

155. Ibid.

156. Ibid.

157. "Fellow Separatist Says Von Brunn's Tone More Violent Lately," *Pittsburgh Post-Gazette*, June 11, 2009.

158. "When James Von Brunn Attempted to Arrest the Fed Chairman," Salon, June 10, 2009.

159. Ibid.

160. Ibid.

161. "Border Vigilante Shawna Forde Sentenced to Death for Home Invasion," *ABC News*, February 22, 2011.

162. Ibid,

163. Ibid.

164. Ibid.

165. www.minutemenamericandefense.org, viewed June 2009.

166. www.sandiegominutemen.org, viewed May 2011.

167. www.minutemenamericandefense.org, viewed June 2009.

168. Ibid.

169. "Chambers Deputy Killed, Suspected Gunman Found Dead," *Houston Chronicle*, July 14, 2009.

170. Ibid.

171. Ibid.

172. Ibid.

173. "Cop Killer Had Over 100 Bombs, Nazi Drawings," MSNBC, July 15, 2009.

174. Ibid.

175. Ibid.

176. "DTx Database Meeting—Thursday, 13 AUG, 1:30 pm," E-mail from DTAD Director, August 14, 2009.

177. Ibid.

178. Ibid.
179. Ibid.
180. Ibid.
181. Ibid.
182. "DTx Database Meeting—Thursday, 13 AUG, 1:30 pm," E-mail from DTAD Director, August 14, 2009.
183. Ibid.
184. Ibid.
185. Ibid.
186. www.start.umd.edu/gtd/, viewed May 2011.
187. www.start.umd.edu/start/about/overview/, viewed May 2011.
188. "DTx Database Meeting.
189. Ibid.
190. Ibid.
191. "DHS Will Discuss Realignment of Intelligence Office," *Government Executive* Magazine, September 24, 2009.
192. Ibid.
193. Ibid.
194. Ibid.
195. Ibid.
196. Ibid.
197. Ibid.
198. Ibid.
199. Ibid.
200. Ibid.
201. Ibid.

CHAPTER 13

1. "Short Biography: Dawn Scalici," Infraguard National Members Alliance Meeting, February 23, 2011.
2. Ibid.
3. "IC Analytic Standards," Reference Card, Analytic Integrity and Standards, Office of the Director of National Intelligence, 2009.
4. "Nominations of Philip S. Goldberg, Assistant Secretary for Intelligence, INR, and Caryn A. Wagner, Undersecretary of Homeland Security, I&A," Select Committee on Intelligence, United States Senate, December 1, 2009.
5. Ibid.
6. Ibid.
7. Ibid.
8. Ibid.
9. Ibid.
10. Ibid.
11. Ibid.
12. Ibid.
13. Ibid.

14. Ibid.
15. Ibid.
16. Ibid.
17. Ibid.
18. Ibid.
19. Ibid.
20. Ibid.
21. Ibid.
22. Ibid.
23. Ibid.
24. Ibid.
25. Ibid.
26. Ibid.
27. Ibid.
28. Ibid.
29. Confirmation Hearing for Caryn A. Wagner, Undersecretary for Intelligence and Analysis at DHS, United States Senate, Homeland Security and Government Affairs Sub-Committee, December 3, 2009.
30. Ibid.
31. Ibid.
32. Ibid.
33. Ibid.
34. Ibid.
35. Ibid.
36. Ibid.
37. Ibid.
38. "DHS Fusion Centers: Tough Tightrope," *Homeland Security Today*, January 3, 2011.
39. Ibid.
40. Ibid.
41. Anonymous DHS Official to Ms. Catherine Herridge, *Fox News*, on May 5, 2009.
42. Secretary Janet Napolitano to Senator John Carter (R-Texas), U.S. House Committee on Appropriations, on May 12, 2009.
43. Secretary Janet Napolitano to Representatives Charlie Dent (R-Pennsylvania) and Christopher P. Carney (D-Pennsylvania), U.S. House of Representatives-Homeland Security Committee, on May 13, 2009.

CHAPTER 14

1. "Daryl Johnson's Performance Appraisal," Memorandum for Record, DTAD Director, November 2, 2009.
2. "Napolitano: The Issue Is 'Turn to Violence,'" Fox News, April 20, 2010.
3. "Napolitano Addresses Resiliency in Speech at 15th Anniversary of OKC Bombing," DHS Press Release, April 19, 2010.
4. Ibid.
5. Ibid.

6. Ibid.

7. Ibid.

8. Ibid.

9. Ibid.

10. Ibid.

11. Ibid.

12. Ibid.

13. Ibid.

14. "Napolitano Urges Vigilance on Antigovernment Extremism during Memorial Ceremony," *Security Management*, April 19, 2010.

15. Ibid.

16. Ibid.

17. Ibid.

18. Ibid.

19. Ibid.

20. "Warrant and Orders of Restoration," Guardians of the Free Republics, March 29, 2010.

21. "Napolitano Urges Vigilance.

22. Ibid.

23. Ibid.

24. Ibid.

25. "Napolitano: The Issue."

26. Ibid.

27. "Napolitano Urges Vigilance."

28. "Napolitano: The Issue."

29. Ibid.

30. Ibid.

31. Ibid.

32. Ibid.

33. "Janet Napolitano: DHS Report on Rightwing Extremism Is 'Ancient History,'" *TPM Muckraker*, September 1, 2010.

34. Ibid.

35. Ibid.

36. Ibid.

37. Ibid.

38. Ibid.

39. "Homeland Security Office Creates 'Intelligence Spam' Insiders Claim," *Center for Investigative Reporting*, Special Report: America's War Within, September 5, 2011.

40. "The Intelligence Spam Machine," *Newsweek*, September 4, 2011.

41. Ibid.

42. Ibid.

43. Ibid.

44. Ibid.

45. Ibid.

46. "Names of Injured Troopers Released after Deadly Shootout," KFVS, September 26, 2008.

47. "ISP Identifies Two Troopers Wounded in Shootout," WMTV, September 26, 2008.

48. Weekly Activity Report, DHS Office of Intelligence Analysis, October 3, 2008.

49. Weekly Activity Report, DHS Office of Intelligence Analysis, January 16, 2009.

50. Ibid.

51. Weekly Activity Report, DHS Office of Intelligence Analysis, December 14, 2008.

52. Weekly Activity Report, DHS Office of Intelligence Analysis, November 14, 2008.

53. Weekly Activity Report, DHS Office of Intelligence Analysis, October 3, 2008.

54. Weekly Activity Report, DHS Office of Intelligence Analysis, March 20, 2009.

55. Weekly Activity Report, DHS Office of Intelligence Analysis, March 27, 2009.

56. Weekly Activity Report, DHS Office of Intelligence Analysis, April 3, 2009.

57. "Arrest Made in Break-Ins," *Jefferson Post*, November 2009.

58. Ibid.

59. Ibid.

60. E-mail message from ATF agent addressed to me, December 9, 2009.

61. "Victor White Denies Shooting Officers," *OAOA*, April 10, 2011.

62. "Page Officer Kills Man in DV Incident," *Arizona Daily Sun*, June 21, 2011.

63. E-mail from law enforcement officer to me, May 28, 2011.

64. Ibid.

65. Ibid.

66. Ibid.

67. Ibid.

68. Ibid.

69. "Representative Gabrielle Giffords Shot in Tucson Rampage; Federal Judge Killed," *Washington Post*, January 9, 2011.

70. "Last of Nine Alleged Cop-Killing Plotters Arrested," *ABC News*, March 29, 2010.

71. "Details Emerge in Alleged Plot to Kill Alaska State Troopers, Judge," *Fairbanks Daily News Miner*, March 11, 2011.

72. Internal Memo from Mr. Richard L. Skinner (DHS Inspector General) to Mr. Homer Pointer (General Counsel, Intelligence Oversight Board), April 2009, p. 7.

73. Ibid.

74. Ibid.

75. Ibid.

76. Ibid.

77. Ibid.

78. "Marshfield Man Charged in Circuit Court with Attempt to Kill Abortion Doctor," *Wisconsin State Journal*, May 27, 2011.

79. Ibid.

80. Ibid.

81. Ibid.

82. Review of Freedom of Information Act Results Concerning I&A Privacy and Intelligence Oversight Violations During 2007–2009, January 2010.

83. Memorandum for Mr. Gus Coldebella (Acting General Counsel) from Mr. Charlie Allen (Undersecretary for Intelligence and Analysis), March 28, 2008.

84. Internal Memo from Mr. Richard L. Skinner (DHS Inspector General) to Mr. Homer Pointer (General Counsel, Intelligence Oversight Board), January 7, 2009.

85. Ibid.

86. Ibid.

87. "Sensenbrenner Request," E-mail from I&A Associate Director for Legislative Affairs, March 3, 2010.

88. Ibid.
89. E-mail from a law enforcement officer to me, June 9, 2011.
90. Ibid.
91. Ibid.
92. Ibid.
93. Ibid.
94. Ibid.
95. Ibid.
96. Ibid.
97. Ibid.
98. Telephone conversation with DHS employee, August 26, 2010.
99. Ibid.
100. Ibid.
101. Ibid.
102. Telephone conversation with DHS employee, August 26, 2010.
103. Islamophobia.org, viewed October 20, 2011.
104. Conversations with multiple DHS employees, June-July, 2010.
105. Ibid.
106. Ibid.
107. Ibid.
108. Ibid.
109. Ibid.
110. Ibid.
111. "Chronology of Extremist Attacks," DT Analytics, viewed October 20, 2011.
112. "91 Killed in Norway Island Massacre, Capital Blast," Fox News, July 23, 2011.
113. Ibid.
114. "Anders Breivik Is Not Christian, but Anti-Islam," *The Guardian*, July 24, 2011.
115. "Killings in Norway Spotlight Anti-Muslim Thought in U.S.," *New York Times*, July 24, 2011.
116. "Norway Attacks Focus Attention on U.S. Rightwing Extremists," *NBC Nightly News*, July 25, 2011.
117. Ibid.
118. Ibid.
119. "Inside the DHS," Southern Poverty Law Center, Intelligence Report, June 17, 2011.
120. "Homeland Security Office Creates 'Intelligence Spam,' Insiders Claim," *Center for Investigative Reporting*, September 5, 2011.
121. Ibid.
122. Ibid.
123. Ibid.
124. "DHS Disputes Claim It Stopped Producing Intel Reports on Rightwing Extremists," *Homeland Security Today*, June 9, 2011.
125. Ibid.
126. "DHS Disputes Claim."
127. Ibid.
128. Ibid.
129. Ibid.

130. Ibid.

131. Ibid.

132. Ibid.

133. "Jailhouse Crock," *American Prospect*, June 16, 2011.

134. Ibid.

135. Ibid.

136. Ibid.

137. Ibid.

138. Ibid.

139. Ibid.

140. Ibid.

141. "Racist Groups Catching Utah's Eye," *Desert News*, September 2, 2002.

142. U.S. v. Leo V. Felton and Erica Chase, United States District Court-District of Massachusetts, February 21, 2001.

143. CRA-USA, Company Website, viewed October 15, 2010.

144. "Roger Mackin," *Bloomburg Businessweek*, Executive Profile, viewed October 25, 2011.

145. "Terrorist Update: Combating the Jihad," America's Truth Forum Website, viewed October 7, 2011.

146. "Norway Shooter 'Inspired' By Robert Spencer and Unabomber," *UK Daily Mail*, July 27, 2011.

147. Multiple articles, Jihad Watch, Robert Spencer Website, viewed October 7, 2011.

148. Multiple programs, Roger Hedgecock Show, XM Satellite Radio Channel 166, 2009–2011.

149. CRA-USA, Company Website, viewed October 15, 2010.

150. "Sued for Terror Watching," America's Truth Forum, viewed October 25, 2011.

151. Ibid.

152. "Friends of Simeon Wiesenthal Center Asked to Condemn Islamophobic Comments," Council on Islamic American Relations-Canada, Press Release, December 9, 2004.

153. Ibid.

154. Ibid.

155. "Islamic Terror Based on Qu'ran: Ex-CIA Official," *Canadian Jewish News*, December 3, 2004.

156. OSINT@yahoogroups.com, Description, viewed January 2011.

157. Multiple posts from Beowulf to OSINT@yahoogroups.com, 2009–2010.

158. "Indigenous-Sovereign," Yahoo! Group, 2009.

159. "The Southern Poverty Law Center Is A Non-Credible, Anti-Conservative Hate Group," Beowulf, Grendelreport@yahoogroups.com, December 2, 2010.

160. Ibid.

161. Multiple posts from Beowulf to OSINT@yahoogroups.com, April 2009.

162. Multiple posts from Beowulf to OSINT@yahoogroups.com, January-February 2011.

163. "Professional 'Anti-Hate' Group Goes to Bed With Reds," Beowulf, OSINT@yahoogroups.com, January 29, 2011.

164. Conversations with law enforcement and intelligence officials, 2010–2011.

165. Statements by Secretary Janet Napolitano to Senator John Carter (R-Texas), U.S. House Committee on Appropriations, on May 12, 2009.

166. Statements by Secretary Janet Napolitano to Representatives Charlie Dent (R-Pennsylvania) and Christopher P. Carney (D-Pennsylvania), U.S. House of Representatives-Homeland Security Committee, on May 13, 2009.

167. "Thank You and Farewell to I&A Staff," E-mail from Bart Johnson, November 18, 2011.

168. Ibid.

169. Conversation with representatives from the Oregon Department of Justice, 2008.

170. "TLO DHS Presentations," E-mail from Detective of the Muskingum County Sheriff's Office, November 22, 2010.

Index

About the Author

Daryl Johnson, an acknowledged subject matter expert in the area of domestic extremism, is the owner of DT Analytics. He has worked as an intelligence analyst for several federal agencies over two decades. For six years, Mr. Johnson was the senior domestic terrorism analyst at the Department of Homeland Security (DHS), Office of Intelligence and Analysis (I&A). During his time at DHS, Mr. Johnson wrote numerous sensitive intelligence reports and briefed a wide range of organizations, including congressional staff; federal, state, and local law enforcement agencies; members of the intelligence community; colleges and universities; and other nongovernment organizations. Mr. Johnson is the primary author of the highly controversial DHS right-wing extremism report dated April 7, 2009.

Prior to his employment at DHS, Mr. Johnson was the subject matter expert on violent antigovernment groups at the Bureau of Alcohol, Tobacco, Firearms, and Explosives (ATF). He provided analytical support during highly sensitive ATF investigations focused on the criminal activities of domestic extremists, such as members of the Ku Klux Klan, antigovernment militias, Christian Identity groups, neo-Nazis, and sovereign citizens. Mr. Johnson has served as a part-time instructor at the ATF National Academy in Glynco, Georgia, for more than a decade, educating and training newly hired special agents on the subject of domestic terrorism.

Mr. Johnson began his federal career as a counterterrorism analyst for the United States Army. He served as a civilian in the Army for several years specializing in CONUS force protection issues. This experience provided him unique insight into domestic right-wing extremist targeting of military personnel for recruitment as well as targeting of military installations by domestic terrorists.

Mark Potok, the author of the foreword and a senior fellow at the Southern Poverty Law Center (SPLC), is one of the country's leading experts on the world of extremism and serves as the editor-in-chief of the SPLC's award-winning quarterly journal, the *Intelligence Report*, its *Hatewatch* blog, and its investigative reports.